Birkhäuser
Basel

D1736772

Birkhäuser
Basel

Extended Urbanisation. Tracing Planetary Struggles

Nitin Bathla, Elisa T. Bertuzzo, Rodrigo Castriota,
Nancy Couling, Alice Hertzog, Nikos Katsikis,
Philippe Rekacewicz, AbdouMaliq Simone, Kit Ping Wong
Edited by Christian Schmid and Milica Topalović

Territories of Extended Urbanisation. Planetary Struggles and Agendas for Action

Introduction

Christian Schmid and Milica Topalović

At the time of writing the last pages of this book, apocalyptic news of migrant tragedies, governance failures, political polarisation, and warfare are inundating the media. Since our international group of scholars started this project in 2017, perceptions of urban stability have been forcefully shattered again and again: exhausted palm oil plantations in Sumatra were burnt to make room for new plantations cloaking Singapore in dangerous fumes; floods swept through the densely settled areas of Bangladesh and Pakistan forcing thousands to resettle; heat waves struck popular holiday destinations in Europe and North America, and forest fires in Canada caused toxic clouds of smoke to choke New York. The entrenched centre-periphery dynamics of stable urban core zones that externalise the crises generated by their own consumption is changing significantly: the turmoil in the peripheries is folding back onto the centres. We argue that destructive developments in both peripheries and centres are aspects of urbanisation.

One of the main motivations of this book, then, is to examine how planetary social and environmental crises are related to urbanisation. Our research perspective stands in contrast to mainstream academia, media, international institutions, state actors, and global enterprises who promote cities and agglomerations as solutions to those crises and present them as the future of humanity; however, they do not acknowledge the planetary character of urbanisation. Such city-centric imaginaries are no longer simply naïve—they are dangerous. Urbanisation needs to be reframed as a multifaceted and contradictory process that is simultaneously productive and destructive and affects both urban centres *and* sparsely settled peripheries. During its historical course, and particularly in the last five decades, urbanisation has unleashed a host of destructive forces leaving a footprint that extends across the planet. For some, this can be seen as "creative destruction" advancing the modernisation of society, the "unintended consequences" of which must be accepted as the price for progress, economic growth, and private profit.

While urban development in the metropolitan centres—"concentrated urbanisation" in our vocabulary—has attracted much attention, "extended urbanisation"—the urbanisation of the peripheries—has remained largely overlooked by mainstream scientific research and public discourse. However, new concepts and engagements with this kind of urbanisation have recently been developed in certain strands of critical and postcolonial urban research, as well as in architecture and urban design. This book contributes to these endeavours, based on insights resulting from ethnographic engagements with many different actors and situations. Most significantly, our interactions with people struggling to establish and protect their livelihoods reinforced our impression of urgency. In conversations with food hawkers along the Lagos-Abidjan corridor, pastoralists in the Arcadian mountains, *camponeses* in the Amazon, workers on oil platforms in the North Sea, villagers in Dongguan and West Bengal, farmers in Iowa, and inhabitants of subaltern settlements in Delhi, we encountered growing political consciousness, struggles for self-determination, and in some cases, organised political movements engaging with and contesting the manifold impacts of planetary crises. Tracing these struggles and resistances against the devastating effects of extended urbanisation became a focus of our research and is the focus and inspiration for this book.

We are convinced that the study of extended urbanisation can give us a better understanding of the interlinked planetary crises. But, in order to engage with these processes, a critical perspective on conventional concepts and theoretical frameworks concerning urbanisation is required. The examples analysed in this book affirm that urbanisation processes unfold both within and beyond centres and agglomerations. A perspective that goes beyond city-centrism does not focus on the facts and statistics that are used to define areas we call "cities" and does not restrict attention to settlements that fulfil the limited criteria of density and population size. In this project, we understand urbanisation as a multidimensional process that produces territories and settlements with implications for the entire planet. We also see it as part of a collective social practice that is neither inevitable nor neutral but intrinsically political. We emphasise the agency involved in the processes of urbanisation and explore the inherent possibilities for changing social practice. Our perspective is directed towards action.

THE PROJECT

This edited volume is a common intellectual project resulting from a collective effort of empirical research and theory building. We selected eight territories to study how processes of extended urbanisation unfold on the ground. These territories are located across North-South and East-West divides to bring different geographies and urban constellations into comparison and dialogue. We were looking for a diversity of study areas, that could allow us to identify and conceptualise different processes of extended urbanisation. When we started this project, most case studies were part of ongoing research projects; thus, the researchers were already familiar with their fields of study. By initiating a transdisciplinary conversation, we analysed how these territories develop, learning from the different experiences, and building a common understanding of urbanisation processes.

What does it mean to carry out research in territories of extended urbanisation? The researchers had to cover vast study areas and often stayed there for long periods of time. They traversed territories on foot, by train and car and applied adapted mobile and multi-sited ethnographic research methods. They also worked with photographs, video, and oral histories. Two of the case studies, Arcadia and the North Sea, build upon prior research that was conducted with architecture students in design studios. Another important instrument brought into this project was an adapted form of radical cartography. It was led by geographer and cartographer Philippe Rekacewicz in collaboration with the researchers. Our main instrument of synthesis were workshops that served as moments of evaluation, comparison, conceptualisation, and theory building. Four workshops took place in Zurich (between 2017 and 2022), two in Singapore (2018), and two at AAG conferences in Boston (2017) and Washington DC (2019). These workshops were generative as we learned from the different positions of the team members, opened up conversations with other researchers, engaged with diverse perspectives, and developed new understandings of the emerging categories and concepts of extended urbanisation, now presented in this collection.

EXTENDED URBANISATION

To contribute to the concept of extended urbanisation,
we worked with a dynamic, multidimensional understanding
of urbanisation, inspired by diverse researchers and thinkers
whose ideas have allowed us to gradually refine; these efforts
are presented in the opening chapter by Christian Schmid.
We further developed these thoughts and concepts during the
research and workshops. We understand urbanisation as a historical process that should not be confounded with the long history
of human settlements and their traces on Earth. Our focus
is on the relatively recent historical phase of urbanisation
as a process linked to the development of capitalism and rooted
in Western anthropocentric rationality and the philosophical
split between society and nature. In many parts of the world,
it is characterised by the industrialisation of society and the
commodification of space, time and experience. The shift from
earlier stages of the development of human territories, including
the establishment of cities, to urbanisation as a dominant, and
potentially planetary, process is not marked by a single event.
Starting with the industrial revolution in the early nineteenth
century and anchored in the core zones of colonial empires,
urbanisation unfolded gradually as an uneven and non-simulta-
neous process affecting both central and peripheral territories.
    The concept of planetary urbanisation captures the latest
chapter of this historical development, resulting from a shift
in the world capitalist system that started at the beginning
of the twentieth century, to fully unfold in the last decades.
This resulted from a major shift of the global accumulation regime
occurring during the long 1980s, based on the globalisation
of financial circuits, the development of global communication
and production networks, the gradual deconstruction of the
Fordist-Keynesian and national-developmentalist regimes of accumulation, the collapse of state socialism, and the subsequent
establishment of an intricate web of global production networks.
In the wake of these processes, the entire planet has become
an arena of extractivism and commodification. Planetary urbanisation produces a "space of effects" consisting of territorial
outcomes such as pollution, the exhaustion of resources, and
the destruction of nature, with grave social consequences. This
space of effects destabilises existing spatial arrangements, often
because neither state actors nor other protagonists can provide
the instruments and regulations to ensure stable or sustainable
"spatial fixes" to such extended processes that often occur
in remote locations. This not only aggravates the climate crisis
and intensifies social and economic crises but erodes the very
conditions that sustain life itself.

THE BOOK

This book presents extended urbanisation as a theoretical concept and a tool for social practice and action. It traces planetary struggles provoked by extended urbanisation in order to increase our capacity to act and challenge the conditions that lead to planetary crises. It outlines strategies of empowerment to achieve social change and self-determination through political networks and everyday practices at different scales and levels. It is a scientific contribution, a theory book, and comprises a collection of well-researched essays. The eight case studies explore and analyse different constellations of extended urbanisation processes, and document the transformations of territories and the social struggles that these sparked and implied. They inform the theoretical propositions concerning the character and forms of extended urbanisation.

The opening chapter by Rodrigo Castriota, "The Mine, the City and the Encampment: Contesting Extractivism in Eastern Amazonia," shows that extractivism has induced various forms of extended urbanisation in Amazonia. In Carajás, the construction of the largest open pit mine in human history and the associated extension of logistics infrastructure led to unprecedented in-migration and urban growth in the Amazon rainforest. Once the mine was completed, most of the workforce was made redundant, as the mine offered permanent jobs to fewer than a hundred workers. Castriota followed the struggles of mining workers who lost their jobs and used their knowledge of the area to squat land in the vicinity of the mine. Amid extreme socio-environmental disruption, new forms of resistance and contestation informed by indigenous and immigrant experiences and practices took hold.

Nikos Katsikis's chapter, "The Horizontal Factory: The Operationalisation of the US Corn and Soy Belt," reconstructs how large parts of the North American Midwest have become a highly specialised hinterland for the primary production of commodities–such as bio fuel, corn syrup, and animal fodder linked to other hinterlands of cattle raring–subjected to an extreme degree of operationalisation. With this term, we denote a process of mechanisation, automation, and exhaustion of ecological surplus in the production of raw materials. This process has led to the gradual depletion of the soil's natural fertility, the pollution of land and groundwater, the loss of jobs, and continuous emigration. The result is a hinterland-of-hinterlands, a highly exploited, emptied, and dehumanised landscape, an exclusive production zone of agricultural commodities.

In "Losing Sea: Abstraction and the End of the Commons in the North Sea," Nancy Couling examines a vast, dispersed, but mostly invisible urbanised realm that stretches across the

North Sea bordering Europe, above and beneath the surface of the water body. The urbanisation of the North Sea is supported by a circulating offshore workforce, which compares to that of a small metropolis. This ocean space is abstractly conceived for resource extraction and then equipped with prefabricated steel and concrete at discrete locations but on an unprecedented scale. This has led to an operationalised and commodified sea space that has replaced the previous sea commons and is now marked by an evacuation of the social.

In "Expropriation and Extended Citizenship: The Peripheralisation of Arcadia," Metaxia Markaki reflects on the future of rapidly depopulating mountainous regions in Greece. Revisiting the mythicised Arcadia on the Greek Peloponnese, she uncovers processes of extended urbanisation in areas that are imagined as "pristine nature" and have even been officially declared as "uninhabited" by state and EU institutions following the Greek crisis. Markaki reports that these landscapes are not "empty" but animated by seasonal activities and movements that see inhabitants maintaining local, regional, and transnational connections to Athens, Albania, Europe, and other regions. For such constellations, she proposes that we give attention to strategies of extended citizenship formed through the reciprocity of social relations connecting centre and periphery.

From Lagos to Abidjan, a metropolitan corridor has emerged along the Gulf of Guinea in West Africa, spanning 1,000 kilometres and bringing together a dense fabric of megacities, towns, and villages. In "Urbanisation through Movement: The Lagos-Abidjan Corridor," Alice Hertzog shows that mobility is inherent to the everyday life of this region. Residents and temporary migrants travel back and forth along the corridor and move from landlocked peripheries towards the coast, seeking opportunities for jobs and income. In the words of Hertzog, these activities "weave" the urban fabric. She analyses how mobilities and movements produce entirely new urban configurations across borders and localities, bridging central and peripheral areas and enabling the often-surprising experience of urbanity in everyday life.

In the outskirts of Kolkata, in a zone where processes of extended and concentrated urbanisation overlap, Elisa T. Bertuzzo explores local processes of domestic industrial production and fierce fights by farmers against the expropriation of their land for the construction of factories and new towns. In "Translocalisation and the Production of Space: West Bengal's Excentric Territories," she finds an example of a different process of the production of space that represents a range of transformations that the inhabitants themselves induce, often financed by remittances earned through temporary and circular migration.

Dongguan was a rural backwater located in the geographical centre of the Pearl River Delta between the Chinese metropolis of Guangzhou and the colonial city of Hong Kong. In the last four decades, an unprecedented urban explosion transformed the Pearl River Delta into the planet's most populous megaregion, setting off a dispersed form of rural industrialisation in Dongguan. In "The Territory and the State: The Urbanisation of Dongguan," Kit Ping Wong reconstructs the contradictory process of extended urbanisation unfolding in the conflictual interplay between state strategies and the counteractions of villagers, who constructed settlements and attracted both investors and mobile migrant labourers. A spectacular process of export-led industrialisation and extended urbanisation ensued, creating the Chinese "world factory." As a result of urban intensification strategies in the last decade, this process was transformed into concentrated urbanisation.

In "The Highway Revolution: Enclosure and State Space in India," Nitin Bathla traces the devastating impact of India's national highway programme setting in motion a cascade of effects based on enclosure of land, from forests, protected nature reserves, and tribal lands to the fertile agricultural belt around Delhi. The resulting corridors of urbanisation have redirected entire settlement systems across the country towards a haphazard form of extended urban development, fuelling the rapid, decentralised urbanisation of India.

These eight case studies are framed by two theoretical texts. The introductory text "Extended Urbanisation: A Framework for Analysis" by Christian Schmid outlines the basic arguments of a general theory of urbanisation, develops the guiding principles of our approach to decentring urban analysis, presents a critique of conventional conceptions in urban studies and urban design, and gives an overview of the different processes of extended urbanisation that we could detect during our research.

In the final chapter "When Extended Urbanisation Becomes Extensive Urbanisation" AbdouMaliq Simone looks from the perspective of the people who are both affected by and coproduce processes of extended urbanisation. He shows how urban dwellers themselves produce urban spaces by their activities and actions. He argues that to be extensive implies to extend, as in the sense of extending a hand and offering something to the functionality of places, bodies, and systems. Extended urbanisation, then, not only signals the progressive unfolding of urbanisation as a set of discrete processes but as a modality of extension, a means through which the operations of multiple systems and actors extend themselves to and through the world.

A TERRITORIAL APPROACH

The eight empirical case studies summarised above were the starting point for the development of a common conceptual framework through a collaborative process. Our discussions and reflections resulted in two major outcomes: first, we revised and refined the analytical framework of extended urbanisation, and second, we developed a vocabulary to grasp a range of extended urbanisation processes. These results are based on and complement three earlier collective research efforts. The projects *Switzerland: An Urban Portrait* (2006) and *The Inevitable Specificity of Cities* (2015), edited by Roger Diener et al., were conducted at ETH Studio Basel and led to the development of a territorial approach to urbanisation based on Henri Lefebvre's theory of the production of space. The third project focused on processes of concentrated urbanisation, based on the comparative analysis of eight large metropolitan territories; it is published in the volume *Vocabularies for an Urbanising Planet: Theory Building Through Comparison* (2023), edited by Christian Schmid and Monika Streule.

Analysing extended urbanisation requires a decentring perspective and involves a thorough recalibration of various concepts to adapt them to the specific problematic. Thus, terms such as urban and rural, planetary, territory, urban fabric, city and non-city, state and state space, territorial regulation, and many others had to be revised. Since this conceptual effort is by necessity an open process, the terms we propose here are revisable, and we invite readers to edit, expand, or enrich these concepts through their own experience.

A key concept underpinning our approach is that of "territory." The term can be misleading in Anglo-American discourse, where it is often reduced to a political geography of state power and offset against the notion of landscape. However, this term has a very different intellectual history and meaning in the context of Roman languages in both Europe and Latin America. In architecture and critical urban studies, this term has rich polysemic connotations. It includes the materiality and life of territories produced by human and non-human activities and labour. In this understanding, territory is a socially appropriated space imbued with social meaning, in which historical production processes, social relations, power constellations and ecologies are inscribed. We incorporated these understandings into Lefebvre's theory of the production of space and analysed urbanisation as a three-dimensional process, including the material production of a territory, territorial regulation, and the experience of urban space in everyday life.

In this triadic thinking, we first understand urbanisation as the *material production of a territory* that transforms built and non-built environments and landscapes. In the course of this process, an *urban fabric* comprising infrastructure and settlements is produced extending from urban centres to territories of primary production, facilitating socio-metabolic processes of industrial production and circulation of goods, energy, information, money and people. We analytically embed the material production of a territory into environmental processes at the planetary scale, and we also see it as enmeshed with ecologies of planetary life, which is itself transformed and obliterated through urbanisation.

In our project, we recognised the great importance of the *movements of people* in the production of territories of extended urbanisation. It is not only the urban fabric that determines urbanisation but also the various forms of movements that pervade a territory. In contrast to agglomerations, where daily commuting prevails, territories of extended urbanisation are marked by different movement rhythms and by longer, more sporadic, and varied forms of mobility, such as practices of temporary migration, whereby people only migrate for a certain time or follow a recurrent pattern of returning regularly to their places of departure. These movements are often induced by the search for income and livelihoods, but they also create networks of interaction and support against peripheralisation and precarisation.

The second dimension of urbanisation is *territorial regulation*, a concept that encompasses the rules that guide the production of the urban fabric and determine the use of the land. Here we realised the great significance of the state space and state actors in the production of territories of extended urbanisation. In recent years, with the rise of massive national and transnational investments and ambitious development strategies, these actors became much more dominant. Intensified interventions by nation-states, international institutions, and corporate actors in the territory correspond to the weakening of more local forms of governance.

In this context, we also encountered the question of *mediation*. The specific role of urban areas is to facilitate a mediation of divergent interests and bring together and moderate the different parts of a territory. However, territories of extended urbanisation offer very different conditions and political and spatial settings than large metropolises, which often have strong metropolitan governments. Because of the fragmented character of the local political entities, this mediating level is therefore usually weak in territories of extended urbanisation. Therefore, regional popular movements and organisations that can mobilise networks of solidarity and support are of particular importance to the creation and defence of participation and self-determination in such territories.

The third dimension of urbanisation we analysed is the question of lived space, or more precisely, the *experience of urban space in everyday life*. These experiences are quite different from concentrated urbanisation, where social density and proximity may allow for direct human encounters. Territories of extended urbanisation are usually marked by sparse population and by large distances between places and centres of activity. The absence of centrality and opportunities for gathering and mutual exchange in everyday life may lead to different social experiences and trajectories of political mobilisation. Social interactions usually proceed in more mediated ways and are generated through movements of people that allow connections to distant places and to each other through various forms of migration and social, political, and cultural organisations and networks. In this way, new popular and self-organised centralities and social movements are coming into existence.

Our cases indicate that people are usually not resisting extended urbanisation as such but respond to contradictions and crises produced by these processes. This results in fights against the expropriation of individual or collective land and other forms of dispossession, displacement, and the loss of jobs and livelihoods, destruction of environments and the foundations of life. At the same time, people are also fighting for better provisions and quality of life under these conditions. These struggles can be understood as assuming a planetary character because they respond to the systematic exploitation and commodification of planetary life and resources. Planetary in this context does not necessarily mean interconnected globally but designates the fact of being entrained within a systematic process of extraction and commodification. At the same time, the term planetary opens a horizon, a potential, and a common perspective.

PROCESSES OF EXTENDED URBANISATION

Based on this analytical framework, we identified and defined a series of dominant *processes of extended urbanisation*. Here we propose a dynamic analysis; we do not analyse static territorial forms but dynamic processes with varied and changing territorial outcomes. The spectrum of urbanisation processes we propose here is not exhaustive; it contains a selection of processes that proved useful in our research and revealed important parallels between seemingly dissimilar territories. This list is therefore preliminary and open.

Processes of extended urbanisation are transforming vast *areas of agricultural production*, which are outside the reach of influence of agglomeration and commuting processes.

Our case studies show that even in very different agricultural territories, such as Arcadia and the US corn and soy belt, a convergence of effects of extended urbanisation are manifest in an ongoing industrialisation of agricultural production, a shift toward monocultures, food-fuel competitions, reliance on migrant labour, and social and ecological desertification.

One widespread process of extended urbanisation we explored in Dongguan is *extended industrial urbanisation*. Today, various forms of peripheral industrialisation are initiated by state strategies that define special economic zones and export processing zones or support global sweatshop regions, back-office locations, data processing facilities, and intermodal logistics terminals. These are often located in periurban areas near large agglomerations, along main transportation corridors, and close to logistics hubs.

In this context, the *production of infrastructure* can itself be understood as a process of extended urbanisation because it leads to de- and re-territorialisation, such as processes of corridor urbanisation and the disintegration of hinterlands. Along motorways and around intersections and bypasses, as in the case of Delhi, countless urban fragments are produced extensively, if unevenly, across large territories, generating an irregular and haphazard urban fabric, which is being at once expanded and blurred.

The precondition for many processes of extended urbanisation is commodifiable land. This land has to be produced through often violent *processes of land enclosure*, which can include dispossession and destruction of traditional forms of land tenure and subsistence economy. While land enclosure can result from other processes of extended urbanisation such as corridor urbanisation or industrial urbanisation, we understand land enclosure as an urbanisation process in itself.

The concept of the *operationalisation of landscapes* brings together the rationalisation and automation of agricultural production, extractivism, energy production, and infrastructure expansion, which are amongst the most dramatic processes of extended urbanisation. The production of operational landscapes enables the procurement and circulation of food, water, energy, and construction materials; the processing and management of waste and pollution; and the mobilisation of labour in support of these various processes of extraction, production, circulation, and management.

The operationalisation of landscapes is often accompanied by extreme forms of rationalisation, which strongly reduces the necessary labour force and thus results in *processes of peripheralisation*. In a similar way, deindustrialisation and changing centre-periphery relations may lead to socio-economic and ecological restructuring, inducing the loss and relocation of economic activities, selective emigration, and depopulation. As a result, permanent settlements are eroding and seasonal or sporadic movements of people to and from central urban areas are becoming more pronounced.

On a general level, extended urbanisation is always implicated in processes of peripheralisation and the production of centralities and thus involves the *restructuring of centre-periphery relationships*. On the one hand, the sequential production of peripherality opens new opportunities for land enclosure, extraction and investment. And on the other, the multiplication of various forms of centrality and their related peripheries across the planet leads to the emergence of large-scale, highly dynamic, and heterogeneous *polynucleated metropolitan zones*, bringing concentrated and extended urbanisation processes together.

In summarising these processes, we realised that extended urbanisation, in general, has a defining double aspect: On the one hand, territories shaped by extended urbanisation are often subjected to the unprecedented increase of extractivism in the broad sense, driven by massive capital investments, particularly by global corporations and nation-states (agribusiness, biotech, mining, energy, transport, logistics, etc.). On the other, this type of rationalisation and automation goes hand in hand with the dramatic reduction in labour power, often resulting in peripheralisation through the devaluation of local activities and the evacuation of the social (in the Amazon, the US corn and soy belt, the North Sea, and Arcadia). These processes have led to rapid commodification in areas that were formerly based on subsistence agriculture and common pool resources. We also note the intrinsic socio-ecological limits to these processes and the exhaustion of both social and natural resources.

At the same time, and in an opposing spatial movement, other territories are becoming more tightly enmeshed into urban networks and are pulled into the gravity field of concentrated urban areas. Here, we observe a divergent trajectory of *intensification of land use and activities*, such the infrastructure frenzy in India, the industrialisation of the Pearl River Delta, the urbanisation of the West African Corridor, and also spontaneous developments fuelled by remittances from circular or periodic migration.

WHAT IS TO BE DONE?

In the course of this collective project, as we met and reflected on our experiences with *camponeses* fighting against a mining corporation in Brazilian Amazonia, the inauguration of a new oil platform in the North Sea arriving from a construction site in Indonesia, and the fight of villagers and supporters against the construction of a car factory in the outskirts of Kolkata, some insights gradually crystallised. They concern the contradictions of extended urbanisation, its implications and struggles, as well as possible alternative pathways and territorial strategies.

The early insights were disheartening: Territories of extended urbanisation appear as battlefields of exploitation and commodification with asymmetric power relations. Regions we worked in are marked by recurrent acts of dispossession, displacement, eviction, and deprivation of people living on and from the land and sea. Entire regions are transformed into landscapes of extraction, leading to deterioration of ecosystems and evacuation of the social, often far away from public attention. Additionally, many forms of extended urbanisation, particularly the construction of urban corridors and the disintegration of hinterlands, imply an enormous waste of resources, leading to the most unsustainable forms of urbanisation.

Our second insight was that urbanisation processes are uneven but also variegated. They can be highly unjust and devastating in social and environmental terms, but there are also inherent potentialities: their outcomes may offer conditions for connection, encounter, and emancipation. This potential could be called, after Lefebvre, differential urbanisation. It is associated with the creation of a differential space, an alternative space rejecting exploitative practices and consumer culture, that defies processes of abstraction and commodification, and enables self-determination and commoning.

The third insight concerns the stereotype that only "big cities" can provide the advantages of urban life. Are there alternatives beyond the big cities? Yes, there are! Several chapters in this book show how people create differential space through their activities and efforts, a space of potential beyond the progressivist mindset of many contemporary metropolises. The creation of self-governed economic circuits and metabolic loops, regenerative ecologies, solidarity networks, and popular centralities as places of meeting and interaction are opening pathways towards different urban futures.

The fourth insight we draw from our discussions and exchanges is that peripheries are not simply areas outside cities and urban life; they are always constituted *relationally* to centralities and other peripheries. As extended urbanisation includes the means to increase connections, it not only generates global connectivity, but also facilitates linking centres and peripheries through social, cultural, political, and economic networks, family ties, and manifold processes of migration and movements. We see a future of multiple belonging and extended citizenship erasing the "urban-rural divide" and connecting centres and peripheries through social practice.

In the course of the project, we repeatedly affirmed the urgency of engaging with the Earth. The conditions for inhabiting the planet are at stake: exhaustion of natural resources, loss of biodiversity, desertification, and evacuation of the social. These are all, to some extent, consequences of extended urbanisation, which are eroding the Earth's vitality. Rather than chasing promises of technocratic fixes, territories of extended urbanisation need to be re-embedded into bio-physical relations based on social and environmental justice and equality. We cannot accept the politics of global apartheid, which are reinforced by the catastrophic and divisive consequences of the current environmental and social crises. We may learn from our case studies that we have to develop connections, reciprocities, international solidarity movements, and mutual understandings in social and ecological terms. The planetary struggles we trace in this book point to some of the possibilities from which collective futures may emerge.

Extended Urbanisation.
A Framework for Analysis

The speed, scale, and scope of urbanisation have increased dramatically in recent decades. Urban research is confronted with urbanisation processes that are unfolding far beyond the realm of agglomerations, extended urban regions, and megaregions. Today, the entire planet is the site and arena of urbanisation processes. Novel patterns of excentric urbanisation are crystallising in agricultural areas, rain forests, and the oceans, challenging inherited conceptions of the urban as a bounded zone and a dense settlement type. However, we are poorly equipped with concepts and theories that allow us to grasp the planetary extension of urbanisation processes and understand the dramatic transformations affecting the most diverse landscapes and territories across the planet.

These observations have sparked fundamental debates about the specificity of the urban. They have catalysed the development of the conception of *planetary urbanisation* as a tool for better understanding the contemporary patterns and pathways of urbanisation. Its analytical core is the distinction between concentrated, extended, and differential urbanisation. While the term *concentrated urbanisation* denotes the formation and growth of agglomerations, resulting in dense urban areas, the term *extended urbanisation* invites us to look at what is seemingly outside of the urban and to study processes of urbanisation "beyond the city" that are transforming sparsely settled areas. The third term, *differential urbanisation*, expresses the potential of urbanisation to generate spaces for encounter and social interaction that create a different urban world. Processes of extended, concentrated, and differential urbanisation should be understood as vectors, not as territories. They may develop on the same territories at the same time, overlapping and permeating each other. In this sense, territories of extended urbanisation are not bounded areas, but territories that are dominated by processes of extended urbanisation, which are often simultaneously also transformed by processes of concentrated and differential urbanisation.

Processes of extended urbanisation are shaping the planet in unprecedented and unpredictable ways, often positioning dynamic and depleting areas side by side. Consequently, territories of extended urbanisation are more varied and complex than might be expected. It is urgent to gain a more comprehensive picture and a systematic understanding of these processes that increasingly determine our planet's destiny. This chapter sheds light on the theoretical, conceptual, and empirical questions that the research on extended urbanisation addresses. It discusses some of these processes and territories that question conventional understandings and boundaries of the urban. It presents an overview of the current research on extended urbanisation and embeds the eight case studies published in this book in the wider context of the rapidly growing scientific literature.

This chapter is divided into four parts; the individual parts are articles in themselves and can be read independently of each other. Part I, "Planetary Urbanisation: An Epistemological Reorientation," outlines the basic arguments of a general theory of urbanisation. It presents a critique of city-centric conceptions, scrutinises the foundational figure in mainstream urban studies of the agglomeration and its hinterland, and sketches out a different conception of urbanisation. Part II, "The Urbanisation of the territory: A Three-Dimensional Framework," develops and explains the guiding principles of our approach to decentring urban analysis. This framework is based on earlier efforts to theorise urbanisation based on Henri Lefebvre's theory of the production of space and inspired by research projects of ETH Studio Basel.[1] The reflections on extended urbanisation result from the collective efforts of the entire research team assembled in this book to better understand extended urbanisation.[2] Part III, "From Concentrated to Extended Urbanisation: The Search for an Elusive Urban Boundary," focuses on the various conceptual attempts to bind the urban and to theoretically and conceptually perpetuate the classic distinction between city and country, which has been constantly destabilised and undermined by the relentless motion of the urbanisation process itself. It presents a critique of conventional conceptions in urban studies and urban design, which have created confusion about the very nature of urbanisation and allowed many processes to remain under the radar of urban analysis. In this situation, the concept of extended urbanisation offers a different approach and methodology for urban analysis and contributes to the development of an entirely new field of urban research. Part IV, "Processes of Extended Urbanisation: An Exploration," gives an overview of the different processes of extended urbanisation that we could detect during our research. Together, these four parts introduce the emerging study of extended urbanisation.

PART I

PLANETARY URBANISATION. AN EPISTEMOLOGICAL REORIENTATION

In recent decades, new urban phenomena emerging across the planet questioned and undermined the familiar canon of concepts and cartographies of the urban. The approach of planetary urbanisation has been developed to precisely address these radical transformations of patterns and pathways of urbanisation. It is based on the hypothesis that urbanisation has acquired a planetary reach and needs a planetary perspective to be adequately understood and analysed. Inspired by Henri Lefebvre's conception of a planetary "urban revolution," it proposes a fundamental epistemological reorientation of our understanding of the urban and urbanisation and demands a radical change of perspective towards a decentring of urban research.[3] At the beginning of the twenty-first century, Roberto Luís Monte-Mór analysed these new phenomena in the Brazilian Amazon and developed the first understanding of extended urbanisation referring to Lefebvre's analysis.[4] In the early 2010s, also directly inspired by Lefebvre's theory, Andy Merrifield, Neil Brenner, and Christian Schmid introduced the concept of planetary urbanisation to the discussion.[5] In the meantime, the concepts of planetary and extended urbanisation have been widely applied and further developed across divergent terrains globally. They also provoked some intense, sometimes highly polemical debates on the appropriate epistemology, conceptualisation, and methodology for urban research today.[6]

The core of the concept of planetary urbanisation is the proposal for an epistemological reorientation of the understanding of urbanisation that is outlined in Part I of this chapter. It starts with a *critique of city centrism* and, thus, a critique of the traditional vision of the city as a nodal, bounded, singular, and universally replicable settlement type that makes it impossible to grasp and understand some of the most pressing urban transformations of our time.[7] To develop an adequate conceptualisation of contemporary urbanisation processes, we have to abandon the classic figure of the urban agglomeration with its agrarian hinterland that has formed the foundations of contemporary urban theory and research. The key argument Brenner and Schmid brought forward is not that agglomerations no longer exist or are no longer central sites and expressions of urbanisation processes. On the contrary, the "power of agglomeration" has been a vital driver of urbanisation since the beginning of the industrial revolution and plays a dominant role in the formation and development of dense urban territories to this day. Instead, the problem is that contemporary approaches continue to focus exclusively on agglomeration processes and obfuscate the most dramatic transformations shaping our planet. Urbanisation encompasses a much broader set of territories, not only dense agglomerations, their proximate hinterlands, and their long-distance networks of connectivity, but also a great diversity of territories "beyond the city" that provide urban areas with labour, energy, food, water, infrastructure, and waste disposal.[8] Therefore, we have to move from an analysis of bounded settlement spaces and urban forms to an analysis of urbanisation processes producing and transforming these forms. For this purpose, Brenner and Schmid proposed a dialectical understanding that brings together three moments of urbanisation in a relational, dynamic, and dialectical framework, including processes of concentrated, extended, and differential urbanisation that are interrelated and mutually constitutive.

CITY CENTRISM: THE NON-CITY AS BLIND FIELD

For a long time, the analysis of urbanisation has been restrained by city-centric conceptions of the urban, focusing on the spatial concentration of population, production sites, infrastructure, and investment within a more or less clearly delineated spatial zone. Despite seriously compromising our collective capacities to decipher and influence urbanisation processes unfolding beyond agglomerations, city centrism only recently attracted broader scrutiny. In their critique of mainstream urban discourses, Brenner and Schmid analyse the long history of city centrism that culminated in the postulation of an "urban age" when UN-Habitat declared that for the first time in history more than half of the world's population was now living in urban areas. This claim has been repeated in various contexts time and again.[9] The urban age discourse drew public attention to the problems and potentials of the growth of "cities" and cast into oblivion other kinds of urban developments in "other parts" of the world.

In a similar vein, Andy Merrifield criticises the concept of the "right to the city," which he considers obsolete in the face of the planetary extension of urbanisation. He asks, "Does it still make any sense to talk about right to *the* city, to the city that's mono-centric and clear-cut about what's inside and what's outside?"[10] Following this argument, Marcelo Lopez de Souza demands a "right to the planet" to address the profound spatial restructuring under capitalism.[11] On their part, Hillary Angelo and David Wachsmuth critique conventional approaches in urban political ecology for adopting a "methodological cityism," which is an overwhelming analytical and empirical focus on the traditional city, "instead of mobilising a Lefebvrian theoretical framework to trouble traditional distinctions between urban/rural and society/nature by exploring urbanization as a global process."[12] From an architectonic point of view, Stephen Cairns shows how city centricity is debilitating our capacities to act and develop alternatives to the dogma of dense, compact, accessible, and mixed-use settlement types.[13]

Despite these criticisms and the increasing difficulties in understanding and grasping contemporary urban phenomena, city centrism still constitutes a major tendency in urban studies and architecture. To this day, the idea that agglomerations represent the privileged or exclusive terrain of urban development remains a core assumption within both mainstream and critical traditions of urban studies. This is particularly evident in economic conceptions of the urban that are based on theories of agglomeration (see below). Demographic and statistical accounts followed this perspective by developing statistical methods to contain the exploding metropolis in an analytical city-centric framework.[14] In a similar way, classical sociological accounts also focused on urban concentration. Georg Simmel theorised the characteristics of the metropolis, contrasting it to small towns and rural life. Continuing this line of reasoning, Louis Wirth made the size of settlements a key criterion of urbanism, which necessarily implies and presupposes a bounding move. Both the Chicago School and later the Los Angeles School—the two most influential Western strands of urbanism—also looked at metropolises that they both epitomised in their books—*The City* (about Chicago) and *The City* (about Los Angeles)—despite their otherwise diverging perspectives.[15] In all these theories and concepts, the urban is seen as a phenomenon of concentration, and the main goal is to fathom the enigma of the effects and consequences of the agglomeration process. Even when urban areas continued to expand, and "urban sprawl" and the "exploding metropolis" became key topics in theoretical and conceptual efforts,[16] these dramatic urban changes were not reflected in new conceptualisations of the urban. Rather, they were addressed by the adjustment of the conceptual "container" of the urban and by extending the radius of the circle defining a "city region." Until recently, both "Western" and "Southern" urban theories evolved along the lines of city centrism, and in a kind of silent convention, the term "city" constituted a common key component of all sorts of new concepts ranging from global city and world city to edge city, megacity, generic city, Southern city, and many more.

Even Henri Lefebvre relied on the term "city" in his earlier texts, as evidenced in his seminal book *The Right to the City,* published in 1968. In one of the most spectacular epistemological shifts in urban studies, he strongly criticised his own concept only two years later in *The Urban Revolution*, where he developed a radically different perspective based on his hypothesis of the complete urbanisation of society. Consequently, he heavily criticised the concept of the "city" as an ideological pseudo-concept and placed the process of urbanisation at the centre of his theory. He declared that the expansion of the urban phenomenon tends to transgress territorial borders and explicitly observed the "prodigious extension of the urban to the entire planet."[17]

In a parallel move, David Harvey, strongly inspired by Lefebvre, changed his focus from an analysis of the city to the theorisation of urbanisation. His ground-breaking book *Social Justice and the City* (1973) was still dominated by theorisations of the city, even though he presented a spectacular paradigm shift from liberal approaches towards a Marxist understanding of the urban. His ambitious theoretical project to introduce (urban) space into Marxist theory culminated in his book *Limits to Capital* (1982), which unfolds an encompassing analysis of the production of the built environment and the circulation of capital. In *Urbanization of Capital* and *Consciousness and the Urban Experience*, both published in 1985, he finally laid down the conceptual core for a fully developed analysis of urbanisation.

Despite these fundamental achievements and the fact that both Lefebvre and Harvey were widely read, discussed, and quoted in the following years and decades, city-centric approaches to the urban largely prevailed. Three core problems are emerging from such conceptions. First, they entail the often-implicit assumption that the urban is a bounded unit. This supposition severely constrains an adequate understanding of the variety of urbanisation processes that are dramatically and rapidly transforming the planet. Thus, the point is not to question specific claims about what happens at the "edge" of the city or discussions on how to define the "boundary of the urban." Instead, the problem is the intellectual act of bounding itself, which is reducing the urban to a territorially defined settlement type.[18]

The second problem is that such conceptions are constructing a contrast between the urban and a putatively non-urban outside that is variously called "rural," "countryside," or "wilderness."[19] We can define the limits of the urban realm in many ways, but we inevitably construct an inside and an outside. Consequently, what happens outside the urban remains under the radar of urban research simply because of the convention that it does not belong to the field of urban studies. As a result, many urbanisation processes shaping the world, often in dramatic ways, remain under-theorised or even unacknowledged. This does not postulate that there is no outside of the urban at all or that concepts of urbanisation must frame all spatial phenomena occurring on the surface of the Earth, as some critics are assuming.[20] Rather, the point is that in asserting an a priori outside of the urban, many urban phenomena are theoretically erased without any possibility to conceptualise them. The distinction between city and non-city not only neglects uneven urban development and the significant variation in the nature of the urban but also results in what Lefebvre called a "blind field." He understands this paradoxical combination of terms as neither a literary image nor a metaphor. It marks what is blinding and what is blinded, what knowledge misconceives and misrecognises. The term also encompasses the power of ideology and the power of language. Lefebvre, therefore, proposes to study the urban as a field of knowledge and as a possibility for action: "On the one hand a path is opened to exploration; on the other there is an enclosure to break out of, a consecration to transgress."[21]

The third problem of city centrism is that urban concentration and agglomeration are treated as one-directional processes that can be understood in isolation from any other processes of territorial transformation. Despite various calls to analyse the urban as a constellation of connections and relations—most famously by Doreen Massey and John Allen[22]—dominant understandings of the city and the urban are still mainly focused on processes of concentration. However, as I will argue in detail below, urban concentration is not possible without an opposite movement of urban extension.

City-centric conceptions and definitions have serious implications and effects, not only in theory but also in practice. The agglomeration paradigm constitutes the basis for UN Habitat's calculation of "urban areas" and also informs its conception of urban sustainability in the *New Urban Agenda,* which does not adequately address urbanisation processes beyond the city.[23] Because of this, it considerably underestimates the degree to which urbanisation contributes to carbon emissions, and it also overlooks the devastating effects of various forms of land enclosures and rural dispossessions as preconditions for the unfolding of extended urbanisation.[24] Furthermore, these conceptions form the basis for the ideological narrative of the *Triumph of the City*, which argues that people have to move to large metropolises in search of prosperity and success.[25] This kind of urban triumphalism engendered a "new metropolitan mainstream" that postulates and disseminates strategies of slum clearance and urban upgrading and imposes norms for urban lifestyles and ways of living, thus legitimising and even promoting strategies of dispossession.[26] This simultaneously entails a devaluation and disempowerment of people living in putatively non-metropolitan or non-urban territories, from peripheral and sparsely populated areas to economically stagnating industrial regions facing decreasing populations, economic decline, and peripheralisation. In the following two sections, I will first problematise the putative "inside" and the crucial concept of agglomeration and then discuss the "outside" and the pertinent but neglected hinterland question.

THE POWER OF AGGLOMERATION

The concept of agglomeration is one of the most fundamental theorems in economic geography and urban planning. It is often seen as a general principle that leads economic activities, people, and infrastructure to cluster in space during successive cycles of capitalist industrial development. Economic geographers Allen Scott and Michael Storper elevated this process

to a kind of universal law: "All cities can be understood in terms of a theoretical framework that combines two main processes, namely, the dynamics of agglomeration/polarisation, and the unfolding of an associated nexus of locations, land uses, and human interactions."[27]

The first description of this process of agglomeration can be found in Friedrich Engels's *The Condition of the Working Class in England.* Here, he makes a clear connection between industrialisation and urbanisation by understanding the capitalist city as the result of the concentration of the means of production and labour power: "The greater the town, the greater its advantages. It offers roads, railroads, canals; the choice of skilled labour increases constantly, new establishments can be built more cheaply, because of the competition among machinists who are at hand, than in remote country districts, whither timber, machinery, builders, and operatives must be brought; it offers a market to which buyers crowd; communication with the markets supplying raw material or demanding finished goods. Hence the marvellously rapid growth of the great manufacturing towns."[28] To this day, this is an almost perfect definition mirrored in most versions of agglomeration economies in one way or another.

Karl Marx, in *Capital: Volume 1,* brought this process into a more general conceptualisation: "The conglomeration of workers, the assembly of different work processes, and the concentration of the means of production thus result simultaneously in a constriction of the spatial sphere (*Raumsphäre*) of labour and an extension of its sphere of effects (*Wirkungssphäre*), which saves a lot of incidental costs (*faux frais*)."[29] Marx postulated that the spatial concentration of the production process increases the productive forces. This idea became fundamental to Lefebvre's understanding of the city as a productive force.[30] We also find here that spatial concentration has not only internal effects, such as the increase in productivity and the reduction of production costs but also external effects by increasing the sphere of influence of agglomerations and industrial production zones.

Many decades later, geographer Alfred Weber called this phenomenon the "force of agglomeration" (*Agglomerationskraft*). He understood it as a process of concentration bringing together people, production processes, and resources, and he distinguished between proper agglomeration forces and incidental forms of agglomeration, such as the concentration of industries following the deposits of ore or coal.[31] His "law of agglomeration" stipulates that a concentration of production lowers production costs. In this context, Weber identified not only agglomerative but also "deglomerative" forces, such as congestion and, notably, increasing land prices in large agglomerations. From these thoughts follow the fundamental principle now known by the term "agglomeration economies."

The analytical figure of dense versus dispersed urban settlements was then used in mainstream economy to show that cities grow faster than non-cities, usually measured in terms of economic and demographic growth. Thus, agglomeration economies became a short-hand explanation for the economic "success" of cities. However, this "mysterious concept of agglomeration" presents considerable empirical and theoretical difficulties, as Pierre Veltz explained.[32] What are the powerful forces that are producing such spectacular changes in urban landscapes? What are the reasons for the concentration of people and economic activities in space leading to the relentless expansion of cities?

The economic literature has brought forward many good reasons for the economic advantages of agglomerations, such as reduced transaction costs, untraded interdependencies, the positive effects of urban governance and institutions, differentiated labour markets and diversified consumption, innovation processes, creativity, uncertainty reduction, and reflexivity.[33] This long list shows that the economic reasons for the power of agglomeration are very diverse, and, importantly, they are also strongly dependent on specific historical situations. While the effect of some agglomeration economies cannot be disputed empirically, they are always specific and elude theoretical attempts

to elevate them to a general principle. Historically, very different patterns of urbanisation have developed, some more dispersed and others more concentrated, some monocentric, others polycentric, and, contrary to the dominant economic narrative, many of the less concentrated urban patterns proved to be highly economically successful, as the famous regions of the *Terza Italia* or southern Germany suggest.

Indeed, there are other reasons for the "growth of cities." In their aspirations to develop their capitals and support (global) command and control centres on their territories, nation-states often play key roles in the agglomeration process but are usually excluded from the analysis. Forced migrations resulting from political and economic crises, armed conflicts, and natural disasters also drive agglomeration processes. Furthermore, there are many examples of urban concentration without "proper" agglomeration economies, particularly in Africa and Asia, such as Lagos or Dongguan, discussed in this book. Why do cities grow? There is a great variety of reasons for the growth of economic activities and population in individual urban territories. Nevertheless, many of these reasons originate outside the economy of agglomeration, and serious questions remain about the systematic logic behind it.

Aside from these reservations about the mechanism of agglomeration economies, two strong theoretical arguments have been mostly excluded from the discussion so far: 1) the question of transport and connectivity and 2) the question of the urban boundary. As Weber recognised, transport costs play a key role in the agglomeration process. However, such costs are relational and take effect in both directions. If they decrease through the applications of new technologies or improvements in infrastructure, they may increase the force of agglomeration because they facilitate movements towards the centre. Although, they may also cause deglomerative effects as newly developed nodes in logistical networks attract activities from main centres. As a result, new centralities are formed that may become cores of agglomeration and concentrated urbanisation. The widely discussed global production networks are not only generating global cities, as Saskia Sassen's famous hypothesis postulates, but also all sorts of new centralities that form, as Veltz has shown, "archipelago economies." Veltz, therefore, rejected the concept of agglomeration and replaced it with a sophisticated conceptualisation of centrality.[34] Furthermore, as I will discuss in Part II of this chapter, various forms of migration and short-term movements reinforce extended urbanisation processes and further blur the significance of agglomeration economies.

The second critical point in relation to the agglomeration paradigm is its one-sided analytical perspective. It constructs an inside and an outside of the agglomeration and thus is entirely dependent on the definition of an urban boundary, even if it is blurred and only vaguely outlined. The argument, brought forward by Scott and Storper, that "the city is to the space economy as a mountain is to the wider topography" misses the point.[35] From a relational perspective on the production of space, there are, by necessity, many relationships between the putative inside and outside these boundaries. Agglomerations cannot be treated in isolation, because they are embedded in a multitude of interactions and networks that stretch far beyond their catchment areas. From this perspective, the agglomeration paradigm seems paradoxical because agglomerations depend entirely on productive hinterlands and cannot even exist without "other" territories that support them.

Therefore, it is in the very nature of agglomeration processes that they generate processes of extension at the same time. What has been largely neglected in all of these concepts and theories is the fact that urbanisation simultaneously entails the transformation of the non-city. It is not possible to concentrate people, means of production, functions, and activities without bringing raw materials, energy, and food into urban areas. They have to be produced "somewhere"—often in regions that are caught in an entrenched spatial division of labour, such as former colonies and peripheral agricultural areas, as already discussed in the context of dependency theory and theories of uneven development.[36] In the same way, people migrating to urban centres are also coming from "somewhere." When they migrate, they do not disappear from their places of origin but instead establish relationships between their new place of everyday life and their place of origin, creating all sorts of connections between city and non-city. The agglomeration cannot exist without a "hinterland," which historically constituted the basic restriction for the growth of cities. We, therefore, have to examine the *question of the hinterland*.

FROM THE HINTERLAND QUESTION TO EXTENDED URBANISATION

The important historical role of the hinterland in the very existence of cities and agglomerations is discussed in many contributions.[37] For a long time in history, the development of a city depended crucially upon the qualities of its localised metabolic support system, particularly the agricultural productivity of its environs and the degree of political and economic control of a sufficiently large hinterland—only very favourable conditions allowed for the growth of cities beyond certain limits. The first problem was always the *metabolic restriction*: To feed an urban population, the generation of an agricultural surplus product is indispensable.[38] As David Harvey states, up until the sixteenth or seventeenth century, the growth of cities, in general, was limited by a very specific metabolic relation to their productive hinterlands: "No matter that certain towns and cities were centres of long-distance trade in luxuries or even that some basic goods, like grains, salt, hides and timber could be moved over long distances, the basic provisioning (feeding, watering and energy supply) of the city was always limited by the restricted productive capacity of a relatively confined hinterland."[39]

Thus, until the industrial revolution, most cities—even the important ones—were relatively small and rarely exceeded 30,000 inhabitants. There were larger cities, but they were either located in very productive environs, in the capitals of powerful empires, or in important global trade centres. As Paul Bairoch calculated, at the end of the eighteenth century, there were less than 90 cities worldwide with more than 100,000 inhabitants.[40] In most cases, large cities were only possible through access to water transport, particularly seaports, for long distant trade but also for supporting the daily needs of a large population. In his epochal work on the Mediterranean, Fernand Braudel carefully analyses and exemplifies this relationship.[41]

The hinterland question was crucial to the flourishing of cities, and this question was treated already in the classic land use model drawn by Johann Heinrich von Thünen in 1826. In his work on the isolated state in relation to agriculture and the national economy, he analysed the differentiation of agrarian land uses in northern Germany in the early nineteenth century considering economic, environmental, and spatial conditions. He imagined a singular large town without access to a navigable river or canal located in the centre of a fertile plain. This central town must "supply the rural areas with all manufactured products, and in return, it will obtain all its provisions from the surrounding countryside."[42] Von Thünen proposed a relatively simple formula connecting land rent, yield per land unit, production expenses, market prices, and freight rates in order to determine the differentiation of land use zones according to their proximity to the town. Since vegetables, fruit, milk, and other dairy products must get to market quickly, they would be produced close to the city. Firewood and timber for fuel and building materials are heavy and difficult to transport and would be produced in the second ring. In the third, fourth, and fifth rings, field crops and livestock are produced in different combinations and intensities until the outer limit of the hinterland is reached. Under these assumptions, von Thünen explained the maximum distance of grain production for the town with a simple example: If the grain is transported by a horse carriage, the horses and drivers need food and will eat from the grain they carry. Once the grain is delivered to the town, there has to be a reserve for provisions on the way back,

and there must also be a profit and land rents to pay. Under the conditions of northern Germany at his time, von Thünen calculated a maximum distance between the town and the agricultural land that serves this town of about 30 miles. Beyond this distance, only cattle could still be produced as the cows could walk on their own feet to the market.

However, von Thünen's ideal static model of the isolated state completely changes within a *dynamic perspective*. As soon as there is an agglomeration process and thus urban growth, this well-ordered hinterland with its radial zones will disintegrate. The hinterland cannot expand in tandem with the growing city, first because the expansion of the agglomeration will consume it and second because much more food and raw materials for the growing population would be needed. By necessity, this leads to the displacement of the hinterland function to distant territories that have to be linked to the growing agglomeration to deliver the necessary resources. In order to start urbanisation, firstly, the hinterland question has to be solved by organising more efficient transport systems and secondly, the agricultural production has to be increased, as these territories now have to serve not only the local economy but also the world market.

THE DISINTEGRATION
    OF HINTERLANDS

For the reasons explained above, cities remained small and decentralised all over the world until the beginning of the nineteenth century. This situation changed fundamentally with the industrial revolution, which allowed a massive increase in the scale of interactions and the transport of food, raw materials, and other products over larger distances. This loosened the dependency of urban areas on their immediate hinterlands. For this reason, the beginning of the urbanisation process is directly related to the industrial revolution. As an illustration, the population of Manchester, the paradigmatic example of a European industrial city, increased from about 20,000 to 300,000 between 1774 and 1841.[43] As we have seen,

Engels explained this spectacular growth through the advantages of agglomeration. But in fact, it was only the massive progress in transport technology, particularly the introduction of railways and steamboats, that made such growth possible. This concerned not only food, but also raw materials as Manchester's production system relied heavily on cotton produced in India and slave labour in North America. The rise of industrial capitalism was thus directly linked to colonialism and imperialism, and the procurement of resources and raw materials became a driver of urbanisation. During the late nineteenth and early twentieth centuries, the development of trading hubs and entrepôt economies in the colonies led to the rapid growth of urban centres, such as Hong Kong, Singapore, and Jakarta, and also centres of mining activities, such as Johannesburg.

But even if innovations and improvements in transport systems allow the supply of large urban territories with food and raw materials, there is still the problem that these products have to be produced for the world market. This requires a fundamental change in agricultural production to massively increase productivity and enable the export of the produced goods. The indispensable precondition for this process is arable land. But this land is not readily available. It must first be removed from the stable type of ownership based on collective or individual inheritance, often small farmers living in a subsistence economy. Thus, a crucial condition for the extension of large agglomerations is the enclosure and commodification of agricultural land.

Marx discussed this process of enclosure under the concept of *ursprüngliche Akkumulation*, which is usually translated as "primitive accumulation" but more precisely means "original accumulation." In chapter 24 of *Capital: Volume 1*, he describes the violent historical process of accumulation that divorces labourers from their means of production and thus creates the "free labourers," who are freed from their chains to the land and the feudal social order but also freed from any means of production of their own, and thus had no other option for survival than

to sell their own labour. For Marx, the classical form of original accumulation, which created both the capitalist and the labourer, happened in the sixteenth century in England in the process of the "enclosure of the commons," through which the agricultural population was dispossessed of its land, its means of production, and its livelihoods.[44] As Goonewardena reminds us, there was a direct connection between enclosure in England at the time of the Industrial Revolution and the parallel developments in the colonies through deportations, the destruction of rural and traditional livelihoods, and the precarity of living conditions.[45] It also has to be stressed that at the same time, slave labour of African descent in the Americas played an essential role in the production of food and raw materials for the world market.

Enclosure and the separation of the farmers from their land was, and still is, a double-edged process, as analysed by Silvia Federici and Álvaro Sevilla-Buitrago.[46] It creates disposable labour on the one hand and the incorporation of land into capital circulation on the other. It also creates a double condition for urbanisation with a mobile labour force to fuel agglomeration and concentrated urbanisation and tradable land for capitalist exploitation. The forceful and often violent expulsion of peasant populations and the commodification and privatisation of land were thus necessary conditions for both capital accumulation and urbanisation. The enclosure of land set a process in motion that abolished the commons but at the same time also dissolved the hinterland of cities. Concomitantly, food, and other agricultural products were transformed into elements of variable capital and ceased to be means of subsistence. They were now commodities produced for the world market.[47]

Marx saw original accumulation as an initial phase of the accumulation process that would soon be replaced by the expanded reproduction of capital that he analysed in *Capital*. Rosa Luxemburg famously opposed Marx's view and insisted on the "other aspect" of capital accumulation: the capitalist exploitation of non-capitalist economies through force, fraud, oppression, and looting. She considered these two sides as organically linked and insisted on the need to look at them together.[48] Returning to these classical debates that are ongoing to this day, David Harvey realised that this process could not be called "original" anymore and introduced the term "accumulation by dispossession" for contemporary processes of commodification and appropriation of surplus value.[49]

Enclosures and dispossession are as urgent as ever in the twenty-first century.[50] In the sense of Luxemburg, we could see various forms of land enclosure today as the "other side of urbanisation" that simultaneously enables and fuels both extended and concentrated forms of urbanisation. Enclosure is a necessary step for the creation of operational landscapes, new spaces of industrial production, and new centralities in the urban periphery (see below). This intrinsic connection underlies the capitalist principle of uneven urban development and the fundamental relationship between domination and dependency. Urbanisation cannot be separated from its other side, the dispossession and commodification of the land, nor the inherent power relations and forms of violence that these processes entail. In this way, an uneven spatial division of labour emerges, imposed and regulated by relations of domination and exploitation.

FROM CITY TO URBANISATION

This overview reveals that a double process was set in motion by the industrial revolution. On the one hand, there was the agglomeration of the means of production and labour power through industrialisation, and on the other was the dissolution of hinterlands via enclosure. From this, we can distinguish two main dynamics that dissolve the city as a bounded unit. First, the agglomeration process leads to the further extension of settlement areas; and second, this process necessitates the enclosure and disintegration of agricultural hinterlands, which are detached from the immediate surroundings of the city and dislocated to specific zones of production, which are linked to agglomerations by networks of information, transport, and logistics.

The starting point of a decentralised analysis is thus to focus on the process instead of the form and to conceptualise urbanisation instead of the city. But how to conceptualise urbanisation? First, we must acknowledge that urbanisation and related concepts such as the city, the urban, and many others are theoretical and not empirical concepts. As with all spatial concepts, or representations of space in Lefebvre's terms, they need a *definition*. Urbanisation, or "the urban" as such, cannot be "seen" without applying a concept that defines what has to be looked at. Urbanisation is a theoretical category, and accordingly, it can be defined in different ways.

It is revealing that the term "urbanisation" was coined at a critical moment in urban history when cities in various parts of the world started to expand beyond the limits imposed by the metabolic restriction discussed above. As Ross Exo Adams and Antonio Lopez de Aberasturi show in detail, it was Ildefonso Cerdà, Catalan engineer, architect, and the urban designer of nineteenth-century Barcelona, who created the neologism *urbanización* to mark the extension of urban spaces beyond the hitherto clearly defined and demarcated boundaries of cities.[51] At that very moment, when the form of the historic city exploded, Cerdà lacked a term to explain what he observed and what he also tried to conceive and design: the extension of cities. He was looking for a term that does not define the city as a political, cultural, or morphological unity but as a general process of extension. He, therefore, used the Latin term *urbe* in the most generic sense to simply designate an ensemble of buildings with no concrete relationship to its size or hierarchical position. He expressed the difference from the term *ciudad* (city), which is rooted in the Latin word *civis*, a citizen of Ancient Rome. The basic idea that urbanisation expresses extension is already embedded in the very first definition of the term urbanisation itself.

In his *Teoría general de la urbanización* from 1867, Cerdà conceived *urbanización* as a double-edged process. On the one hand, it expresses the moment of an almost unlimited extension of settlement areas and the physical process in which the city extends potentially unhindered over the territory; on the other, he used this term to designate a universal model for the building of cities in design terms. What is fascinating in this conception is the fact that it conceives urbanisation as both an analytical term and a design strategy, imagining an almost endless extension of the built-up area. For Cerdà, *urbanización* includes both a passive and an active meaning. For instance, a territory might be urbanised, but an actor can also urbanise a territory. This term was soon imported into the French language and later also into English. In the Anglo-American scientific discourse, however, urbanisation came to mean movement to cities or growth of settlements, usually in terms of population.[52]

A hundred years later, when urbanisation was approaching the "critical point" in which the entire planet was potentially affected by urbanisation processes, Henri Lefebvre proposed his hypothesis of the complete urbanisation of society. He used the inspiring metaphor of "implosion–explosion," borrowed from atomic physics, to express the contradictory double process of concentration and extension that is transforming both rural and urban areas. With his intervention, he presented a new understanding of urbanisation and opened up a new field of inquiry. However, while he understood urbanisation as a total phenomenon and distinguished levels and dimensions of the urban, he left us without a further differentiation that would allow us to identify and analyse particular urbanisation processes.

A similar and related understanding was developed in Latin America, where, since the 1960s, debates on urbanisation have flourished. In parallel to Lefebvre, Peruvian sociologist Aníbal Quijano developed a broad understanding of urbanisation as a multidimensional and encompassing process of transformation across the entire society. In the Latin-American context, he also understood urbanisation as a process related to dependency on the capitalist world system. Brazilian geographer Milton Santos approached urbanisation from the perspective of the production of space. And in the 1980s, Roberto Luís Monte-Mór developed his concept of extended urbanisation based on Lefebvre's theory.[53]

David Harvey, for his part, although strongly influenced by Lefebvre's hypothesis, embedded urbanisation into Marx's theory of the circulation of capital and looked at it from the perspective of the process of the production of the built environment, that is to say, the construction of housing, production sites, and infrastructure with all the attendant social implications. Harvey concluded that increasing investments into the built environment lead to the "urbanisation of capital." This conceptualisation could be understood as a political-economist reformulation of Lefebvre's encompassing thesis of the complete urbanisation of society.

CONCENTRATION, EXTENSION, AND DIFFERENTIATION

While these contributions fundamentally changed our understanding of the urban and urbanisation, they did not allow us to approach and analyse urbanisation processes in detail. This was the motive and reason for a range of theoretical and methodological inventions that together formed the planetary urbanisation approach. The concept of planetary urbanisation understands urbanisation as a reciprocal process in which both the urban centres and the hinterlands change in tandem with each other. Urbanisation is seen as an interplay between three mutually constitutive moments: 1) concentrated urbanisation, 2) extended urbanisation, and 3) differential urbanisation. These three moments are dialectically interconnected and mutually constitutive; they are analytically distinguished to offer an epistemological basis for a reinvented conceptualisation that transcends the limitations and blind spots of mainstream concepts of urbanisation.[54]

The moment of concentrated urbanisation is directly related to agglomeration processes through which people, economic activities, and infrastructure cluster together in space. Obviously, agglomerations remain central arenas and engines of urban transformation. However, we understand agglomeration in a different way than the economic mainstream sketched out above—not as a bounded territory but as an open process of concentrated urbanisation that is always related to extended and differential urbanisation. Urban concentration is not possible without extended urbanisation. Every urban centre inevitably has a hinterland. With the growth of agglomerations, this hinterland expands further outwards, drawing ever-more remote areas into the urban process. It is finally dissolved and dislocated to distant peripheries into specialised zones of production of food and raw materials. Urbanisation can therefore be understood as the simultaneity of processes of concentration and extension. Any form of urbanisation generates not only the spatial concentration of people, means of production, and infrastructure that leads to concentrated urbanisation but also inevitably and simultaneously causes a proliferation and expansion of the urban fabric, resulting in extended urbanisation.[55] Labour, food, water, energy, and raw materials must be brought to urban centres, requiring logistical systems ranging from transport to information networks. Conversely, areas that are characterised by extended urbanisation can also develop into new centralities and urban concentrations. Thus, concentration and extension are inextricably related, with each existing in a dialectical relationship to one another.

The dialectic of concentrated and extended urbanisation contains the intrinsic potential of differential urbanisation. In fact, the relentless transformation of the urban fabric opens up possibilities for creating a different urban world and potentially turns both concentrated and extended urbanisation processes into differential urbanisation. But whereas in territories of concentrated urbanisation, differences are often generated in direct encounters of people, this interaction does usually proceed in a more mediated way in territories of extended urbanisation. Here, differences are generated through movements of people that allow connectivity to distant places and to each other through various forms of migration and social, political, and cultural organisations and networks. In this way, new popular and self-organised centralities may come into existence.

This conceptualisation connects the three moments of urbanisation in a relational, dynamic, and dialectical framework that is not a one-sided and one-directional process but multi-dimensional and contradictory. This conception gives equal analytical emphasis to each term within the dialectics of concentrated, extended, and differential urbanisation, which results in a co-constitutive, mutually transforming dynamic. Urbanisation is thus conceived as an evolving force field in which the three moments of urbanisation continually interact to produce historically specific forms of socio-spatial organisation and uneven development. The modalities and characteristics of these three different vectors of urbanisation are analysed in Part II.

PART II

THE URBANISATION OF THE TERRITORY. A THREE-DIMENSIONAL FRAMEWORK

The study of processes of extended urbanisation is still at its beginning. For a long time, these processes were excluded from analysis by the constricted and one-sided representation of urban space and a selective acknowledgement of urban reality. As shown in Part I, the explicit or implicit dogma of the urban as a bounded settlement space has reached its limits. A decentring of the analytical perspective is needed. The concepts of extended, concentrated, and differential urbanisation avoid this bounding move and allow an open exploration and analysis of the multitude of urbanisation processes that are transforming the world. In light of this, we propose to shift the focus of analysis from urban territories to urbanisation processes and to grasp urbanisation as a process that is continuously reshaping these territories.

Decentring urban research has various consequences. It requires redirecting the view toward supposedly non-urban areas and examining how they have been affected by urbanisation processes. In other words, the investigation should not proceed from an urban centre and then slowly move "outwards" but rather examine the urban transformations of a territory, and in so doing, also include, from the very beginning, those areas usually designated as non-urban. It is important to note that this outside, the non-urban, is not always the "rural." It includes mountains, deserts, forests, and oceans. In this sense, Lefebvre's thesis of complete urbanisation was only a starting point for an encompassing analysis of urbanisation anywhere on the planet.

The concept of planetary urbanisation thus proposes a profound reorientation of urban analysis that not only concerns the analysis of extended urbanisation but also affects the analysis of concentrated and differential urbanisation. Instead of examining an urban territory, we have to focus on the production of this territory and identify and analyse particular urbanisation processes shaping this territory. While the analysis of concentrated urbanisation is presented in detail in the book *Vocabularies for an Urbanising Planet: Theory Building through Comparison*, edited by Christian Schmid and Monika Streule,[56] I look in this chapter particularly at processes of extended urbanisation. The following framework for analysis is based on Lefebvre's theory of the production of space and has been developed in the context of the project "Specificity" by ETH Studio Basel.[57] This framework has been further revised by the collective effort of the entire research team that created this book.[58]

THE CONCEPT OF EXTENDED URBANISATION

Processes of urban extension and the question of the outside of the urban have sparked scholarly debates in architecture and urban studies for years. They have been provoked by a plethora of empirical observations that generated disruptions, interferences, and obfuscations of city-centric conceptualisations and made it necessary to adapt theories and concepts, often by extending the perimeters of observation. Many city-centric approaches already expressed and conceptualised certain aspects and facets of extended urbanisation and tried to find ways to integrate them into more conventional understandings of the urban. However, a conceptual framework for analysing such processes and a broader understanding of extended urbanisation have been missing.

In the 1990s, Terry McGee coined the term *desakota* for densely populated agricultural zones outside large urban centres in Asian monsoon areas.[59] This term is derived from Indonesian *desa* (village) and *kota* (city) and is inspired by the typical Indonesian *kampungs* (villages) that are urbanised through intensification and extension by the people and can develop into lively urban neighbourhoods. As McGee observed in Indonesia, desakota zones form a patchwork of urbanised villages and rice fields beyond the periurban zone more than 30 kilometres from the metropolitan core, often stretching along corridors between agglomerations. Desakota zones might then be followed by densely populated agricultural areas dominated by wet-rice production and sometimes also by sparsely populated "frontier regions." Starting from the example of Indonesia, McGee developed an entire typology of desakota regions in Japan, China, India, and South East Asia that was further elaborated in *The Extended Metropolis,* edited by Norton Ginsburg, Bruce Koppel, and Terry McGee.[60] This work resulted in the definition of the "extended metropolitan region." While this conceptualisation is still tied to a city-centric perspective, it tries to grasp and conceptualise important aspects of extended urbanisation.

The term "extended urbanisation" was first introduced by Roberto Luís Monte-Mór in his seminal work on the urbanisation of the tropical rain forest in Amazonia, Brazil. He noted that this region was not a rural region or "pristine jungle" as it was often portrayed. Monte-Mór describes mining, agriculture, cattle ranching, and forest extraction activities not as rural activities. He instead uses the term extended urbanisation to indicate their profoundly urban nature, even in the face of unstable migrant populations and precarious urban infrastructures, small towns with muddy roads, and palm-tree huts popping up in farming and mining areas amidst the tropical forest.[61] For Monte-Mór, the concept of extended urbanisation expresses a particular social spatiality in which isolated areas are connected and rearticulated. Directly inspired by Lefebvre, he analyses the extension of socio-spatial relations as a dialectical unity of urban centres and the urban fabric. He observes how extended urbanisation penetrates along roads and highways, electric power lines, and communication networks into hitherto non-urbanised spaces, as well as into industrial regions and the islands of rural life in the hinterlands of the big metropolises. In this way, he identifies the extension of urban forms, processes, and practices far beyond cities and agglomerations, integrating rural into

urban-industrial spaces. Thus, mining areas and timber industries, settlements and colonisation projects, and numerous concentrations of commerce and services spread over the territory, combining oppositional spaces—the jungle and the urban fabric—and linking these spaces directly to metropolitan centralities. "The urban phenomenon has reached Brazil's farthest and wildest frontier," Monte-Mór concludes.[62]

Independent of these efforts, Brenner and Schmid developed a similar concept of extended urbanisation without knowing about the ongoing Latin American discussion. Like Monte-Mór, Lefebvre inspired us and we introduced the term to designate forms of urbanisation unfolding beyond the "urban boundary," contributing to and resulting from agglomeration processes. And in a different but related way, we understood it as an analytical concept that is dialectically linked to processes of concentrated and differential urbanisation. In our dialectical conception, extended urbanisation includes the transformation of territories usually located far beyond dense population centres to support the everyday activities and socio-economic dynamics of urban agglomerations. This process results from the most basic socio-metabolic imperatives associated with urban growth—the procurement and circulation of food, water, energy, and construction materials; the processing and management of waste and pollution; and the mobilisation of labour power to support processes of extraction, production, circulation, and management. This involves the ongoing construction and reorganisation of relatively fixed and immobile infrastructures and the enclosure of land from established social uses in favour of privatised, exclusionary, and profit-oriented modes of appropriation for resource extraction, agribusiness, logistics functions, and other activities.[63]

In recent times, extended urbanisation has also been used as a generic umbrella term designating any kind of urban development beyond urban core areas, lumping together extended urbanisation with processes as different as suburbanisation, periurbanisation, and exurbanisation.[64] In other words, in this conception, extended urbanisation designates all sorts of urbanisation processes outside of central urban areas, which blurs and obliterates all distinctions between these processes. This is not just a game of words, as concepts are central elements of analysis and theory, which need careful elaboration and clear definition. Thus, Brenner and Ghosh insist that extended urbanisation "cannot be reduced to the spillover of city-like spaces into peri-urban fringes or contiguous hinterlands."[65] As has become clear in Part I of this chapter, the concept of extended urbanisation was developed to express a qualitatively different process than the expansion of more or less dense settlement spaces, which are still part of concentrated urbanisation. It focuses on sociospatial transformations that underpin and enable agglomeration processes and their resulting wide-ranging, potentially devastating political-ecological impacts across the planet.

The introduction of the concepts of planetary and extended urbanisation has initiated a broad discussion and opened up the field of urban studies to analyses of the entire planet, thus following Lefebvre's call for a renewed urban research: "It is the analyst's responsibility to identify and describe the various forms of urbanisation and explain what happens to the forms, functions, and urban structures that are transformed by the breakup of the ancient city and the process of generalised urbanisation."[66] Along these lines of argumentation, various research efforts have applied the concept of extended urbanisation to investigate a wide variety of urbanisation processes and their economic, social, and political consequences.

DE-CENTRING URBAN ANALYSIS: METHODS, PROCEDURES, AND APPROACHES

Within traditional approaches to urban analysis, extended urbanisation is not discernible. Its recognition is excluded by definitional procedures that declare many forms of extended urbanisation as belonging to the rural or, more broadly, the non-urban realm. Thus, analysing extended urbanisation first requires reversing the dominant perspective

in urban studies. The main goal is no longer to examine various forms of settlement space, spheres of influence, or catchment areas of large agglomerations but to take a comprehensive look at the (urban) transformation of the entire territory. This means decentring the focus of analysis, looking from an ex-centric position, one that starts anywhere and asks where to find traces of urbanisation. It is necessary to examine the diversity of urban manifestations that are inscribing themselves onto territories and turning them into urbanised landscapes. By taking this perspective, urban areas are no longer treated as bounded entities but as open zones: the entire area must be systematically scrutinised. A typical example of this decentred perspective is Marcel Meili's essay "Is the Matterhorn City?"[67]

What does it mean for urban research to epistemologically abandon the urban boundary? In order to examine such extended urban constellations, new methods and procedures of inquiry are needed, along with modes of analysis and mapping that are capable of tracing the multi-dimensional nature and plural determination of urban territories. This means carefully screening the territory to detect traces of urbanisation and trying to grasp changes in the patterns of urbanisation involving smooth transitions and abrupt fault lines, superimpositions, and entanglements of urbanisation processes. Exploring territories of extended urbanisation conveys a very specific kind of experience. Criss-crossing large areas and following the movements of people imposes a different way to orient yourself in the territory, which is unfamiliar for urban studies and full of surprises. Mapping becomes an indispensable method to cope with the large territories to be examined, and various methods of mobile and multi-sited ethnography can be applied, as described in the contributions to this book.[68]

Before the term extended urbanisation was coined, ETH Studio Basel developed a specific research approach to examine such extended urbanising territories. The project *Switzerland: An Urban Portrait* played a pioneering role in developing an appropriate methodology.

The involved research teams selected and analysed small sections of the Earth's surface with a specific set of qualitative methodologies. In a second step, they expanded these punctual insights to provide an encompassing analysis of the entire territory. Cartography played a central role in this task, making it possible to expand individual results to cover the entire surface area of the examined territory. Thus, in the Swiss portrait, it was possible to identify a range of areas that were located clearly outside agglomerations but nevertheless showed traces of various urbanisation processes. These areas were labelled "quiet zones" and "Alpine fallow lands," avoiding the terms rural and urban.[69]

In this way, ETH Studio Basel developed a territorial approach that not only examines how compact forms of the city dissipate through manifold processes and interrelationships within a regional configuration but aims to gain a comprehensive understanding of the urban transformation of the entire territory. Over several years, ETH Studio Basel analysed various forms of extended urbanisation, such as the subtle changes occurring in the still largely agrarian Nile Valley, the massive urban transformations generated by tourism on the Canary Islands, and the urbanisation of the area surrounding Mount Vesuvius near Naples. The following project "Territory" analysed large segments of Earth's surface stretching across several hundred kilometres in the mining region of Minas Gerais in Florida and the Italian Peninsula from Rome to the Adriatic, in the desert area around Muscat, and in the extended environs of Hanoi.[70]

In a similar and related project, Milica Topalović and her team examined the urbanisation of Singapore's hinterland. In the most radical move of decentring the analytical perspective, they engaged the metaphor of the "eclipse" by masking the entire territory of the city-state to make visible all those areas that were concealed so far by the "bright lights" of this global city. The team showed how a densely woven urban fabric came into existence around Singapore, forming a fragmented and splintered extended urban region. But beyond this still relatively compact regional urbanisation, an even larger region can be identified, comprising large parts of South East Asia, as supplying water, food, and sand for the various landfills, as well as cheap and heavily controlled (and gendered) labour. Finally, the planetary hinterland appears to supply all sorts of inputs, raw materials, and labour power.[71]

Nikos Katsikis comprehensively analysed the urbanisation of these global hinterlands, revealing the great variety of landscapes of extended urbanisation, and showed that they constitute most of the planet's surface and are inhabited by at least half of its human population.[72] In their analysis of the hinterlands of the Capitalocene, Brenner and Katsikis sketch out major transformations of non-city spaces to capture the relational interplay between agglomerations and the recomposition and dislocation of the former hinterlands that underpin urban expansion, as well as its wide-ranging, potentially devastating political-ecological impacts across the planet.[73]

Neil Brenner and the Urban Theory Lab tested the concept of extended urbanisation in the alternative mapping project *Extreme Territories of Urbanisation,* which investigates putative outsides, the zones that are commonly represented as rural, remote, wild, and/or untouched by human impact. They looked at regions such as the Amazon, the Arctic, the Gobi Desert, the Himalayas, the Pacific Ocean, the Sahara, Siberia, and even the urbanisation of Earth's atmosphere through satellite systems. The urbanisation of the oceans has already been analysed in more depth. The volume edited by Nancy Couling and Carola Hein explores and discusses the multi-layered process of the urbanisation of the North Sea, and the chapter by Nancy Couling in this book gives a detailed account of how the North Sea has become almost entirely urbanised. She shows how this process can be analysed with precisely the same theoretical and conceptual framework as other territories of extended urbanisation.[74]

In Latin America, Monte-Mór's analysis of the urbanisation of Amazonia marked the starting point for an in-depth analysis of extended urbanisation, which generated a range of essential contributions. Rodrigo Castriota and João Tonucci explore and further develope the concept of extended urbanisation on the tracks of Monte-Mór's theorisation. Miguel Kanai shows how attempts to globalise Manaus in the midst of the Amazon rainforest precipitated territorial restructuring and socio-spatial change far beyond the city's boundaries. Japhy Wilson and Manuel Bayón analyse contested urbanisation processes in the Ecuadorian Amazon.[75] Another well-developed field of research is concerned with the operationalisation of resource extraction, pioneered by Martín Arboleda's analysis of the devastating effects of mining in the Atacama Desert and further developed in his subsequent texts on the planetary ramifications and consequences of the mining industry. Furthermore, the edited volumes *Beyond the Megacity* by Nadine Reis and Michael Lukas and *Emerging Urban Spaces* by Philipp Horn, Paola Alfaro d'Alençon, and Ana Claudia Duarte Cardoso show the great breadth of current research on extended urbanisation with a mainly postcolonial orientation.[76]

Political ecology is another important strand of the analysis of extended urbanisation. A classic in this field is Erik Swyngedouw's study on the urbanisation of water in Guayaquil, Ecuador. Starting from Angelo and Wachsmuth's critique of cityism, the concept of extended urbanisation has opened the field for further investigation of ecology and metabolism.[77] In their analysis of the political ecologies of emergent infectious disease, Brenner and Ghosh show how urbanisation processes have profoundly transformed the very bio-geophysical environments upon which the metabolism of urban life depends, often in destructive, even catastrophic ways, by creating more-than-human political ecologies. These high-intensity, agro-industrial, and extractive landscapes are being subsumed into global circuits of capital.[78] All these observations make it possible to further develop the concept of extended urbanisation and to present a more precise account and definition of various aspects of this process.

THEORISING EXTENDED URBANISATION

From a general point of view, urbanisation can be seen as an encompassing but uneven transformation of the Earth's surface. However, this is not to say that the traces of earlier phases completely disappear. Urbanisation is not—like a footprint in the sand—the direct expression of general social development. The territory is never "empty" or "primal." It is always already occupied by people with their social practices, and it bears material marks and remnants as well as fragments of social and political structures of earlier phases of development. Each successive round of urbanisation encounters the results of earlier phases of the production of space and transforms them anew. André Corboz uses the metaphor of a *palimpsest* to express this process of inscription: The territory is repeatedly worked and reworked, continually overwritten with a new texture until it resembles an old, perforated, and worn parchment.[79]

Lefebvre defines urbanisation as a comprehensive transformation of society that he analyses as a *total phenomenon*. Thus, urbanisation includes the construction of settlements, production sites, logistics facilities, and infrastructure and the development of economic, social, and cultural networks that span and permeate urban space. It is based on global financial, informational, technical, and logistical systems and networks and is thus embedded in the capitalist world system in one way or another. From a general perspective, Lefebvre understands urbanisation as a *process of abstraction*—a given space is transformed into a technologically determined, abstract space—a *second nature*. In this process, "nature" serves as raw material for the production of abstract space. In a society's interaction and confrontation with natural forces, a second nature is produced, which finally is accepted as a given and appears almost as a natural foundation of human activities, despite being determined by concrete social relations that materialised during the course of the urbanisation process. In this way, not only material structures, such as settlements, road patterns, infrastructure grids, property boundaries, and centre-periphery relations, but also power relations are incorporated into the territory. The production of urban space incorporates social relations into the material surface of the planet—this is one of Lefebvre's central propositions on the production of space.[80]

This second nature produces *new scarcities* (*nouvelles raretés*), as Lefebvre calls them: Certain once scarce goods are becoming comparatively abundant due to industrial production, while once abundant "natural" goods, such as vegetation, air, light, and water, which previously had no value because they were not products, became scarce. Everything affected by scarcity has a close relationship to the Earth: the resources of the land (soil, water), those beneath the earth (petroleum, ore), and those above it (air, light), along with products that depend on these resources, such as plant and animal products and energies of various kinds. Since it is no longer possible to take them directly from the inexhaustible reservoir of nature, they now have to be produced and are increasingly drawn into the capitalist process of capital circulation. They become commodities themselves whose use must be paid for.[81] Jason W. Moore goes in a similar direction with his concept of "cheap nature," asserting that capitalism organises nature, including human nature, to create cheap labour, food, energy, and raw materials.[82] This line of thought is the starting point for the conceptualisation of extended urbanisation: The production of food and raw materials for a world market is a central aspect of the industrialisation and operationalisation of landscapes that lead to the consumption and (creative) destruction of nature, and thus also contributes to the contemporary planetary crises of climate, biodiversity, and food.

According to Lefebvre, the history of urbanisation can be understood as a history of socially produced abstraction, turning the *space of nature* (*espace nature*) into abstract space. In this process, space as such becomes a commodity. As Lefebvre explains, the *commodification of space* goes much further than simply selling space "bit by bit." The entire space, including the subsoil and the volumes above the ground and no longer just the land, becomes *exchange value*. This also includes the people living in this space and actually producing it—they become part and parcel of the space that is sold and bought. But exchange implies interchangeability; by becoming a commodity, social space assumes an apparently autonomous reality, made comparable to other things, such as a quantity of sugar or coal.[83] Today, the commodification of social space potentially encompasses the entire planet. This applies both to densely populated agglomerations that are developing into highly commodified and exclusive metropolises as well as to territories of extended urbanisation, which are being enclosed, commodified, and operationalised for agricultural production, the extraction of raw materials, and energy production, which are often degraded, depleted, and destroyed in the process (see Part IV of this chapter).

THE THREE-DIMENSIONAL PRODUCTION OF EXTENDED URBANISATION

These reflections on abstraction, second nature, and commodification of space relate to the general aspects of urbanisation. However, to grasp and analyse concrete, specific urban situations, we have to understand how abstract, general processes materialise in concrete places and form a concrete totality, a specific urban territory with its own features and specific patterns and pathways of urbanisation.

This poses the question of how the abstract and the concrete are related. As we have explained elsewhere, urbanisation (as well as the urban, the city, etc.) is not an empirical but a theoretical category; it is a theoretical abstraction based on general considerations.[84] But what we encounter on the ground are always concrete phenomena. In empirical research, we start from certain observations in specific locations and bring them into conceptualisation, which means that we construct a representation or a concept. As noted in Part I of this chapter, the concept of urbanisation should not be reduced to simply the growth of cities but needs to be understood as a multidimensional process. As mentioned, Lefebvre did not develop a detailed theory of urbanisation that would allow us to further distinguish different urbanisation processes. But in *The Production of Space*, he presented a sophisticated theorisation of the dimensions of the production of space, expressed in a double triad. From a phenomenological point of view, this is perceived, conceived, and lived space; from a linguistic perspective, these are urban practices, representations of space and spaces of representation.[85] Slightly modifying this dialectical grid, we can distinguish three dimensions of urbanisation: 1) The material production of urban space, 2) the production of territorial regulations, and 3) the production of urban experiences in everyday life.[86]

Firstly, we can analyse how a spatial practice produces a *material territory* that can be perceived by the five senses. Spatial practice creates connections and a system of networks and leads to the formation of centres and peripheries. It produces an urban fabric that covers increasing parts of the territory and enables as well as hinders social actions. Because centrality generates privileged and potentially productive places, it is always contested.

Secondly, we can explore how urbanisation is conceived, planned, and controlled. This is directly related to the representation of urban space and, thus, to how urban units are defined and demarcated. We subsume these aspects under the term *territorial regulation*, which encompasses the rules that guide the production of the built environment, determine the use of the land, and also dictate what will be localised in which part of the territory. This trans-scalar process of territorial regulation is highly complex and dynamic because it brings together a wide variety of contradictory social forces and is, in most cases, highly contested.

Thirdly, we have to consider the question of lived space, or more precisely, the *experience of urban space* in everyday life. This depends on the social forces that create an urban space by initiating interactions and relationships between people and places. It is related to the production of meaning and generates spaces of representation that are linked to symbolisms and (collective) experiences. In this process, specific patterns of social, economic, and cultural differentiation evolve that can be seen as a main element of the specificity of an urban territory.

This three-dimensional conception of urbanisation resonates with David Harvey's approach that starts from a critical political economy of space and regards urbanisation as the process of the production of the built environment. However, as urbanisation unfolds, it is not only the space economy that changes but also the common understanding and the social meaning of the urban. Consequently, Harvey also analysed the urbanisation of consciousness and the production of an urban experience.[87]

THE MATERIAL PRODUCTION OF URBAN SPACE

The first dimension shaping urbanisation is the material transformation of the territory. The production of a specific territory starts with its appropriation through human activities that generate traces and artefacts, which initially are ephemeral but increasingly condense and solidify. More persistent material patterns develop over a long period of time, sometimes over centuries. In this way, what Lefebvre calls an "urban fabric" (*tissue urbain*) is formed. It gradually emerges, thickens, spreads out across the territory, and transforms both urban and rural areas. Lefebvre does not define this term clearly nor limit its meaning only to morphology. The urban fabric, he explains, forms the economic basis of urban society, the *material support* through which urban life pervades rural areas.[88]

This concept of the urban fabric initiated a broader understanding of planetary and extended urbanisation.[89] A whole urban system of material objects and infrastructure is realised as part of this fabric: roads, highways, train lines, canals, ports, shipping lanes, airports, pipelines, high-voltage lines, and logistics, energy, and information systems.[90] The urban fabric is based on the microelectronic revolution, the introduction and expansion of the World Wide Web, the far-reaching effects of smartphones and social media increasing the mobility of people, the massive expansion of air traffic, and the introduction of intermodal containers, allowing for the direct transition from waterways to railways and roads. The building and maintenance of this logistical infrastructure require substantial long-term investments. Therefore, the full planetary extension of urbanisation only arrived with the globalisation of the international financial system. It also necessitates regulations and agreements allowing for the smooth and frictionless movement of goods, capital, information, and corresponding state policies. Only on this basis does the establishment of global production networks with sophisticated supply chains become possible.

The continuous expansion and thickening of the urban fabric make it possible to increase the scale of interactions and extend the metabolic support systems of urban areas. This loosens the dependency of agglomerations on their immediate hinterlands and advances the process of urbanisation until it reaches a planetary scale. Accordingly, territories of extended urbanisation are often affected by infrastructure-led developments; in this context, Miguel Kanai and Seth Schindler speak of an "infrastructure scramble"[91] (see Part IV of this chapter). These processes are exemplified in this book by the "highway revolution" in India that generates corridor urbanisation (Bathla) and the almost complete operationalisation of the North Sea through oil extraction, wind farms, and shipping lanes (Couling).

The extension of the urban fabric facilitates all kinds of *movements* of people that crisscross the territory and, in doing so, bind it together and create new forms of interaction. While concentrated urbanisation induces centripetal movements towards urban agglomeration nodes, territories of extended urbanisation are usually characterised by longer, more sporadic, and varied forms of mobility. Various practices of circular or temporary migration develop, whereby people only migrate for a certain time or follow a recurrent pattern of returning regularly to their places of departure. AbdouMaliq Simone understands movements in a very broad sense as a multifaceted strategy of urban survival, reflecting the increasing material unavailability of specific urban territories as platforms on which to constitute a stable and coherent social existence.[92]

Alice Hertzog's analysis of the West African Corridor in this book highlights the great variety of movements by people searching for opportunities, operating small businesses, crossing borders to take advantage of fluctuations in prices and exchange rates of currencies, connecting widely ramified social networks, and maintaining extended family ties. With these movements and their related activities, people create a polycentric and multi-scalar social reality, thus contributing to the generation of extended urban territories.

The urban fabric is more or less tightly woven, with smaller and larger interstices between the strands of its mesh. It contains hubs and nodes with intense interactions while interactions at the outer reaches fade. Therefore, one of the most important aspects of the urban condition is the *dialectic of centres and peripheries*: urban centres never exist without diverse peripheries that supply food and raw materials, water, and energy; they function as dumping grounds or provide recreational areas and serve for ideological and mental compensation. The periphery is not just a "natural space," "countryside," or "non-city," but a relational space that can be defined through its relationship with the centres that dominate it. In every territory, centres and peripheries form a specific pattern that manifests itself on any scale—from the neighbourhood to polycentric urban regions up to the global system of metropolises—thus creating multi-scalar realities.

For this reason, Pierre Veltz has replacedthe concept of agglomeration with a relational conception of centrality.[93] As he shows, centres become increasingly interconnected and economically specialised as a result of globalisation, thereby forming complex networks that are generating new centralities at nodes of transport networks, at places with certain economic, cultural, or scenic qualities, in emerging tourist regions, or even in favourably located peripheries, where, for example, special economic zones are created. Veltz calls these new territorial configurations "territories by networks," which replace the former "territories of networks." They are no longer clearly defined units within a nested hierarchy but interconnected condensation nuclei in an immense and indecipherable network on a planetary scale. In this sense, networks have a double effect: they increase both centrality and global connectivity. Therefore, networks are driving extended urbanisation. At the same time, they also push concentrated urbanisation, when nodes of networks develop into centralities and huge agglomerations. Depending on the situation, very different forms of the urban fabric evolve. Whatever the concrete pattern may be, the urban fabric has a dual character: It forms a structure that guides action and predefines further development, and it facilitates processes of interaction, but it also channels them and thus impedes and sometimes even precludes alternative options of development.

As David Harvey has shown the production of the urban fabric is determined by the *dialectics of fixity and motion*, the contradiction between the dynamics of urbanisation and the permanence, the persistence of the spatial structures it produces.[94] On the one hand, the urbanisation process tends to overcome all spatial barriers and create ever closer connections between more and more areas, thereby accelerating the exchange of people, goods, and information. On the other hand, the urban fabric is immobile and rigid, and its production requires massive long-term capital investments that need a long time to generate profits. This is one of the key reasons why urbanisation manifests such a high degree of path dependency. The built environment cannot be changed without causing massive destruction and devaluation of existing investments. Sooner or later, the built environment and, thus, the urban

fabric will come into conflict with the ever-evolving dynamics of socio-economic and technological change.[95] This may have dramatic consequences when an existing urban fabric becomes obsolete and devalued, and once flourishing regions are left behind, facing decline and peripheralisation, as is the case in industrial areas that turn into brownfield sites. Technological innovations and automation can also devalue existing settlement structures, such as the rationalisation and operationalisation of extraction sites, causing a dramatic reduction of their labour force, thus devaluing material and social infrastructure, as is the case in the Carajás mine in Amazonia (see Castriota in this volume).

With the new centralities, new peripheries are formed in a reciprocal movement, and many previously agrarian and industrial areas sometimes face dramatic processes of *peripheralisation*. The transformation, commodification, and sometimes even complete destruction of centralities not only affect the residents and businesses of these places but directly or indirectly concern the entire population of an urban territory. As a result, a complex urban topography emerges, characterised by the simultaneity of processes of peripheralisation and centralisation. This dynamic particularly affects territories of extended urbanisation, as the discussion in Part IV of this chapter will show. While processes of extended urbanisation have an inherent tendency towards peripheralisation, the evacuation of social energies, the loss of population and jobs, and the homogenisation and reduction of social wealth, they also open up possibilities for the development of new connections and centralities. Lefebvre's call for a right to centrality in *The Urban Revolution* expresses these different moments; it demands the right of access to the material and immaterial resources of centrality, to the possibilities and opportunities an urban centre can offer—the right to a renewed urbanity. The struggle for the creation, maintenance, and defence of popular centralities created by the people plays an important role in both territories of concentrated and extended urbanisation.

THE PRODUCTION OF TERRITORIAL REGULATIONS

As has become evident in the preceding subsection, the urban fabric of a territory has a determining character. It guides social activities, suggests certain actions, hinders or prevents others, and can be understood as a material incorporation of instructions. This means that social relations inscribe themselves into a territory, solidifying and creating an urban fabric that, in turn, determines human actions by "allocating a space" to them by defining their possibilities and limitations in space and time. Although, crucially, it is not only materiality that is a determinant but also the rules that pertain to this materiality and the power that is protecting and enforcing those rules.[96] Power is thus incorporated into any territory in a wide variety of ways. This, in turn, raises the further question of how a territory is controlled and how urbanisation processes are guided and steered.

The rules and procedures that guide urbanisation arise from specific constellations of social forces, which generate and develop specific forms of *territorial regulation*. In the broadest sense, territorial regulations establish how a territory may be used and appropriated. This concept refers directly to the French regulation approach, which understands "regulation" as a set of explicit and implicit "rules of the game" that apply in a particular field.[97] Territorial regulations allocate places for activities and determine what people are allowed to do and where.[98] The framework of rules that constitutes territorial regulation is complex since it includes not only the formal and informal agreements and rules in the realms of construction and architecture, urban development and design, and spatial and urban planning; it also concerns the procedures and modalities of decision making and the social processes of negotiation that affect the use of the territory. Of central importance are rules regulating land and housing markets, patterns of ownership, and the various land rights regimes, but also the organisation of daily life and the use of public spaces. Territorial regulations result in norms and ideals determining how people should live, what is beautiful and what is ugly, and so on. Norms and rules are often applied subconsciously, and specific forms of problem-solving develop that people regularly return to.

Territorial regulations are not static but dynamic and often contested; rules are often being challenged and breached, the land is occupied, used and transformed, and various forms of informality and illegality may evolve. Thus, contradictory and complex arrangements of regulation may develop, and sometimes regimes of formal legislation coexist with traditional rules or customary rights.[99] The spectrum of forms of territorial regulation is vast, which is also one of the main reasons urban territories are so distinctive. As a consequence, territorial regulations can be very difficult to research and are generally hard to understand for people not familiar with the local context.

It turned out in our research that territories of extended urbanisation are particularly demarcated by a clash between designated rural and urban regulations. Territories that are defined as urban may be subjected to different rules than those designated as rural. Planning laws often limit land use of rural areas to agricultural production and related activities. This opens up all sorts of tactics to either evade or violate land use restrictions or to find ways to officially turn rural land into urban land, generating massive windfall profits as the rent on urban land is usually much higher. State actors often play vital roles in the land game. Such strategies and struggles play key roles in the urbanisation of China and India and are further discussed in the contributions by Kit Ping Wong and Nitin Bathla in this book.

In peripheral and sparsely settled zones, local and regional governments often lack resources, and thus the nation-state has much stronger leverage than in large agglomerations with strong city governments. Territories of extended urbanisation are often determined by national strategies, which aim to homogenise legislations and procedures and push the implementation of infrastructure and real estate projects. Because of this, extended urbanisation is often shaped and enforced by a wide range of specific *state strategies*. These strategies seek to facilitate urbanisation by attacking traditional and collective land rights and promoting the financialisation of land, opening up vast territories for capital accumulation through enclosure and expropriation. This creates the conditions for continued urban expansion through massive investments into the urban fabric.[100] As Gavin Shatkin shows, such projects may generate enormous profits for national and international investors and also political and personal gains for state actors. Sai Balakrishnan calls areas along Indian urban corridors "zones of variegated sovereignty" because of the complexity of regulatory arrangements. And Rodrigo Castriota's contribution to this book on the mining projects in Carajás highlights the multiple roles of the state as owner, legislator, and controller.

Of particular importance to extended urbanisation are strategic infrastructural projects, such as high-speed railways, highway systems, and complex infrastructural initiatives that impose an overarching logic on the territory, such as the "Plan Puebla Panama," a cross-border infrastructure project for southern Mexico and Central America that was ultimately abandoned.[101] More recently, China's "One Belt, One Road" initiative became not only a driver for investment and political domination but also opened up vast territories for commodification and urbanisation.[102] Nitin Bathla shows how the Indian state launched an immense highway program that opens up huge areas across the country for extended urbanisation. In all these cases, extended urbanisation was not primarily generated through the spillover of agglomeration processes but through encompassing state strategies that are propelling the urbanisation of a territory. These processes of enclosure, expropriation, and dispossession are so violent that they often provoke fierce struggles and massive protest movements[103] (see Part IV of this chapter).

All these examples show that state actors play critical roles in the advancement of extended urbanisation. The planetary spread of urbanisation is only possible through the massive intervention of nation-states, their manifold infrastructure projects, and their regulatory control; nation-states often strongly support and push for the enclosure and commodification of land. In this context, Lefebvre argues that a new space has emerged on a planetary scale, which he calls "state space" (*espace étatique*). In this process, states became the agents that direct and monitor the production of space, control the national resources, the organisation and planning of the entire territory, and design, launch, and finance megaprojects and massive infrastructure systems—usually hand in hand with private capital and corporate investors. The state is not necessarily homogenous. It has different scales, origins, and actors with sometimes conflicting interests. In this way, state space is not a unified power but a contradictory and fragmented entity.[104]

In his book *New State Spaces*, Brenner further develops this concept and applies it to the analysis of emerging regional urban configurations.[105] In her contribution to this book, Kit Ping Wong details how the Chinese state decided and launched extended rural urbanisation in Dongguan, which was then implemented by local towns and village collectives in a contradictory and sometimes turbulent process. And Nancy Couling explains how ocean space has been turned from an open space and a vast commons into a territory of extended urbanisation through military, regulatory, and material interventions by several nation-states to possess and operationalise ocean space.

In Lefebvre's analysis, state space and particularly the worldwide system of state spaces—together with the world market—constitute a general level of social reality. He contrasts this far order or *general level* of social reality with the near order, the *private level* of everyday life. In between these two levels, Lefebvre places an intermediate, mediating one that he identifies as the *urban level*. His thesis is that in the wake of urbanisation, this intermediate urban level tends to be pulverised by the interaction of the private and the general levels. While the state attacks from above and tries to control and plan the entire national territory and seeks to homogenise this territory and thus suppress the specificity of places and locations, corporate capital moves from below, from the private level, by commodifying, standardising, and fragmenting everyday life. In this process, the urban level tends to disappear, losing its mediating capacity.[106] In territories of extended urbanisation, this mediating level is usually particularly weak because of the fragmented character of the local political entities. Therefore, regional popular movements and organisations that can organise and mobilise networks of solidarity and support are of particular importance to the creation and defence of participation and self-determination in such areas.

THE PRODUCTION OF URBAN EXPERIENCES IN EVERYDAY LIFE

In Lefebvre's analysis, one of the main contradictions of urbanisation is the confrontation between *abstract* and *differential space*. While the production of a second nature includes a process of industrialisation and commodification and thus leads to homogenisation and abstract space, urbanisation also creates the conditions of a different space, a space of meeting and encounter, a differential space, where differences come to light and interact with each other. In such a space, separations and space-time distances are replaced by oppositions, contrasts, superimpositions, and the juxtaposition of disparate realities.[107] Urban space can be defined as a place where differences know, recognise, and explore each other and affirm or negate each other. However, difference as the generating force of the urban can only unfold when different people and activities come together. In other words, through centrality. But centrality requires social interaction and thus mediation so that it is accessible to all parts of society. Likewise, centrality as a place of meeting and encounter can also contribute to mediation. And finally, differences presuppose mediation so that they can flourish and enter into a productive exchange. In this sense, in Lefebvre's dialectics of the urban,

difference, centrality, and mediation are mutually related and constitutive.

According to a widely shared assumption, these qualities can only develop in dense and diverse urban spaces. It seems that only in "cities" can differences unfold, centrality flourish, and mediation become effective. This assumption led Mark Davidson and Kurt Iveson, in their critique of planetary urbanisation, to ask: Can we give up the city as a political project?[108] But Lefebvre already gave a dialectical answer to this question half a century before when he explained that urbanisation could be a devastating, homogenising force, but it also has the inherent potential to disrupt borders and limitations, increase exchanges, give people access to material and immaterial resources, create new centralities, and enable differences to flourish. This potential is expressed with the concept of differential urbanisation. It is important to understand that differential urbanisation can result from both concentrated and extended urbanisation.

A closer look reveals that differences can develop in a twofold manner: On the one hand, they result from the totality of interactions and relationships between different people with their own histories, experiences, knowledge, abilities, and needs that are coming together in a specific place. On the other, differences can also be generated by networks. As urbanisation overcomes all kinds of borders, it can link previously distant and separate areas and connect and articulate different (near and far) places and situations. As Alice Hertzog shows in the example of the West African Corridor in this book, mobility and movements can create new centralities and places of encounter and thus foster difference and urbanity. The crucial question, however, is precisely how such urban experiences unfold and develop and how people adapt to or resist processes of extended urbanisation.

The Latin American discussion places great importance on this political aspect of extended urbanisation. Monte-Mór has shown that the development of urban practice accompanied extended urbanisation in Brazil.

The struggles for control of the collective means of reproduction and the claims for citizenship that emerged in the 1970s in the larger urban centres began to extend to more remote places in the 1980s. Today, urban social movements in Amazonia also include, among others, indigenous peoples, rubber tappers, and landless workers.[109] Similarly, in his research on operational landscapes of resource extraction in Colombia and Chile, Arboleda shows that these processes drive marginalisation and dispossession and enable opportunities for encounters between previously isolated communities or individuals, generating new centralities. The strong social mobilisations in many parts of Latin America against mining, agribusiness, logging, energy, and oil extraction projects also created new forms of solidarity between local communities and national and international advocacy networks, linking operational landscapes and large urban agglomerations in mutually transformative ways. Arboleda notes, "It is precisely in the opening of avenues for increased communication and interaction where the emancipatory promise of planetary urbanisation lies."[110] In the same vein, Stefan Kipfer shows how resistance by indigenous peoples to a pipeline project that connects a tar sand extraction site in the Canadian province of Alberta to global markets is able to also connect various struggles along the pipeline, from the production site to metropolitan and interstitial spaces. Wilson explains how the mere planning of the Plan Puebla Panamá (see above) sparked widespread local resistance, which in turn also forged new links between different groups and organisations, such as the movement fighting against airport development on the outskirts of Mexico City and the resistance against the Isthmus of Tehuantepec Megaproject in southern Mexico.[111] Several contributions to this book trace conflicts sparked by extended urbanisation: Castriota follows the struggle of mining workers who lost their jobs and used their knowledge of the area to squat land in the vicinity of the mine. Bertuzzo refers to the massive struggles against projects to construct new factories on the outskirts of Kolkata, in Nandigram and Singur, as an example of struggles against the transformation of agricultural land. And Bathla examines struggles against the completion of a highway project in Delhi. Many more struggles and also various forms of "quiet" resistance should be taken into consideration. However, we must be aware that examples of successful mobilisations have to be juxtaposed with many other moments in which processes of extended urbanisation are brutally enforced by politics, police, and military, leading to displacements, dispossession, and marginalisation.

TOWARDS A RELATIONAL UNDERSTANDING OF URBANISATION PROCESSES

The theoretical framework presented here allows us to draw some initial conclusions on the processes of extended urbanisation. The proliferation of the urban fabric and the production of planetary connectivity through the massive extension of transport and communication infrastructure is enabling all sorts of movements and connections that transform territories in various ways. State strategies actively promote, support, guide, and launch processes of extended urbanisation to open up new territories for commodification and capital accumulation. As a result, the urban fabric spreads further to cover increasingly remote places, whether agricultural land, rainforests, or sea spaces.

These developments spark struggles for the re-appropriation of land and livelihoods across the landscapes of extended urbanisation, which can thus be understood as struggles against the devastating forces of planetary urbanisation and abstract space and for self-organisation and self-determination. These struggles are demanding and realising differential space through their resistance and create alternative networks and popular centralities. In this sense, they are not demanding a "right to the city" anymore, but a "right to difference" or a "right to space" in Lefebvre's words, or a "right to the planet," as formulated by Marcelo Lopez de Souza.[112] These planetary struggles for access to the material and immaterial resources and for recognition and self-determination in everyday life play out in very different ways.

All these processes and actions produce territories of extended urbanisation that are not bounded areas but open zones. They are often transformed by several overlapping and imbricating processes.

Territories of extended urbanisation are thus constituted by a wide range of urbanisation processes and result in a great variety of territories marked by different socio-spatial situations in everyday life. In Part IV of this book, I will have a closer look at the different processes of extended urbanisation we were able to identify in our case studies.

PART III

FROM CONCENTRATED TO EXTENDED URBANISATION. THE SEARCH FOR AN ELUSIVE URBAN BOUNDARY

The concept of extended urbanisation was developed to address urgent questions raised by the observation of a variety of new phenomena and processes that could not be explained by existing concepts in urban theory. Within classical approaches, extended urbanisation is not visible because it is excluded by the very definition of the city as a bounded unit. As a consequence, the question of the urban boundary has haunted urban research since its beginnings, as empirical findings continuously undermined and challenged traditional concepts of the city, indicating that some urbanisation processes extend beyond the supposed urban borders. This raised the question of how to grasp these processes and, consequently, how to theoretically delimit urban areas and define "the city." The goal of Part III is to discuss the range of explicit and implicit answers to this question in urban theory and research and to evaluate the conceptual limits of those answers. If we want to understand extended urbanisation, it is crucial to carefully analyse the problematic of the urban boundary because it gives us many hints on the modalities and the differences between extended and concentrated urbanisation.

The idea of the urban boundary has hampered the analysis of extended urbanisation in many ways and influenced how urban theory interpreted, named, and analysed urbanisation processes and urban forms. Notably, two binary conceptions have impeded the problematisation of the urban boundary: the urban-rural binary and the city-suburb binary. The question of city and countryside and the related difficulties of distinguishing rural and urban areas have sparked extensive debates in the histories of urban and rural studies, which are too extensive to analyse here in detail. However, it is essential to note that the rural usually served as the defining criteria for the identification of the outer boundary of the urban, and this made it almost impossible to apprehend extended urbanisation. There were always processes of extended urbanisation, but these were obfuscated by this binary conception and thus not noticed nor further analysed.

The second important binary that impedes the recognition of extended urbanisation is the distinction between city and suburb or between urban centre and urban periphery. This binary has become an epistemological trap, as it has constructed two types of the urban—a kind of inner-city urban and a seemingly antagonistic outer-city urban. This construction had considerable, long-standing effects and structured the analysis of urban settlements. However, a closer look reveals that this dualism and the internal boundary that it involves are, in many cases, irrelevant or even do not exist. Contemporary urban territories are much too complex and differentiated just to divide them into two different parts. A further consequence of this conceptual binary is that it presupposes a third term: the rural. After all, if there is an inner and an outer city, or city and suburbia, there must also be something beyond—the non-city, the countryside. Both parts, the urban core and the urban periphery, are accordingly bound in the superordinate concept of agglomeration, and this binary leads, again, to the trap of city centrism.

However, the urbanisation of what is "outside" the urban continued to destabilise the very core of the concept of the city for many decades. The relentless extension of settlement areas and the increasing global connectivity led to various forms of urban sprawl. Migration processes, global production networks, metabolic relations, and all sorts of spillover effects transgressed the putative urban boundaries, and the urban and the rural became increasingly enmeshed in shared processes and activities. Throughout the history of urban studies, new concepts and terms have been created to grasp these emerging processes. They highlighted connections and interdependencies and

identified catchment areas, commuter zones, labour markets, and production clusters to define various expanded urban units and city regions, such as functional urban regions and metropolitan regions. These definitions served different purposes and found a wide range of practical applications, and they can still be useful to a certain degree. However, they have to be inserted into the broader context of the urbanisation of the planet.

THE URBAN AND THE RURAL, THE CITY AND THE COUNTRYSIDE

Any analysis of urbanisation is confronted with an important theoretical obstacle—the concept of the rural. While the idea of the city as a bounded unit has haunted urban studies, the imagination of a rural-urban dichotomy has also severely limited the analysis of urbanisation. The two concepts are directly related: If the urban boundary demands a distinction between urban and non-urban areas, the non-urban is often regarded as the rural. It is indeed astonishing to see how persistent the reference to the rural has been in urban studies. It is still strongly present in current debates and often related to mythical images and simplifying preconceptions, and in many cases, it is also laden with strong ideological meaning. Most surprising, however, is the fact that the content of the rural is often taken for granted. The rural seems to be immediately understandable without requiring any further analysis or definition, to be applicable to all possible situations, a supposed universal constellation persisting since the beginning of human history.

However, if we look at territories or landscapes considered rural today, we are confronted with a disturbing variety of situations. These range from persisting subsistence economies to highly industrialised and operationalised zones of agricultural production, from peripheralised regions marked by emigration and shrinking economic activities to urban park landscapes in metropolitan areas, and from agricultural landscapes destroyed by enclosure and commodification to peri-urban zones affected by gentrification and megaprojects. It is questionable what keeps such different situations together and whether it is useful to subsume them under the single category of "the rural."

As argued above, it has to be considered that the rural, like the urban, is a theoretical concept, which is always based on explicit or implicit definitions and assumptions. A closer look reveals that these definitions vary enormously over time and space. It is thus crucial to remind ourselves that depending on the situation and theory, quite different definitions of the city and the urban exist and coexist. The same applies to the rural and the countryside. For the field of *rural studies*, as Keith H. Halfacree shows, the definition of the rural has been in dispute since the beginning of the twentieth century.[113] Criteria used for its definition vary widely and include the dominance of agricultural production, low population density, the absence of large cities, a certain way of life or cultural form, the prevalence of certain traditions, lifestyles and forms of socialisation, the relative autonomy of rural communities, as well as many more. Already half a century ago, Henri Mendras highlighted the paradox that such criteria refer directly to the urban: "The peasant is defined in relation to the city. If there is no city there is no peasant, and if the society is entirely urbanized there is no peasant either."[114]

Other approaches focus on identity and define the rural as a representation of space framing social life. Nevertheless, such definitions postulate a rupture between the perceived and the lived, or the material and the imaginary, and sometimes implicitly admit that there might be a material process of urbanisation that is imagined or represented as "rural."[115] The rural is also an important category of national, regional, and urban planning, thus linked to territorial regulation. In this case, the rural-urban distinction has direct consequences for land use, forms of governance, strategies of spatial development, the availability of subsidies, and the organisation of social reproduction. This is particularly of great relevance in China and India (as expounded by Wong and Bertuzzo in this volume).

In contrast, in the field of *urban studies,* the rural is often simply defined as the non-city. In fact, many approaches only define the city and relegate all the rest of the inhabited territory to the category of the rural. Many scholarly writings do not even offer any definition of the rural, and it is therefore highly unclear what they understand by urban and rural at all. Accordingly, it remains equally nebulous what the urban-rural relationship might be, which is, like the rural itself, often treated as universal and conceptualised as *the* urban-rural relation or contradiction. This contradiction, however, is not universal but differs fundamentally in different societies. As Marx and Engels analysed, the relationship between town and country changed fundamentally from Western antiquity to the European Middle Ages and then again with emerging capitalism.[116] Lefebvre built on this periodisation and identified the surprising sublation (*Aufhebung*) of the rural-urban contradiction in his thesis on complete urbanisation. Wingshing Tang criticised Lefebvre's generalisation and pointed out that the rural-urban relationship in contemporary China fundamentally differs from Lefebvre's account. There, relations between rural and urban are strongly related to China's specific power relations and institutional forms of territorial control.[117] A closer examination reveals that the relationship between urban and rural areas—if we want to keep this binary conception at all—depends on concrete situations and circumstances, conditions and constellations, traditions, forms of land ownership and territorial regulations, and political and ideological orientations. It is not universal but inevitably specific.

Further problems are generated by the imbrication of urban and rural realms. Maintaining notions of separate urban and rural lifeworlds is highly doubtful since these are effectively interconnected in many ways. The "classic" migration from rural to urban areas alone, which still accounts for much of the growth of agglomerations, establishes long-lasting relationships between the places of origin and the destinations of migration.[118] Moreover, in large parts of the world, processes of circular and temporary migration have long established close ties and relationships between rural and urban areas, which are now multiplied and further differentiated by the creation of planetary connectivity through revolutions in transport and communication (see Part IV of this chapter).

Finally, we have to look at the consequences of urbanisation processes that transgress all sorts of borders, transforming both the rural and the urban. In this process, the rural is integrated and inscribed into the urban, but the urban is also inscribed into the rural. Despite his hypothesis of the complete urbanisation of society, Lefebvre insisted that the transformation of the rural-urban contradiction does not mean that the rural reality completely disappears. On the contrary, the rural continues in many ways, even intensifies, and is incorporated into urban life as material reality, as a social form, as a representation of space, as a political instrument, or ideological concept.[119]

Indeed, imprints of the rural in urban territories are well-known and experienced in everyday life. For instance, the specific land regime of indigenous villages has strongly influenced the high-rise development of Hong Kong. The narrow, winding street patterns originating from rural land use are still a nuisance for daily contemporary life in the outer boroughs of London or the banlieues of Paris. The persisting village structure, as well as entrenched political power relations dating back to the Middle Ages, are determining recent urbanisation processes in the extended region of Zurich. Customary rural rights are strongly influencing the urban development of Lagos, and the Kampungs that turned from rural to urban villages play a key role in Jakarta, to give just some examples.[120] This shows that the rural enters urbanisation in many ways; it is inscribed and incorporated through legal regulations, land rights, plot boundaries, customs, traditions, and all sorts of material structures and artefacts. But we should not characterise these phenomena as an amalgamation of the rural and the urban. They are, in fact, part of how the production

of space proceeds, namely by incorporating and thus preserving spaces produced under preceding social formations (as seen in Part II of this chapter).

On the other hand, urbanisation is also radically transforming rural areas, a fact that is widely acknowledged today in rural studies. As early as 1967, in his widely discussed book *The Vanishing Peasant*, Henri Mendras observed the industrialisation and urbanisation of agriculture in France. Three decades later, Farshad Araghi presented a history of global depeasantisation and deruralisation as part of the political history of capitalism.[121] And today, we are discussing the operationalisation of agricultural landscapes on a planetary scale. The concept of the rural is not really helpful in understanding these processes; instead, a turn towards the *agricultural question* may open the way to extended urbanisation. We will look at the relationship between agricultural landscapes and urbanisation at the beginning of Part IV.

SUBURB AND URBAN PERIPHERY

The analysis of extended urbanisation is confronted with a second theoretical obstacle arising from another binary conception: The distinctions between city and suburb or the urban centre and the urban periphery. Cerdà distinguished between *urbe* and *suburbe* in his famous text, and like the term urbanisation, "suburbanisation" was adopted in Anglo-American literature. In the North American context, the paradigmatic "suburb," as it developed after the Second World War, used to be a monofunctional accumulation of middle-class detached houses with front and backyards as the material support of a "suburban way of life." However, the city-suburb distinction poses considerable difficulties on conceptual grounds and in empirical research. Suburbs can be defined politically as municipalities beyond the central city; geographically as being located at the edge; morphologically as less dense than the urban core; socially as relatively homogenous; and functionally as lacking central facilities and activities. Suburbs are also defined as places with a lifestyle that is clearly different from an urban lifestyle. Many of those criteria are, of course, dubious assumptions or stereotypes. In fact, the suburb was never the universal model that Anglo-American urban studies were pretending. The volume *What's in a Name?* edited by Richard Harris and Charlotte Vorms, and Christian Topalov's summary of the project of a multilingual dictionary of urban concepts present a wide range of terms for urban configurations at urban peripheries ranging from *banlieue, borgata, reparto, barrio, favela,* and many more.[122] Yimin Zhao reflects on improper urban vocabularies and insufficient translations at the example of the urban periphery of Beijing.[123] The large research project "global suburbanisms" led by Roger Keil gives an illuminating impression of the multitude of urban forms and the great diversity of patterns and pathways of urbanisation developing in urban peripheries all over the world.[124] Unsurprisingly, attempts to use the terms "suburbanisation" and "suburbanism" as umbrella terms for all possible processes and urban forms beyond the urban core have posed major problems and received various criticisms. On the one hand, these terms construct a dualism or even a contradiction between city and suburb. On the other, they subsume the wide variation of urban forms and urbanisation processes evolving worldwide in peripheral urban areas under one Western concept.[125]

The city-suburb binary was further destabilised when researchers detected a range of "new urban phenomena" in the 1980s that questioned the "familiar" Western forms and shapes of the urban. New business districts and centralities emerged, called variously urban villages, outer cities, or edge cities,[126] driven by neoliberal politics and the massive extension of transport and information networks, allowing for more flexible production of urban space and a much higher variability of land use patterns. Furthermore, parts of the urban periphery were soon engulfed by the constantly expanding urban areas and thus not located at the edge of agglomerations anymore. These urban transformations led to a paradigm shift in Western urban studies, which foregrounded the

emergence of new polycentric urban forms, ex-centric urban developments, and political and social fragmentation, turning the metropolis inside out and outside in and thus generating an urban form famously called *exopolis* by Edward W. Soja.[127] At the same time, the urban periphery densified and became more diverse, with more "urban" characteristics and features, such as attractive public spaces, public transport, and even processes of gentrification and displacement of low-income people; these processes were labelled with terms like "post-suburbanisation" or "urban intensification."[128] Furthermore, as a result of the ongoing urban explosion, new urban fragments popped up across all continents, and new towns, technopoles, export processing zones, megaprojects, and bypass urbanisms emerged in various urban peripheries.[129]

Recently, a very different understanding of the urban periphery has been introduced into the Anglo-American discourse through translations of older texts and new interventions from Latin America. As Michael Lukas and Nadine Reis reconstructed, in the 1950s, when massive urbanisation in Latin America began in earnest, the term *peripheral urbanisation* was introduced in scholarly debates.[130] This term was originally linked to the dependency theory and thus to uneven socioeconomic development on a global scale. Thus, the term periphery had a double meaning: dependent on Western countries and located at the periphery of urban centres. In this way, Aníbal Quijano analysed the urbanisation of the economic structure of Latin America and the marginalisation of rural migrants in the peripheries of the dependently industrialised urban centres—this was conceptualised at the time as the "periphery of the periphery."[131]

The concept of peripheral urbanisation has been recently revived by a new discussion initiated by Theresa Caldeira. She uses this term in a different sense, namely as a metaphor to characterise pervasive urban spaces in the global South that are produced differently than those of North Atlantic urbanisms. She looks particularly at spaces that are inherently unstable and contingent, produced mainly through auto construction and unfolding transversally in relation to official logics. Caldeira explicitly does not understand periphery as a spatial category because it "does not simply refer to a spatial location in the city … but rather to a way of producing space that can be anywhere."[132] This conception is gaining traction in global urban studies, and further destabilises ideas of an urban-suburban binary. It also illustrates the impossible mission of finding any kind of coherence in the conceptualisation of urbanisation processes in urban peripheries across the world.

It is important to understand that all these forms of urbanisation, whether they are called suburbanisation or peripheral urbanisation, are processes of concentrated urbanisation because they lead to the agglomeration of people (residents, migrant workers, visitors etc.), jobs, investments, infrastructure, functions, and activities. The identification and delimitation of these agglomerations did not pose major analytical problems as long as urban areas were still morphologically demarcated from their surroundings in relatively clear ways—even if the surrounding areas were not necessarily non-urban. The concept of agglomeration in this classical sense also played a central role in critical urban studies. Manuel Castells regarded the agglomeration as the basic unit of the reproduction of labour power, and David Harvey defined the unit of the urban by the work day, and thus by the agglomeration defined as the maximal extension of the daily commuter zone.[133]

Still today, most concepts and definitions of the urban are strongly influenced by this form of agglomeration, which is commonly treated as the primary unit of urban analysis. In order to contain the multiple and contradictory developments at the urban periphery described above, the concept of agglomeration was stretched and finally replaced by the concept of the urban region, based on the analysis of overarching catchment areas. According to Richard Forman, a functional urban region could be vaguely defined as an urban centre's area of influence or as the area of active interactions between a centre and its surroundings,

whereby a significant drop in the rate of flows and movements could determine its outer boundary, which leads us back to the discussion of Scott and Storper's definition of agglomeration in Part I of this book.[134] As we have seen, the main problem is not finding a pragmatic solution for identifying the urban boundary but the *idée fixe* of the urban boundary as such.

THE URBANISATION OF THE PERIPHERY

With the worldwide urban explosion during the long 1980s, urbanisation processes began spreading beyond agglomerations and urban regions, stretching further and further out to remote territories. Thus, new terms and concepts were developed, reflecting a wide variety of situations and observations. The most generic term to designate this process is "periurbanisation." In distinction to the "urban periphery," which means the periphery of the urban, periurbanisation designates the (gradual) urbanisation of the periphery, and thus, in contrast to the suburban, which is often fully built up, the periurban still shows the strong influence of agricultural production and village life. In the late 1970s, the term *périurbanisation* was introduced in France to precisely designate areas beyond the relatively dense and compact banlieues. It focused on the dispersed settlements scattered over the territory as extensions of villages and towns, often inhabited by low-income or middle-class people that were looking for access to affordable single-family homes. They settled in predominantly agricultural areas, attracted by lower land prices, a "green" environment, and improved road connections while commuting to central urban areas. These newcomers first changed the socioeconomic composition of these areas and soon also the settlement patterns themselves. Today, periurban areas often contain all sorts of infrastructure and facilities, from energy production, storage and logistics to recreation areas and golf courses. In North America, similar processes have been analysed under the rubric of "exurbanisation." Here, poor and wealthy people migrate from large agglomerations to often sparsely populated areas beyond the "urban frontier" in search of cheap land and "nature."[135] In Africa and Asia, the term periurbanisation has been used since the 1990s, applying a wide range of definitions, including criteria such as topography, demography, land use, and economic and social dynamics. The main focus of the studies was on processes and conflicts related to access, control, and use of land-based resources.[136]

Around the turn of the twentieth century, the use of the terms periurban and periurbanisation in scientific publications grew exponentially, reflecting the massive transformation of these zones, particularly in Africa and Asia, which had become strongly affected by all sorts of urban extensions, from popular settlements to urban megaprojects and large-scale infrastructure developments. John Friedmann summarised the periurban as "encounters of an ever-expanding urban" with the rural surrounding of large cities.[137] These processes are often highly dynamic and sometimes change rapidly, making it even more difficult to isolate and define specific situations at a given time. In a very detailed recent study, Alexander Follmann analyses the analytical confusion that these processes create, shows the difficulty of using periurbanisation as an umbrella term for the wide spectrum of emergent urban situations across the globe, and calls for the development of much more specific conceptualisations and terms.[138] Exactly along this line of thought, the team of Paula Meth, Tom Goodfellow, Alison Todes, and Sarah Charlton made a fascinating comparison of peripheral urban areas in four African territories and developed a typology of five logics grasping very different situations that stretch out clearly into territories of extended urbanisation.[139]

The proliferation of these peripheral urbanisation processes has resulted in the development of increasingly heterogeneous urbanised landscapes across the planet, with centres and peripheries scattered over the territory. Thus, in architecture and urban design, an old question resurfaced: What is the new form of the city? In a very general way, cultural anthropologist Marc Augé observed the proliferation of "non-places" (*non-lieux*), places without proper identities, relations, and histories, and architect Rem Koolhaas provoked heated debates about the "generic city."[140] More specifically, the new form of urbanising territories is well illustrated by the concept of the "100 mile city" by architecture critic Deyan Sudjic, who tries to grasp the almost endless conglomeration of urban fragments, and the "in-between city" (*Zwischenstadt*) brought forward by urban designer Tom Sieverts, describing a zone characterised by a state between "place and world, space and time, city and country."[141] Architectural historian André Corboz identified the new urban form as *ville-territoire* (city-territory) that no longer forms a de-limitable unit but rather a sprawling, polycentric urban region where the old city centres lose their historical functions, and the peripheries take on new meaning. What evolves in this process is an encompassing form of the city, a place of the discontinuous, the heterogeneous, the fragmentary, being in constant transformation.[142] Similar ideas can also be found in the concept of the *città diffusa* inspired by the dispersed settlement patterns emerging in northern Italy, particularly in the Veneto and in Milan.[143] Influenced by both concepts, urbanist Paola Viganò developed the concept of a "horizontal metropolis," which she particularly understands as a concept that can be applied to find new design solutions for urban settlements offering an alternative to concepts of the compact city and strategies of urban densification.[144]

We can clearly understand these new urban forms as the result of the complex interaction of various urbanisation processes, in which both vectors, concentration and extension, interweave and overlap. Most of these periurban configurations have aspects of hinterlands, providing agricultural production and water supply and containing all sorts of infrastructure. At the same time, they function as spillover basins for the further extension of agglomerations. However, the crucial point is that many concepts still presume a vast field of non-urban areas beyond these periurban territories, which they not further treat and illuminate in their analysis. So, even if the urban boundary does not play an important role in these accounts anymore, it is still present as an invisible and unexpressed condition for the urban.

THE EXTRA-LARGE SCALE: MEGALOPOLIS, MEGAREGION AND METROPOLISATION

What happens when urbanisation processes stretch even further, connecting several neighbouring agglomerations and extended urban regions? In this last section of Part III, we look at urban configurations on an even larger scale, when extensively urbanised interdependencies are being consolidated within extremely large, polynucleated megaregions that often traverse multiple national boundaries. Such mega-scaled urban constellations have been recognised for over a century within the field of architecture and urban studies, from Patrick Geddes to Jean Gottmann and Constantinos Doxiadis. Historically, they were mainly produced through massive and fast industrialisation in certain core regions of capitalism. In 1915, planner Patrick Geddes identified large polycentric urbanised regions, which he called "conurbations."[145] He coined this term to describe the emerging spatial entity constituted by the coalescence of several industrial towns and cities in the United Kingdom. According to his analysis, this is mainly the result of large coal deposits that offered a cheap energy supply resulting in the clustering of factories. As Alfred Weber had already recognised, it was advantageous to place steel factories close to coal mines because it is much cheaper to use coal, which is fully consumed in the process, on the spot, instead of transporting it to another location. The heavily industrialised German Ruhr area offers another example of this relationship.

Half a century later, French geographer Jean Gottmann analysed the then-largest urban zone of the world along the East Coast of the United States between Boston and Washington—the famous BosWash—that he labelled "megalopolis."[146] This name directly refers to the ancient Greek town at the foothills of Arcadia that was named *Megalopoli*, a "very large city" by their founders, in the hope it would become the largest of the Greek cities (see also Markaki in this volume). As Gottmann observed, large industrial plants had long left the BosWash area, which subsequently specialised in urban economies dominated by urban and suburban modes of life and land occupations. This gave Gottmann the idea that this megalopolis represented early signs of a new urban global order shaped by urbanisation: "The long accepted opposition between town and country has therefore evolved toward a new opposition between *urban regions*, of which Megalopolis is certainly the most obvious and advanced case, and *agricultural regions*, the largest and most typical of which is found in the grain-growing Great Plains."[147] The corn and soy belt in the North American Midwest—currently the world's largest zone of operationalised agricultural production—is analysed by Katsikis in this volume.

Architect and town planner Constantinos Doxiadis developed an even more encompassing approach.[148] In the 1960s, he began with a systematic investigation of megalopolitan configurations across the world. He concluded that centripetal forces of agglomerations and centrifugal forces of major transportation corridors, economic clusters, and topographical features such as coastal areas combine to create a large-scale, mesh-like urbanisation pattern that could be developed to cover the foremost habitable areas of the world. If well planned, he believed it could become a successful "Ecumenopolis," a fusion of different megalopolises. As Katsikis argues, this utopian analysis could be interpreted as the first formulation of planetary urbanisation, which also imagines a possible urbanistic project.[149]

Since the long 1980s, similar extra-large urban formations have been developing with unprecedented speed across the planet, particularly in Asia, but also in Latin America and Africa. Urban regions are interweaving, networked through processes of globalisation and metropolisation, forming polycentric, multi-layered, and multi-scalar landscapes with overlapping catchment areas often stretching over multiple regional and national boundaries. In recent years, the term "megaregion" has become an umbrella term to mark such developments.[150] Many names have been proposed for these configurations, and similar to the other urbanisation processes and urban forms discussed above, the scientific debates are very confusing. Often, research focuses only on the physical extension of such extended urban landscapes. A widely quoted but strongly simplified version was presented by Richard Florida and his team using satellite night light images to identify contiguous large-scale urban zones without even analysing their internal functional connections.[151] However, the superficial observation that urban areas are clustered together in physical proximity does not necessarily imply that they are tied together by intense interactions and functional relationships. Thus, such concepts are often generated through extrapolation and generalisation of limited data and the selective use of parameters and characteristics.

A different conceptualisation of large-scale urban developments was introduced in France with the term *metropolisation*. This concept looks not at agglomerations but focuses instead on centralities as defining elements of new urban formations. Consequently, it is less interested in boundaries but much more in connections. Pierre Veltz summarises the basic figure of this concept: The globalised economy is organised in encompassing networks of production and consumption, which coalesce in metropolitan nodes generating specific regional effects of agglomeration and multiplication of centralities and multi-scalar urban realities. This leads to uneven spatial development between well-connected city cores and "inner peripheries."[152] In the ambitious comparative project *The Polycentric Metropolis* led by Peter Hall and Kathy Pain, several research teams explored such networked areas in Europe, in which multiple nodes are linked together and coalesced to form large metropolitan territories comprising dense patterns of overlapping networks that radiate globally as well as regionally.[153] In this analysis, the outer border of the urban area is less important than the inner structure, the connections, and the nodes. In their edited volume *Post-Metropolitan Territories*, Alessandro Balducci, Valeria Fedeli and Francesco Curci present the results of an ambitious research project analysing very different examples of multi-scalar regional urbanisation in Italy, based on the territorial approach to urbanisation.

To conclude this discussion, it must be emphasised that whatever the definition of such megaregions may be, they always imply and incorporate all sorts of peripheries and areas of extended urbanisation. Once located at the edge of the urban, these peripheries might now be "in-between" amid complex urban territories in which "outside" and "inside" are entangled and enmeshed.

CONCLUSION: THE QUESTION OF THE OUTSIDE (OF THE URBAN)

Urbanisation has produced many different urban forms across the world, including the spread of built-up areas in peripheral territories, the proliferation of settlements along transport axes, and the creation of new centralities and megaprojects in remote places. Furthermore, the incessant increase of planetary connectivity is leading to heterogeneous territories comprising villages, dense new settlements, and large agricultural zones. In such territories, processes of concentrated, extended, and differential urbanisation may proceed at the same time, forming new complex landscapes with varied characteristics. Therefore, some concepts discussed above include aspects of extended urbanisation.

However, many of these concepts still presume that urbanisation is a spatially confined phenomenon and that a vast non-urban realm extends beyond urban territories—a realm that is usually not further illuminated by urban analysis. Thus, during the course of the history of urban studies, many new urban forms have been identified that are marked by various combinations of concentrated and extended processes of urbanisation. But their analysis has been trapped by the city-centric perspective and the prevailing concepts of concentration and boundedness of the urban. Whether high-lighting monocentric or polycentric forms, they still share the attempt to delimit the units of the urban universe. In this sense, territories of extended urbanisation are often not "new" territories or landscapes but the result of long-standing developments. However, they can be recognised and distinguished only by a different, de-centring analytical perspective on these landscapes.

The question of the outside of the urban that was raised by the concept of planetary urbanisation and the call for an "urban theory without an outside" put forward by Brenner has led to lengthy debates, bringing up all sorts of more or less sophisticated philosophical reflec-tions about the basic problem of the "outside" in general, and the question as to whether every-thing should be called urban today.[154] Neglected and concealed in these debates is the very prac-tical need for a decentred perspective on the urban. Therefore, it is crucial to go one step further, to cross the "urban boundary" and gain a comprehensive understanding of the urban transformation of the entire territory. In one of his latest articles, Edward W. Soja, who was so strongly engaged in the discovery of new urban forms and constellations, concluded: "Today, it can be argued that every square inch of the world is urbanised to some degree."[155]

PART IV

PROCESSES OF EXTENDED URBANISATION. AN EXPLORATION

One of the key findings of the project which we are reporting in this book is that territories of extended urbanisation are very diverse and often highly differentiated, with contradictory or even paradoxical processes developing side by side. These territories are often highly dynamic and may take divergent pathways to urbanisation. While some develop towards peripheralisation, others become centralities and agglomerations themselves. They could become fully operationalised landscapes hollowed out and emptied of social activities, facing the loss of jobs, population, and social energies, or they could densify, intensify, and turn into polycen-tric metropolitan landscapes.

Following the analytical framework presented in Part II, I focus here not on entire territories but on urbanisation processes. The concept of urbanisation processes is analysed in detail in the volume *Vocabularies for an Urbanising Planet*, edited by Schmid and Streule, which presents a series of concepts for processes of *concentrated urbanisation*. This Part IV engages now with processes of *extended urbanisation*. Our own research presented in this book yielded a great wealth of insights into the modalities, patterns, and pathways of extended urbanisation. The rapidly increasing number of other research efforts contributed additional important findings. Together they allow us to propose a series of processes of extended urbanisation. This list is not exhaustive; it contains a selection of possible processes that proved useful for our own research and revealed important parallels between seemingly dissimilar territories. It partly overlaps with a preliminary list of phenomena of planetary urbanisation sketched out by Brenner and Schmid.[156]

The first group of processes presented here is related to the *agrarian question*. Processes of extended urbanisation are often transforming areas of agricultural production; however, as I have explained in Part III, the rural-urban binary is not a useful conceptualisation for understanding urbanisation processes. Instead, as is well known in rural studies, the agrarian question offers a much more productive perspective for analysing the dramatic transformations of huge territories which are not directly related to agglomerations and commuting processes. These transformations result from various processes of migration and movements facilitated by increased connectivity and improved transport infrastructure, enabling decentralised forms of wealth creation and income.

A widespread process of extended urbanisation is *extended industrial urbanisation.* This process existed already at the beginning of industrialisation in the late eighteenth century. Today, various forms of peripheral industrialisation are initiated by state strategies that promote special economic zones and export processing zones or support global sweatshop regions, back-office locations, data processing facilities, and intermodal logistics terminals. These processes are often located in periurban areas near large agglomerations, along main transportation corridors, and close to logistics hubs.

Another process, *extended urbanisation through infrastructure production* is leading to various forms of de- and reterritorialisation, such as processes of corridor urbanisation and the disintegration of hinterlands. Along motorways and around intersections, countless urban fragments are mushrooming extensively, if unevenly, across large territories, generating an irregular and haphazard urban fabric, which is being at once expanded and blurred.

The precondition for many processes of extended urbanisation is commodifiable land. This land has to be produced through often violent processes of *land enclosure*, which include dispossession and destroy traditional forms of land tenure and subsistence economy. While land enclosure can result from other processes of extended urbanisation like corridor urbanisation or extended industrial urbanisation, we understand land enclosure here as an urbanisation process in itself.

The concept of the *operationalisation of landscapes* brings together the rationalisation and automation of agricultural production, extractivism, energy production, and infrastructure development, which belong to the most dramatic processes of extended urbanisation. The production of operational landscapes results from the most basic socio-metabolic imperatives associated with urban growth—the procurement and circulation of food, water, energy, and construction materials; the processing and management of waste and pollution; and the mobilisation of labour power in support of these various processes of extraction, production, circulation, and management.[157]

The operationalisation of landscapes is often accompanied by extreme forms of rationalisation, which strongly reduces the necessary labour force and thus results in processes of *extended peripheralisation*. In a similar way, deindustrialisation and uneven development may also induce the loss and relocation of economic activities, leading to selective emigration and depopulation. As a result, permanent settlements are eroding and seasonal or sporadic movements of people to and from central urban areas are becoming more pronounced.

On a general level, extended urbanisation always implies the restructuring of centre-periphery relationships. With the multiplication of various forms of centrality and their related peripheries over the planet, large-scale, highly dynamic, and heterogeneous *polynucleated metropolitan zones* are emerging, bringing a wide range of concentrated, extended, and differential urbanisation processes together.

These different urbanisation processes obviously overlap and reinforce one another. They are also mediated through contextually specific regulatory-institutional arrangements, state and corporate strategies, everyday practices, and socio-political struggles.

URBANISATION AND
THE AGRARIAN QUESTION

Any analysis of extended urbanisation inevitably involves an engagement with the complex relationship between urbanisation and agricultural areas. Agricultural land has undergone a wide variety of urban transformations since the industrial revolution. Long neglected, these transformations have received increasing attention in both urban and rural studies in recent years and have sparked a wide range of discussions. Consequently, a number of critical *urban scholars*, such as Shubhra Gururani, Sai Balakrishnan, Swarnabh Gosh, and Ayan Meer, have called for greater engagement with the agrarian question in urban studies, explicitly linking critical agrarian studies with extended urbanisation.[158] Conversely, scholars of *rural studies* have given more attention to extended urbanisation processes, as Kasia Paprocki discusses in detail.[159] This makes revisiting the rural-urban relationship discussed in Part III indispensable, with a focus this time on the agrarian question.

The distinction between the rural and the agrarian question has sparked various debates, which it is not possible to explore here in detail. Suffice it to mention that the discussion of the agrarian question has a long history, starting with the famous texts by Karl Kautsky and Vladimir Lenin, who discussed and promoted the industrialisation of agricultural production, going all the way to recent discussions about whether the agrarian question is still relevant in times of globalisation and urbanisation, or more precisely, which aspects of this question are still relevant.[160] While Henry Bernstein looks at the question of labour and observes a crisis of reproduction because peasants and rural workers are increasingly struggling for their means of livelihood, Philip McMichael focuses on the global corporate food regime and the struggle for food sovereignty, and Martín Arboleda investigates the sphere of circulation and asks who controls the way agriculture is produced.[161] As we will see, all of these three perspectives are highly relevant for extended urbanisation. In this context, the agricultural question particularly appears in 1) the operationalisation of agricultural territories, 2) the enclosure (and thus erasure) of agricultural land, and 3) the extension of urban settlements into areas of agricultural production. While the

first two points are discussed in the following subsections, here I will illuminate the third point, the development of settlement spaces in agricultural territories.

Basically, urban transformations of agrarian landscapes can be approached from two different perspectives: If we look from the *centre* of an agglomeration, we detect processes of concentrated urbanisation radiating centrifugally towards the outskirts and gradually fading with greater distance from the centre. If we look from a *de-centred* perspective, we detect other, less obvious forms of urban transformation that often seem to be spontaneous. The question arises whether these territories, in which extended and concentrated urbanisation processes overlap and intermingle, are still rural, already urban, or even something else.

I discussed the first city-centric perspective in Part III with terms like peri- and exurban territories. These territories manifest the strong influence of agglomeration processes, while agricultural production still plays a dominant role. They are also crucial for water and energy supply, waste disposal, recreation, and tourism. At the same time, they are becoming places of residence for diverse high- and low-income groups commuting to central areas; furthermore, they are increasingly used for all sorts of infrastructural facilities and urban megaprojects. Thus, they are hybrid territories transformed by overlapping processes of concentrated and extended urbanisation and are often framed as transition zones, as rural-urban or urban-rural interfaces. The most common assumption is that they are both spatial and temporal transition zones that will become "fully" urbanised sooner or later. However, this might be a premature assumption, as the balance between agricultural and urban uses is sometimes quite stable and lasting. For such zones, Terry McGee has introduced the term desakota, discussed in Part II. In his research on Indonesia, Stephen Cairns proposes the term "urban-rural hybrid" to avoid developmentalist assumptions that see rural areas on the fringes of agglomerations inevitably giving way to urbanisation that is "fully formed." His project is to explore and support strategies that could protect and preserve "non-urban conditions" in these areas.[162] With similar concerns, Shubhra Gururani has chosen the term "agrarian urbanism" to express situations in which agrarian and urban dynamics sustain and coproduce each other.[163]

A second perspective on such territories reveals a very different picture: If we approach them from an ex-centric position, we detect underlying processes of extended urbanisation, which are masked by concentric processes of concentrated urbanisation and are, therefore, often overlooked. In the research project "Territory," the team of ETH Studio Basel investigated various remote areas far away from agglomerations. It observed in the densely settled Nile Valley a slow, gradual, and initially almost unnoticeable transformation of villages and small towns generated by the everyday mobility of local people.[164] Other territories in the Red River Delta around Hanoi and on the peripheries of Minas Gerais in Brazil—located beyond the commuter distance to urban centres and thus not or only weakly related to agglomeration processes—showed urbanisation processes through the solidification and extension and the construction of new buildings that have an urban appearance. A similar observation is described by Yu Zhu for the eastern coastal region of China with high population densities and improved transport and communication conditions far from agglomerations and not related to rural-urban migration. She calls this form of urbanisation that is produced by the people themselves, to accommodate manufacturing and other non-agricultural activities "in situ urbanisation."[165] It could also be discussed under the rubric of extended industrial urbanisation (see the next section).

Likewise, the team of Robbin van Duijne, Jan Nijman, and Chetan Choithani observed in Bihar and West Bengal dispersed emergent urban formations that result from densification, expansion, and amalgamation of built-up environments in the absence of significant local agglomeration. These areas are marked by a rapidly declining agricultural sector and the emergence of a consumption-oriented local economy. A closer analysis revealed that the wealth enabling these transformations is created by circular labour migration that however no longer relates to the seasonal agricultural cycle, from which livelihoods have become almost entirely divorced. The team introduced the concept of *injected urbanism* to denote a form of urbanisation that is exogenously generated through remittances and thus depends on economic activities elsewhere, abroad and domestically.[166] For instance, this "elsewhere" could be a tenement town located in an urban corridor close to Delhi, where temporary labour migrants from Bihar are kept in a state of permanent insecurity, precarity, and exploitation, as analysed by Nitin Bathla.[167] This example illustrates in a shocking way how two very different forms of extended urbanisation are directly related and how corridor urbanisation in Delhi fuels injected urbanism in Bihar through sporadic and precarious labour migration.

This example points to a process that is well-known but has been neglected for a long time in urban studies: the urbanising effect of migration. On the one hand, remittances from rural-urban migration, and often also circular and other forms of temporary migration, are invested in the place of origin of the migrants. These processes, which developed in many agrarian areas across the world, have been researched for a long time in rural studies. Deborah Potts provides an exemplary analysis of rural-urban linkages to secure livelihoods for Sub-Saharan Africa.[168] In her ethnographic fieldwork, Elisa Bertuzzo followed migrant labourers from West Bengal to southern India and described different forms of sporadic migrations that she calls "translocalisation."[169] Kasia Paprocki goes in a similar direction in proposing an alternative reading of urbanisation resulting from multiple local and translocal social movements that fight for livelihoods and futures that could persist independently of relationships with large cities. She advocates counter-hegemonic political imaginaries that are developed in agrarian communities in the search for other political visions.[170]

On a much broader scale, the extensive research project on *subaltern urbanisation* by Partha Mukhopadhyay, Marie-Hélène Zérah, and Eric Denis explored and defined urbanisation processes beyond urban agglomerations in India.[171] They used the term "subaltern urbanisation" to highlight the multiple local and translocal flows that are shaping urbanisation processes that could exist independently of relationships with large cities. This concept highlights the contribution made by the people on their own that is independent of the elite, resulting in diffuse forms of urbanisation. It brings together quite different situations that are systematised in a typology: "The influenced town" is located close to metropolitan centres; the "micropolis" is a conglomeration of entrepreneurial small towns outside the direct influence of large centres; small "market towns" are usually statutory towns catering to the needs of agricultural areas. The fourth category, "emerging small towns," describes rapidly urbanising villages that are developing towards larger settlements, whose workforce is moving away from the agrarian sector.

This ongoing discussion highlights the great diversity of extended urbanisation in agricultural territories. It indicates that a detailed differentiation of the involved processes is necessary and that we have to clarify which processes are addressed by our conceptualisations. There is first the process of *the production of urban space* and its various modalities, which can be examined from different angles: subaltern urbanisation highlights the role of the people; in situ urbanisation focuses on the absence of agglomeration effects; and injected urbanism looks at the origin of the resources fuelling the urban transformation and thus considers the variation of migration processes. Further urbanisation processes will be analysed in the remainder of this chapter: the *process of enclosure* of agricultural land and the related mechanisms, pointing to power relations, territorial regulations, and land rights; and finally, the *agrarian question* in the proper sense as a social production process that is facing commodification and operationalisation.

EXTENDED INDUSTRIAL URBANISATION

An often-overlooked process of extended urbanisation is related to the industrialisation of areas located outside agglomerations. As is well known, industrialisation historically not only affected cities, but also followed the availability of energy, raw materials, and cheap labour, thereby often stimulating decentralised pathways of urbanisation. Thus, in eighteenth-century Europe, the so-called "domestic system" combined home work with agricultural production in predominantly poor, rural areas, tapping the availability of cheap labour. Early industrialisation in parts of Europe, particularly in alpine regions and Scandinavia, followed water courses in peripheral areas, leading to a much more decentralised urbanisation pattern than the classic Manchester model suggests.[172]

In the twentieth century, industrial rural urbanisation was often induced by state developmental strategies, which tried to promote economic growth in relatively poor peripheral regions. Tellingly, the starting point of Lefebvre's engagement with the urban question was not the transformation of the Paris region that he would analyse in detail later but the state-led construction of the new town of Mourenx close to his hometown Naverrenx. Following the discovery of a natural gas deposit amidst the French Pyrenees, a gas-processing and aluminium plant, along with several chemical factories, were constructed together with an entire town consisting of working-class neighbourhoods and houses for the managers. This industrial town never developed into a major agglomeration and is still a small settlement with about 7,000 inhabitants today. But the building of such a new town *ex nihilo* in a rural socioeconomic context came as a shock to Lefebvre and served him as a paradigmatic example of the fundamental transformation caused by urbanisation.[173]

Today, forms of peripheral industrialisation are initiated on much larger scales by state strategies that define special economic zones and export processing zones or support global sweatshop regions, back-office locations, data-processing facilities, and intermodal logistics terminals. They are often located in periurban areas in the vicinity of large agglomerations, but sometimes also along main transportation corridors and close to logistics hubs. These forms of industrialisation are often detached from direct agglomeration effects and show certain similarities to urbanisation through resource extraction (see below). Basic conditions for such zones are usually a certain degree of connectivity and the availability of cheap labour, land, and capital. However, capital is mobile, and labour power can also be found in distant villages (often female workers) and through various forms of temporary migration, which developed on a massive scale in China and India. During further development, some of these zones are transforming into areas of concentrated urbanisation or becoming integrated into metropolitan regions.

In the 1990s, Gillian Hart researched the formation of globally linked industrial districts in former Bantustan areas of South Africa and traced the continuing salience of agrarian histories there in a process that she called "rural industrialisation." In a comparative analysis, she found similar developments in East Asia, particularly South Korea. In this context, she criticised the "core-centric" contemporary literature on industrial restructuring that was not able to address the divergent local trajectories of peripheral industrialisation and their related histories of dispossession.[174]

One of the most extreme examples of large-scale rural industrialisation is Dongguan, a county in the middle of the Pearl River Delta, presented by Kit Ping Wong in this book. Until the early 1980s, Dongguan was a classical agrarian hinterland of Guangzhou (the former Canton). As Wong shows, the rapid extended industrialisation and urbanisation of the entire county was not the result of agglomeration or spillover processes but a complex progression of extended urbanisation launched by the Chinese state and implemented by the interplay of the county government, the town governments, and the village collectives.[175] This process started in the 1980s and was driven by the

Chinese economic strategy of industrialisation and urbanisation initiated by Deng Xiaoping. In this process, an entire rural county was converted into an "urban" territorial system. In 1988, the county was declared a prefecture city, and town governments and village collectives were given their own administrative jurisdictions and collective land. In a contradictory and conflictual interplay with state strategies, the villages attracted investors and mobile-migrant labourers and started a spectacular process of export-led industrialisation that created the famous Chinese "world factory." Rural characteristics were embedded into the urbanisation process, generating highly scattered and fragmented urban spaces. This extended form of urbanisation finally turned into concentrated urbanisation, consuming and transforming most of Dongguan's agricultural land. As if in a time-lapse, this example illustrates the pathway of extended urbanisation in a rural county towards concentrated urbanisation and finally to the complete urbanisation of the entire territory in only three decades.

EXTENDED URBANISATION THROUGH INFRASTRUCTURE PRODUCTION

One of the main drivers of extended urbanisation is the massive increase of connectivity on all territorial scales. Urban theorists have long recognised transport-based urban development patterns, but in the last decades, these patterns reached a new level in that the historically unprecedented production of planetary connectivity involves the almost endless proliferation of infrastructural spaces, connecting metropolitan regions with each other and with zones of extraction and primary production.

This infrastructure boom is generating unexpected impacts. Along motorways and around intersections, countless urban fragments are mushrooming extensively, if unevenly, across large territories, generating an irregular and haphazard urban fabric, which is being at once expanded and blurred. This leads to the juxtaposition of often disjointed urban elements, as very different urban fragments might be located side by side without being functionally linked. This results in a dysfunctional socio-spatial structure with unprecedented dimensions, creating all sorts of disturbances and negative effects. Under such conditions, agglomeration economies are only partially effective because the various economic functions and activities are often thrown together in a wild mélange and thus develop only tenuous synergies and interrelationships.

Miguel Kanai and Seth Schindler show how a global development policy consensus to foster economic growth in peripheral regions through infrastructure-led developments has generated an "infrastructure scramble." Numerous state actors and global agencies make massive investments in infrastructure connectivity, often linking resource frontiers and urban systems—often across national borders—to articulate value chains geared toward extracting resources, logistical integration, and industrial production. These investments have grave effects because, on the one hand, the new roads often bypass existing areas and thus foster peripheralisation, and on the other, they generate all sorts of novel urbanisation processes.[176] Typical outcomes are urban corridors developing along large-scale infrastructure developments. Sai Balakrishnan analyses in detail India's first economic corridor along the Mumbai–Pune Expressway that functions as a spine along which special economic zones, smart cities, and other "zones of variegated sovereignty" develop. In this process, volatile conflicts have erupted over land reallocation from agricultural to industrial and urban use in economic corridors and their attendant new towns.[177]

An extreme form of this kind of extended urbanisation by infrastructure production is the devastating outcome of India's national highway program, which is analysed in this book by Nitin Bathla. Similar to the programmes in Western countries before and after the Second World War, but in much more extensive dimensions, India's highway network stretches over the entire subcontinent. Bathla shows how this programme

unleashes a cascade of effects, such as the enclosure of all sorts of land, from the fertile agricultural belt around Delhi to protected nature reserves, forests, and tribal lands. The highway programme redirects entire settlement systems towards a decentralised and haphazard form of urban development. With the evolution of this process, extended urbanisation has become an instrument for the enclosure of non-urban land, fuelling the rapid, decentralised urbanisation of India.

Not only the construction but also the planning of such corridors and large infrastructure projects can have tremendous influences on urbanisation processes and are often used as a vehicle for massive transformations through extended urbanisation. Examples of this are the Plan Puebla Panama and the Manta-Manaus multi-modal transport corridor analysed by Wilson and Bayón.[178] On a much larger scale, China's Belt and Road initiative, launched at the end of 2013 by Chinese President Xi Jinping, has unleashed countless urbanisation processes in various parts of the world and also in China and has been widely researched and discussed in several disciplines.[179]

ENCLOSURE AS AN URBANISATION PROCESS

One of the crucial preconditions and consequences of these and many other processes of extended urbanisation is to prepare and open up agricultural land for commercial use. This process of enclosure often provokes fierce resistance from small farmers fighting for their land. In Part I of this chapter, land enclosure stood historically at the very beginning of both capitalism *and* urbanisation. Marx treated the enclosure of the commons in the context of original accumulation and saw it as the initial process of the accumulation of capital that would soon be replaced by the extended reproduction of capital. However, as we have seen, enclosure continues to play an important role in the development of capitalism, and to this day, it is a crucial precondition for the mobilisation and commodification of land, whether for resource extraction, agribusiness, logistics functions, or otherwise. In generating commodifiable land and disposable labour, enclosure destroys traditional forms of land tenure and subsistence economy and enables production for the (world) market. More than ever, migrant labourers play a key role in all sorts of urban economies driving both concentrated and extended urbanisation.

It could thus be argued that the enclosure of agricultural land is itself a process of extended urbanisation. Sevilla Buitraga developed exactly this thesis. He follows the historical moment of parliamentary enclosure in England and shows that it was deploying a new spatial rationality that mobilised the reorganisation of the territory as an instrument for the production of a new social order. In this process, the relationship between the city, the countryside, and international networks was radically reconfigured. State action played a key role in this process.[180]

The way in which land is enclosed, commodified, and opened up for various urbanisation processes is, of course, today very different from the model of parliamentary enclosure in England described by Marx. As Silvia Federici states, a process of "new enclosures" started in the late 1970s and early 1980s as a result of China's economic transition and the imposition of structural adjustment programs by the World Bank and the IMF on large parts of the former colonial world in the wake of the "Third World" debt crisis.[181] The role of state actors is crucial in gathering large swathes of land through expropriation and various forms of dispossession. Particularly in China and India, the transformation of rural into urban land has become a general strategy of state-driven urbanisation. Gururani traces the recent round of land enclosure in India back to the 1980s, when the urbanisation of agrarian land became a key strategy to bolster economic growth and attract foreign direct investment in metropolitan commodification and de-agrarisation.[182] Michael Levien developed the concept of "regimes of dispossession" to better understand the different modalities of dispossession during historical development. While the

postcolonial Indian state dispossessed land mostly for public-sector industry and infrastructure, the adoption of neoliberal economic policies in the early 1990s prompted state governments to become land brokers for private real estate capital, and particularly for the creation of special economic zones. The enclosure of land often sparks fierce opposition and what Levien calls "land wars" that erupt across India, with farmers resisting the state's forcible transfer of their land to capitalists.[183]

The process of land enclosure is confronted with highly uneven agrarian land markets and a great variation of land ownership. Thus, Balakrishnan, who analysed the transition of agrarian land markets to real estate development in the context of the Mumbai-Pune corridor, discovered that primary agricultural cooperatives had been reorganised into real estate companies by agrarian elites as an entry point into an urbanising economy. She calls this process "recombinant urbanisation"; this concept focuses on the institutional mechanisms through which differentiated agrarian property regimes combine with neoliberal reforms to produce new geographies of uneven development. In this process, "collisions and collusions" between landed property and urban real estate occur that can turn into fierce struggles. This complex process does not necessarily lead to marginalisation, precarisation, and displacement; it can also enrich villagers and rural populations.[184] A similar situation developed in China, where villagers also became shareholders of real estate companies, as explained by Kit Ping Wong in this book. A very illuminating overview of land dispossession in China and India can be found in a special issue of the *Journal of Peasant Studies*.[185]

The modalities of land enclosure are highly influenced by the dominant mode of territorial regulation. In many countries, agricultural land is protected by national planning laws that do not allow its transformation to industrial or urban uses. This opens up multiple options for illegal land transformations or bypassing existing rules and regulations. As Gavin Shatkin has shown in his analysis of Asian urban megaprojects, turning officially designated rural land into urban land generates huge windfall profits for developers and political and personal gains for state actors.[186] This leads to various forms of "bypass urbanism," an urbanisation process that cuts short or circumvents existing territorial regulations and planning procedures and takes advantage of certain "flexibilities" and legal "grey spaces" in regulatory systems, often including direct and indirect forms of corruption.[187]

Thus, to this day, enclosure plays a key role in urban development and agricultural land transformation. Farshad Araghi directly links "the great global enclosure of our times" and global depeasantisation. He identifies a global strategy of enclosure-induced "accumulation by displacement," which results in global deruralisation on the one hand and, on the other, peripheral urban expansion fuelled by the deproletarianised and homeless surplus labour populations produced in this process.[188]

OPERATIONALISATION OF LANDSCAPES

Once the land is privatised and commodified, it can become further functionalised and operationalised for all sorts of production processes. In this way, industrial production zones and urban corridors may develop, as shown above. Other territories, often located far beyond dense population centres, are transformed into specialised zones of primary commodity production and large-scale logistical infrastructure. The term "operationalisation of landscapes" has been introduced by Nikos Katsikis and Neil Brenner to designate a process in which territories are subsumed under the logic of capital accumulation for the production of energy, raw materials, all sorts of agricultural outputs, and for infrastructure and waste disposal. These zones are embedded into transnational production networks and intermeshed within the planetary logistical space mediated through the abstract space of the world market.

These "hinterlands of the capitalocene," as Brenner and Katsikis call them, are no longer staging grounds for specific urban regions.

They are spatially dissociated and functionally decoupled from direct links with the metropolitan areas and serve as metabolic support systems and processing zones for the global metropolitan network as a whole. The capital-intensive process of operationalisation usually goes hand in hand with thorough rationalisation and automation, thus dramatically reducing the necessary labour power for the production process. The operationalisation of landscapes is therefore marked by the decrease of the organic composition of capital, as living labour is replaced by machines, equipment, and infrastructure. In this process, the territory becomes completely industrialised and functionalised to form large-scale, territorialised ecological machinery or "horizontal factories," as Katsikis calls them in his contribution to this volume.[189]

Sandro Mezzadra and Brett Neilson developed an interesting conceptualisation of "operations of capital." Drawing from a wide range of theoretical sources, they understand the contemporary capitalist world as constituted by a web of operations, particularly finance, logistics, and extraction operations. Each of these operations is predicated on a set of conditions that it cannot produce itself since operations necessarily involve the labour of subjects that cannot be reduced to capital. At the same time, these operations impinge on extant human and nonhuman environments.[190] If we speak of the operationalisation of landscapes, then we look precisely at the way in which these environments are functionalised to serve as "material support" (in the Lefebvrian sense) for various types of operation. Accordingly, we can distinguish several forms of operationalisation that are often difficult to separate: the operationalisation of landscapes for agricultural production, resource extraction, energy production, and logistical operations.

The *operationalisation of agricultural production* results in the production of food and feed to all sorts of raw materials, from bio-fuel to inputs for various industrial processes. In his contribution to this book, Nikos Katsikis shows the long operationalisation process of North America's largest agricultural zone, the corn and soy belt in the Midwest. He follows the transformation of a landscape, once associated with the iconic image of endless prairies and huge bison flocks, now a fully operationalised zone of agrarian, industrial production, so devoid of people and animals that even the insects are systematically extinct in these landscapes. This extreme form of agro-industrial transformation has resulted in an entire production system that delivers energy, fertilisers, pesticides, genetically modified seeds, machinery, materials, transport, and logistics. Katsikis shows how this entire system is constantly driven towards further rationalisation and automation until it becomes a huge factory-like material device combining a great variety of operations that spread out over a huge surface of the earth. At the same time, this system is reducing the input of labour power to the point where living labour is almost entirely replaced by machinery. This, in turn, destroys the livelihoods of a large part of the local population, which causes the lasting emigration of people and the degradation of basic social infrastructures and thus leads to the peripheralisation of the entire region. Furthermore, the operationalisation of agricultural production has accelerated the exhaustion and depletion of soil fertility and thus adds to the current environmental, food, and biodiversity crisis.[191]

This development finally results in a complete decoupling of the production process from urban life. This is quite different from William Cronon's analysis of *Nature's Metropolis*. He documents how at the very moment when agricultural production began to transform, the prairies and the Midwest were ruralised, and Chicago became an urban centre. In his book, he presents one common history of the metropolis and its vast extended hinterland. The output of this hinterland was transported to Chicago, that functioned as a logistics hub, an industrial processing zone with its infamous meat factories, the famous Pullman factory to produce railroad cars, the Chicago Board of Trade, one of the world's oldest futures and options exchanges, and the related financial activities.[192] Today, this direct relationship between the metropolis and its hinterland is dissolved, as the production system of the Midwest is directly linked to global markets.

Research on the operationalisation of agricultural production has illuminated ever-new aspects of this process in recent years. Thus, Gastón Gordillo looks at the operationalisation of genetically engineered soybean production in Argentina's Gran Chaco region through the lens of the metropolitan infrastructure, which reveals the imperialistic nature of this kind of extended urbanisation. Kasia Paprocki shows how the introduction of shrimp aquacultures as an anticipatory adaptation strategy to climate change in Bangladesh's delta region has led to ecological degradation and the dispossession of local rice farmers. It has produced an operational landscape that literally causes the ruination of the practices of production and social reproduction through which communities in this region have historically sustained themselves.[193] Milica Topalović and Hans Hortig analyse the transformation of tropical forests and agrarian land into operationalised territories of industrial palm oil production in South East Asia and explore how architects, urban designers, and landscape architects can address the challenges arising from agro-industrial production.[194]

The operationalisation of food production on a planetary scale could not work without the development of a global system of agro-industrial production and circulation. This necessitates the implementation and enforcement of market rules about what kind of food has to be produced and also the standardisation of food consumption through global rules, state regulations, and subsidies. On the basis of regulation theory, Harriet Friedmann and Philip McMichael developed the concept of the "food regime," which links international relations of food production and consumption to historical forms of accumulation.[195] The current global corporate industrial regime of "cheap food" has eroded smallholder economies, advanced global depeasantisation, and triggered the struggle for food sovereignty that has become a broad and lasting planetary movement.[196]

Finally, Arboleda turns to the sphere of exchange and examines the role that investment banks, pension funds, logistics companies, supermarkets, consumers, and laboratories have in the organisation of agro-food systems, highlighting the supply chain capitalism that dominates today's global production networks. With the example of Walmart Chile, he shows how large retail chains directly influence agricultural production. He also shows how new formations of political struggle have emerged in Chile that target ports, warehouses, roads, and other infrastructures of connectivity to influence primary-commodity production.

The relationship between operationalisation and global production networks also applies to energy production. Carola Hein reconstructs the emergence of a "palimpsestic global petroleumscape" in which corporate and public actors have built the physical and financial flows of petroleum into encompassing material and representational landscapes that became essential parts of modern society and everyday lives.[197] Hajar Ahmad Chusaini, Imam Buchori, and Jawoto Sih Setyono apply this concept to their analysis of the transformation of the urban fabric in the Cepu region in Indonesia.[198] In a touching essay, Japhy Wilson tells the inside story of an otherwise unreported revolt on a remote extractive frontier in the Ecuadorian Amazon in 2017, in which mestizo, Afro-descendant, and indigenous workers and communities confronted the combined forces of a multinational oil company and a militarised state. The evolving battle bears witness "to the fleeting emergence of an insurgent form of political universality" by subaltern subjects.[199] Today, energy landscapes rapidly extend towards desert, mountain, and ocean spaces to produce "green energy" in extensive wind farms and solar plants.

In a similar way, *operationalisation through extractivism* is covering ever larger proportions of the planet's surface, leaving behind natural and social wastelands. From a historical perspective, the extraction of raw materials was often a strong driver of processes of concentrated urbanisation. Mining used to be very labour-intensive and, therefore, often led to the formation of huge agglomerations. Famous examples are the industrial belts along coal deposits that became core agglomerations of the industrial revolution in Europe and North America and mining places that developed into large metropolises, such as Johannesburg or Belo Horizonte. However, as Rodrigo Castriota shows in this book, this relationship between extractivism and urban development has changed radically in the last decades. Rationalisation and automation made places of resource extraction, which are largely devoid of human labour, leaving workers without jobs and turning mining boom towns into ghost-like peripheries.

In his book *Planetary Mine*, Arboleda places this process of resource extraction in the context of planetary connectivity and analyses the sprawling infrastructural systems that connect sites of extraction to factories in export processing zones, precarious migrants and industrial workers, metropolitan consumer markets, and financial circuits and reflects on the possibility of revolutionary subjectivity.

In parallel, the *operationalisation of transports and logistics* is needed to produce planetary connectivity. This involves constructing airports, motorway networks, and high-speed trains and particularly the introduction of the intermodal container, as Nancy Couling shows in this book. This has enabled the efficient and smooth transport of materials and products across different modes of transportation, easily changing from ship to rail and truck.

This led not only to the operational landscapes of global transportation but also to the automation of harbours. Once the most important generators of urban agglomerations, huge transfer sites and cosmopolitan meeting places connecting people, information, and goods, harbours have become operational landscapes.[200] One of the most striking examples is the new deep-water container port on an island south of Shanghai, which was expected to fuel the Lingang New Town planned nearby with new activities and functions. It was initially believed that the port would promote the development of a port-related economy, bringing about clusters of maritime business services and industries, logistics, as well as a resident population. As part of Shanghai's New Town program, a port city was therefore proposed to be constructed in Nanhui. The idea was known as "the port works for the city, the city prospers for the port."[201] To the great astonishment of planners and politicians, this fully automated harbour with less than a hundred workers created almost nothing more than traffic jams of container trucks, and the plans had to be completely revised.

In her chapter on the operationalisation of the North Sea in this book, Nancy Couling analyses the overlapping and entanglement of different forms of operationalisation, from transport and logistics to resource extraction, energy production, and fishing, to examine how almost the entire North Sea became a fully operationalised space not only on its surface but affecting the entire volume of the sea. The transformation of a huge commons into an operationalised space can be seen as the ultimate commodification of space, the maximal homogenisation and destruction of pre-existing differences and qualities that leaves almost no spaces for social processes but results in the complete evacuation of the social. The alliance of capital and state space leaves nothing else than empty landscapes, what Couling describes as the loss of sea, loss of commons, and finally, loss of social life and "nature."

EXTENDED PERIPHERALISATION

As we have seen, urbanisation is characterised by uneven development and trans-scalar centre-periphery relationships. Therefore, it not only increases land use pressure and urban extension but may also generate adverse effects when more remote areas are bypassed by economic development or the operationalisation of landscapes dramatically reduces employment. In many ways, peripheralisation thus represents the "reverse side" of urbanisation, resulting in strong and lasting emigration, which is often highly selective, the stagnation or relocation of economic functions, the draining of social

activities, the loss of livelihoods, and the degradation of social, cultural, and economic networks, often setting in motion a self-reinforcing process of decline.

While the theorisation of centre-periphery relationships has a long history and was extensively discussed in the 1960s and 1970s in the context of the debate on the capitalist world system and dependency theory, the concept of peripheralisation was only recently applied in wider contexts. It shifts the focus from a structural analysis of centre-periphery relations towards a dynamic conceptualisation of urbanisation. It was used in the context of deindustrialisation processes, particularly for the analysis of declining industrial regions in Europe and North America and of sparsely populated areas in Eastern and Southern Europe.[202] Other forms of peripheralisation are emerging in urban territories, particularly in post-proletarian areas, similarly marked by deindustrialisation and economic crisis.[203]

Processes of peripheralisation are also a widespread feature of extended urbanisation. They affect very different situations and occur on the large as well as the small scale. They emerge in "meshes" in the urban fabric, as "in-between spaces" and pockets of poverty, but also as extended "fallow lands" and double (or multiple) peripheries that are decoupled from centralities.[204] Paradoxically, peripheralisation can also be a consequence of operationalisation, as shown above for the corn and soy belt in the North American Midwest. Nancy Couling describes this process as the evacuation of social activities in the North Sea. New transport connections can also lead to bypassing and peripheralisation of entire regions, as Kanai and da Silva Oliveira show for Roraima in Brazil's extreme north.[205]

Our example in this book is Arcadia, the idealised landscape in the Peloponnese treated as a rural periphery by national politics. Metaxia Markaki analyses the long-standing emigration towards Athens that resulted in the almost complete depopulation of parts of this mountainous area. Long left behind and neglected by the nation-state, new state strategies have started to intervene in recent years. As Markaki shows, a far-reaching administrative reform particularly targeted Greek peripheries and considerably accelerated peripheralisation, installing a state space of low resolution, low governance, and low cost and preparing peripheralised regions to become operationalised for "green" energy production. However, accounts of "emptiness" are often strongly influenced by static perspectives regarding territories as given containers. A dynamic perspective reveals that these landscapes are not empty but animated by manifold activities as people have kept strong ties to their place of origin and thus maintain connections between the dominating capital, Athens, and its periphery. Furthermore, peripheralised areas have a strong potential for appropriation and reappropriation by very different social groups and practices.

THE PRODUCTION OF
POLYNUCLEATED
METROPOLITAN ZONES
Finally, as discussed in Part III, the question of the large scale returns to the foreground with examples of conurbations, megalopolises, and megaregions. Yet, these concepts are mainly defined by the sheer size of the territories observed and the extension of the urban boundary, not by their dynamics and internal structure. In contrast, we are focusing here on particular polycentric multi-scalar constellations that are integrating several global and regional centres, their catchment areas, and various peripheries in their spheres of influence. While new centralities are emerging in parts of these territories, they also expand outwards, integrating existing centralities, such as smaller cities and towns, into the metropolitan networks. These zones often cross national and regional borders and are thus generating urban differentials through cross-border dynamics. This creates all sorts of movements crisscrossing the zone that lead to the formation of complex multi-scalar centre-periphery relationships. While connections between centres are consolidated and intensified, processes of peripheralisation are also

occurring in areas that are left behind and in emerging in-between spaces that are bypassed by high-speed transportation and are experiencing a decrease in connectivity.

By far, the largest of these urban constellations is the Pearl River Delta, with the entrenched centre of Guangzhou (Kanton) and the former colony of Hong Kong as historical cores. As Wong shows in her overview, the People's Republic of China launched an unprecedented industrialisation of the entire region as part of its political opening and economic transition at the end of the 1970s. While China was developing rapidly growing city-territories—with Shenzhen and Dongguan the most prominent of them—it also took control over the financial global centre of Hong Kong in 1997, thus advancing a strong process of cross-border metropolisation.[206]

The Gauteng City-Region in South Africa, nearly 200 kilometres in diameter, is another paradigmatic example of this kind of extended urbanisation. Lindsay Howe examines the "spatiality of poverty" that is created by the dynamics between main urban centralities such as Johannesburg and Pretoria and regional-scale peripheries established by the legacy of mining and apartheid. Today, a large number of people reside on the extreme peripheries of this region, which are so geographically remote that transit dominates everyday life. Howe sheds light on various forms of popular agency, as people negotiate both local and regional-scale spaces in pursuit of opportunities and create new "popular centralities" as they exercise their agency to move across the region and produce alternative forms of space.

The case study in our book illustrates these processes with the example of the West African Corridor. Despite its name, it is not a corridor, but a 1,000-kilometre extended zone, that stretches over five countries between Lagos and Abidjan, with its main axis along the coast, connecting the main centralities of Accra, Lomé, and Cotonou, and extending far towards the north into the Sahel, integrating rural areas in various ways into the urban fabric. Armelle Choplin analyses this process in her book

Concrete City through the lens of the production, circulation, and consumption of cement, which is literally and metaphorically binding this huge region together. She follows the itinerary of cement bags from the production plant to the plot and observes the actors involved in the cement chain, showing how state actors are launching large-scale projects, global cement companies are investing in promising markets, and local people are developing their personal construction sites. In a complementary analysis presented in this book, Alice Hertzog explores the emerging metropolitan condition along this corridor by following the circulation of people and goods. She analyses the complex relationships that emerge through mobilities and movements that are producing entirely new urban configurations across borders and localities, bridging urban and rural areas and enabling the often-surprising experience of urbanity in everyday life.

CONCLUSION: HOW URBANISATION CHANGES THE PLANET

The overview of the recent scholarly literature presented in this section testifies to the breadth of analyses of extended urbanisation. They form a quickly expanding field of study that goes far beyond the classic understanding of urban studies, crossing borders to various other fields and disciplines, thus offering openings in different directions. The focus of the analysis presented here is on the identification and conceptualisation of different *urbanisation processes*, which resulted in a necessarily incomplete and still preliminary list of processes: urbanisation of agricultural areas; extended industrial urbanisation; extended urbanisation through infrastructure production; enclosure as urbanisation process; operationalisation of landscapes; extended peripheralisation; and production of polynucleated metropolitan zones. The identification of these processes can help to grasp the quite diffuse and disruptive phenomenon of extended urbanisation.

In order to better understand the full dynamics of contemporary urbanisation, we have to think about the different urbanisation processes in their relationships to each other. Urban territories are often dominated and transformed by specific combinations of urbanisation processes. Processes of concentrated, extended and differential urbanisation are not mutually exclusive and may exist side by side. It is, therefore, important to maintain a dynamic view of urbanisation. In this way, it is possible to analyse the sometimes highly volatile dynamics of urbanisation processes in their mutual interactions.

At the same time, it is also important to problematise the devastating effects that extended urbanisation may generate. These processes are often accompanied by massive and brutal interruptions of people's everyday lives and livelihoods, leading to violent displacements and dispossessions. They are usually aimed at the commodification of space, resulting in the production of an abstract space. As processes of enclosure, operationalisation, and peripheralisation show, abstraction is a real, material process with concrete effects and consequences, such as the homogenising and standardising of everyday life and the evacuation of the social. At the same time, many processes of extended urbanisation are devastating our planet, aggravating the most dramatic and existential threats, from the climate crisis to the biodiversity and the food crisis. The de-centring analytical perspective of planetary urbanisation reveals the full dimensions of extended urbanisation, often resulting in the most unsustainable way to develop urban spaces. For example, the cement industry is one of the world's largest emitters of greenhouse gases, and the unregulated and scattered distribution of industrial plants, real estate projects, and all sorts of facilities along urban corridors and across disintegrated hinterlands multiply energy consumption for private transportation. These observations suggest that city-centric approaches not only become instruments for creating allegedly sustainable urban islands of prosperity for the rich, but also shield this other side of urbanisation from view.

This situation urgently demands the development of alternatives to these kinds of urbanisation processes. Many struggles at very different places and on different levels and scales have been arising against extended urbanisation in recent times, struggles by Indigenous people, peasants, workers, and migrants, for land, food, jobs, and livelihoods. There are countless acts of resistance against large-scale projects, blocking streets and occupying land, but also unspectacular everyday struggles, such as creating facts on the ground by constructing houses to defend the land. The production of settlements and neighbourhoods is often the work of the subaltern in both central and peripheral areas, and the demand for self-determination is universal. Many of these struggles have long been generating connections and networks between peripheries and metropoles, creating popular centralities, places for meeting and encounter, advancing difference and communality. It is urgent to go beyond the urban and non-urban binary and to link these still often separated struggles with each other in the fight for a different planet.

ENDNOTES

1   Schmid, *Henri Lefebvre and the Theory of the Production of Space*, and "Specificity;" Diener et al., *The Inevitable Specificity of Cities*.

2   For an earlier version of this part see Schmid, "Analysing Extended Urbanisation."

3   Lefebvre, *Urban Revolution*.

4   Monte-Mór, "What is the Urban in the Contemporary World?"

5   Merrifield, *The New Urban Question;* Brenner and Schmid, "Planetary Urbanization"; Brenner and Schmid, "Towards a New Epistemology"; Brenner, *Implosions/Explosions*; Schmid, "Journeys through Planetary Urbanization."

6   For critiques of the concept of planetary urbanisation see Scott and Storper, "The Nature of Cities"; Peake et al., "Placing Planetary Urbanisation in Other Fields of Vision"; Davidson and Iveson, "Beyond City Limits." For illuminating insights into different aspects of the planetary urbanisation debate, see Buckley and Strauss, "With, Against and Beyond Lefebvre"; Angelo and Goh, "Out in Space"; Goonewardena, "Planetary Urbanization and Totality"; Addie, "Stuck Inside the Urban."

7   Brenner and Schmid, "Urban Age in Question."

8   Brenner and Schmid, "Towards a New Epistemology."

9   Brenner and Schmid, "Urban Age in Question"; UN Habitat, *World Cities Report*.

10   Merrifield, "The Right to the City," 475.

11   Lopes de Souza, "Right to the Planet."

12   Angelo and Wachsmuth, "Urbanizing Urban Political Ecology," 16.

13   Cairns, "Debilitating City-Centricity," 115.

14   Brenner and Schmid, "Urban Age in Question."

15   Park et al., *The City*; Scott and Soja, *The City*.

16   Whyte, *The Exploding Metropolis*.

17   Lefebvre, *Urban Revolution*, 169.

18   Brenner and Schmid, "The Urban Age in Question."

19   Brenner, "Introduction."

20   Roy, "What Is Urban about Critical Urban Theory?"; Jazeel, "Urban Theory with an Outside."

21   Lefebvre, *Urban Revolution*, 30.

22   Massey, *Space, Place and Gender*; Allen, *Lost Geographies of Power*.

23   UN-Habitat, *New Urban Agenda*.

24 See e.g. Angelo and Wachsmuth, "Why Does Everyone Think Cities Can Save the Planet?"

25 Glaeser, *Triumph of the City;* Brugmann, *Welcome to the Urban Revolution.*

26 Schmid, "Henri Lefebvre, Right to the City."

27 Scott and Storper, "The Nature of Cities," 1.

28 Engels, *The Condition of the Working Class in England,* 326.

29 Marx, *Capital,* Vol. 1, 446. Translation by author from MEW 23, 348.

30 See Schmid, *Henri Lefebvre and the Theory of the Production of Space,* 410–414.

31 Weber, *Theory of the Location of Industries.*

32 Veltz, *L'économie d'archipel,* 74.

33 Scott, *Regions and the World Economy;* Storper, *The Regional World;* Amin and Thrift, "Neo-Marshallian Nodes in Global Networks"; Phelps and Ozawa, "Contrasts in Agglomeration"; Krätke, *The Creative Capital of Cities.*

34 Veltz, *L'économie d'archipel.*

35 Scott and Storper, "The Nature of Cities," 7.

36 Amin, *Accumulation on a World Scale;* Quijano, "The Urbanization of Latin American Society". Friedmann, "The Future of Urbanization in Latin America"; Massey, *Spatial Divisions of Labour;* Smith, *Uneven Development.*

37 See e.g. Braudel, *The Mediterranean;* Cronon, *Nature's Metropolis.*

38 This is a fact that is affirmed by Scott and Storper. See "The Nature of Cities," 5.

39 Harvey, "Cities or Urbanisation?" 44.

40 Bairoch, 11.

41 Braudel, *The Mediterranean.*

42 Thünen von, *The Isolated State.*

43 Schmidtgall, *Friedrich Engels,* 88.

44 Marx, *Capital Vol. 1,* 741–744.

45 Goonewardena, "The Country and the City."

46 Federici, *Re-enchanting the World;* Sevilla-Buitrago, "Urbs in Rure."

47 Marx, *Capital Vol. 1,* 761, 773–774.

48 Luxemburg, *The Accumulation of Capital,* 452–453.

49 Harvey, *The New Imperialism.*

50 See e.g. Hart, "Denaturalizing Dispossession".

51 Cerdá, *General Theory of Urbanization 1867;* Adams, "Natura Urbans, Natura Urbanata"; Lopez de Aberasturi, "Pour une lecture de Cerdá."

52 Brenner and Schmid, "Urban Age in Question."

53 Quijano, "The Urbanization of Latin American Society"; Santos, *The Nature of Space;* Monte-Mór, "Modernities in the Jungle." See also Vegliò, "Postcolonizing Planetary Urbanization"; Lukas and Reis, "Old and New Dimensions of Peripheral Urbanization."

54 For this section, see Brenner and Schmid, "Towards a New Epistemology."

55 Brenner and Schmid, "Towards a New Epistemology," 154.

56 Schmid and Streule, *Vocabularies for an Urbanising Planet.*

57 Schmid, *Henri Lefebvre and the Theory of the Production of Space* and "Specificity;" Diener et al., *The Inevitable Specificity of Cities.*

58 An earlier version of this Part II is published in Schmid, "Analysing Extended Urbanisation."

59 McGee, "The Emergence of Desakota Regions in Asia."

60 Ginsburg et al., *The Extended Metropolis.*

61 Monte-Mór, *Modernities in the Jungle,* 6–7, 13.

62 Monte-Mór, *Modernities in the Jungle,* 7.

63 Brenner and Schmid, "Towards a New Epistemology," 167.

64 See e.g. Connolly et al., "Extended Urbanisation and the Spatialities of Infectious Disease."

65 Brenner and Ghosh, "Between the Colossal and the Catastrophic," 881.

66 Lefebvre, *The Urban Revolution,* 17.

67 Meili, "Is the Matterhorn City?" See also Schmid, "Travelling Warrior and Complete Urbanization in Switzerland".

68 Streule, "Doing Mobile Ethnography."

69 Diener et al., *Switzerland: An Urban Portrait.*

70 Diener et al., *The Inevitable Specificity of Cities;* Diener et al., *Territory.*

71 Topalović, *Hinterland: Singapore Beyond the Border.*

72 Katsikis, "From Hinterland to Hinterglobe."

73 Brenner and Katsikis, "Operational Landscapes,"; Brenner and Katsikis, "Is the Mediterranean Urban?"

74 Couling and Hein, *Urbanisation of the Sea.*

75 Arboleda, "In the Nature of the Non-city," "Spaces of Extraction, Metropolitan Explosions," and *Planetary Mine.*

76 Monte-Mór and Castriota, "Extended Urbanization"; Castriota and Tonucci, "Extended Urbanization in and from Brazil"; Kanai, "Capital of the Amazon Rainforest," and "On the Peripheries of Planetary Urbanization"; Wilson and Bayón, "Concrete Jungle," and "Black Hole Capitalism"; Wilson, *Reality of Dreams.*

77 Swyngedouw, *Social Power and the Urbanization of Water;* Angelo and Wachsmuth, "Urbanizing Urban Political Ecology"; Kaika et al., *Turning up the Heat.*

78 Brenner and Ghosh, "Between the Colossal and the Catastrophic."

79 Corboz, "The Land as Palimpsest."

80 Lefebvre, *Production of Space,* 84, 123, 128, 334, 409.

81 Lefebvre, *Production of Space,* 329; see also Lefebvre, *Urban Revolution,* 151, 161.

82 Moore, *Capitalism in the Web of Life.*

83 Lefebvre, *Urban Revolution,* 155; Lefebvre, *Production of Space,* 336–337.

84 Brenner and Schmid, "Towards a New Epistemology"; Schmid, *Henri Lefebvre and the Theory of the Production of Space.*.

85 See Schmid, "Henri Lefebvre's Theory of the Production of Space."

86 Lefebvre, *Production of Space.*

87 Harvey, *Consciousness and the Urban Experience.*

88 Lefebvre, *Right to the City,* 71.

89 See for examples Brenner, *New Urban Spaces;* Merrifield, *The New Urban Question.*

90 Lefebvre, *Production of Space,* 402–403.

91 Kanai and Schindler, "Infrastructure-led Development."

92 Simone, *For the City Yet to Come,* 118.

93 Veltz, *L'économie d'archipel.*

94 Harvey, *Limits to Capital;* see also Brenner, "Between Fixity and Motion" and Brenner, *New Urban Spaces.*

95 Harvey, *Limits to Capital,* xvi, 422.

96 Lefebvre, *The Production of Space,* 57, 120.

97 Lipietz, "Accumulation, Crises, and Ways Out"; Leborgne and Lipietz, "New Technologies, New Modes of Regulation."

98 DuPasquier and Marco, *Régulation Fordiste et post-Fordiste en Suisse;* Schmid, "Specificity and Urbanization."

99 This is particularly visible in the process of plotting urbanism. See Karaman et al., "Plot by Plot."

100 Brenner, *New Urban Spaces.*
101 Wilson, "Plan Puebla Panama."
102 Sidaway and Woon, "Chinese Narratives on One Belt, One Road."
103 Levien, *Dispossession Without Development.*
104 Lefebvre, *State, Space, World,* 223–253.
105 Brenner, *New State Spaces.* See also Brenner, *New Urban Spaces.*
106 Lefebvre, *Urban Revolution,* 97–98.
107 Lefebvre, *The Urban Revolution,* 96, 125, 173–174.
108 Davidson and Iveson, "Beyond City Limits."
109 Monte-Mór, *Modernities in the Jungle.*
110 Arboleda, "Spaces of Extraction, Metropolitan Explosions," 107.
111 Wilson, "Plan Puebla Panama."
112 Lopes de Souza, "Right to the Planet."
113 Halfacree, "Locality and Social Representation."
114 Mendras, *The Vanishing Peasant,* 7.
115 Phillips et al., "The Gentrification of a Post-industrial English Rural Village."
116 Marx and Engels, *The German Ideology,* 64.
117 Tang, "Town-Country Relations in China "; see also Wong, in this volume.
118 See e.g. Potts, *Circular Migration.*
119 Lefebvre, *Urban Revolution,* 103; Lefebvre, *Right to the City,* 71–72, 120.
120 Tang, "Where Lefebvre Meets the East"; Schmid, "Planetary Urbanization in Zürich"; Karaman et al., "Plot by Plot"; Simone, *Jakarta: Drawing the City Near.*
121 Araghi, "Global Depeasantisation."
122 Harris and Vorms, *What's in a Name?*; Topalov, "The Naming Process."
123 Zhao, "Jiehebu or suburb?"
124 See e.g. Keil and Wu, *After Suburbia.*
125 See e.g. Schmid et al., "Towards a New Vocabulary of Urbanisation Processes"; Bartels et al., "Towards Situated Analyses of Uneven Peri-Urbanisation."
126 See e.g. Garreau, *Edge City.*
127 Soja, *Thirdspace.*
128 See e.g. Teaford, *Post-Suburbia*; Nüssli and Schmid, "Beyond the Urban-Suburban Divide."
129 Datta and Shaban, *Mega-urbanization in the Global South*; Murray, *Urbanism of Exception*; Sawyer et al., "Bypass Urbanism."
130 Lukas and Reis, "Old and New Dimensions of Peripheral Urbanization."

131 Quijano, "The Urbanization of Latin American Society"; see also Vegliò, "Postcolonizing Planetary Urbanization."
132 Caldeira, "Peripheral Urbanization," 4.
133 Castells, *The Urban Question*; Harvey, *Urbanization of Capital.*
134 Forman, *Urban Regions,* 6; Scott and Storper, "The Nature of Cities."
135 See e.g. Taylor and Hurley, *A Comparative Political Ecology of Exurbia.*
136 Mbiba and Huchzermeyer, "Contentious Development: Peri-Urban Studies in Sub-Saharan Africa."
137 Friedmann, "Becoming Urban"; see also Friedmann and Sorensen, "City Unbound: Emerging Mega-conurbations in Asia."
138 Follmann, "Geographies of Peri-Urbanization in the Global South."
139 Meth et al., "Conceptualizing African Urban Peripheries."
140 Augé, *Non-Place*; Koolhaas, "Generic City."
141 Sudjic, *100 Mile City*; Sieverts, *Cities Without Cities.*
142 Corboz, *Vers la ville-territoire.*
143 Indovina, *La Città diffusa.*
144 Viganò et al., *The Horizontal Metropolis.*
145 Geddes, *Cities in Evolution,* 25.
146 Gottmann, *Megalopolis,* 4.
147 Gottmann, *Megalopolis,* 215.
148 Doxiadis, *Ekistics: An Introduction to the Science of Human Settlements*; Doxiadis and Papaioannou, *Ecumenopolis: The Inevitable City of the Future.*
149 For a thorough analysis of the concepts of Gottmann and Doxiadis, see Katsikis, "From Hinterland to Hinterglobe."
150 Harrison and Hoyler, *Megaregions*; Friedmann and Sorensen, "City Unbound: Emerging Mega-conurbations in Asia."
151 Florida et al., "The Rise of the Mega-Region."
152 Ascher, Veltz, *L'économie d'archipel.*
153 Hall and Pain, *The Polycentric Metropolis.*
154 Brenner, "Introduction: Urban Theory Without an Outside"; Roy, "What is Urban about Critical Urban Theory?"; Jazeel, "Urban Theory With an Outside."
155 Soja, "Regional Urbanization and the End of the Metropolis Era," 285.
156 Brenner and Schmid, "Planetary Urbanization" and "Towards a New Epistemology."

157 Brenner and Schmid, "Towards a New Epistemology," 167.
158 Balakrishna and Gururani, "New Terrains of Agrarian–Urban Studies"; Gosh and Meer, "Extended Urbanisation and the Agrarian Question."
159 Paprocki, "The Climate Change of Your Desires."
160 Kautsky, *On the Agrarian Question.*
161 Bernstein, "Is There an Agrarian Question in the 21st Century?"; McMichael, "Historicizing Food Sovereignty;" Arboleda, "Towards an Agrarian Question of Circulation."
162 Cairns, "Debilitating City-Centricity."
163 Gururani, "Cities in a World of Villages."
164 Diener et al., *Territory.*
165 Zhu, "Beyond Large-City-Centred Urbanisation"; Zhu, "In Situ Urbanization in China."
166 van Duijne et al., "Injected Urbanism?"; van Duijne and Nijman, "India's Emergent Urban Formations."
167 Bathla, "Planned Illegality."
168 Potts, *Circular Migration.*
169 Bertuzzo, *Archipelagos: From Urbanisation to Translocalisation.*
170 Paprocki, "The Climate Change of Your Desires."
171 Denis and Zérah, *Subaltern Urbanisation in India*; Mukhopadhyay et al., "Subaltern Urbanisation."
172 See e.g. Schmid, "Planetary Urbanization in Zürich."
173 Lefebvre, "Les nouveaux ensembles urbains"; Stanek, *Henri Lefebvre on Space,* 106–116.
174 Hart, "Multiple Trajectories", and "Denaturalizing Dispossession."
175 See also Wong, "Territorially-Nested Urbanization in China."
176 Kanai and Schindler, "Infrastructure-led Development" and "Peri-urban Promises of Connectivity."
177 Balakrishnan, "Recombinant Urbanization" and *Shareholder Cities.*
178 Wilson, "Plan Puebla Panama"; Wilson and Bayón, "Fantastical Materialisations."
179 See for example, Safina et al., "Rescaling the Belt and Road Initiative in Urban China."
180 Sevilla-Buitrago, "Urbs in Rure," 240.
181 Federici, *Re-enchanting the World.*
182 Gururani, "Cities in a World of Villages."
183 Levien, "Politics of Dispossession"; Levien, "From Primitive Accumulation to Regimes of Dispossession"; Levien, *Dispossession Without Development.*

184	Balakrishnan, "Recombinant Urbanization"; Balakrishnan, *Shareholder Cities.*
185	Joel Andreas et al., "Rural Land Dispossession in China and India."
186	Shatkin, *Cities for Profit.*
187	See for example, Sawyer et al., "Bypass Urbanism."
188	Araghi, "Accumulation by Displacement"; see also Ghosh and Meer, "Extended Urbanisation and the Agrarian Question," 1108.
189	Brenner and Katsikis, "Operational Landscapes: Hinterlands of the Capitalocene."
190	Mezzadra and Neilson, *The Politics of Operations,* 67.
191	Moore, *Capitalism in the Web of Life.*
192	Cronon, *Nature's Metropolis.*
193	Cordillo, "The Metropolis"; Paprocki, "All That Is Solid Melts into the Bay."
194	Topalović, "Palm Oil"; Hortig "Plantation Technologies"; Pratama et al., "Extended Urbanization through Capital Centralization."
195	Friedmann and McMichael, "Agriculture and the State System."
196	For more details on this broad and widely discussed field, see McMichael, "Historicizing Food Sovereignty"; Patel, "Food Sovereignty"; Gosh and Meer, "Extended Urbanisation and the Agrarian Question."
197	Hein, *Oil Spaces.*
198	Chusaini et al., "Petroleumscapes and the Urban Fabric."
199	Wilson, "We Are All Indigenous!"; Wilson, *Extractivism and Universality.*
200	Braudel, *The Mediterranean;* Hesse, *The City as a Terminal;* Hein, "Oil Spaces."
201	This account is reported as part of a comparative research project on Johannesburg, Shanghai, and London, see Robinson et al., "Financing Urban Development, Three Business Models."
202	See for instance, Fischer-Tahir and Naumann, *Peripheralization;* Kühn and Bernt, "Peripheralization and Power."
203	See for instance, Kockelkorn et al., "Peripheralization through Mass Housing Urbanization."
204	Diener et al., *Switzerland.*
205	Kanai and da Silva Oliveira, "Paving (through) Amazonia."
206	Wong, "Hong Kong, Shenzhen and Dongguan: Cross-border Urbanisation."

BIBLIOGRAPHY

Amin, Ash, and Nigel Thrift. "Neo-Marshallian Nodes in Global Networks." *International Journal of Urban and Regional Research* 16, no. 4 (1992): 571–587.

Amin, Samir. *Accumulation on a World Scale: A Critique of the Theory of Underdevelopment.* New York: Monthly Review, 1974.

Adams, Ross Exo. "Natura Urbans, Natura Urbanata: Ecological Urbanism, Circulation, and the Immunization of Nature." *Environment and Planning D: Society and Space* 32, no. 1: 12–29.

Addie, Jean-Paul. "Stuck Inside the Urban with the Dialectical Blues Again: Abstraction and Generality in Urban Theory." *Cambridge Journal of Regions, Economy and Society* 13, no. 3 (2020): 575–592.

Andreas, Joel, Sunila S. Kale, Michael Levien, and Qian Forrest Zhang. "Rural Land Dispossession in China and India." *The Journal of Peasant Studies* 47, no. 6 (2020): 1109–1142.

Allen, John. *Lost Geographies of Power.* Oxford: Blackwell, 2003.

Angelo, Hillary, and Kian Goh. "Out in Space: Difference and Abstraction in Planetary Urbanization." *International Journal of Urban and Regional Research* 45, no. 4 (2021) 732–744.

Angelo, Hillary, and David Wachsmuth. "Urbanizing Urban Political Ecology: A Critique of Methodological Cityism." *International Journal of Urban and Regional Research* 39, no. 1 (2015): 16–27.

———. "Why Does Everyone Think Cities Can Save the Planet?" *Urban Studies* 57, no. 11 (2020): 2201–2221.

Araghi, Farshad A. "Accumulation by Displacement: Global Enclosures, Food Crisis, and the Ecological Contradictions of Capitalism." *Review* (Fernand Braudel Center) 32, no. 1 (2009): 113–146.

———. "Global Depeasantization, 1945–1990." *The Sociological Quarterly* 36, no. 2 (1995): 337–368.

Arboleda, Martín. "Towards an Agrarian Question of Circulation: Walmart's Expansion in Chile and the Agrarian Political Economy of Supply Chain Capitalism." *Journal of Agrarian Change* 20, (2020): 345–363.

———. "In the Nature of the Non-city: Expanded Infrastructural Networks and the Political Ecology of Planetary Urbanisation." *Antipode* 48, no. 2 (2016): 233–251.

———. *Planetary Mine: Territories of Extraction under Late Capitalism.* London: Verso, 2020.

———. "Spaces of Extraction, Metropolitan Explosions: Planetary Urbanization and the Commodity Boom in Latin America." *International Journal of Urban and Regional Research* 40, no. 1 (2016): 96–112.

Augé, Marc. *Non-Places: Introduction to an Anthropology of Supermodernity.* Translated by John Howe. London: Verso, 1995.

Bairoch, Paul. *Cities and Economic Development: From the Dawn of History to the Present.* Translated by Christopher Braider. Chicago: University of Chicago Press, 1988.

Balakrishnan, Sai. "Recombinant Urbanization: Agrarian–Urban Landed Property and Uneven Development in India." *International Journal of Urban and Regional Research* 43, no. 4 (2019): 617–632.

———. *Shareholder Cities: Land Transformations Along Urban Corridors in India.* Philadelphia: University of Pennsylvania Press, 2020.

Balakrishnan, Sai, and Shubhra Gururani. "New Terrains of Agrarian–Urban Studies: Limits and Possibilities." *Urbanisation* 6, no. 1 (2021): 7–15.

Balducci, Alessandro, Valeria Fideli, and Francesco Curci eds. *Post-Metropolitan Territories: Looking for a New Urbanity.* London: Routledge, 2017.

Bartels, Lara Esther, Antje Bruns, and David Simon. "Towards Situated Analyses of Uneven Peri-Urbanisation: An (Urban) Political Ecology Perspective." *Antipode* 52, no. 5 (2020): 1237–1258.

Bathla, Nitin. "Planned Illegality, Permanent Temporariness, and Strategic Philanthropy: Tenement Towns Under Extended Urbanisation of Postmetropolitan Delhi." *Housing Studies* 37, no. 6 (2022): 868–888.

Bertuzzo, Elisa. *Archipelagos: From Urbanisation to Translocalisation.* Berlin: Kadmos, 2019.

Bernstein, Henry. "Is There an Agrarian Question in the 21st Century?" *Canadian Journal of Development Studies/Revue Canadienne d'études du développement* 27, no. 4 (2006): 449–460.

Brenner, Neil. "Between Fixity and Motion: Accumulation, Territorial Organization and the Historical Geography of Spatial Scales." *Society and Space* 16, no. 4 (1998): 459–481.

———.*Critique of Urbanization: Selected Essays.* Basel: Birkhäuser, 2016.

———.ed. *Implosions/Explosions: Towards a Study of Planetary Urbanization.* Berlin: Jovis, 2014.

———.*New State Spaces: Urban Governance and the Rescaling of Statehood.* Oxford: Oxford University Press, 2004.

———.*New Urban Spaces: Urban Theory and the Scale Question.* New York: Oxford University Press, 2019.

———."Introduction: Urban Theory Without an Outside." In *Implosions/Explosions: Towards a Study of Planetary Urbanization*, edited by Neil Brenner, 14–30. Berlin: Jovis, 2014.

Brenner, Neil, and Swarnabh Ghosh. "Between the Colossal and the Catastrophic: Planetary Urbanization and the Political Ecologies of Emergent Infectious Disease." *Environment and Planning A: Economy and Space* 54, no. 5 (2022): 867–910.

Brenner, Neil, and Nikos Katsikis. "Is the Mediterranean Urban?" In *Implosions/Explosions: Towards a Study of Planetary Urbanization*, edited by Neil Brenner, 428–459. Berlin: Jovis, 2014.

———."Operational Landscapes: Hinterlands of the Capitalocene." *Architectural Design* 90, no. 1 (2020): 22–31.

Brenner, Neil, and Christian Schmid. "Planetary Urbanization." In *Urban Constellations*, edited by Matthew Gandy, 10–13. Berlin: Jovis, 2011.

———."Towards a New Epistemology of the Urban?" *City* 19, no. 2–3 (2015): 151–182.

———."The 'Urban Age' in Question." *International Journal of Urban and Regional Research* 38, no. 3 (2014): 731–755.

Braudel, Fernand. *The Mediterranean and the Mediterranean World in the Age of Philip II*, Vol. 1. New York: Harper, 1972.

Brugmann, Jeb. *Welcome to the Urban Revolution: How Cities Are Changing the World.* New York: Bloomsbury, 2009.

Buckley, Michelle, and Kendra Strauss. "With, Against and Beyond Lefebvre: Planetary Urbanization and Epistemic Plurality." *Environment and Planning D: Society and Space* 34, no. 4 (2016): 617–636.

Cairns, Stephen. "Debilitating City-Centricity: Urbanisation and Urban-Rural Hybridity in Southeast Asia." In *Routledge Handbook of Urbanization in Southeast Asia*, edited by Rita Padawangi, 115–130. New York: Routledge, 2019.

Caldeira, Teresa. "Peripheral Urbanization: Autoconstruction, Transversal Logics, and Politics in Cities of the Global South." *Environment and Planning D: Society and Space* 35, no. 1 (2017): 3–20.

Castells, Manuel. *The Urban Question: A Marxist Approach.* Translated by Alan Sheridan. London: Edward Arnold, 1977 [1972].

Castriota, Rodrigo, and João Tonucci. "Extended Urbanization In and From Brazil." *Environment and Planning D: Society and Space* 36, no. 3 (2018): 512–528.

Cerdà, Ildefons. *General Theory of Urbanization 1867.* New York: Actar Publishers, 2018.

Choplin, Armelle. *Concrete City: Material Flows and Urbanisation in West Africa.* Chichester: Wiley & Sons, 2023.

Chusaini, Hajar Ahmad, Imam Buchori, and Jawoto Sih Setyono. "Petroleumscapes and the Urban Fabric: A Study of Hinterland Development in Cepu, Indonesia." *Planning Perspectives* (2023, forthcoming).

Connolly, Creighton, Roger Keil, and S. Harris Ali. "Extended Urbanisation and the Spatialities of Infectious Disease: Demographic Change, Infrastructure and Governance." *Urban Studies* 58, no. 2 (2021): 245–263.

Corboz, André. "The Land as Palimpsest." *Diogenes* 31, no. 121 (1983): 12–34.

———.*Vers la ville-territoire.* Bern: Paul Haupt, 2001.

Couling, Nancy, and Carola Hein, eds. *Urbanisation of the Sea: From Concepts and Analysis to Design.* Rotterdam: NAI010 Publishers, 2021.

Cronon, William. *Nature's Metropolis: Chicago and the Great West.* New York: W.W. Norton, 1991.

Datta, Ayona, and Abdul Shaban, eds. *Mega-urbanization in the Global South: Fast Cities and New Urban Utopias of the Postcolonial State.* London: Routledge, 2017.

Davidson, Mark, and Kurt Iveson. "Beyond City Limits." *City* 19, no. 5: 646–664.

Denis, Eric, and Marie-Hélène Zérah, eds. *Subaltern Urbanisation in India.* New Delhi: Springer India, 2017.

Diener, Roger, Manuel Herz, Jacques Herzog, Marcel Meili, Pierre de Meuron, Christian Schmid, and Milica Topalović, eds. *The Inevitable Specificity of Cities.* Zurich: Lars Müller Publishers, 2015.

Diener, Roger, Liisa Gunnarsson, Mathias Gunz, Vesna Jovanović, Marcel Meili, Christian Müller Inderbitzin, and Christian Schmid, eds. *Territory: On the Development of Landscape and City.* Zurich: Park Books, 2016.

Diener, Roger, Jacques Herzog, Marcel Meili, Pierre de Meuron, and Christian Schmid. *Switzerland: An Urban Portrait.* Basel: Birkhäuser, 2006.

Doxiadis, Constantinos A. *Ekistics: An Introduction to the Science of Human Settlements.* New York: Oxford University Press, 1968.

Doxiadis, Constantinos A., and J.G. Papaioannou. *Ecumenopolis: The Inevitable City of the Future.* Athens: Athens Center of Ekistics, 1974.

Duijne, Robbin Jan van, and Jan Nijman. "India's Emergent Urban Formations." *Annals of the American Association of Geographers* 109, no. 6 (2019): 1978–1998.

Duijne, Robbin Jan van, Jan Nijman, and Chetan Choithani. "Injected Urbanism? Exploring India's Urbanizing Periphery." *Economic Geography* 99, no. 2 (2023): 161–190.

DuPasquier, Jean-Noël, and Daniel Marco. *Régulation fordiste et post-fordiste en Suisse depuis 1937.* Geneva: Unité pour l'étude de la régulation en Suisse, 1991.

Engels, Frederick. "The Condition of the Working Class in England." In *Karl Marx, Frederick Engels: Collected Works*, Vol. 4, 295–583. New York: International Publishers, 1975 [1845].

Federici, Silvia. *Re-enchanting the World: Feminism and the Politics of the Commons.* Oakland CA: PM Press, 2018.

Florida, Richard, Tim Gulden, and Charlotta Mellander. "The Rise of the Mega-Region." *Cambridge Journal of Regions, Economy and Society* 1, no. 3 (2008): 459–476.

Follmann, Alexander. "Geographies of Peri-Urbanization in the Global South." *Geography Compass* 16, no. 7 (2022): e12650.

Forman, Richard T.T. *Urban Regions: Ecology and Planning Beyond the City.* Cambridge: Cambridge University Press, 2008.

Friedmann, Harriet, and Philip McMichael. "Agriculture and the State System: The Rise and Decline of National Agricultures, 1870 to the Present." *Sociologia Ruralis* 29, no. 2 (1989): 93–117.

Friedmann, John. "Becoming Urban: Periurban Dynamics in Vietnam and China—Introduction." *Pacific Affairs* 84, no. 3 (2011): 425–434.

———."The Future of Urbanization in Latin America: Some Observations on the Role of the Periphery." *Papers of the Regional Science Association* vol. 23, (1969): 161–174.

Friedmann, John, and André Sorensen. "City Unbound: Emerging Mega-Conurbations in Asia." *International Planning Studies* 24, no. 1 (2019): 1–12.

Garreau, Joël. *Edge City: Life on the New Frontier.* New York: Doubleday, 1991.

Geddes, Patrick. *Cities in Evolution: An Introduction to the Town-Planning Movement and the Study of Cities.* London: Williams and Norgate, 1915.

Ginsburg, Norton, Bruce Koppel, and Terry G. McGee, eds. *The Extended Metropolis: Settlement Transition in Asia.* Honolulu: University of Hawaii Press, 1991.

Glaeser, Edward. *Triumph of the City: How Our Greatest Invention Makes Us Richer, Smarter, Greener, Healthier, and Happier.* New York: Tantor, 2011.

Goonewardena, Kanishka. "The Country and the City in the Urban Revolution." In *Implosions/Explosions: Towards a Study of Planetary Urbanization,* edited by Neil Brenner, 219. Berlin: Jovis, 2014.

———."Planetary Urbanization and Totality." *Environment and Planning D: Society and Space* 36, no. 3 (2018): 456–473.

Gordillo, Gastón. "The Metropolis: The Infrastructure of the Anthropocene." In *Infrastructure, Environment, and Life in the Anthropocene,* edited by Kregg Hehterington, 66–94. Durham: Duke University Press, 2019.

Gosh, Swarnabh and Ayan Meer. "Extended Urbanisation and the Agrarian Question: Convergences, Divergences and Openings." *Urban Studies* 58, no. 6 (2021): 1097–1119.

Gottmann, Jean. *Megalopolis: The Urbanized Northeastern Seaboard of the United States.* New York: Twentieth Century Fund, 1961.

Gururani, Shubhra. "Cities in a World of Villages: Agrarian Urbanism and the Making of India's Urbanizing Frontiers." *Urban Geography* 41, no. 7 (2020): 971–989.

Halfacree, K. H. "Locality and Social Representation: Space, Discourse and Alternative Definitions of the Rural." *Journal of Rural Studies* 9, no. 1 (1993): 23–37.

Hall, Peter, and Kathy Pain, eds. *The Polycentric Metropolis: Learning from Mega-City Regions in Europe.* London: Earthscan, 2006.

Harris, Richard, and Charlotte Vorms, eds. *What's in a Name? Talking about Urban Peripheries.*Toronto: University of Toronto Press, 2017.

Harrison, John, and Michael Hoyler, eds. *Megaregions: Globalization's New Urban Form?* Cheltenham: Edward Elgar, 2015.

Hart, Gillian. "Denaturalizing Dispossession: Critical Ethnography in the Age of Resurgent Imperialism." *Antipode* 38, no. 5 (2006): 977–1004.

———."Multiple Trajectories: A Critique of Industrial Restructuring and the New Institutionalism." *Antipode* 30, no. 4 (1998): 333–356.

Harvey, David. "Cities or Urbanisation?" *City* 1, no. 1–2 (1996): 38–61.

———.*Consciousness and the Urban Experience: Studies in the History and Theory of Capitalist Urbanization.* Baltimore: Johns Hopkins University Press, 1985.

———.*The Limits to Capital.* Oxford: Blackwell, 1982.

———.*The New Imperialism.* Clarendon Lectures in Geography and Environmental Studies. Oxford: Oxford University Press, 2005.

———.*The Urbanization of Capital: Studies in the History and Theory of Capitalist Urbanization.* Baltimore: Johns Hopkins University Press, 1985.

Hein, Carola, ed. *Oil Space: Exploring the Global Petroleumscape.* New York, NY: Routledge, 2022.

Hesse, Markus. *The City as a Terminal: The Urban Context of Logistics and Freight Transport.* Franham: Ashgate, 2008.

Horn, Philipp, Paola Alfaro d'Alençon, and Ana Claudia Duarte Cardoso, eds. *Emerging Urban Spaces: A Planetary Perspective.* Cham: Springer, 2018.

Hortig, Hans. "Plantation Technologies: More-Than-Human Histories of Operationalisation in the Palm Oil Production Territories of Johor State, Malaysia." In *Footprint 33: Situating More-Than-Human Ecologies of Extended Urbanisation.* TU Delft, 2023 (forthcoming).

Indovina, Francesco, ed. *La Città diffusa.* Venezia: Daest, 1990.

Jazeel, Tariq. "Urban Theory with an Outside." *Environment and Planning D: Society and Space* 36, no. 3 (2018): 405–419.

Kaika, Maria, Roger Keil, Tait Mandler, and Yannis Tzaninis, eds. *Turning Up the Heat: Urban Political Ecology for a Climate Emergency.* Manchester: Manchester University Press, 2023.

Kanai, Juan Miguel. "Capital of the Amazon Rainforest: Constructing a Global City-Region for Entrepreneurial Manaus." *Urban Studies* 51, no. 11 (2014): 2387–2405.

———."On the Peripheries of Planetary Urbanization: Globalizing Manaus and Its Expanding Impact." *Environment and Planning D: Society and Space* 32, no. 6 (2014): 1071–1087.

Kanai, J Miguel, and Seth Schindler. "Infrastructure-Led Development and the Peri-Urban Question: Furthering Crossover Comparisons." *Urban Studies* 59, no. 8 (2022): 1597–1617.

———."Peri-Urban Promises of Connectivity: Linking Project-Led Polycentrism to the Infrastructure Scramble." *Environment and Planning A: Economy and Space* 51, no. 2 (2019): 302–322.

Kanai, J. Miguel, and Rafael da Silva Oliveira. "Paving (through) Amazonia: Neoliberal Urbanism and the Reperipheralization of Roraima." *Environment and Planning A* 46, no. 1 (2014): 62–77.

Karaman, Ozan, Lindsay Sawyer, Christian Schmid, and Kit Ping Wong. "Plot by Plot: Plotting Urbanism as an Ordinary Process of Urbanisation." *Antipode* 52, no. 4 (2020): 1122–1151.

Katsikis, Nikos. "From Hinterland to Hinterglobe: Urbanization as Geographical Organization." PhD diss., Harvard University, 2016.

———."Two Approaches to 'World Management': C.A. Doxiadis and R.B. Fuller." In *Implosions/Explosions: Towards a Study of Planetary Urbanization,* edited by Neil Brenner, 480–504. Berlin: Jovis, 2014.

Kautsky, Karl. *On the Agrarian Question.* Translated by Pete Burgess. London: Zwan Publications, 1988 [1899].

Keil, Roger and Fulong Wu, eds. *After Suburbia: Urbanization in the Twenty-First Century.* Toronto: University of Toronto Press, 2022.

Kipfer, Stefan. "Pushing the Limits of Urban Research: Urbanization, Pipelines and Counter-Colonial Politics." *Environment and Planning D: Society and Space* 36, no. 3 (2018): 474–493.

Krätke, Stefan. *The Creative Capital of Cities: Interactive Knowledge Creation and the Urbanization Economies of Innovation.* Chichester: Wiley, 2011.

Koolhaas, Rem. "The Generic City." In *S, M, L, XL*, edited by Rem Koolhaas and Bruce Mau. Rotterdam: 010 Publishers, 1995.

Leborgne, Danièle, and Alain Lipietz. "New Technologies, New Modes of Regulation: Some Spatial Implications." *Environment and Planning D: Society and Space* 6, no. 3 (1988): 263–280.

Lefebvre, Henri. *The Production of Space.* Translated by Donald Nicholson-Smith. Oxford: Blackwell, 1991 [1974].

———."Les nouveaux ensembles urbains. Un cas concret: Laq-Mourenx et les problèmes urbains de la nouvelle classe ouvrière." *La Revue française de sociologie*, no. 1–2 (1960): 186–201.

———.*The Right to the City.* In *Writings on Cities*, edited by Eleonore Kofman and Elizabeth Lebas, 63–182. Oxford: Blackwell, 1996 [1968].

———.*The Urban Revolution.* Translated by Robert Bononno. Minneapolis: University of Minnesota Press, 2003 [1970].

Lipietz, Alain. "Accumulation, Crises, and Ways Out: Some Methodological Reflections on the Concept of Regulation." *International Journal of Political Economy* 18, no. 2 (1988): 10–43.

Lopes de Souza, Marcelo. "From the 'Right to the City' to the Right to the Planet." *City* 19, no. 4 (2015): 408–443.

Lopez de Aberasturi, Antonio. "Pour une lecture de Cerdá." In Ildefonso Cerdá, *La théorie générale de l'urbanisation*, 13–63. Paris: Les éditions de l'imprimeur, 2005.

Lukas, Michael, and Nadine Reis. "Old and New Dimensions of Peripheral Urbanization in Latin America." In *Beyond the Megacity: New Dimensions of Peripheral Urbanization in Latin America*, edited by Nadine Reis and Michael Lukas, 3–53. Toronto: University of Toronto Press, 2022.

Luxemburg, Rosa. *The Accumulation of Capital.* New York: Monthly Review Press, 1968.

Marx, Karl. *Capital: A Critique of Political Economy,* Vol. 1. Translated by Ben Fowkes. London: Penguin Books, 1976 [1867].

Marx, Karl, and Frederick Engels. "The German Ideology." In *Karl Marx, FrederickEngels: Collected Works*, Vol. 5. New York: International Publishers, 1975 [1845].

Massey, Doreen. *Space, Place and Gender.* Minneapolis: University of Minnesota Press, 1994.

———.*Spatial Divisions of Labour: Social Structures and the Geography of Production.* Basingstoke: Macmillan, 1984.

Mbiba, Beacon, and Marie Huchzermeyer. "Contentious Development: Peri-Urban Studies in Sub-Saharan Africa." *Progress in Development Studies* 2, no. 2 (2002): 113–131.

McGee, Terry G. "The Emergence of Desakota Regions in Asia: Expanding a Hypothesis." In *The Extended Metropolis: Settlement Transition in Asia*, edited by Norton Ginsburg, Bruce Koppel, and Terry G. McGee, 3–25. Honolulu: University of Hawaii Press, 1991.

McMichael, Philip. "Historicizing Food Sovereignty." *The Journal of Peasant Studies* 41, no. 6 (2014): 933–957.

Meili, Marcel. "Is the Matterhorn City?" In *Implosions/Explosions: Towards a Study of Planetary Urbanization*, edited by Neil Brenner, 103–108. Berlin: Jovis, 2014.

Mendras, Henri. *The Vanishing Peasant: Innovation and Change in French Agriculture.* Translated by Jean Lerner. Cambridge, MA: MIT Press, 1970 [1967].

Merrifield, Andy. *The New Urban Question.* London: Pluto Press, 2014.

———."The Right to the City and Beyond." *City* 15, no. 3–4 (2011): 473–481.

Meth, Paula, Tom Goodfellow, Alison Todes, and Sarah Charlton. "Conceptualizing African Urban Peripheries." *International Journal of Urban and Regional Research* 45, no. 6 (2021): 985–1007.

Mezzadra, Sandro, and Brett Neilson. *The Politics of Operations: Excavating Contemporary Capitalism.* Durham: Duke University Press, 2019.

Monte-Mór, Roberto Luís. "Modernities in the Jungle: Extended Urbanization in the Brazilian Amazonia." PhD diss., University of California, Los Angeles, 2004.

Monte-Mór, Roberto Luís. "What is the Urban in the Contemporary World?" *Cadernos de Saúde Pública* 21, no. 3 (2005): 942–948.

Monte-Mór, Roberto Luís, and Rodrigo Castriota. "Extended Urbanization: Implications for Urban and Regional Theory." In *Handbook on the Geographies of Regions and Territories*, edited by Anssi Paasi, John Harrison, and Martin Jones. Cheltenham: Edward Elgar, 2018.

Moore, Jason. *Capitalism in the Web of Life.* London: Verso, 2015.

Mukhopadhyay, Partha, Marie-Hélène Zérah, and Eric Denis. "Subaltern Urbanization: Indian Insights for Urban Theory." *International Journal of Urban and Regional Research* 44, no. 4 (2020): 582–598.

Murray, Martin J. *The Urbanism of Exception.* Cambridge: Cambridge University Press, 2017.

Nüssli, Rahel, and Christian Schmid. "Beyond the Urban-Suburban Divide: Urbanization and the Production of the Urban in Zurich North." *International Journal of Urban and Regional Research* 40, no. 3 (2016): 679–700.

Paprocki, Kasia. "All That Is Solid Melts into the Bay: Anticipatory Ruination and Climate Change Adaptation." *Antipode* 51, no. 1 (2019): 295–315.

———."The Climate Change of Your Desires: Climate Migration and Imaginaries of Urban and Rural Climate Futures." *Environment and Planning D: Society and Space* 38, no. 2 (2020): 248–266.

Park, Robert E., Ernest W. Burgess, and Roderick D. McKenzie. *The City.* Chicago: University of Chicago Press, 1925.

Peake, Linda, Darren Patrick, Rajyashree N. Reddy, Gökbörü Sarp Tanyildiz, Sue Ruddick, and Roza Tchoukaleyska. "Placing Planetary Urbanization in Other Fields of Vision." *Environment and Planning D: Society and Space* 36, no. 3 (2018): 374–386.

Phelps, Nicholas A., and Terutomo Ozawa. "Contrasts in Agglomeration: Proto-Industrial, Industrial and Post-Industrial Forms Compared." *Progress in Human Geography* 27, no. 5 (1 October 2003): 583–604.

Phillips, Martin, Darren Smith, Hannah Brooking, and Mara Duer. "The Gentrification of a Post-Industrial English Rural Village: Querying Urban Planetary Perspectives." *Journal of Rural Studies* 91 (April 2022): 108–125.

Potts, Deborah. *Circular Migration in Zimbabwe and Contemporary Sub-Saharan Africa.* Rochester, NY: Boydell & Brewer, 2010.

Pratama, Isnu Putra, Haryo Winarso, Delik Hudalah, and Ibnu Syabri. "Extended Urbanization through Capital Centralization: Contract Farming in Palm Oil-Based Agroindustrialization." *Sustainability* 13, no. 18 (2021): 10044.

Quijano, Aníbal. "The Urbanization of Latin American Society." In *Urbanization in Latin America: Approaches and Issues*, 109–153. New York: Anchor Press, 1975.

Reis, Nadine and Michael Lukas, eds. *Beyond the Megacity: New Dimensions of Peripheral Urbanization in Latin America.* Toronto: University of Toronto Press, 2022.

Robinson, Jennifer, Philip Harrison, Jie Shen, and Fulong Wu. "Financing Urban Development, Three Business Models: Johannesburg, Shanghai and London." *Progress in Planning* 154 (2021): 100513.

Roy, Ananya. "What Is Urban about Critical Urban Theory?" Urban Geography 37, no. 6 (2016): 810–823.

Safina, Astrid, Leonardo Ramondetti, and Francesca Governa. "Rescaling the Belt and Road Initiative in Urban China: The Local Complexities of a Global Project." *Area Development and Policy* (2023, forthcoming).

Santos, Milton. *The Nature of Space.* Translated by Brenda Baletti. London: Duke University Press, 2021.

Sawyer, Lindsay, Christian Schmid, Monika Streule, Pascal Kallenberger. "Bypass Urbanism: Re-ordering Center-Periphery Relations in Kolkata, Lagos and Mexico City." *Environment and Planning A, Economy and Space* 53, no. 4 (2021): 675–703.

Schmid, Christian. "Analysing Extended Urbanisation: A Territorial Approach." In *Urbanisation of the Sea*, edited by Nancy Couling and Carola Hein, 93–106. Rotterdam: NAI010 Publishers, 2021.

———.*Henri Lefebvre and the Theory of the Production of Space.* London: Verso, 2022.

———."Henri Lefebvre, the Right to the City, and the New Metropolitan Mainstream." In *Cities for People, Not for Profit: Critical Urban Theory and the Right to the City*, edited by Neil Brenner, Peter Marcuse, and Margit Mayer, 42–62. New York: Routledge, 2012.

———."Henri Lefebvre's Theory of the Production of Space: Towards a Three-Dimensional Dialectic." In *Space, Difference, Everyday Life: Reading Henri Lefebvre*, edited by Kanishka Goonewardena, Stefan Kipfer, Richard Milgrom, and Christian Schmid, 27–45. New York: Routledge, 2008.

———."Journeys through Planetary Urbanization: Decentering Perspectives on the Urban." *Environment and Planning D: Society and Space* 36, no. 3 (2018): 591–610.

———."Planetary Urbanization in Zürich: A Territorial Approach for Urban Analysis." In *The Suburban Land Question: A Global Survey*, edited by Richard Harris and Ute Lehrer, 90–121. Toronto: University of Toronto Press, 2018.

———."Specificity and Urbanization: A Theoretical Outlook." In *The Inevitable Specificity of Cities*, edited by Roger Diener, Manuel Herz, Jacques Herzog, Marcel Meili, Pierre de Meuron, Christian Schmid, and Milica Topalović, 287–307. Zurich: Lars Müller Publishers, 2015.

———."Travelling Warrior and Complete Urbanization in Switzerland: Landscape as Lived Space." In *Implosions/Explosions: Towards a Study of Planetary Urbanization*, edited by Neil Brenner, 138–155. Berlin: Jovis, 2014.

Schmid, Christian, Ozan Karaman, Naomi C. Hanakata, Pascal Kallenberger, Anne Kockelkorn, Lindsay Sawyer, Monika Streule, and Kit Ping Wong. "Towards a New Vocabulary of Urbanisation Processes: A Comparative Approach." *Urban Studies* 55, no. 1 (2018): 19–52.

Schmid, Christian and Monika Streule, eds. *Vocabularies for an Urbanising Planet: Theory Building through Comparison.* Basle: Birkhäuser.

Schmidtgall, Harry. *Friedrich Engels Manchester-Aufenthalt, 1842-1844.* Trier: Karl-Marx-Haus, 1981.

Scott, Allen J. *Regions and the World Economy: The Coming Shape of Global Production, Competition, and Political Order.* Oxford: Oxford University Press, 1998.

Scott, Allen J., and Michael Storper. "The Nature of Cities: The Scope and Limits of Urban Theory." *International Journal of Urban and Regional Research* 39, no. 1 (2015): 1–15.

Scott, Allen J., and Soja Edward W., eds. *The City: Los Angeles and Urban Theory at the End of the Twentieth Century.* Los Angeles: University of California Press, 1996.

Sevilla-Buitrago, Álvaro. "Urbs in Rure: Historical Enclosure and the Extended Urbanization of the Countryside." In *Implosions/ Explosions: Towards a Study of Planetary Urbanization*, edited by Neil Brenner, 236–259. Berlin: Jovis, 2014.

Shatkin, Gavin. *Cities for Profit: The Real Estate Turn in Asia's Urban Politics.* Ithaca, NY: Cornell University Press, 2017

Sidaway, James, and Chih Yuan, Woon. "Chinese Narratives on 'One Belt, One Road' in Geopolitical and Imperial Contexts." *Professional Geographer* 69, no. 4 (2017): 591–603.

Sieverts, Thomas. *Cities Without Cities: An Interpretation of the Zwischenstadt.* London: Spon Press, 2003.

Simone, AbdouMaliq. *For the City Yet to Come: Changing African Life in Four Cities.* Durham: Duke University Press, 2004.

———.*Jakarta: Drawing the City Near.* Minneapolis: University of Minnesota Press, 2014.

Smith, Neil. *Uneven Development: Nature, Capital, and the Production of Space.* Cambridge, MA: Blackwell, 1984.

Soja, Edward W. "Regional Urbanization and the End of the Metropolis Era." In *Implosions/Explosions: Towards a Study of Planetary Urbanization,* edited by Neil Brenner, 276–287. Berlin: Jovis, 2014.

Soja, Edward W. *Thirdspace: Journeys to Los Angeles and Other Real-and-Imagined Places.* Cambridge, MA: Blackwell, 1996.

Streule, Monika. "Doing Mobile Ethnography: Grounded, Situated and Comparative." *Urban Studies* 57, no. 2 (2020): 421–438.

Storper, Michael. *The Regional World: Territorial Development in a Global Economy.* New York: Guilford, 1997.

Stanek, Łukasz. *Henri Lefebvre on Space: Architecture, Urban Research, and the Production of Theory.* Minneapolis: University of Minnesota Press, 2011.

Sudjic, Deyan. *The 100 Mile City.* New York: Harcourt Brace & Company, 1992.

Swyngedouw, Erik. *Social Power and the Urbanization of Water: Flows of Power.* Oxford: Oxford University Press, 2004.

Tang, Wing-shing. "Town-Country Relations in China: Back to Basics." *Eurasian Geography and Economics* 60, no. 4 (2019): 455–485.

———."Where Lefebvre Meets the East: Urbanization in Hong Kong." In *Urban Revolution Now: Henri Lefebvre in Social Research and Architecture,* edited by Łukasz Stanek, Christian Schmid, and Ákos Moravánszky, 71–91. Farnham: Ashgate, 2014.

Taylor, Laura E., and Patrick T. Hurley. *A Comparative Political Ecology of Exurbia: Planning, Environmental Management, and Landscape Change.* Cham, Switzerland: Springer, 2016.

Teaford, Jon C. *Post-Suburbia: Government and Politics in the Edge Cities.* Baltimore, MD: Johns Hopkins University Press, 1997.

Thünen, Johann Heinrich von. *The Isolated State.* Translated by C.M. Wartenberg. New York: Pergamon Press, 1966.

Topalov, Christian. "The Naming Process." In *What's in a Name? Talking about Urban Peripheries,* edited by Richard Harris and Charlotte Vorms, 36–67. Toronto: University of Toronto Press, 2017.

Topalović, Milica, ed. *Hinterland: Singapore beyond the Border.* Basel: Birkhäuser, forthcoming.

Topalović, Milica. "Palm Oil: A New Ethics of Visibility for the Production Landscape." *Architectural Design* 86, no. 4 (2016): 42–47.

UN-Habitat (United Nations Human Settlement Programme). *The State of the World's Cities Report 2006/2007.* London: Earthscan for UN-Habitat, 2007.

———.*New Urban Agenda.* United Nations Conference on Housing and Sustainable Urban Development (Habitat III) in Quito, Ecuador, 2016. United Nations, 2017.

Vegliò, Simone. "Postcolonizing Planetary Urbanization: Aníbal Quijano and an Alternative Genealogy of the Urban." *International Journal of Urban and Regional Research* 45, no. 4 (2021): 663–678.

Veltz, Pierre. *Mondialisation, villes et territoires: L'économie d'archipel.* Paris: Presses Universitaires de France, 1996.

Vigano, Paola, Chiara Cavalieri, and Martina Barcelloni Corte, eds. *The Horizontal Metropolis: Between Urbanism and Urbanization.* Cham, Switzerland: Springer, 2018.

Weber, Alfred. *Theory of the Location of Industries.* Translated by Carl J. Friedrich. Chicago: University of Chicago Press, 1929 [1909].

Whyte, William H. Jr, ed. *The Exploding Metropolis.* Berkeley: University of California Press, 1993.

Wilson, Japhy. *Extractivism and Universality: Inside an Uprising in the Amazon.* New York, NY: Routledge, 2023.

———."Plan Puebla Panama: The Violence of Abstract Space." In *Urban Revolution Now: Henri Lefebvre in Social Research and Architecture,* edited by Łukasz Stanek, Christian Schmid, and Ákos Moravánszky, 113–131. Farnham: Ashgate, 2014.

———.*Reality of Dreams: Post-neoliberal Utopias in the Ecuadorian Amazon.* New Haven, CT: Yale University Press, 2021.

———."'We Are All Indigenous!' Insurgent Universality on the Extractive Frontier." *Capitalism Nature Socialism* 33, no. 3 (2022): 120–137.

Wilson, Japhy, and Manuel Bayón. "Black Hole Capitalism." *City* 20, no. 3 (2016): 350–367.

———."Concrete Jungle: The Planetary Urbanization of the Ecuadorian Amazon." *Human Geography* 8, no. 3 (2015): 1–23.

———."Fantastical Materializations: Interoceanic Infrastructures in the Ecuadorian Amazon." *Environment and Planning D: Society and Space* 35, no. 5 (2017): 836–854.

Wong, Kit Ping. "Territorially-Nested Urbanization in China: The Case of Dongguan." *Eurasian Geography and Economics* 60, no. 4 (2019): 486–509.

———."Hong Kong, Shenzhen and Dongguan: Cross-border Urbanisation." In *Vocabularies for an Urbanising Planet: Theory Building through Comparison,* edited by Christian Schmid and Monika Streule, 84–106. Basle: Birkhäuser.

Zhao, Yimin. "Jiehebu or Suburb? Towards a Translational Turn in Urban Studies." *Cambridge Journal of Regions, Economy and Society* 13 (2020): 527–542.

Zhu, Yu. "Beyond Large-City-Centred Urbanisation: In Situ Transformation of Rural Areas in Fujian Province." *Asia Pacific Viewpoint* 43, no. 1 (2002): 9–22.

———."In Situ Urbanization in China: Processes, Contributing Factors, and Policy Implications." *China Population and Development Studies* 1, no. 1 (2017): 45–66.

The Mine, the City, and the Encampment. Contesting Extractivism in Eastern Amazonia

When the plane begins its descent towards the Carajás Airport, the view of the endless rainforest covering the mountain range is thrilling. It evokes the illusion of an idyllic Amazonian stereotype of vast green, dehumanised landscapes that underlie the global imaginary of the region. But this is only because the airport is located inside the Carajás National Forest, a federal conservation unit of 411,000 hectares that protects not only the rainforest, but also several mining complexes and their supporting infrastructures, such as open pit mines, roads, company towns, railroads, and the airport itself.

As I land in the northern sector of the National Forest, surrounded by the dense rainforest, it becomes clear that nature does the job of building a wall, insulating the extractivist operations and infrastructures. [Fig. 1] After all, unless one knows how to handle the heat, the humidity, and the hundreds of animal and plant species that live here, walking through the rainforest might not be a good idea. Tourists and passengers are allowed to enter the National Forest only to access guided tours and the

airport. All other entrances and exits are exclusive to Vale S.A., which was once a Brazilian state company, and today is the third largest transnational mining group on the planet. [Fig. 2–3]

A few kilometres away, in the southern sector of the National Forest, lies Vale's most recent development: the S11D Mining Complex, the largest open pit mine in human history. During its construction from 2011 to 2016, the S11D created more than 45,000 jobs in mining, attracting a mass of migrants to Canaã, previously a town of 30,000 residents. After the mining complex started operating in 2017, less than 100 workers were required to run the mine due to the high level of automation, instantly leaving tens of thousands unemployed. Some residents left the city, leaving behind their houses and their neighbourhoods; some rushed to find other work opportunities, causing changes in the urban economy; and some became *camponeses* and occupied plots of land in the agricultural zone of the municipality, often close to zones of logistics and extraction, hence becoming a direct threat to their former employer.

Fig. 1

This chapter explores urbanisation processes that followed the construction of the S11D. My goal is not to discuss mining itself but what happens *around* the mining complex, *in response to* it, and *in spite of* it. What kinds of cities and towns emerge in response to a vast mining enterprise within the domains of the rainforest? What kinds of extended materialities and capacities are mobilised by the state, the mining company, and the "urban majorities" that co-produce urbanisation?[1] If we understand extractivism as a driver of urbanisation, how, then, do the different generations of mining technology induce different forms of urbanisation? In what ways centres and peripheries are reorganised and recast, and what forms of contestation emerge in response?

By anchoring the analysis on Lefebvre's notion of "levels of reality and analysis", especially in relation to the extension of the ediating character of urbanisation towards the non-city, I propose a radical decentring of the urban analysis by exploring, beyond the city, what other mining-induced forms of extended

urbanisation are taking place.[2] I emphasise the role of the encampments and the experience of their residents in the rural zone of the municipality to unveil different perspectives of what urbanisation might look like from the "outside." I describe the boom-and-bust process of the mining town that led to rural land occupations by hundreds of families and how these residents relate to and are embedded within extractivist urbanisation even kilometres away from the urban centre. In doing so, I argue that extended urbanisation works both as an extension of the state and capital strategies, and as an open-ended transformative process, as a means through which subjectivities nurtured on the level of everyday life are expressed, often in contesting and generative ways.[3]

The first section of this chapter thus presents the theoretical ground resulting from my broader research to help the reader navigate the text and subsequent empirical sections.[4] The second section presents a brief geohistorical introduction to the region, highlighting that the theoretical framework of extended urbanisation

Fig. 2

Fig. 3

is particularly useful in the Amazonian context to interpret the various rounds of state and capital colonisation in the 1970s and 1980s. The third section discusses how extraction induced the emergence of cities and towns, roads, railroads, mines, and other socio-spatial transformations that have usually followed the expansion of extractive projects in the region.

The remaining sections derive directly from my fieldwork in Carajás, conducted in 2018 and 2019. The fourth section presents the North Sierra and the South Sierra of Carajás and their contrasting extractivist temporalities and urban trajectories. The fifth section examines the urbanisation of the urban centre of Canaã, which hosts the majority of the migrant labour employed in the S11D. The final section presents stories of the "non-city," focusing on agrarian encampments founded by former town residents who, in the process of becoming peasants (*camponeses*), established new forms of appropriating the extended materialities of extractivism and new political subjectivities related to its contestation. In doing so, my goal is to decentre perspectives on urbanisation not only by training analytical attention to non-city spaces but also by positioning myself and narrating everyday life and struggles of the *camponeses* that would otherwise remain unnoticed by city-centric urban research and theory.

CONCEPTUAL OPENINGS:
URBANISATION, EXTRACTIVISM
AND LEVELS OF ANALYSIS

In 1970 Henri Lefebvre pioneered the conceptualisation of the extended character of urbanisation, assuming these processes are induced by industrialisation. They are not restricted to the expansion of industrial cities but also involve the spreading of an urban-industrial fabric, simultaneously absorbing and eroding agrarian life through numerous and diverse "disjunct fragments."[5] Thus, Industrialisation induced processes of "extended urbanisation" generating material, ecological, and socio-political

F. 1   Aerial view of the Carajás National Forest.

F. 2   Carajás National Forest: The main gate.

F. 3   Carajás National Forest: Internal roads.

transformations beyond dense settlement areas.[6] Lefebvre argued that to grasp the generative and transformative character of the urban, it is necessary to move beyond the "blind field" of industrialism, which shapes our conceptions and representations of the urban and urbanisation.[7]

In this chapter, I propose an alternative, more precise, and geographically specific hypothesis of induction, moving from industrialism to "extractivism."[8] Given its importance in the Amazonian and Latin American contexts, I explore urbanisation processes driven by extractivism, considering the role of state and capital in its planning and production as well as the everyday dynamics and popular practices that contest and co-produce urbanisation.

Although many recent contributions analyse the workings of extraction globally, the literature in urban studies aimed at interrogating the relationship between extractivism and urbanisation is still incipient.[9] Besides, in spite of the insights such contributions convey, their focus is mostly on city-making and agglomeration dynamics—examples of "methodological cityism."[10] Thus, my intent is to show how extractivism induces not only concentrated but also extended forms of urbanisation.

I foreground the role of mining, with its extended extractive assemblies, as a crucial driver of urbanisation in Eastern Amazonia. In addition to the actual extraction sites, these activities demand logistical, hydroelectric, and other energy infrastructures, as well as communication and transportation apparatuses. These assemblies shape the formation of cities and towns, villages, encampments, and other forms of larger and smaller centralities fundamental to extended urbanisation.[11] Here, extraction entails both the emergence of such centralities—their making and remaking through everyday practices, movements, and struggles—and their destruction or radical reorganisation. These extended extractivist assemblies are also subject to popular appropriations and contestations that take advantage of their own "leaks."[12] All of these materialities and flows are constitutive of processes of extended urbanisation, whether or not they have concentrated urban forms (towns, cities, metropolises) as their actual *or* virtual outcome.

It is important to notice that, beyond their immediate material implications, urbanisation processes need to be understood, particularly in the Amazonian context, as a form of mediation between different "levels of analysis and social reality," following Lefebvre's (1970) crucial formulation.[13] In this perspective, the urban is conceptualised as a mediating level between two other levels of social reality: the general level of abstract social relations of state and capital and the private level of concrete dynamics of everyday life. The general level comprises the domains of capital and the state as "will" (of those who hold power and design political strategies) and as "representation" (as ideologies and conceptions of power). The private level comprises the concrete, contradictory, and contestatory dynamics of everyday life, of dwelling, and of lived experience, and is subjected to both domination and radical appropriation.[14]

In this conception, the urban level is shaped by both the projections and materialisations of abstract strategies and general social relations on the one hand, and of everyday forms of contestation and appropriation by various social groups on the other. The urban, thus, needs to be understood as a battleground of struggle and contestation. It is both a means through which capital and state logics violently penetrate everyday life and through which an everyday "reservoir of radical-utopian subjectivity" contests and destabilises the same concrete abstractions.[15]

Though this framework has been used, especially in Latin America, to analyse extended urbanisation, an explanation of why the notions of level and mediation are crucial for understanding these processes has been lacking.[16] Here, I briefly foreground three interrelated arguments on the mobilisation of the Lefebvrian methodological apparatus to the study of extended urbanisation. First, the *extension of urbanisation* entails the *extension of mediation*. Urbanisation advances beyond city limits often as particular projections of state and capital: a company town, a mining complex, a logistical corridor, or even a unit of conservation. These "top-down" developments, in turn, are met by everyday dynamics of migration, movement, and circulation; in this way, for example, movements of people searching for jobs in mining provinces have entailed the emergence of the "boom towns of the Amazon."[17] Beyond cities and towns, extended urbanisation transforms diverse areas that formerly supported local dynamics like grazing landscapes, *quilombos*, riverine communities, agrarian settlements, and villages of various kinds. Take, for example, indigenous lands and villages in Eastern Amazonia that were crossed by extractivist and logistical developments and experienced displacement and resettlement as a result of the reorganisation of territories and the recasting of centres and peripheries.[18]

Secondly, in non-city geographies, both the projections of the general level and the "counter-projections" on the mediating level are often different, in quantitative and qualitative terms, from their city counterparts.[19] The ways in which state and capital "show up" in the geographies of extended urbanisation are not the same as in cities; and the ways people appropriate and contest them are different too. For instance, in Canaã's countryside, mining infrastructure works are less regulated, police violence (often forwarded by Vale's private security) is more extreme and brazen, and evictions are more brutal, precisely because both Vale and the prefecture understand these landscapes as "off the radar." An example is Vale's relationship with different tentacles of the Brazilian State (environmental agencies, regulatory bodies, police, and law) which allows the company to extend its violence and territorial control in rural areas in ways that would be unthinkable in large urban centres. Illustrative is also the difference between the creation of a park in the centre of Belo Horizonte to displace homeless people and the creation of a conservation unit in Carajás to displace hundreds of peasants living near mining areas; both are examples of environmental "conservation"

that occlude intentions generated at the general level and projected into the territory.

Finally, the levels of analysis have to be understood as levels of abstraction. Although the mediation between the levels leads to the penetration of everyday life by abstract objects, rhythms, and logics, the *distinction between* the levels— that is, the very criteria of their determination— is given by degrees of abstraction.[20] The general level comprises the most general and abstract relationships, and its projections onto the mediating urban level engenders an "abstract space."[21] The private level, on the other hand, "is the ground in which all other levels of social reality are rooted."[22] The levels of abstraction suggest different rationales associated with each level: from the "concrete rationality" of everyday practices to the "abstract rationality" of hegemonic actors of space production (the authoritarian state, the planner, the developer).[23]

Through the levels of abstraction, we can understand how extended urbanisation is also composed of processes of operationalisation, i.e., how the multiple "operations of capital," particularly those related to extraction and logistics, are mediated and territorially instantiated.[24] Abstraction produces and brings into relation a fully automated mine, a fully industrialised agricultural landscape, a fully controlled seascape of oil extraction, and a fully protected unit of conservation in the heart of the Amazon—all of which are temporarily deprived of everyday dynamics through which the fissures of abstract space would be explored and disrupted, turned into something else, unplanned, unpredicted, and unanticipated.[25]

In this chapter, I foreground the importance of the extension of these mediations through urbanisation, highlighting its qualitative differences in city and non-city environments, the projections and counter-projections that co-produce urbanisation, and the levels of abstraction involved in the production of space. This conceptual apparatus is particularly useful, as I present in the next two sections, to understand the multiple rounds of colonisation in Amazonian history.

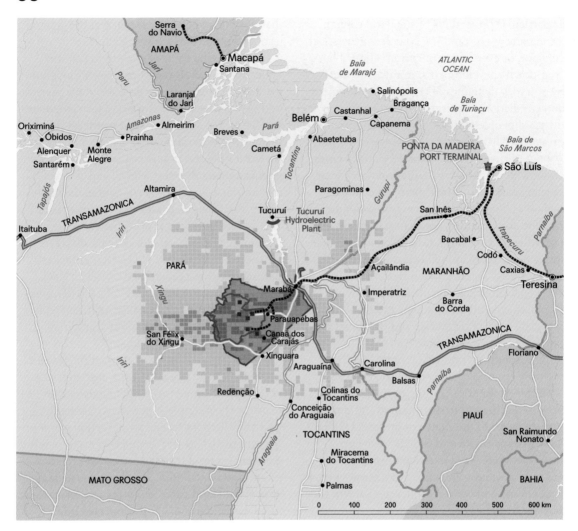

Legend

- Urban centres
- Road network
- Transamazonica
- Conservation areas (rain-forest and indigenous land)
- Former Marabá municipal area in the 1980s, now divided into six municlpalities
- Railways
- Transshipment port

MINING LEASES AROUND CARAJÁS REGION

- Granted to Vale
- Granted to other companies
- Mining site (open and closed)

EASTERN AMAZONIA
AND THE MINING REGION OF CARAJÁS
Fig. 4

STATE COLONISATION, FRONTIER EXPANSION, AND EXTENDED CITIZENSHIP IN AMAZONIA

The Brazilian Amazon encompasses two-thirds of the country's territory. Its regional resourcefulness—nearly half of the world's remaining tropical forests, a quarter of the world's fresh water and one-third of the world's known species—has been recurrently instrumentalised by modern-colonial narratives of an unexplored territory of hidden and boundless riches. After independence in 1822, the state incurred multiple colonisation efforts emanating from the hegemonic south-central regions of the country.[26] In addition to the many "marches to the west" in the nineteenth and early twentieth centuries, state efforts to integrate the Amazon into the national and world economy massively increased in pace and scale in the 1960s.[27] Until then, despite the political and economic control that metropolises such as Belém and Manaus exerted in the region, the Amazon could be characterised as an "urban archipelago" of disarticulated cities and towns.[28]

The military regime (1964–1985) changed that trajectory through violent and authoritative strategies and policies, securing the role of the Amazon as the frontier for land colonisation, agribusiness, resource extraction (mining, logging, hydrocarbons), and hydropower production. Through a series of migration policies, colonisation projects, regional economic plans, and incentives for extractive activities, the military attempted to subsume the Amazon to capital and state interests. Beyond ravaging and plundering, these large extractive and infrastructural interventions also functioned as forms of "internal colonisation" that hold to the present and are central to understanding the historical geographies of urbanisation in extractivist Amazonia in relation to the industrialising south-east region.[29]

The state's goal was twofold: first, to exclude, either by dispossession or extermination, the Amazonian autochthone majorities that populated the region; and second, to extract and export regional resources at an unprecedented pace, brutality, and scale. These interventions were carried out by the authoritarian state and national and foreign capital—mining companies, contractors, large-scale loggers, banks, and others—engendering environmental plunder and displacement of Amazonian majorities. Simultaneously, migration policies and promises of cheap land, work opportunities, and abundant resources drove large masses of south-central residents to the Amazon. Cities, towns, and neighbourhoods quickly emerged while oversight, regulation, and control were almost absent, leading to chaotic settlement and land use patterns and social and environmental tragedies in the clashes between migrant "pioneers" and the peoples of the forest.[30]

In this context, the notion of "Frontier Amazonia" was developed to denote transformations and spatio-temporal clashes in that part of the Amazon that was more brutally and intensely occupied in the first decades of the military regime.[31] It was the analysis of Frontier Amazonia that led Monte-Mór to formulate the concept of extended urbanisation, drawing on Lefebvre.[32] Even deep in the Amazon, social processes and spatial forms seemed connected to the urban-industrial realm as the "general conditions of production," formulated by Lojkine and Topalov.[33] [Fig. 4] Those conditions, formerly constrained to cities and metropolitan regions, gradually extended to spaces usually seen as determined by local and everyday dynamics. The concept of extended urbanisation responded to the need to understand the formation of "concentrated urban nuclei" and the entanglements and ramifications of the "extended urban fabric," including centralities and sub-centralities created, articulated, and reorganised with significant territorial differentiations and socio-environmental consequences.[34]

In Frontier Amazonia, it became clear that urbanisation not only engendered the equipment of the territory in urban-industrial terms but also *mediated* different temporalities, from pre-Columbian societies to modern capitalism, often separated by short territorial distances.

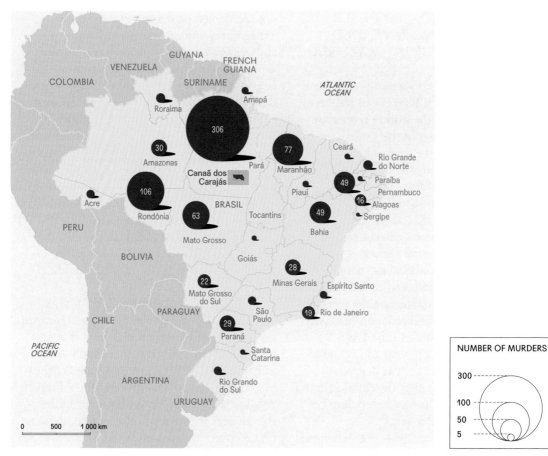

MURDERS IN THE COUNTRYSIDE
DUE TO LAND CONFLICTS, 1997–2019
Fig. 5

In the process of intense frontier occupation after 1970, several late encounters between the modern forces of urban-industrial developmentalism and pre-[Columbian] groups of Índios, some of them never before contacted by "civilised men," took place in Frontier Amazonia as bulldozers and axes assaulted the jungle with highways, towns and villages. The Suruís and Cinta-Largas, in Rondônia, and the Panarás and Caiapós, in Mato Grosso's Nortão and southern Pará, were some of the groups of Índios forced to face the civilisation brought along with roads, colonisation projects, cattle ranches, *gold mining, logging, and other frontier activities.*[35]

This "superimposition of temporalities" embedded within the extended urbanisation of Frontier Amazonia was expressed in violent land conflicts.[36] Although the Brazilian state advanced several colonisation projects[37] by advertising free or cheap land to south-central migrants, the vast majority of incomers were never able to secure a piece of land in the region, instead attempting to earn their livelihoods through land occupation, often in conflict with traditional peoples, mining companies, project developers, and ranchers. In the 1970s and 1980s, the intensity of these struggles increased, leading to a record number of murders, tortures, and massacres in Frontier Amazonia, especially in the state of Pará. [Fig. 5]

The "fight for land" consolidated as the central political feature of the region.[38] A wide range of struggles and forms of contestation emerged against large-scale projects and land concentration assembling landless peasants, traditional communities, and most "peoples of the forest" in organised and well-articulated social movements that transcended the regional scale.[39]

The role of extended urbanisation in the articulation of diverse social groups and political demands—urban and rural unions, indigenous peoples, rubber tappers, tap miners, religious groups, political parties, and many others— led Monte-Mór to conceptualise a concomitant process of "extended citizenship": a particular kind of re-politicisation of space related to the urban praxis radiating from large urban-industrial centres. This theorisation reveals how, despite colonisation efforts by state and capital, urbanisation is always also marked by (re)appropriations, contestations, and radical transformations nurtured at the level of everyday life. It highlights the "multitemporal heterogeneities" that both compose and result from extended urbanisation, which is an open-ended spatial process, never fully predictable, no matter how strong the disciplinary powers of state and capital may seem.[40]

Although urban scholars have shown for a long time that urbanisation processes are crucial for interpreting historical and contemporary Amazonia, the reverse also holds true: the Amazon region is important for contemporary urban studies to subvert inherited concepts and theories and to unveil possible futures that remain off the radar.[41] It is of particular importance to show that studies of cities and towns are insufficient in exploring the drivers and implications of urbanisation, particularly in relation to extractivism. In this sense, the region of Carajás presents a privileged lens for the study of such relations and for illuminating (extended) urban futures.

EXTRACTIVISM AND URBANISATION IN CARAJÁS

The construction of Brasília was crucial for the colonisation of the Amazon. In 1960, the conclusion of the Belém-Brasília Highway paved the way for both the implementation of large extractivist projects and for settling migrant populations. Mining and cattle ranching combined with cheap land and public financial incentives laid the foundation for land colonisation throughout the 1960s and 1970s. South-eastern Pará was one of the first frontier regions to be colonised, largely due to mining activities in Carajás, the mountain range forming a complex of plateaus between the Itacaiúnas and Parauapebas rivers. [Fig. 6] These plateaus hold one of the greatest mineral deposits on Earth, discovered by The United States Steel Corporation in the 1960s and explored by Vale since the 1970s.

Although tap-mining (*garimpo*) was an important activity responsible for large migration inflows since the 1950s, large-scale mining operations were the strongest force behind urbanisation in the region. Throughout the 1980s and 1990s, the concentration of jobs and state-capital apparatuses in this forested region led to several economic booms causing cities and towns to grow in size and number.[42] As new urban centres formed, new municipalities were constituted. The entire region of south-eastern Pará, for example, was previously one single municipality, Marabá. [Fig. 7]

Localised energy and water infrastructures (hydropower plants, waterways), transportation (roads, railways), and waste management (tailing dams) also induced growth and the emergence of new centres. The Tucuruí Hydropower Plant (1981) in Carajás entailed the expulsion of many indigenous, *quilombola*, peasants, and riverine communities and the displacement of 6,000 families involved in fishing, agriculture, and gathering.[43] More than 2,800 km² were flooded for the construction of the dam, further generating soil erosion, gas emissions, and loss of water-life.[44] The Carajás Railroad (1986) was (and still is) responsible for numerous land conflicts along its 993 kilometre route running between Carajás and

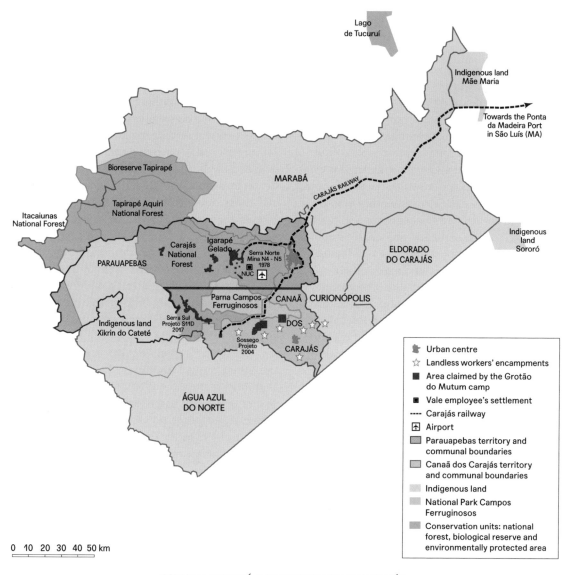

SOUTH-EAST PARÁ AND THE REGION OF CARAJÁS:
MINING, INDIGENOUS LANDS, AND PROTECTED AREAS
Fig. 6

Vale's port through indigenous, peasant, and *quilombola* lands, conservation units, and archaeological sites.[45] Several metal mining industries and agribusiness enterprises settled along the Carajás Railroad for locational advantages, and pig iron mills were installed in centres such as Açailândia (MA), Marabá (PA), and Santa Inês (MA), which bolstered logging in response to the mills' charcoal demand.[46]

These infrastructural assemblages—mine, railroad, hydropower plant, and port—still support Vale's operations today. Most of them were constructed in the context of the "Project Great Carajás" (PGC) launched in 1980 by the military regime to deepen the exploration of Eastern Amazonian natural resources. The entire project area encompassed more than 900,000 km², more than 10% of the Brazilian

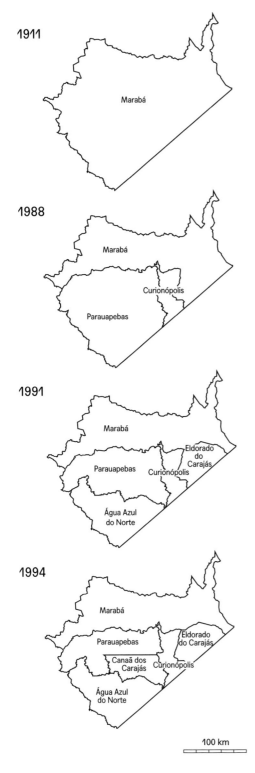

1911

1988

1991

1994

100 km

THE CONSTITUTION OF MUNICIPALITIES
AND URBAN CENTRES IN SOUTH-EAST PARÁ
Fig. 7

territory. In its attempts to subordinate Eastern Amazonia to the foreign and national capital, it unleashed incalculable social and ecological disruptions.[47] Extractive, financial, and administrative businesses were attracted to the region by the enhanced infrastructures, financial incentives, lack of pollution and deforestation controls, labour supply, and lack of trade union organisation. Although advertised as a broad development programme with diversified economic activities, the PGC mostly produced the extractivist infrastructure that, today, is either owned or controlled by Vale S/A. This company was founded as a state company in 1942 and privatised for just 3.3 billion dollars in 1997; today, it is the third largest mining group on the planet.

I have presented the historical geographies of extractivism in Carajás in relation to urbanisation for three reasons. First, to reassert the idea that extractivism can induce urbanisation in manifold ways, not only around the extraction sites but also related to their supporting infrastructures—highways, hydropower plants, railroads, and company towns. By agglomerating state and capital apparatuses, infrastructure, and jobs, extractivism creates concentrated nuclei giving rise to urban economies. However, these extended materialities do not necessarily crystalise in the forms of cities, rather they reorganise the entire territory through population displacement and environmental resource plunder.

Secondly, these projects are examples of general state and capital strategies and logics projected and materialised at the urban level. They unsettle and disrupt ecologies, communities, and forms of everyday life that often did not have any relations with the general order). The *Xikrin* people, for example, inhabited the region that today corresponds to south-eastern Pará since the eighteenth century. For the past five decades, they have lived in a constant battle with Vale and the state due to logistic projects in their lands, river contamination, mining explosions, and several other disruptions to their ecosystems and cultural landscapes.[48] Together with other Amazonian majorities—*quilombolas, seringueiros, quebradeiras-de-coco, camponeses, ribeirinhos, sem-terra, faxinalenses*—they are forced to operate within the abstract logic of the "general level," manifesting in meetings and negotiations, hearings and inspections, protests, and demonstrations.

Finally, these projections and mediations are not restricted to the conventional repertoire of material imaginaries in urban studies—roads and buildings, cities and towns, concrete and cement. They can also be expressed, as Lefebvre noted, in sites of nature preservation.[49] The Carajás National Forest, discussed in the next section, is a good example of how abstract strategies are mediated and territorially instantiated; in other words, how large territories can be operationalised through environmental regulation.

THE CARAJÁS NATIONAL FOREST AND TWO HISTORICAL MOMENTS OF EXTRACTIVISM

The area that today corresponds to the Carajás National Forest has been explored by Vale since the 1970s. The conservation unit was created in 1998, less than one year after the company was privatised. Formally, Vale only holds a seat in the Forest's managing board, which is controlled by a federal environmental agency. One of the managers in the agency has declared that the privatisation of the mineral "deposits, the territory, would have been a bigger scandal," thus, "this arrangement was made, which [created] the conservation unit in 1998." In practice, Vale has full control of the area.[50] [Fig. 8]

Other authors have used terms like "green shield" and "green belt" to refer to the Forest's function in protecting Vale's operation in a region marked by land conflicts and occupations.[51] I have shown elsewhere that the Forest fulfils several other functions.[52] It regularises Vale's illegal land acquisition while signalling to national and international speculators an ostensible institutional security, reinforcing the legal formalisation of appropriated land, the right to property, and the commodification

and financialization of land.[53] Since public agencies are formally in charge of the conservation unit, it transfers the costs and the legal responsibility of protection to the state. It works as an instrument of dispossession of landed groups settled in the area. It gives an alibi and helps fulfil the legal requirements for mining activities since the conservation units are not usually the equivalents of environmental destruction. It creates a massive environmental marketing campaign supported by popular representations of "preserving nature in the Amazon."

While demonstrating how operationalisation can be enacted through environmental regulation, the Carajás National Forest also illustrates two distinct historical moments of extractivism and extended urbanisation in the two *sierras* of the mountain range, both explored by Vale. The North Sierra contains infrastructures built in the 1970s and 1980s, which operate to this day using the old technological model. In contrast, the South Sierra mine utilises a "fourth generation technology" allowing for completely automated operations, thus inducing a different kind of urbanisation.[54]

NORTH SIERRA: THE OLD MODEL

In the North Sierra, Vale has been extracting iron, manganese, copper, chromium, nickel, cassiterite, tungsten, and gold since 1978. The materials are transported to Vale's port through the Carajás Railroad, which penetrates the "preserved" rainforest. [Fig. 9] The North Sierra hosts the Carajás Airport and a company town built in the 1970s. Regionally known as "Vale's neighbourhood" (Bairro da Vale), the company town is well equipped with infrastructure, urban services, and facilities, which are exclusive to Vale's high-ranking employees.[55]

Immediately after the main gate is the centre of Parauapebas, a city that sprung from Vale's operations in the late 1970s. At the time, operating with older technologies, this mine required more human labour, engendering a massive flow of migrants into the city emerging "at the foot of the mountain." In contrast to the planned and structured company town set amid

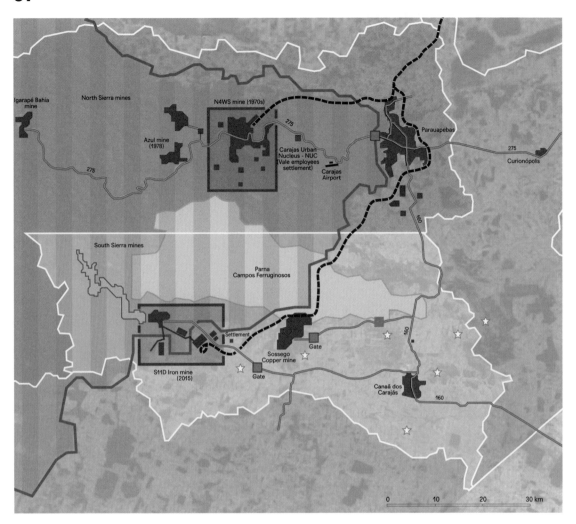

Igarapé Bahia mine

North Sierra mines

N4WS mine (1970s)

Azul mine (1978)

Carajas Urban Nucleus - NUC (Vale employees settlement)

Carajas Airport

Parauapebas

Curionópolis

South Sierra mines

Parna Campos Ferruginosos

Settlement

Sossego Copper mine

Gate

Gate

S11D Iron mine (2015)

Canaã dos Carajás

■ Urban centres
☐ Area of the two main mining complexes
■ Mining sites (open and closed)
■ Guarded entrance gates to the mining sites
☆ Landless workers' encampments
■ Area claimed by the Grotão do Mutum encampment
---- Carajás Railroad
— Road network
Parauapebas territory
Canaã dos Carajás
Conservation areas
National Park Campos Ferruginosos

0   10   20   30 km

THE NORTH SIERRA AND SOUTH SIERRA MINING REGIONS
IN THE CARAJÁS MOUNTAIN RANGE
Fig. 8

THE N4WS MINE

THE COMPANY TOWN

THE AIRPORT

Fig. 9

the rainforest, Parauapebas was a precarious "city of subcontractors."[56] From 1983 to 1989, its population grew from 1 to 53,000 people living mostly on informally occupied land and auto-constructed houses. While the population boom was followed by growing unemployment, illiteracy, prostitution, and criminality, Vale and the state institutions pressed on with extractive activities despite rising social and political problems.[57]

Today the city of Parauapebas has 200,000 residents. It is the fifth largest city of the state of Pará and Brazil's main exporter of raw materials extracted at the North Sierra, which are expected to continue until 2048. Although

Parauapebas has outgrown its initial capacities and is no longer merely a city of migrant mining workers, Vale's historic influence continues to dominate. Parauapebas' everyday rhythms of: traffic congestions and street movements follow the change of labour shifts in the mine. Also, the decisions on public expenditures are mostly aimed at improving Vale's operations, expressing the city's dependence on mining royalties and mining jobs.[58]

Parauapebas is a classic example of historic entanglements between urbanisation and extraction, as in numerous other examples in Eastern Amazonia. The construction of the *Transamazônica Highway* in the 1960s paved the way for several

PARAUAPEBAS

F. 9   The North Sierra–the old model: extended assemblies of extractivist urbanisation–the forest, the mine, the company town, the airport, and the city of Parauapebas.

cities and towns to emerge along its route.[59] The proliferation of tap-mining (*garimpos*) has also induced the formation of several other urban centres, the most emblematic being *Serra Pelada*.[60] Furthermore, the relationship between extractivism and urbanisation has been analysed in a wide range of geographies around the world.

    The case of Parauapebas and the North Sierra also clarifies the strong entanglement between the extraction technology and the rhythms and pathways of urbanisation. The technology of the 1970s applied in Parauapebas required much more labour than contemporary technologies. Therefore, it generated particular movements and spatialities

in an environment of flexible circulation, functional and spatial mobility of labour, and new kinds of "extensionalities."[61] The patterns and pathways of urbanisation of Parauapebas are thus entwined with older forms of operations in extraction, logistics, and management; the role of the state was different, as were rationalities, movements, and expectations. In this respect, Parauapebas stands in sharp contrast to the contemporary socio-spatial transformations taking place in the neighbouring municipality of Canaã in the South Sierra.

F. 10   The South Sierra: the S11D
iron complex, the Sossego copper
mine, and the town of Canaã
dos Carajás.

THE SOUTH SIERRA:
THE COMPLETE AUTOMATION
OF MINING

Constructed between 2011 and 2016, the S11D Complex in the municipality of Canaã in the South Sierra is, as Parauapebas in the North Sierra, also located in the domains of the National Forest. [Fig. 10] It is the largest open-pit mine in human history and was constructed relatively quickly through high-technology module assemblage, allowing for the simultaneous construction of logistics, ore separation, and processing facilities. The operation involves mobile excavators extracting iron ore and feeding dozens of kilometres of conveyor belts that transport the ore to the processing plant. Instead of fixed crushers and off-road trucks that would require human labour throughout the extractive procedure, this system uses mobile crushers and long-distance conveyor belts and treadmills—a scheme Vale proudly advertises as the "Truckless System." The company invested more than 14 billion dollars in the complex, which includes the extension of the Carajás Railroad, new energy transmission lines, iron ore processing modules, long-distance treadmills, transportation tunnels, roads, and bridges.[62] The entire assemblage is completely detached from Canaã's urban centre.

However, the massive amounts of materials, resources, and bodies needed to assemble one of the largest mining interventions in the world also entailed the transformation of the urban centre. Over five years (2011–2016), the project opened up more than 45,000 jobs positions in Canaã, a town of 30,000 residents, back in 2010. Local

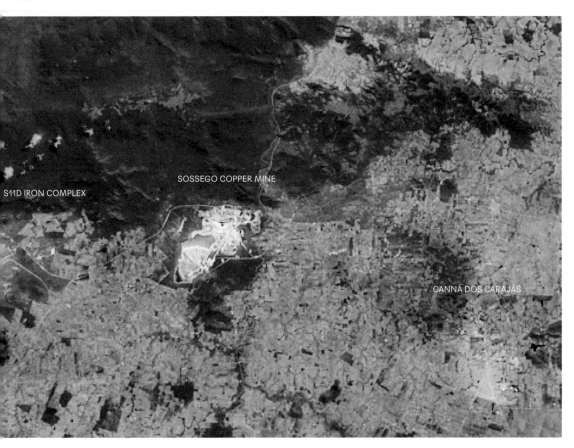

S11D IRON COMPLEX

SOSSEGO COPPER MINE

CANÃA DOS CARAJÁS

Fig. 10

public officials, union representatives, and business owners share the estimate that over 40,000 people settled here during the time of the mine construction.[63] Though many worked in activities of provisioning for the booming urban economy, most migrants were absorbed in the construction of the mining complex, hired either directly by Vale or by third-party companies. With the launch of the operation and the dispatch of the first batch of iron ore in 2017, the vast majority of employees and subcontractors were fired. When I arrived in Canaã in April 2018, the mine was able to operate with less than 100 workers.[64]

The full automation of mining and the low demand for predominantly specialised and highly skilled labour brings the question of operationalisation to the forefront: this is a landscape marked by increasing levels of abstraction—manifestations of the abstract logics of state and capital. The technological model based on automation demands only a fraction of labour compared to the model based on older technologies, thus inducing different forms of urbanisation, unfolding at both the urban and everyday levels. What happened to the tens of thousands of people who are now unemployed? How did Canaã manage to accommodate tens of thousands of new residents in such a short period of time? How did residents experience these changes, and how did they secure their livelihoods amidst the mass unemployment crisis?

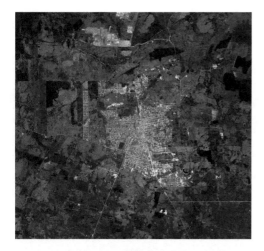

2011

2018

CANAÃ'S URBAN CENTER
Fig. 11

CANAÃ: THE BOOM AND BUST CYCLE OF THE MINING TOWN

Canaã dos Carajás is one of the most extreme and disruptive cases of entanglement of advanced technologies of extractivism with pathways and rhythms of "concentrated urbanisation."[65] Between the S11D's launch in 2011 and April 2018, when I first arrived the town rapidly expanded. [Fig. 11] It became evident to me that Canaã's urban decay following the massive unemployment crisis was as acute and dramatic as its preceding growth when it doubled its previous population.

Instances of violence escalated quickly. The post office was robbed twice in three months, with the subsequent kidnapping of two employees on one of the occasions. Multiple bank break-ins, blown-up ATM terminals, and home invasions fed the local news, together with rising prostitution, drug trafficking, and gun violence, all recurrent features of mining towns.[66] The prefecture claimed it didn't have the means to provide an appropriate response to the urban decay, despite the fact that it raised more than BR$ 184 million (42 million US dollars) that year from mining royalties. Despite the popular support for the recently re-elected mayor, residents believed that corruption was the only plausible explanation for the fact that the largest mining project on the planet was unable to generate any form of local develop-ment. In February 2018, a state judge ordered the mayor's suspension from office for a period of 180 days due to a highly overpaid contracting of a consultancy firm. A few weeks later, he resumed duty with no further explanations, causing an uproar in local politics.

People appeared shocked at Canaã's grim reality and recalled the "good times" with a mixture of nostalgia and regrets for not having bought a certain piece of land, not having conducted business in a certain direction, or not having accepted a job offer elsewhere. They did not regret, however, settling in Canaã even though the horizon was now harsher. Some residents attempted to convince me that there was no better place to be over the previous years.

F. 11   The rapid expansion of Canãa, between 2011 and 2018, before the dramatic decline.

It was as if they wanted me to agree with a simple rationale: if you settle in a place experiencing such tremendous growth, you will make money.

Hotel owners, moto-taxi drivers, merchants, storekeepers, waiters, informal settlers, public officers, and many other participants of the local economic game always made sure in each conversation that I understood how extraordinary Canaã's economic life was between 2011 and 2016. Hotels were full, many were under construction, and various schemes for accommodation arose daily. Supermarkets were crowded with two-hour queues at the cashiers. Moto-taxi drivers were making their usual monthly income in a single day. Stores and restaurants were constantly packed, and their hardest task was not selling, but managing inventories.

Even those who came to Canaã to find work in mining took advantage of this fleeting phase of economic prosperity. Ricardo from Tucuruí lived in Parauapebas before coming to Canaã in 2012. He and his wife both took mining-related technical courses. "I was in the initial cohort of 20,000 people working in the S11D project." In ten months, he earned enough money to buy a small piece of land. "Five years ago, I was paid twice the money that technicians receive today." As he gradually expanded his networks, he calculated that opening a clothing store would be a better deal. Since 2015, he managed to finish his house and save some money, but is now in the process of shutting down the store. "It's all falling, like an avalanche, from the top down, hitting all levels." He had enough money to keep the eight square metres store running for another year since the rent was declining. "It started with 1,500 in 2015. It reached 1,000 last year. Now the owner brought it down to 750, but I don't want it." Many other stores and houses in town went through similar episodes. "I've never seen the rent go down while the tenant is still in, but that's what's happening! Nowadays, you could even rent a good house for 300–400."

Ricardo's story is not an exception. Real estate development was perhaps the clearest expression of the boom and the decay of Canaã, echoing the construction of the S11D. From 2011 in-migration exceeded accommodation capacities. With rent prices skyrocketing, housing quickly became the main concern for migrants, developers, and the local administration, and a hot market for exogenous actors. Canaã's representatives added multiple extension areas to the urban perimeter to accommodate new housing projects.[67] However, even from the technocratic point of view of planners, urbanists, and consultants, the planned expansions bore "no logic."[68] Several interviewees mentioned illicit schemes behind the conversion from rural to urban land, ultimately selectively implemented for exorbitant profits.

In this context, mobilising the urban as a "governmental category" entailed multiple shifts of urban forms with land conversion enabling land parcellation.[69] New urban allotments became the most popular housing alternative for migrants, gradually filling up the ever-expanding edges of Canaã. In partnership with private regional contractors, rural landowners built basic sanitation in areas marketed and sold as "planned neighbourhoods." Buyers committed to building their own houses in addition to paying relatively cheap monthly instalments for their 300-m² lots. As the majority of migrants had income security through mining-related employment, the combination of auto-construction and monthly instalments for land became the prevalent model of housing provision.[70] [Fig. 12]

Moving through Canaã from the centre outwards, larger houses mix with commercial and service facilities, followed by residential allotments. These first, more central developments are denser, and the loose arrangement of programmes and buildings does not follow clearly defined neighbourhood boundaries. The properties do not have fences around them, and the houses are usually neither plastered nor painted. Even older buildings are often found side-by-side with areas of environmental vulnerability and soil erosion, sometimes inhabited by squatters. Moving toward Canaã's edges, the infrastructures begin to dissipate into fragmented roundabouts, roads that abruptly end in dust or bushes, and unfinished and often abandoned houses. The landscape is punctuated by precarious auto-constructed bars, shops, and evangelical temples, only identifiable through plastic banners on their brick facades. Signs "for sale," "for rent" and even "trade for motorcycle" are more frequent on houses in the periphery, many of which have no ceilings or walls. Moving further, there is still some infrastructure but almost no houses. The landscape comprises streetlight poles and low grass; under a green sales booth, two people with matching shirts protect themselves from rain and sun. [Fig. 13]

These landscapes express the rhythms of high-technology extractivism imposed on migration, housing, and urbanisation. Because private developers were aware that the housing market would tumble after the completion of the mine, the task of building the houses was transferred to the buyers. In a boom-and-bust economy, private developers rushed to parcel and sell the land without adding any construction value as there was no time for it to be realised. While a higher technological level of mining operations engenders a faster urbanisation process, human capacities for automated construction remain largely the same. The construction of large mining complexes requires tens of thousands of workers, but the demand for low-skilled labour, indispensable during the construction of the mine, is eliminated in the operation phase due to high levels of automation. Highly skilled labour, however, is permanent, less numerous, and well-paid.

The steady demand for highly skilled labour is also expressed in housing patterns at Canaã's edges. In sharp contrast to the landscape of residential allotments, but contiguous to it, is *Residencial Vale*, a development launched by a partnership comprising Vale, the regional contractor Buriti, and VBI Real Estate; the last being a private equity real estate investment firm headquartered in São Paulo. The settlement hosts Vale's high-ranking engineers and officials in hundreds of identical double-story houses in sober colours equipped with cameras and security systems. [Fig. 14]

Fig. 12

Fig. 13

Fig. 14

This project was not an isolated intervention, however. Vale was also responsible for the construction of several townhouses, materialising the company's strategies at the urban level. A company manager took me on a tour of various completed and ongoing works that "Vale did for Canaã": parks, schools, hospitals, the building for the municipal fair, the judicial court, as well as avenues and streets that were either expanded or paved. Vale also has its own community centre, the "Casa de Cultura," promoting free activities for local residents, including music lessons, a playground, and art exhibitions. The centre's manager clarified that its funding comes from Rouanet Law, a federal fiscal incentive programme that allows companies to redirect their taxes into cultural activities. In fact, that was also the case for most of the aforementioned social projects of Vale in Canaã: they were funded by controlling and redirecting mining royalties (taxes) from the local prefecture.[71] Besides the control over public funds, Vale's inscriptions throughout the city speak of different forms of power the company exerts over everyday life. According to Cândido, the company's employees have distinct social credentials for accessing goods and services in Canaã.[72] In hospitals, for example, wearing the company's uniform guarantees a care priority, regardless of the severity of the illness. Local activists and organisers have also emphasised that the company's financial and operational support in the construction of Canaã's civil court amplified its influence in the local judiciary.

Canaã's urban centre expresses the level of precarity, peripherality, and segregation that is predominant across Latin American cities. It also displays the agglomerative dynamics that are expected of booming mining towns,

F. 12 Billboards advertising 300-m² allotments at low monthly instalments.

F. 13 Peripheral landscapes of subdivisions in Canaã.

F. 14 The twin houses of the *Residencial Vale*, for high-ranking company officials.

Fig. 15

particularly given the dimension of this particular mine. Housing and urban expansion respond to the capitalist imperatives of reproducing the labour force while allowing regional developers and contractors to extract quick profits through rural-to-urban land conversion and speculation.[73] This boom town also shows that the technological level of mining is intertwined with the production of urban space, mostly auto-constructed by migrant majorities seeking new opportunities in these centres, generating ghost-like peripheries once full automation is ready to take place, which also exemplifies how the general, urban, and private levels operate with one another. While Canaã's urban centre seems to move towards an uncertain future, a key question remains to be answered: What happened to the workers that became dispensable and were expelled from the production process of the automated mine? In search of an answer, the next section will turn to the non-city geographies of Canaã.

CONTESTING EXTRACTIVISM: LANDLESS PEASANTS, RESISTANCE, AND THE POLITICS OF URBANISATION BEYOND THE CITY

In this section, I speak to this complexity by presenting the case of landless encampments in the rural zone of Canaã, in conflict with Vale and the local state. Although they are situated outside Canaã's formal urban perimeter, they are inextricably intertwined with urbanisation processes, both within the urban core and across the extended urban fabric. I also analyse how extended forms of urbanisation penetrate these agrarian territories and even provide opportunities for urban migrants that previously lived in the booming urban centre.

THE FIGHT FOR LAND
The historical struggles for land in Brazil are referred to as the "fight for land" (*luta pela terra*). Some interpretations qualify these

F. 15   Producing food at the encampment.
F. 16   The Carajás railroad at the
        southern border of the Rio Sossego
        encampment.

Fig. 16

struggles as organised actions of rural workers articulated by social movements that basically consist in occupying agricultural land, producing food and resisting evictions. Other interpretations look at a larger set of social groups (e.g., riverine and indigenous peoples, *quilombolas*, migrants, people affected by dams, rural workers), and a broader set of intersectional movements.[74] Several accounts trace the conflicts between the landless and the landowners (ranchers, merchants, companies, banks) and the chronicle of murders, tortures, and massacres that mark the country's history and, in particular, the Amazon.[75]

The migratory movements of the 1970s to Amazonia, and the expansions of large-scale extractivist projects in the same period, boosted land conflicts and extended the scale of these struggles. Social movements formed that soon exceeded the local level and dedicated themselves to the fight for land and agrarian reform on the national level. Migrants regularly struggled against armed militias deployed by large ranchers who claimed extensive portions of land and used all kinds of scams to "prove" their land titles and obtain control over the land. Land-grabbing, known as *pistolagem*,[76] and document falsification were so entrenched that some areas in Eastern Amazonia, both in and outside cities, are said to have "multiple floors," i.e., multiple faked titles, and thus multiple "owners," of the same land. Among the innumerable forms of land scams, *grilagem*[77] is the usual denomination for the practice of falsifying documents, followed by violent expulsions. In the 1970s, *grilagem* and *pistolagem* were practised frequently, most often by ranchers. Today, these practices are carried out by soy exporters, cattle ranchers, mining companies, and even municipal administrations. Dispossession is a diversified and complex phenomenon, coupled with the judicialization of land struggles, criminalisation of social movements, and the involvement of private security companies and police forces.

ENCAMPMENTS: OCCUPATION
AND ENDURANCE

Until the 1990s, agriculture and cattle rearing were the most important economic activity in Canaã. With the start of explorations of mineral deposits, agrarian economies began to decline[78] and rural land prices to rise. Today, many ranchers still control vast agricultural areas and are thus able to profit from booming land prices resulting from new "discoveries" of mineral deposits, exploration works, and the ensuing urban extensions. Some of these lands have almost no "productive use"; the few cattle or sparse crops on these fields are rather used as a means of "flagging" control over an area and deterring landless occupation. Despite such efforts, several occupations took place in 2015 when the S11D neared completion and tens of thousands of workers lost their jobs in mining and the broader urban economy. With high unemployment and deteriorating living conditions in the urban centre, hundreds of residents made a radical and concerted movement towards the occupation of agrarian lands and founded seven encampments in Canaã's rural area, each ranging from 20 to 100 km² (5,000 to 25,000 acres).

Rural occupation and encamping are long-established practices in Brazil, especially since the consolidation of the Landless Workers Movement (MST) in the 1980s.[79] Initially, the goal of the settlers in Canaã was just to occupy the land successfully, begin growing food, and resist eviction. But growing food needs technical and environmental requirements, knowledge, skills, and a set of agricultural inputs. [Fig. 15] Furthermore, it needs an appropriate communal organisation: the settlers have to elect their coordinators, who work internally as leaders managing resources and relationships and act externally as representatives of the community in meetings and negotiations. While handling the tumultuous congregation of families and individuals of various backgrounds and relationships, coordinators also need to be in touch with public authorities and negotiate the formalisation of the settlement.

These are all requirements of becoming a camponês. The term has a historical and political meaning, particularly in the context of the struggle for land. It literally means "peasant," but here I use it in Portuguese for its political meaning.[80] Once people identify as camponês, there is no way back to the city. They become "marked cards" in the urban socioeconomic game as explicit and tacit barriers are created for getting a job or accessing basic services. In order to tackle exclusion and criminalisation, camponeses' social movements and activists try to bring public opinion to their side, providing a high standard of food production, food security, food diversity, and lower prices.[81] These efforts are not always noticed. "People from 'the street' [the city] don't know where their bread comes from, but they anyway call us lazy, invaders, criminals," a camponês told me. Here, I have chosen three encampments to illustrate some of the problems and challenges often shared among the camps. A detailed account of these encampments can be found elsewhere.[82]

The encampment Grotão do Mutum gathered 150 families. They occupied an area that Vale knowingly bought from a grileiro: a large ranch including thousands of hectares of public land that its previous owner "illegally fenced in." When Vale went to Canaã's court[83] to evict the camponeses, it was requested to present the appropriate property titles. The company, however, did not have the land scripture and presented a mere contract of purchase between them and the previous owner, a classic example of grilagem. When the judge refused to proceed with the eviction without proof of ownership, Vale argued that the families should be evicted because the area would be used for the creation of the Campos Ferruginosos National Park (PARNA), an environmental "counterpart" of S11D. [Fig. 8] In the judicial process, Vale stated that "if the current situation of the property is not resolved [...] and the area is not destined for the conservation of biodiversity, as determined by the environmental licensing of the S11D project, the enterprise itself may have problems issuing an operating license."[84]

In other words, the company was arguing that if the 150 landless families were not removed from that area, it would not be able to create the park and, therefore, would not have its environmental license to mine *in another area.* The judge accepted the company's appeal and ordered the eviction of the community in 2016 without any proof that the land legally belonged to Vale. Eight families managed to occupy a much smaller piece of land nearby, hoping that their judicial appeal to get back to their land will someday be heard and processed. In 2017, PARNA was finally established. The presidential decree that created the park, states that more than 19,000 hectares were "donated" by the company—the same area that was once fenced by the rancher and then illegally sold to Vale— and explicitly states that federal environmental agencies allow Vale to run transmission lines, gas pipelines, and other extractive installations through the park. This example shows how environmental regulation can be operationalised according to mining interests and how crucial it is for the company to exert its territorial control within the boundaries of "legality."

In another part of the municipality, the encampment *Rio Sossego* faces different issues. It is located near both the S11D main gate and the highly surveyed Carajás railroad that transports ores to Vale's port in Maranhão. [Fig. 16] Therefore, *camponeses* face more frequent and violent forms of abuse, surveillance, and control. They report different forms of everyday harassment and humiliation by "one of Vale's police forces." They use this formulation because enforcements and interventions are enacted by the National Guard (federal), the Military Police (state), the Civil Police (municipal), the Company of Special Operations (regional), and Vale's private security. Guards and drones are constantly circulating around the camp and taking pictures, "keeping a record of who we are," a *camponês* told me. "We've had beatings, suffocations, mild injuries, and fatalities. We all know we can't walk alone." "They have also arrested a comrade for fishing in the river, saying he was breaking the environmental law." The river, however, like many other nearby water

Fig. 17

F. 17   Collective facilities in the encampment: kitchen, church and auditorium.

sources, was severely poisoned by Vale's mining residues. Water toxicity has already produced multiple cases of skin rashes and diseases.

The encampment *Monte Sião* was formed in an area that was Canaã's municipal dumping ground. Their antagonist is not Vale but the prefecture of Canaã, which bought an extremely overpriced piece of land from someone that, as in the previous example, did not have a property title in the first place. Once aware of the irregularity, 89 families rushed to occupy the area, which meant they would live side by side with massive piles of urban garbage. After being evicted twice from this area, they managed to get the property documents with the assistance of social movements and could prove that the prefecture's transaction was illicit. Now they are filing a lawsuit against the Federal Agrarian Agency to reverse the prefecture's acquisition and to formalise their settlement. Until this process is decided, the prefecture cannot evict them, at least formally. However, the families still face many mechanisms of threats and dispossession: crops are burned down and destroyed, leaders are co-opted, and networks with the city are disrupted.

In order to fight evictions and to cope with all the challenges and threats, *camponeses* count on the strong support of regional social movements and unions, which offer all kinds of assistance. They visit the encampments to offer educational courses on broader social and political questions and help develop strategies of mobilisation and organisation. These encounters help to form new leaders and coordinators and to embed *camponeses* into other movements and agendas, expanding their networks of struggle and care. Other social movements offer courses on agricultural techniques for specific types of land, including the use of appropriate tools, fertilisers, irrigation systems, etc. [Fig. 17]

Through these networks, social movements also offer legal assistance, as most of the *camponeses* are living under threats and lawsuits. Lawyers and activists in different cities contact residents and coordinators to inform them about new injunctions, the timetables of various processes in agencies and courts, and any new

lawsuits filed against them. During a lunch at the encampment, Junior, a young leader, received a WhatsApp message from an activist lawyer with good news regarding the previous arrest of a fellow *camponês*. He explained, "Internet is very important here because sometimes Vale files a suit in the morning and the police [are] already here by the afternoon [...] Of course, our own lawsuits against them take at least six months to be processed." He told me that the internet connection in his camp is better than in the city because of their proximity to the mines. After our lunch, he loosened his overalls and took off his white boots for a well-deserved rest and told me about the perils of life and work at the encampment. To relax at night, he told me, he watches his favourite series. He is a huge fan of Netflix's *La Casa de Papel*, claiming it is "almost as good as Game of Thrones."

Carlos is one of many *camponeses* who have lived in many different cities across the country. Some grew up on farms and moved to find work in larger cities before coming to Canaã. Others have spent most of their lives working in factories and construction sites or in extractivist projects such as S11D. It is precisely the intermixture of experiences, ideas, networks, and the presence of long-established national and regional social movements that makes the encampment a place of difference, resourcefulness, and endurance. Assembling the skills and experiences that each individual *camponês* (migrant, peasant, factory worker, farmer) brings to the table generates a huge potential. While some learn how to work the land, others learn how to fight for it. The enormous flexibility and mobility of *camponeses*, both spatially and functionally, and their ability to engage in complex social and technical situations creates the conditions to both produce their own infrastructure and take advantage of the existing extractivist infrastructure. It also creates the conditions, as I will explore in the next section, to appropriate these extractive materialities in order to contest them.

INTERRUPTING PLANETARY EXTRACTIVIST INFRASTRUCTURE

All mining infrastructures explicitly produced for extractivism can have alternative uses. The roads constructed by Vale to connect the mine and town, allowing the circulation of vehicles and workers for mining operations, are also used by *camponeses* to occupy land, to sell their food products, and to receive visits by activists and social movements for political engagements and socialising. Communication, energy, and transportation networks provide the means for the camps to communicate with each other and external collaborators. But, most importantly, Vale's mines, roads, and railroads have become a permanent terrain for political contestation.

"Vale is in our hands," a *camponês* told me. After months of fieldwork and collecting hundreds of testimonies on the seemingly seamless veneers of Vale's power and control, I was particularly struck by this statement. "We know everything. We built that mine!" he emphatically insisted, calling my attention to how the company actually provided the means for the *camponeses* to protest and fight against the company. In other words, Vale trained the same people it is now trying to expel. After all, the *camponeses* know the entire mining complex, the location of each facility, and the schedule of trucks, employees, and machines. They have built (and know how to unbuild) tracks, roads, and bridges that lead everyone and everything in and out of the mine. They know the capacity and the schedule of each wagon, how long it takes to reach the port, and the estimates of Vale's hourly losses if the railroad stops. They know how much land Vale "owns" in the region, and they can assess that their own land claims are financially irrelevant to the company. By occupying the road to the S11D, the Carajás railroad and by the sheer eventuality of other occupations with costly repercussions for Vale, the *camponeses* were able to suspend or postpone injunctions and evictions. Importantly, this is how they can assert their own collective demands and secure a seat at the negotiating table.

Fig. 18

F. 18 At the first National Meeting of the "Movement for the Popular Sovereignty in Mining," in May 2018, social movements, communities, and activists marched to the Carajás National Forest main gate to protest against Vale's crimes and abuses not only in Carajás, but throughout the country.

The same logistical apparatus that secures the interconnectivity between territories of extended urbanisation and the large urban agglomerations that form the contemporary global metropolitan system also exposes its vulnerability. In Eastern Amazonia, landless *camponeses*—as well as other historically marginalised groups—are able to play with the logistical interconnectivity of planetary urbanisation. In a contradictory way, extractive logistical infrastructure is what put them "in the game." As much as the operational assemblages of extractivism can fulfil their functions according to well-known profit-oriented intentionality, neither Vale nor the state anticipated what was likely to happen: they were providing the means for new political subjects and modes of collective action to use that same infrastructure to fight for their political rights. [Fig. 18]

In this context, it becomes clear that the mediating character of (extended) urbanisation also works "the other way around" as "counter-projections" that emanate from everyday life.[85] For several decades, indigenous peoples, landless peasants, and other Amazonian majorities have marched to large cities (especially Brasília) for political demonstrations, to make their demands heard, and to find a mediation between their everyday struggles and the abstract actors against which they fight. These activities and actions include a large range of modalities of mediation enabled by extended urbanisation and show how the process of operationalisation can be mediated and territorially instantiated; how power, state control, and capital's projections can be challenged; how these extended materialities can be appropriated in unanticipated ways and/or how they can contribute to transformations in the socio-political terrain.

This is not to say that *camponeses* are "anti-extractivist" or "anti-capitalist"; they are not, at least not initially. They are mobilising, occupying, negotiating, cooperating, sowing, and reaping based on immediate necessities. However, there is always room for individual interests to match collective interests, as individuals are increasingly able to see themselves and

the actors they cooperate with or fight against in a different way. The capacity of encampments to gather these heterogeneous experiences and perspectives engenders a stronger sense of self-consciousness, empowerment, and endurance, often in relation to a broader movement or question that transcends the level of everyday life, such as the fight for the land, for agrarian reform, for food security, etc.

Ultimately, *camponeses*, *índios*, riverines, *quilombolas,* and other Amazonian majorities have something to say about urbanisation that nobody else does. They have a lot to say about nature, sustainability, agriculture, and land but also about infrastructure, social mobilisation, territorial regulation, housing, politics, and streaming platforms. Of course, these voices and perspectives that are continuously created, threatened, and reinvented outside of cities might take some time to be heard, as city-centric approaches to urbanisation are excluding these perspectives from being considered.

BETWEEN EXTRACTION AND REBELLION: EXTENDING URBAN MEDIATIONS

In this chapter, I discussed the historical geographies of Eastern Amazonia as a privileged terrain for the study of urbanisation in relation to extractivism. Through the Lefebvrian notion of levels of social reality, I analysed the historical rounds of Amazonian colonisation with particular attention to the region of Carajás and the contemporary urban transformations in Parauapebas and Canaã dos Carajás in the wake of the construction of massive mining projects. I have suggested that the transformations in mining towns are inextricably intertwined with the technologies and rhythms of extractivism. Although both Canaã and Parauapebas are expressions of the precarity and peripherality that characterise mining centres, the differences in mining technologies and operations have generated distinct processes of urbanisation.

Furthermore, extractivism has induced not only the formation of cities and towns but also of abandoned and unfinished settlements, violent and precarious neighbourhoods in cities, as well as extended materialities, practices, and subjectivities, such as those taking place in the landless encampments in their struggle against Vale and the prefecture.

In these encampments, we find a radical alternative form of political struggle, work, and inhabitation that embodies both the fight for land in the Amazon and the contingencies of urban life under twenty-first-century extractivism. Necessities and practices at the level of everyday life engender unanticipated uses and (re)appropriations of the same extractive assemblies that are used for operationalising the region. It is precisely because of the opportunities encountered by urban majorities for remaking their livelihoods and for contesting abstract logics and interventions from the capital and the state that different levels of abstraction should be considered in the study of extended urbanisation. Importantly, the ways in which the general level projects itself onto the urban level are dramatically different in cities and geographies of extended urbanisation, as demonstrated by how the capital and the state "show up" in the non-city as police forces, eviction injunctions, as private guards, and violent infrastructure.

By being attentive to how the mediations embedded within urbanisation processes—both in their vital and pervasive senses—are extended to non-city domains, urban research can bring elements that are apparently dispersed in the inquiry of urbanisation without the inherited empirical and disciplinary boundaries. The levels can bring together both lived experience and state and capital; both the critique of political economy and the embodied experiences of field research; they can bring into conversation and articulation, the city, countryside, forest, village, and mining geographies that are increasingly shaped by contemporary urbanisation. But most importantly, the analysis of urbanisation through the levels of analysis can bring to the forefront a perspective of urbanisation that is not centred in the voices of city dwellers but also of peasants, villagers, *quilombolas*, riverine, indigenous peoples, and many other groups across the planet whose lives and spaces have been deeply transformed by extended urbanisation.

114

ENDNOTES

1   Simone, "The Urban Majority and Provisional Recompositions in Yangon."
2   Lefebvre, *The Urban Revolution.*
3   Goonewardena, "The Urban Sensorium."
4   A more complete account of my perspective of extended urbanisation—that draws upon its classical formulations but attempts to move the debate forward—as well as the full story of Carajás is available in my PhD dissertation, see Castriota, *Urbanização Extensiva na Amazônia Oriental: escavando a não-cidade em Carajás.*
5   Keil, "Extended Urbanization."
6   Monte-Mór, "Urbanization, colonization and the production of regional space in the Brazilian Amazon," *Modernities in the Jungle,* "Extended Urbanization and Settlement Patterns in Brazil"; Brenner and Schmid, "The 'urban age' in question".
7   Lefebvre, *The Urban Revolution*; see also Monte-Mór, *Urbanização, Sustentabilidade, Desenvolvimento.*
8   Gudynas, *Extractivismos*; Svampa, "Commodities consensus."
9   Gago and Mezzadra, "A Critique of the Extractive Operations of Capital"; Mezzadra and Neilson, *The Politics of Operations*; Arboleda, *Planetary Mine*; Andrade, *Spaces and Architecture of Extractivism*; Ruiz, "Territory, Sustainability, and Beyond"; Marais et al., "Mining Towns and Urban Sprawl in South Africa."
10   Angelo and Wachsmuth, "Urbanizing Urban Political Ecology."
11   Monte-Mór, "Modernities in the Jungle"; Kipfer, "Pushing the limits of urban research."
12   Simone and Pieterse, *New Urban Worlds: Inhabiting Dissonant Times.*
13   There are many readings of Lefebvre's discussion of the levels of reality and analysis, see especially Martins, *Henri Lefebvre e o retorno à dialética*; Shields, *Lefebvre, Love and Struggle*; Brenner, "The Urban Question," "Henri Lefebvre's critique of state's productivism"; Elden, *Understanding Henri Lefebvre,* "Mondialisation Before Globalization"; Goonewardena, "The Urban Sensorium"; Goonewardena et al., *Space, Difference, Everyday Life*; Merrifield, *Henri Lefebvre: A Critical Introduction*; Schmid, *Henri Lefebvre and the Theory of the Production of Space*; Kipfer "Why the Urban Question Still Matters"; Kipfer et al., "Henri Lefebvre: Debates and controversies"; Stanek, *Henri Lefebvre on space*; Butler, *Henri Lefebvre: spatial politics*; Kipfer et al., "Henri Lefebvre: debates and controversies,"; Costa et al., *Teorias e Práticas Urbanas: condições para a sociedade urbana*; and Fraser, *Towards an Urban Cultural Studies.*" I have provided elsewhere a critical account of this literature while stressing at length the implications of Lefebvre's levels for a broader understanding of extended urbanisation, see Castriota, *Urbanização Extensiva na Amazônia Oriental.*
14   Lefebvre, *Critique of Everyday Life, The Right to the City, The Production of Space.*
15   Goonewardena, *The Urban Sensorium,* 66; Stanek, "Space as Concrete Abstraction."
16   See Monte-Mór, *Modernities in the Jungle*; Arboleda, "In the Nature of the non-City."
17   Godfrey, "Boom Towns of the Amazon."
18   Hall, *Developing Amazonia*; Silveira, *Transformations in Amazonia*; Malheiro, *O que Vale em Carajás?.*
19   Goonewardena, "The Urban Sensorium."
20   See Lefebvre, *Critique of Everyday Life,* 412–416.
21   Lefebvre, *The Production of Space.*
22   Shmuely, "Totality, hegemony and difference," 217.
23   Stanek, *Henri Lefebvre on Space,* 142–143.
24   Mezzadra and Neilson, "Extraction, Logistics, Finance," "Operations of Capital", *The Politics of Operations.*
25   See Katsikis, this volume; see Couling, this volume.
26   Heckenberger et al., "The Legacy of Cultural Landscapes in the Brazilian Amazon," 197.
27   Monte-Mór, *Modernities in the Jungle.*
28   Santos, *O Trabalho do Geógrafo no Terceiro Mundo.*
29   Casanova, *Colonialismo interno (uma redefinição)*; Malheiro, *O que Vale em Carajás?*
30   Monte-Mór, *Modernities in the Jungle.*
31   Hecht and Cockburn, *The Fate of the Forest*; Schmink and Wood, *Conflitos sociais e a formação da Amazônia.*
33   Monte-Mór, "Urbanization, colonization and the production of regional space in the Brazilian Amazon," *Modernities in the Jungle.*
33   Lojkine, *O Estado Capitalista e a Questão Urbana*; Topalov, *La Urbanización Capitalista.*
34   Monte-Mór, "Urbanization, Colonization and the Production of Regional Space in the Brazilian Amazon."
35   Monte-Mór, *Modernities in the Jungle,* 59.
36   Castriota, *Urbanização Planetaria ou Revolução Urbana?*; Castriota and Tonucci, "Extended Urbanization in and from Brazil."
37   See Hecht and Cockburn, *The Fate of the Forest* and Monte-Mór, *Modernities in the Jungle* for a broader account of colonisation projects in Frontier Amazonia. Hall, *Developing Amazonia* presents the geo-history of these projects in south-eastern Pará and Pereira, *Colonização e conflitos na Transamazônica* discusses the case of Marabá, Carajás' "regional capital."
38   Pereira, *Do posseiro ao sem terra*; Michelotti, *Territórios De Produção Agromineral.*
39   Hecht et al., "The Social Lives of the Forest."
40   Monte-Mór, *Modernities in the Jungle.*
41   Castro, *Cidades na Floresta*; Heckenberger et al., "Pre-Columbian Urbanism, Anthropogenic Landscapes, and the Future of the Amazon"; Kanai, "On the Peripheries of Planetary Urbanization."
42   Godfrey, "Boom Towns of the Amazon."
43   The Tucuruí HPP is essential for supplying several regional extractive projects. Its construction was led by state company Eletronorte and costed 7.5 billion dollars. In 1982–1983, there were 30,000 people working on the construction of the plant which, when finally completed in 1984, was the fourth largest in the world.
44   Silva Júnior and Petit, *Hidrelétricas na Amazônia.*
45   See Hall, *Developing Amazonia*; Silveira, *Transformations in Amazonia*; Coelho e Cota, *Dez Anos da Estrada de Ferro Carajás*; The Carajás Railroad was constructed between 1980 and 1986, initially with 892 km of extension, to connect the Carajás Mine (1978) to the Ponta da Madeira port (1986) in São Luís (MA).

46 Carneiro, *A exploração mineral de Carajás*.

47 For broader assessments of the Project Great Carajás see Hall, *Developing Amazonia*; and Coelho, *Projeto Grande Carajás*.

48 Gordon, *Economia Selvagem*; Santos, *Xikrín versus Vale*.

49 Lefebvre, *The Urban Revolution*, 79.

50 Barros, *A Mirada Invertida de Carajás*.

51 Santos, *Território em Transe*; Barros, *A Mirada Invertida de Carajás*.

52 Castriota, *Urbanização Extensiva na Amazônia Oriental: escavando a não-cidade em Carajás*.

53 See Santos, *Mineração e Conflitos Fundiários no Sudeste Paraense*.

54 Gudynas, *Extractivismos*.

55 Coelho, *A CVRD e o Processo de (Re)Estruturação e Mudança na Área de Carajás (Pará)*; see also Hall, *Developing Amazonia*.

56 Roberts, "Subcontracting and the Omitted Social Dimensions of Large Development Projects."

57 Coelho, *A CVRD e o Processo de (Re)Estruturação e Mudança na Área de Carajás (Pará)*; Palheta da Silva, *Território e mineração em Carajás*.

58 Coelho, *Projeto Grande Carajás*. In 2019 the City Hall collected more than BR$ 680 million (US$ 154 million) in mining royalties. Data from the latest demographic census (2010) shows that nearly 10% of Parauapebas' labour force is directly employed in the extractive sector, not to mention third party companies involved in the broader supply chain.

59 Schmink and Wood, *Conflitos sociais e a formação da Amazônia*.

60 Godfrey, "Boom Towns of the Amazon."

61 Simone, "Without Capture."

62 Vale S.A., *Complexo S11D*.

63 This estimate is shared by public officers, union representatives, retailers and other Canaã residents. Official numbers are estimates based on linear parameters and do not capture such demographic surges. The underestimate of population data is clear when compared to electoral data: according to the Brazilian Institute of Geography and Statistics, the 2018 estimated population of Canaã is 36,000 *residents*; however, according to the Superior Electoral Court, there were 339,000 *voters* in Canaã in the same year.

64 It is difficult to estimate the exact amount of people working in the complex, as a Vale manager revealed in an interview. He suggested that due to the truckless system, the need for human labour is almost zero. Other sources, however, suggest that at least 100 workers are necessary for the mine to operate (see Cardoso et al., "Canaã dos Carajás: A laboratory study concerning the circumstances of urbanization, on the global periphery at the dawn of the 21st century."

65 Brenner and Schmid, "Towards a New Epistemology of the Urban?"

66 Gudynas, "Extractivismos En América Del Sur y Sus Efectos Derrame."

67 See Cruz, *Mineração e Campesinato em Canaã dos Carajás*; Cândido, *A cidade entre utopias*.

68 Cardoso et al., "Canaã dos Carajás: A laboratory study concerning the circumstances of urbanization, on the global periphery at the dawn of the 21st century."

69 Roy, "What is Urban About Critical Urban Theory?"; Whereas a rural land plot's minimum size is 20,000 m², the urban land in Canaã can be parcelled into 300 m² lots. Rural landowners were able to obtain substantial profits as the average price of urban lots increased 965% between 2001 and 2014, see Bandeira, *Alterações Sócio-Espaciais no Sudeste do Pará*.

70 Caldeira, "Peripheral Urbanization"; Holston, *Insurgent Citizenship*.

71 Juliana Barros, *A Mirada Invertida de Carajás*, 185 has framed Vale's "corporate social responsibility" policies in Carajás as a form of "territorial domination" masked as "assistance," where putative forms of education and community organisation "constitute the expansion of corporate power."

72 Cândido, *A cidade entre utopias*.

73 Castells, *The Urban Question*.

74 Pereira, *Do posseiro ao sem terra*; Gonçalves, *(Re)politizando o conceito de gênero*; Welch and Sauer, "Rural Unions and the Struggle for Land in Brazil."

75 Pereira, and Afonso, "Conflitos e Violência no Campo, na Amazônia Brasileira"

76 The term "pistolagem" would translate literally to "pistoling," meaning the practice of using a pistol, a firearm. The name attributed to the hitman—professional murderers hired to kill, torture or threaten—is "pistoleiro."

77 The term comes from a technique of producing an aging effect on a paper, which consists in placing false documents inside a box with crickets (*grilos*) to make them yellowish, due to insects' excrement, and gnawed. In his historical summary of the land question in Brazil, Holston, "*Insurgent citizenship*" discusses several forms of land scams.

78 Since the early 2000s, Vale S.A. has established three other mining projects in Canaã: *Projeto Sossego*, *Projeto Níquel do Vermelho* and *Projeto 118*. Although they are not comparable to the S11D in terms of size, volume and intensity they contributed to a historical transition from an agrarian to an extractivist economy

79 There are several accounts of the MST in English, but here I highlight its role in fostering education opportunities and coordinating rural production (Pahnke, "The Changing Terrain of Rural Contention in Brazil"), in strengthening democracy in Brazil (Carter, "The Landless Rural Workers Movement and Democracy in Brazil") and in creating alternatives to capitalist relations of production and property (Diniz and Gilbert, "Socialist Values and Cooperation in Brazil's Landless Rural Workers' Movement").

80 The term *camponês* has a historical and political meaning, particularly in the context of the *struggle? for land*. The MST reasserts the term "as an expression of values linked to environmental preservation and biodiversity, food production, especially for local markets, food sovereignty, cultural diversity and, above all, criticism of an agricultural model based on agribusiness (understood as an export-oriented, high-tech, large-scale production based on monocultures controlled by large trading companies and inputs suppliers). For the MST, the term *camponês* refers to the utopia of a more egalitarian and supportive society" (Medeiros, *A luta por terra no Brasil e o Movimento dos Trabalhadores Rurais sem Terra*, 5). The camps I have worked with in Canaã are not affiliated with the

MST, but to the STTRCC (Union of Men and Women Rural Workers of Canaã). They nevertheless position their practices of land occupation and food production within the broader context of the *fight for land* and agrarian reform and identify themselves as *camponeses*.

81 Although there is no aggregate organisation of food production, camps produce more than 40 types of fruits and vegetables without the use of pesticides. Average prices dropped since the first camp harvests in 2015, which increased food supply substantially. The price of a 50 kg sack of manioc flower—a central component of local and regional diet—decreased from BR$ 400 in 2014 to BR$ 150 in 2017.

82 Castriota, *Urbanização Extensiva na Amazônia Oriental: escavando a não-cidade em Carajás*.

83 Eviction injunctions in agrarian land cannot be processed in local (urban) courts, so the fact that Vale went to Canaã's court is both illegal and a proof of its influence on the municipality (see Santos, *Mineração e Conflitos Fundiários no Sudeste Paraense*).

84 Ação Possessória 0014461-68.2015.8.14.0136. See Santos, *Mineração e Conflitos Fundiários no Sudeste Paraense,* 88.

85 Goonewardena, "The Urban Sensorium."C

BIBLIOGRAPHY

Andrade, Alejandra E. "Space and Architecture of Extractivism in the Ecuadorian Amazon Region." *Cultural Studies* 31, no. 2–3 (4 May 2017): 307–330.

Angelo, Hillary and David Wachsmuth. "Urbanizing Urban Political Ecology: A Critique of Methodological Cityism." *International Journal of Urban and Regional Research*, 39, no. 1 (2014): 16–27.

Aráoz, Horácio M. *Mineração, genealogia do desastre: O extrativismo na América como origem da modernidade*. São Paulo: Editora Elefante, 2020.

Arboleda, Martín. *Planetary Mine: Territories of Extraction under Late Capitalism*. London: Verso Books, 2020.

———."In the Nature of the Non-city: Expanded Infrastructural Networks and the Political Ecology of Planetary Urbanisation." *Antipode*, 48, no. 2 (2015): 233–251.

Bandeira, Alex de O. *Alterações Sócio-Espaciais no Sudeste do Pará: a mudança de terra rural para solo urbano na cidade de Canaã dos Carajás*. Master Thesis, Universidade Federal do Pará, 2014.

Barros, Juliana N. *A Mirada Invertida de Carajás: a Vale e a mão-de-ferro na política de terras*. PhD Diss., Universidade Federal do Rio de Janeiro, 2018.

Brenner, Neil. "The Urban Question: Reflections on Henri Lefebvre, Urban Theory and the Politics of Scale." *International Journal of Urban and Regional Research*, 24, no. 2 (2003): 361–378.

———."Henri Lefebvre's Critique of State's Productivism." In *Space, Difference, Everyday Life: Reading Henri Lefebvre*, edited by Kanishka Goonewardena, Stefan Kipfer, Richard Milgrom and Christian Schmid, 231–249. New York, London: Routledge, 2008.

Brenner, Neil and Christian Schmid. "The 'Urban Age' in Question." *International Journal of Urban and Regional Research*, 38, no. 3 (2013): 731–755.

———."Towards a New Epistemology of the Urban?" *City*, 19, no. 2-3 (2015): 151–182.

Butler, Chris. *Henri Lefebvre: Spatial Politics, Everyday Life and the Right to the City*. New York: Routledge, 2012.

Caldeira, Teresa. "Peripheral Urbanization: Autoconstruction, Transversal Logics, and Politics in Cities of the Global South." *Environment and Planning D: Society and Space* 35, no. 1 (2017): 3–20.

Cândido, Lucas. *A cidade entre utopias: o Neoliberalismo e o Comum na produção contemporânea do espaço urbano amazônico*. Master Thesis, Universidade Federal do Pará, 2018.

Cardoso, Ana C. D, Lucas Cândido and Ana Carolina C. M. "Canaã dos Carajás: A laboratory study concerning the circumstances of urbanization, on the global periphery at the dawn of the 21st century." *Revista Brasileira de Estudos Urbanos e Regionais*, 20, no. 1 (2017): 121–140.

Carneiro, M. "A exploração mineral de Carajás: um balanço trinta anos depois." *Revista Não Vale v. I, Justiça nos Trilhos*, (2014): 16–30.

Carter, Miguel. "The Landless Rural Workers Movement and Democracy in Brazil." *Latin American Research Review*, 45 (2010): 186–217.

Casanova, Pablo G. "Colonialismo interno (uma redefinição)." In *A teoria marxista hoje: problemas e perspectivas*, edited by Atílio A. Boron, Javier Amadeo, and Sabrina Gonzáles, 395–420. Buenos Aires: CLACSO, 2002.

Castells, Manuel. *The Urban Question: A Marxist Approach*. London: Edward Arnold, 1979.

Castriota, Rodrigo. "Urbanização planetária ou revolução urbana? De volta à hipótese da urbanização completa da sociedade." *Revista Brasileira de Estudos Urbanos e Regionais*, 18, no. 3 (2016): 507–523.

———.*Urbanização Extensiva na Amazônia Oriental: escavando a não-cidade em Carajás*. PhD Diss., Universidade Federal de Minas Gerais, 2021.

Castriota, Rodrigo, and João Tonucci. "Extended Urbanization in and from Brazil." *Environment and Planning D: Society and Space*, 36, no. 4 (2018): 512–528.

Castro, Edna. *Cidades na Floresta*. São Paulo: Annablume, 2009.

Coelho, Maria C., and Raimundo G. Cota. (eds). *Dez Anos da Estrada de Ferro Carajás*, Belém: UFPA-NAEA, 1997.

Coelho, Tádzio. P. Projeto Grande Carajás: *Trinta anos de desenvolvimento frustrado*. Belém: iGuana, 2015.

Coelho, Maria C. "A CVRD e o Processo de (Re)Estruturação e Mudança na Área de Carajás (Pará)." In *10 anos da Estrada de Ferro Carajás*, edited by Maria C. Coelho and Raimundo Cota G., 51–78. Belém: UFPA/NAEA, 1997.

Corrêa, Wilson G. *A Ação do GETAT na região Sul e Sudeste do Pará.* Master Thesis, Universidade Federal do Sul e Sudeste do Pará, 2016.

Costa, Geraldo M., Heloisa Costa and Roberto L. M. Monte-Mór (eds). *Teorias e Práticas Urbanas: condições para a sociedade urbana.* Belo Horizonte: C/Arte Editora, 2015.

Cruz, Thiago M. *Mineração e Campesinato em Canaã dos Carajás: o avanço cruel do capital no sudeste paraense.* Master Thesis, Universidade Federal do Sul e Sudeste do Pará, 2015.

Diniz, Aldiva S., and Bruce Gilbert. "Socialist Values and Cooperation in Brazil's Landless Rural Workers' Movement." *Latin American Perspectives*, 40, no.4 (2013): 19–34.

Elden, Stuart. *Understanding Henri Lefebvre.* London: Continuum, 2004.

———."Mondialisation Before Globalization: Lefebvre and Axelos." In *Space, Difference, Everyday Life: Reading Henri Lefebvre*, edited by Kanishka Goonewardena, Stefan Kipfer, Richard Milgrom, and Christian Schmid, 80–93. New York: Routledge, 2008.

Fraser, Benjamin. *Towards an Urban Cultural Studies: Henri Lefebvre and the humanities.* New York: Palgrave Macmillan, 2015.

Gago, Verónica, and Sandro Mezzadra. "A critique of the extractive operations of capital: toward an expanded concept of extractivism." *Rethinking Marxism*, 29, no. 4 (2018): 574–591.

Godfrey, Brian J. "Boom Towns of the Amazon," *Geographical Review*, 80, no. 2 (1990): 103–117.

Gonçalves, Renata. "(Re) politizando o conceito de gênero: a participação política das mulheres no MST." *Mediações-Revista de Ciências Sociais*, 14, no. 2 (2009): 198–216.

Goonewardena, Kanishka. "The Urban Sensorium: Space, Ideology and the Aestheticization of Politics." *Antipode*, 37, no. 1 (2005): 46–71.

Goonewardena, Kanishka, Stefan Kipfer, Richard Milgrom, and Christian Schmid (eds). *Space, Difference, Everyday Life: Reading Henri Lefebvre.* New York: Routledge, 2008.

Gordon, Cesar. *Economia Selvagem: Ritual e mercadoria ente os índios Xicrin-Mebêngôkre.* Rio de Janeiro: Editora UNESP/ISA, NUTI, 2006.

Gudynas, Eduardo. *Extractivismos: ecología, economía y política de un modo de entender el desarrollo y la naturaleza.* Cochabamba: CEDIB, 2015.

———."Extractivismos En América Del Sur y Sus Efectos Derrame," *La Revista*, Boletín, no. 76 (2015): 13–23.

Hall, Anthony L. *Developing Amazonia: Deforestation and Social Conflict in Brazil's Carajás Programme.* Manchester: Manchester University Press, 1989.

Hecht, Susanna B., Kathleen D. Morrison, and Christine Padoch (eds). *The Social Lives of Forests: Past, Present, and Future of Woodland Resurgence.* Chicago: University of Chicago Press, 2014.

Hecht, Susanna B., and Alexander Cockburn. *The Fate of the Forest: Developers, Destroyers, and Defenders of the Amazon.* London: Verso, 1989.

Heckenberger, M. J., Russell, J. C., Fausto, C. ... and Kuikuro, A. "Pre-Columbian urbanism, anthropogenic landscapes, and the future of the Amazon." *Science*, 321 (5893) (2008): 1214–1217.

Heckenberger, Michael J., J. Christian Russell, Joshua R. Toney and Morgan J. Schmidt. "The Legacy of Cultural Landscapes in the Brazilian Amazon: Implications for Biodiversity." *Philosophical Transactions of the Royal Society of London B: Biological Sciences*, 362, no. 1478 (2007): 197–208.

Holston, James. *Insurgent citizenship: Disjunctions of Democracy and Modernity in Brazil.* New Jersey: Princeton University Press, 2007.

Kanai, Juan Miguel. "On the Peripheries of Planetary Urbanization: Globalizing Manaus and Its Expanding Impact." *Environment and Planning D: Society and Space* 32, no. 6 (2014): 1071–1087.

Keil, Roger. "Extended Urbanization: 'Disjunct Fragments' and global suburbanisms." *Environment and Planning D: Society and Space*, 36, no. 3 (2017): 494–511.

Kipfer, Stefan. "Why the Urban Question Still Matters: Reflections on Rescaling and the Promise of the Urban." In *Leviathan undone: Towards a Political Economy of Scale*, edited by Roger Keil and Rianné Mahon, 67–85. Vancouver, Toronto: UBC Press, 2009.

———."How Lefebvre Urbanized Gramsci: Hegemony, Everyday Life, and Difference." In *Space, Difference, Everyday Life: Reading Henri Lefebvre*, Kanishka Goonewardena, Stefan Kipfer, Richard Milgrom, and Christian Schmid, 193–211. New York: Routledge, 2008.

———."Pushing the Limits of Urban Research: Urbanization, Pipelines and Counter-colonial Politics." *Environment and Planning D: Society and Space*, 36, no. 3 (2018): 474–493.

Kipfer, Stefan, Parastou Saberi, and Thorben Wieditz. Parastou Saberi and Thorben Wieditz. "Henri Lefebvre: Debates and Controversies." *Progress in Human Geography*, 37, no. 1 (2012): 115–134.

Lefebvre, Henri. *The Urban Revolution.* Minneapolis, London: University of Minnesota Press, 2003 [1970].

———.*Critique of Everyday Life: The One-volume Edition.* London, New York: Verso, 2014.

———.*O Direito à Cidade.* São Paulo: Centauro, 1999 [1968].

———.*The Production of Space.* Oxford: Blackwell, 1991 [1974].

Lojkine, Jean. *O Estado Capitalista e a Questão Urbana*, São Paulo: Martins Fontes, 1981.

Malheiro, Bruno. *O que Vale em Carajás? Geografias de exceção e r-existência pelos caminhos do ferro na Amazônia.* PhD Diss., Universidade Federal Fluminense, 2019.

Marais Lochner, Stuart Denoon-Stevens, and Jan Cloete. "Mining Towns and Urban Sprawl in South Africa." *Land Use Policy*, 93 (2020): 103953.

Martins, José S. *Henri Lefebvre e o retorno à dialética.* São Paulo: Hucitec, 1996.

Medeiros, L. S. *A luta por terra no Brasil e o Movimento dos Trabalhadores Rurais sem Terra.* SAEI: Secretaria de Acompanhamento e Estudos Institucionais, 2009.

Merrifield, Andy. *Henri Lefebvre: A Critical Introduction.* New York: Routledge, 2008.

Mezzadra, Sandro, and Brett Neilson. "Extraction, Logistics, Finance: Global Crisis and the Politics of Operations." *Radical Philosophy*, 178, (2013): 8–18.

———."Operations of Capital." *South Atlantic Quarterly*, 114, no. 1 (2015): 1–9.

———.*The Politics of Operations: Excavating Contemporary Capitalism*. London: Duke University Press, 2019.

Michelotti, Fernando. *Territórios De Produção Agromineral: Relações de Poder e Novos Impasses na Luta pela Terra no Sudeste Paraense*. PhD Diss., Universidade Federal do Rio de Janeiro, 2019.

Monte-Mór, Roberto L. "Urbanization, Colonization and the Production of Regional Space in the Brazilian Amazon." In *16th Inter-American Congress of Planning* (Sociedade Interamericana de Planificación: SIAP), San Juan, Porto Rico, 22–26 August 1988.

———.*Modernities in the Jungle: Extended Urbanization in the Brazilian Amazonia*. PhD Diss., University of California Los Angeles, 2004.

———."Extended Urbanization and Settlement Patterns in Brazil." In *Implosions/Explosions: Towards a Study of Planetary Urbanization*, edited by Neil Brenner, 109–120. Berlin: Jovis, 2014.

———."Urbanização, Sustentabilidade, Desenvolvimento: complexidades e diversidades contemporâneas na produção urbano." In *Teorias e Práticas Urbanas: Condições para a sociedade urbana*, edited by Geraldo M. Costa, Heloísa Costa, and Roberto L. Monte-Mór, 55–70. Belo Horizonte: C/ Arte Editora, 2015.

Pahnke, Anthony. "The Changing Terrain of Rural Contention in Brazil: Institutionalization and Identity Development in the Landless Movement's Educational Project." *Latin American Politics and Society*, 59(3) (2017): 3–26.

Palheta da Silva, João M. *Território e mineração em Carajás*. Belém: GAPTA/UFPA, 2013.

Pereira, Airton R. *Do posseiro ao sem terra: a luta pela terra no sul e sudeste do Pará*. Recife: Editora UFPE, 2015.

———."Colonização e conflitos na Transamazônica em tempos da ditadura civil-militar brasileira." In *Culturas e dinâmicas sociais na Amazônia Oriental brasileira*, edited by Airton Pereira, H. Anjos, and I. Silva, 143–167. Belém: Paka-tatu, 2017.

Pereira, A. R. and J.B. Afonso. "Conflitos e Violência no Campo, na Amazônia Brasileira." In *CPT – Comissão Pastoral da Tera (org.), Conflitos no Campo Brasil,* edited by Comissão, 183–188. Goiânia: CPT Nacional, 2018.

Roberts, J. T. "Subcontracting and the Omitted Social Dimensions of Large Development Projects: Household Survival at the Carajás Mines in the Brazilian Amazon," *Economic Development and Cultural Change*, 34, no. 4 (1995): 735–758.

Roy, Ananya. "What is Urban About Critical Urban Theory?" *Urban Geography* 37, no. 6 (2015): 810–823.

Ruiz, Germán A. "Territory, Sustainability, and Beyond: Latin American Urbanization through a Political Ecology." *Environment and Planning E: Nature and Space*, no. 3 (2020): 786–809.

Santos, Milton. *O Trabalho do Geógrafo no Terceiro Mundo*. São Paulo: Edusp, 2008 [1978].

Santos, Jorge L. R. *Xikrín versus Vale: direitos olvidados*. PhD Diss., Universidade Federal do Pará, 2013.

———."Território em transe: a Floresta Nacional de Carajás." In *Anais do V Encontro Nacional da Associação Nacional de Pós-Graduação e Pesquisa em Ambiente e Sociedade (ANPPAS)*, Florianópolis, Brasil, 2018. Accessed Feb 2, 2019. http://www.anppas.org.br/encontro5/cd/artigos/GT16-43-16-20100903195758.pdf.

Santos, Andréia S. S. *Mineração e Conflitos Fundiários no Sudeste Paraense*. Master Thesis, Universidade Federal Do Sul e Sudeste Do Pará, 2018.

Schmid, Christian. *Henri Lefebvre and the Theory of the Production of Space*. London: Verso, 2022.

Schmink, Marianne, and Charles H. Wood. *Conflitos sociais e a formação da Amazônia*. Belém: EDUFPA, 2012.

Shields, Rob. *Lefebvre, Love and Struggle: Spatial Dialectics*. London: Routledge, 1999.

Shmuely, Raymond W. A. "Totality, Hegemony and Difference: Henri Lefebvre and Raymond Williams." In *Space, Difference, Everyday Life: Reading Henri Lefebvre*, edited by Kanishka Goonewardena, Stefan Kipfer, Richard Milgrom, and Christian Schmid, 212–230. New York: Routledge, 2008.

Simone, AbdoulMaliq. "The Urban Majority and Provisional Recompositions in Yangon: The 2016 Antipode RGS-IBG Lecture." *Antipode*, 50, no.1 (2017): 23–40.

———."To Extend: Temporariness in a World of Itineraries." *Urban Studies*, 57, no. 6 (2020): 1127-1142.

Simone, AbdoulMaliq, and Edgar Pieterse. *New Urban Worlds: Inhabiting Dissonant Times*, Cambridge: Polity Press, 2017.

Silva Júnior, C.; Petit, P. "Hidrelétricas na Amazônia: impactos energéticos, sociais e ambientais." In *Culturas e dinâmicas sociais na Amazônia Oriental brasileira*, edited by Airton Pereira, H. Anjos, and I. Silva, 307–332. Belém: Paka-tatu, 2017.

Silveira, Semida. *Transformations in Amazonia: The spatial reconfiguration of systems*. Royal Institute of Technology, Department of Infrastructure and Planning, Stockholm, Sweden, 1993.

Stanek, Łukasz. *Henri Lefebvre on Space: Architecture, Urban Research, and the Production of Theory*. Minneapolis, London: University of Minnesota Press, 2011.

———"Space as Concrete Abstraction." In *Space, Difference, Everyday Life: Reading Henri Lefebvre*, edited by Kanishka Goonewardena, Stefan Kipfer, Richard Milgrom, and Christian Schmid, 62–79. New York: Routledge, 2008.

Svampa, Maristella. "Commodities Consensus: Neoextractivism and Enclosure of the Commons in Latin America." *South Atlantic Quarterly*, 114, no. 1 (2015): 65–82.

Topalov, Christian. *La urbanización capitalista: algunos elementos para su análisis*. Colômbia: Edicon, 1979.

VALE S. A. "Complexo S11D." Accessed 16 June 2017.

Welch, Clifford A., and Sérgio Sauer. "Rural Unions and the Struggle for Land in Brazil." *The Journal of Peasant Studies* 42, no. 6 (2015): 1109–1135.

IMAGE CREDITS

All photography from author unless otherwise stated.

All maps from Philippe Rekacewicz with author unless otherwise stated.

F. 4   Sources: GéoComunes; Environmental Justice Atlas; Instituto Brasileiro de Geografia e Estatistica (IBGE); Sâmia Nunes et al. "Potential for Forest Restoration and Deficit Compensation in Itacaiúnas Watershed, Southeastern Brazilian Amazon", *Forests* 10, no. 5 (2019): 439.

F. 5   Comissão Pastoral da Terra, Massacres no Campo, https://www.cptnacional.org.br/mnc/index.php

F. 8   Sources: GéoComunes; Environmental Justice Atlas; Instituto Brasileiro de Geografia e Estatistica (IBGE)

F. 9   Google Earth

F. 10   Google Earth

F. 11   Google Earth

The Horizontal Factory.
The Operationalisation of
the US Corn and Soy Belt

We all live in the city.
We all live in the country.
Both are second nature to us.[1]

WHAT IS THE CORN BELT?

"Imagine how much food
we could produce."[2]

The words of Don, a farmer who spent more
than seven decades of his life in south-west Iowa,
sounded quite paradoxical, considering
we were standing amidst a green sea of corn-
fields just outside Corning, Iowa. A largely
continuous farming zone extended for hundreds
of miles around, stretching from the state of
Iowa to Illinois, Indiana, southern Michigan,
western Ohio, eastern Nebraska, eastern South
Dakota, and southern Minnesota. This is the
Corn Belt,[3] [Fig. 1] a landscape where 80 million
acres of cropland cover more than two-thirds
of the land, producing more than 30% of all

corn and more than 20% of all soybeans in the
world. I had been slowly immersed in this landscape as I drove west from Chicago to meet
Don. I crossed endless corn and soy fields that
were only interrupted by grain storage towers,
elevators, biofuel plants, and windmills. The
uncanny feeling was amplified by the apparent
minimal presence of living organisms, from
humans to free ranging animals, or even insects,
making the landscape feel less like an agricultural "countryside," and more like a "horizontal
factory." What kind of landscape was that,
and how could it be conceptualised?
      The Corn Belt is undoubtedly a highly
industrialised, monofunctional landscape
of agricultural hyperproduction, consistently
calibrated towards a particular set of outputs.
In an early map from 1949, the United States
Department of Agriculture (USDA) defined
the Corn Belt as a region producing "predominantly feed and livestock."[4] [Fig.3] This relationship between grains, feed, and livestock has
historically and continues to define the nature of
the Corn Belt. While the Corn Belt has emerged,

and subsequently transformed, as an agricultural system configured to cultivate grains for animal feed, more recently, the system has also been geared towards the production of biofuel. In fact, while US corn production has almost doubled over the past three decades, the increased volume has been driven predominantly by the increase in bioethanol production, while the production of animal feed remained rather static.[5] [Fig. 6] Whether producing feed, or biofuel, the Corn Belt is hardly producing any food. Don was right.

How has such a vast area been configured in this way? To answer this question, we first need to contextualise the type of landscape the Corn Belt is within the global agri-food system. The analysis [Fig. 1–2] unveils a stark contrast in the composition of global cropland areas. On the one hand, specialised, cash-crop systems producing feed (such as corn and soybeans) dominate Western industrialised agricultural systems; on the other hand, areas predominantly producing food for direct human consumption (such as rice and wheat) dominate the global South.[6] The Corn Belt is, of course, highlighted as a seminal zone of the former. These landscapes can be characterised as "hinterlands of hinterlands" as they do not directly support human populations but supply zones of dense livestock concentrations. [Fig. 4] Depending upon high direct and indirect inputs of energy (mainly in the form of machine fuel, fertilisers, and pesticides), they can be seen as metabolic systems converting energy into livestock. In doing so, they rely on (so far) cheap energy to sustain a rather inefficient nutritional exchange due to the low-calorie conversion of livestock.[7]

To complicate things even more, with increasing percentages of soy and corn yields directed to biofuel production, the recent metabolic structure of the Corn Belt can also be seen as a system metabolising one form of energy into another. Thus, positioning the Corn Belt within the food, feed, and energy nexus reveals its configuration's metabolic "irrationality": High-input farming transforms crops into nutritionally inefficient livestock and biofuels that embody more energy than they contribute. Why would such a huge area be sacrificed in producing this

particular set of outputs through a significantly wasteful set of metabolic processes?

The Corn Belt has never been shaped by a meaningful metabolic logic but rather by the capitalist search for profit. It has always been and remains a profitable landscape. Or even better, an assemblage of landscapes, consisting of a system of spatial elements, configured and reconfigured, crystallised and "creatively destroyed" in search of profit maximisation.[8] This assemblage of profit landscapes extends beyond the sea of farms and monocultures. It comprises grain storage facilities and feed-production plants; ethanol and biofuel distilleries, fertiliser factories, pesticide plants, and seed production facilities; animal feeding operations and meat packing plants, windfarms, electricity grids, and natural gas pipelines; the rail corridors, highway networks, and intermodal freight nodes. [Fig. 5] The constant pressure to renegotiate the social, technical, and natural capacities of this assemblage in order to offer bundles of profitable commodities to the global markets, leads to increasing industrialisation, infrastructuralisation and intensive monofunctional specialisation, turning the landscapes that compose it into more and more operational landscapes: metabolic landscapes operationalised for the extraction of capitalist profit through shifting bundles of human and more-than-human systems.[9]

This contribution investigates the emergence, development, and eventual exhaustion of the operational landscapes of agricultural production across the US Corn Belt system, focusing on the state of Iowa. Building upon a historical geography of operationalisation of the Corn Belt, this contribution aims to reveal the socio-ecological struggles behind

F. 1   The corn and soy belt in the US revealed by the overlay of high corn (red) and soybean (blue) cultivation frequencies over a period of ten years (2008–2018).

F. 2   The global distribution of agricultural crop production for food (blue) and feed (brown) in 2015.

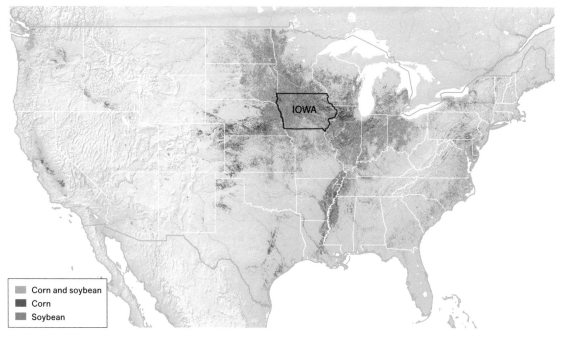

THE US CORN AND SOY BELT
Fig. 1

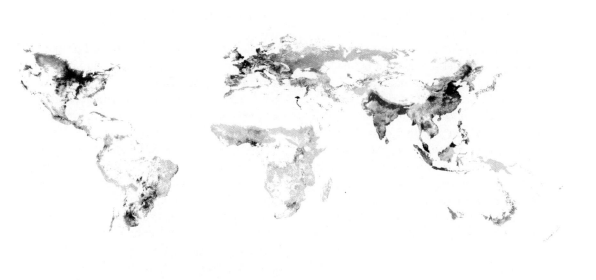

A SPECIALISED AGRICULTURAL
TERRITORY IN A GLOBAL CONTEXT
Fig. 2

Fig. 3

the constant race for increases in productivity, reflected on the exhausted soils, the contaminated hydrological systems, the genetically modified plants and animals, the shrinking settlements, and the still-persistent family farmers, who struggle to maintain their livelihood under the pressure of increasingly oligopolistic commodity chains. Behind the record-high yields are rapidly approaching yield plateaus, massive subsidies, extensive depopulation, and environmental degradation; signs of an overall exhaustion of the capacity to displace and obscure the negative externalities of capitalist agriculture and eventually reproduce and reinvent itself.

F. 3   The Corn Belt defined by the USDA in 1949: a specialised agricultural area producing feed grains and livestock.

F. 4   The Corn Belt as a cash-crop system producing animal feed and supplying zones of dense livestock concentrations.

LANDSCAPE OPERATIONALISATION IN THE CAPITALOCENE

The operationalisation of the Corn Belt can only be understood within the context of constructing a globalised, capitalist hinterland, that is part of the metabolic geographies of planetary urbanisation. The concept of operational landscapes aims to help conceptualise the complex processes of extended urbanisation that construct the material basis of contemporary urban life. Following Neil Smith, under capitalist development, the reproduction of material life is deeply interwoven with the production and reproduction of surplus value.[10] In the age of capital, the Capitalocene, and under conditions of planetary urbanisation, this relationship is generalised, amplified, and intensified.[11] Not only does the inherently expansive nature of capitalism constantly scan Earth for new opportunities to extract surplus value, but the continuous concentration of human populations and economic activities in agglomeration zones and other areas of

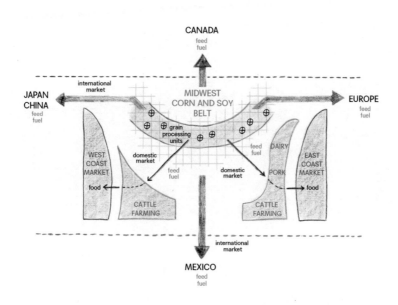

THE CORN BELT AS "HINTERLANDS OF HINTERLANDS"
Fig. 4

concentrated urbanisation depends upon a web of multiscalar, geo-metabolic interdependencies that extend across the planetary terrain. As this planetary urban metabolism is interwoven with the capitalist search for surplus value, it operationalises a wide variety of landscapes around the world, landscapes of primary production (agriculture, mining, forestry), circulation (transport, communication), and waste disposal.

Operational landscapes are the metabolic "hinterlands" of the Capitalocene, the landscapes that constitute the material basis of the urbanised geographies of planetary urbanisation.[12] As operational landscapes are predominantly dedicated to the production and circulation of primary commodities, they are deeply interwoven with more-than-human systems. They are the terrains where nature becomes "a universal means of production in the sense that it not only provides the subjects, objects, and instruments of production but is also in its totality an appendage to the production process."[13] Nature is produced through the operationalisation of landscapes, but also production across the operational

landscapes happens through nature. Thus, operational landscapes play a central role in putting nature at work in the production and circulation of surplus value as part of the capitalist world ecology.[14]

The concept of the ecological surplus, introduced by Jason Moore, allows for a more precise investigation of this exact process.[15] Central to the concept is a distinction between labour and work, both of which are mobilised in the process of capitalist production. For Moore, capitalism not only extracts value from the exploitation of paid work (wage labour) but also through unpaid work or work embedded in the process of reproducing the labour force. What is important, however, is that unpaid work is not restricted to humans: it can also refer to processes of the natural environment. For example, the growth of a plant, photosynthesis in general, geological processes that produce minerals, and the water cycle all require some kind of "work" to be performed. This is work that, when appropriated through the production process, remains unpaid. Based on this concep-

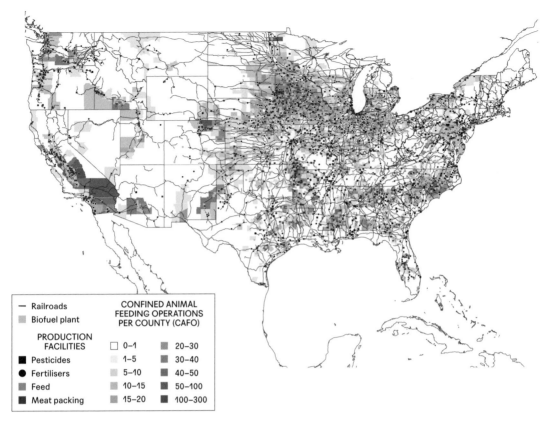

THE OPERATIONAL ASSEMBLAGE
OF THE EXTENDED CORN BELT SYSTEM
Fig. 5

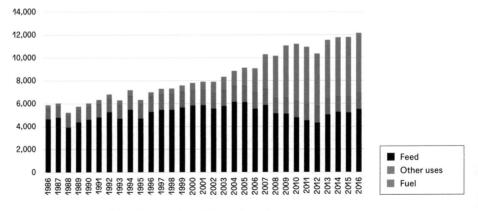

US CORN PRODUCTION 1986–2016
Fig. 6

tualisation, the ecological surplus is defined as the ratio between the actual capital investment in paid work (wage-labour), fixed capital, and raw materials over the unpaid work that is mobilised through it from human and more-than-human agents.

The struggle for the successful appropriation of this unpaid work is what has historically allowed, and still allows, capitalism to develop upon the exploitation of what Moore frames as the "four cheaps": labour power, food, energy, and raw materials. It also guides the multidimensional operationalisation of production and circulation landscapes across scales and territories. As primary production is to a large degree grounded to the specificities of natural geographies and natural processes, the construction of operational landscapes of primary production can be conceptualised as a constant effort to extract ecological surplus across two frontiers: On the one hand, through the expansion of geographical frontiers, allowing access to areas of untapped resources; and on the other hand, through the conquest of the biochemical frontiers (such as through genetic engineering), allowing access to the processes of natural work, and thus its exploitation. The "frontier condition" can be conceptualised as a condition that allows the maximisation of ecological surplus and the appropriation of high amounts

of unpaid work for relatively low amounts of capital investment. As nature's capacity to contribute free work to the system is exhausted and negative externalities are generalised, the ecological surplus has the tendency to fall.[16] Resource deposits are exhausted, soils cannot be replenished, and forests are logged, all leading to the need to substitute the exhausted "productivity" of natural systems through capital investment, which decreases the amount of ecological surplus and leads to pressure to reinvent novel bundles of the four cheaps. The endless search for profit through the constant reconfiguration of the four cheaps allow for high degrees of ecological surplus that construct and reconstruct assemblages of operational landscapes for primary production.

The shifting nexus between food, feed, and fuel, largely shaping the structure of agricultural systems, can thus be contextualised within this broader framework of the four cheaps. A generic scheme of operationalisation of primary production landscapes would see initial investments in surveying and transport to allow for the expansion of geographical frontiers, which, as they are slowly exhausted, would lead to increased investment in mechanisation and inputs to sustain productivity. With their initial ecological surplus exhausted, these landscapes would then depend more and more on the appropriation of new frontiers elsewhere across the geographical and geochemical domain. For instance, in agriculture, the exhaustion of the initial fertility of the soil would be countered through mechanisation, or expansion over biochemical and geographical frontiers around certain inputs (fertilisers, pesticides, energy), with high ecological surpluses in energy production eventually sustaining a high input agricultural metabolism, which would sustain cheap food and cheap labour, and thus a multitude of other opportunities for appropriating ecological surplus elsewhere in the system.

The question of the construction of the Corn Belt can thus be framed in a way that connects it to shifts in the composition of ecological surplus. An initial phase of expansion over

F. 5   The operational assemblage of the extended Corn Belt system: the map reveals the concentrations of corn and soybean cultivation, density of animal feeding operations, feed production facilities, pesticide and chemical production facilities, seed production facilities, bioethanol and biofuel plants, and railway networks.

F. 6   Corn production for feed, fuel, and other uses in the US, 1986–2016: the overwhelming majority of corn is geared towards the feed and fuel industry, with a minor percentage going to direct consumption, mostly in the form of corn syrup. Corn production has doubled from 7 billion bushels in the early 1990s to around 14 billion today, but most of the increase has been due to the rising demand for biofuels.

previously uncultivated lands in the Midwest allowed for the exploitation of an extremely high ecological surplus. This was made possible mostly through investment in transport infrastructure, which was soon followed by a continuous trend towards exhaustion through the gradual depletion of the soil's natural fertility. This has led to a continuous intensification of the production process through commodified inputs, such as energy and fertilisers, to compensate for it, which took advantage of areas of ecological surplus across distant geographies or geochemical developments. The exhaustion of several different bundles of ecological surplus across the Corn Belt has left one last frontier able to still contribute unpaid work into the system: the social structure of and around the family farm.

The role and nature of human work in the construction of the Corn Belt is very much connected to the persistence of the family farm as the dominant unit of production. Given its extreme degree of industrialisation, it might appear surprising that Corn Belt agriculture is, and has always been, predominantly based on family farms. It is thus crucial to offer a framework for understanding the role of the family farm in the construction of the Corn Belt. Following Harriet Friedmann, it is important to distinguish between the family farm, as a form of production, operating within a capitalist mode of production.[17] The form of production refers to the basic unit of productive organisation—the farm—and the particular social relations around it, and the range of techniques. The family farm, as a form of production, is embedded within a broader set of relationships dominated by the market logic of the various phases of the capitalist mode of production. Nevertheless, the family farm is not a capitalist unit of production (such as the enterprise) but rather a household unit of production (although there is a certain tendency to treat and even celebrate the farmers of the Corn Belt as entrepreneurs). The major difference is twofold: The family farm does not rely on waged labour relationships since almost all labour is done by members of the household, and it is not driven solely by profit, but rather by the goal of reproducing its personal and productive consumption base. Personal consumption refers to the costs of social reproduction, and productive consumption to the reproduction of the inputs of the production process (seeds, fertilisers, etc.). In this case, both are part of the same pool.

The blurred boundary between personal and productive consumption is also influenced by the particular condition of agricultural production, which theoretically allows (or allowed) a series of these processes to be internalised. With the cultivation of food, some part of personal consumption could be initially provided by the farm itself (theoretically even leading to complete subsistence). At the same time, the productive basis could be reproduced within the farm, as seeds used for the next crop or manure used as fertiliser. As it will be discussed, the history of the Corn Belt can be traced following the constant commodification of the elements of the productive and reproductive basis of the family farm, through constant corporatisation of all processes, except for the farmland itself. At the basis of these processes, we can try to trace shifts in the nexus of labour power, food, energy, and raw materials, which theoretically could have been part of a subsistence mode of existence, but under capitalism, have become part of the continuous search for profit.

In this struggle, the work relations within the farm constitute the last frontier of ecological surplus within the Corn Belt: As the household form of production has a much larger dedication to ensuring its reproduction and given the blurred lines between costs of social and productive reproduction, it allows for a much higher adaptability to shocks in the capitalist relations that surround it, through high degrees of self-exploitation. For Friedmann, this particular combination of factors has offered the family farm a certain robustness and competitive advantage over other capitalist organisations of agricultural production, allowing it to proliferate as the dominant unit. At the same time, as it was positioned within capitalist systems of production, the multiple combinations of the labour power, food, energy, and raw materials it allowed, and the high degree of self-exploitation, offered several opportunities for extracting ecological surplus, which was then gradually exhausted by the commodification of almost all involved metabolic relations.

Building upon these two frameworks, the history and contemporary anatomy of the Corn Belt that follow are largely focused on unpacking the processes of exhaustion of ecological surplus within the Corn Belt and the dependence upon new frontiers of ecological surplus beyond its boundaries until it has reached its last frontier, the family farm.

GEOGRAPHICAL EXPANSION AND THE ORIGINS OF THE CORN BELT SYSTEM

Central to the history of the operationalisation of the Midwest is a narrative that describes the expansion of farming over an extensive, virgin, fertile land, following an almost "natural" process.[18] But the "fertility" of the Corn Belt, and thus its capacity to contribute ecological surplus, has been a much more dynamic condition, reshaped over long periods of time by geology and climate, but also, to a large extent, socio-technically constructed. The basis of the fertility of the Corn Belt is the soil, which is the result of two main processes: The depositions of several phases of glacial advances and the decomposition of tall and thick grassland that dominated for the past thousand years.[19] This combination has created thick layers of topsoil with a structure and texture able to absorb large quantities of water. The porosity allows the circulation of air and, thus, the reproduction of the microorganisms responsible for metabolising the necessary nutritional elements for the plants.[20] Thus, the agricultural suitability of Corn Belt soils is not so much due to rich organic matter content (like in tropical soils), which was very early exhausted, but due to their structure and texture, making them still efficient under the more recent use of fertilisers.

While the latest glacial advance defines the latitudinal limit of the Corn Belt to the south, the average rainfall and levels of humidity largely define the longitudinal limit to the west, completing an "environmental envelope" of rainfed agriculture over fertile soils. But in the absence of human activity and agricultural cultivation, humidity, and annual rainfall also affect the prevalence of forests or prairies. Interestingly, the levels of humidity and precipitation across the Corn Belt could largely support the existence of more forested vegetation types. But when the first Western explorers appeared in the late seventeenth century, what they observed was extensive grassland prairies with scattered woodlands. What they were interpreting as pristine nature was actually an already anthropogenic "second nature."[21] Over hundreds of years, the native tribes had co-produced the grasslands together with nature by helping the prairie penetrate the forest through land clearings, and preventing the forest from reconquering the prairie, given the climatic conditions.[22] It was not just the work of nature that contributed to the high initial ratio of ecological surplus to the arriving settlers, but also the work of the indigenous populations. The eventual violent expulsion of the native tribes by the Western settlers would not only mean the expropriation of their lands but also the appropriation of generations-long embodied labour that their ancestors had contributed.

If the glacial deposits and the hydrological systems of the Mississippi and Missouri basins form the geographic basis of the Midwest and the contemporary Corn Belt, it was the corridors crossing the Appalachian range and the Ohio River valley that largely defined the trajectories of settlement towards the Midwest, but also the trajectories of diffusion of the model of Corn Belt agriculture. According to the geographer John Hudson, the origins of the model of cultivating feed for the fattening of livestock, the model that still defines the essence of Corn Belt agriculture, can be traced back to early nineteenth-century West Virginia. From there, it would eventually migrate westwards, together with the expansion of the frontier.[23] This system could be characterised as cash-crop farming, but in this case, crops were not sold in the form of grain but in the form of livestock, either cattle or hogs.[24] In the early versions of the system, animals were the main commodity (besides the purchase of agricultural tools), both forward and backward in the chain: animals were bought as stock from grazing areas, then fed corn on the farm to gain weight rapidly, and eventually sold for cash.

The central role of livestock in the early logistics of the system can be associated with the restrictions of the early configuration of the food, feed, and fuel nexus in the absence of adequate transportation means. Crops are bulky commodities, costly to transport to the market. Embodied in the form of animals, the value of crops can literally walk to the market, consuming only some amount of the weight gained and feed used. Although both cattle and hogs were often raised on the same farms, their different metabolisms positioned them in very different roles in the system. Cattle were much more efficient at covering larger distances without losing considerable weight than hogs, which offered a more extensive line of products when processed (from lard to bacon).

Thus, the early nineteenth-century version of the Corn Belt system largely reflected the interplay between geography and the metabolism of hogs and cattle. The majority of the population was still concentrated in the east, along the Atlantic coast, while the majority of cattle were raised in the west, beyond the Appalachian mountains. Cattle walked eastward in large herds to the early Corn Belt farms that were at an intermediate location across the Miami and Ohio valleys, where they were fattened with corn. They then walked further east to the major markets, such as Philadelphia.[25] Processing facilities, mostly for swine products, were initially spread across the waterways of the Ohio valley, through which they could also be transported in barrels all the way down the Mississippi River, which already constituted the major north-south trade corridor.

The early Corn Belt farm suggested a system of mixed farming. The dominant cultivation model involved the rotation between corn, which was used for animal feed, wheat, which was used for household consumption (and to a certain degree as a cash crop sold to local mills), and oats, used to feed the draft animals, mostly horses. The livestock was fed in what could be described as an open feedlot, with cattle contained in open pens, feeding off stacks of corn, with hogs coming after them and consuming what was left behind. Animal waste was, to a large extent, used as manure and the whole farm had a considerable degree of self-sufficiency in terms of reproducing both the personal and productive consumption of the family that worked it. Feed for livestock and food for the family was largely produced at the farm (which also had dairy cows and chickens). The commodified relationships included the acquisition and selling of livestock, as well as the land itself.

While the early Corn Belt farm was already directed towards the production of exchange values, this particular metabolism also offered a certain robustness that allowed the family farm to respond to the volatilities of the market and to environmental risk. Depending on the level of production, the farmers still had some flexibility regarding what portion of the crop they would feed to cattle or hogs or even sell directly to the market and what portion of the production would be diverted to personal consumption. Significant pressure came mostly from the demand side, securing adequate markets in a state of limited transport options. But as the Corn Belt moved north and west, and levels of specialisation increased, a rescaled, splintered Corn Belt system eroded the internal, circular metabolism of the open feedlot farm, with more and more relationships of personal and productive reproduction becoming commodified.

Fig. 7

LAYING THE GROUND
INFRASTRUCTURES OF
COMMODIFIED METABOLISM

Two major developments around the turn of the nineteenth century largely set the base infrastructures that facilitated the relocated, rescaled, specialised, and further commodified metabolism of the Corn Belt: The Public Land Survey System (PLSS) that served as the major tool for commodifying and transferring expropriated land from indigenous tribes to Western settlers; and the development of the railway network, which not only reshaped patterns of accessibility, but also acted as a device of land speculation and capital concentration setting the tone for the continuous corporatisation of the Corn Belt. What was also introduced with these two developments was the crucial and entangled roles both of state and corporate actors in the development of the Corn Belt.

    The Land Ordinance of 1785 marked the beginning of the PLSS and is the basis of the familiar checkerboard pattern of the mid-western United States.[26] The conception and implementation of the PLSS are probably the most lucid examples of what Henri Lefebvre highlighted as the production of "abstract space."[27] What was eventually produced through surveying,

quantification, and systematic representation was a space of exchange, not use value; a spatial condition favouring homogenisation, interchangeability, repetitiveness, and the erasure of difference, experiential visual, temporal, and sensual spatial relations. A space constitutive of the capitalist mode of production while, at the same time, reflective of capitalist power. A little more than three decades after the Enclosures Act in the UK, the PLSS formalised processes of enclosure at a previously unseen continental scale. The processes appropriated not just the land and embodied labour of indigenous populations, but also eradicated cultural values and historical practices of environmental coexistence and care, opening the way for ecological deterioration.[28]

    The PLSS plates reveal this homogenised, but at the same time, centrally planned and hierarchically structured space of abstraction. [Fig. 7] Concealed were not just the socio-natural complexities that characterised

F. 7   Public Land Survey System (PLSS) plates for Marion County (left) and Washington township within Marion County (right) showing the subdivision of properties during the 1880s.

indigenous inhabitation, but also the variations of natural geography. At the same time, the system introduced a well-articulated idea not just of social order but also of the scales and forms of social and economic interaction that were neatly prescribed through the nested hierarchies of the PLSS grid. Based on this logic that celebrated Cartesian space, and with minimal ground surveying, the PLSS subdivided (on paper) almost the entire area west of the Ohio River in townships of 36 square miles, which were further subdivided into 36 parcels of 640 acres (64,000 m²). In what could be characterised as the biggest land grab and land sale in human history since the end of the eighteenth century, these land subdivisions sold to the new settlers, offering both an incentive for new farmers to move west and a valuable income to the new state that was in financial distress. By 1868, when the Homestead Act provided the remaining agricultural land for free, less than 3% of land in core Corn Belt states such as Iowa was still available.[29]

But the theoretical rationality suggested by the Public Land Ordinance's checkerboard system was severely challenged in its implementation, and the actual settlement pattern of the Midwest rarely happened in an "orderly" fashion. Land speculation, already embedded in the original lower limit of 640 acres, distorted the presumed goal of creating a nation of self-sufficient farmers. Not only was the amount required to obtain it unaffordable for most farmers, but also the minimum purchasable area was more than ten times larger than what would be needed to support a family and impossible to cultivate to its full extent given its limited labour force.[30] Even the subsequent lower limits of 160 and 80 acres were still too much for a family to afford and efficiently work. The exuberant sizes reflected the interests of the East Coast and often overseas investors and opened a cycle of widespread land speculation, which led to intensified and unsustainable cultivation practices.[31] Farmers who were often heavily indebted to purchase the land were urged to produce more agricultural commodities, often exhausting the land, only to quickly

sell it off and move further west to take advantage of higher ecological surplus.

At the same time, the homogeneous checkerboard grid was laid over a highly variable natural geography, leading early farmland development to leapfrog over extensive areas and concentrate at the edges of wooded zones (as wood was the main source of construction materials and energy), along major river systems (as they provided the only means of transportation), and away from zones that had poor drainage and required extensive investment in infrastructure.[32] Thus, the general direction of the north and west expansion of the Corn Belt in the early nineteenth century was not one of continuous, organised development. Rather, it was an unstable meshwork of pockets and corridors, mostly concentrated along waterways.

The gradual infilling and extensive homogenisation of the midwestern landscape were only made possible through the development of the railways in the mid-nineteenth century, which also completely reoriented the major trade routes of the Corn Belt. In its initial configuration, grain trade occurred along the Mississippi River, with St. Louis being the major transportation hub and New Orleans the major port connecting the Midwest to the world. By the 1850s major railway corridors linked Chicago directly to New York and the East Coast, with a secondary radial network extending around it, penetrating the Midwest.[33] This fuelled further expansion on agricultural land that was often less favourable and required higher investment but promised higher revenues through better access to markets. Overall, the railways decisively enhanced cash crop farming. Walking livestock to the market was not the only option anymore. Grain could be shipped directly to the market as a commodity.

But as the superimposition of the PLSS grid reflected the dominance of state power, so did the rapid expansion of the railways introduce its interplay with the interests of corporate actors. The private companies that developed the railways in exchange for long stretches of land along the lines also boosted migration and settlement since they had a dual incentive to draw population to the regions they crossed. They could benefit both from the sale of agricultural land and from increased volume in freight traffic.[34] By the late nineteenth century, railways were the dominant mode of transporting grains and livestock across the Midwest. Their confluence in Chicago created an unprecedented concentration of the livestock industry around its terminals, reflecting the exuberant concentration of capital that characterised the Gilded Age.

Further centralisation and intensification of the industry were fuelled by the introduction of the refrigeration car in the late nineteenth century. This allowed meat processing operations to function all year round (and not just during the colder months), something that pushed farmers to speed up a continuous supply of livestock. The concentration and intensification of processing and manufacturing led to the generalisation of wage labour relations in the major agglomeration zones of Chicago and Saint Louis, where surplus value was extracted through their exploitation, as lucidly documented by Upton Sinclair.[35] At the same time, family farmers were increasingly getting caught up in the vicious cycle of overproduction, struggling to keep extracting ecological surplus out of a landscape that was already becoming exhausted. While still in control of the land, the family farm was engulfed fully within—and dependent upon—the emerging and increasingly corporate agri-food system without it ever becoming a corporate entity itself. This indirect "corporatisation" of the family farm continued to characterise Corn Belt agriculture ever since.

The Gilded Age signified the crystallisation and dominance of corporate capitalism that would become the dominant force in the operationalisation of the Corn Belt, while at the same time started recalibrating the role of the state away from distributive politics and toward regulative and redistributive solutions to the ensuing problems of overaccumulation that would become increasingly pressing in the early twentieth century.[36] By then, the Corn Belt had expanded north and west to Indiana, Wisconsin, Michigan, and Minnesota, and by the mid-twentieth century, it had largely stabilised in an area that roughly corresponds to its contemporary limits. Expansion was largely over, as was the initial phase of exploitation of high ecological surplus connected to the fertility of previously uncultivated land. After the 1920s, a long period of intensification and specialisation unravelled.

SPECIALISATION AND THE SPLINTERING FEEDLOT

Starting in the early twentieth century, the different elements of the Corn Belt metabolism that were once largely consolidated in a single farm were becoming decoupled. A threefold transformation of specialisation, rescaling, and splintering unfolded, together with the continuing industrialisation and commodification of the means and inputs of production, leading to more and more capital-intensive forms of production.

In the initial Corn Belt farm, besides the land and the cattle that had to be acquired, most other inputs for production, such as seeds, hogs, and manure (used as fertiliser), could be reproduced off the farm. Nevertheless, even during the first phases of cultivation of the mid-western grasslands, improved equipment was needed to plough the thick, hard-to-penetrate, sod-covered soil. Family farms did not have a shortage of land but rather, a shortage of labour. The invention of the steel plough by John Deere in Iowa unleashed a wave of innovation and production in agricultural machinery that directly addressed this problem. A farm's only means of increasing production was to extend the reach of human labour through mechanisation, thus acting as catalysts for the creation of an agro-industrial production complex that emerged in the Midwest during the early twentieth century.[37]

But the growth of productivity, both in manufacturing and in agriculture, also meant that farmers were entering a vicious cycle. As they invested more capital, they had to produce more revenue, and the only way to do that was to produce more crops. This led to problems of overproduction and surplus, pushing prices down to where they could only respond by producing more and investing more capital since the labour supply of the family farm was inelastic. A crises of overproduction emerged, most notably in the 1920s and 1930s, constituting a continuous challenge for the region.[38]

Continuous mechanisation was also decisive for the specialisation and rescaling of agricultural production. As obtaining farming equipment required significant investment, the only way to offset the high costs was to disperse them over higher production acreages.[39] This also meant that, as equipment was often specific to certain crops, it became more and more cost-efficient to concentrate on one specific crop. Most importantly, mechanisation allowed family farms to escape their labour limitations. Before the diffusion of tractors, the acreage that could be planted was defined by the capacity to mobilise human and animal labour during the specific weeks of planting and harvesting (in spring and fall). For the family farm, this set a quite particular upper limit, which was pushed upwards with mechanisation.

Along with the general upscaling of farming operations, the shift from solar-powered farms (through photosynthesis) to fossil fuel-powered farms also released significant amounts of land to monoculture. As farms were initially horse-powered—and early agricultural equipment required a large amount of horse-power—a significant part of the production of the farm, mostly oats, was feed for the reproduction of draft animals.[40] But by 1950, almost all farms had at least one tractor, which also meant that producing feed for the draft animals was removed from the farm rotation, allowing for further specialisation. However, this also meant that besides the costs of machinery, one more input was commodified and added to the cost structure of the farm. Fuel for the tractors could not be produced on site as the feed for the horses had been, and agriculture started depending heavily on the provision of cheap energy.

As oats were removed from the rotation, a completely novel crop was imported from Asia,

introduced as an alternative cash crop to help deal with problems of surplus corn production: soybeans. Soybeans were introduced in the 1930s and were often combined in annual rotations with corn since they helped restore the fertility of the soil that corn cultivation exhausted.[41] In 1930, only a few years after their introduction, more than 3 million acres of soybeans were planted across the United States, and by 2018 soybean acreage matched the acreage of corn.[42] Similar to corn, soybeans are used for the production of animal feed (and, more recently, biofuel). But in contrast to corn that could (at least initially) be directly consumed on the farm, soybeans needed to be crushed in order to produce protein-rich oil. Therefore, soybeans could only be traded as a cash crop, not used directly on the farm to feed animals, and this required an industrial facility to process them.

At the same time, livestock production was rapidly upscaled and transformed into a closed system detached from the farm, operating through industrialised facilities in increasingly specialised locations. In 1900 more than 60 million hogs were dispersed in over 4 million farms across the US, with the majority concentrated in the Corn Belt. In 2012 there were just 60,000 farms with hogs, roughly the same number of hogs (60 million), but now farms had at least 1,000 hogs on average. A similar consolidation and upscaling happened with cattle. In 1900, there were around 40 million animals dispersed over 4 million farms across the United States, and in 2012, just over 900,000 farms were feeding more than 90 million animals.[43]

While hog production was concentrated in areas of northern Iowa and Illinois, after WWII, cattle production started moving farther west, closer to the grazing areas that produced cattle stock. The dominance of truck transport, especially after the 1970s, with the development of the Interstate Highway system, allowed the meatpacking and processing industry to decentralise. Abandoning large cities not only meant more efficient logistics but also escaping labour disputes with strong labour unions, as well as stricter environmental regulations that were starting to emerge.[44]

The decentralisation of the meatpacking industry enhanced the concentration of feedlots around it, contributing to their general upscaling and the eventual domination of large-scale confined animal feeding operations (CAFOs) that largely emerged out of a new type of operation: the dry feedlot. The dry feedlot could be largely considered as a machine for fattening cattle. Its operations fed anywhere from 1,000 to more than 50,000 animals, each in densely packed, grassless compartments with specially mixed blends.[45] The CAFOs (both for hog and cattle) were a decisive step, not only in the upscaling of the livestock industry but also in the decoupling of the integrated metabolism that originally characterised the Corn Belt system. Feed was not grown but purchased, and manure was not recycled as fertiliser, but concentrated as waste, creating severe environmental problems.

The effects of economies of scale started significantly transforming the structure of the Corn Belt farm towards larger-scale, specialised, cash-crop monocultures. As the total harvested area remained largely the same, farms got bigger and bigger, and the mode of production became increasingly capital-intensive while relying on less and less labour. Large farms, able to benefit from economies of scale, came to dominate Corn Belt (and US) agriculture, while acreage per farm and farmer increased exponentially.

INTENSIFICATION AND HOMOGENISATION BEYOND THE LAND

The continuous specialisation of the Corn Belt was starting to create a set of largely homogenised operational landscapes. But the homogenisation was not only due to the similar types of crop plantations and the concentrations of similar types of livestock. It was also due to the elimination of the biological variation of plants and animals. Since the early nineteenth century, the biological selection process at the farm level had reduced the hundreds of varieties of corn once found across the American continent to only a handful. Among them, the Southern Dent variety dominated, since it was delivering adequate yields, but most importantly its kernels were soft shelled, so animals could consume it directly without further processing.[46]

Productivity concerns also defined the selection of dominant livestock breeds. Farmers sought breeds that could gain weight rapidly on a corn diet and generate lean pieces of meat. However, before the diffusion of the railways, the ability of animals to walk to the market without losing considerable weight was also favoured. A handful of breeds ended up dominating the US livestock industry. In the cattle industry, Hereford and Angus still dominate the market. In hog production, breeds that were able to gain a lot of weight and produce a lot of leaner meat dominated, such as the Yorkshire, Duroc, Berkshire, and Hampshire.[47] Moreover, as CAFOs started spreading, livestock was bred for more efficient fattening and responding better to the vitamin supplements and antibiotics that became necessary in the abnormally densely stocked feeding pens.

While livestock has been highly modified through breeding, genetic modification of animals has generally been avoided, something that has not been the case with the development of seeds. Despite cross-pollination experiments by farmers at the farm level, corn yields had reached a plateau by the early 1900s. After the 1920s, efforts to develop higher yielding varieties started becoming more systematic, amplified by institutional actors, such as agri-cultural universities, and the research stations of the United States Department of Agriculture (USDA).[48] Through self-breeding, the first generations of hybrid seeds allowed for increases in yield and more sturdy plants that performed better under mechanised farming. But as hybrid seeds were self-pollinated (every plant reproducing itself), they were very weak in maintaining their productivity after the first generation. A system of specialised farms emerged for producing and supplying farmers with the hybrid seeds they now had to buy before every planting cycle. As a result, one more input was commodified and had to be added to the cost structure of the family farm.

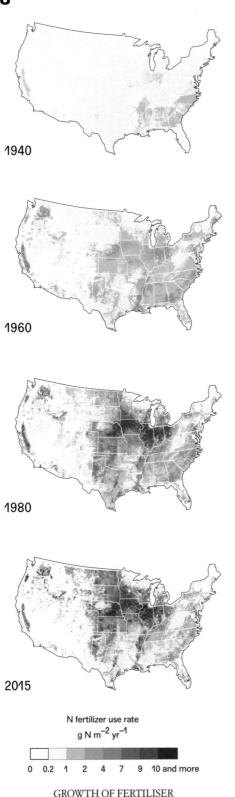

1940

1960

1980

2015

N fertilizer use rate

$g \, N \, m^{-2} \, yr^{-1}$

0   0.2   1   2   4   7   9   10 and more

GROWTH OF FERTILISER
CONSUMPTION
Fig. 8

While hybrid seeds were only trying to improve seed productivity through still largely natural crossbreeding methods, after the late 1980s, and especially during the 1990s, bioengineering was used to modify the DNA of plants directly. Genetic modifications are aimed at improving the productive capacity of plants and addressing the complex problems emerging from the intensification of chemical inputs. Modifications were aimed at making plants more resistant to herbicides and pesticides or repelling and exterminating insects and bacteria, so that fewer chemicals would be used. Continuous hybridisation kept improving the capacity of plants to absorb nutrients from the soil and allowed for higher and higher densities of planting. In the late nineteenth century, corn fields across the Corn Belt had a density of around 10,000 plants per acre and every acre could produce around 40 bushels of corn. By 2017, densities were up to 35,000 plants per acre, and yields were up to 200 bushels.[49] Within a century, the same amount of land was hosting three times more plants, producing five times more corn. Similar to the overcrowded livestock feedlot, the overcrowded corn (or soybean) field, became part of a high-input metabolism.

None of the yield increases would be possible without the development and production of synthetic fertilisers. In the initial Corn Belt metabolism, the cycle of replenishing the soil included animal manure that was produced on the farm, which would soon be complemented by industrially produced fertilisers, which helped add the phosphorus (P) and nitrogen (N) necessary for plant growth. Early fertiliser production in the nineteenth century was centred either around mining N- and P-rich soils across the planet or around the by-products of the livestock industry (for example, grinding P-rich animal bones). Early twentieth-century mechanisation was accompanied by a considerable increase in the application of these industrially produced fertilisers that were still directly linked to biological and geological processes and had a natural organic base. This metabolic link would also break after the 1930s with the generalisation of the synthetic production of N-based fertilisers from non-organic sources (mostly natural gas). The diffusion of the application of ammonia and urea-based fertilisers after WWII led to an unprecedented intensification of production and a critical modification of the nutrient and energy cycle, affecting not only the quality of soils but also the hydrological and atmospheric systems that were directly and indirectly connected to the Corn Belt's metabolic cycle as nitrates started leaking into the water system. [Fig. 8]

By the turn of the second millennium, the Corn Belt system, once tightly consolidated around the family farm, was spatially decoupled into specialised production landscapes across the United States. Certain regions—mostly across southern Illinois and Iowa—specialised in soybean production, while Iowa, Nebraska, and northern Illinois specialised in corn production, and several farms in northern Iowa, Illinois, and eastern Nebraska focused on swine. Cattle production was dispersed to Texas, Nebraska, Kansas, California, and Oklahoma. Moreover, as all metabolic relationships around the farm were commodified, corporate control over the complex commodity chains was turning the Corn Belt into a profit landscape, with the farm as a mere conduit. It was basically circulating capital in the form of inputs and outputs. In this capital-intensive system of high revenues, the farm was becoming less and less significant.

CORPORATISATION AND THE GEOPOLITICAL ECONOMY OF OPERATIONALISATION

Perhaps it is not so surprising then, that under the contemporary highly industrialised model of Corn Belt production, farms across the Midwest, are still not predominantly owned by corporations, but rather by families.[50] In Iowa and Illinois—the centre of the Corn Belt—more than 85% of the farms are still family-run.[51] But owning and operating the land is diminishing in importance, as profit is not emerging from it but through it. In the initial configuration

of the Corn Belt system, most of the value came from the soil, and most productive factors could be reproduced off the farm, giving farmers relative control. Seeds, livestock (hogs), fertiliser (manure), draft animals, and farm animals (such as chickens) could be largely reproduced on site. With the industrialisation of the Corn Belt system and the rescaling and splintering of its metabolism, all inputs became commodified and controlled by increasingly oligopolistic corporate structures. Family farms became squeezed into a treadmill that imposed both downward pressure (on the demand side) and upward pressure (on the supply side) while undertaking all the risks of growing plants and animals.

The oligopolistic concentration of the US agribusiness has been remarkable on both ends. On the demand side, livestock production has been one of the older fields of oligopolistic control, with collusion between the big meat-packers dating back to the nineteenth century. In the early twenty-first century, four corporations (Tyson, Cargill, Swift, Smithfield) control more than 85% of the beef-packing and processing industry, and around 70% of the pork-packing and processing industry, while Smithfield and Cargill dominate the feedlot industry. Animal feed plants are also largely consolidated, with the four biggest companies (Land O'Lakes, Cargill, ADM, and Heiskell) controlling around 40% of the market.[52] Soybeans and ethanol production, which were initially presented as alternative markets to farmers, are also mainly controlled by the same companies, with soybean crushing dominated by ADM, Cargill, and Bunge, who control more than 70% of the market. ADM and Cargill also control almost 40% of ethanol production. At the same time, more than 60% of the US corn and soybean seed market has been

F. 8 Growth of fertiliser consumption across the US between 1940, 1960, 1980 and 2015: more than 5 million tonnes of N based fertilisers were applied systematically across the Corn Belt almost every year after 2010, roughly corresponding to 50 kg per acre of farmland.

controlled by only two companies, Monsanto (now owned by Bayer) and Du Pont/Pioneer, who also hold the majority of patents related to genetically modified seeds. Similar concentration has characterised the fertiliser industry. Mosaic, a company controlled by Cargill, together with CF Industries, have been responsible for more than 60% of US production, competing with Canadian Nutrien. Finally, Du Pont, Monsanto (Bayer), and Syngenta (Novartis) are also dominating the agricultural chemicals market (herbicides and insecticides).[53]

Furthermore, several of these companies that often compete in the same sector are forming (formal or less formal) partnerships across sectors, creating what has been described as agri-food "clusters."[54] These clusters facilitate the entire process, from genetic engineering to fertiliser and chemical application, grain trade, feed, and livestock, even as far as the supermarket. These bundles are presented to the farmers as either best practices to increase productivity or as parts of contractual agreements, reducing farms into fully controlled, intermediate steps in the production process. Contract farming started to dominate the livestock industry in the late twentieth century (especially poultry). Livestock producers have to undertake investment in fixed capital to develop feedlots, only to raise feedstock that they do not even own, under contracts that also prescribe the feeding process, feed, antibiotics, hormones, and a fixed price for the final output. Given the licensing agreements that often accompany the use of genetically modified seeds, and the precision required in the combination of inputs for their best performance (specific fertilisers, pesticides, etc.), contract agriculture has also started to penetrate the corn and soybean cultivation sector.

But even with increased capital inputs, farmers see diminished returns with initial productivity gains quickly exhausted, and several experts expect yield plateaus in corn and soybean production.[55] In fact, certain physical limits have been reached and are difficult to surpass. For example, the density of corn plantations is so extreme that it is challenging the capacity of the soil to physically support, process, and deliver moisture and nutrients, despite intense fertilisation. As the limits of soil and plant productivity are reached, agribusiness corporations are aiming to further increase productivity through the very precise, specialised, and integrated coordination of all means of production. Geospatial technologies and increased automation have a central role in this new paradigm of "precision agriculture."[56] Through the use of remote sensing, geospatial information is collected regarding the conditions of the soil, plants, atmosphere, and weather. This data is then used to define the planting of seeds, the application of fertilisers and chemicals, and, eventually, the harvesting process. Through GPS tracking, the location of machinery is also monitored and could lead to models of completely automated farming.[57]

With the agricultural machinery market in the United States largely saturated, these companies are pushing toward a structural shift in the business model of industrial farming, turning it into a service industry. Consulting through this accumulated geospatial knowledge and "expertise" is the more productive combination and application of the already assembled bundles of corporate commodities, thus providing an instantly consumed service commodity, integrating all others. Under the rubric of sustainability, since precision agriculture promises more efficient use of inputs (such as fertilisers and chemicals), farmers are threatened to lose the last non-commodified asset that they could still claim to master: their grounded, experiential knowledge of the situated complexities of cultivation of their farm. Precision agriculture is the last paradigm in the Corn Belt's long industrialisation process that started with a phase of mechanisation and was followed by a biochemical phase that unleashed the use of fertilisers and chemicals, leading to the final phase of genetic modification. Every phase promised advancements in productivity but was also signalling the exhaustion of previous gains.

In all these various phases, the tendency towards corporatisation has always been

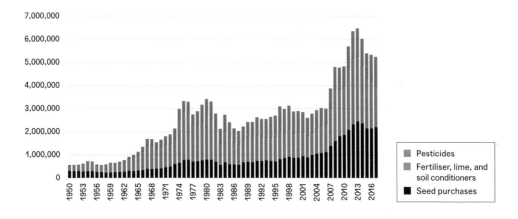

COST STRUCTURE OF IOWA FARMS
Fig. 9

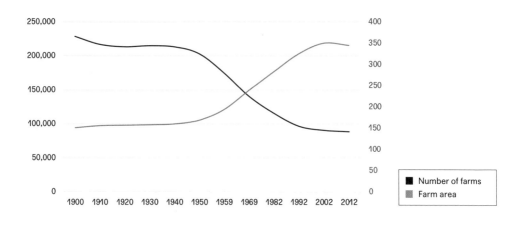

THE CHANGING SCALE OF FARMING IN IOWA
Fig. 10

F. 9   The operating costs of Iowa farms rose from an average of around $160 in the mid-1990s to $240 in 2015. The costs for seeds increased more than three times, from around $30 to $100, and the costs of fertilisers more than two times, from $50 to $120. In 2017, cultivating an average-size 350 acre farm in Iowa required on average over $200,000, with the major variable costs at around $40,000 for seeds, $50,000 for fertilisers, and $20,000 for pesticides.

Depending on the yield and the price received, the average farm would see a revenue of no more than $240,000.

F. 10   The average farm size increased from 150 acres in 1900 to 350 acres in 2017. But these numbers are distorted by small farms close to agglomeration zones that are often just part-time farms and are not the ones driving production. Out of the 80,000 farms in Iowa, more than 75% of the land is operated by no more than 20,000

farms that are larger than 500 acres and dominate the landscape in the counties in the north and west, but also parts of the south. Around 8,000 of these farms are larger than 1,000 acres and operate almost 50% of all land. With this significant rescaling of farm operations, Iowa has lost more than 60% of its farms over the past century, with more than 120,000 disappearing since 1900 and more than 80,000 since 1960.

interwoven with the role of the federal government, instrumentalised largely through the USDA. Until the early twentieth century, the USDA was only indirectly contributing to the development of farming practices by advising and educating farmers. But after the crises of overproduction in the 1920s, the USDA established its central role in commanding the agricultural economy, which, for most of the twentieth century, was centrally planned.[58] The USDA started intervening directly in agricultural commodities markets with New Deal measures that introduced production ceilings as agricultural surpluses were becoming a structural problem. At the same time, the federal government was becoming instrumental in the process of agricultural industrialisation, either by investing directly in infrastructure or by subsidising investment in mechanisation and agricultural research.

After the two World Wars, two lines of policies were combined to address both internal problems of overproduction and geopolitical goals. The United States used its hegemony to establish an adequate system of world markets to channel its surpluses.[59] The most significant expression of capitalist power in the shaping of this "food regime" is that food and agriculture products were completely excluded from the General Agreement on Tariffs and Trade (GATT), and US surpluses were channelled through non-market, state-to-state exchange mechanisms in the form of food aid.[60] In this way, food aid served domestic agricultural policy—by solving the chronic problem of overproduction—and allowed the United States to pursue foreign policy goals in the context of the Cold War.

After the mid-1990s, and the inclusion of agricultural commodities in the GATT, agricultural policies in the United States changed dramatically, opening the way to the establishment of what has been coined as a "corporate food regime."[61] Instead of trying to regulate supply, starting with the 1996 Freedom to Farm act, the federal government encouraged farmers to produce as much as possible, securing that they could cover their costs as market-based

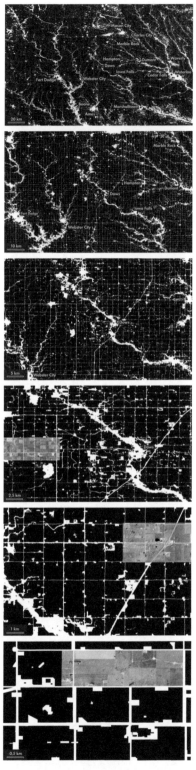

SCALES OF OPERATIONALISATION
ACROSS IOWA
Fig. 11

Fig. 12

loss-assistance payments were introduced.[62] These payments complemented the market prices in case they were too low, based on the historical production estimates of the farms, and thus encouraged farms that were historically overproducing to continue doing so. As this significant change in policies allowed for the market prices of agricultural commodities to drop, the ones that were subsidised were not really the farmers, but rather the corporations on both ends of production. On the demand side, the feed, livestock, and grain processing industries benefited by reducing the costs of their inputs, and on the supply side, seed, chemical, and fertiliser companies could benefit from the increasing demand without the reduced prices being reflected in the costs they imposed. The emphasis on biofuels in the early twenty-first century further enhanced this process by adding yet another subsidised outlet.

The system of subsidies at the beginning of the twenty-first century was, in fact, devised to sustain a flow of massive inputs to the farm, and cheap outputs from it, to be used as inputs to the livestock and food processing industry and, more recently, the energy sector. Through a lengthy interplay of corporate and state power, the landscapes of the Corn Belt have been transformed into a horizontal factory, turning the farm into a conduit in the process of capital circulation. The increasing entanglement of the Corn Belt farmer into more and more complex, closed and precise systems of commodified flows of production dissolves the illusion of the long-celebrated entrepreneur farmer. Farmers

F. 11   Cultivation areas cover more than 85% of the total area of the state of Iowa, following the checkerboard grid introduced by the PLSS. Only roads, surface water, and settlement areas disrupt the continuous carpet of corn and soybean farming.

F. 12   Aerial view of the Public Land Survey grid over Iowa.

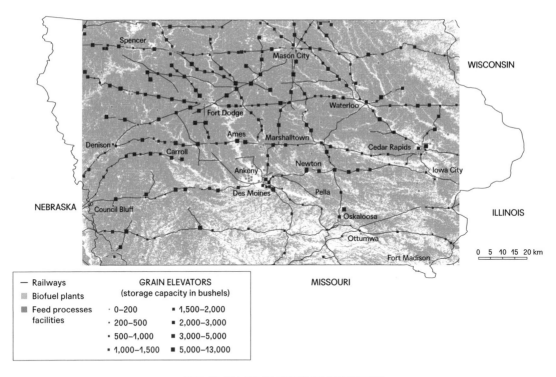

GRAIN ELEVATORS
(storage capacity in bushels)

· 0–200	▪ 1,500–2,000
· 200–500	▪ 2,000–3,000
· 500–1,000	▪ 3,000–5,000
▪ 1,000–1,500	▪ 5,000–13,000

0 5 10 15 20 km

THE GRAIN COMMODITY CHAIN IN IOWA
Fig. 13

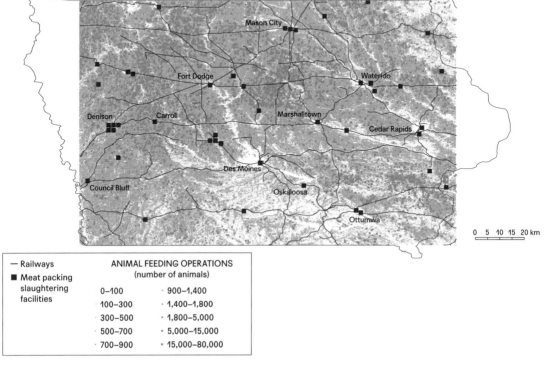

Railways
Meat packing slaughtering facilities

ANIMAL FEEDING OPERATIONS
(number of animals)

0–100	· 900–1,400
100–300	· 1,400–1,800
· 300–500	· 1,800–5,000
· 500–700	· 5,000–15,000
· 700–900	· 15,000–80,000

0 5 10 15 20 km

THE LIVESTOCK COMMODITY CHAIN IN IOWA
Fig. 14

across the Corn Belt might still own the land, but under the contemporary mode of the corporatisation of Corn Belt agriculture, the soil is just a seedbed through which expensive inputs (bought from oligopolies) are turned into cheap outputs (sold to oligopolies). The farmer handles exuberant amounts of capital but is left with thinning returns and, at the same time, is solely undertaking all the risk. As the constant commodification of inputs has led to steep increases in cultivation costs across the Corn Belt, average farm income (adjusted for inflation) has remained largely stagnant, even as productivity has increased.[63] [Fig. 9]

Although not necessarily owned by any corporation, the operational landscapes across the Corn Belt are perhaps even more corporate than the typical central business district in any American city; it is a landscape where corporate capital has tried and exhausted ecological surplus out of various bundles of social, technical, and natural systems. The last frontier of ecological surplus has also been the most persistent unit in the Corn Belt system. This is the family farm itself; its reproduction is threatened by thinning profit margins, the prospect of full automation, and the overall erosion of its surrounding social fabric. [Fig. 10]

ANATOMY OF AN OPERATIONAL LANDSCAPE

These transformations are deeply embedded and reflected in the physical configuration of the Corn Belt landscape. Perhaps in no other area is this more evident than across the state of Iowa. With a human population of just over 3 million, Iowa's area is covered almost completely by farmland, with more than 30 million acres of corn and soybeans covering more than 85% of its territory. This extensive farmland produces more corn than any other US state and is only second to neighbouring Illinois in the production of soybeans. Indeed, crossing the northern counties of Iowa, the intensive use of the land is striking. It seems that almost every square metre

Fig. 15–17

F. 13 Major elements of the grain commodity chain in Iowa: farming areas, grain elevators, feed processing facilities, biofuel and bioethanol plants, and railways.

F. 14 Major elements of the livestock commodity chain in Iowa: animal feeding operations, meat packing and processing facilities, and railways.

F. 15 Genetically modified seeds waiting to be planted in a farm close to Corning, Iowa.

F. 16 Machine shed in a farm close to Corning, Iowa.

F. 17 Farm and farmstead close to Corning, Iowa.

Fig. 18

of land is in some way operationalised, either put into production or hosting a functional facility central to the Corn Belt system. The sense of a highly rational, instrumentalised, and machinic landscape is amplified by the regularity imposed by the subdivisions of the Public Land Survey system. [Fig. 11–12]

As the secondary system of state and county roads largely follows the boundaries of the original townships, county roads create parcels of 6x6 miles, subdivided by smaller (often dirt) roads every mile. The one-mile squares were originally meant to host four 160-acre farms. But as the farms in Iowa have grown bigger and bigger, and farmland consolidated into larger plots, farms have been eradicated and become more sparsely spaced. From an original density of around four farms per square mile, one might now often drive for more than a mile to see a farmhouse, and most structures that are found across

the fields are not farmhouses, but rather metal boxes that host either grain or hog and poultry feedlots. [Fig. 11–12]

The regular checkerboard pattern of roads and farms is only slightly disrupted by the transport corridors of railways and interstate highways that organise the circulation of agricultural commodities. The five major railway corridors that intersect Iowa from east to west still form the backbone of Corn Belt logistics. These lines enable efficient, bulk transport and are positioned with grain elevators so that corn and soybeans can be collected, stored, and eventually loaded on railcars. They also connect to major grain processing facilities for ethanol, biofuel, and feed manufacturing plants. [Fig. 13] The same is the case for fertiliser, pesticide, and chemical plants, as well as meat-packing and processing facilities. [Fig. 14] It is quite easy to reconstruct the dominant commodity chain of corn and soybeans from this linear network of nodes and connections. From the farm, the farmer transports the grain by truck to the closest grain elevator or to the

F. 18   Hog feedlot in Pocahontas
        County, Iowa.

closest biofuel or feed-manufacturing facility, whichever offers the better price. From this point on, the farmers largely lose track of what happens to their produce as it is processed, loaded, and transported. Similarly, finished livestock is transported by truck to one of the meatpacking and processing facilities as new livestock enters. Overall, although the farmers operate in a global context, they experience only a local part of the chain. The rest of the process is completely concealed.

The farm remains the basic unit of production, but it is transformed into a small factory, and the major structures dominating its landscape are not the farmhouse, but rather the clusters of grain bins that are used to store corn or soy (and thus address the volatilities of the market), and the huge machine sheds that have replaced the stable or barn, and house hosting the collection of machinic equipment necessary to operate the farm. [Fig. 15–17] These structures often dwarf the farmhouse, which in the case of cash-crop farms, is still on site, something that is rarely the case when it comes to livestock operations. Hog and poultry feedlots are the most dominant in Iowa (especially in the north) and are housed in specialised, elongated metal buildings, often clustered in parallel lines, and built upon a covered manure lagoon, where animal waste is collected and deposited. [Fig. 18] Animals are rarely seen since they are confined, and their presence can be ascertained only through the distinctive odour. Neither are people since they are not necessary. This is predominantly a machine landscape, designed to put mostly nature—not humans— to work.

Indeed, visiting one of the machine sheds in a typical farm reveals how it is possible to need a mere couple of human labour hours to produce more than 200 bushels of corn per acre. [Fig. 16] What is most impressive is not so much the army of machines, consisting of giant combines and tractors with planting and spraying arms and large and smaller trucks, but the fact that all this equipment can be operated and assembled by a single person. This spans the whole process from planting

and harvesting to loading grains into trucks. Considering that the capital invested in purchasing this equipment lies at the levels of several hundred thousand dollars (combines can cost more than half a million), it is apparent that farms on the scale of 500 acres are at the lower end of the size needed to produce enough revenue to sustain this model. Fuel tanks for the machinery and natural gas infrastructures for drying the grain in the corn bins reflect the high-energy dependency of Corn Belt farms, while containers of nitrogen fertilisers are a reminder of the exhausted fertility of the soil.

Since there are no animals grazing there are no fences, only signs with the seed company brands signifying the genetically modified variations that were planted. [Fig. 15] This also largely explains one more element that becomes noticed by absence: insects. It is striking that even in the middle of the summer, standing among billions of plants, there are only a few insects buzzing around. This results from insect-repellent variations of corn and soybean seeds acting as embodied insecticides. The obvious risk of environmental catastrophe is supposed to be addressed by the seed companies—they are supposed to place anti-insect genes in only small percentages of the plants, so insects are not completely eradicated.

What finally concludes the impression of a machinic landscape "void" of life, but full of productive capacity, is the apparent absence of humans. Across the state of Iowa, less than 100,000 people are working in agriculture, putting into production an estimated 80 million animals (cattle, hogs, and chickens), 400 billion corn plants, and 500 billion soybean plants.[64] The general change in the organic composition of capital towards more capital-intensive (and less labour-intensive) agricultural practices has led to farmland consolidation, farms being eradicated and upscaled, and animal breeding concentrated in larger and larger CAFOs. As populations working in agriculture and living on, or close to, farms diminish, the pattern of settlement and communal structure in Iowa is severely transformed towards a much more centralised form of inhabitation. More than 80%

of the population lives around the four major agglomeration zones. These zones include the area around the capital of Des Moines in the centre, the agglomeration corridors along the Cedar and Iowa rivers in the east, and a zone around the Nebraskan city of Omaha at the very south-western border of Iowa.

But similar to the rest of the Corn Belt states, the settlement pattern in Iowa has been much more decentralised and structured around the farm as the basic settlement unit. Around 1900, more than 60% of the population was not living in any form of concentrated settlement (towns, cities, or villages of any form and size). Rather, they lived on individual farmsteads that hosted more than one million people. At the time, there were less than 30 settlements with more than 5,000 inhabitants and most of the population was spread over a quite decentralised network of small towns. [Fig. 19] This regular and quite homogenous settlement pattern largely reflected the subdivisions of the Public Land Survey System, which also enabled a pattern of density and territorial organisation. As the land was commodified through townships, certain sections within the townships were reserved for the public in order to host social infrastructures, such as schools and cemeteries. Since these parcels were in predefined lots that were around the centres of the townships, they affected the regular organisation of settlements around them. Moreover, as townships were further aggregated to form counties, settlements that were closer to the centre of the counties were preferred as county seats so that the civil functions located there could be easily accessible from all parts of the county.[65]

The development of the railways, in most cases complemented this underlying structure, linking several of the more central settlements and amplifying their role. The construction of the railways also largely standardised the infrastructural layout of the towns, introducing a sequence of grain elevators that became central parts of the settlements and their economic life. Grain elevators and the associated infrastructure were often positioned on the north part of the rails. At the same time, the remaining economic activity was often extended to the south, as railways typically crossed the settlements along an east-west axis. This structure suggested a dispersed and rather hierarchical geography of central places, the basis of which was the family farm.

The economy of the small towns that were dispersed among the farms largely revolved around the metabolism of the Corn Belt system and served as markets for agricultural equipment, seeds, and fertilisers. They also hosted public services like schools, banks, and post offices, in so much as they were hubs for agricultural storage and transport, and these amenities were necessary. Moreover, they also offered complementary labour markets to the members of the family farm, allowing them to have employment outside the farm. Naturally, the upscaling of farms and the associated decline in farm population led to the gradual erosion of this settlement pattern after the 1930s and especially after the 1960s. For almost every decade after the 1950s, Iowa saw more than 70% of its counties lose population. Around 20 out of 99 counties lost more than 30% of their populations, some close to half, while the only counties that gained population were near the major agglomeration centres that continued to grow—similar to the trend in the settlement dynamics. Since 1960, around 60% of all settlements in Iowa have been shrinking, with several of them losing more than half of their population. Decades of depopulation have left more than half the counties in Iowa almost empty, with densities of less than ten people per square kilometre, leading to a downward spiral where depopulation means unbearable living conditions for those who remain, leading to even more depopulation.

At the same time, however, the more counties become depopulated, the more operational they become for the corporate metabolism of the Corn Belt. Several counties that have lost half their populations have increased their productivity. For example, since the 1950s, Adams County has lost more than three-quarters of its farms and farmers but has been producing four times more corn. Such counties represent extreme examples of operational landscapes

Fig. 19

that are almost devoid of any social activity. They are dedicated almost completely to primary production, shaped by a lean, industrialised functionality where all operations are precisely prescribed, like parts of a horizontal factory.

The ongoing process of operationalisation, leading some of Iowa's counties in these extreme, almost ultimate stages of performativity, is interwoven with a dual process of centralisation and peripheralisation. This process has largely reshaped the initially decentralised pattern or settlement into a rather distinct set of depopulated but highly productive operational landscapes surrounding the four major agglomeration zones that continue to grow in terms of population and economic activity: the area around the capital of Des Moines, the agglomeration zones forming around Iowa City, Cedar Rapids, and Waterloo across the Iowa and Cedar rivers and of course around the city of Davenport on the Mississippi River, as well as the areas around Omaha and Sioux City on the border with Nevada. [Fig. 20] Major operations of agricultural corporations such as Pioneer (seed manufacturing) and John Deere (tractors) are concentrated around these agglomerations

and along the corridors connecting them, reflecting through their spatial concentration also the market consolidation of agricultural manufacturing businesses that used to be much more dispersed across the less centralised settlement. Corporate agribusiness is shaping both agglomeration zones and the extended operational landscapes of Iowa.

INHABITING AN OPERATIONAL
    LANDSCAPE

As farm employment has remained rather static (when not decreasing), the jobs created by the increasingly corporate agribusiness economy

F. 19   Lithography, perspective view of John D. Rivers' stock farm in Des Moines Township, Iowa, 1875. The town of Dallas is seen in the back, while farms dot the landscape. The mixed farming of cattle, pigs, and feed cultivation is supported by early mechanised means.

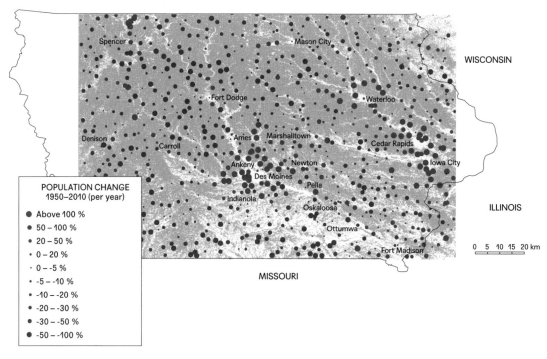

POPULATION CHANGE IN IOWA
Fig. 20

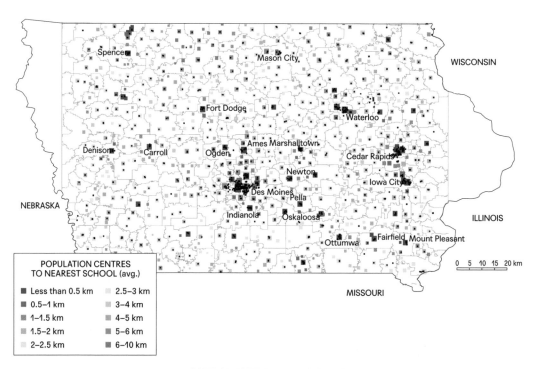

SCHOOL DISTRIBUTION IN IOWA
Fig. 21

Fig. 22

Fig. 23

F. 20 Per cent change in settlement
       population in Iowa, 1950–2012:
       population growth is limited
       to the central agglomeration
       of Des Moines and the corridors
       of the Cedar and Iowa rivers
       in the East, leading to a clustering
       of the population around the major
       cities and a hollowing out of the
       in-between farming zones.
F. 21 Distribution of schools and school
       districts in Iowa, and distance
       of settlement from the nearest
       school, 2015.
F. 22 Davis Avenue, looking south,
       Corning, Iowa.
F. 23 Music fair in Pocahontas county
       on a Saturday afternoon, Iowa.

suggest a growing penetration of wage labour relationships that concentrate around the major agglomeration zones and extend to the smaller towns of the depopulated Iowa counties. In fact, for counties such as Pocahontas, or Buena Vista, with populations in the range of 10,000 or 20,000, the operation of a biofuel refinery, a soybean mill, a seed production facility, or a meat processing plant is crucial for the employment of the thinning population, and especially for their fragile towns. For example, a medium-sized biofuel factory, such as the Valero plant next to Albert City (population 700), can employ around 100 people, a significant percentage of the workforce.

The combination of the sparsely populated counties and the growing significance of the operations of agribusinesses, as the sole employment opportunities has led to increased competition between the struggling counties to attract corporate investment and the relocation of plants, but also to a high precarity in the labour market. A striking example is the case of Cherokee county, one of the most depopulated counties in north-west Iowa, which has lost more than 50% of its population since the 1950s. Since 2014, Tyson Foods closed its meat processing plant near the city of Cherokee (population 4,900), laying off more than 450 people, and has since refused to allow any competitors to take over the plant, thus largely keeping the city hostage.[66] The "we are hiring" banners that are very often hanging at the entrance of seed processing facilities or biofuel and feed mills signify both the prevalence of this model and the underlying dependencies it creates. Within this context, the existence of (or proximity to) less precarious employers, such as medical services, and of course, city and state jobs (schools, postal service, etc.), can often prove a decisive factor for the prospects of Iowa's small towns.

But the more the population retreats, the more difficult it becomes for cities and counties to sustain such functions, impacting the daily life of the local communities. The consolidation of school districts and the closing of schools offers a striking indicator in this respect, with Iowa losing more than 4,000 schools since the 1950s, making access to education increasingly challenging for those left behind. [Fig. 21] Equally decisive, both for the labour market and for the standard of living, has been the restructuring and rescaling of retail functions. Once concentrated along the main streets of the agricultural towns, most retail has consequently moved either closer to highway entrances or completely eradicated and replaced by shopping centres, positioned even further away in selected locations. Thus, walking along the few blocks that used to constitute the commercial centre of the main street, even in the central towns and county seats, is an uncanny experience, often accompanied by zero encounters with people, closed shops, and a relative surprise when a business is still running. [Fig. 22] Still, quite a few of the towns manage to concentrate basic retail (clothing, furniture, giftshops) and service options (accounting, real estate, insurance, banks) and recreational facilities, even movie theatres, while the occasional local pub, or bar, is often the only place that is still full of people.

Besides the few general supply stores and low-cost stores that often remain in the centre of towns, most everyday retail takes place along state roads and highway intersections. The diffusion of corporate retail chains adds a sense of genericity with McDonalds, Burger King, and Subway weakening the sense of any local character or the feeling of being in "the countryside." Especially the existence of large retailers, such as Walmart, is often considered an advantage, both for the jobs created and the shopping options they are believed to offer. They function as a magnet that can attract growth to surrounding communities. The penetration of corporate America can also be seen as an ironic reflection of the commodified relationships that characterise the food, feed, and fuel nexus: a Big Mac consumed in Corning, Iowa, could be very well conceived to contain some of the local landscape in it, but only after the corn harvested in one of its farms, concludes a long journey across the operational landscapes of the US agri-food system.

With the rescaling of production and retail, and the retreat of social infrastructures, living in Iowa's small-town communities has several negative elements of larger and denser agglomeration zones without any of their advantages. From a high dependency on the automobile to the penetration of generic corporate chains, the inhabitants of the depopulated counties of the Iowan operational landscapes have, in some respects, a quite similar experience to every other citizen of suburban America. But at the same time, they have to face a deficit of social infrastructures, retail, entertainment, and recreational options, and the lack of economic and cultural versatility of larger cities, further aggravated by environmental problems (such as water population), and the negative externalities of industrial agriculture (especially those associated with CAFOs, such as waste and odour).

Nevertheless, while these problems are often acknowledged, most inhabitants are rather conscious of what they see as a trade-off between the difficulties of inhabiting an increasingly operational landscape and the persistence of several elements of "rural" or "countryside" living. Indeed, stronger community bonds, the ability to better manage time, and a closer relationship to the land, contribute to the robustness of the local communities, while informal economies continue to thrive even under the pressure of ever more pervasive wage labour relations. In fact, the liveliness that the small Iowan towns are missing is to be found in the numerous smaller or larger town and county fairs and community festivals, which are quite common, especially during the summer months. From simple food and music fairs to more radiant specialised thematic events (often related to popular leisure activities, such as reconstructions of vintage agricultural machinery), these events reflect and strengthen community ties and animate the otherwise dormant landscapes. [Fig. 23]

The same community and family ties play an important role in the persistence of a complex web of multivariate, often informal economic activities that are directly interwoven with the seasonality and the diverse needs linked to farming. While farming activities are concentrated around specific periods of time—mostly during spring (planting) and fall (harvesting)—the maintenance and management of the farm and the model of the farmer/entrepreneur require a multitude of tasks that are often outsourced through family or community networks in the form of informal, part-time jobs. From accounting tasks to construction work and equipment installation and maintenance, the basic economic functions of agricultural production are diffused through various employment opportunities in local communities.

This exact condition offers a certain robustness to the socio-economic structure of the local communities. It could also be seen as the final frontier of ecological surplus for the capitalist mode of agricultural production, as these often-informal relations between agricultural production and social reproduction provide several degrees of elasticity for local communities to absorb the volatility of agricultural markets. They also allow high degrees of self-exploitation, not limited to the farms themselves, but diffused to the whole community within which they are embedded, thus absorbing economic pressures that allow profits to be accumulated elsewhere along the agricultural commodity chains. Revisiting Harriet Friedman, who highlighted this mechanism at the level of the family farm, perhaps it makes more sense to consider this elasticity at the level of the whole community within which it is positioned.[67] But as local communities are eroded through depopulation, even this last frontier for the appropriation of ecological surplus seems to be exhausted.

FRONTIERS OF EXHAUSTION

Operational landscapes are landscapes that depend highly on the appropriation of ecological surplus for the extraction of surplus value. As bundles of human and more-than-human natures are appropriated and eventually exhausted in the search for profit, operational landscapes are transformed by the continuous search for the next "frontier" of accumulation. The more these frontiers are exhausted, the more operational landscapes tend towards a complete commodification of all the relationships that construct them. And vice versa, high degrees of commodification signify the exhaustion of ecological surpluses, which are basically operational landscapes that have reached a "mature" or "saturated" state.

The Corn Belt can be undoubtedly characterised as an operational landscape that has reached such a state. A landscape where frontiers of ecological surpluses have been gradually exhausted. The initial appropriation of high-ecological surpluses was based on the extraction of the socio-natural work that was embedded into the mid-western soil. As this frontier was gradually exhausted, productivity gains started becoming more and more dependent upon a high-input metabolism that unfolded together with the mechanisation of the means of production. In turn, this high-input metabolism reflected the struggles to assemble frontiers of cheap energy that fuelled industrial farming and pushed chemical innovation in fertilisers and pesticides. Genetic engineering in crops signified an additional level in the exploitation of biochemical frontiers, which increasingly challenged the sensitive state of ecological systems.

Achieving a balance with nature has proven an elusive task. Since 2011, superbugs (such as the corn rootworm) have been observed to develop resistance to genetically modified crops and have actually evolved into stronger breeds as a result of the modified seeds.[68] Similarly, the emergence of superweeds able to resist herbicide treatment occurred even earlier, around 2005. Superweeds and superbugs only confirm the downward spiral of environmental disruption that has accelerated in the past decades, only to amplify historically persistent problems of soil erosion and nitrogen pollution.[69] Soil erosion problems are as old as the mechanisation of agriculture in Iowa in the 1920s, and nitrate diffusion problems date back to the intensification of fertiliser application after the 1960s. Soil erosion is most prevalent in the west and southwest, where the terrain is hillier, since erosion is directly related to slope. While the negative effects of soil erosion are directly linked to the area of the farm, nitrogen pollution through extensive fertiliser use has extensive and multiscalar negative externalities.

Since the late 1970s, nitrogen from fertilisers leaking through the soil has entered Iowa's hydrological system as converted nitrates, which are poisonous to drink and cause oxygen depletion through eutrophication in aquatic ecosystems. Over the past decades, the intensification of nitrate pollution problems has forced water suppliers to install water treatment systems to remove nitrates, costing millions of dollars. Furthermore, polluted water from Iowa has made its way to the major water corridors of Missouri and Mississippi, and through them, to the Gulf of Mexico. This contributes to the recurrent emergence of a "dead zone" close to the Mississippi delta—a hypoxic zone leading to massive fish kills, biodiversity reduction, and the fishing industry's destruction.[70] Ironically, it is through the underground infrastructure of tilling that has been placed under the glacial depression of the Des Moines Lobe to improve draining that most of the nitrate-polluted water is leaking into the system. Equally ironic is that the Mississippi River carries the pollutants to the gulf yet is the main waterway through which nitrogen fertilisers are shipped north from the clustered processing plants in its mouth, around New Orleans, completing a destructive cycle.

Superbugs and superweeds, soil erosion, and nitrate pollution are all signs of an exhausted landscape, where attempts to increase productivity are releasing complex and often unpredictable sets of negative externalities. These negative externalities are often spatially or systemically offset and are unaccounted for in the costs of production. But as the ecological surplus contributed by the work of nature has been continuously exhausted, the family farm as a form of production, but also as a source of ecological surplus (through the self-exploitation of its members), has been also challenged. As the productive landscape of Iowa has been continuously depopulated, relationships of social reproduction have been largely commodified and disassociated from the reproduction of the productive elements of farming, a common pool that used to add to the robustness of the family farm model. It is not just nature that has been in a state of exhaustion in Iowa, but also several communities, especially in northern and southern areas.

As the operational landscapes of Iowa are deeply interwoven into globalised networks of production, they become elements of geopolitical struggles and capitalist power, revealing the indifference of capitalism's global search for profit to local ideologies, cultures, and political beliefs. The latest shocks in the soybean markets, inflicted by the growing trade tension between China and the United States, had a severe impact on Iowan soy exports, revealing the weak positionality of local farmers within the global agri-food dependency scheme. Spending several hours in front of their computers monitoring the prices of commodities, they have the illusion that they have agency in the global market. Yet, while they produce more than one-third of the global output they are mere subjects of commodity markets set by hedgers, traders, speculators, and political opportunists. Ultimately, they can only drive their produce to the closest grain elevator with reassurance that federal subsidies will cover their losses. Occupied with trying to decipher the right choices for the upcoming cycles of production, out of an increasing amount of information, they fail to realise that their choices are not real but prescribed within a corporate pallet of commodified product bundles and that perhaps they are the last generation of farmers able to reproduce the model of the family farm. Not surprisingly, when asked if his children would continue the family farming business, Don replied that his son was planning to set up a business that would sell the last remaining foundation of the Corn Belt farm: the soil.[71]

ENDNOTES

1   Cronon, *Nature's Metropolis: Chicago and the Great West*, 385.

2   Conversation with Don Vogel in Corning, IA, 2 July 2018.

3   United States Department of Agriculture (USDA) *Quick Stats 2.0.*

4   Bureau of Agricultural Economics, "Generalized Types of Farming in the United States: Including a list of counties in type-of-farming regions and subregions."

5   In its latest phase, it has been the "green energy" transition that has been largely driving the intensification of production across the Corn Belt. Historic data from: United States Department of Agriculture (USDA), *Quick Stats 2.0.*

6   Banerjee, "Food, Feed, Fuel: Transforming the Competition for Grains."

7   While dairy production has a reasonable efficiency rate of calorie conversion (around 40%), for poultry and pork this goes down to 10% and for beef to a mere 3%. Direct energy consumption on the farm depends upon the mechanisation of cultivation processes (such as the use of tractors, harvesters, etc.), but also storage (drying grains in grain elevators), and indirect consumption depends upon energy embodied in the chemicals, fertilisers, pesticides, and seeds, which are used as inputs (especially nitrogen fertilisers that use natural gas as the main input). See: Banerjee, "Food, Feed, Fuel: Transforming the Competition for Grains; "Cassidy, "Redefining Agricultural Yields: From Tonnes to People Nourished per Hectare."

8   Harvey, *The Limits to Capital.*

9   For an initial framing of the concept of operational landscapes, see: Katsikis, "The 'Other' Horizontal Metropolis: Landscapes of Urban Interdependence,"; Katsikis, *From Hinterland to Hinterglobe.*

10   Smith, *Uneven Development: Nature, Capital, and the Production of Space.*

11   Moore, *Capitalism in the Web of Life: Ecology and the Accumulation of Capital.*

12   Brenner and Katsikis. "Operational Landscapes: Hinterlands of the Capitalocene."

13   Smith, *Uneven Development: Nature, Capital, and the Production of Space.*

14   Moore, *Capitalism in the Web of Life: Ecology and the Accumulation of Capital.*

15   Moore, *Capitalism in the Web of Life: Ecology and the Accumulation of Capital.*

16   Moore, *Capitalism in the Web of Life: Ecology and the Accumulation of Capital.*

17   Friedmann, "World Market, State, and Family Farm: Social bases of household production in the era of wage labour."

18   See for example: Denevan, "The Pristine Myth: The Landscape of the Americas in 1492."

19   The latest glacial advance that shaped much of the topography of the Corn Belt, the Wisconsin Episode, retreated fairly recently, around 12,000–14,000 years ago. For an overview of the history of Corn Belt landforms in Iowa see: Prior, *Landforms of Iowa.*

20   Veenstra, "Fifty Years of Agricultural Soil Change in Iowa."

21   For a discussion of first and second nature in relation to the Midwest see: Cronon, *Nature's Metropolis: Chicago and the Great West*; in relation to urbanisation processes see: Luke, "Urbanism as Cyborganicity: Tracking the Materialities of the Anthropocene."

22   For a discussion of this position see: Sauer, "A Geographic Sketch of Early Man in America."

23   Hudson, *Making the Corn Belt: A Geographical History of Middle-western Agriculture.*

24   Hart, "The Middle West."

25   Hudson, *Making the Corn Belt: A Geographical History of Middle-western Agriculture.*

26   Johnson, "Gridding a National Landscape."

27   Lefebvre, *The Production of Space.*

28   For a critical overview of the role of enclosures in processes of planetary urbanisation see: Sevilla-Buitrago, "Capitalist formations of enclosure: Space and the extinction of the commons"; In the context of extended urbanisation see: Nancy Couling (this volume) and Rodrigo Castriota (this volume).

29   Hart, "The Middle West."

30   Parcels of land were sold for $2 per acre for a minimum of 640 acres in East Coast markets. When most of the Midwest was being settled, after 1820, land law allowed acquiring a minimum of 80 acres for $1.25 per acre, in 1840 a minimum of 40 acres. For a detailed discussion see: Bogue, *From Prairie to Corn Belt: Farming on the Illinois and Iowa prairies in the nineteenth century.*

31   Shannon, *The Farmer's Last Frontier: Agriculture, 11860–1897*

32   Hudson, *Making the Corn Belt: A Geographical History of Middle-western Agriculture.*

33   Cronon, *Nature's Metropolis.*

34   Cronon, *Nature's Metropolis.*

35   Sinclair, *The Jungle.*

36   Schneirov, "Thoughts on Periodizing the Gilded Age: Capital Accumulation, Society, and Politics, 1873–1898."

37   Page and Walker, "From Settlement to Fordism: The Agro-industrial Revolution in the American Midwest."

38   Hart, *The Changing Scale of American Agriculture.*

39   For example, an early Ford tractor that cost around $600 when introduced in the early 1920s, would cost around $8 per acre if harvesting an 80-acre farm, but only $4 per acre if operated on a 160-acre farm. See: Cochrane, *The Development of American Agriculture: A Historical Analysis.*

40   In 1910, there were around 1.5 million horses on farms in Iowa and 1.4 million in Illinois, and every farm could have up to 7 or 8 horses. United States Department of Agriculture (USDA), *Quick Stats 2.0.*

41   Soybeans are legumes and capture and store nitrogen in the soil, which is in heavy demand by corn plants.

42   United States Department of Agriculture (USDA), *Quick Stats 2.0.*

43   United States Department of Agriculture (USDA), *Quick Stats 2.0.*

44   Cochrane, *The Development of American Agriculture: A Historical Analysis.*

45   For a general discussion on industrial livestock production see: Weis, *The Ecological Hoofprint: The Global Burden of Industrial Livestock.*

46   Clampitt, *Midwest Maize: How Corn Shaped the US Heartland*

47   Hudson, *Making the Corn Belt:*

A Geographical History of Middle-western Agriculture.

48   True, *A History of Agricultural Experimentation and Research in the United States, 1607–1925: Including a History of the United States Department of Agriculture.*

49   Hart, *The Changing Scale of American Agriculture.*

50   Even after 2010, family owned and operated farms in the US, accounted for more than 95% of all farms, operated close to 90% of all farm area, and accounted for more than 85% of all agricultural production. United States Department of Agriculture (USDA), *Quick Stats 2.0.*

51   Duffy and Johanns, *Farmland Ownership and Tenure in Iowa, 2014.*

52   Hendrickson and Heffernan, "Concentration of Agricultural Markets."

53   Lang and Heasman, *Food Wars: The Global Battle for Mouths, Minds and Markets.*

54   Hendrickson and Heffernan, "Concentration of Agricultural Markets."

55   Andersen and Pardey, "The Rise and Fall of U.S. Farm Productivity Growth, 1910–2007."

56   Bronson and Knezevic, "Big Data in Food and Agriculture."

57   Corporations such as the tractor and combine manufactures, John Deere and New Holland, are establishing control centres that collect data, monitor the tractors and combines, and could be eventually used to command fleets of driverless farming machines. See: McBratney, "Future Directions of Precision Agriculture."

58   McMichael, "A Food Regime Genealogy."

59   McMichael, "A Food Regime Genealogy."

60   Carolyn, Effland, and Conklin. *The 20th Century Transformation of US Agriculture and Farm Policy.*

61   McMichael, "Global Development and the Corporate Food Regime."

62   Carolyn, Effland, and Conklin. *The 20th Century Transformation of US Agriculture and Farm Policy.*

63   Hart, *The Changing Scale of American Agriculture.*

64   United States Department of Agriculture (USDA), *Quick Stats 2.0.*

65   Johnson, "Gridding a National Landscape."

66   Article in *Des Moines Register*, 19/9/2018: https://eu.desmoines-register.com/story/money/business/2018/09/19/tyson-foods-cherokee-iowa-plant-iowa-food-group-moves-justin-robinson-pork-beef-chicken-pro-cessing/1356962002/.

67   Friedmann, "World Market, State, and Family Farm: Social Bases of Household Production in the Era of Wage Labour."

68   See for example the Iowa State University report from 2018: https://www.ent.iastate.edu/dept/faculty/gassman/files/page/files/2018_ent_report.pdf.

69   Patel and Moore, *A History of the World in Seven Cheap Things: A Guide to Capitalism, Nature, and the Future of the Planet*.

70   Turner et al., *Corn Belt Landscapes and Hypoxia of the Gulf of Mexico*.

71   Soil trade for landscaping, greenhouses, and even the replenishment of soil erosion has become a growing practice.

BIBLIOGRAPHY

Alston, J., M. Andersen, and P. Pardey. "The Rise and Fall of U.S. Farm Productivity Growth, 1910–2007." *Staff Paper P15–02,* St. Paul: Department of Applied Economics, University of Minnesota, 2015.

Banerjee, Arindam. "Food, Feed, Fuel: Transforming the Competition for Grains." *Development and Change* 42, no. 2 (2011): 529–557.

Bogue, Allan G. *From Prairie to Corn Belt: Farming on the Illinois and Iowa Prairies in the Nineteenth Century.* Chicago: Ivan Dee, 1963.

Brenner, Neil, and Nikos Katsikis. "Operational Landscapes: Hinterlands of the Capitalocene" *Architectural Design* 90, no. 1 (2020): 22–31.

Bronson, Kelly, and Irena Knezevic. "Big Data in Food and Agriculture." *Big Data & Society 3,* no. 1 (2016).

Bureau of Agricultural Economics, "Generalized Types of Farming in the United States: Including a List of Counties in Type-of-Farming Regions and Subregions" in *Agriculture Information Bulletin* No. 3. USDA, 1949.

Cassidy, E. S., West, P. C., Gerber, J. S., & Foley, J. A., "Redefining Agricultural Yields: From tonnes to people nourished per hectare." *Environmental Research Letters,* 83, 2013.

Clampitt, Cynthia. *Midwest Maize: How Corn Shaped the US Heartland.* Champaigne: University of Illinois Press, 2015.

Cochrane, Willard W. *The Development of American Agriculture: A Historical Analysis.* Minneapolis: University of Minnesota Press.

Cronon, William. *Nature's Metropolis: Chicago and the Great West.* WW New York: Norton & Comapny, 2009.

Denevan, William M. "The Pristine Myth: the Landscape of the Americas in 1492." *Annals of the Association of American Geographers,* 82, no. 3 (1992): 369–385.

Dimitri, Carolyn, Anne Effland, and Neilson C. Conklin. *The 20th Century Transformation of US Agriculture and Farm Policy.* USDA Report No. 1476-2016-120949, 2005.

Duffy, Michael, and Ann M. Johanns. *Farmland Ownership and Tenure in Iowa 2014.* Extension and Outreach Publications, Iowa State University, 2014.

Friedmann, Harriet. "World Market, State, and Family Farm: Social Bases of Household Production in the Era of Wage Labor." *Comparative Studies in Society and History* 20, no. 4 (1978): 545–586.

Hart, John Fraser. "The Middle West." *Annals of the Association of American Geographers* 62, no. 2 (1972): 258–282.

———.*The Changing Scale of American Agriculture.* Charlottesville: University of Virginia Press, 2003.

Harvey, David. *The Limits to capital.* London: Verso Books, 2018 (1982).

Hendrickson, Mary, and William Heffernan. *Concentration of Agricultural Markets.* Columbia, Missouri: Department of Rural Sociology, University of Missouri, 2007.

Hudson, John C. *Making the Corn Belt: A Geographical History of Middle-western Agriculture.* Bloomington: Indiana University Press, 1994.

Johnson, Hildegard. "Gridding a National Landscape." In *The Making of American Landscape. New York,* edited by Michael P. Conzen. London: Routledge, 2010, 142–161.

Katsikis, Nikos. "The 'Other' Horizontal Metropolis: Landscapes of Urban Interdependence," in *The Horizontal Metropolis Between Urbanism and Urbanization*, edited by Paola Viganò, Chiara Cavalieri, and Martina Barcelloni Corte, Berlin: Springer, 2018, 23–45.

———.*From Hinterland to Hinterglobe.* Doctoral Dissertation, Harvard GSD, 2016.

Lang, Tim, and Michael Heasman. *Food Wars: The Global Battle for Mouths, Minds and Markets.* London: Routledge, 2015.

Lefebvre, Henri. *The Production of Space.* Blackwell: Oxford, 1991.

Luke, Timothy. "Urbanism as Cyborganicity: Tracking the Materialities of the Anthropocene." *New Geographies* 6 (2015): 38–51.

McBratney, Alex, et al. "Future Directions of Precision Agriculture." *Precision Agriculture* 6, no. 1 (2005): 7–23.

McMichael, Philip. "A Food Regime Genealogy." *The Journal of Peasant Studies* 36, no. 1 (2009): 139–169.

———."Global Development and the Corporate Food Regime." *New Directions in the Sociology of Global Development.* Emerald Group Publishing Limited, 2005, 265–299.

Moore, Jason W. *Capitalism in the Web of Life: Ecology and the Accumulation of Capital.* London: Verso Books, 2015.

Page, Brian, and Richard Walker. "From Settlement to Fordism: The Agro-industrial Revolution in the American Midwest." *Economic Geography* 67, no. 4 (1991): 281–315.

Patel, Raj, and Jason W. Moore. *A History of the World in Seven Cheap Things: A Guide to Capitalism, Nature, and the Future of the Planet.* Oakland: University of California Press, 2017. Prior, Jean Cutler. *Landforms of Iowa.* Iowa: University University of Iowa Press, 1991.

Sauer, Carl O. "A Geographic Sketch of Early Man in America." *Geographical Review* 34, no. 4 (1944): 529–573.

Schneirov, Richard. "Thoughts on Periodizing the Gilded Age: Capital Accumulation, Society, and Politics, 1873–1898." *The Journal of the Gilded Age and Progressive Era* 5, no. 3 (2006): 189–224.

Sevilla Buitrago, Alvaro. "Capitalist Formations of Enclosure: Space and the Extinction of the Commons." *Antipode* 47, 4 (2015): 999–1020.

Shannon, Fred A. *The Farmer's Last Frontier: Agriculture, 1860–1897.* Routledge, 2017.

Smith, Neil. *Uneven Development: Nature, Capital, and the Production of Space.* Athens, GA: University of Georgia Press, 2010.

Sinclair, Upton. *The Jungle.* Create Space Independent Publishing Platform, 2014 (1906).

True, Alfred Charles. *A History of Agricultural Experimentation and Research in the United States, 1607–1925: Including a History of the United States Department of Agriculture.* US Department of Agriculture, 1937.

United States Department of Agriculture (USDA), *Quick Stats 2.0.* U.S. Department of Agriculture, National Agricultural Statistics Service, Washington D.C. https://quickstats.nass.usda.gov/

Veenstra, Jessica. *Fifty Years of Agricultural Soil Change in Iowa.* Doctoral Dissertation, Iowa State University, 2010.

Weis, Tony. *The Ecological Hoofprint: The Global Burden of Industrial Livestock.* London: Zed., 2013.

IMAGE CREDITS

All photography from author unless otherwise stated.

All maps from Philippe Rekacewicz with author unless otherwise stated.

F. 1 Bureau of Agricultural Economics. "Generalized Types of farming in the United States: including a list of counties in type-of-farming regions and subregions." In: Elliot, F.F. (Ed.), *Agriculture Information Bulletin* No. 3. USDA, 1950.

F. 2 Cassidy, E. S., West, P. C., Gerber, J. S., & Foley, J. A. (2013). "Redefining agricultural yields: from tonnes to people nourished per hectare." *Environmental Research Letters, 8*(3), 34015.

F. 3 Bureau of Agricultural Economics. "Generalized Types of farming in the United States: including a list of counties in type-of-farming regions and subregions." *Agriculture Information Bulletin* No. 3. USDA, 1949.

F. 5 USDA National Agricultural Statistics Service, USDA-NASS, Washington, DC: USDA Cropland Data Layer, USDA 2017; Agricultural Atlas of the United States; USGS The National Map: National Boundaries Dataset, Geographic Names Information System, National Structures Dataset, and National Transportation Dataset; United States Environmental Protection Agency, ECHO Detailed Facility Report.

F. 6 USDA National Agricultural Statistics Service. NASS – Quick Stats, 2017.

F. 7 Atlas of Marion County, Iowa, 1901. Iowa University Libraries Digital Library

F. 8 Cao, P., Lu, C., and Yu, Z.: "Historical nitrogen fertilizer use in agricultural ecosystems of the contiguous United States during 1850–2015: application rate, timing, and fertilizer types." Earth Syst. Sci. Data, 10, 969–984,

F. 9 USDA National Agricultural Statistics Service NASS – Quick Stats, 2017.

F. 10 USDA National Agricultural Statistics Service NASS – Quick Stats, 2017.

F. 11 USDA National Agricultural Statistics Service, USDA-NASS, Washington, DC: USDA Cropland Data Layer, 2018.

F. 13 USDA National Agricultural Statistics Service, USDA-NASS, Washington, DC: USDA Cropland Data Layer, 2018; USGS The National Map: National Boundaries Dataset, National Transportation Dataset; United States Environmental Protection Agency, ECHO Detailed Facility Report; Iowa Geodata portal, State of Iowa Office of the Chief Information Officer; Iowa DOT open geodata portal, Iowa Department of Transportation.

F. 14 USDA National Agricultural Statistics Service, USDA-NASS, Washington, DC: USDA Cropland Data Layer, 2018; USGS The National Map: National Boundaries Dataset, National Transportation Dataset; United States Environmental Protection Agency, ECHO Detailed Facility Report; Iowa Geodata portal, State of Iowa Office of the Chief Information Officer; Iowa DOT open geodata portal, Iowa Department of Transportation.

F. 19 A. T. (Alfred Theodore), 1839–1900, Rumsey Collection

F. 20 U.S. Census Bureau, Population Division: County Population in Iowa by Year.

F. 21 Iowa Geodata portal, State of Iowa Office of the Chief Information Officer and Iowa Department of Education.

Losing Sea. Abstraction and the End of the Commons in the North Sea

It was much bigger than I expected . . .
it was like a full city in the middle of the
North Sea and I felt very small.[1]

The Process Electrician worked at Ekofisk for
35 years, since he was 19 years old. He described
his first offshore impressions, how he loved both
his job and the working environment and how
he developed strong bonds with workmates. The
regular office job he tried once just didn't suit
him and he couldn't wait to head back offshore.

In December 1969, Ekofisk became the
North Sea's first major oil discovery on the
Norwegian continental shelf. It turned out to
be a giant reservoir and was developed rapidly
into a complex of eight fields with over
30 different installations, including a sub-sea
storage tank the size of a city block, leisure
facilities, and accommodation for workers from
over 50 different professions. "Ekofisk City,"
as it was called, was located in the extreme
south-west corner of the Norwegian continental
shelf, 280 kilometres from Stavanger, in waters
70 to 75 metres deep.[2] [Fig. 1]

The North Sea hosts a working life that
goes beyond standard formats. The longevity,
operational density, and functional complexity
of the Ekofisk fields, including its residential
components, challenge inherited understandings
of urbanisation. In the early 1970s, a new type
of space was produced offshore, marked by
giant clusters of steel and concrete, with long
distances to land and extreme on-site spatial
restrictions. These places emerged above
petroleum-rich geological formations located
up to 3,200 meters below the sea's crust. They
were far removed from established places
of work or settlement. During the construction
phase, 7,000–8,000 workers were based at
Ekofisk—a population four times that of most
Norwegian coastal towns. Ekofisk has been the
singularly most important place for the
Norwegian economy. It earned Norway 190
billion US dollars between 1974 and 2004. This
amount is equivalent to 20% of Norway's total
oil and gas production during this period.[3]
The discovery of the Ekosfisk field marked
the beginning of a new oil economy, manifested

Fig. 1

by the Government Pension Fund of Norway, otherwise known as the "Oil Fund." Despite the current process of North Sea decommissioning, the oil economy is still omnipresent.

Today the Ekofisk complex is a cultural artefact that has outlived its original life expectancy. While some parts are currently being dismantled, the Ekofisk South field is still being developed, making Ekofisk the longest-producing field on the North Sea. Due to its remarkable place in Norwegian history, the Ekofisk complex has been recognised by the Norwegian Directorate for Cultural Heritage as a technical-industrial monument.[4]

At the Ekofisk complex, all three "dimensions of urbanisation" conceptualised by Henri Lefebvre and further articulated by Neil Brenner and Christian Schmid are manifest: the explicit forms of territorial regulation that enabled its emergence, the physically constructed "urban fabric"—it is the North Sea's most concentrated agglomeration of material installations and pipelines—and the highly regulated practices of everyday working life.[5]

Yet despite these characteristics, sites like Ekofisk City and numerous other manifestations of extended urbanisation in the North Sea are unfamiliar and enigmatic in urban terms. They contradict conventional notions of the urban, such as density, diversity, and centrality, and they exemplify a specific operationalised and industrialised territory located at a carefully maintained distance outside public visibility and consciousness.

This chapter tells the story of intensifying urbanisation processes in the North Sea. These processes enabled national governments and industrial enterprises to take possession of the entire sea and fill it with a particular type of urban fabric exemplified by Ekofisk, which requires organised labour relations to operate and maintain it. The sea space has become a place where capitalist practices accumulate, thereby inducing accumulated forms of loss; the loss of the sea as a socio-cultural space,

F. 1   Ekofisk complex, North Sea.

as a space of human labour, as a commons, and finally as a space of balanced ecosystems.

The historical overview in the first section charts the role of the sea in western European socio-cultural and economic relations from the Roman Empire to the Second World War. The central nexus of trading activity moved from the Mediterranean to the North Sea during this period, where the sea was increasingly exploited in the service of the expansion of empires and the commodity economy. It began to be conceptualised and mapped in a rational way, illustrating the transformation of the sea from an animated space full of geographic features and human experience to an efficient, neutralised trading highway. By the seventeenth century, the sea was losing its socio-cultural significance, followed by its importance as a place of work in the twentieth century as containerisation and air travel began to make large sections of maritime labour redundant.

The second section examines how the urbanisation of the North Sea began in earnest after the Second World War. The North Sea played a major role in the conflicts of both World Wars, and the military domination meant that the sea had been largely cleared of civilian activities—the state had gained a major role in organising and controlling the sea commons. International post-war conventions not only resulted in the regulation of sea space but also paved the way for creating a state space, determining resource use in vast exclusive economic zones at the expense of the sea commons. The way these zones consumed the sea space entirely in the North Sea, resulted in the loss of the sea commons.

The abstract state enclosures in the North Sea established the basis for further planning and operationalisation for oil and gas and, more recently, wind-energy industries. The third section illuminates this process and how the urban fabric described above for Ekofisk was constructed for a dedicated workforce under strict codes, rhythms, and spatial constriction.

In 2018, the *New York Times* published the article "Losing Earth: The Decade We Almost Stopped Climate Change," about the years 1979–1989 when the effects of climate change were already understood, but scientists, politicians, and activists did not manage to finalise a global framework to reduce carbon emissions.[6] This chapter's title, *Losing Sea*, is in reference to this poignant article. It demonstrates how processes of extended urbanisation in the North Sea, although facilitating unprecedented economic gains for northern Europe, have resulted in an ecologically degraded marine habitat and immeasurable loss.

INHABITING THE SEA: A BRIEF HISTORY

The transformation of society's relationship to the sea over the long timespan between the Romans and the end of the Second World War is examined in this section. During this period, the leading trading region shifted from the Mediterranean to the North Sea. The nation-state emerged with colonial ambitions realised through the domination of maritime space, which was then heavily occupied by military activities in both World Wars. The world capitalist economy became increasingly dependent on long-distance maritime networks, culminating in the post-war container revolution. These events set up the conditions for the urbanisation of the sea, an urbanisation process paralleled by the systematic emptying of the sea's traditional socio-cultural significance.

EARLY MARITIME TERRITORIALISATION FROM MARE NOSTRUM TO MARE LIBERUM

Before the development of road networks in Western Europe, waterways were the major logistical routes for exchanging goods, people, and knowledge.[7] It was across the water that connections were established and sustained between important regional centres whose wealth frequently depended more on international trade than their hinterlands. Between 700 and 1,600, and before the rise of the nation-state, people were constantly migrating around the North Sea; the Anglo-Saxons came to England in the fifth century from Germany and Denmark and continued to settle; the Vikings travelled and settled all around the region, and the Shetland Islands were under Norwegian rule from the ninth to the fifteenth century.[8] Traces of language, music, arts, and architecture testify to constant circulation—the material culture of marine societies around the North Sea was more similar than diverse and coastal cities had more in common with their opposite shores than with their hinterlands.[9] Wealth gained through trade was physically manifested in the built environment, and around the sixteenth century, literacy rates were higher on the coasts than inland.[10] The common sea space supported and facilitated this exchange. Such evidence of the sea's critical role in commercial and socio-cultural dynamics has long been recognised. Still, until recently, the sea has not been considered integral to urbanisation processes.

Historically in Europe, kingdoms or political entities ruling over coastal land that partially enclosed seas used the concept of *Mare Nostrum* (Roman for "our sea"), where sea and land were integrated into a territorial whole. The Mediterranean unified under Roman rule from 31 BC to 200 AD is a well-known example. Also, when the rule of the Norwegian Kings extended to Greenland and Iceland from the tenth to thirteenth centuries, they aimed for a similar concept: *Mare Clausus* (closed sea). At that time, Greenland was thought to extend to Svalbard, and Svalbard to Novaya Zemlya, thereby closing the "Northern Sea" dominion (*Mare Septentrionalis*).[11] The difference between *Mare Nostrum* and *Mare Clausus* could be slight, depending on the exertion of power to claim exclusive rights and access. While the Norwegian Kings tried to establish a *Mare Clausus* by preventing foreign ships from entering and trading during this period, according to Steinberg, the Romans developed a doctrine of stewardship, claiming *imperium* (right to command) in the Mediterranean, but not *dominium* (right to own). For the Romans, the sea, a *res communis* was a thing that by nature was common to all and therefore governed according to *jus gentium* (common law), and not *jus civile*—the law applied to Roman citizens on land.[12]

The sixteenth-century Mediterranean was the focus of Fernand Braudel's ground-breaking work, which accomplished the first comprehensive history of a western European maritime space, including port cities and hinterlands.[13] His work contributed to a specific spatial dimension, considering the Mediterranean's climate and geography together with its central focus on the economic life of maritime trade. It became the most important historical precedent for conceptualising maritime space connecting a system of cities. Braudel describes the Mediterranean's centre of power during the fifteenth and sixteenth centuries as an "urban quadrilateral," comprising the four main centres of Venice, Milan, Genoa, and Florence. Venice disposed of a limited hinterland, and in order to achieve continuous expansion, markets were sought through overseas trade. The powerful influence of the Venetian Republic and its integrated trade and communication systems encompassed the Mediterranean and beyond, including the most prosperous ports, a series of secondary urban centres, and peripheral areas—each operating with different dynamics but all part of a widespread economic system. The sea is drawn into urbanisation processes as a major feature and the facilitator of a dilating, coherent space of extended urban relations. Braudel argues for the Mediterranean as an *économie-monde*— an extensive network of economic exchange comprising an economically autonomous section of the planet.[14]

For Braudel, the Mediterranean also clearly demonstrates the inextricable link between long-distance trade and the expansion of capitalism, exemplified by the Italian city-states sometime around the thirteenth century.[15] Manuel de Landa continued this line of thought, referring to maritime port cities connected by the medieval Baltic, Mediterranean, and North Seas, which were not interested in accumulating territory, but rather "exhibited the kind of weightlessness or lack of inertia that we associate with transnational corporations today."[16] In the seventeenth century, the dominance of Venice in European trade declined in favour of northern Europe, and the central nexus of activity migrated from the Mediterranean to the North Sea. The dynamics of this shift have been discussed thoroughly by historians. It has been linked to the deliberate undercutting of high-quality Venetian products by the English and the rapid expansion of the Dutch and then English colonial empires.[17]

The North Sea was a geographical region distinct from the Mediterranean with its own cultural and economic history. Control of trade around the North Sea had changed hands over the centuries, from the Frisians (first to the eighth century) to the Vikings (eighth to tenth century), and subsequently to the Hanseatic League (at its height between the twelfth and fifteenth centuries). These groups were highly skilled navigators who could find their way in the fog and knew the seasons and the difficult North Sea storms, tides, and currents. Norse sagas tell how the indigenous Sámi people— who were excellent navigators—built the boats that proved such a success for the Vikings. The North Sea measures around 600 kilometres at its widest part, a distance Viking vessels easily crossed in four to five days. It was a topographical zone filled with human activity linked to specific seascape characteristics communicated through narratives of first-hand experience— for example, detailed knowledge about the rich local fishing grounds. Competing ruling feudal states sometimes attempted to annex these grounds as territorial extensions under their power, the Nordic Kings being one such example.

The North Sea was also marked by fierce independence from political domination before the rise of the nation-state. This is true for the Frisians, who today are still proud of "Frisian Freedom"; since the ground was poor and difficult to farm, foreign rulers were never interested in owning it, and the Frisians remained independent until the sixteenth century. Likewise, the Hanseatic League was an independent business confederation of 200 coastal and river ports throughout the Baltic and the North Sea regions, united as free trading cities in the interests of commerce, without ambitions of territorial expansion.

But by the seventeenth century, Dutch trading companies had expanded beyond the North and Baltic Seas, initially pursuing the lucrative spice trade but also aiming to overthrow the Portuguese control and monopoly on strategic trading posts and maritime routes. Succeeding Spain and Portugal, they established the Dutch colonial empire in Africa, North and South America, India, the Middle East, China, Japan, and Indonesia. Their greatest maritime rival, the UK, was pursuing similar ambitions. In this context of competing for territorial claims at sea linked to trade, in 1609, the Dutch lawyer Grotius formally articulated the principle of "freedom of the seas for all" in his book *Mare Liberum*.[18] Vested interest in trade was Grotius' primary motivation, but he embellished this commercially grounded idea with ethical arguments, insisting that this freedom was in the general interest of humankind. The publication also pointed to the English monarchy, which threatened to take over large maritime areas as a sovereign right. *Mare Liberum* suited the commercial importance of the sea for both parties—they could continue their expansion of trade across seas unimpeded by territorial claims. It remained the guiding principle for all seas for over 300 years until after the Second World War and the adoption of the United Nations Convention on the Law of the Sea (UNCLOS).

Mare Liberum was intended to facilitate worldwide capitalist expansion and colonisation by European powers through maritime means. It was further enabled by the combined technological improvements in ocean navigation, which Braudel named among the three great technical revolutions from the fifteenth to the eighteenth century, alongside artillery and the printing press.[19] These developments meant that during the seventeenth and eighteenth centuries, empires were established based on oceanic rather than terrestrial dominance, and international relations were configured

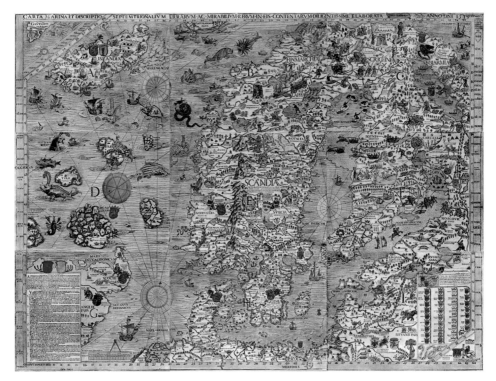

Fig. 2

worldwide rather than in regional systems, including the global imbalances that emerged as a result.[20]

THE MAKING OF
"THE GREAT VOID"

The rise of the nation-state and its domination of trade and commerce throughout the North Sea and beyond—first by the Dutch and then the English empires during the sixteenth to the nineteenth centuries—set a parallel process of socio-cultural evacuation in motion. Rather than the obviation of state power, the expanding transnational networks were the very expression of it. As Michael Miller put it: "In nearly every instance when global processes can be identified, it is possible to locate a state presence or the advancement of the state."[21] The international consensus to maintain a *Mare Liberum* for trade prioritised the abstraction of the sea to a horizontal transport surface across what Steinberg calls the "great void" rather than a differentiated seascape supporting coastal life.

This was a space within which European sea powers exerted and consolidated their political and economic strength, primarily through trade, with a military escort if required.[22]

Cartographic abstraction served the void conceptualisation of sea space and the subjugation of local knowledge; up to the sixteenth century, maritime maps had incorporated narrative features, expressing both real and imagined experiences at sea. The "Carta Marina" map of the northern lands by Swedish ecclesiastic Olaus Magnus, portrays an animated sea, illustrating not only accurate geographic information from different sources, including the cartographer's own experience, but also sailor's descriptions of marine features such as the maelstrom off the Norwegian coast, and mysterious sea creatures. [Fig. 2] By the seventeenth century, with the rise of the early modern state and when rational science began to influence cartography, the sea became increasingly featureless, emptied of such imaginaries.[23] Carta Marina also illustrates portolan lines—diagonals emanating from centre points and representing up to 32 wind directions—which were the main navigational aids at sea from the medieval to the early modern period. Sea maps from the seventeenth century lost the multitude of portolan lines and increasingly adopted abstract, gridded lines of latitude and longitude, even though longitude was still only a concept that could not be accurately measured.[24] As Wood stated, "cartographic control" took over the sea "to give the elusive idea of the state concrete form."[25] Pre-existing maritime histories and beliefs were overwritten, and places were renamed or erased into blankness. Through these practices, socio-cultural seas were the first to be lost to imperial expansion and colonisation all over the globe.

THE GEOPHYSICAL
NORTH SEA

Processes of urbanisation in the North Sea are tightly linked to its geophysical properties. This is a shallow but stormy subdivision of the Atlantic Ocean, located between 51 and 61 degrees north. [Fig. 3] Covering an area of 575,000 km², it is around 970

kilometres long and 580 kilometres wide, and with an average depth of just 95 metres, it is a "shelf" sea, mostly lying on the continental shelf (see below). The maximum depth of 700 metres occurs in the Norwegian trench, running along the Norwegian coastline.

The southern part of the North Sea is only 20–40 metres deep, with depths increasing northwards at around 58 degrees north. This bathymetric feature retraces the outline of the higher parts of prehistoric "Doggerland," named after the Dogger Bank—an area of shallow waters located in the middle of the North Sea—which was a vast, low-lying plain with river valleys and a large population of Mesolithic people, washed over and submerged by the sea around 10,000 years ago.[26] Settlements around the North Sea are faced with constant storms and flooding, so they were originally established close to natural estuaries, sheltered ports or higher ground. Nearly all great northern European ports—for example, Hamburg, Rotterdam, and previously London—are located on tidal rivers, providing shelter from the open sea and links to the hinterland.[27] The seabed in the southern North Sea is mainly sandy

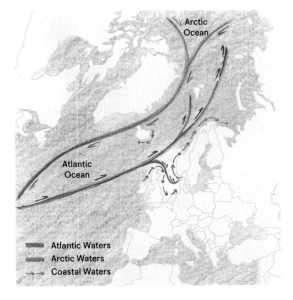

THE NORTH SEA: A POCKET OF THE
ATLANTIC OCEAN
Fig. 3

F. 2   Carta Marina, Olaus Magnus, 1539.
F. 3   Altantic Ocean and the North
          Sea with main currents.

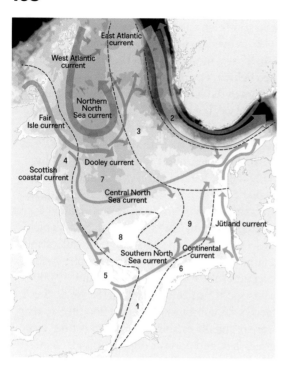

1 Channel water,
  warm, 35% salinity
2 Skagerrak water,
  low salinity
3 Transition water (2–7),
  surface salininty
4 Scottish coastal water
5 English coastal water,
  vertical mixing
6 Continental coastal
  water, low salinity
7 North Atlantic water
  35.2 salinity
8 Mixture of types
  1, 4, 5, 6
9 East-west
  salinity increase

NORTH SEA CURRENTS
AND HYDROGRAPHIC REGIONS
Fig. 4

and once boasted abundant oyster beds since removed through centuries of trawling. This sandy substrate and the proximity to dense urban areas have recently made it a favoured offshore wind farm development site.

Salinity, temperature, currents, and bathymetric characteristics have resulted in a complex oceanography, naturally divided into nine hydrographical regions according to different water masses. [Fig. 4] The North Sea ecosystem is nutrient-rich due to inflow from major European rivers—Elbe, Rhine-Meuse, Humber, and Thames—and oceanic inflow from the Atlantic, producing one of the world's most abundant fishing grounds. Wind-driven currents contribute to the dominant counter-clockwise water circulation, which ensures a continuous distribution of nutrients and organisms. Areas of coarse substrate on the seabed are important for spawning fish, particularly herring. Until the 1970s, captive fisheries harvested up to 4 million tonnes in the North Sea annually.[28]

Thousands of metres below the surface, the composition of ancient sedimentary layers has also become crucial for the urbanisation of the North Sea, determining the spatial configuration of oil and gas installations. Continental shelves are a continent's submerged periphery; hence they collect organic deposits from both the land and the sea. In addition, the geology of the North Sea is made up of a series of buried basins, which support the accumulation of vast sedimentary layers from surrounding landmasses.[29] Petroleum was formed due to the particular North Sea conditions during the late Jurassic/early Cretaceous period when geological rifts occurred, tectonic plates moved apart, and sediments were deposited along rift margins.[30] This was followed by a rise in sea level and the burial of the Jurassic rock containing hydrocarbons, creating the major geological features of the Viking Graben and the Central Graben, down the middle of the North Sea, where much of the North Sea petroleum has been discovered.[31]

LOADING AND EMPTYING
THE SEA

Human activity has taken place around specific spaces produced by the North Sea's geophysical properties: fishing grounds and hydrocarbon formations, but also its interconnected transport surface and the space for offshore wind. Since Braudel, and as pointed out by philosophers, historians, and human geographers, Western academic thought has been overwhelmingly terrestrial, lacking the imagination to embrace the space of the sea, let alone analyse processes of urbanisation there.[32] The socio-cultural sea has been preserved in its otherness in European maritime societies. It is cognitively separate from land in both antagonistic and complementary ways, as archaeologist Westerdahl has specifically shown of prehistoric northern Europe.[33] This otherness appears more recently in Nordic folklore. While several of the marine activities in the North Sea listed above can be easily identified prehistorically, Hatch reminds us, "When a landscape has true cultural value … engagement moves beyond simple exploitation. Cultures invest their maritime landscapes with ritual and symbolic depth." [34]

As the world capitalist economy became increasingly dependent on long-distance maritime networks in the nineteenth and twentieth centuries, and as the exploitation of marine resources expanded exponentially, the sea as a space of human labour was the second sea to be lost. Until the mid-twentieth century, and before its subsequent rapid industrialisation, the North Sea supported a sizeable human labour force; it was crossed by numerous passenger ferries, hosted a large fishing fleet, and shipping and port operations required manual work. Port workers in London—the world's busiest port in tonnes until the Second World War—numbered 54,000 in 1925 and, although diminished, still 28,722 in 1960.[35]

However, two transformative events occurred in 1956: the Pan Am transatlantic jet service was introduced on the same day as a converted tanker carried 58 truck trailers from Newark to Houston—the predecessor of the contemporary container ships.[36] The subsequent evacuation of the large-scale public presence in the sea, the rapid standardisation and mechanisation of the shipping industry geared to containers, and the discovery of offshore oil transformed the nature of urbanisation in the North Sea and seas around the world. These factors, combined with the parallel beginnings of global maritime planning initiatives, signalised the historical moment when the urbanisation of the sea began in earnest.

Containerisation revolutionised maritime transport and reorganised world labour relations through a new international division of labour and a shift to cheap production regions. Over 90% of all goods travel across the ocean in containers. But containerisation turned the sea into what Alan Sekula calls "The Forgotten Space." Not only were containers impenetrable, anonymous, odourless, revealing nothing of their contents, but working lives at sea were banished to a liquid no-mans-land. Sekula stated, "100,000 invisible ships, 1.5 million invisible seafarers binding the world together through trade." [37] Sekula's work traces the social spaces of the shipping industry in the urbanised sea, both internally sharply controlled and obscured from the outside. As the sea was increasingly loaded with goods and vessels, it was also being emptied of social activities, legal rights, and the historically respected culture of seamanship.

THE SEA AS TERRITORY

The recognition of sea regions as territories in their own right is critical to the understanding of sea space in relation to urban dynamics. If the sea is understood and treated as a territory, urbanisation processes can be analysed at a range of scales and can consider the notion of *seascape* in both its cultural and geophysical dimensions. Within the tradition established by Claude Raffestin, where territory is considered a socially appropriated space, Bernard Debarbieux proposed an understanding of the territory as a dynamic set of conditions needed to support a social community.[38] With specific reference to my analysis of the Barents and Baltic Seas, I defined maritime territory as formed through the interactions between geophysical, biological, and socio-economic layers.[39] Such a fluid, relational perspective enables critical examination of both the sea territory as a spatial entity with specific characteristics and the largely hidden exploitive practices and movements within them.

Parallel to cultural landscapes, cultural seascapes are produced by mutually transformative interactions between human activity and the natural environment. Specific characteristics of *seascapes*—the depth and salinity of the water, the seafloor composition, and their capacity to sustain marine life or resource-driven maritime activities—have steered human interaction. Thus dredging, trawling, dumping of waste, shipwrecks, laying of mines, detonations to clear munitions, drilling, and injections of carbon have contributed to a continuous moulding and transformation of these very seascapes over time.[40] It is imperative to extend the concept of territory "beyond terra," in particular to oceans, to gain a clearer understanding of the economic activity and political power being exerted in such unbounded places undergoing continual transformation.[41] Together, the design and research projects described below highlight the exploitation through capitalist industrialisation, the infrastructural density, the extent of segregation, levels of state control, and the resulting public retreat that characterises contemporary urbanised sea territories.

After Braudel's work on the Mediterranean, significant spatial perspectives that encompassed sea spaces and a shift of focus from the land to the sea were first seen in association with systems thinking. Bringing land and sea together in one comprehensive understanding of world systems was one of the aims of the visionary architect, inventor, and designer Richard Buckminster-Fuller. This included potential flows and the design of an equitable distribution of energy and resources that could, together with technological advances, solve society's burgeoning problems. The "one-ocean-world" version of Fuller's Dymaxion map aimed to broaden the narrow historical perspective that prioritised small continents (30%) over

the vast ocean (70%) and to promote fluidity, interconnectivity, and dynamics in place of the prevailing static, entrenched, and isolated "landlubber" world-view.[42] [Fig. 5]

Resource flows across the world's oceans have become hallmarks of the capitalist system. As Sloterdijk affirms, ocean space has been the "natural media of unrestricted capital flow."[43] Maritime transport systems reveal the central contradiction of capitalist urbanisation: it is simultaneously fixed and in motion. As identified by Harvey and Brenner, the de-territorialising aspect of capital, its "drive toward spatial expansion, temporal acceleration and relentless spatiotemporal restructuring," is only possible through the production of more permanent, "fixed," physical infrastructure, resulting in a massive extension of the built environment on land and sea.[44] Fixed offshore facilities and supporting infrastructure for the maritime transport of oil, containerised goods, and communications are primarily out of sight yet comprise a vast, uneven template of cables and pipelines on the seafloor. At the same time, physical modifications are continuously being made to the seafloor along dedicated heavy maritime traffic routes.[45] The invisibility of these systems enables the capitalist illusion of smooth, uninterrupted flows to persist. The "vast logistical landscape" of the ocean is the subject of still unrecognised material, political, and ecological significance, according to landscape architect Pierre Bélanger.[46]

In addition to shipping, industrial exploitation of the sea is continuously advancing, even into what the WWF describes as Europe's last intact marine ecosystem, the Barents Sea. Ironically, the alarmingly rapid depletion of sea ice has massively increased the strategic territorial role of this sea space. It has been opened up for exploitation by the new Northern Sea Route across the Arctic Ocean, a part of the north-east passage that lies entirely in Russia's exclusive economic zone, and by releasing new petroleum exploration licenses in increasingly ice-free areas. Design research at the EPFL Laboratory Basel highlighted the mounting geopolitical pressure to transform the Barents Region into

Fig. 5

an extractive "province," setting the planning processes and construction of the required infrastructure in motion.[47]

The Mediterranean has also changed dramatically and turned into what Stefano Boeri and John Palmesino called "the solid sea," a complex, stratified, and highly controlled space through which people, information, and materials move.[48] Their research identified mutually exclusive trajectories that seldom offer the possibility of any kind of exchange. Although the authors began with understanding the sea basin as a liquid continent, "the only certain territory" was a volatile region of shifting borders. The resulting view of the Mediterranean was of "a 'Solid Sea,' a territory ploughed by predetermined routes and insuperable boundaries and subdivided into strictly regulated bands of water. A solid space, crossed at different depths and in different directions by distinct flows of people, goods, information, and money."[49] Subsequently, the deadly hardening of the Mediterranean's borders in response to migrant crossings has been precisely documented in the work of Forensic Oceanography—a specialist group within the Forensic Architecture research agency at Goldsmiths, University of London. "Liquid violence" is their term for the state practices of militarising the EU border but renouncing rescue obligations at the same time.[50]

The fragmentation and separation of contemporary sea space recognised by Boeri and Palmesino found unequivocal resonance in other regions. The once open, fluid archipelago comprising Singapore and regions of Malaysia and Indonesia is today divided by the proliferation of maritime borders designed to secure vital shipping functions and prevent the informal exchange of people and goods. Milica Topalović and her team demonstrate how the role of the connective sea is reversed to a "carceral" space of separation.[51] Tightly controlled borders also determine the reclaimed Singapore coastline, completely transformed to accommodate the needs of the military, port functions, and the petrochemical industries. As a result of the reconfiguration of coastal and maritime space for commercial and industrial purposes, the public has also been forcibly withdrawn from the sea. Topalović's *Hinterland* research revealed how only 7.5% of the Singapore coastline is accessible to the public.[52] The organisation of settlements

F. 5   A variation of Fuller's Dymaxion projection to show a continuous "One Ocean."

has been disconnected from relations to the sea and is evolving according to the dominant land-based logic. Hence, the experience of the sea has also retreated from the public consciousness.

Parallel to this work, the theory of planetary urbanisation provided a theoretical framework for empirical research and design within which the global ocean was implicated.[53] Neil Brenner's *Extreme Territories of Urbanization* included cartographic studies on the Pacific Ocean, representing previously undetected levels of urbanisation, not only on the ocean surface through global shipping but also across the continental shelves and the deep seabed. For the first time, the ocean was identified as an urbanised realm, not in relation to the population density within a territorial space, but rather in terms of its infrastructural networks and widely dispersed concentrations of intense activity. In my research, I recognised such patterns of dispersed intensity as indicators of the urbanised sea.[54] These are spaces of extended urbanisation, mostly remote from established settlements but connected through robust delivery systems since settlements depend on this connection for vital resources.

Critical reflection on urbanisation processes in the North Sea has been rare, despite, or perhaps because of, its highly industrialised state. One exemplary contribution is "Future Commons 2050," a speculative project that recognises the imminent threat to the sea commons by offshore economic zones. In response, the project proposes that the economic zone in Belgium be transformed into an official "Maritime Commons," a radical proposal based on socio-ecological and ethical rather than economic concerns.[55] My North Sea research published with Carola Hein, "The Urbanisation of the Sea: From Concepts and Analysis to Design," responds to this lack of critical analysis. We show how conceptualising the sea as an urbanised realm is a vital tool to track, confront, and reveal hidden processes, spatial discontinuities, and rarely noticed state planning decisions. Particularly in the face of the ecological crisis, it is crucial to link the understudied sea to the land across the land-sea urban continuum.[56]

THE ABSTRACTION OF THE NORTH SEA

The industrialisation of the North Sea advanced rapidly after the Second World War, which marked the moment when the urbanisation of the sea began in earnest. But this type of urbanisation demanded more than accelerating industrial processes; it required a full state apparatus to transform the very nature of the sea space, render it abstract rather than "natural," and then perform operations of homogenisation. This meant fundamentally transforming a complex, differentiated, *living and contingent* space, resulting in one of the most contradictory examples of abstract state space in the Lefebvrian sense. This section explains how military activities took over the North Sea (along with other seas worldwide) as an extension of state sovereignty after the war through the establishment of exclusive economic zones. By forming this new state space, the sea commons in the North Sea were eliminated entirely.

IT STARTED WITH FISH[57]

Transfiguration of the North Sea into an abstract space of state management results from a process that ironically started with fish and an unpredictable, volatile form of extraction that, aquaculture excluded, still depends on a healthy marine ecosystem. Not only did industrialisation and excessive exploitation of North Sea resources first appear in the fishing sector, but the push for regulation to secure exclusive national control over resources led to the introduction of a systematic series of restrictions.

Fishing is the extraction of "wild" biomasses from the sea. Fishing technology in Europe gradually developed with beam trawling and well boats appearing at the beginning of the fourteenth century, which held a tank and could deliver fresh fish to Hamburg and London from the central North Sea.[58] Medieval technologies of sail, oar, hook, trap, and net prevailed in the eighteenth and mid-nineteenth centuries until the advent of the steam engine in the 1880s expanded vessel size, enabling fishing further offshore and in deeper waters. Diesel replaced steam in the early twentieth century, with further increases in size and power and advancements in net materials from hemp and cotton to monofilament.

These developments caused what Holmes calls the "Great Acceleration" in post-war fishing, parallel to the sharp increase of resource use and the human planetary footprint in other sectors.[59] He links this exponential increase directly to the war, which led to the improvement of navigation technologies, vessel size, and power.

Until the Second World War, European fishing areas were rarely spatially defined. Fishing was carried out in a *Mare Liberum*. However, it was both the industrialisation and commodification of the industry and the emergence of territorial claims on fishing grounds that pre-empted the demand to extend territorial sovereignty out to sea in the form of exclusive economic zones. Holm claims that the advent of "ocean management"—a new centralised, abstracted, standardised form of territorial regulation in the space of the sea—was also a direct result of the Second World War. Wartime geopolitics around the strategic position of Iceland, where increasing German presence resulted in the 1940 invasion by British forces, led to the Icelandic declaration of independence in 1944. With this autonomy came the proclamation of a separate, exclusive fishery zone of 12 nautical miles beyond its territorial sea during the 1950s.[60] This launched the "cod wars" with the UK, which was finally settled in 1975 and demonstrated the state's increasing interest in spatially defined fishing grounds and maritime borders. Recent Brexit disputes demonstrate the ongoing conflict around the still highly lucrative UK fishing industry and the importance of state borders, which may or may not align with commercial quantities of fish.

THE MILITARISATION
OF THE NORTH SEA

Until after the Second World War, the formal spatial regulation of the sea was limited to a narrow coastal strip originally as wide as the reach of a cannon shot, to which a nation's sovereign rights extended. Defence practices were carried out within this strip of the territorial sea, and the protection of merchant's vessels was expected. Beyond the territorial sea lay the "high seas" or international waters, which were not yet regulated or otherwise defined but understood as long-term "voids" that could also be appropriated for military purposes if required. This "neutral," non-developable void offered a realm external to the land ruled by monarchs and governments, which could be appropriated for their displays of military power and outright warfare. The rivalry between the Dutch Republic and England culminated in the Anglo-Dutch wars of the mid-seventeenth to the late eighteenth centuries. Other major North Sea battles were the Battle of Jutland (1916) and the Battle of the Atlantic (1939–1945) between Germany and Britain.

During both world wars, the North Sea was mined and otherwise exploited for military purposes, thereby reducing and excluding the civilian component and reconceiving, physically constructing, and occupying the sea as an abstract, strategic military space. Battles, mines, and blockades were aimed at severing enemy supply lines since urban centres on both sides of the North Sea relied on these extended maritime delivery systems. Still recognised as the high seas and not yet divided into its surrounding nations, the North Sea hosted the conflict for land-based power, transforming the geography of its "international waters" into a labyrinth of mines, patrol lines, and potential U-boat locations. Miller states of the First World War: "The maritime history of the war thus emerges, ironically, as the pivotal factor in a conflict centred on colossal land battles."[61]

The First World War "North Sea Mine Barrage" stretched from the Orkney Islands to Norway, and together with minefields in the English Channel, aimed to prohibit German U-Boats from leaving the North Sea and sabotaging important Atlantic supply lines from the US to the UK. [Fig. 6] The German strategy to destroy enemy supply lines through U-boat attacks on escorted merchant ships in the North Atlantic was again deployed in the Second

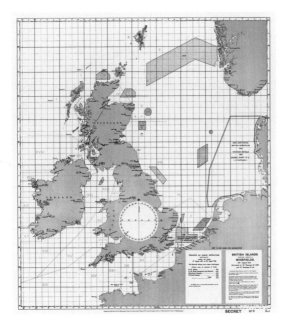

F. 6   British Islands: approximate
position of minefields, 1918.
Hydrographic Department of
the Admiralty.

Fig. 6

World War, supported by using "Marine-quadratkarten," which were coded military maps where geography was subordinated to a secret numbered grid. The North Sea "quadrat" (square) was coded as "AN" and divided into 81 smaller numbered squares.

The legacy of military presence in the North Sea and other seas across the world has had long-lasting implications and given the state a dominant role in maritime affairs. After the Second World War, the North Sea *international waters* were gradually eliminated. Mounting international concern about the continued presence of nuclear-powered submarines and military plans to place antiballistic missile systems on the seabed, alongside an alarming reduction of fish stocks, increased pollution, and national ambitions to control marine resources, contributed to the reassessment of the *Mare Liberum* doctrine by the United Nations. This resulted in a series of international conventions and, ultimately, the entire sea being given over to industrial activities. While ostensibly initiated for peaceful democratic purposes, it "turned into a global diplomatic effort to regulate and

write rules for all ocean areas, all uses of the seas, and all of its resources," as the UN itself concedes.[62]

THE ENCLOSURE OF
THE SEA COMMONS

Directly after the end of the Second World War, President Truman declared that all natural resources on the US continental shelf would be subject to US jurisdiction. This claim was an unprecedented extension of sovereignty into sea space and a historic event that influenced the UN's decision to take action.[63] Truman was prompted by Japanese salmon fisheries off the Alaskan coast and sustained pressure from the petroleum industry, pushing to explore further offshore. During the war, new technology had been developed both in the fishing and petroleum industries, and particularly relevant for the oil industry, steel was again more readily available. A series of similar claims from other nations directly followed that of the United States.

In response to these claims, the first United Nations Conference on the Law of the

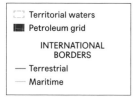

Territorial waters
Petroleum grid

INTERNATIONAL BORDERS
— Terrestrial
— Maritime

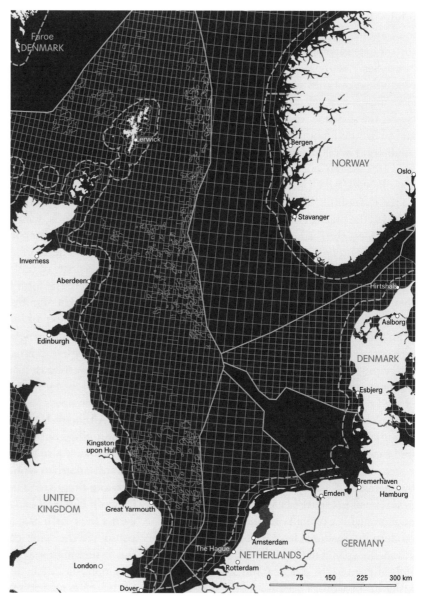

NORTH SEA PETROLEUM GRID
Fig. 7

Sea was held in Geneva in 1956 and established four separate conventions governing the use and definition of sea space.[64] For example, the Convention on the Continental Shelf (1964) was explicitly defined according to the possibility of resource exploitation; hence, the world's continental shelves were earmarked as new extractive territories from the outset.[65] Once this Convention was in place, national legislation moved quickly to establish international maritime borders and thereby facilitate petroleum exploration. In 1964 a grid of coordinates across the North Sea was established by the UK in collaboration with Norway, based on quadrants of 1-degree latitude by 1-degree longitude. In the first UK licensing round in 1965, 394 blocks subdivided within these quadrants were licensed to 22 applicants, thereby launching a half-century of extensive petroleum exploration in the North Sea.[66] With the exception of Germany, all North Sea countries adopted the grid as an efficient means of accelerating offshore exploration; hence, the seascape was geometrically organised and swiftly commodified for the extraction and production of oil and gas. [Fig. 7]

In 1982 the four previous conventions were consolidated in the United Nations Convention on the Law of the Sea (UNCLOS), which included the precise definition of a radical new state space—the Exclusive Economic Zone (EEZ). This zone extends from baselines along the coast to 200 nautical miles offshore, overlapping the previous commons of the High Seas, thereby greatly reducing what had previously been "international waters" at the global scale. With this convention, the sea emerged as a *new type of state space* of vast proportions. Unimpeded by the property rights and long-term forms of habitation that have accumulated on land, the sea offered the state abundant space to manoeuvre. For Lefebvre, state space displays "a rationality of unification [...] used to justify violence," a unification that tends towards homogeneousness, which is subsequently perceived as a consensus by the public.[67] The global dimension of this new type of sea space became an historic precedent, arguably exemplifying the first rules of modern international law.[68] It also illustrates the advancing spatial demands of the state ostensibly aligned to the practical purpose of keeping order in the world's oceans and seas. The wholesale absorption of expansive areas of sea space into state-controlled extractive zones, justified through motives of peace-keeping and improving maritime spatial coordination between rivalling nations, is a primary example of such unification.

Campling and Colas have described the establishment of the formal instrument of the EEZ as "the single greatest enclosure in human history."[69] An enclosure of this nature is usually ascribed to large-scale privatisation and commodification of property on *land*. Using the example of seventeenth-century English parliamentary enclosure, Sevilla-Buitrago argues that this is an important historical form of extended urbanisation, which gathered previously autonomous (relatively) rural areas into new spatial-social relations for extraction and accumulation.[70] The collective use and management of the commons was an essential aspect of pre-capitalist land-use arrangements, comparable to the sea commons of the *Mare Liberum*. The sea was not a site for human habitation. Still, traditional fishing communities around the North Sea interacted daily in common fishing grounds, which were not subject to formalised ownership or static regimes of control. Therefore, the establishment of EEZs is part of the history of colonial capitalism in the form of the enclosure of sea as on land. The significance and unprecedented nature of the expansion of sovereign rights into the common sea space reached a crescendo in the twentieth century by dramatically extending capitalist maritime space and setting up conditions for the establishment of operational seascapes.

Although UNCLOS was a reaction to mounting conflict around resource extraction, it also comprised the last step towards an urban world "without an outside," to quote Brenner.[71] The fluid gap or "void" between exploitable *land* territories closed across the North Sea; today, EEZs have consumed the water completely. Together, the former high seas comprised the largest commons on Earth. Subsequent to the notions of the sea as a socio-cultural space, then as a space of human labour, the sea commons were the third type of sea to be lost through processes of extended urbanisation. They were dramatically reduced because of the UNCLOS while areas of sovereign space were extended, ripe for new forms of capitalist exploitation, which, once established, were refitted to suit successive industrial requirements. Nationalised, bounded, and over-exploited regional seas, one of the last planetary frontiers for state expansion with mounting spatial conflicts, have become state spaces to be "managed" and planned.

A NEW STATE SPACE

The new state space of the North Sea was intangible, defined only by abstract coordinates and subdivided with grids. The grid is an age-old rational and generic planning device of colonisation and a powerful vehicle of extended urbanisation.[72] It has been implemented throughout history to impose a superficial layer of imperial order on unknown territories, irrespective of geography. Likewise, in the North Sea, governments had little information about what was below the water surface or on the seabed at sites offered for petroleum exploration. Wave heights and weather conditions affecting potential structures in the stormy North Sea had not been systematically recorded. North Sea waters presented the most demanding offshore environment for oil and gas so far, surpassing previous technical limits of, for example, the calmer seas of the Persian Gulf.

My conclusions about the petroleum grid in the Barents Sea also apply to the North Sea; "The grid establishes an immutable, orthogonal, and highly resilient referential layer, presupposing the possibility of development anywhere within its range," while in theory, the water column still remained a dubious "common" rented out to transient oilrigs.[73] As abstract political devices, the borders and grids of offshore economic zones are also highly resilient; their positions result from state negotiations, but once set, activities within them can be transformed as required by capitalist projects. The current transformation of the North Sea from oil and gas to wind energy, discussed in the next section, exemplifies this process.

The homogeneous, easily extendable North Sea petroleum grid exemplifies Lefebvre's notion of abstract space.[74] Lefebvre clarifies that the state, having gained its sovereignty through latent or overt violence, accumulates wealth, land, and in this case, sea. Imposing administrative divisions "aggressed all of nature" according to the rationality of accumulation.[75] Lefebvre argues that the political principle of unification (of legislation, culture, knowledge, and education) is imperative to this project, without which it cannot be realised. In the North Sea, national interventions worked hand in hand with the demands of global oil corporations to establish a "unified" referential space of extraction. This principle of unification explains the simultaneously abstract and concrete character of state space. Passing for *absence*, the abstract space constructed by the state in the North Sea conceals the *presence* of operational procedures and their physical results.[76] Lefebvre distinguishes "three formants" of abstract space, the *geometric,* the *optical,* and the *phallic,* which both imply and conceal one another.[77] The geometric formant is expressed in homogenous, Euclidean space; the optical format promotes the dominance of the visual, simulating full reality also to conceal; and the phallic formant is expressed through the power and violence of symbolic objects and icons. Particularly pertinent to the North Sea are the geometric and optical formants.

Geometric formant: The power of the geometric formant lies in reducing social space to a Euclidean abstraction by flattening three dimensions to a two-dimensional plane.[78] The complexity of the geophysical North Sea, as previously described here, is irrelevant to the petroleum grid. In the early stages of the Ekofisk development, it was not clear how oil could be transported to the Norwegian mainland, given the topography of the Norwegian trench with depths up to 700 metres directly adjacent to the coastline. Pipeline technology had not advanced sufficiently to master such depths but only became possible later.[79]

Following the establishment of EEZs in 1984, littoral countries began the process of planning these zones, designating areas for a range of uses such as transport routes, offshore wind parks, sand extraction, military exercise zones, and protected areas. EU Directive 2014/89 required that all European countries present marine spatial plans for their EEZs by 31 March 2021.[80] The production of such plans has developed into a fully-fledged discipline called "Marine Spatial Planning," led by the state and initially following simplified, two-dimensional planning methods inherited from land, thereby not considering the motion, depth, or volume of the marine environment. Exploiting the *economic capacity* of the sea space, rather than addressing the ecological balance, has emerged as the main objective of such plans. In the German EEZ, environmental assessment reports are used to ascertain if exploitative activities within protected natural areas result in adverse effects. Assessments of long-term cumulative effects—as in the exponential increase in offshore wind parks—demand technocratic calculations whose accuracy is not guaranteed. But the EU has established a series of "Blue Growth" objectives, which aim to expand and exploit the economic potential of the maritime industries in Europe through a variety of planning instruments.[81] "Blue-green" has replaced "Green" in much official literature around the transition to renewable energy production and sustainable development. At the same time, the ecological condition of European seas continues to decline.

Despite the production of increasing quantities of maritime data, the reduction of complexity permeates state-led planning initiatives in the sea. Political scientist and anthropologist James C. Scott regards abstract standardised units of measurement and cadastre plans as an unequivocal exercise of power and control that inevitably cannot be thoroughly upheld.[82]

Optical formant: Lefebvre's optical formant of abstract space deceives and conceals through the domination of vision over other senses leading to a different kind of simplification: "that which is merely seen is reduced to an image."[83] The open sea provides the possibility to experience space in one of its most abstract forms. While the sea's topographical features are located on the seafloor, invisible from the surface, the sea surface appears devoid of spatial information. As Howard and Rogers argue, there is a lack of "visual depth cues," which mediate between the body and the environment, transmitting information on scale and distance.[84] The surface of the open sea is also characterised by a lack of enclosure, augmented by the ultimate boundary of the horizon itself, which like a horizontal curtain, enables objects

and landmarks to slip behind it. From the natural human viewpoint, this occurs at a distance of just under 5 kilometres; hence the abstract spatial experience of the sea is one of continuous opening and unfolding but also of concealment.[85] The horizon, and what may lie beyond it, has stimulated human imagination and spirituality throughout time, described, for example, by author Didier Maleuvre as "a shifting line where perception trails off" and thematised by artist Hiroshi Sugimoto as the meeting place of water and air: "so very commonplace are these substances … yet they vouchsafe our very existence."[86] [Fig. 8]

Observation of the horizon dividing sea and sky is the defining visual experience of "seascapes." The common usage of the word seascape corresponds closely to the concept of landscape as a pictorial view, which according to landscape researchers is still the predominant understanding.[87] Although the German *Landschaft* and the Dutch *landshap* were originally a unit of political organisation, when the English term *landscape* was imported at the end of the sixteenth century, it meant at first only Dutch landscape painting.[88] Capturing the sea through paintings followed the genre of landscape painting, although at a later date.

This understanding of seascapes has entered into planning considerations around the North Sea, referring to the visual preservation of an uninterrupted horizon, for example, in the case of Dutch and German planning policies.[89] In Germany, offshore wind production has been politically driven and allocated large areas in Europe's first legislative Marine Spatial Plan in 2009. But wind turbines have been kept at a minimum of 32 kilometres from the coast, with visible hub heights limited to 125 metres to preserve the visually open seascape.[90] In the case of the Wadden Sea UNESCO World Heritage site—itself, a cultural landscape extended and modified over hundreds of years of human intervention—a visually constructed "ring of nature" is preserved around the coastal edge.[91] Beyond lies an energy zone capable of producing 6,436 MW, equal to 8.3% of total German electrical power production.[92]

Fig. 8

Due to the location of geological formations containing hydrocarbons in the North Sea, a sprawling combination of rigs, platforms, and infrastructure for the petroleum industry emerged far offshore, removed from the North Sea's visual seascape.[93] This is the North Sea's offshore "petroleumscape," a term developed by urban and architectural historian Carola Hein to define the palimpsestic, ubiquitous spatial formation serving the petroleum industry that is deeply embedded in our landscapes in ways beyond pure infrastructure yet remains hidden from ordinary life. According to Hein's research, the petroleumscape does more than simply steer flows; it transitions smoothly between the different layers of ports, industrial enterprises, administration, retail, and infrastructure creating lasting narratives that provide a "feedback loop" that perpetuates oil dependency.[94] Discussing the invisibility of the petroleumscape, we concluded, "Corporations and nations control the spaces of oil and gas in secrecy and concealment, making it extremely difficult to *site* as well as *sight*[...] The industry is a multinational giant without a face, both ostensibly liberated from and inextricably implicated in state operations." [95]

Back on shore, the effect of "pure spectacle" described by Lefebvre in relation to the optical formant is most palpable at Scheveningen, where surfers paddle out from the shore, framed by the Port of Rotterdam's industrial silhouette. [Fig. 9] An urban seafront has been conceived and constructed as a backdrop and a place from which to view the lively spectacle of a crowded beach with a string of leisure facilities. Vessels heading in and out of Rotterdam plough the horizon. Offshore, just beyond the territorial waters, two munitions dumping sites organised after the Second World War lie submerged, their metallic coatings slowly corroding, becoming "ticking time bombs." [96] In the Netherlands, the contradictions and deceptions of a "purely visual space" are most evident in the face of the heavy

F. 8   Hiroshi Sugimoto, Seascape
Rügen, Baltic Sea, 1996.

Fig. 9

industrial use of the limited North Sea space; the foreground seascape, preserved as a visual metaphor for leisure and relaxation, upstages the blurred perception of the background industrial activities.[97]

THE OPERATIONAL SEASCAPE

The transformation of the North Sea into a state space, organised around abstract borders and a unifying petroleum grid, enabled governments and companies to further optimise the space for industrial production. This led to the construction of an operational seascape composed of pipelines, cables, sea lanes, and offshore installations for wind farms and oil fields. Katsikis and Brenner describe operationalised landscapes as the capital-intensive, highly industrialised, and densely equipped hinterlands of the *Capitalocene* that, primarily for primary production, are laid out for maximum efficiency and are intermeshed with one another through complex extended global linkages.[98]

THE OFFSHORE URBAN FABRIC
The urbanised North Sea shows different types of technical installations and enclosures: cables, pipelines, and the industrial activities of oil, gas, and wind energy, as well as proposed marine protected areas. [Fig. 10] While the combined vessels for fishing, heavy shipping routes, and constantly circulating offshore

petroleum servicing make a dense spatial imprint on the North Sea, these activities are not represented in this map since the objective is to draw attention to the multitude of fixed elements, which represent a marked spatial departure from the long-standing "fluid" maritime industries. The piecemeal, fragmented industrial logic of this space is apparent; operations are organised around national territories and are not coordinated. Offshore installations and their infrastructures have emerged over time; as new oil and gas discoveries were made, the offshore urban fabric was extended and adapted according to the technological limits and short-term practical and economic considerations only. It was never clear during the first phases of development how large complexes such as "Ekofisk City" would grow. The abstract unified state space of the sea afforded the conditions for unlimited and uncoordinated expansion irrespective of the sea's inherent geophysical properties.

North Sea governments not only authorised the large-scale operationalisation of sea space for production purposes but, in particular in the case of the UK, also aimed to attract the interest of petroleum companies through rapid preparation of the territory for exploration. This operational seascape is closely aligned with the traits of operational landscapes. It includes the production of a comprehensive system of encompassing territorial regulations, the physical construction of offshore installations, the laying of infrastructure to deliver supplies through

Territorial waters
Petroleum grid
Marine protected areas
Wind energy

OFFSHORE
INFRASTRUCTURE
Oil and gas platforms
Pipelines
Main cables

INTERNATIONAL
BORDERS
Terrestrial
Maritime

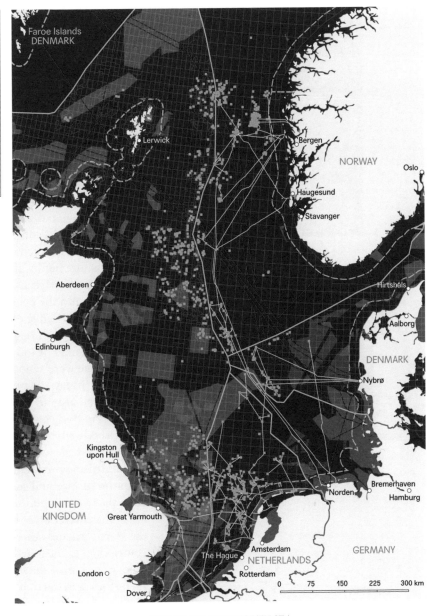

THE URBANISED NORTH SEA
Fig. 10

pipelines, cables, and shipping lanes, the securing of landings for delivering offshore resources into downstream networks, and the continuous displacement of a large rotating workforce.[99] While organised around the regular grid, the operational seascape is uneven and hugely distorted, at once thinly stretched over large distances and extremely compacted at industrial nodes. It is mostly invisible and kept out of sight from the recreational and contemplative "visual" seascape and served either by permanently moving vessels or undersea conduits.

The above map of the urbanised North Sea presents an unfamiliar geography of offshore industrial operations, with places frequently named after Norse gods on the Norwegian side

Fig. 11

Fig. 12

of the continental shelf and birds on the UK side, in an appeal to a national cultural imagination. Between 1972 and 2010, the Norwegian Petroleum Directorate presided over the naming of oilfields in a deliberate effort to link these strange new geographic places with thousands of on-site construction workers and heroic, nationalistic Norse mythology. Place names such as Frigg, the goddess of love and the wife of chief Norse god Odin, or Gannet, a beautiful yellow-headed seabird, are pure abstractions, disconnected from the geophysical characteristics of the sea or navigational conditions. [Fig. 11] Early nineteenth-century North Sea maps included features such as the Dogger and other offshore banks, the Norwegian trench, indications of the seabed composition, depth soundings, and the course of important vessels.[100] Knowledge of the sea space was socially acquired through physical engagement, and place names of towns and cities around the sea edge were synonymous with the life of the sea. Today, the petroleum delivery system is organised around secured, obscure coastal landings nobody has heard of, removed from established settlement sites. Technology has also enabled the long, deep, sometimes horizontal drilling procedures to fully disconnect both the surface and seabed "geography" from the hydrocarbon source far below.[101]

The extraction of hydrocarbons from the North Sea and other global sites has directly contributed to the fourth and ultimate form of loss; the loss of the sea's ecological balance. As historical extraction sites reach maturity—meaning full depletion of oil and gas resources—the petroleum industry continues to earmark deeper, colder, more technologically extreme sites while investing in other forms of energy extraction in the sea space. Wind-energy pilot projects executed by Equinor—the new name for Norwegian Statoil, which avoids any allusion to oil extraction—are a prime example. Carbon emissions from fossil fuels have led to expanding seawater, rising sea temperatures, and the destruction or transformation of local ecosystems. The North Sea is warming, cod are migrating further north to cooler waters,

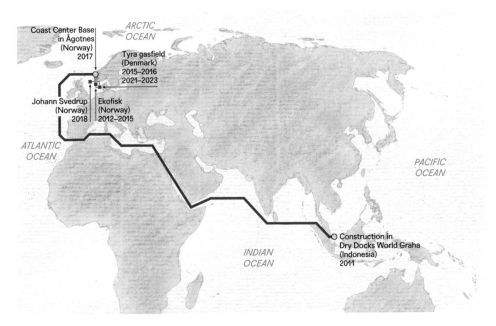

THE CIRCULATION OF AN ACCOMMODATION RIG
Fig. 13

invasive species are thriving, and more frequent storm surges are observed, resulting in destruction and flooding around the North Sea perimeter, partly in densely populated areas.

EVERYDAY LIFE ON THE RIG

The operational seascape is not yet fully automated on the North Sea and still requires a large human workforce. A Lefebvrian "lived space" is therefore anchored by a highly specific everyday existence offshore. Life on a rig echoes the distorted, uneven nature of the offshore urban fabric itself and is rigidly organised in extreme spatial confinement and intense bursts of time.

Offshore rigs are temporary by definition—they are vessels constructed for a lifespan of around 25 years, during which they will work in different fields. Once an unfamiliar sight, unemployed rigs stranded at landings have become more common around the North Sea in recent years, bringing the scale of otherwise inaccessible and rarely visible North Sea oil operations into public range.

I arrive at the accommodation rig *Haven*, moored at a 7 hectare site not far from Bergen, Norway. Owned by a firm originally established to serve Ekofisk, this service base for offshore industries offers quays adjacent to water 50 metres deep; the extension of the Norwegian trench provides deep-water docks inside some fjords. *Haven* is a jack-up accommodation rig with a maximum capacity of 443 occupants—the largest of this type currently in operation in the North Sea and requires a deep dock. Jack-up rigs work like a woodpecker screwdriver in reverse; on arrival at its destination, the legs are levered down notch by notch to the required depth. *Haven* has been stationed at the base for several months while strengthening and lengthening work on its legs is carried out in addition to providing new spud cans—the huge suction pads that attach the rig to the seafloor. Time is running, the work is over schedule, and overshooting the original estimate of $100 million. The pinch is being felt all over in the offshore industries. Owned by Jacktel, a subsidiary of Master Marine, founded in 2009 and registered in Oslo, *Haven* is rented out for specific periods according to awarded contracts. Therefore, it is an itinerant vessel sailing under the Cyprus flag and constantly looking for work. Different contracts mean different water depths; therefore, lengthening work can be required.

Haven was constructed in 2011 at Dry Docks World-Graha on the Indonesian island of Batam, itself a special economic zone serving global manufacturing industries, set up under Singaporean management. [Fig. 12] It was immediately mobilised to the Ekofisk field, after which she served in the Danish North Sea until 2015. Following structural improvements, *Haven* provided accommodation at the state-of-the-art Johan Sverdrup oilfield, located on the Norwegian continental shelf at water depths of 115 metres and ceremoniously opened by the Norwegian Prime Minister on 7 January 2020. Following structural adjustments at a different Norwegian base, *Haven's* next contract is for 20 months at the Danish North Sea field Tyra, which is undergoing redevelopment. While decommissioning of some of the over 8,000 structures in the North Sea (including platforms, pipelines, and wells) is already underway, selected projects such as the Johan Sverdrup field have been freshly completed. It is one of the five largest oilfields on the Norwegian continental shelf, cited by Equinor as "one of the most important industrial projects in Norway in the next 50 years." [102] [Fig. 13]

Offshore operations are carried out by a myriad of service companies with limited contracts; rig workers of all professions, including engineering, catering, maintenance, and cleaning (amongst others), do not work directly for oil companies but for separate contracting companies. Precarity is built into the operational logic of offshore oil and gas extraction. The continuous circulation of people, materials, finance, and machines, imperative to the ongoing capitalist project of North Sea oil and gas, leaves no time or space for continuity, responsibility, or concern. Temporariness, therefore, serves as a systematic means to maintain fluid, flexible, unchallenged operations while successive contracts add up to long-term

activities at sea *simultaneously*. The longevity of a field is not determined by the license but rather by the exploitable quantities of oil or gas. Regulations have been developed to enable both the rapid abandonment of unprofitable fields and the full exploitation of lucrative fields.

Rigs occupy privatised and securitised zones, inaccessible to the general public and only connected to the North Sea urban fabric by specific pathways, some of which lead to part-time homes for thousands. According to current data, about 60,000 itinerant workers comprise the North Sea's oil and gas population. [Fig. 14] The rituals of physical and psychological preparation for a ride of up to two hours and a separation from land life of two to three weeks begins at restricted heliport gateways. Workers describe how tension is already building up in families a week before flying out.

Crews will board *Haven* in a two-week on/four-week off rhythm according to the Norwegian system, or three weeks on/three weeks off according to the UK system. Oil workers explain how the extreme life on a rig becomes normal; you get used to its particular sway within half a day, and some claim that the main difference to land is the highly regimented rhythm penetrating every minute of the day and night. Curiously, rig-life is described by a worker as being like a "rest home" not because it is relaxing but because a strict schedule dictates working days from 5:30 am to 10:30 pm with minimal deviations of time and space. [103] Daily routines are ingrained, and tasks are frequently repetitive, making it challenging to maintain concentration. This type of environment leaves nothing to chance. Many rigs have reached an age where they require urgent maintenance. This work must be carried out at the same time as production continues and therefore requires an increased workforce on an already crowded rig. During maintenance, two-bed cabins are shared by three rotating workers, called "hard-lie" in offshore jargon. The tightening of profit margins in the industry is reflected in tightening spatial conditions for offshore workers, who, on the UK continental shelf, for example, are now required to change

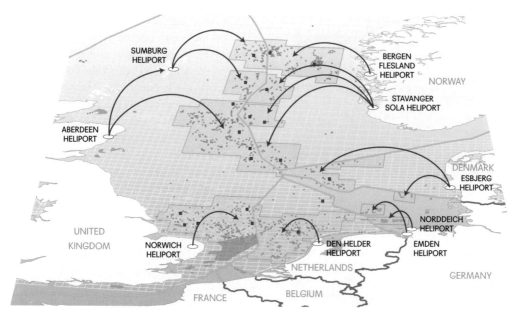

THE CIRCULATION OF OFFSHORE LABOUR
Fig. 14

from the previous two weeks on/two weeks off, to a three-week rhythm. Worker's unions have protested that this rhythm is a serious danger to health, and in 2019 a strike took place on four platforms run by the French company Total. Further strikes by other platform groups followed, and oil companies were forced to go into negotiations with worker's unions about improving offshore conditions.

Platforms stand above the 30 metres wave safety margin. In normal weather the sea is visible far below but also all around. You can hardly hear it because the rig is a noisy place with 24-hour production. A crane operator described what he could see from his position high up in the cab: storms coming through, an occasional whale, seals, gannets, and kestrels picking off small migratory birds. Some workers seek out the sea and embrace the experience, relishing the strange North Sea weather and the unique feeling of being suspended between sky and sea. But for many, the sea remains in the background, perceived as vast and dangerous. Yet, for those who love the sea, even at 280 kilometres offshore, it is difficult to catch a

glimpse during their daily indoor work routine. A rig sounds and smells metallic. Hard security lighting illuminates cold, smooth surfaces. This is an unforgiving built environment, which workers know could easily be much improved if oil companies so desired. The requirements of *working* are prioritised over the requirements of *living*.

Haven's neighbour at the base is a semi-submersible drilling rig floating on wide pontoons. The sea heaves restlessly at the rig's lowest level, temporarily caged inside a space between the pontoons called the *moonpool*. [Fig. 15] Here, the grip of steel feels precarious in the face of the pulsing North Sea, yet the persistent socio-cultural imprints of human work overlay this otherwise technical and wholly artificial environment; human habitation and imagination are captured by the way a fragment of the contained sea is named after the reflection of the moon.

F. 14 Offshore workers commute through specialized heliports to North Sea "neighbourhoods"

Fig. 15

Fig. 16

F. 15   The moonpool.
F. 16   The mirage of active oilfields,
        unidentified rig, North Sea, 2019.
F. 17   The arrival of the Brent Delta
        topside at Hartlepool, UK.
        May 2017.

THE WASTELAND

Both active and decommissioned platforms appear on the horizon when sailing through the industrial wasteland on one of the last remaining ferries crossing the North Sea. The active fields looked like an improbable mirage of floating industrial cathedrals. [Fig. 16] The Frigg field made history by straddling the UK/Norway North Sea border. Fully decommissioned in 2010 after a six-year process, Frigg's concrete gravity foundations, one around 100 metres in diameter, are still in place and make a strange ensemble protruding from the sea surface. They are an urban residue for which we have no name or conceptual foundation. The abstract space in the North Sea is mutating into new "formants" of wasteland space, although we have hardly noticed it unfolding. Its material legacy is not so easily dislodged from the sea; while floating and jack-up rigs can relocate, the support systems of pipelines, cables, and concrete foundations to which they were attached mostly remain in place, successively taken over by marine life.

Some scientists say removing structures like Frigg is more harmful to the marine environment than leaving them in place. In the last 50 years, a diverse range of species has adapted to the strange mineral substrates that provide new habitats. Jørgensen argues that not only have planning instruments failed to realise that the North Sea is fully urbanised, but they also insist on the temporary nature of installations despite continuous construction work in the last 50 years. However, if the urban sea is seen as something more permanent, a more careful consideration of the emerging ecosystems could be achieved.[104]

On 2 May 2017, the 24,200-tonne, 130-metre topside from Brent Delta, a Shell-operated field in the northern North Sea, arrived at the UK port of Hartlepool to be dismantled and sold as scrap metal by the British company Able UK. Topsides are the part of a platform above the waterline, which have been severed from their concrete foundations and, in this case, lifted onto a barge and transported back to shore. Such operations are full of superlatives: the heaviest offshore lift onto the world's largest barge and the first major piece

Fig. 17

of infrastructure to be decommissioned in the North Sea. [Fig. 17] The Brent field on the UK continental shelf was one of the first to be discovered and began production in 1976. Therefore, it was also one of the first to be dismantled. It was located 186 kilometres north-west of Lerwick in the Shetland Islands in water depths of 140 meters.

By law, decommissioned offshore facilities must be brought back to land. In the North Sea, over 800 structures will be up for decommissioning over the next twenty years. Hartlepool has a legacy of maritime industries that have suffered economic decline; the thriving shipbuilding and steelwork industries experienced setbacks after heavy bombing in the Second World War, and the subsequent de-industrialisation and closure of the British Steel Corporation in 1977 contributed to the highest levels of unemployment in the UK at the time. The Brent Delta topside contains 17,000 tonnes of steel, enough to build the Eiffel tower twice over, 98% of which is being recycled. But apart from the steel, the arrival of the Brent Delta enabled

daily life offshore to be brought into a local field of vision. It had been a part-time home for thousands of workers, was worn, slightly old-fashioned, a bit rusty, and had developed a certain patina coated with emotion: As journalist Lusher reported: "In the canteen, the tables were lined up in one long row, decorated with plastic flowers. A manager told me they had held a special dinner to mark their final night on the Delta—with the table layout resembling the painting of the Last Supper." [105]

OPERATIONALISATION
    OF THE WIND
        After the fifty years of North Sea oil and gas launched at Ekofisk in 1969, most "easy oil" had already been extracted, and production is declining. My research shows how selected new activities linked to wind energy production, CO_2 capture and storage, and potentially hydrogen storage and distribution are recolonising and retrofitting the operational seascape originally laid out for hydrocarbons.[106] As objectives for reducing northern European

CO_2 emissions fail to be reached and the areas required for increased wind energy can no longer be found on land, the North Sea is now earmarked for offshore wind-energy production on a grand scale. The wholesale expansion of the North Sea's post-oil wind-energy production demonstrates how the hydrocarbon enclosure has rapidly reoriented to renewables in the brief half-century of depleting those very resources. According to the development scenarios tested by the project Energy Odyssey 2050, the North Sea can potentially accommodate 90% of European energy demand by the year 2050.[107] The spatial impact of such a scenario, however, would be overpowering. Renderings of this possible future show the North Sea consumed by dispersed, luminous, pulsing nodes extending out from the coastlines. A sea completely operationalised for the production of renewable wind energy, which would be landed at a series of unfamiliar coastal sites.

Offshore wind energy is a highly technical industry relying on state administration of tracts of sea space even larger than blocks within the petroleum grid. It requires the production and delivery of specialised components, continuous construction and dismantling to upgrade efficiency through scaling-up, and a substantial workforce to operate and maintain the system. The offshore wind industry had grossly underestimated the required maintenance and is now erecting accommodation rigs for staff rotating on a two-week basis. These new ways of living and working at sea are technical in nature, carried out in a rigidly laid-out sea, inflexible to shifting conditions, and closing off increasingly large areas. The configuration of a wind park is based on the geometry of turbine spacings, which are proportional to their height. Therefore, wind park areas expand exponentially according to turbine size. Applying a 500 metres safety zone around the projected number of North Sea wind parks would potentially produce both an energy territory and a no-fishing zone of 12,000 km² by default, given that these areas are also restricted to fishing.[108] Greater pressure on fish stocks in non-restricted zones is predicted as a result. Fishers who know

the sea argue that the long-term ecological effects of the vast expansion of offshore wind parks have not been considered. And they notice that wind patterns have changed, and no one knows how this will affect the water circulation patterns of the North Sea itself.

RECONNECTING TO THE SEA

This chapter shows how offshore activities in the North Sea are inextricably linked to land-side urban development in a reciprocal process operating across the land-sea threshold and mobilising people, vessels, materials, finance, and legal instruments. These operations perform vital functions for highly urbanised northern Europe and are interlocked into global economic networks. North Sea maritime activities are strictly programmed and regulated to extend, perpetuate, and intensify systems of delivery and exchange to urban agglomerations. Vast tracts of sea space and dedicated coastal sites are planned and reorganised, daily, and weekly human rhythms are strictly set, and unprecedented volumes of materials are transported across its surface, fixed to the seafloor and again dismantled in ongoing cycles.

Industrialisation has caused the social space of the sea to be replaced by a space of extraction—biomass (marine life), hydrocarbons, and wind energy—and the movement of goods, while selected shoreline spaces are redesigned to offer "leisure" and to artificially intensify the seaside experience. The conceptualised map of the urbanised North Sea illustrates this reversal. Clusters of fixed petroleum infrastructure form a series of dispersed centralities down the middle of the North Sea on which development is focused and around which operations and movements circulate. These sites are extended centres of action controlled by landside headquarters and government departments. [Fig. 18] When less dominated by industrial functions, the sea's periphery forms a ring towards the coastlines, where the sea can be experienced as a cultural space and consumed in a pre-industrial visual form, expressly preserved for this purpose. In this

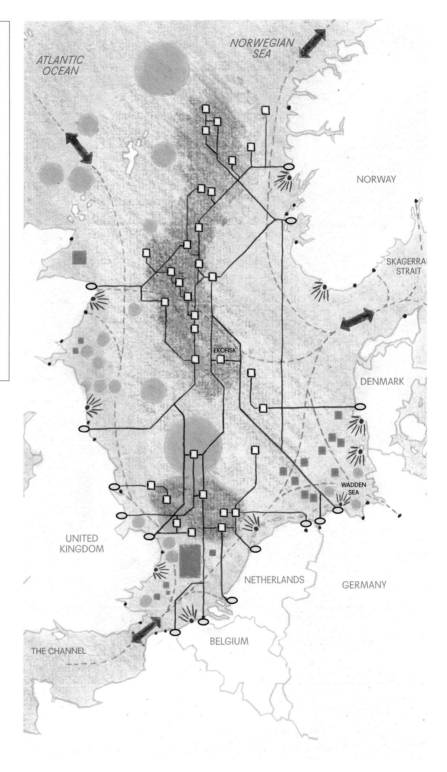

CENTRES

High concentration of industrial activities and human circulation

Oil and gas infrastructure (platforms and pipelines)

PERIPHERY

Maritime territory with less intense activity but still impacted by the centres

Marine protected areas

Windparks

INTERFACE LAND/SEA

Coastal waters linking the industrialised and urbanised North Sea, and other water bodies

Industrial infrastructure, interface between sea and land

Cultural sites, recreation and visual consumption of the sea space

Main merchandise transport routes and connections

NORWEGIAN SEA

ATLANTIC OCEAN

NORWAY

SKAGERRA STRAIT

EKOFISK

DENMARK

WADDEN SEA

UNITED KINGDOM

NETHERLANDS

GERMANY

BELGIUM

THE CHANNEL

THE REVERSAL OF CENTRE AND PERIPHERY
IN THE URBANISED NORTH SEA
Fig. 18

Fig. 19

way, we continue to uphold an artificial culture/ nature conceptual divide within maritime space while industrial residue has long been fully absorbed into the North Sea's biochemical composition.

This process of urbanising the North Sea has been a process of loss; the loss of the socio-cultural sea, the loss of the sea for human labour, the loss of the sea as commons, and the loss of the ecological sea. The reinforcement of the peripheral leisure sea facilitates an illusion

F. 19 Bird Station- an alternative to decommissioning. The North Sea rig Gyda is decommissioned and transformed into a bird station where migrating birds can rest, nest, and receive care if injured, and bird-watchers can observe at close range. Zoelie Millereau-Dubesset BAS 2020.

of concealing these lost seas—until storm surges of increasing force and frequency pound the North Sea coastlines.

What is the outcome of this loss? Instead of unfolding complexity, diversification, and interconnectivity, which could generate social conditions comparable to those found in urban environments, extended urbanisation in the North Sea does *not* produce urban qualities, offer social interaction spaces, or promote synergies. Instead, this urbanisation process gathers the discrete and inert loads of industrial production while pushing selected layers of socio-cultural meaning to its very edge. The cultural links between social life and new technological workplaces offshore are tenuous. In contrast to the North Sea's heterogeneous oceanographic features, and complex ecological system, resource management is increasingly streamlined, rigid, and subject to technological abstraction and operationalisation. All sectors are tightly controlled by the state in collaboration with multinational companies or other organisations wielding power. This resonates with Lefebvre's critique of the attack on the urban from the state level: "a global project to subject the national territory to a process of 'development' controlled by industrialisation," where "the urban is reduced to the industrial" and where the places to assert rights have also been eroded.[109]

The grave ecological condition of the planet's *one ocean* is an urgent consequence of extended urbanisation, and the evacuation of the social sea has facilitated unchecked industrial expansion. As a result, we are now losing the sea to climate change. It is, in fact, within these very relations that organic reactions, not in a social but in an ecological sense, have occurred out of the control of grids, directives, and planning efforts. Long-range pollutants, such as microplastics, are transported by currents through a *borderless* ocean.

In the North Sea, the "urban" must also face its own specific mode of transformation of nature. Having arrived at an understanding of the current situation through research and analytical work, it is the further task of

architectural, urban, and territorial design to set the processes of *reconnecting to the sea* in motion. Urban theorist Roberto Luis Monte-Mor has also provided some important responses. He argues that the intimate relationship between urban ecology and the environmental question is not yet well understood and that we should also work to rebuild and *reproduce* the relationships between built and natural space. "We must confront extended urbanisation with extended naturalisation if we are to deal not only with urban and environmental problems at the micro-level of everyday life but also with the global aspects of environmental and social crises."[110]

Reimagining the damaged sea with its more-than-human inhabitants is one way of assuming responsibility. Bird Station is a project that aims to reconnect people to the transformed, living sea space. [Fig 19] We can bridge the widening public gap engineered by the industrial-technological take-over through engagement and education. Reconnecting to the sea will require a major transdisciplinary effort and, in particular, a host of powerful and enticing creative visions.

ENDNOTES

1   *Oljeliv/Offshore ID.*
2   Kvendseth, *Giant Discovery.*
3   Gjerde, "Ekofisk Industrial Heritage."
4   Sandberg and Gjerde, "Preserving Norway's Oil Heritage."
5   Lefebvre, *The Production of Space*; Brenner and Schmid, "Towards a New Epistemology of the Urban?"; Diener et al., *The Inevitable Specificity of Cities.*
6   Rich, "Losing Earth."
7   Engel et al., *OverHolland*, 10.
8   Pye, *The Edge of the World.*
9   Ayers, *The German Ocean.*
10 Blass, *The Naked Shore.*
11 Theutenberg, *Mare Clausum et Mare Liberum.*
12 Steinberg, *The Social Construction of the Ocean.*
13 Braudel, *The Mediterranean and the Mediterranean World.*
14 Braudel, *Civilization and Capitalism.*
15 Braudel, *Civilisation and Capitalism*
16 De Landa, *A Thousand Years of Nonlinear History*, 128.
17 Rapp, "The Unmaking of the Mediterranean Trade Hegemony."
18 Grotius, *Mare Liberum.*
19 Braudel, *Civilization and Capitalism.*
20 Mancke, "Early Modern Expansion."
21 Michael B. Miller, *Europe and the Maritime World*, 8.
22 Steinberg, *Social Construction.*
23 As mapped by Dutch cartographer Frederik de Wit, for example, *Nova Orbis Tabula in Lucem Edita* by De Wit, c. 1665.
24 Sobel, *Longitude.*
25 Wood, *Rethinking the Power of Maps*, 31.
26 Spinney, "Searching for Doggerland."
27 Miller, *Maritime World.*
28 ICES, "Greater North Sea Ecoregion."
29 Chapman, *North Sea Oil and Gas.*
30 "CO2 Storage Atlas Norwegian North Sea."
31 UK Department of Energy and Climate Change, "Petroleum Prospectivity of the Principal Sedimentary Basins on the United Kingdom Continental Shelf."
32 Lambert, Martins, and Ogborn, "Currents, Visions and Voyages"; Anderson and Peters, *Water Worlds.*
33 Westerdahl, "The Maritime Cultural Landscape."
34 Hatch, "Material Culture and Maritime Identity."

35 Miller, *Maritime World.*
36 Miller, *Maritime World.*
37 Sekula and Burch, *The Forgotten Space.*
38 Debarbieux, *Social Imaginaries of Space*, Raffestin and Butler, "Space, Territory, and Territoriality."
39 Couling, "Ocean Space and Urbanisation."
40 For a discussion on the material transformation of territory over time, see Schmid, "Analysing Extended Urbanisation: A Territorial Approach."
41 Steinberg, Peters, and Stratford, *Territory Beyond Terra.*
42 Fuller, "Fluid Geography," 119.
43 Sloterdijk, *In the World Interior of Capital*, 43.
44 Brenner, "Between Fixity and Motion"; and Brenner, *New Urban Spaces.*
45 Couling and Hein, "Blankness."
46 Bélanger, "The Other 71 Percent."
47 Gugger, Couling, and Blanchard, *Barents Lessons.*
48 Boeri and Palmesino, "Around a Solid Sea."
49 Boeri and Palmesino.
50 Heller and Pezzani, "Forensic Oceanography. Mare Clausum. Italy and the EU's Undeclared Operation to Stem Migration across the Mediterranean."
51 Topalović, Hortig, and Krautzig, *Sea Region. Singapore, Johor, Riau Archipelago.*
52 Topalović et al., *Hinterland.*
53 Brenner and Schmid, "Planetary Urbanization."
54 Couling, "Nine Principles of Ocean Urbanization in the Baltic Sea."
55 Geldof and Janssens, "The Future Commons 2070."
56 Couling and Hein, "The North Sea."
57 Borgese, "Oceanic Circle."
58 Roberts, *The Unnatural History of the Sea.*
59 Holm, "World War II and the 'Great Acceleration' of North Atlantic Fisheries."
60 Iceland, although independent, was closely aligned to Denmark, which was already occupied by Germany.
61 Miller, *Maritime World*, 213.
62 UN, "United Nations Convention on the Law of the Sea (A Historical Perspective)."
63 United States Government, "1945-Truman-Proclamation-No.-2667.Pdf."

64 Convention on the Territorial Sea (1964), the Continental Shelf (1964), the High Seas (1962), and Fishing and Conservation of Living Resources of the High Seas (1966).
65 United Nations, "Convention on the Continental Shelf."
66 Kemp, *The Official History of North Sea Oil and Gas.*
67 Lefebvre, *The Production of Space,* 282.
68 Theutenberg, "Mare Clausum et Mare Liberum."
69 Campling and Colás, "Capitalism and the Sea," 780.
70 Sevilla-Buitrago, "Urbs in Rure."
71 Brenner, "Introduction: Urban Theory Without an Outside."
72 See also Katsikis, this volume.
73 Couling, "Urbanization of the Ocean," 245.
74 Couling and Hein, "Blankness."
75 Lefebvre, *The Production of Space,* 280.
76 Lefebvre, 289.
77 Lefebvre, *The Production of Space,* 285.
78 Lefebvre, 285.
79 Kvendseth, *Giant Discovery.*
80 European Parliament and the Council of the European Union, "Directive 2014/89/EU Establishing a Framework for Maritime Spatial Planning."
81 European Commission, "Report on the Blue Growth Strategy Towards More Sustainable Growth and Jobs in the Blue Economy."
82 Scott, *Seeing Like a State.*
83 Lefebvre, *The Production of Space,* 286.
84 Howard and Rogers, *Perceiving in Depth.*
85 Couling, "Formats of Extended Urbanisation in Ocean Space."
86 Maleuvre, *The Horizon*; and Sugimoto.
87 Prominski, "Landschaft."
88 Olwig, Kenneth R. *Landscape, Nature, and the Body Politic.*
89 Dutch Ministry of Infrastructure and the Environment and Dutch Ministry of Economic Affairs, "Policy Document on the North Sea 2016–2021."
90 BSH, "Anlage Zur Verordnung Über Die Raumordnung in Der Deutschen Ausschließlichen Wirtschaftszone in Der Nordsee (AWZ Nordsee-ROV) Vom 21. September 2009."
91 Couling, "Extensions and Viscosities in the North Sea"; see also Castriota, this volume.

92 Eckert, "German North Sea Wind Capacity Rose Almost to 2020 Target Last Year – TenneT."
93 Couling, "The Offshore Petroleumscape."
94 Hein, "Oil Spaces."
95 Couling and Hein, "Blankness"; see also Wilson and Pendakis, "Sight, Site, Cite."
96 Franzen, "Ticking Time Bombs on the Bottom of the North and Baltic Sea | DW | 23.08.2017."
97 Lefebvre, *The Production of Space,* 286.
98 Brenner and Katsikis, "Operational Landscapes."
99 Katsikis, "On the Geographical Organization of World Urbanization."
100 See, for example, the 1796 map of the "North Sea with the Kattegat from the Chart of Messrs. De Verdun, Borda and Pingre" by William Faden.
101 Couling, "Extractive Geometries."
102 See, https://www.equinor.com/en/what-we-do/johan-sverdrup.html.
103 A home for the elderly.
104 Jørgensen, "The Anthropogenic Seascape and the Energy Transition."
105 Lusher, "Brent Delta."
106 Couling, "The Offshore Petroleumscape."
107 Sijmons and Hajer, "IABR."
108 Equal to 1.6% of the North Sea area; ICES, "Greater North Sea Ecoregion?"
109 Lefebvre, *The Urban Revolution,* 94.
110 Monte-Mór, Roberto Luís, "Extended Urbanization," 118.

BIBLIOGRAPHY

Anderson, Jon, and Kimberley Peters, eds. *Water Worlds: Human Geographies of the Ocean.* Farnham: Ashgate, 2014.

Ayers, Brian. *The German Ocean. Medieval Europe around the North Sea.* Studies in the Archaeology of Medieval Europe 6. Sheffield: Equinox, 2016.

Bélanger, Pierre. "The Other 71 Percent." *Harvard Design Magazine* 39, no. F/W 2014 (2014).

Blass, Tom. *The Naked Shore: Of the North Sea.* London: Bloomsbury, 2015.

Boeri, Stefano, and John Palmesino. "Around a Solid Sea." *ARCHIS Flow,* no. 5 (October 2002).

Borgese, Elisabeth Mann. "The Oceanic Circle: Governing the Seas as a Global Resource." Tokyo: The Club of Rome, 1998.

Braudel, Fernand. *Civilization and Capitalism: 15th-18th Century.* Translated by Siân Reynolds. New York; Cambridge [etc.]: Harper & Row, 1981.

———.*The Mediterranean and the Mediterranean World in the Age of Philip II.* Vol. 1. New York: Harper, 1972.

Brenner, Neil. "Between Fixity and Motion: Accumulation, Territorial Organization, and the Historical Geography of Spatial Scales." *Environment and Planning D: Society and Space* 16, no. 4 (1998): 459–481.

———."Introduction: Urban Theory without an Outside." In *Implosions / Explosions: Towards a Study of Planetary Urbanization,* 14–30. Berlin: Jovis, 2014.

———.*New Urban Spaces: Urban Theory and the Scale Question.* New York NY: Oxford University Press, 2019.

Brenner, Neil, and Nikos Katsikis. "Operational Landscapes: Hinterlands of the Capitalocene." *Architectural Design* 90, no. 1 (2020): 22–31.

Brenner, Neil, and Christian Schmid. "Planetary Urbanization." In *Urban Constellations,* edited by Matthew Gandy. Berlin: Jovis, 2011.

———."Towards a New Epistemology of the Urban?" *City* 19, no. 2–3 (4 May 2015): 151–182.

BSH. "Anlage Zur Verordnung Über Die Raumordnung in Der Deutschen Ausschließlichen Wirtschaftszone in Der Nordsee (AWZ Nordsee-ROV) Vom 21. September 2009." Bundesanzeiger Verlag GmbH, 21 September 2009.

Campling, Liam, and Alejandro Colás. "Capitalism and the Sea: Sovereignty, Territory, and Appropriation in the Global Ocean." *Environment and Planning D: Society and Space* 36, no. 4 (6 November 2017): 776–794.

Chapman, Keith. *North Sea Oil and Gas: A Geographical Perspective.* Problems in Modern Geography. Newton Abbot a.o: David & Charles, 1976.

Norwegian Petroleum Directorate. *CO2 Storage Atlas Norwegian North Sea.* Stavanger: NPD, 2011.

Couling, Nancy. "Extensions and Viscosities in the North Sea." In *The Urbanisation of the Sea: From Concepts and Analysis to Design,* edited by Nancy Couling and Carola Hein, 189–203. Rotterdam: nai010, 2020.

———."Formats of Extended Urbanisation in Ocean Space." In *Emerging Urban Spaces- A Planetary Perspective,* edited by Philipp Horn, Paola Alfaro d'Alençon, and Ana Claudia Duarte Carduso, Cham:Springer, 2018

———."Nine Principles of Ocean Urbanization in the Baltic Sea." In *The Baltic Atlas,* 172–179. Berlin: Sternberg Press, 2016.

———."Ocean Space and Urbanisation: The Case of Two Seas." In *The Urbanisation of the Sea: From Concepts and Analysis to Design,* edited by Nancy Couling and Carola Hein, 189–203. Rotterdam: nai010, 2020.

———."The Offshore Petroleumscape: Grids, Gods and Giants of the North Sea." In *Oil Spaces: Exploring the Global Petroleumscape,* edited by Carola Hein, 109–126. New York: Routledge, 2022.

———."Urbanization of the Ocean; Extractive Geometries in the Barents Sea." In *Infrastructure Space.* LaFargeHolcim Forum for Sustainable Construction. Berlin: Ruby Press, 2016.

Couling, Nancy, and Carola Hein. "Blankness: The Architectural Void of North Sea Energy Logistics." *Footprint* 12, no. 23 (2018).

———."The North Sea: New Perspectives on the Land-Sea Continuum." In *The Urbanisation of the Sea: From Concepts and Analysis to Design,* 6–15. Rotterdam: nai010, 2020.

Debarbieux, Bernard. *Social Imaginaries of Space*. Cheltenham, UK; Northampton MA, USA: Edward Elgar, 2019.

Diener, Roger, Manuel Herz, Jacques Herzog, Marcel Meili, Pierre de Meuron, Christian Schmid, and Milica Topalović, eds. *The Inevitable Specificity of Cities: Napoli, Nile Valley, Belgrade, Nairobi, Hong Kong, Canary Islands, Beirut, Casablanca*. Zürich: Lars Müller, 2015.

Dutch Ministry of Infrastructure and the Environment and Dutch Ministry of Economic Affairs. "Policy Document on the North Sea 2016–21." Dutch Ministry of Infrastructure and the Environment, December 2015.

Eckert, Vera. "German North Sea Wind Capacity Rose Almost to 2020 Target Last Year–TenneT." *Reuters*, 13 January 2020.

Engel, Henk, Esther Gramsbergen, Henk Hoeks, and Reinout Rutte, eds. *OverHolland 10: The Transformation of the Landscape of the Western Region of the Netherlands (9th to 21st Century)*. OverHolland: Architectural Studies for Dutch Cities 10/11. Amsterdam: Sun Publishers or Faculty of Architecture TU Delft, 2011.

European Commission. "Report on the Blue Growth Strategy Towards More Sustainable Growth and Jobs in the Blue Economy." Commission Staff Working Document. Brussels: European Commission, 31 March 2017.

European Parliament and the Council of the European Union. "Directive 2014/89/EU Establishing a Framework for Maritime Spatial Planning." European Union, 23 July 2014.

Franzen, Harald. "Ticking Time Bombs on the Bottom of the North and Baltic Sea | DW | 23.08.2017." *DW.COM*, 23 August 2017.

Fuller, Richard, Buckminster. "Fluid Geography." *American Neptune- A Quarterly Journal of Maritime History and Arts* IV, no. 2 (April 1944).

Geldof, Charlotte, and Nel Janssens. "The Future Commons 2070: The Ethical Problem of the Territorialization of the North Sea," 2014. https://publications.lib. chalmers.se/records/full-text/230581/local_230581.pdf.

Gjerde, Kristin, Ø. "Ekofisk Industrial Heritage – How to Document and Communicate a Large Technical-Industrial Monument at Sea." Minneapolis, MN, 2005. https://www.academia.edu/3715 5653/Ekofisk_Industrial_ Heritage3.doc

Grotius, Hugo. *Mare Liberum, Sive de Jure Quod Batavis Competit Ad Indicana Commercia Dissertatio*. Dutch Republic: Lodewijk Elzevir, 1609.

Gugger, Harry, Nancy Couling, and Aurélie Blanchard, eds. *Barents Lessons. Teaching and Research in Architecture*. Zürich: Park Books, 2012.

Hatch, Heather, E. "Material Culture and Maritime Identity: Identifying Maritime Subcultures Through Artifacts." In *The Archaeology of Maritime Landscapes*, edited by Ben Ford. When the Land Meets the Sea. New York: Springer-Verlag, 2011.

Hein, Carola. "Oil Spaces: The Global Petroleumscape in the Rotterdam/ The Hague Area." *Journal of Urban History*, 13 February 2018,

Heller, Charles, and Lorenzo Pezzani. "Mare Clausum: Italy and the EU's Undeclared Operation to Stem Migration Across the Mediterranean." *Forensic Architecture* (2018).Holm, Poul. "World War II and the "Great Acceleration" of North Atlantic Fisheries." *Global Environment* 5, no. 10 (1 January 2012): 66–91.

Howard, Ian P., and Brian J. Rogers. *Perceiving in Depth*. Oxford: Oxford University Press, 2012.

ICES. "Greater North Sea Ecoregion: Ecosystem Overview." ICES Ecosystem Overviews, 2018.

———."Greater North Sea Ecoregion: Fisheries Overview." ICES Fisheries Overviews. Copenhagen: ICES, 30 November 2018.

Jørgensen, Anne-Mette. "The Anthropogenic Seascape and the Energy Transition: The Need for a New Perspective on Marine Nature and Human-Made Structures." In *The Urbanisation of the Sea: From Concepts and Analysis to Design*, edited by Nancy Couling and Carola Hein. Rotterdam: nai010, 2020.

Katsikis, Nikos. "On the Geographical Organization of World Urbanization." *MONU*, Geographical Urbanism, 20 (2014).

Kemp, Alex. *The Official History of North Sea Oil and Gas: Vol. I: The Growing Dominance of the State*. Abingdon, Oxon: Routledge, 2013.

Kvendseth, Stig, K. *Giant Discovery. A History of Ekofisk through the First 20 Years*. Norway: Phillips Petroleum Company, 1988.

Lambert, David, Luciana Martins, and Miles Ogborn. "Currents, Visions, and Voyages: Historical Geographies of the Sea." *Journal of Historical Geography*, Historical Geographies of the Sea, 32, no. 3 (July 2006): 479–493.

Landa, Manuel de. *A Thousand Years of Nonlinear History*. New York: Zone Books, 1997.

Lefebvre, Henri. *The Production of Space*. Translated by Donald Nicholson-Smith. Oxford, UK etc: Blackwell, 1991.

———.*The Urban Revolution*. Minneapolis: University of Minnesota Press, 2003.

Lusher, Adam. "Brent Delta: A North Sea Giant Gives up Its Secrets." *Inside Energy, Shell Global*, 19 July 2019. https://www.shell.com/inside-en-ergy/brent-delta-north-sea-oil-gas. html.

Maleuvre, Didier. *The Horizon: A History of our Infinite Longing*. Berkeley: University of California Press, 2011.

Mancke, Elizabeth. "Early Modern Expansion and the Politicization of Oceanic Space." *Geographical Review* 89, no. 2 (1 April 1999): 225–236.

Miller, Michael B. *Europe and the Maritime World: A Twentieth-Century History*. New York: Cambridge University Press, 2012.

Monte-Mor, Roberto Luis. "Extended Urbanization and Settlement Patterns in Brazil: An Environmental Approach." In *Implosions / Explosions Towards a Study of Planetary Urbanization*, 109–120. Berlin: Jovis, 2014.

Oljeliv/Offshore ID. Norwegian Petroleum Museum, 2018. https://www. norskolje.museum.no/en/ how-is-life-with-mum-working-off-shore/.

Olwig, Kenneth R. *Landscape, Nature, and the Body Politic: From Britain's Renaissance to America's New World*. Madison: University of Wisconsin Press, 2002.

Prominski, Martin. "Landschaft." In *Über Den Zwischenraum // Zum Wandel Des Ästhetischen Interresses*, edited by Christophe Gilot, Anette Freytag, Susanne Hofer, and Albert Kirchengast. ETH Zürich, Departement Architektur, ILA, 2011.

Pye, Michael. *The Edge of the World: How the North Sea Made Us Who We Are.* London: Penguin Books, 2015.

Raffestin, Claude, and Samuel Butler. "Space, Territory, and Territoriality." *Environment and Planning D: Society and Space* 30, no. 1 (1 February 2012): 121–141.

Rapp, Richard T. "The Unmaking of the Mediterranean Trade Hegemony: International Trade Rivalry and the Commercial Revolution." *The Journal of Economic History* 35, no. 3 (1975): 499–525.

Rich, Nathaniel. "Losing Earth: The Decade We Almost Stopped Climate Change." *The New York Times*, 1 August 2018, sec. Magazine. https://www.nytimes.com/interactive/2018/08/01/magazine/climate-change-losing-earth.html.

Roberts, Callum. *The Unnatural History of the Sea.* Washington D.C: Island Press, 2007.

Sandberg, Finn, H, and Kristin Gjerde Ø. "Preserving Norway's Oil Heritage." In *Artefacts: Studies in History Science and Technology*, 150–167. Smithsonian Institution Scholarly Press, 2017.

Schmid, Christian. "Analysing Extended Urbanisation: A Territorial Approach." In *The Urbanisation of the Sea: From Concepts and Analysis to Design*, edited by Nancy Couling and Carola Hein, 189–203. Rotterdam: nai010, 2020.

Scott, James C. *Seeing Like a State: How Certain Schemes to Improve the Human Condition Have Failed.* The Institution for Social and Policy Studies. New Haven, CT: Yale University Press, 2008.

Sekula, Allan and Nöel Burch. *The Forgotten Space*, 2010. http://www.theforgottenspace.net/static/notes.html. Accessed 12 December 2022.

Sevilla-Buitrago, Alvaro. "Urbs in Rure: Historical Enclosure and the Extended Urbanization of the Countryside." In *Implosions / Explosions Towards a Study of Planetary Urbanization*, 236–259. Berlin: Jovis, 2014.

Sijmons, Dirk, and Maarten Hajer. "IABR. 2050: An Energetic Odyssey." Accessed 20 September 2019. https://iabr.nl/en/projectatelier/Atelier2050.

Sloterdijk, Peter. *In the World Interior of Capital: For a Philosophical Theory of Globalization.* Cambridge: Polity, 2013.

Sobel, Dava. *Longitude: The True Story of a Lone Genius Who Solved the Greatest Scientific Problem of His Time.* London: Fourth Estate, 1996.

Spinney, Laura. "Searching for Doggerland." *National Geographic Magazine*, December 2012.

Steinberg, Philip E. *The Social Construction of the Ocean.* Cambridge Studies in International Relations 78. Cambridge [etc.]: Cambridge University Press, 2001.

Steinberg, Philip E., Kimberley Peters, and Elaine Stratford, eds. *Territory Beyond Terra.* Geopolitical Bodies, Material Worlds. London: Rowman & Littlefield International, 2018.

Theutenberg, Bo Johnson. "Mare Clausum et Mare Liberum." *ARCTIC* 37, no. 4 (December 1984).

Topalović, Milica, Hans Hortig, and Stefanie Krautzig, eds. *Architecture of Territory. Sea Region. Singapore, Johor, Riau Archipelago.* Zürich: ETH Zürich DArch, FCL Singapore, 2015.

Topalović, Milica, Martin Knüsel, Martin Jäggi, and Stefanie Krautzig, eds. *Hinterland: Singapore, Johor, Riau.* Zürich: ETH Zürich DArch, 2013.

UK Department of Energy and Climate Change. "Petroleum Prospectivity of the Principal Sedimentary Basins on the United Kingdom Continental Shelf." UK Department of Energy and Climate Change, December 2013.

UN. "United Nations Convention on the Law of the Sea (A Historical Perspective)." 1998. https://www.un.org/Depts/los/convention_agreements/convention_historical_perspective.htm#Historical%20Perspective. Accessed 3 March 2023.

United Nations. "Convention on the Continental Shelf," 29 April 1958.

United States Government. "1945-Truman-Proclamation-No.-2667.Pdf." 1945. https://cil.nus.edu.sg/wp-content/uploads/2017/08/1945-Truman-Proclamation-No.-2667.pdf. Accessed 3 March 2023.

Westerdahl, Christer. "The Maritime Cultural Landscape." *International Journal of Nautical Archaeology* 21, no. 1 (1992): 5–14.

Wilson, Sheena, and Andrew Pendakis, eds. "Sight, Site, Cite. Oil in the Field of Vision." *Imaginations: Journal of Cross-Cultural Image Studies*, Sighting Oil, 3, no. 2 (6 September 2012).

Wood, Denis. *Rethinking the Power of Maps.* New York: Guilford Press, 2010.

IMAGE CREDITS

All photography from author unless
otherwise stated.

All maps from Philippe Rekacewicz
with author unless otherwise stated.

F. 1   Courtesy of Jan Berghuis, 2019
F. 2   Full colour facsimile of the original
        1539 edition, courtesy of the James
        Ford Bell Library, University
        of Minnesota
F. 4   Currents from: Paramor, O.A.L.,
        Allen, K.A., Aanesen, M.,
        Armstrong, C., Hegland, T.,
        Le Quesne, W, Piet, G.J., et al.
        "MEFEPO North Sea Atlas."
        Liverpool: University of Liverpool,
        2009. https://www.liverpool.ac.uk/
        media/livacuk/mefepo/docu-
        ments/wp1/atlases/
        NS_Atlas_English.pdf.
        Hydrographic regions from:
        Huthnance, J. M. "Physical
        Oceanography of the North Sea."
        Ocean and Shoreline Management,
        North Sea: Environment and
        Sea Use Planning, 16, no. 3
        (1 January 1991): 199–231
F. 5   After Richard Buckminster Fuller,
        1944. Courtesy of Michael
        Paukner, 2009
F. 6   Library of Congress, Geography
        and Map Division
F. 7   GIS data from: Rijkswaterstaat
        (NL), Danish Energy Agency (DK),
        Norwegian Petroleum Directorate
        (NO), Oil and Gas Authority (UK)
F. 8   © Hiroshi Sugimoto, courtesy
        Fraenkel Gallery, San Francisco
F. 10   GIS data sources as Fig 7, and
        DEFRA, EMODNET, GEBCO,
        OSPAR, CONTIS, EEA, Marine
        Regions & Natural Earth Data
F. 17   © North News & Pictures Ltd.,
        UK
F. 19   Courtesy of Zoelie Millereau-
        Dubesset, Bergen School
        of Architecture, 2020

Expropriation and Extended Citizenship. The Periphalisation of Arcadia.

Et in Arcadia Ego, "Me too in Arcadia," wrote Johann Wolfgang von Goethe in his travelogue on the Italian countryside in 1786.[1] In 1873, Arcadia re-emerged as a feral myth of naked Nymphs and the satyr-like god Pan in a painting by William-Adolphe Bouguereau, and as the pastoral ideal of a shepherd peacefully scooping water under the shade of a bush in the 1836 painting by Thomas Cole. The Arcadian landscapes reappear at the centre of the cosmopolitan life of late nineteenth-century Berlin on the murals of Café Bauer. In 1909, Shaftesbury Theatre London hosted the musical *The Arcadians,* introducing a metropolitan audience to a group of idyllic peasants who wished to transform the wicked metropolis into a land of truth and simplicity. [Fig. 1] Today, Arcadia is ubiquitous. Its name stands on the billboard of a university campus in Pennsylvania, a city in Los Angeles County, an immigrant's club in Brooklyn, and a hotel in the Greek mining town of Megalopolis. Heterogeneous and dispersed in space and history, how do all these "Arcadias" relate to each other? And what is the common place they recall?

This chapter examines the actual region of Arcadia, a mountainous landscape located at the core of the Peloponnese peninsula in Greece. It is a place where extended urbanisation is unfolding under a rural and bucolic backdrop, where idyllic images cloak social struggles and dispossessions, and recent economic and environmental crises are accelerating the deregulation and depopulation of peripheral areas. In contemporary Arcadia, land expropriations and the enclosure of commons and agricultural land are silently unfolding under the pretext of green development and energy transition, while a consistent policy of emptying and flattening the mountain region has been enabling regional re-articulations and the redistribution of power and wealth, allowing processes of capital to proceed. This is a tale of peripheralisation.

This chapter draws upon archival and ethnographic fieldwork conducted in the landscapes of Mount Mainalo, located at the core of "mountainous Arcadia,"[2] between 2017 and 2021. The multi-sited fieldwork took place

Fig. 1

F. 1   The "Arcadians" musical
at Shaftesbury Theatre,
London, 1909.

in bureaucratic and logistical spaces, olive groves, villages, pastures, and the forest. There, I collected qualitative information, including oral histories, everyday experiences, and counter cartographies that narrate an "invisible" landscape under extreme pressure for transformation.

In this chapter, I depart from the Western myth of Arcadia and unpack it as the fabrication of an imaginary "urban outside" and a spatial and temporal frontier enabling multiple extensions. I then return to the actual Arcadia, where a peripheral landscape can be understood as a contemporary urban outside. Over the last decades, the region has been drained of a permanent population and related social and economic structures. It has been systematically peripheralised, eventually becoming dependent on national and international centralities. As I narrate this history, I reconstruct its emptying in relation to a "filling-in" that manifests simultaneously elsewhere. I then examine the transformation of Greek state space, especially during the Greek debt crisis, allowing me to observe how extended urbanisation unfolded as part of a more extensive process of peripheralisation. This process currently exceeds the scale of the nation-state and the region and reclaims peripheralised territories when coupled with resistance and extended forms of citizenship. Overall, this chapter works towards developing a relational understanding of urbanisation. It focuses

on processes that polarise and generate unevenness, such as inhabited and uninhabited lands, developing and left-behind places, and centres and peripheries forming relationally in different geographies and scales. The chapter suggests peripheralisation as a process of extended urbanisation, which manifests as interwoven and interdependent with processes of centralisation. Peripheralisation reinvents places as "outsides," eventually marginalising, subordinating, and enclosing them. This work mainly entails an urgent call for revisiting peripheralised and arcadised lands and their ecological margins to unveil such processes that uncontrollably occur there. It occurs to me that our generation's most crucial social and ecological struggles are staged in such peripheral lands. Thus, this work defends those fragile, socioecological fabrics that, although latent and under extreme pressure, continue to present, persist, and resist.

THE MYTH OF THE OUTSIDE

Arcadia has been constructed as a myth of an urban outside. In this view, it is an outer frontier constantly negotiated, reconceived, and reconfigured. Progressively, Arcadia has transpired in literature and arts as an imaginary trope, a spatial and temporal frontier marking the beginnings of (modern) time and (anthropogenic) culture.

ARCADIA AS A SPATIAL AND TEMPORAL FRONTIER

Pausanias, the second-century AD Greek traveller and geographer, encountered the region of Arcadia, describing it as a land far from the sea and surrounded by mountains.[3] He recounted how in the "ancient world," *Arkades*, the inhabitants of Arcadia, were believed to be the descendants of Pelasgians, the oldest clan of ancient Greece. Pausanias stated that *Arkades* were thought to have sprouted from the ground, binding Arcadia to autochthony and the idea of an archaic time.

"Sweet is the voice of the goat, sweet the shepherd's flute," wrote Theocritus, the founder of bucolic poetry, in his third-century BC oeuvre *Idylls*, celebrating for the first time in Greek poetry the everyday life of pastoralists in Sicily. Yet, his poetry was not addressed to the shepherds and landscapes it described. As a city poet, his bucolic poetry offered an idealised representation of an imaginary pastoral world for a city audience. Twentieth-century art historian Erwin Panofsky accounts how this urban myth about rural origins was translocated to Arcadia two centuries later in Latin art and literature. During the Roman Republic, pastoral poetry took further shape as a critique and a counter-narrative to corruption and vice in the city of Rome. "Blissful is the man who cultivates his land, free from city's usurers and the power of city elites," wrote Horace (30 BC).[4] However, it was Virgil, in his *Bucolics* (or *Eclogues*, 37 BC), who translocated the pastoral ideal and reinvented Arcadia, initially known in the Roman world through the narrations of the Arcadian immigrant Polybius as a remote, rocky place with "meagre goats and frugal shepherds,"[5] as a utopia with an actual topos. Synthesising the image of Sicilian pastoral landscapes (from Theocritus), with the nostalgic fascination of a distant rural homeland (from Polybius), Virgil painted an alternative: Arcadia as "a realm sufficiently remote from everyday Roman life to defy any realistic interpretation, yet sufficiently saturated with visual concreteness to appeal directly to the inner experience of the reader."[6] He opened *Bucolics* with an image of city warfare,

where the Roman countryside and pastures were exhausted by the metropolis's exploitation.

Since then, Arcadia has emerged as a relational topos, an urban myth for an idealised "outer" land and a constitutive "urban other." This myth has been crafted upon the conflictual condition of the "familiar far" as a nostalgia for a place not yet reached but already experienced. In this myth, distance and groundedness matter. Locating rootedness and origins in this outside legitimises illusive rights for appropriating a shared pre-urban world. The myth of the outside lays the groundwork for possible extensions and occupations.

ARCADIA AS A COLONIAL FRONTIER

As the colonial mission approached "Port Royal" (Matavai Bay, Tahiti) in April 1769, Sir Joseph Banks noted the beauty and blissfulness of the coasts, the abundance of shade and fruits, and the welcoming kindness of the indigenous populations. As he wrote in his diary, "The image we saw was the truest picture that imagination can form of an *Arcadia* … of which *we were going to be the kings.*"[7] [Fig. 2] The first French colony in Canada was officially named *Acadie* in reference to the mythical Arcadia. The Western depiction of Arcadia, often nestled within the imagery of Paradise, re-emerged as one of the foundational imaginaries promoting the colonisation of the new world.[8] Emptying the land, declaring it as *terra nullius* (nobody's land), helped metaphorically annihilate the rights of its indigenous inhabitants. This colonial gaze entails a severe provocation and an immense power of extensionality, a way to conquer by idealising or to enclose by *arcadising*. We can claim that the myth of Arcadia is a myth about extensions. To extend (εκ-τείνω) means to create distance, to create ground (ἐκ-ταση). An extension is relational; it implies a centre from which to come and a vector towards which to go. In this way, the myth of the outside resides in the firm belief in the eternal possibility of extending territory, and entails the acts that will enable such extensions.

Fig. 2

F. 2   Tahiti Revisited, Maitavie Bay
in the Island of Otaheite, Tahiti.
William Hodges, 1776.

AN ACT OF PERIPHERALISATION

Looking at Titian's 1508 painting, the *Pastoral Concert*—one of the first bucolic Renaissance paintings—it occurs to me that the Arcadian myth entails an act of abstraction. A group of bourgeois musicians and their naked female company occupy the foreground, while a shepherd and his goats fade into the background. Merged with the trees, the shepherd has become part of the landscape, an abstract pastoral world, a symbolic scenography to stage higher concepts. [Fig. 3] The fabrication of the Arcadian myth entails an act of invisibilisation and, thus, dispossession. It removes the material complexity of an actual locus to serve a more idealised depiction: the water springs, the species of Mediterranean trees, and the mythic figure of Pan and the Nymphs. Elements of ecosystems and social formations have been used but reduced, emptied of their meaning and complexity, while others remain invisible. For instance, the Arcadian painting *Pan and Syrinx* (1615) depicts a city arising in the far distance, [Fig. 4] while in *Landscape with Satyr Family* (1507), an amplified depth highlights the distance, constructing the "urban far." Thick trunks, bushes, and pronounced naturalist elements suggest the urban outside. It is a peripheral landscape, cast as an extension and experienced as a dialectical opposition through an external narrative projected from afar. It occurs to me that the Arcadian myth itself involves a geographical act, *an act of peripheralisation*. The imaginary of Arcadia eventually extends to variegated landscapes beyond urban centres, nature reserves, rural areas, or tourist destinations, re-establishing each as "idyllic urban exteriors." What struggles, land claims, and dispossessions may lie hidden under such a frozen image of an urban outside?

PERIPHEREIA—ANATOMY OF A PERIPHERY

It is late evening on Easter Eve. We are stuck in a huge traffic jam on the outskirts of Athens. The lanes leading to the city are empty; cars are lined up in the other direction towards Peloponnese. Drivers and passengers patiently

Fig. 3

Fig. 4

F. 3   The Pastoral Concert, Giorgione
and/or his disciple Titian,
1509–1510. Merged with the trees,
the shepherd has become part
of the landscape.

F. 4   Pan pursuing Syrinx, Hendrick
van Balen the Elder and Follower
of Jan Brueghel the Elder, 1615.
A city arises in the distance,
constructing the "urban far."

Fig. 5

F. 5   On the highway to Peloponnese.
Entering the mountain is a bodily
experience.

wait with their car headlights turned on.
A massive urban exodus is underway. [Fig. 5]
Three hours' drive south of Athens, Arcadia
is part of the *periphereia* of Greece, the urban
outside. *Periphereia* and *eparchia* (province)
signify "the rest of Greece." They are perceived
as geographies of less privilege in a nation-state
with a long-standing policy of centralisation
in the capital. Through a prolonged rural exodus,
especially during the 1960s and 1970s, the
Athens metropolitan region grew into the Attica
basin, reaching around 4 million inhabitants, a
third of the country's population. In the process,
it stripped the periphery of people and resources.

Today, these peripheral landscapes pulsate
seasonally. Often seen as remnants of a dissolving
rural world returning to the wilderness, they
acquire the role of destinations for tourists and
urban dwellers as lands to escape to. They tell
a history of a *generalised process of peripheralisation*, which evolved alongside the growth of
the capital city of Athens. Nevertheless, Athens
maintains a persistent yet ambivalent link
to its periphery. The Athenian peasants that once
inhabited it, unable to respond to the speed
of modernisation and urbanisation, have cultivated an ambiguous relationship with their rural
origins, weaving complex and ambivalent links
between the exploding capital and its shrinking
periphery. These are the same people lining
up on the highway on Easter Eve. They are not
tourists but urban dwellers returning to their
villages and family homes. [Fig. 6]

CONDENSED HISTORY
The highway cuts through the various
strata of the urban fabric covering the Attica
basin. It follows the coastline, leaving behind
Athens' centre and its dense western suburbs.
Industrial plants, a port, an oil refinery, electricity poles, and logistics areas mark the edge
of the Thriasio Plain, the vast infrastructural
backbone of Athens. On this route, thick layers
of mythologies and histories unveil toponyms
and archaeological spots, places known from
antiquity. Elefsina reminds us of the Eleusinian
Mysteries, the most famous of the secret religious rites of ancient Greece and the agrarian

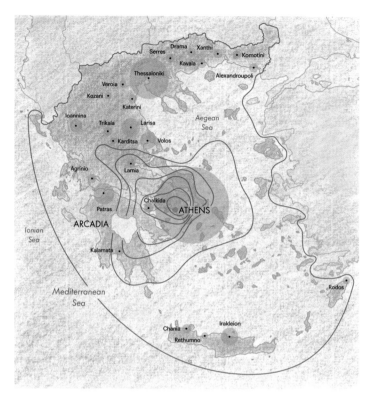

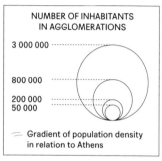

NUMBER OF INHABITANTS
IN AGGLOMERATIONS

3 000 000

800 000

200 000
50 000

Gradient of population density
in relation to Athens

WHERE IS THE PERIPHERY?:
THE ATHENS–ARCADIA DENSITY ENVELOPE
Fig. 6

myth of Persephone.[9] Kakia Skala recalls the travels of Theseus while Corinth, Argos, and Stymphalia herald the labours of Heracles. Loutro Elenis is the bath of the most beautiful woman of the ancient world. Thiva, Mycenae, Epidaurus, and Olympia will follow. As we drive down this highway through the Peloponnese, known as the origin of Greek antiquity and the foundational land of the modern nation-state, narrating these histories, we revive the imaginary of a deeper temporality that has been condensed. Yet, it is still present in contemporary landscapes.

As I perform this indigenous historiography,[10] I wonder: Whose histories do I narrate? Have they been projected onto the periphery and narrated by the urban centre? Certain histories appear more central, and some temporalities more glorified than others, such as the Greek antiquity and its national neoclassical revival.

However, others have remained untold and marginal, like the long Ottoman past or contemporary urban transformations.[11] In the periphery, I need to challenge my own "cityism" and ways of seeing. I am keenly aware they were shaped in the city centres and centralised institutions of Athens and Europe. Questioning established methodologies and ways of knowledge building is imperative when encountering and analysing these other histories that have remained untold.

F. 6   The Greek "periphery", known as periphereia or eparchia in Greek, encompasses all territories laying "outside" the few main urban centres of the country. The term reflects the geography of an over centralised nation-state and a generalised process of peripheralisation.

DEEP TIME

Industrial plants, transport networks, heroes, and myths cram together at the Isthmus of Corinth, the long bridge over the artificial canal that connects the Ionian and Aegean Seas. The bridge pronounces the exodus from Attica, and after the isthmus, the highway splits. Highway 8A follows a narrow piece of land along the northern coast, forming an almost continuous extension of the metropolitan region of Athens to Patras and its international port. Highway EO65 heads south through valleys and plateaus, bypassing the mountains through an infrastructural space punctuated by local urban centralities. The mountains of the Peloponnese appear as silhouettes in the distance, behind which lies Arcadia. They are part of a broader peripheral landscape: Greece, including the islands, is mountainous. [Fig. 7]

Geologically, Greece emerged during the Alpine orogeny phase, rising as the continuous landmass of Aegis (Αιγηίδα) from the Tethys Sea. This landmass then partially sank again, with its valleys becoming the Aegean Sea and its mountaintops forming the islands. [Fig. 8] The Peloponnese emerged as part of the Alpine orogenic fold and marked the southern climax of a mountain range. Colloquially known as the *backbone of Greece*, it runs centrally from the south to the north and continues with the Pindus Hellenides in northern Greece and southern Albania and the Balkan Dinarides, outlining a transnational space with historical, cultural, and ecological links.[12] With peaks reaching 1,500 to 2,000 metres above sea level, the Peloponnese holds in its pleats, valleys, plateaus, ridges, and cliffs the rich and variegated core where Arcadia is located. Towards the south, the mountainous fold descends towards the Aegean Sea, shaping the valley of Sparta and the olive plains of Kalamata.

THE SENSORIUM OF AN
        IMMATERIAL URBAN FABRIC

As we follow the road south, fragments of the urban fabric mingle with agricultural fields, summer houses, vegetable stands, and billboards for provincial events. Tuning on the car radio, a competition of radio stations from Athens and the periphery produces a strange polyphony of interruptions. This interference of sounds occurs because of the refraction of radio waves in the mountainous topography: local news, folk music, classic rock, church prayers, and sudden silences blend into one another. The capital's soundscape is renegotiated and slowly fades while the surrounding agglomeration of urban fabric dissolves. All sorts of trucks pass by transporting petrol, milk, yoghurt, honey, cheese, and livestock. This landscape is fragmented yet interconnected and does not emerge as an outer land of the capital city but as a field of flows. We are crossing a space of manifold relations and re-articulations as well as a field of tensions and multiple extensions.

As we exit the highway, curling up the winding road, a warning sign informs us that sheep and goats might be crossing. We have to slow down. The landscape is changing as we approach Mount Mainalo. This name is derived from the ancient myth of μαίνος, the mythological *divine mania, the orgy, and force* that is believed to have given birth to the wilderness. Mainalo was at the heart of ancient Arcadia and was considered the mythical home of Pan, the half-human, half-goat protector of the shepherds and a lover of the Nymphs.

THE URBAN FABRIC SURROUNDING
        MOUNT MAINALO

Today, Mount Mainalo forms the core massif of the Peloponnese. It is bypassed by major transport arteries, and its foothills are surrounded by local centralities, urban settlements, and infrastructure. The plateau of Tripolis offers fertile agricultural plains and is located at an altitude of 600 metres. It hosts a town of approximately 30,000 inhabitants and provides a key centrality of services, such as schools, hospitals, regional administration, a logistical hub, and an infrastructural corridor. Further south, it stretches towards the plateau of Megalopolis, the "big ancient polis," where the remnants of its ancient theatre, parliament, and stadium coexist alongside a huge open-pit coal mine. The lignite extracted from this coal

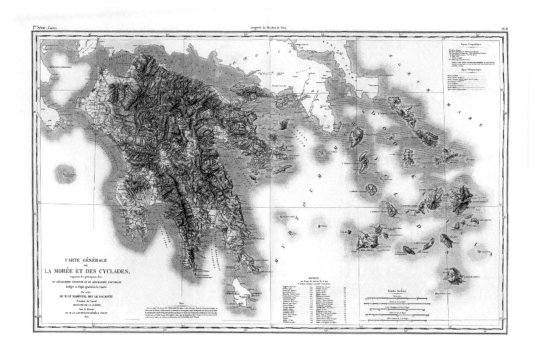

Fig. 7

Fig. 8

F. 7 The peripheral landscapes of
Greece are mountainous:
General Map of the Peloponnese
and the Cycladic Islands by
the French scientific-military
Morée Expedition, 1828–1832.

F. 8 The geological birth of a
mountainous territory. The
palaeogeography of Greece from
the Miocene to the present
(land is depicted in orange, sea
and lakes in blue).

THE URBAN FABRIC SURROUNDING
MOUNT MAINALO
Fig. 9

mine is burnt locally in Greece's second-biggest state-owned energy plant. In the south and west of Mount Mainalo, the Alfeios River collects water in Arcadia and flows to the Ionian Sea. The topography smoothens towards the extensive agricultural plains of Elia, where we find the archaeological site of Olympia. The Ionian coastal zone hosts beaches, resorts, local summer settlements, and ecological reserves. It also includes the growing provincial towns of Pyrgos and Amaliada and the cruise port of Katakolon, which is used mostly for daily tourists visiting Olympia. [Fig. 9–10]

"Entering" the mountain is a bodily experience. Bodies sway synchronised, tuning in to the tempo of this bigger geological form that now infolds, pleats, and cracks, making space for us to move through its interior. Mainalo is a dynamic karst landscape of water-soluble limestone that formed gorges, caves, springs, and still unexplored underground currents. We are not outside the mountain anymore, but in the midst of it, in the heart of an *ex*-centric territory. More than a mere "periphery of," it acquires its own complexity, temporality, and form. The road is now empty, and we drive in silence and darkness. The crowd has disappeared, spreading gradually into the villages located along the way. At times throughout the year, many of these villages are virtually empty. The smallest village has less than five permanent inhabitants, while the largest has as many as 600. But on a day like this, all the houses are full. We arrive at Stemnitsa, where a billboard at the entrance of the village reads: "Permanent inhabitants: 191. Summer months: 850."[13]

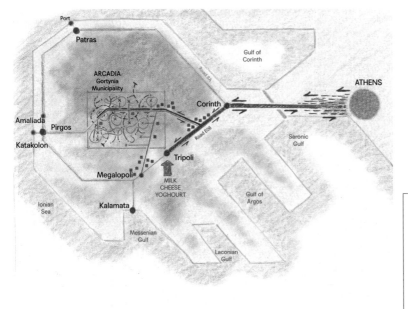

ARCADIA: A PULSATING
PERIPHERAL LANDSCAPE
Fig. 10

EMPTYING: A HISTORY
OF PERIPHERALISATION

"This mountain was once the centre. We were never peasants here. We were burghers [urban citizens, *astoí*]." Nena, a permanent inhabitant, proudly narrated to me at her guest house, "Belleiko" in Stemnitsa. Belleiko is her family name, referring to wealthy silversmiths, bell-makers, and later wealthy immigrants in the United States. It is now the name of her guest house, which was crafted by local stone builders who drew upon architectural influences from northern Greece and testified to a cosmopolitan culture and taste. Stemnitsa is one of the peri-forest villages located at the forest fringes of Mainalo, whose inhabitants have a history of craftsmanship and share a special relationship with the forest.

On the slopes of Mainalo, the colours start to change slightly to olive, brown, and deep green. The different colours indicate three distinct altitudinal zones and, thus, three diverse ecosystems. Olive groves grow up to 600 metres, hosting fields and agriculture. A forest of Greek firs (*Abies cephalonica*) starts at 1,000 metres and engulfs the alpine meadows. In between is an unfertile zone of steep slopes with kermes oaks and shrubs and a peri-forest zone of craft villages. Most of them flourished during the Ottoman Era, profiting from the proximity to different landscapes and resources, such as the woods, creeks, gorges, bushes, pastures, and the energy potential of the springs and mountain water streams. They developed mixed economies in which agriculture and livestock

F. 9   Mount Mainalo at the heart of Arcadia forms the core massif of the Peloponnese. It is bypassed by major transport arteries, and its foothills are surrounded by local centralities, urban settlements, and infrastructure.

F. 10   The relation of a capital-city and its periphery, depicted through movements and flows.

farming complemented proto-industrial activities, commerce, and proto-urban economies.

Unlike the lower plains, which could be tamed and exploited by the Ottoman Empire and where life was militarised and ruralised, the mountain space could retain partial autonomy. Rough, infertile, and challenging to access and discipline, the area was ruled by a taxation regime that allowed its inhabitants economic freedom "as long as they would pay taxes and would not revolt."[14] From the thirteenth century onwards, the population gradually agglomerated, and small villages emerged from a landscape of dispersed family-based transhumance settlements in the Arcadian region. By the end of the eighteenth century, these villages had prospered, and the population reached several thousands of inhabitants, each specialising in a different craft (silversmith in Stemnitsa, gunpowder in Dimitsana, leather-making in Zatouna, stonemasonry in Langadia, and so on). Some of these villages emerged as early commercial centres, concentrating local commerce and trading local products. These locales cultivated a Greek bourgeois that was distinguished in terms of their wealth, ownership, culture, and education. As the merchants and craftsmen extended their activity far beyond the montane region to the Balkans, Istanbul, and Central Europe, the villages developed a cosmopolitan culture with material and intellectual extensions. Coming in contact with advanced ideas of liberalism and nationalism cultivated in Western Europe at the time, they developed political ideals of national autonomy, freedom, and sovereignty. In 1907, the Arcadian craft villages of Mainalo (known as the region of Gortynia) had reached a population of approximately 50,000 inhabitants, holding an essential economic, political, and intellectual role for the Greek population of Ottoman Greece.

The dynamism that developed in the mountainous regions during this era would support some of the most important changes of the centuries to follow. These mountainous communities would offer the social and economic capital to support the war for national independence in the early nineteenth century. Through successive waves of migration, the same regions would later provide the human demand for the urbanisation of Athens (the new national capital), as well as for the growth of other international urban centres. They would also provide the labour for the industrialisation of the Peloponnese plains and, in a broader sense, support the industrialisation of Europe. The emptying of the mountainous landscapes occurred relationally with the same processes of accumulation, concentration, and centralisation that occurred elsewhere. Their histories illuminate that peripheralisation was not an inevitable process, but rather the result of a strategic policy with historical and political roots that can be traced back from the end of the Ottoman era to the present.

PERIPHERALISATION AS A PROJECT: A CAPITAL AND ITS PERIPHERY

The first round of peripheralisation started with the foundation of the independent Greek nation-state in 1821. The nation-building process required new geography and architecture to unify a heterogeneous territory and its multi-ethnic population under one common national narrative. It was materialised through the invention of a new capital city as a potent symbol of national unity, subordinating and homogenising all other regions as peripheries. Echoing the European intellectual elites calling for a revival of the ancient Greek world, this policy aimed at erasing traces of the "oriental" Ottoman past. The ancient cities of Athens, Sparta, and Megalopolis went from ruins and hamlets to revived, new centralities. However, the strong social and economic structures that developed in the mountain regions of the Peloponnese were not recognised. They were seen as insignificant and antagonistic traces of an Ottoman past and, therefore, potentially politically dangerous due to their partial autonomy and were pushed to the margins. In 1870, both the Peloponnese and the Greek mainland were renamed *eparchia* (province, sub-governance). In the following decades, the introduction of terms such as *peripheria* (periphery) and *upaithros* (open-air) went hand in hand with the systematic dissolution of local authorities. The laying of train and road networks at the national scale at the end of the nineteenth century largely bypassed the montane core of the Peloponnese, assigning it as an urban "void" as part of the spatial division of labour of an emerging urban geography oriented towards the new flourishing centres.

HISTORY OF MIGRATIONS

The formation of the Greek nation-state led to the first wave of migration of mountainous populations to the plains. The transfer of Ottoman agricultural land to the ownership of the Greek nation-state as "National Lands" (Εθνικές Γαίες) opened the pathway for the valorisation of the plains and the intensification of agricultural production.[15] Simultaneously, growing links with the markets of industrialising Central Europe linked the Peloponnese with new economic geographies through the ports of Patras and Kalamata. Particularly between 1863–1890, the monoculture of olives and raisins, nicknamed "black gold," flourished in the fertile plains of north-west Peloponnese, often replacing subsistence farming. The mountainous regions provided labour for the intensification of agriculture in the plains. The seasonal movements and social networks that developed between the mountains and the plains during this period still exist today.[16] At the end of the nineteenth century, a crisis in raisin commerce triggered another large wave of migration of the mountainous population towards the United States of America. By 1922, when the United States closed its borders, imposing restrictions upon migration, about 600,000 Greeks had migrated there.[17] They were colloquially referred to as "Brooklides" due to Brooklyn being their entry port in the United States, even though the migration routes extended further, in unexpected directions, even to Cuba.[18] These diasporic communities maintained strong ties with their roots in the Greek mainland and would often repatriate after a few decades. There are historical references to a strong "bridal trade" that developed between Chicago and the Arcadian villages at the time.[19]

As critical urban historian Gewrgios M. Sariyannis accounts, the "growth and empowerment" of Athens was accompanied by the "drastic economic and political weakening of the periphery."[20] In Greece in the early nineteenth century, the political strength and the revolutionary potential of the periphery was strongly pronounced in the aftermath of the war for national independence. On the one hand, the concentration of power in Athens allowed the local governing elites to gain political control over the country. On the other hand, it facilitated foreign interference by Central European forces (particularly Germany) in gaining political control over the young Greek state. The urbanisation of Athens further intensified after World War I, when Athens absorbed the massive wave of refugees from Asia Minor following the Greco-Turkish War of 1919–1922. The Nazi occupation during World War II and the fierce civil war that followed harmed the social and material fabric of the periphery. The guerrilla war turned the Arcadian mountains into a battlefield and devastated its rural sphere. These conditions, along with the consistent centralisation policy of the coming decades—the strategic industrialisation of only a few selected centres in the country[21] and a radical change in building regulations that further pushed the urbanisation of Athens[22]—triggered a massive exodus of rural populations, especially between the 1960s and 1970s. The waves of migration further weakened the social and economic dynamics of the mountain areas.

Yet, departures were coupled with returns, embedding the mountain regions into a new geography, where movements weave an extended and trans-local territorial web of social and economic relations. One of the traces of these links can be seen in the numerous epigraphs of donors present in all villages of the mountainous region: statues, fountains, public squares, restorations of buildings carrying names of Arcadians who left, telling the long history of migration. At the same time, in Athens, Europe, and North America, migrant community clubs were

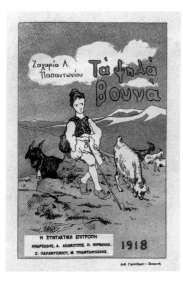

Fig. 11

Fig. 12

F.11 The famous children's novel by
Zacharias Papantoniou, the High
Mountains, published in 1918 as
a 3rd grade reading book, recounts
the experiences of a group of
children who spend their summer
vacation experiencing the forest
and the local communities in
the mountains–an example of how
the mountainous agricultural
hinterland of Greece became
gradually the subject of a "peculiar
internal orientalism" (Drinis).

F. 12 Family Giannis Giwnis at Leivadi,
Arcadia, Dekapedaugoustos (15th
August), ca. 1943. In contrast to the
simplifications occurring in various
representations, the photograph
reveals the richness and socio-
economic complexity present in
the communities of the periphery.

emerging as the counterpart of these memorials
and donations. It is apparent when standing in
the Arcadian villages that an absence here meant
a presence there. This highlights a spatial duality
of persisting social and economic relationships
challenging the notional and geographic binaries
of the city and village, centre and periphery,
bridging geographical distances, and generating
unexpected relations and links.

"ARCADISATIONS"
      The richness and complexity of this
extended mountainous geography remained
hidden under a narrative progressively building
up in capital cities and European centres,
through art and literature, often in synergy
with the developing epistemes, natural sciences,
archaeology, and historiography.[23] In this narrative, the mountainous Greek periphery is
represented, on the one hand, as an idealised
outer land, where antiquities are unearthed
in the purity of the rural world as evidence
of a shared European history. On the other
hand, they are remnants of the Ottoman past,
a decaying, recessed sphere that needs to
modernise and meet the European spirit and
contemporary standards. Eli Clare explains the
contradiction entailed in this Western perspective. What is "natural" is seen simultaneously
as an ideal and as an underdeveloped "other,"
trapping bodies and places in this oxymoron.[24]
Gradually, the mountainous agricultural hinterland of Greece became the subject of a "peculiar
internal orientalism," as Drinis explains,[25]
"a virgin land to venture, explore, and conquer
in quest of the origins of Greek and Western
culture."[26] Representations by urban populations
depicted an exotic, underdeveloped land
destined for leisure and escape and its inhabitants as the "noble savages" of the European
continent.[27] These narratives radically simplified
these landscapes while idealising and homogenising their diverse multi-ethnic populations.
[Fig. 11–12] They basically employed these
myths for strategic political means and linked
them to territorial claims for the young Greek
nation. And perhaps more generally, for the
whole Western world.

In the 1920s, tourism had already appeared as a bright prospect for the mountainous regions. In the 1950s, the montane landscape's social, economic, and productive structures gradually dissolved. In their place came a collective reinvention of the region as an ideal vacation destination for urban dwellers looking to retreat from modern life, experience nature, or gain insight into folklore and religion. In the 1990s, Arcadia was again rediscovered as a winter landscape and an alternative destination for holidays, especially the craft villages of Dimitsana, Stemnitsa, Langadia, and Vitina, which turned into new tourist centralities easily accessible from Athens. It was established as a contemporary land of urban escapism, a venture into the "wilderness and a city-fallback." In the following decades, the entanglement of Greece in global politics, economies, and markets would decompose the mountainous region's social and economic coherence, especially during the Greek debt crisis. In the aftermath of the financial crisis of 2007–2008, the Greek state faced a debt crisis. "The Crisis," as it was colloquially known, was aggravated by a series of sudden reforms and austerity measures that led to impoverishment and the loss of income and property, which created a humanitarian emergency. Overall, the Greek economy suffered the longest recession of any advanced mixed economy to date.[28] As a result, the Greek political system was upended, social exclusion increased, and hundreds of thousands of well-educated people left the country. This crisis pushed peripheralisation to new dimensions.

The urban gaze, which has idealised Arcadia and its landscape, is the same gaze that now empties it. It selectively sees the region as an untouched landscape, offering archaeological findings and folklore figures of villagers and shepherds while "invisibilising" the productive structures, conflicts, dispossessions, and less-dominant worldviews. Today, this image of Arcadia remains frozen, perceived as a stagnant rural periphery where narratives of emptiness persist. Here, peripheralisation intertwines with "arcadisation" as an act of imaginative blindness and a consequential act of reinvention in subordination.

ON PERIPHERALISATION

Periphery, *peripheria,* etymologically derives from the Greek verb *peri–pherw* (περι-φέρω), literally meaning "to carry around," and describes a relation that unfolds around a centre. The word originated in the mathematics of antiquity, where it meant the perimeter of a circle. Later, it appeared in physics as the "turning spin."[29] In twentieth-century geography and sociology, it denoted "a radius, the fringe, or the situating at the fringe."[30] Along these lines of thought, peripherality is expressed as a distance from a centre—of power, accessibility, and economics. It establishes a relational position in an overarching system, a spatial, economic, or governmental regime. More than an absolute location, it relationally determines the outer sphere of something, which, in turn, indicates a spatial and temporal inequality or unevenness. *Peripherw, peripheromai* (περιφέρομαι) also means to roam around without a purpose, without a goal. The word hints at a condition of dependency, a process of losing narrative coherence; it describes a subject designed to gravitate around the core. Periphery is more than a place; it is an action, *to peripheralise,* and a process, *peripheralisation.*[31]

PERIPHERALISATION, A MULTIDIMENSIONAL AND MULTISCALAR PROCESS

While the process of peripheralisation has found only limited attention so far, the term periphery has been used widely within the disciplines of economy, geography, sociology, urban studies, and political science. Yet, a comparative literature review by Kühn and Bernt reveals that it lacks a universal or comprehensive definition.[32] Through the multiplicity and shared strings of this literature, one element becomes clear: It is a multidimensional phenomenon that unfolds in space and time and can only be explained relationally, with reference to the interaction of different socio-spatial dimensions (economic, social, and political) and through different scales (regional, national, and transnational).[33] In the following section,

I outline a brief literature review, which by no means aims to be conclusive but offers a broad overview for this chapter.

In economics and historical geography, the work on peripheries refers to different scales. In the 1960s, both dependency theory and world-systems theory analysed the structural position of "third-world" economies. Dependency theorists like Oswaldo Sunkel, Samir Amin, and André Gunder Frank critically interrogated the systematic relations of dominance and dependence between centres and peripheries. They conceptualised the shift from colonial to imperialist-industrial dependency. Immanuel Wallerstein's theory on the capitalist world system divided the planet into three zones—the core, the semi-periphery, and the periphery.[34] The peripheral zone included countries that heavily relied upon exports of raw materials and imports of advanced machinery and technologies from the developed core countries. It was through the application of this theory in a European context that the term peripheralisation was first introduced.[35]

Nitz used the term *primary peripheralisation* in reference to the redistribution of labour and raw materials from national to international economic systems. He also coined *descending peripheralisation* to refer to how this process diminishes the influence and well-being of former core regions.[36] This definition shifts the focus from a static conceptualisation of the periphery as a geographical location to the analysis of a dynamic and contradictory economic, political, and social process. Increasing socio-spatial inequalities have led to a revival of the term peripheralisation in recent urban and regional research, particularly for the analysis of declining industrial regions in Europe and North America and sparsely populated areas in eastern and southern Europe.[37]

Radical geography developed another strand of the analysis of spatial differentiation and fragmentation. Doreen Massey interrogated the capitalist economy's fundamental tendency to produce a spatial division of labour marked by stark social inequalities between rich and poor regions.[38] Neil Smith's ground-breaking work *Uneven Development: Nature, Capital and the Production of Space*[39] conceptualised the production of spatial and temporal unevenness as a "systemic process of economic and social development, endemic to capitalism." This literature was developed further by Costis Hadjimichalis,[40] who provided important insights into the capitalist entanglement with the uneven production of trans-scalar geographies and transnational spaces.

THE PERIPHERAL TURN IN URBAN STUDIES

In recent years, Ren has observed a "peripheral turn" in urban studies, which is characterised by a deliberate spatial, social, political, and analytical shift away from the centre.[41] The relevance of the periphery has become integral to urbanisation as scholars shift their analytical lens from privileged urban centres to suburbs, small towns, sprawling hinterlands, and the global South more generally. It is especially pertinent in Latin America, where a rich scholarship in "writing urban history from the margins" has been deployed for a long time.[42] Peruvian sociologists Aníbal Quijano and John Friedmann brought forward various key concepts such as dependent urbanisation, informality, and marginality.[43] In 2017, anthropologist Teresa Caldeira introduced the concept of *peripheral urbanisation* to investigate the logics of urban production that differ from those found in the global North. Caldeira explores auto-construction processes, seeking an emancipatory potential for urban processes to occur away from the centres of control and power. She argues that "peripheral urbanisation does not simply refer to a spatial location in the city—its margins—but rather to a way of producing space that can be anywhere …"[44] What makes this process peripheral is not its physical location but rather the crucial role of residents in the production of space and how as a mode of urbanisation, it unfolds transversally in relation to official logic and amidst political contestations.[45] According to James Holston, peripheral urbanisation reveals insurgent portraits of citizenship in an era of global urban peripheries.[46] "Periphery is everywhere," AbdouMaliq Simone contends, as he brings forward the periphery as a "platform" of "anticipatory urban politics" and its subversive ways of spatial production, movements, bodies, and spaces.[47]

THE QUESTION OF PERIPHERALISATION WITHIN EXTENDED URBANISATION

How do peripheries form? And how does urbanisation generate processes of peripheralisation? These questions of the periphery reappear with new relevancy in the analytical light of extended urbanisation. Seeing peripheralisation through the urban lens entails an immense analytical potential to bridge a fragmented discourse and open new perspectives on the very question of the periphery and of the urban more generally.

On the one hand, literature on peripheralisation has emerged in various fields, even if the term has been used in a somewhat fragmented and unsystematic manner, describing the "symptoms" of broader processes without fully deploying its important analytical potential. Some examples include the discourse on shrinking cities in Germany,[48] the revival of the terms peripheralisation and marginalisation in the discussion on the current increase in sociospatial inequalities in Europe,[49] the analysis of the integration of Balkan countries as new members of the European Union and their new role as economic peripheries,[50] discussions on energy peripheralisation[51] and topics of environmental inequality and the formation of wastelands.[52]

On the other hand, several efforts have started to analyse processes of peripheralisation through the lens of urbanisation. Some have remained within metropolitan regions or at the fringes of the urban fabric,[53] while others have addressed heterogeneous territories engaging with the concept of extended urbanisation. In 2021, in the special issue *Engaging the Urban from the Periphery,* Gururani, Kennedy, and Sood invoked the concept of the periphery to attend to India's diverse forms of extended urbanisation that unfold not only on the edges of metropolitan regions but also in smaller towns and settlements enmeshed with agrarian and rural rhythms.[54] They pointed to crucial land and governance contestations and the need for methodological and theoretical openings to explore such territories. The recent publications *Beyond the Megacity*[55] by Lukas and Reis and *After Suburbia*[56] by Keil and Wu call for a reconceptualisation of the extant concepts of peripheral urbanisation and the suburban, respectively, in relation to the theoretical openings of planetary and extended urbanisation. These approaches have included non-city territories where the urban fabric extends in various forms: small towns, sprawling and intensifying agricultural regions, and extractive and operationalised hinterlands. Yet, the question remains: have we gone as far as we could?

The concept of peripheralisation under the light of extended urbanisation allows us much more than going beyond metropolitan edges to explore other territories of urban growth. It enables approaching territories that have so far escaped urban imaginaries and analyses but have been subsumed within the processes of peripheralisation: the mountain peaks of the Swiss Alps,[57] the transnational hinterlands of Singapore,[58] the landscapes of Arcadia in Greece,[59] and subsequently, less accessible and sparsely populated areas, depopulating mountainous and archipelagic regions, emptying forests, and diminishing seas (see Nancy Couling's chapter in this volume).

Understanding peripheralisation as a relational process of urbanisation entails immense potential. It enables the exploration of the production of space beyond the growth of the urban fabric and the operationalisation of landscapes within cycles of shrinking and degradation, and the drainage of social, economic, and cultural resources. Such moves open new fields and crucial questions: Who are the actors, and what places are involved? To what extent can we view peripheralisation as not just an economic or social process but as an ecological one involving human and non-human interactions? And how does peripheralisation open new

Fig. 13

F. 13   Arcadian villages.

alternative possibilities for processes of appropriation, interaction, and networking—can it become a socioecological project in itself? Exploring peripheralisation as a process of extended urbanisation allows the investigation of multiple scales and dimensions through a consistent relational lens. Secondly, it offers links between dissimilar fabrics that share similar experiences and relates to other urbanisation processes unfolding at the planetary scale. Lastly, and most importantly, it opens new imaginaries and a new sensorium for seeing and including the full potential and socioecological role of long-marginalised places while seeking subversive modalities and emancipatory potential.

"TO GOVERN FROM AFAR"— STATE SPACE AND NEW SCALES OF PERIPHERALITY

Vytina, November 2021. The Forestry Department of Mount Mainalo is in turmoil today. It is hosted within the former Forestry School, an impressive neoclassical building located in one of the villages at the fringes of the fir forest. "Agriculture and Forestry is the future of this country," wrote Panyotis Triantafyllidis in 1862, donating his fortune to form agricultural schools in the newly founded Greek nation-state. Today, the school stands empty, closed since the 1980s. The Triadafyllidis Fund was trimmed during the crisis, while most local youths have left for better prospects in Greek cities or abroad. The department is underequipped, its duties radically reduced during the last years of the crisis or transferred to urban services (i.e., fire protection) or left to private responsibility (i.e., wood cutting). The state has progressively abandoned its obligation to the forest. This was especially accentuated during the global pandemic. During this period, the legal framework of forest protection was radically weakened by deregulation, which "liberated" once-protected lands and invited private actors to invest under the pretext of green energy and strategic environmental importance.

The head forester is especially confused today. Her department has just been transferred

Fig. 14

F. 14   The Mount Mainalo forest:
        commons, community pastures
        and peaks burnt in forest fires
        where a wind park is now planned.

from the Ministry of Agriculture and Food
to the new Ministry of Environment and Energy.
The decision is contradictory, as Mainalo is
considered one of Greece's oldest "inhabited,
harvested" forests.[60] The oral testimonies
I collected describe a "productive, edible"
forest, offering water, grazing lands, and
harvests of many kinds while still functioning
as a commons. "Now, they say that the mountain
is uninhabited for tourists and windmills to
stroll around," and she points at a pile of papers
on her desk. "Lately, there have been dozens
of applications for energy operations and green
investments in the forest. Water dams, wind
turbines, photovoltaics. The scale is industrial.
The location is random. There is no state planning, no environmental study, and no industrial
zoning. Companies can choose any public land
and apply for and receive EU funding for the
energy transition. For wind turbines, they prefer
the burnt parts of the forest. They are cheaper,
and they face less resistance," she says as she
points to a peak burnt in 2006. "Those peaks
are naked, since. Such fir forests cannot be
restored. They were created in much cooler
climatic eras. Now it's over. The mountain was
not uninhabited. It was emptied." I remember
leaving Mainalo with a bad feeling. The forest,
emptied of service structures, state care, and
legal protection, was now under extreme pressure. [Fig. 14]

"HOLLOWING OUT"—
THE KALLIKRATIS PLAN
AND THE STREAMLINING
OF THE STATE
            In May 2010, at the peak
of the Greek debt crisis and as the country
signed the first Memoranda of Understanding
with the International Monetary Fund (IMF)
and its European Partners, the PASOK
government under prime minister George
Papandreou voted for a major administrative
reform named the Kallikratis Plan—New
Architecture of Self-administration and
Decentralised Administration.[61] This was one
of the most far-reaching administrative reforms
in the history of the modern Greek state.[62]

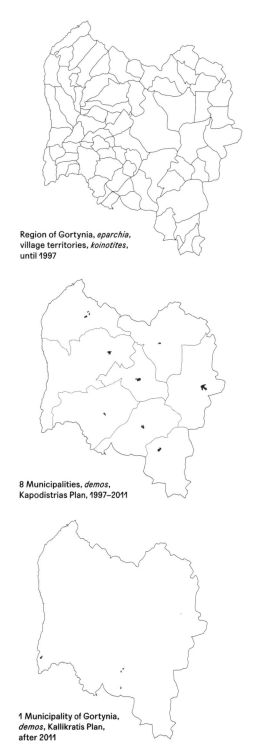

Region of Gortynia, *eparchia*,
village territories, *koinotites*,
until 1997

8 Municipalities, *demos*,
Kapodistrias Plan, 1997–2011

1 Municipality of Gortynia,
demos, Kallikratis Plan,
after 2011

MERGING MUNICIPALITIES IN ARCADIA
Fig. 15

The government presented it as a necessary remedy to the hypertrophic, over-centralised Greek nation-state and its costly public sector. It included the fusion of public services and the abolition of public schools and hospitals, particularly affecting peripheral regions. In the following years, the term *Kallikratis* became synonymous with an encompassing state policy of restructuring and peripheralisation.

Above all, the reform had massive local and governmental consequences. It radically interfered with the complexity of the extant territorial structure, merging and enlarging local administrative units. The previous structure was composed of a nested system of *koinotites* (communes) and *demos* (municipalities) as the first and second levels of governance, organised in the larger self-governed units of prefectures and provinces that had crystalised during several historical and political phases. Complex and bureaucratic, yet thick in meaning and memory, this structure provided a small-scale territorial grain, expressing nuanced differences, specificities, origins, conflicts, and polarities. The severe rural exodus of the 1970s had already challenged the scale and meaning of this system. At the same time, the entry of Greece into the EU in 1981 signalled an attempt to rationalise and align with the administrative structures of the other member states. This policy was reflected in the first administrative reform, the Kapodistrias Plan, in 1997. Under the dramatic debt crisis of 2008 and the massive political pressure of an alleged emergency situation, the Kallikratis Plan introduced more radical changes to the territorial structure and governance, drastically simplifying the previously complex yet precise territorial system.[63] Arcadia's core is overseen by the new megamunicipality of Gortynia, which includes a heterogeneous territory of 1,190 km², spanning an altitude of 160 to 2,000 metres. [Fig. 15] Following austerity politics, local services such as schools, post offices, healthcare facilities, and local authorities have been dramatically reduced and concentrated in a few new local centralities.[64] In contrast, other vital services, such as animal health care and agricultural departments, have been moved to Tripolis.

Large parts of the mountain region, deprived of their autonomy, increasingly depend on connections to these centralities and rely on a web of movements for survival. Cars, trucks, and buses enable interconnections and access to services, reflecting the peripheralisation of the region at a local scale. The mobility bans between regions during the two years of the global pandemic and the recent boost in fuel prices due to global instability have raised significant concerns about accessibility to services for the inhabitants of Arcadia.

The Kallikratis Plan also entailed a broader process of peripheralisation at the national level. Under the narrative and policy of correcting the hyper-trophic public sector, the plan foresaw a reduction in the state to play only a mediating role between global and local levels of governance. It abolished the self-governed prefectures and provinces and created new regions with "decentralised administrations." In synergy with other reforms, the state as a governmental entity was hollowed out and had its responsibilities for welfare and social services reduced.[65] In this sense, the Kallikratis Plan did not, as it announced, reduce centralisation in favour of the self-governance of the regions. Instead, it constructed a territorial and governmental architecture that facilitates the rearticulation of regions within broader scales of governance. Dimitropoulos explains that this policy aligns with a globally emerging governance model where nation-states participate in international formations, delegating a large part of their powers concerning policymaking, regulation, and planning to levels beyond the state.[66] In short, the reforms install an ever-growing global interventionism at the local level and a policy that attempts to build territories that can be governed from afar.

F. 15   After the Kallikratis Plan (2011), Arcadia's core is overseen by the new mega-municipality of Gortynia, which includes a heterogeneous territory of 1.190 square kilometres, spanning an altitude of 160 to 2000 metres.

Mainalo is full of empty schools,[67] indicating the successive waves of elimination of public services in the mountainous region. The slimming of public services and the radical changes in local governance occurred as part of a broader policy of austerity. This policy eventually opened up "unused" land for private investments of global capital, revealing a new role for the state as a facilitator of commodification, often by simply retracting and abandoning and enabling de-commoning and land grabbing through new regulations. Since 2011, all high schools in Gortynia, located at the heart of Mainalo, have been merged into one. A mother of two told me in Stemnitsa: "Vytina, where the high-school students were moved to, is located on the other side of the mountain. In between so many gorges, dales, and turns. Can you imagine the conditions during winter, with snow and ice? If you measure the distance on a map with a straight line, Vytina doesn't seem so far, just 30 kilometres away, but this is where topography needs to be considered. Kallikratis turned our mountain flat."

"FLATTENING"— A STATE STRATEGY FOR MOUNTAINOUS REGIONS.

The new emerging scales of governance are accompanied by simplification and abstraction. Narratives and representations of "flatness" are used as instruments for the production of space. In the administrative definition of Kallikratis, the new municipality of Gortynia is declared rural (*agrotikos demos*) and flat (*pedinos demos*), despite its intrinsic heterogeneity and complexity. [Fig. 16–17] Almost 90% of the Greek territory, predominantly mountain areas and islands, are lumped together in the category "flat," which represents a profound distortion of the topographic image of the country.[68] According to the previous classification under the 1997 Kapodistrias Plan, 60% of Greek municipalities were declared mountainous or semi-mountainous. The problems with the new classification are obvious when considering that the term "mountain areas" (*ορεινότητα)* carries not only specific historical and social meanings but also entails specific economies and challenges that

KAPODISTRIAS PLAN
1997–2011

KAPODISTRIAS PLAN 1997–2011

KALLIKRATIS PLAN 2011

KALLIKRATIS PLAN 2011

■ Mountain municipality
■ Flat municipality

■ Primary
■ Secondary
■ Tertiary

MUNICIPAL CLASSIFICATION ACCORDING
TO TOPOGRAPHY
Fig. 16

MUNICIPAL EMPLOYMENT ACCORDING
TO ECONOMIC SECTOR
Fig. 17

require appropriate territorial strategies. Flattening, as an administrative act, erases the complexity and allows the implementation of standardised territorial strategies designed for other territories. It saves state expenses and reduces the required state support. It affects everyday life, the distribution of resources, and public services. "Sooner or later, we will need to move away for the kids to make it to school," a shepherd from Langadia recounted. It triggers dispossessions, relocations, and concentrations, eventually generating an actual geography of flatness.

"Your land is too rocky, too thorny. Pastures have to be flat and grassy," said the EU techno-crats to the Arcadian shepherds, disqualifying traditional grazing slopes and invisibilising their activities, according to oral testimony from official authorities that I collected. "The Greek veterinar-ians presented anatomic drawings of the saliva and peptic system of the goat, yet technocrats were still not convinced." The land is now characterised as abandoned, re-wildered, and unused. Flatness as an image denotes, more broadly, the progressive dissolution of inherited coherences of the social fabric and productive structures. It constitutes an act of violent simplification of a complex, vulner-able territory, its entanglement with multiscalar geographies, the deletion of rich local narratives, and the preparation of an empty ground available to be rewritten with new, more relevant stories. Flattening is, in this sense, an act of producing *terra nullius*.

"CHARTING"—RATIONALIZING THE LAND

In the *Kafeneio* of Kapelitsa, at the west foot of Mainalo, old Greek men and immi-grant workers from Albania are sitting around a table. They are talking about some of their co-villagers who moved to Athens a few years ago to find brides and are now renting their family fields to the remaining locals. Sophia, who lived half of her life in Bulgaria, and is now the wife of the owner of this *Kafeneio*, is serving coffee. Surprised and sceptical about my presence, the regulars asked me to submit their complaints to the government. They think I am a journalist

or a public servant. A few days ago, another Athenian from the ministry appeared here, inves-tigating the borders of their olive groves. He showed several satellite images and asked for plot lines and proofs of land ownership.

During my visit in 2019, agricultural land was still uncharted here. Small and dispersed micro-properties with olive trees covered exten-sive landscapes at the lower foot of Mainalo. [Fig. 18] The plot boundaries in this fragmented land circumscribe family trees and dowries and tell migration histories. [Fig. 19] Proofs of ownership are difficult to provide and often contested: hand-written wills, wedding contracts, and Ottoman documents. This structure of agricultural land dates back to the historical context of land acquisition under Ottoman Rule,[69] a national strategy of undefined land ownership to avoid big private concentrations (with a few exceptions) coupled with a favouring of micro-appropriations, especially prominent in the Peloponnese. By 1892, the German traveller Alfred Philipson noted that "here, almost everyone holds a small piece of land, there is no aristocracy, neither proletariat."[70] Instead, there is still today a characteristic Greek peasant family household caring for its own reproduc-tion, performing practices that often transcend capitalist, profit-orientated logic and structures.[71] The profound socio-political extensions of these conditions were critically documented in 1855 by the Greek politician Pavlos Kalligas in the portrait of a state and of a whole society— justice and penalty, taxation and governance, corruption, power and class, the agricultural question—unfolding out of this specific and conflictual relation to land.[72]

F. 16   The Kallikratis Plan has classified only 9,23% of the 325 country's municipalities as "mountainous."

F. 17   The Kallikratis Plan abstracts and simplifies regional complexities, as the previous image of a multi-occupational mosaic is replaced by a territory with few purely agricul-tural areas and smaller agricultural municipalities are merged with urban centralities.

Fig. 18

This is actually the third effort to establish an agricultural cadastre in the area. The official charting of lands has been a major imperative for Greece during the years of the crisis and an absolute priority of governmental policies. Per an article in the *New York Times* in May 2013, uncharted land and unresolved land claims have been a big obstacle to the "recovery" of the Greek economy. The extensive charting operation, which is still ongoing, includes the formation of an "agricultural land cadaster" and traces all micro-ownership in parallel with the formation of "forest cartas," which track state and privately owned land with traces of re-forestation after agricultural abandonment. The charting operation is expected to radically change the status quo of land ownership in Greece.

"We had no maps here. No cadastre," one of the old men tells me in the *Kafeneio* of Kapelitsa. "We did not need to measure the dimensions of the fields. We knew that from this root to this root, it belonged to my grandfather. From this stream to that big tree, it belonged to somebody else." His words exhume a different knowledge of the land: social layers, older metric perceptions, counting without plots and orientating without borders. As he sketches a diagram of local fields on paper, I understand that even with no map, the charting of this land still exists in the community, in the informal agreements between those who harvest and care for it. *Uncharted land*—chaotic at first glance and as scattered and dispersed as its community. One person is the owner, whereas another is the one who tends to it. The land here is not flat, measured, or clearly allotted. Accessible only through unpaved pathways, it remains unpredictable and slow. *Irrational land*—its absurdity does not allow someone who comes from afar to understand, to manage, to buy, and to sell it. In a strange way, this "irrationality" seems to protect it. This land remains undefined and has resisted being modernised, valorised, and commercialised.

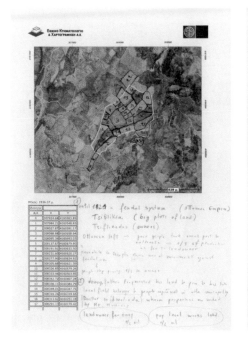 

Fig. 19

"GRABBING"—SILENT LAND EXPROPRIATIONS FOR ENERGY TRANSITION

In October 2021, I returned to Kapelitsa. An uncontrollable fire during the summer devoured the olive groves, destroying their *kapeli* (local hill with ideal conditions for qualitative olive cultivation). The regulars at *Kafeneion* explain that a Spanish company attempted to buy the whole area of burnt land and create a photovoltaic park. Taking advantage of the disappointment of the villagers, they offer five times its value, but the operation remains unsure, delayed by the absence of a land register and the social complexity of land ownership. Meanwhile, in the forestry department, the applications for investments pile up as private companies gain interest in the installation of green energy plants in the forest and on public land that is amply available and offered to them for free.

In his book *Debt Crisis and Land Grabbing*, Costis Hadjimichalis points out that the Greek debt crisis coincides with increased international interest in land accumulation and land-revenue monopolies. Mainalo is no exception. Under the narrative of green development and the pretext of climate emergency, an unprecedented operation of land grabbing, enclosure, and privatisation is currently underway in the majority of Greek mountains and islands, including forests and protected areas. What is at stake is the abundant land owned and managed by the state covering most peripheral landscapes in Greece, which is rooted in the specific historical context of the land distribution of the nineteenth century. Today this land covers almost 60% of the surface of the country. [Fig. 20] State properties had already been brutally targeted in the last decade when the Greek debt crisis was used to unleash massive privatisations of state-owned resources, land,

F.18   Olive farming in Arcadia is still based on family labour.

F. 19   Land Cadaster: The ongoing formation of an agricultural land cadaster has been a major imperative for Greece during the years of the crisis.

Public land
60%

Micro property
private and church
40%

LAND-GRABBING:
THE ABUNDANT STATE PROPERTY AT STAKE
Fig. 20

and infrastructure.[73] Today, the question of land unexpectedly intertwines with energy transition operations, requiring extensive surfaces and staged now in peripheral landscapes, which are called to acquire roles of green energy providers. Meanwhile, the electricity bill for Greek households has been rising monthly: green energy costs more, and local consumers eventually pay for its infrastructure. Is this energy truly for us, or did we just become the expensive green battery for Europe? In Arcadia, regional governance is being gradually dissolved. We experience a state space of low resolution, low governance, and low cost, a deregulated space where capital operations can now proceed less controlled and obtruded. In this space, however, moments of self-regulation and actions of resistance can also occur.

ASTOCHORIKOS: AN EXTENDED CITIZENSHIP

Mount Mainalo, 2 February 2016. Music is playing on the radio, and potatoes, tomatoes, and onions dangle as a truck follows the mountain road through snow and fog. Kostas, a travelling grocer, departs every Wednesday from Tripolis: the distances are long and services scarce. "People will complain if I don't go. Sometimes they ask for favours, bring some batteries for a watch, or

fix the plumbing. They are old, you see." Kostas is a vendor on wheels and not the only one. There is a fisherman, a hairdresser, some bakers, a doctor, and a travelling priest. Vendors on wheels bind the Arcadian villages together. They replace waning services and connect to local towns. Movements emerge as an everyday practice that keeps a dispersed social fabric together. A technique for survival, especially at this time of the year, indicates that everyday mountain life depends on the extension to other localities.

Athens, 15 August, every year. The capital is hot and deserted. Bars are closed, streets are silent, and there is an abundance of free parking spots in the city centre. This is the best season for burglars of any kind. The inhabitants are all on mountains and islands, their villages of origin. The Athenian vacuum of *Dekapenaugustos* is a story of temporary flight. People will return only at the end of the summer season in early September. The absence of people indicates a presence elsewhere. Athens and its periphery form an interesting complementarity. When the one is full, the other is empty; when the one is marked by presence, the other is marked by absence. The same population inhabits both places and experiences both conditions. Rather than separate, the capital and the villages, the centre and the periphery are interwoven, extending deeply into each other in a manner that a map or a geographical model could not predict. They indicate a dual appearance, a double belonging enabled by a movement, a seasonal rituality of returns, and a periodic manner of inhabitation.[74]

Kapelitsa, 11 November 2016. It is already late. We are descending from Mainalo in complete darkness when, in the middle of nowhere, a luminous, vibrant space pops up. People are waiting in queues in front of piles of bags. A loud machinic sound and an acidic smell reveal the conundrum: We have arrived at an olive mill, and the luminous celebration marks the peak of the harvest season. Families from the neighbouring villages and towns, accompanied by relatives, friends, and their kids, bring the freshly picked varieties of Olympia or Koroneiki olives to the mill. It is an action required to achieve the extra-virgin type of olive oil. In the middle of the night, this generic logistic space is turned into the liveliest public space in the community. The olive harvest is a season of return, and harvesting is a family business. Such olive trees cover most of the semi-mountainous landscapes of Greece. They massively sprouted in the 1980s and 1990s, replacing subsistence cultivations rendered residual after the rural exodus. Yet, inherited land was reallotted multiple times over the generations and has been reconfigured to serve a seasonal agricultural occupation. Fragmented and dispersed like the community that harvests it, it allows city dwellers to return seasonally, remaining active in the rural sphere. Metallic buckets of extra-virgin olive oil travel to Tripolis, Athens, Zurich, and its namesake, Arcadia, in New York. This fragmented "irrational land" seems not so irrational at this time of the year. Mirroring the demographic specificity of the periphery, it enables seasonal returns and extended productive links to agricultural production. People can return and will return to inhabit, cultivate, and harvest as long as this land still belongs to them.

Contrary to what official demographics indicate, Arcadia does not remain static and depopulated throughout the year. It experiences seasonal tides that occupy and transform it instantly. In a seemingly depopulated region,

Fig. 21

F. 20   Under the narrative of green development and the pretext of climate emergency, an unprecedented operation of land grabbing, enclosure, and privatisation is currently underway in Greece.

F. 21   Sunivenstents: photovoltaic plants emerging in the olivegroves.

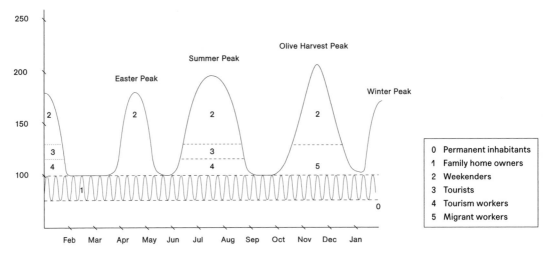

TIDAL INHABITATION
Fig. 22

moments of urbanity emerge, and various temporalities appear. These visitors are not tourists. They are Athenians, former immigrants, olive tree and family homeowners, seasonal migrants or regional workers who return in different rhythms to engage in social and political life. They maintain houses and productive land, participate, care, and belong as they tidally reinhabit the periphery. [Fig. 22–23]

A SHARED EXTENDED SPACE

Stathis Damianakos, a prominent Marxist sociologist and researcher of agriculture life

F. 22   Arcadia's seasonal tides of inhabitation, while in the background, the permanent population continues to decline.

F. 23   The world interacts with Arcadia which interacts with the world. Much more than a depopulating peripheral land, Arcadia emerges as part of a shared collective ground which stretches across an extended geography of the urban/ rural sphere. It is in these extensions that a form of fluid commons emerges, and it is from the right to this extended geography that the right *to an extended citizenship* unearths.

in Greece, wrote, "We are not simply dealing with a situation of 'dual' or 'secondary' residence reserved for holidays and weekend leisure. The uncertainty of allocating [to the urban or rural sphere] this fluid part of the population comes from the real equivalence that remains between two environments of social and spatial belonging that involve all the social living conditions of individuals: economic activities, political relations, sociocultural identities."[75] Analysing the demographical statistics of three mountain villages in Pindos (northern Greece) in the 1980s, he argues against the image of a static depopulating mountainous sphere painted by official demographic statistics. He asserts that the villages are inhabited in a tidal manner, painting the portrait of a hybrid citizen that he calls *Astochorikos. Astos* means a dweller of a city (in Greek: *asty*), but also a burgher. *Chorikos* denotes the dweller of a village (in Greek: chorio) and, more generally, of the rural sphere, the peasant. The figure of Astochorikos, the urban-rural citizen, the *villageois-citadin* in French, offers an alternative to dominant binary conceptions of urban *or* rural inhabitants.

Damianakos borrowed this term from K.D. Karavidas, a sociologist and prominent researcher of the Greek agricultural economy,

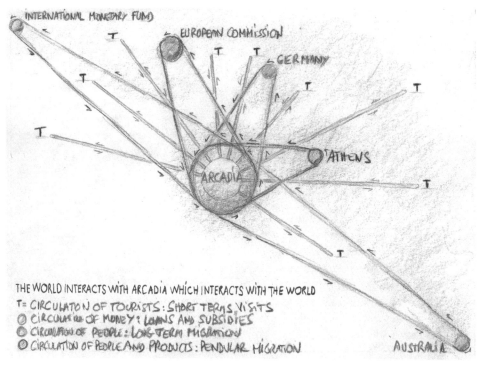

INTERNATIONAL MONETARY FUND

EUROPEAN COMMISSION

GERMANY

ATHENS

ARCADIA

THE WORLD INTERACTS WITH ARCADIA WHICH INTERACTS WITH THE WORLD

T= CIRCULATION OF TOURISTS: SHORT TERMS VISITS
Ⓞ CIRCULATION OF MONEY: LOANS AND SUBSIDIES
Ⓞ CIRCULATION OF PEOPLE: LONG-TERM MIGRATION
Ⓞ CIRCULATION OF PEOPLE AND PRODUCTS: PENDULAR MIGRATION

AUSTRALIA

ARCADIA AS A GLOBAL ACTOR AND PART
OF A SHARED EXTENDED SPACE
Fig. 23

who analysed this hybridity in the 1930s. In his work *Rurals (Αγροτικά)*, Karavidas identified the "mixed urban-rural family" as a specific socio-economic form of the Greek peasantry amongst other pre-capitalist productive structures in the Balkans (i.e., *zadruga, tseligato, chiflik*).[76] Karavidas referred to micro land owners as those who lived in cities but still kept productive links with rural land in retaining property, cultivating it with the help of relatives or other villagers, and thus remained politically and economically active in the rural sphere. On the other hand, he observed strong social and geographical mobility, both inter- and intra-generationally, generating a variety of incomes and socio-professional statuses in the extended family. He thus stated the difficulty of classifying these families according to existing scientific categories, as their activities challenged Western imaginaries of separate and antagonistic worlds: a purely rural society, anchored

in the land and sealed from modernity, and a diversified and mobile urban society orientated towards progress. Tackling this ambiguity, he introduced the figure of Astochorikos.[77] The figure of Astochorikos allows us to imagine an extended form of citizenship and outlines a space in which the rural and urban spheres permeate each other. Within this space, movement does not appear as a privilege of the urban dweller but rather as a shared social practice enabling access to a common urban-rural sphere.

MOVEMENTS

Movements are nothing new for Greece and many other places worldwide (see the chapters by Alice Hertzog and Elisa Bertuzzo in this volume). They emerge as a continuation of traditional practices developed by mountainous and insular communities. The seasonal travels of merchants, craftsmen, and shepherds, the reoccurring returns and repatriations of migrants,

Fig. 24

F. 24   "Against Nature's Looting. Fight for the Earth and Freedom." Protester's banners in the Periseri-Lakmos, Epirus region, Greece, June 2020. Social movements and portraits of an extended insurgent citizenship emerging in the "uninhabited" mountains.

and various forms of circular migration structured the traditional economies. They created a particular geography in which movement bridged realms traditionally understood as contrasting or even oppositional. These societies developed an economy that took advantage of broader territorial networks but, at the same time, was also grounded on the stability of families and villages in the rural sphere, securing social reproduction and serving as points of reference and return. What is intriguing in these traditional communities is that, like in many other places globally, movements do not appear as an antagonistic condition. What makes them different from nomadic societies is that they experience a double presence, a double belonging. The figure of Astochorikos helps grasp such historical practices but also demystifies movements occurring in contemporary peripheral landscapes. It is interesting to observe the persisting, inherited characteristics of movements in Arcadia. Although many other structures and productive processes shrink and decrease, the practice of movement sustains, becoming a dominant process. It is a different kind of inhabitation, extended and tidal;[78] networks and flows still enable relationality and extensions in a productive sense, generating a different type of citizenship and hybrid subjectivities that claim rights by participating in the production and reproduction of these landscapes. As a regular at the Kafeneion of Stemnitsa pointed out: "Can you imagine what would happen if the returns were to stop? Only the ice cream truck would remain, bringing ice cream to tourists in a thematised, empty mountain park." Movements are thus essential for the production of the peripheral region as a social space.

Since 2019, pressure for the enclosure of depopulating mountainous regions has been gradually increasing, while the legal framework of environmental protection has been radically weakening. At this critical moment, hybrid communities have unexpectedly surfaced. Groups that still use the land as commons, hikers, scientists, and archaeologists have formed to understand, inform, and support local communities, organise themselves in more extensive networks and stop dispossession and commodification. They have developed a language in which land and nature acquire a political meaning. "We walked to the tops. We defended our rights to free the mountains, land, and nature. We met virtually over Zoom when physical gatherings were banned during the pandemic. We filed legal objections against the installation of wind turbine parks on mountaintops and uninhabited islands. We sometimes stopped them," a participant in the movement said.[79] Such struggles share features of urban struggles and resistances against the enclosure of commons. It is unclear to me where these people come from, how they gathered, and how long they will resist. They have emerged as citizens of an extended territory to join and support these local struggles. [Fig. 24]

PERIPHERALISATION, AN ORDINARY PROCESS OF EXTENDED URBANISATION

The people of Arcadia and other depopulating landscapes share a collective ground, stretching across an extended geography of the urban/rural sphere. The city is commons, and commons are the practices of commoning, explains Stavros Stavrides.[80] Therefore, we can imagine this extended ground as composed of a specific form of commons, produced, maintained, and shared by different social networks, enabled by the synergy of conditions that are usually antagonistic. Urban yet rural, moving yet fixed, remote yet connected, each manifests an extended territory that enables exchange and mutuality, movement and participation. They empower links to both cities and peripheral lands, extended forms of dwelling and belonging. They challenge official demographics and the idea of depopulation generated by a purely quantitative calculation of permanent inhabitants. They are presenting an alternative to the narrative of emptied—and now uninhabited—peripheral lands, and they reveal fragile and neglected social and territorial structures that enable relationality and extension in a productive sense. These fluid commons offer the right to transcend dualisms. They uncover a space to defend a claim to the rights to both the city and the countryside. It is from the right to extended geography that the right *to extended citizenship* emerged.

This text could have very well concluded in 2019, when it was first drafted, by marking the officially pronounced end of the Greek debt crisis. The change to an even more neoliberal government, the outbreak of the global pandemic and health crisis in 2020, and the occurrence of extreme wildfires in the summer of 2021 as part of the aggravating climate crisis accelerated latent processes and phenomena. The demand for green energy regimes led to the enclosure of public land while the "uninhabited" narrative was instrumentalised for dispossessions in various Greek islands and mountain areas, making the full extent of ongoing peripheralisation processes visible. These observations

advocate for a radical reconceptualisation of the experience of the periphery at various spatial scales. Peripheralisation is not a static spatial condition but emerges as a dynamic, multidimensional, and trans-scalar process that generates geographies of uneven development.

To extend means to govern from afar. Learning from the Arcadia case, peripheralisation entails processes of hollowing out, emptying, and flattening, which violently shape unevenness and dependencies at multiple scales. It operates entangled with the fabrication of imaginaries, acts of abstraction and invisibilisation. It intertwines with narratives of emptiness and the imaginary production of idyllic outsides. Consequently, peripheralisation creates conditions for other processes of extended urbanisation, such as the enclosure of commons and the operationalisation of landscapes (see the chapters by Nitin Bathla, Nancy Couling, and Nikos Katsikis in this volume). In this sense, different processes of extended urbanisation coexist and unfold in relation to each other.

The production of these territories is put forward through moments of crisis (financial, ecological, health, etc.), offering the pretext for the politics of exception to unfold and eventually fixating and installing a permanent context of deregulation.[81] In this process, the state emerges as a crucial actor, and the reorganisation of state space plays a key role. It retracts the responsibility of care and governance and mediates to enable local access to global stakes.

Yet, *to extend does not always mean to expand and dominate. It may also mean to de-centre, to relate, and to touch.* "Invisible things are not necessarily not-there; a void may be empty, but it is not a vacuum. Certain absences are so stressed, they call for attention," Toni Morrison argues.[82] Parallel to dominant forces that peripheralise, disarticulate, and subordinate, the periphery reveals itself as a field of knowledge, extensions, relations, and re-articulations that require a different way of thinking about continuities and on notional, bodily, and interspecies extensions.

On my journey to Arcadia, I noticed that the locals knew little about the idealised Arcadia of the West. They spoke of other myths connected to their place and the land. Geomythologies about ancient water creatures illustrating the mountain hydrogeology; stories about a Mycenaean censer found buried in a field; about the acorn-eating inhabitants of the Arcadian forest; about the local olive fruit which, when hand-picked, is the healthiest in the world; myths re-engaging human bodies to land histories, ecologies, and multi-species metabolisms. Which are ultimately the stories we want to share about peripheral lands? Perhaps those stories narrate *how to extend* tales otherwise latent in the everyday practices and self-narratives of mountainous regions that persist outside existing classifications. Ex-centric territories entail an immense liberating potential when seeing the periphery as *a space of de-centring, not knowing, and unlearning*[83] to re-narrate possible relationships between places, people, and the rest of nature. As contemporary social and ecological challenges brutally unfold, increasingly staged on the fragile ecologies of peripheralised landscapes, Arcadia, and to a great extent all territories under processes of extended urbanisation, testifies that alternatives persist. It narrates ways to resist and means for working towards socioecological repair. Is there anything left from Arcadia that still nourishes our urban imaginary and that could be a tale of a different kind? One of extended insurgent citizenship, of contested fluid commons, of urban innovation that emerges from "uninhabited" peripheral lands, and of uncanny ways of seeing that allow us to *mountanise mountains* and *islandise*[84] *islands* as *ex*-centric counterparts of a shared extended urban space.

ENDNOTES

1 Von Goethe, *Italian Journey*.
2 Unlike ancient Arcadia, which was located solely at the mountainous core of Peloponnese, the contemporary regional unit of Arcadia spans the eastern Aegean coasts of Peloponnese. It consists of the "mountainous Arcadia" (ορεινή Αρκαδία) and the "coastal Arcadia," including five heterogeneous municipalities. In this text, I use the word Arcadia to refer to mountainous Arcadia, where ancient Arcadia was located and I focus on its core massive, namely Mount Mainalo and the municipality of Gortynia.
3 Pausanias, *ΑΡΚΑΔΙΚΑ* is one of his ten travelogue books *Description of Greece* (Ἑλλάδος Περιήγησις, *Hellados Periegesis*).
4 Horace, "Epode 2." Translation mine.
5 Olalla, *Eudaimon Arcadia*.
6 Panofsky, *Et in Arcadia Ego*.
7 Banks, "1769 April 13. Arrival Port Royal Bay." Emphasis mine.
8 Marx, *The Machine in the Garden*.
9 The Eleusinian Mysteries were initiations held every year at the Panhellenic Sanctuary of Elefsina in ancient Greece, based on an old agrarian cult, rooted in religious practices of the Mycenean period. The mysteries represented the myth of Persephone, daughter of Demeter, goddess of Earth, who was abducted in winter by Hades to the underworld and returned to the earth in spring.
10 In reference to Watkins, *Indigenous Archaeology*.
11 For more on this discourse, see also Hamilakis, "Indigenous Hellenisms/Indigenous Modernities"; Hamilakis, "Decolonizing Greek Archaeology"; Hamilakis, *The Nation and Its Ruins*; Peckham, *National Histories, Natural States*.
12 For the historical and cultural continuities of the Balkan's mountainous space, see also Nitsiakos, Ο Ορεινός Χώρος της Βαλκανικής.
13 The billboard was found at the Arcadian village Raptis: "Permanent inhabitants: 192. Summer months: 850." For the narrative purposes of this chapter, it is freely attributed to the village Stemnitsa with adjusted numbers.
14 Oral testimony (nn) in ERT, "Παραδοσιακά Επαγγέλματα στη Γορτυνία," 1989, 09:52.

15 After Greek National Independence, the land of the Ottoman State, institutions and big land owners were transferred to the ownership of the new Greek state. Nevertheless, it was not directly distributed to the farmers, due to political concerns of land concentration in the hands of a few families and the creation of a land-oligarchy. Furthermore, the promise of land distribution to the peasants acted as an incentive to support the central government, at the same time that the land had been encroached upon by them and cultivated illegally. The first agricultural reform happened in 1871 and the second in 1881. For the question of National Lands, see also Psychogios, *Το Ζήτημα Των Εθνικών Γαιών*.

16 Drinis, "Μετασχηματισμοί Και Αναπαραστάσεις."

17 Drinis, 215.

18 Drinis, 215, footnote 219.

19 Psychogios, *Προίκες, Φόροι, Σταφίδα και Ψωμί*, 165.

20 Sariyannis, *Athens 1830–2000*, 13.

21 Sariyannis.

22 Issaias, "The Absence of a Plan as a Project."

23 Peckham, *National Histories, Natural States*; Raffestin, "The Rural Origins of European Culture."

24 Clare, "Notes on Natural Worlds."

25 Drinis, "Μετασχηματισμοί Και Αναπαραστάσεις," 208.

26 Raffestin, "The Rural Origins of European Culture."

27 Drinis, "Μετασχηματισμοί Και Αναπαραστάσεις," 208.

28 Oxenford and Chryssogelos, "Greek Bailout."

29 Vogt, "Ubi Leones/Wo Nichts."

30 Kühn and Bernt, "Peripheralization and Power."

31 Schmid and Markaki, "Peripheralisation."

32 Kühn and Bernt, "Peripheralization and Power."

33 Kühn, "Peripheralization."

34 Wallerstein, *World-Systems Analysis*.

35 Nolte, *Europäische Innere Peripherien*.

36 Nitz, "Der Beitrag Der Historischen Geographie."

37 For example, see Copus, "From Core-Periphery"; Herrschel, "Regional Development, Peripheralisation"; Sassen, "Recomposition and Peripheralization"; on East Germany, see note 48; on Balkan regions, see note 50.

38 Massey, *Spatial Divisions of Labour*.

39 Smith, *Uneven Development*.

40 Hadjimichalis, *Uneven Development and Regionalism*.

41 Ren, "The Peripheral Turn."

42 For more on the Latin American discourse, see also Reis and Lukas, *Beyond the Megacity*.

43 Quijano, *Los Movimientos Campesinos Contemporáneos*; Castells, *The Urban Question*; Kentor, "Structural Determinants of Peripheral Urbanization"; Friedmann, "The Future of Urbanization in Latin America"; Jaramillo González, "Heterogeneidad Estructural En El Capitalismo"; Duhau, "La Investigación Urbana y Las Metrópolis Latinoamericanas."

44 "[…] nor does peripheral refer to macro relations of uneven development, as in world system theory."

45 Caldeira, "Peripheral Urbanisation."

46 Holston, "Insurgent Citizenship."

47 Simone, "People as Infrastructure"; Simone, "Ritornello."

48 Lang, "Shrinkage, Metropolization and Peripheralization in East Germany"; Naumann and Fischer-Tahir, *Peripheralization*; Kühn, Bernt, and Colini, "Power, Politics and Peripheralization"; Bernt and Colini, "Exclusion, Marginalization and Peripheralization"; Leibert and Golinski, "Peripheralisation."

49 Kühn, "Peripheralization."

50 Lang et al., *Understanding Geographies of Polarization and Peripheralization*; Ehrlich, Kriszan, and Lang, "Urban Development in Central and Eastern Europe."

51 O'Sullivan, Golubchikov, and Mehmood, "Uneven Energy Transitions."

52 Blowers and Leroy, "Power, Politics and Environmental Inequality."

53 Howe, "Processes of Peripheralisation"; Kockelkorn et al., "Peripheralization through Mass Housing."

54 Gururani, Kennedy, and Sood, "Engaging the Urban from the Periphery."

55 Reis and Lukas, *Beyond the Megacity*.

56 Keil and Wu, *After Suburbia*.

57 Diener et al., *Switzerland–An Urban Portrait*.

58 Topalović, "Hinterland."

59 Topalović et al., *ARCADIA*; Markaki, "Arcadia."

60 Pausanias, *ΑΡΚΑΔΙΚΑ*.

61 Law 3852/2010, ΦΕΚ 87 A/7 June 2010.

62 For more on Kallikratis Plan, see also Υπ. Εσωτερικών, "Νομοσχέδιο" and "Αιτιολογική Έκθεση"; Υπ. Οικονομίας και Οικονομικών, "Επικαιροποιημένο Πρόγραμμα Σταθερότητας και Ανάπτυξης."

63 The Kallikratis Plan entirely abolished the institution of *communities* at the first level of local government and reduced 1,034 municipalities to 325.

64 Namely at the villages of Dimitsana, Langadia, Vitina, and Tropaia.

65 Konstatatos, Spourdalakis, and Hadjimichalis, "Στη Συγκυρία της Κρίσης."

66 Akrivopoulou, Dimitropoulos, and Koutnatzis, "The Kallikratis Program."

67 Zacharopoulos, *Από το Κρυφό Σχολειό στο Ολοήμερο Σχολείο*.

68 Kyriakopoulou, "Από Τον Καποδίστρια Στον Καλλικράτη."

69 For the question of National Lands, see note 15.

70 Tsoukalas *Έξάρτηση καὶ Ἀναπαραγωγή*, 79.

71 Drinis, "Μετασχηματισμοί Και Αναπαραστάσεις," 179. He cites Karavidas, *Αγροτικά*; Psychogios, *ρoίκες, Φόροι, Σταφίδα και Ψωμί*; Petmezas, *Η Ελληνική Αγροτική Οικονομία*, 41.

72 Kalligas, *Θάνος Βλέκας*.

73 The privatisation of Greek public state-owned assets has been prescribed via the memoranda of agreement signed between the Greek state, the International Monetary Fund, and the European partners. It was carried through the constitution of the "Hellenic Republic Asset Development Fund (TAIPED)," following the model of "Treuhandanstalt," implemented for the privatisation of public assets of East Germany in the 1990s.

74 Damianakos, *Villageois et Citadins de Grèce*, 199.

75 Damianakos, "Les équivoques de la statistique." Translation mine.

76 Karavidas, *Αγροτικά*.

77 Although Karavidas' work on Greek rural spaces had been commissioned by the Greek Ministry of Agriculture, it was persistently neglected and eventually accidentally lost. Karavidas published the work on his own expense but with no effect on the official planning and agricultural policy of the Greek state.

78 Topalović et al., *ARCADIA*.

79 Oral testimony (nn). My interview on 26 April 2021.

80 Stavrides, *Common Space*.

81 Schmid and Markaki,

82 "Peripheralisation."
Morrison, "Unspeakable Things Unspoken."

83 Martínez, Di Puppo, and Frederiksen, *Peripheral Methodologies.*

84 The term "islandisation (νησιωτικοποίηση)" was introduced as a critical concept against the touristification of the Greek Aegean islands. See Lykourioti Iris, "Κριτικό πνεύμα: Γιατί χρειαζόμαστε τη νησιωτικοποίηση," in TA NEA, 21 August 2022; Kallis, "Islandizing the City," in *In Defense of Degrowth*, 211.

BIBLIOGRAPHY

Akrivopoulou, Christina, Georgios Dimitropoulos, and Stylianos-Ioannis G. Koutnatzis. "The 'Kallikratis Program': The Influence of International and European Policies on the Reforms of Greek Local Government." *Istituzioni del Federalism: Rivista di Studi Giuridici e Politici* 3 (2012): 653–693.

Banks, Sir Joseph. "1769 April 13. Arrival Port Royal Bay." In *The Endeavour Journal of Sir Joseph Banks, 1768–1771* (Project Gutenberg of Australia eBooks: 2005).

Bernt, Matthias, and Laura Colini. *Exclusion, Marginalization and Peripheralization: Conceptual Concerns in the Study of Urban Inequalities*, no. 49. Leibniz Institute for Research on Society and Space (IRS), 2013.

Blowers, Andrew, and Pieter Leroy. "Power, Politics and Environmental Inequality: A Theoretical and Empirical Analysis of the Process of 'Peripheralisation.'" *Environmental Politics* 3, no. 2 (June 1994): 197–228.

Caldeira, Teresa PR. "Peripheral Urbanization: Autoconstruction, Transversal Logics, and Politics in Cities of the Global South." *Environment and Planning D: Society and Space* 35, no. 1 (2017): 3–20.

Castells, Manuel. *The Urban Question: A Marxist Approach*. Vol. 1. London: Edward Arnold, 1977.

Clare, Eli. "Notes on Natural Worlds, Disabled Bodies, and a Politics of Cure." *Disability Studies and the Environmental Humanities: Toward an Eco-Crip Theory* 7 (2017): 242–268.

Copus, Andrew K. "From Core-Periphery to Polycentric Development: Concepts of Spatial and Aspatial Peripherality." *European Planning Studies* 9, no. 4 (1 June 2001): 539–552.

Damianakos, Stathis. "Les équivoques de la statistique: dépeuplement et double appartenance sociale en Épire (1961–1991)." *Strates. Matériaux pour la recherche en sciences sociales* 10 (2001).
———.*Villageois et Citadins de Grèce: L'autre et Son Double*. Ladyss, 2001.

Diener, Roger, Jacques Herzog, Marcel Meili, Pierre de Meuron, and Christian Schmid. *Switzerland–An Urban Portrait: Vol. 1: Introduction; Vol. 2: Borders, Communes–a Brief History of the Territory; Vol. 3: Materials*. Basel; Boston: Birkhäuser, 2006.

Dimitropoulos, Georgios. "The 'Kallikratis Program': The Influence of International and European Policies on the Reforms of Greek Local Government." SSRN Scholarly Paper. Rochester, NY: Social Science Research Network, 1 June 2012.

Drinis, Ioannis. "Μετασχηματισμοί Και Αναπαραστάσεις Του Ορεινού Χώρου (Από Τον 19ο Αιώνα Μέχρι Σήμερα): η Περίπτωση Της Δημητσάνας." PhD Thesis, Πανεπιστήμιο Ιωαννίνων. Σχολή Φιλοσοφική. Τμήμα Ιστορίας και Αρχαιολογίας, 2013.

Duhau, Emilio. "La investigación urbana y las metrópolis latinoamericanas." *RAMÍREZ VELÁZQUEZ, BR y PRADILLA COBOS, E. Teorías sobre la ciudad en América Latina. México DF, México, Universidad Autónoma Metropolitana* (2013).

Ehrlich, Kornelia, Agnes Kriszan, and Thilo Lang. "Urban Development in Central and Eastern Europe – Between Peripheralization and Centralization?" *DisP-The Planning Review* 48, no. 2 (2012): 77–92.

Friedmann, John. "The Future of Urbanization in Latin America: Some Observations on the Role of the Periphery." In *Papers of the Regional Science Association* 23, 161–174. Springer, 1969.

Gururani, Shubhra, Loraine Kennedy, and Ashima Sood. "Engaging the Urban from the Periphery." *South Asia Multidisciplinary Academic Journal* 28 (2021).

Hadjimichalis, Costis. *Uneven Development and Regionalism: State, Territory, and Class in Southern Europe*. London: Croom Helm, 1987.

Hamilakis, Yannis. "Decolonizing Greek Archaeology: Indigenous Archaeologies, Modernist Archaeology and the Post-Colonial Critique." In *A Singular Antiquity: Archaeology and Hellenic Identity in Twentieth-Century Greece*, Μουσείο Μπενάκη, 2008, 273–284.
———."Indigenous Hellenisms/Indigenous Modernities: Classical Antiquity, Materiality, and Modern Greek Society." In *The Oxford Handbook of Hellenic Studies*, Hellenic Studies. Oxford: Oxford University Press, 2009.

———.*The Nation and Its Ruins: Antiquity, Archaeology, and National Imagination in Greece.* Oxford: Oxford University Press, 2007.

Herrschel, Tassilo. "Regional Development, Peripheralisation and Marginalisation–And the Role of Governance." *The Role of Regions* (2011): 85–102.

Holston, James. "Insurgent Citizenship in an Era of Global Urban Peripheries." *City & Society* 21, no. 2 (2009): 245–267.

Horace. "Epode 2." In *Odes and Epodes.* Edited and translated by Niall Rudd. Loeb Classical Library 33. Cambridge, MA: Harvard University Press, 2004.

Howe, Lindsay. "Processes of Peripheralisation: Toehold and Aspirational Urbanisation in the GCR." *Antipode* 54, no. 6 (2022): 1803–1828.

Issaias, Platon. "The Absence of a Plan as a Project: On the Planning Development of Modern Athens: 1830–2010." In *The City as a Project*, edited by Pier Vittorio Aureli, 292–333, Berlin: Ruby Press, 2013.

Jaramillo González, Edgar Samuel. "Heterogeneidad Estructural En El Capitalismo: Una Mirada Desde El Marxismo de Hoy," Bogotá: Universidad de los Andes–Facultad de Economía–CEDE, 2012.

Kalligas, Pavlos. *Θάνος Βλέκας.* Vol. 29. Pelekanos Books, 2015 [1855].

Kallis, Giwrgos. *In Defense of Degrowth.* https://indefenseofdegrowth.com. Accessed 19 January 2023.

Karavidas, Kostas D. *Αγροτικά*, Athens: Papazisis, 1931.

Keil, Roger, and Fulong Wu. *After Suburbia: Urbanization in the Twenty-First Century.* Toronto: University of Toronto Press, 2022.

Kentor, Jeffrey. "Structural Determinants of Peripheral Urbanization: The Effects of International Dependence." *American Sociological Review* (1981): 201–211.

Kockelkorn, Anne, Christian Schmid, Monika Streule, and Kit Ping Wong. "Peripheralization through Mass Housing Urbanization in Hong Kong, Mexico City, and Paris." *Planning Perspectives* (2022): 1–39.

Konstantatos, Haris, Michalis Spourdalakis, and Costis Hadjimichalis, "Στη Συγκυρία της Κρίσης: Η Τεράστια Διοικητική-Πολιτική Αναδιάρθρωση του Καλλικράτη και η Λογική της 'Αποκένωσης' του Κράτους." Ενθέματα, 2010. enthemata.word-press.com. Accessed 21 January 2023.

Kühn, Manfred. "Peripheralization: Theoretical Concepts Explaining Socio-Spatial Inequalities." *European Planning Studies* 23, no. 2 (2015): 367–378.

Kühn, Manfred, and Matthias Bernt. "Peripheralization and Power: Theoretical Debates." *Peripheralization: The Making of Spatial Dependencies and Social Injustice* (2013): 302–317.

Kühn, Manfred, Matthias Bernt, and Laura Colini. "Power, Politics and Peripheralization: Two Eastern German Cities." *European Urban and Regional Studies* 24, no. 3 (2017): 258–273.

Kyriakopoulou, Natalia. "Από Τον Καποδίστρια Στον Καλλικράτη: Μεθοδολογικό Πλαίσιο Αξιολόγησης Διοικητικών Περιφερειών Με Χρήση Μεθόδων Ποσοτικής Χωρικής Ανάλυσης Σε Περιβάλλον GIS." Diploma Thesis, Σχολή Αγρονόμων και Τοπογράφων Μηχανικών, Εθνικό Μετσόβιο Πολυτεχνείο, 2011.

Lang, Thilo. "Shrinkage, Metropolization and Peripheralization in East Germany." *European Planning Studies* 20, no. 10 (2012): 1747–1754.

Lang, Thilo, Sebastian Henn, Kornelia Ehrlich, and Wladimir Sgibnev. *Understanding Geographies of Polarization and Peripheralization: Perspectives from Central and Eastern Europe and Beyond.* London: Palgrave Macmillan, 2015.

Leibert, Tim, and Sophie Golinski. "Peripheralisation: The Missing Link in Dealing with Demographic Change?" *Comparative Population Studies – Zeitschrift Für Bevölkerungswissenschaft* 41, no. 3–4 (2016): 255–284.

Markaki, Metaxia. "Arcadia. An Urban Portrait. Tracing Processes of Urbanisation on the Greek Mountains." PhD Thesis, ETH Zurich, Department of Architecture, Landscape and Urban Studies Institute, ongoing.

Martínez, Francisco, Lili Di Puppo, and Martin Demant Frederiksen, eds. *Peripheral Methodologies: Unlearning, Not-Knowing and Ethnographic Limits.* Anthropological Studies of Creativity and Perception. Abingdon, Oxon; New York, NY: Routledge, 2021.

Marx, Leo. *The Machine in the Garden*, New York: Oxford University Press, 2000 [1964].

Massey, Doreen. *Spatial Divisions of Labour: Social Structures and the Geography of Production.* London and Basingstoke: Macmillan International Higher Education, 1995.

Morrison, Toni. "Unspeakable Things Unspoken: The Afro-American Presence in American Literature (L990)." *A Turbulent Voyage: Readings in African American Studies* 246 (2000).

Naumann, Matthias, and Andrea Fischer-Tahir. *Peripheralization: The Making of Spatial Dependencies and Social Injustice.* Springer Science & Business Media, 2013.

Nitsiakos, Basilēs G. Ο Ορεινός Χώρος της Βαλκανικής, Αθήνα: Πλέθρον, 2000.

Nitz, Hans-Jürgen. "Der Beitrag Der Historischen Geographie Zur Erforschung von Peripherien." *Europäische Innere Peripherien Im 20. Jahrhundert* (1997): 17–36.

Olalla, Pedro. *Ο Ελαίμων Αρκαδία.* Η Σαγήνη ενός Μύθου στον Πολιτισμό της Δύσης, ROAD, 2005.

O'Sullivan, Kate, Oleg Golubchikov, and Abid Mehmood. "Uneven Energy Transitions: Understanding Continued Energy Peripheralization in Rural Communities." *Energy Policy* 138 (2020): 111–288.

Oxenford, Matthew, and Angelos Chryssogelos. "Greek Bailout: IMF and Europeans Diverge on Lessons Learnt." https://www.chatham-house.org/2018/08/greek-bailout-imf-and-europeans-diverge-lessons-learnt. Accessed 20 August 2018.

Panofsky, Erwin. "Et in Arcadia Ego: Poussin and the Elegiac Tradition." In *Philosophy and History, Essays Presented to Ernst Cassirer* edited by Klibansky, Raymond and Paton H. J., Oxford: Clarendon Press, 1936, 295–320.

Pausanias, ΑΡΚΑΔΙΚΑ. In αυσανίου Ελλάδος Περιήγησις – Αχαϊκά – Αρκαδικά. Τόμος IV. Εκδοτική Αθηνών, 2016.

Peckham, S. R. *National Histories, Natural States: Nationalism and the Politics of Place in Greece* London: I.B. Taurus, 2001.

Petmezas, Sokrates. *Η Ελληνική Αγροτική Οικονομία κατά τον 19ο αιώνα. Η Περιφερειακή Διάσταση*. Ηράκλειο: ΠΕΚ, 2003.

Psychogios, K. Dimitris. *Προίκες, Φόροι, Σταφίδα Και Ψωμί: Οικονομία Και Οικογένεια Στην Αγροτική Ελλάδα Του 19ου Αιώνα/*. Εθνικό Κέντρο Κοινωνικών Ερευνών, 1987 [1995].

―――.*Το Ζήτημα των Εθνικών Γαιών*, Αγροτική Τράπεζα της Ελλαδός, 1994.

Quijano, Aníbal. *Los Movimientos Campesinos Contemporáneos En América Latina*. Ed. Latina, 1967.

Raffestin, Claude. "The Rural Origins of European Culture and the Challenge of the Twenty-First Century." *Diogenes* 42, no. 166 (1994): 1–22.

Reis, Nadine, and Michael Lukas. *Beyond the Megacity: New Dimensions of Peripheral Urbanization in Latin America*. Toronto: University of Toronto Press, 2022.

Ren, Xuefei. "The Peripheral Turn in Global Urban Studies: Theory, Evidence, Sites." *South Asia Multidisciplinary Academic Journal* 26 (2021).

Sariyannis, G. *Athens 1830–2000: Urban Development, Planning and Transports*. Athens: Symmetry Editions, 2000.

Sassen-Koob, Saskia. "Recomposition and Peripheralization at the Core." *Contemporary Marxism* 5 (1982): 88–100.

Schmid, Christian, and Metaxia Markaki. "Peripheralisation: The Production of Ex-Centric Places as an Ordinary Process of Extended Urbanisation." In RC21 Athens. Panel 26, 2022.

Simone, AbdouMaliq. "People as Infrastructure: Intersecting Fragments in Johannesburg." *Public Culture* 16, no. 3 (2004): 407–429.

―――."Ritornello: 'People as Infrastructure.'" *Urban Geography* 42, no. 9 (2021): 1341–1348.

Smith, Neil. *Uneven Development: Nature, Capital, and the Production of Space*. Athens, GA: University of Georgia Press, 2010.

Stavrides, Stavros. *Common Space: The City as Commons*. New York: Bloomsbury Publishing, 2016.

Topalović, Milica. "Hinterland: Singapore and Urbanisms beyond the Border." *Kerb: Journal of Landscape Architecture* 24 (2016): 98–99.

Topalović, Milica, Metaxia Markaki, Karoline Kostka, Fabian Kiepenheuer, and Lukas Wolfensberger. *ARCADIA: A Journey into the Pastoral. Studio Report*. ETH Zurich D-ARCH Architecture of Territory, 2017.

Tsoukalas, Konstantinos. *Εξάρτηση και Αναπαραγωγή. Ο Κοινωνικός Ρόλος τών Εκπαιδευτικών Μηχανισμών στήν Ελλάδα (1830–1922)/*.Ü Αθήνα: Θεμέλιο, 1987 [1977].

Vogt, Matthias Th. "Ubi Leones/Wo Nichts Als Löwen Hausen. Zum Begriff Und Problem Der Peripherizität." *Peripherie in Der Mitte Europas. Schriften Des Collegium Pontes* (2009): 9–45.

Von Goethe, Johann Wolfgang. *Italian Journey: 1786–1788*. London: Penguin, 1992.

Wallerstein, Immanuel. *World-Systems Analysis: An Introduction*. A John Hope Franklin Center Book. Durham, NC: Duke University Press, 2004.

Watkins, Joe. *Indigenous Archaeology: American Indian Values and Scientific Practice*. Lanham, MD: Rowman & Littlefield, 2000.

Υπουργείο Εσωτερικών. Πρόγραμμα Καλλικράτης: Νομοσχέδιο, Αθήνα: Βουλή των Ελλήνων, 2010.

Υπουργείο Εσωτερικών. Πρόγραμμα Καλλικράτης: Αιτιολογική Έκθεση. Αθήνα: Βουλή των Ελλήνων, 2010.

Υπουργείο Οικονομίας και Οικονομικών. Επικαιροποιημένο Πρόγραμμα Σταθερότητας και Ανάπτυξης, Αθήνα: Βουλή των Ελλήνων, 2009.

Zacharopoulos, Ioannis G. Από το "Κρυφό" Σχολειό στο Ολοήμερο Σχολείο. Ένα Χρονικό της Πρωτοβάθμιας Εκπαίδευσης στην Αρκαδία (1821–2010). Τρίπολη: Νομαρχιακή Αυτοδιοίκηση Αρκαδίας, Σύλλογος Εκπαιδευτικών Πρωτοβάθμιας Εκπαίδευσης Νομού Αρκαδίας, 2010.

Urbanisation through Movement. The Lagos-Abidjan Corridor

Nina wakes at 3:30 am five days a week to cook for her food stall in the Lagos-Abidjan Corridor. Cheap and cheerful restaurants like Nina's are synonymous with roadside urbanism all across West Africa. They are called *maquis* in Benin, *Mama's Puts*, *Food is Ready*, aka *Bukkas* in Nigeria, and *Chop Bars* over in Ghana. Nina prepares the food and packs it into two plastic thermal containers. Then, along with her middle-aged sister, caregiver for children always with an infant or two in tow, piled on two moto-taxis with all their day's stock, coolers expertly balanced, and a block of ice carefully wrapped to protect it from the sun. The site they are heading to is a few hundred metres from the toll booth and happens to be a perfect location for feeding hungry truckers. It is also a good vantage point from which to observe everyday mobility and contemplate how this mobility produces extended urban spaces along the Lagos-Abidjan Corridor. After all, to the east, the road continues straight to Cotonou, Porto Novo, and Lagos; to the west are Lomé, Accra, and, several hundred kilometres further, Abidjan.

Out on the highway, the empty frame of Nina's maquis awaits them. The open structure of the maquis is slightly set back from the road. It is made from bamboo, wooden panels, corrugated iron sheets, and a rapidly deteriorating cement floor. Upon arrival, Nina and her team transform it into a roadside diner. The floor is swept, tarpaulins folded away, and a child is sent to pump water. They fetch the wooden table from the back, cover it in a plastic floral tablecloth, and sprinkle it with kerosene to keep the flies away. They rope a piece of nylon lace over the window and unpack the toothpicks and bottle openers, the palm wine and plastic jugs. Under a makeshift counter, Nina stashes away the portions of mashed yam and corn dough, smoked fish, boiled spicy eggs, and Fulani cheese, all prepped and hidden under several layers of bed sheets to keep the dust, flies, and sun off. Her sister lays out her goods for sale: toothbrushes, sweets, pills and medicine, soft drinks, and disposable plastic bags of whisky. She breaks the ice to cool the 50 centilitre plastic bags of water she will be selling as she

Fig. 1

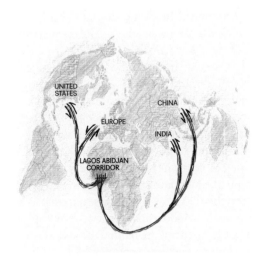

THE WEST AFRICAN CORRIDOR
IN A GLOBAL CONTEXT
Fig. 3

F. 1   Vendors await traffic at the toll
       booth.
F. 2   Map of the West African Corridor
       from Lagos to Abidjan.

stands on her toes, extending a handful
of bags up into a trucker's cab or through
a bus window.

All around, vendors are setting up for
the day in anticipation of the traffic that will
pass through. [Fig. 1] There are women selling
watermelons, mangos, piles of limes, and pastoralists primed with buckets of fresh cheese
that will later be pressed against the tinted
windows of passing four-by-four vehicles.
A handful of teenage boys are cycling from
the Fan Milk ice cream depot in the periphery
of Cotonou, working on commission. They
can be spotted from a mile off in their blue
jackets, with iceboxes mounted on the front
of their bikes, blowing their shrill bicycle horns.
Between the lanes of the toll booth, girls are
selling bread, madeleines, and peanuts while
women are preparing glasses of crushed ice
and concentrated milk, and men are pitching
racks of pirated CDs. The vendors and hustlers
are ready for a long day's work, hopeful for
a good day's business.

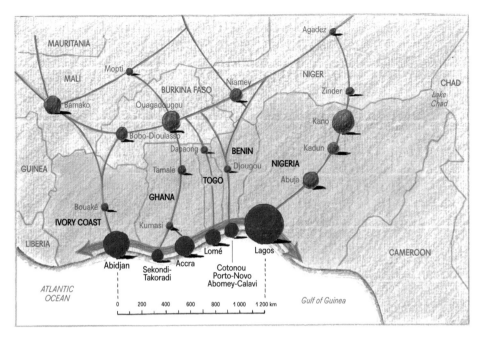

THE WEST AFRICAN CORRIDOR
Fig. 2

At the toll booth, like many locations along the corridor, all sorts of people will pass through, loiter or bump into each other. For Nina and her colleagues, there's no knowing what opportunities the road will bring today. A bus of school children on an outing? A pastor with his flock of followers? A delegation of civil servants on a donor-funded training seminar? Or maybe Ghanaian traders en route to Lagos with cash to spare? Most likely, familiar faces will stop for a chat and gossip, and strangers will order food in pidgin English. Here, people will slow down, take a break, catch some sleep, and have something to eat.

The toll booth is one of many stops along the Lagos-Abidjan Corridor. Situated in Benin between Lomé and Cotonou, it is not quite in either periphery, and it is far away from the bustling districts of Lagos or Abidjan. This chapter starts here, at the toll booth. As a starting place, it does not contain any premature definitions or aspirations of what the corridor could be, should be or will be. The toll booth is never a final destination in itself, and nobody sets out in the morning, intent on eating at Nina's

maquis. Instead, they end up here, side-lined as they order yams and fish, watching traffic pass as they rinse their hands and tuck in.

THE LAGOS-ABIDJAN CORRIDOR

Starting from the toll booth in Benin, this contribution explores the polycentric development of the Lagos-Abidjan Corridor, notably the role that migration and mobility play in underpinning urban development between its major city hubs. [Fig. 2] It positions this mobility within a larger historical context that has seen traders, the displacement of slaves, and the forced migration of African labour under colonialism shape this space since the fifteenth century. [Fig. 3] This chapter suggests that to grasp the role of contemporary mobility within urbanisation, theories of extended urbanisation must be "mobilised." This mobilisation involves both operationalising theories and addressing modes of urban development

Fig. 4

through the lens of movement. This chapter adopts a methodology that sticks to the road, considering how transactions between road-side communities and travellers transform urban fabric.

Following on from an initial appraisal of the Lagos-Abidjan Corridor, the second section presents findings from the field, or more precisely, from the highway. These explore several processes by which mobility and also immobility contribute to the emergence of an urban corridor. The third and final section pinpoints some of the contradictions between the daily production of space and current political framings of urban development and migration along the corridor. In doing so, it suggests a roadmap for a politics of extended urbanisation along the Lagos-Abidjan Corridor that anticipates the requirements of those travelling along it with the needs of those residing in its wake.

F. 4   Urbanisation, caught between
        an eroding coastland and lagoons
        prone to flooding

A POLYCENTRIC DEVELOPMENT BETWEEN BACKLOGS AND SYNERGIES

The Lagos-Abidjan Corridor is one of the fastest-growing mega-regions in the world. Along the Gulf of Guinea in West Africa, a number of urban areas are coming together to form a remarkable polycentric corridor. [Fig. 4] It spans 1,000 kilometres from Lagos in Nigeria to Abidjan in the Ivory Coast, passing through the Beninese cities of Porto Novo and Cotonou, the Togolese capital Lomé, and the Ghanaian capital Accra. Strung together by a coastal highway, the corridor is made up of major cities but also market towns, ports, borders, and villages.[1] Urbanisation along the corridor includes centres and peripheries with varying densities, built forms, and commercial usages. This territory, whilst opening up new development paths, also brings substantial challenges in governance and sustainability.

In West Africa, much urbanisation is still to occur. The region is experiencing the highest rate of urban growth on the continent, and it is predicted that it will soon be home to more than 50 million people.[2] Over the course of the past decades, a shift has occurred from city-based urbanisation towards the emergence of city regions, urban corridors, and mega-urban regions.[3] In the case of the Lagos-Abidjan Corridor, the "mushrooming" of settlement along the Gulf of Guinea is forming one of the most significant urban corridors in Sub-Saharan Africa. The relevance of such megaregions is only set to increase, and a recent study by the OECD predicts that, given the evolution of population settlement, the emergence of such urban forms will intensify.[4] These new morphologies require new tools for both practitioners and researchers and raise vital questions for urban research.[5]

The cities along the corridor have long-standing backlogs in terms of investment and infrastructure. Examined one by one, the United Nations observes that they have "exhibited incongruous physical development, absence of a resilient tax base and a general lack of sustainable economic development patterns." Such issues have been reinforced by poor policy and interventions, as well as Structural Adjustment Programmes.[6] Yet in West Africa, much hope in solving current-day challenges is pinned on the future of the Lagos-Abidjan Corridor. For the commissioner of the Economic Community of West African States (ECOWAS), the corridor is vital in stimulating economic growth and eliminating poverty.[7] Indeed, the Lagos-Abidjan Corridor clearly has far more potential when compared to the sparsely populated and under-developed northern hinterland. This potential is further consolidated by the relative security and wealth of the coastline, which already centralises economic infrastructure and political institutions, as compared to the increasing poverty and ongoing security crisis in the Sahel.[8]

The proximity between the main cities along the corridor is flagrant, with Cotonou at no more than 150 kilometres from Lagos and 350 kilometres from Accra. In this sense, the corridor's potential lies in the high levels of diversity and synergies encountered along the coast. The urban areas along the corridor might have experienced common deficits, but each has a specific trajectory and is highly differentiated. This differentiation, in terms of anglophone or francophone spaces, produces opportunity in and of itself as people travel up and down the corridor in search of opportunity. Yet while the corridor is embedded within the Economic Community of West African States (ECOWAS) that seeks to promote the free circulation of people and goods along the corridor, it is also disjointed by national borders.[9] These borders, while disruptive, also produce possibilities for exchange and trade by creating a difference, for example, in currencies or available goods. For AbdouMaliq Simone, the Lagos-Abidjan Corridor is an obvious example of how all kinds of transactions could be maximised, "taking advantage of niche markets, differentials in national regulatory structures, and singular economic histories to ply various small and medium-scale trades." This would, in turn, require regional urban development planning to productively connect cities and towns across national borders and rural-urban divides.[10]

MIGRATION, MOBILITY, AND MOVEMENT

The urban corridor between Lagos and Abidjan is a space of heightened mobility as people travel along the interstate highway crossing the various national borders that cut across the corridor. It is tricky to quantify regional mobility and migration in West Africa, given the informal flow of people and goods that are hard to measure with administrative and statistical tools.[11] Furthermore, migration paths in West Africa are multipolar and shift directions depending on the economic context, with people moving rapidly in response to market fluctuations or political contexts to the decline of some places and increasing potential of others.[12] Most of the migration in West Africa is regional, with regional flows accounting for 84% of movements. This is seven times more than migration flows from West Africa to other parts of the world.[13] The West African region also has the highest number of inter-regional and international migrants

Fig. 5

F. 5   Airplane advertisement promoting
       the proximity of capitals along
       the corridor.
F. 6   A map of the Slave Coast, 1789.

in Africa, a figure of 8.4 million, representing 2.8% of the population.[14]

In West Africa, mobility remains a strategy in the face of high poverty levels, the absence of a welfare state and economic vulnerabilities that create high levels of volatility.[15] This, in turn, has shaped the emergence of urban spaces where mobility determines urban livelihoods. Migrants are often blamed for urban poverty, with governments trying to reduce or control rural-urban migration to the detriment of migrants and other low-income residents.[16] This is equally mirrored by numerous development corporations that have reproduced the sedentary bias of colonial administrations, seeking to keep migrants in their place.[17] For Debbie Potts, "One outcome of livelihood vulnerability has been an increased propensity for mobility, not just into towns, but out of them as well."[18] Much of the mobility within West African cities can be accounted for not just through classic theories of rural push and urban pull but also through the increasing urban push.[19] Entrenched patterns of economic problems, insecurity of urban life, and threats of destitution all constitute drivers for circular migration. This is the kind of "strategic nomadism" Oliver Bakewell, and Gunvor Jónsson describe for Lubumbashi, where African migrants constantly move back and forth between the city and other locations.[20]

All along the Lagos-Abidjan Corridor, the social capital of relationships is vital for the production of livelihoods, and mobility is a crucial means to enrich and nurture these inter-human contacts. Interactions, such as those occurring at the toll booth, far from being just for the sake of themselves, are deeply embedded in urban subjectivities. [Fig. 5]

This chapter is grounded within a broad scholarship of mobility in West Africa.[21] It combines mobility and migration within the same analytical frameworks of Oliver Bakewell, Loren Landau, and AbdouMaliq Simone and chooses to adopt mobility or movement rather than migration as its lens of analysis.[22 / 23] In the West African context, producing clear-cut categories of movements remains a struggle. When is a journey a fluid mobility, a stable form of migration, or the tipping point between the two, when migration requires mobility or mobility leads to migration?[24] Indeed, when writing about the city of Dakar, the anthropologist Caroline Melly suggests that mobility is an enduring, elusive, and collective value that both embody expectations of migration and exceeds the binary geographies of arrival and departure.[25]

The mobility turn, of which Mimi Sheller and John Urry are key proponents, has promoted the study in social sciences of the interdependencies between the movements of people, information, images, and objects and increasingly called attention to the theoretical possibilities of moving beyond sedentary conceptualisations of place and movement.[26] This marks a shift from studying practices rooted in place to care-

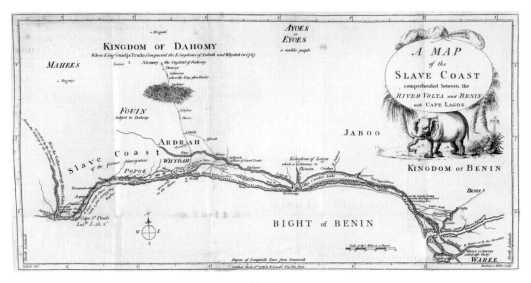

Fig. 6

fully considering the many mobility practices that make up everyday life. It brings to the fore an emphasis on fluidity and motion, drawing together various forms of movement and circulation and highlighting interdependent forms of mobility that organise social life around movement, distance, and absence.[27] From this perspective, as Mimi Sheller and John Urry write, places are tied into networks of connections "that stretch beyond each such place and mean that nowhere can be an island."[28] This resonates strongly in the context of West African urbanisation, where livelihoods are underpinned and sustained through mobility and where, as Loren Landau observes, planetary urbanisation is made real through "micro-level socialites, individual and familial projects."[29]

ANCIENT LAGOONS AND
FORCED DISPLACEMENT

Whilst the scale and intensity of urbanisation along the Lagos-Abidjan Corridor are new, the connections and movements along the coast are well established. Historically, traders and travellers have navigated the waterways creating a network of coastal lagoons along the Guinea Gulf.[30] Dating back to the fifteenth century, this extensive system

of lagoon networks enabled people to move along the gulf while avoiding the rough Atlantic coastline.[31] Described by the historian, Law as an "important medium of lateral communication," these networks once connected the Volta River in modern-day Ghana to the Niger Delta, allowing caravels and canoes to circulate rapidly, trading slaves, sugar, and gold.[32]

Traders and merchants have moved for centuries between cultural groups, establishing lateral communication along the West African coastline. Since then, the coastline has been shaped by a series of departures and returns, the most significant of these being the trafficking of slaves from Ouidah and later the return of enfranchised Afro-Brazilians who played a dominant role in the development of urban centres along the coast.[33] [Fig. 6] These returnees, referred to as the Agudas, settled, for example, in Porto-Novo, a former Portuguese slave-trading port founded in the sixteenth century. Equipped with trans-border networks and both social and economic capital, many Agudas went into trade and commerce, affiliating themselves with the urban Yoruba civilisation, developing strong ties with current-day Nigeria, and embedding themselves in trade networks dating back to pre-colonial times.[34]

MID XVIII—MID XIX CENTURY
The Kingdom of Dahomey at the Heart of the Slave Trade

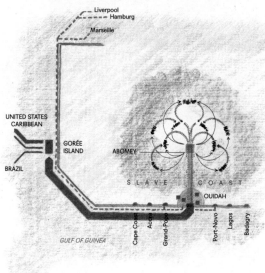

MID XIX—MID XX CENTURY
The Colonisation Period and the Agudas Return

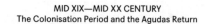

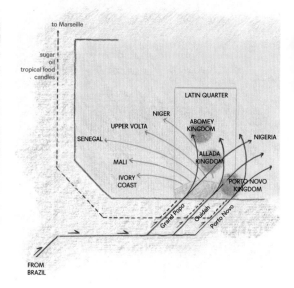

---- Trade route linking
Dahomey to Europe

SLAVE ROUTES

⌒ Removal of inhabitants
from the interior and forced
displacement to the port of
Ouidah

▬ Transport of slaves by ship

▨ Sphere of influence
of the Abomey kingdom's
"palace town."

▪ Forts and facilities belonging
to colonial and slave powers

---- Trade route between Dahomey
and Marseille

⇀ Return of Agudas (enfranchised
slaves from Brazil)

→ Dispatch of lettered elite from
Dahomey for administrative
support

⬸ Development of urban
armature along the coast with
the arrival of Agudas

● The three initial kingdoms
becoming a French
protectorate and colony

Other waves of mobility and return have followed. [Fig. 7] These include the displacement of African workers under colonialism to meet the economic and administrative needs of imperial powers and, more recently, the plight of refugees in the post-independence period.[35] These groups created and maintained strong links, often of a kinship or ethnic nature, between places of origin and destination. For example, during the Biafra war in Nigeria from 1967–1970, refugees fled the civil conflict to seek refuge in Benin, as did political refugees fleeing electoral violence under the dictatorial rule of the Gnassingbé family, which has "won" all six presidential elections in Togo since the 1990s. The displacement of both Togolese and Nigerian refugees in the period of post-independence reinforced trans-border trade that remains central to the urban economies and a structural part of livelihoods along the coast. In each period, ancient, colonial, or post-colonial, mobility, rather than settlement, has played a defining role in the creation of urban hubs along the corridor. Today, the lagoons are harder to navigate and overgrown with water lilies. [Fig. 8] In their place, the highway connects the various urban centres and has become the main backbone of the region.

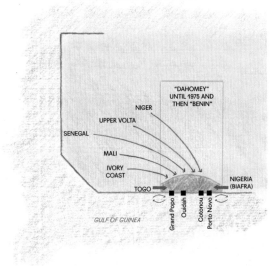

AFTER THE 1960s
The Post-Colonial Era
The Development of the Corridor

"DAHOMEY" UNTIL 1975 AND THEN "BENIN"

NIGER

UPPER VOLTA

SENEGAL

MALI

IVORY COAST

TOGO

NIGERIA (BIAFRA)

Grand Popo · Ouidah · Cotonou · Porto Novo

GULF OF GUINEA

→ Return of the Beninese diaspora

Development and urbanisation of the coastal area

Refugee population flows fleeing the Biafra war in Nigeria and political violence in Togo: permanent links maintained with countries of origin

MAPPING WAVES OF CONSECUTIVE DISPLACEMENT
Fig. 7

MOBILISING THE CONCEPT OF EXTENDED URBANISATION

This chapter focuses on how contemporary mobility patterns produce extended urbanisation. This is, for instance, the case at the toll booth, where travellers and passengers are contributing to the production of urban space in an unbuilt section of the corridor. It argues that mobility is key to producing urban space in this region, especially outside the urban centres.

The highway along the corridor allows us to observe how everyday urban life is closely tied to being on the move. There are two sides to this picture: first, the people who are actually travelling, and second, those dwelling along the highway, who are reliant on this passage of people and goods in order to sustain their livelihoods. In this sense, the highway is not a road that simply passes through the countryside, connecting cities, but rather a piece of infrastructure that urbanises the land it crosses.

Indeed, advocates of planetary urbanisation have argued that major transportation corridors contribute to the "blurring and rearticulation of urban territories" and produce expansive catchment areas that stretch beyond any single metropolitan region and cross

Fig. 8

multiple national boundaries.[36] This description of an interdependent and polynuclear urban megaregion is a fairly accurate portrait of the urbanisation processes at play along the Lagos-Abidjan Corridor. But to further mobilise the concepts of planetary and extended urbanisation, attention must be drawn to how mobility and immobility occur within the corridor and how this, in turn, produces specific urban forms.

This chapter "mobilises" the concept of extended urbanisation and looks at how new forms of urbanisation can be captured through a close, ethnographic analysis of mobility. This is done by working on a cross-section of spaces that have previously been considered as either urban or rural. In the following, I will explore the potential for thinking through modalities of urbanisation that are produced through mobility as opposed to settlement. For Henri Lefebvre, movement, notably commuting, is one of the core elements that produce urban space, as people move over territory and urbanise both their place of residence and work.[37] However, the movement along the Lagos-Abidjan Corridor encompasses a much wider spectrum of mobility than commuting, including, for instance, trans-border trade, hustling, and labour migration.

The question arises as to how mobility contributes to the emergence of an urban corridor in the absence of manufacturing industries and a formal job market. How are roadside communities along the highway leveraging mobility, and what happens when this mobility slows, when traffic and passengers come to a stop, be it through sudden breakages or planned pitstops? We discuss the various encounters and transactions along the corridor between roadside dwellers and people on the move. Is the highway just a highway, or is it creating an opportunity for urban livelihoods, a certain density and diversity that is contributing to the creation of urban spaces? This hypothesis mirrors initial observations at the toll booth. As traffic slows down, urban form emerges from the simultaneity of events, perceptions, and elements to the bringing together and meeting of people and things. These everyday

F. 8   The floating village of Ganvié on the outskirts of Cotonou: one of many along the corridor.

F. 9   Sand for sale to be used in the building sector.

F. 10   A neighbourhood chief observes construction work to limit the erosion in his constituency.

Fig. 9

Fig. 10

practices create a certain number of contradictions with extant territorial regulation, be it regional integration, spatial planning, or migration management. The chapter examines how these contradictions play out, for example, in the case of regional development strategies that seek to improve the road infrastructure to enable traffic and goods to flow more freely, while local communities are encouraging traffic to slow down and spend money, enabling them to capture resources as they flow by.

A THOUSAND KILOMETRES OF URBANISATION OFF THE MAP

African urban studies have spent too long on the periphery of urban scholarship. Indeed, whilst the Lagos-Abidjan Corridor has played an important role in the political imaginary of post-colonial regional integration, it has received little scholarly attention. An exception to this is the work undertaken by Armelle Choplin, a geographer whose recent work has sought to elucidate the current forms of urbanisation through the production and consumption of cement along the urban corridor.[38] [Fig. 9]

Yet, we still know so little about this corridor, especially when compared to other urban megaregions, like BosWash along the north-eastern US coast of the United States, the SanSan between San Francisco and San Diego, the Pearl River Delta, the Rio de Janeiro–Sao Paulo conurbation, or the Gauteng City Region in South Africa.[39] This also reflects how traditionally, urban research has focused on individual cities along the Gulf of Guinea rather than the dynamics and urban processes that cut across them. This has privileged knowledge production on national capitals, historical cities, and larger trading cities along the coast while overlooking research on more extended metropolitan areas. In contrast, the study of Lagos, for example, is flourishing, emerging as a dynamic sub-field of its own.[40] Meanwhile, significant urban research is being undertaken in Accra.[41] Less can be said of Lomé and Cotonou. Indeed, up until now, little attention has been paid to what is happening in less populated sites in-between the capital cities.[42]

There are three possible explanations as to why this substantial area, nearly 1,000 kilometres of urbanisation, has remained off the map in the field of urban research. The first is that it is difficult to define the exact boundaries of the corridor. In itself, it is not an established administrative unit, and the exact territory it covers is debatable. The borders of the corridor vary depending on the interlocutor; policy reports at times refer to the Lagos-Abidjan Corridor, whilst researchers also speak of the Lagos-Accra Corridor and other multilateral organisations refer to the GILA, the Greater Ibadan-Lagos-Accra Corridor.[43] Although the endpoints of the corridor are contested, it is even harder to define the corridor's width. It thickens and thins, for example, with the coastal highway shifting from two to eight lanes. At times the metropolitan expansion appears to be only a sliver of row houses lining the road. At other times it bulges, pulling in market towns and suburbs. One would think it would be easier to draw a fixed boundary for the corridor along the coast. But this, too, is shifting due to rapid erosion, the causes of which include the extraction of sand for the building sector, coastal infrastructure, rising sea levels, and strong currents. [Fig. 10]

A second obstacle to a more encompassing urban scholarship is the colonial legacy of alternating anglophone and francophone countries. Academic collaborations, training and studying abroad, and teaching exchanges continue to privilege connections between former colonies and old powers. The linguistic geographies have resulted in anglophone scholars focusing on urban spaces in Nigeria and Ghana, whilst francophone scholars are predominant in studies of Benin, Togo, and the Ivory Coast. In turn, both urban theories and empirical findings remain too often confined to either Anglo or Franco communities. Universities along the Gulf of Guinea teach and publish in either French or English but rarely both, and their work is seldom translated. This hampers discussions on the joint processes of urbanisation that cut across these colonial divides. Rare are the scholars such as Amandine Spire, who considers

Fig. 11

a more diverse cross-section of Anglo and Franco spaces in her analysis of strangers in the cities of Accra and Lomé.[44]

There is a third possible explanation for the lack of scholarship on this urban corridor. Researchers observing that there are still rural areas between the capital cities have, at times, come to the premature conclusion that this indicates there is no metropolitan region. Indeed, when there are breaks in the cemented landscape, the corridor looks, at times, deceptively rural. However, upon closer inspection, one observes a pile of construction sand by the road, a hand-painted advertisement for video production, or a blue landowner's sign, which all point to urban processes at play. Venturing into the villages, many of the rural dwellers are absent, busy in town trading or working as motorbike taxi drivers. One of the dangers of maintaining the conception of a rural-urban dichotomy is that these places are not considered to be participating in the emergence of extended urbanisation, and are used as arguments against the hypothesis of an urban corridor running between Lagos and Abidjan.

METHODOLOGICAL CONSIDERATIONS FOR STAYING ON THE ROAD

The urban corridor is a territory that mirrors contemporary urbanisation patterns described by Andy Merrifield as "shapeless, formless and apparently boundless, riven with new contradictions and tensions that make it hard to tell where borders reside and what's inside and what's outside."[45] In this space, my research sticks to the highway between Lagos and Abidjan that has become the backbone of this corridor and provides a material surface to work from. More specifically, it focuses on the Beninese section of the corridor, drawing on eighteen months of ethnographic fieldwork undertaken in the context of my doctorate and in policy analysis for the Swiss Development Cooperation.[46] This chapter can be read alongside the web-

F. 11   Road sweepers after their morning shift at the tollbooth.

Fig. 12

Fig. 13

F. 12 *Zémidjan* motorbike taxis navigate traffic and perilous road conditions.

F. 13 A petrol smuggler takes a break; his motorbike has been converted to navigate the road system between Nigeria and Benin.

documentary *Parcours de Migrants* produced in 2021, which showcases the voices of both people, along with policymakers, academics and cartographers who address current trends in mobility and urbanisation along the Lagos-Abidjan Corridor.[47]

The territories of extended urbanisation along this corridor are far more expansive than a mere strip of road, at times stretching north to encompass commuter towns and lagoon settlements and bulging when passing through towns and villages. But the interstate road acts as a backbone, connecting the various localities, and channelling movement along the coast. It is a vector for extended urbanisation as people move up and down at various tempos, sometimes coming to a standstill, willingly or not.

Sticking to the road is to "think infrastructurally" and to consider the physical networks, goods, and people who move through the territory.[48] As Brian Larkin puts it, "infrastructures

are matter that enables the movement of other matter," even when that matter is people.[49] The road is positioned theoretically as an infrastructure of extended urbanisation, a physical form that controls speed and direction and enables various groups to capitalise on the movement. The road privileges, facilitates, and legitimates certain forms of movement and resulting urban forms while limiting others. This chapter builds on the anthropology of roads and, particularly in the African context, extends agency to include the various material features of the road, the asphalt, or the hole.[50] Roads, as connectors between various urban centralities, are an ideal entry point to understanding how urbanity occurs outside the city. As an analytical device, roads focus attention on the in-between places and, like extended urbanisation, explode the idea of a bounded urban site. Furthermore, roads as infrastructure are assemblages that bundle together various scales and rhythms of mobility as everyday commuters travel side by side with once-in-a-lifetime pilgrims.

THE PRODUCTION
OF AN URBAN CORRIDOR:
A VIEW FROM THE HIGHWAY

Shaped by boom and bust, the Lagos-Abidjan Corridor is constantly re-enacted as people travel up and down, weaving their trans-local lives into the urban fabric. And it's not just people on the move, the territory itself is also shifting. On the one hand, coastal erosion edges away neighbourhoods due in part to the trade in the sand for construction along the beaches. On the other hand, new pieces of land appear as residents pour cement into the bog-land around the lagoons to reclaim land and get a footing on the corridor. Drawing on fieldwork observations in Benin, this section explores how mobility along the Lagos-Abidjan Corridor shapes urbanisation processes. It does so by focusing on the interstate highway, examining both its materiality and the various immobilities that occur along it. It asks how mobility, congestion, and interruptions to journeys are producing urbanity. How are people crafting a livelihood from this road? Are they street hawkers or roadside boutiques? [Fig. 11] And how are specific strategies seeking to make a living from the people and goods that flow along the corridor also replicated on the level of state and local governance?

FROM DIRT TRACK TO ASPHALT:
ROAD SURFACES AS
URBAN ACCELERATORS
The highway along the Lagos-Abidjan Corridor is one of the few asphalt surfaces in the coastal area. Even in the capital city of Cotonou, only a handful of strategic avenues connecting the port to the airport and presidential palace are asphalted. Locally, there is a strict spatial hierarchy that distinguishes between different road surfaces: right at the bottom is *la piste* (dirt tracks), followed by a slightly improved category of the road: *le von* (the French colonial acronym for *Voie d'Orientation Nord*, North-Orientated Road), then *le pavé* (paved road), and at the top of the typology, *le goudron* (asphalted road). [Fig. 12–13]

Access to the main road with a *goudron* increases the price of land. The price of plots varies depending on how close they are to the *goudron,* a detail that is mentioned in all real estate advertisements. For example, research by Gisèle Glele in the periphery of Cotonou noted that in 2010 prices for a standard plot of land far away from a road were around 700 USD, while average prices of plots adjacent to an asphalted road were 2,200 USD.[51] Up and down the corridor, land on each side of the Lagos-Abidjan highway has been snapped up through speculation because the asphalt makes it highly accessible, and living on the edge of a highway is a considerable advantage. In this sense, the highway is producing extended urbanisation, creating an incentive for people to settle on each side of the road, drawn by the prospect of more accessible transport and connectivity.

At times the roads leading off the highway are upgraded, and their status shifts from dirt track to cobbled street to asphalted road. At other times this is done in response to higher levels of circulation or imposed by urban planning—it also often coincides with the prestige and political power of those who reside along it. The asphalting of a road is embedded within everyday urban governance practices *and* local corruption. This became evident during fieldwork when the Beninese First Lady inaugurated her charity in one of the wealthier neighbourhoods in Cotonou. It was originally on a *von* but was rapidly upgraded to a *pavé* in order to better connect the foundation to the main artery, the *goudron.*

Asphalt is a rare, and therefore precious and notable feature when it appears in the urban landscape. On top of structuring land prices and demonstrating power, the smooth surface of the goudron also enables a whole series of urban practices that take place along it: roller-blade teams practice, young Lebanese men race their flashy sports cars up and down, and housewives

lie washing out on edge, along with batches
of fish and peppers to sun-dry on the tarmac.

POTHOLES AND HOLD UPS: WHEN
DELAYS PRODUCE URBANITY

The surface quality of the roads
in the region is far from permanent and can
quickly deteriorate due to bad weather, potholes,
accidents, poor engineering, and embezzled
maintenance funds. Given these fluctuations,
the quality of road surfaces is a critical concern
to people on the move and the constant topic
of conversation and press articles. This is understandable, given that the deterioration of a road
surface can lead to everyday life being completely re-routed as people try to fit their sched-
ules around the ensuing traffic jams.

Congestion is an ever-present feature
of urban life along the Lagos Abidjan Corridor.
In African cities, people get stuck in traffic,
but their projects, aspirations, and futures also
get stuck. Writing about Cotonou, Armelle
Choplin and Riccardo Ciavolella speak of a city
where all the roads are jammed, geographically
at the bridges, roundabouts, and crossroads,
but also socially, as people try to get into school
or the job market.[52] Along the corridor, nothing
flows freely; people and things get caught up,
stuck in traffic, or break down. Caroline Melly's
work on Dakar is key to theorising stagnation
as a marker of contemporary urbanisation.[53] She
argues that the bottleneck or the *embouteillage*
has been a defining feature of life and policy
in Dakar. In her terms, the bottleneck signifies
an era in which "urban and global mobilities
are both intensely valorised and increasingly
regulated, restricted and deferred." And she
describes the bottleneck as an unpredictable,
widely generative, "critical urban force
that often exceeds management, planning
and intervention."[54]

Such bottlenecks are often caused by holes
in the road. Holes are common on the highway
and play a prominent role in the collective imagination. Locals refer to Cotonou as "Coto-trou,"
le trou meaning both holes, and places of little
significance, outside the glare of the megacities.
For the anthropologist Filip De Boeck, the hole

becomes a meta-concept of African urbanism,
reflecting material ruination, sites of erosion,
and social decay in the city.[55] Nonetheless, these
holes also generate activity along the road and,
at times, are even dug out by youths, who set
up ad-hoc check-points and then ask for contributions to "repair" the road.

As traffic slows down around the hole,
all types of activities emerge. An example of this
road-hole phenomenon is captured in Nigeria
by the author and journalist Ryszard Kapuscinski
in describing, "The edges of the hole have
become a centre of attraction, generating curi-
osity and encouraging initiative. Thanks to this
god-forsaken hole, this place, this sleepy deadly
suburban ruin… transforms spontaneously, into
a dynamic neighbourhood, full of life
and noise. Social life gets colourful, the edge
of the abyss becomes a place of encounters,
of discussion, a children's playground."[56] Holes,
breakdowns, and pitstops along the corridor
become opportunities and potential encounters
that generate urbanity from Lagos to Abidjan.

One day at the toll booth, a loaded bus
hurtling down the corridor en route to Lagos
broke down. It was an absolute wreck of a
vehicle, and it took days for the driver to find
the right replacement piece and fix the engine.
Many of the passengers, unwilling or unable
to pay for another ticket, got stuck for several
days, which, in turn, kept all of the vendors
at the toll booth busy for several days. At the
maquis, Nina sold out completely, jumping
on a motorbike at midday to restock from home.
The shack was so full of Nigerians streaming
Nollywood sitcoms on their mobile phones that
Nina's sister had to shoo them out, setting up
a bench for them under the mango tree so she
could sweep the floor. Much like the hole, the
breakdown created a moment of ephemeral
urbanisation, creating a veritable neighbourhood
that disappeared as quickly as it had appeared
once the bus was repaired.

The obstacle—be it a hole in the
asphalt, traffic lights, speed bumps, customs
check-points, a crashed lorry, or a toll-booth—
enables urban bystanders to collect the
dividends of immobility as people alongside

the road find ways to seek out a living and make a little money from their location on the highway. As those on the move get stuck, there are people waiting, ready to barter services, wash and repair cars, and sell petrol from large glass demijohns, plastic bags of fried manioc snacks, tomatoes, hot peppers, salt, dried fish, and haircuts.

ROAD HAWKERS AS A VITRINE OF EXTENDED URBANISATION

The road provides a site along which to barter and trade goods. And as traffic slows down, roadside dwellers display their wares, hoping to entice clients as they travel past. Trade along the corridor transforms the roadside into a series of sales points, from shacks to sturdy constructions. Be it a simple basket, a wooden stall, or a makeshift metal shed, these structures are subtle indicators of urbanisation along the corridor that relies on the mobility and immobility of people travelling between the urban hubs. As one nears the urban centres, these ephemeral roadside stalls become individual shops set back from the highway, turning into long rows of one-story storefronts.

These roadside shops announce the aspirations and urban futures at play. The various goods on sale speak of urban consumer trends as fabric vendors display yards of bold wax fabric to be cut and tailored. Bright yellow facades indicate "mobile money" shops for immediate cash transfers and phone data. Hardware stores announce the price of cement, plastic piping, and Chinese solar panels. Furniture makers line up wooden beds and three-piece sofa suites, facing the road, their price scribbled in chalk onto the fake leather. These material goods respond to the growing market of urban households along the corridor seeking to equip and furnish their new homes.

The shop fronts are overlaid with another series of vitrines—those of the street vendors, who move in and out of the cars, expertly carrying glass display cabinets. They make the most of the cars and buses at a standstill at roundabouts and traffic lights. They pitch gadgets, books, political pamphlets, maps, car accessories, mouse traps, and the latest CDs of Lagos dance tunes. They weave in and out of the vehicles and often target the minibuses' open side doors, which become shop windows used to display goods. In this sense, the road is much more than a surface that is travelled. It is a place for trade and interaction where goods are pitched and sales are made. Items are passed through windows and considered while prices are bartered. People often do this just to pass the time, as passengers window shop in a drive-through bazaar of imported goods. Road congestion incites people to inhabit the road differently and leads travellers to combine travel with window shopping. The manner in which various groups inhabit the road along the corridor points to the role of movement and how it structures opportunity along this linear, polycentric region. Up and down the corridor, various groups are looking, in the absence of formal employment, to capitalise from the resources and people moving along the corridor either by speeding them up or by slowing them down. This includes individual traders, community groups, and local governments, who are all taking their share of roadside businesses.

OPERATING IN THE ENTREPÔT STATE

The Lagos-Abidjan Corridor, or more precisely, the taxation of goods that are imported and then transported along it, is a key source of revenue for the Ivory Coast, Ghana, Togo, Benin, and Nigeria. For the geographer John Igué, Benin functions as an "état-entrepôt," a warehouse state that relies on goods and resources that circulate within its borders as opposed to internal production.[57] This strategy relies on generating income through customs taxes in the absence of manufacturing industries and producer services.

However, the central state is not the only one collecting customs taxes along the road. All along the corridor, local leaders use the roadside location of their constituencies to generate revenue from the corridor. Such practices hook onto opportunity as it passes by, overturning the logic of point-to-point logistics or economies of scale. Rather than delivering services to facilitate the fluid transport of goods, fees are extracted by delaying and side-tracking goods and people. Nina at her *maquis* can only generate an income because the toll both delays and interrupts the journey of those travelling along the highway, and the same applies to many other communities residing along the corridor. From the perspective of these locations, the corridor is not just connecting hubs and crossing borders. It is also distributing resources along its edges where it disposes of residues, people, things, and money.

One such place is PK10, a neighbourhood that got its name because it is situated 10 kilometres out of Cotonou (*Point Kilométrique 10*). It is located between the port of Cotonou and the Nigerian border and occupies a gap between the highway and the coastline. The neighbourhood is a mix of high-end residential units, informal settlements, industrial warehouses, and a university campus. As I spent time with the neighbourhood chief, shadowing him in his daily duties, I learned of an intricate scheme for the neighbourhood to generate money from the corridor.

The neighbourhood is strategically situated by a second toll booth. This one, much like the toll booth Nina works at, charges a high fee for lorries once their weight is over a certain threshold. However, local officials have devised a workaround so that the lorry drivers can avoid paying the fee. They would instead pay a smaller fee to the locals from PK10, letting them pocket the difference. Heavily-loaded lorries could pull into warehouses in PK10, where local young men off-load the goods onto several small pickups. These pickups then cross the toll, paying only a nominal fee. The empty lorry also drives through, paying only a nominal fee, and on the other side, the young men reload the goods onto the lorry. The whole operation takes time and labour, countering the logistics of economies of scale. However, in this *état* speed and fluidity are no longer a priority, as money can be made by slowing down the circulation of goods.

These processes are highly codified and organised and are far from random interventions along the highway. One morning I accompanied the neighbourhood chief, who was summoned to the district chief's office. His superior had noticed the revenue from the warehouse operation decreasing and had sent out his men to investigate. An assistant had diligently noted every lorry that was coming in and out. There were clear discrepancies with the sums he had been receiving. "It's not rigorous," he admonished his colleague, "my men on the ground carefully checked." He went on to read from a schoolbook the number plates of the vehicles that had not been declared properly. "Things need to straighten up around here." The PK10 chief apologised profusely, nodding in agreement. The arrangement in place makes money for the truckers themselves, the constituency directly on the roadside, and the wider district—some of which is reinvested in local services to cover neighbourhood costs, all whilst reducing the money collected at the toll booth intended to fund road maintenance. It is both a case of budgetary imagination and the everyday corruption at play in West Africa. In a context where there is little local formal employment and, therefore, a reduced tax base, local authorities, just like vendors, are turning to the corridor to generate income.

[IM]MOBILITY AS A DRIVER OF CORRIDOR URBANISATION

The corridor produces urbanity both through mobility and also through these moments of immobility. On the highway, journeys are slowed down by congestion and breakages that slow down travel and keep people stuck in traffic jams. This means that, more often than not, journeys along the Lagos-Abidjan Corridor are marked by moments of immobility. Trips start and stop as passengers get stuck in traffic, wait for busses to fill up, queue to cross borders, are pulled aside by police agents, or have their cars break down.

On the one hand, there is a porosity between road transit and roadside communities. The various pitstops and the road design favour numerous interactions between travellers and local dwellers. Unlike highways elsewhere, the

Fig. 14

highway along the Lagos-Abidjan Corridor has no identified exits, crash barriers, constant speed limits, or lay-bys. It is not separated from the urban neighbourhoods. It moves through physical dividers. At any moment, drivers can pull into the cities, towns, and villages that line the road. At some moments, to tame the road, communities have added improvised speed bumps and pedestrian crossings to navigate the fracture the road creates when it cuts through localities. For those residing along the corridor, there is an imposed proximity created by congestion and the fact that neighbourhoods extend onto the road, often occupying the asphalted surface, seeking to engage with those travelling through. Indeed, this highway doesn't bypass villages and towns but runs straight through them. In this way, urban life comes right up to the edge of the road and then over it, as school children skip over the highway and vendors hustle in the middle.

Various levels of governance along the corridor rely on this immobility to collect revenue from goods travelling through the territory. This is one example of how territories situated between the major cities along the corridor generate revenue from stalling mobility along the corridor. Interruptions in the flow of people and goods contribute to creating moments of ephemeral urbanity but also highlight the many political challenges facing the governance of mobility and immobility in such territories of extended urbanisation.

In terms of classic development economics, a good road is a road that flows, but for roadside communities, there can also be a vested interest in slowing down and creating breakages in the transit. Working from the road can help identify these moments of slowing down, which in turn creates a certain form of urbanity. This density may be fleeting, disappearing once again as soon as the engines start up. Whereas it might not be in the best interest of road maintenance, everyday corruption along the corridor does

F. 14   The tollbooth manager
generates enough income
to keep two young wives.

Fig. 15

maintain local communities, who have identified and sought to capture revenue as the trucks roll past. [Fig. 14] These are all moments of extended urbanisation, where various strategies of stalling materialise infrastructurally as a vitrine, a warehouse, or a hole, and in turn, sustain extended urbanisation.

ROADMAPS FOR A POLITICS OF EXTENDED URBANISATION

The empirical observations of both the materiality of this road and everyday practices along it can shed light on the current contradictions within existing political initiatives to control both territories and movement along the corridor. Here we move from the various elements along the road, such as a toll booth, a hole, or shock absorbers, to consider the political implications of mobility and immobility along this linear and transnational urban space. We suggest here that everyday movements along the corridor are

deviating from official roadmaps and challenging current territorial regulations.

The mobility of people along the corridor raises fundamental questions about the constitution of politics in this emerging urban configuration. The urban extends over borders, blurring the boundaries of municipalities, ethnic groups, and linguistic zones and, in doing so, muddles the associations between political power and defined spatial areas. Along the Lagos-Abidjan Corridor, people move in and out of different political territories, at times showing a yellow vaccine card, at others bribing a border guard to cross between constituencies. This large, emerging urban space transcends the unities of political action and encompasses various national and ethnic territories. This third section considers how various political actors are addressing regional integration, territorial planning, and migration management in this context. It asks how stakeholders on various scales exert power when both the social and spatial basis it seeks to govern are continually shifting.

REGIONAL INTEGRATION
AS A SHARED ASPIRATION

There is an initial tension here between interregional intentions to increase fluidity and local tactics that seek to slow down traffic, for example, in PK10, where the local community tries to make a living out of the road. Thus, on a regional level, development projects seek to increase the fluidity of traffic along the corridor, whilst local communities seek to slow down the traffic in order to generate revenue for side-of-the-road and border towns.

There are concerted inter-governmental efforts to maintain good road surfaces and increase the fluidity of persons and goods along the corridor in order to boost the West African economy. Governance bodies are very aware that on a regional level, 75% of the economic activities occur along the corridor.[58] One such body is the Economic Community of West African States (ECOWAS), which promotes the free circulation of people and goods within its 15 member countries. The maintenance and development of the road are one of the largest infrastructure projects in ECOWAS and part of a wider trend of promoting regional integration in West Africa. The World Bank, African Development Bank, German Development Agency, and Japanese Development Agency are all funding improvements to accelerate the integration and growth of regional exchanges, reduce obstacles and barriers in the ports, rationalise the borders, and reduce the cost of goods by reducing the cost of transport.

Another central body is the Abidjan-Lagos Corridor Organisation. The organisation was founded with US funds from the Millennium Challenge. Its original mandate was to prevent the aids epidemic from spreading via truckers and sex workers along the corridor. The organisation has since broadened in scope and today seeks to improve transport dynamics within the corridor and facilitate intra-regional trade and competitive industries. One such measure is the monitoring of roadblocks that seeks to put pressure on states to reduce the number of obstacles for those moving up and down the corridor. They also monitor the condition of the road and the amount of time it takes truckers to cross the various borders with their goods. The main objective here is to improve the flow of traffic; however, it pays little attention to the urbanisation of territories situated along the highway and their needs in terms of access and resources.

The tension between attempts to produce a fluid transit space and local interests is exemplified at Kraké, the coastal border post between Nigeria and Benin. [Fig. 15] The European Union has funded the construction of a large border infrastructure that would combine the customs processes for both countries, speeding up and regularising transit. However, much like another large border infrastructure in Malainville with Niger, the border post, at the time of writing, had still not been inaugurated. Every day transit and customs controls continue to take place in a series of shacks along a dirt track. There is an unspoken reticence from local actors to open the new border post that would effectively bring a stop to many of the informal practices by local officers, but also local community leaders and elders that levy additional costs on those passing through. [Fig. 16] For some travellers and traders, it is also convenient to be able to bribe local officers to cross the border without paperwork or with undeclared goods. In this regard, they have little to gain from opening a formalised border post. Again, contrary to regional development strategies, opportunities are leveraged by roadside communities when traffic slows along the corridor.

TERRITORIAL PLANNING AND
THE PROBLEM WITH CLUSTERS

A second contradiction arises from a mismatch between conceptions and urban realities. While the conurbation continues to grow and merge spaces, territorial planning focuses on individual bounded units. Policymakers, spatial planners, and international agen-

F. 15   Border check-point at the Benin-Nigeria border.

Fig. 16

Fig. 17

cies maintain a focus on cities as the panacea of urban development and often contain their strategies within city limits or national borders rather than considering the transnational urbanisation processes cutting across the corridor.[59] Territorial strategies developed in Nigeria, Benin, Togo, and Ghana overlook the corridor's relevance and potential for growth and development. Like much research, these planning exercises are often trapped within the limits of methodological nationalism, failing to draw on regional and transnational dynamics.

One such example is the Beninese national territorial development plan, launched in 2016. It presents a development scenario structured around regional poles, radiating from secondary cities throughout the country, "structuring each pole around one or more towns as driving forces, with specific potentiality and vocations."[60] The Beninese territorial plan appropriates the notion of the pole from French urban planning that introduced the concept of clusters, or *pôles de compétitivité,* as a legal instrument for urban planning in 2002. Due to the circulation of dominant urban planning models from France to francophone West Africa, the document overlooks the significance of the urban continuity along the coast and its relevance within a larger urban territory. Consequently, the Beninese coastline, which spans just 120 kilometres, is divided into the South-East Pole, South Pole, and South-West Pole, each centred on a city and given a specific role. In the document's accompanying cartography, there are no connections between the various regions along the corridor. The neighbouring nations are left as one grey expanse, leaving no opportunity to account for the territorial role of Togo or Nigeria despite the importance of trans-border exchanges. The absence of trans-border spatial planning is systematic of the region's national planning documents

that often overlook urban growth along the corridor, along with the dependencies on trade and circulation. [Fig. 17]

Slicing the corridor into distinctive functional units connected to their respective national hinterlands prevents planning authorities from anticipating how the corridor will thicken and grow as it expands north and as new constructions fill in the gaps in the urban fabric. Furthermore, it prevents national authorities from developing strategies that draw on territorial synergies along the corridor. The Beninois government, for instance, is currently seeking to boost the tourism sector and attract European tourists to its heritage sites, floating villages, and beaches.[61] This is of limited success, but just down the road, in Lagos, there is an emerging market of middle-class urbanites with higher disposable incomes seeking to escape the megacity, its pollution, and "go-slow" traffic for short breaks. Residents in Lagos consider Benin a calmer, safer, and more provincial location and would be a strategic clientele to target. In Benin, decentring policies away from France could enable planners and policymakers to identify potential opportunities in neighbouring countries and build strategies to develop complementary territorial agendas.

MIGRATION MANAGEMENT AND CONTAINMENT STRATEGIES

Efforts to improve regional integration and territorial planning appear at odds with the lived experience of the corridor on the ground. The same can be said for migration management policies, which, again, produce a contradiction between the discursive framework of policy-making and the everyday experience of mobility along the corridor. Indeed, whereas the vast majority of migration is made up of inter-regional mobility, the political focus remains on departures to Europe. The presence of strangers is part of everyday urbanity, creating encounters as people seek out opportunities along the various sites on the corridor. ECOWAS has sought to legislate this movement. In 1979, it passed the first protocol for free movement and residence for West African citizens, and in 2000

F. 16 A female trader transports goods across the Benin-Nigeria border during the rainy season.

F. 17 The facade of a building demolished in an urban planning operation.

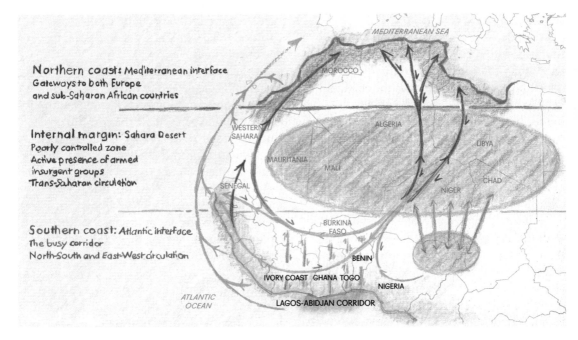

Northern coast: Mediterranean interface
Gateways to both Europe
and sub-Saharan African countries

Internal margin: Sahara Desert
Poorly controlled zone
Active presence of armed
insurgent groups
Trans-Saharan circulation

Southern coast: Atlantic interface
The busy corridor
North-South and East-West circulation

MEDITERRANEAN SEA

MOROCCO
ALGERIA
LIBYA
WESTERN SAHARA
MAURITANIA
MALI
SENEGAL
NIGER
CHAD
BURKINA FASO
BENIN
IVORY COAST GHANA TOGO
NIGERIA
ATLANTIC OCEAN
LAGOS-ABIDJAN CORRIDOR

TWO MIGRATION COASTLINES
Fig. 18

introduced an ECOWAS passport to facilitate crossing borders. The passport has had limited uptake, and so far, Benin is the only country along the corridor to have adopted it.

However, given the current preoccupation of Western aid donors with inter-continental African migration, there is a risk that the fluidity of movement is reframed as problematic to align with current regimes of containment. This, in turn, would overlook the key role mobility plays in enabling urban futures in West Africa. There is a danger that these regional forms of mobility are interpreted within the narrow European perspective on international migration, especially given the current securitisation and criminalisation of international African migration.

The mismatch between everyday mobility along the coast and the dominant discourse from international partners was made tangibly during fieldwork en route from Lagos to Cotonou. Sitting in a *Tokpa* minibus, I was hurtling down the corridor heading to the Dantokpa market. The sliding door was jammed open, primed for new passengers to scramble on, and the ticket boy, keen on maintaining capacity at 150%, leant out of the bus, shouting the destination out to potential travellers. Sitting in the back on retro-fitted wooden benches, babies got passed over, more bundles of goods squeezed in, and we squabbled over change for the tickets. Coming into Cotonou, we slowed down in traffic alongside a billboard plastered with a public awareness campaign.

The billboard featured a cartoon image of a flimsy boat overloaded with black people, accompanied by the slogan *Non à l'Emigration!* and stamped with the European Union logo. The image was designed for the illiterate and drew on tropes that have become omnipresent in the media, referencing the dangers of crossing the Mediterranean. Looking out from the minibus window, the discrepancy between the everyday experience of mobility in West Africa and the European Union's policy messages were salient. Here travel is more likely to occur in a run-down minibus moving along the corridor than in a dingy floating across the Mediterranean.

During the slave trade, black bodies left this coast in boats, but today, only petrol smugglers and fishermen launch their crafts out over the waves. The Gulf of Guinea is largely unmonitored, and it is an ordinary coast with unspectacular, un-policed mobility that rarely makes headlines, unlike the images of the North African coastline with barbed wires, coast guards, and radars. [Fig. 18]

In a later interview with a government official working on migration, he recognised that the poster addressed the wrong target group, and if someone was really set on migrating, a billboard would do little to dissuade them. But "Bon! It's the vision of the European Union, we are trying to change it a little, but remember, the EU contributes a lot of aid to Benin and is one of our key technical partners." Along with the securitisation of movement and externalisation of migration management, development aid is being tied in with containment strategies, seeking to "keep people in their place." [62] Following the 2015 migration "crisis," official development aid delivered along the corridor is increasingly mandated to improve life opportunities in Africa and prevent migration to Europe. Up until now, migration in many of the corridor countries has not been a salient political issue, with the exception of xenophobic outbreaks, for example, in the Ivory Coast. However, imaginaries, discourses, and projects are increasingly informed by the European fear of mobile Africans. Messages such as these circulate the idea that the movement of people is problematic and overlooks the importance of mobility in shaping the localities along the corridor.

CONTRADICTIONS AND CONFLICTS IN THE GOVERNANCE OF THE LAGOS–ABIDJAN CORRIDOR

In the three instances of regional integration, territorial planning, and migration management, the experiences of the urban majority along this corridor are not aligned with government discourse and policy, creating various tensions between official representations and everyday practices of mobility and immobility along the corridor. Metaphorically, territorial regulation and everyday life are driving in opposite lanes of the corridor, either ignoring each other as they pass or crashing when the inconsistencies no longer compute. Identifying the contradictions within these instruments enables us to understand why these politics are failing to deliver for this territory of extended urbanisation. If traffic is sped up along the road without considering the interests of road-dwelling communities, then there is a possibility that these communities will nevertheless seek to slow it down and create moments to trade. If territorial planning fails to account for the spatial dynamics along the corridor, it will produce isolated urban development projects that overlook regional synergies and the potential of leveraging difference and opportunity, as is the case of the tourism strategy in Benin. Finally, if migration policy is only preoccupied with migration towards Europe and how to deter it, it will overlook the real challenges, vulnerabilities, and advantages of inter-regional mobility.

It is of little surprise that the European Union and European interventions feature in these contradictions, such as building unused border posts, exporting urban planning notions, or designing ill-fitting migration campaigns. This reflects a framing of mobility issues and territorial planning that conform to tacit European understandings of how this corridor should be governed and post-colonial tendencies to replicate various political instruments, as in the notion of competitive clusters. Understanding these contradictions paves a path to alternative strategies of action that take into account the interests of road-dwelling communities, for whom the road might be a key source of income. These strategies should consider trans-border exchange and how various scales of mobility are enabling livelihoods up and down the road.

THE [IM]MOBILITIES OF EXTENDED URBANISATION

Researchers observing still-unbuilt areas between the capital cities along the Lagos-Abidjan Corridor have, at times, concluded that this is not indicative of a metropolitan region.

Indeed, when there are breaks in the cemented landscape, the corridor looks deceptively rural. For example, Amandine Spire refers to the desa-kota concept, which Terry McGee proposed for urban developments in South East Asia's rice landscapes to characterise the corridor.[63] Is it "at the crossroads of the city and the country?" she asks. Or is this hypothesis too risky? What to make of the village settlements, the coconut plantations, and the fields of yams that are between the major cities?[64] One answer would be that these diverse spaces are all participating at different degrees and speeds in the emerging space of extended urbanisation along the Lagos-Abidjan Corridor. And perhaps a focus on either rural or urban settings has slowed down the development of a more comprehensive research agenda, overlooking how individuals forge livelihoods across multiple locations, contributing to their transformation and ongoing urbanisation.

The Lagos-Abidjan Corridor is not the sum of the cities along it, nor is it a transnational West African Bos-Wash. This chapter sets out to decentre studies of urbanity in West Africa. As Milica Topalović proposes[65], it eclipses the major capitals and skirts around the predominant city-centrism and Western frameworks of urban analysis. It is a study of African mobility that moves outside the city centres into other urban spaces to examine how movement produces urban form in its interstices.

The road takes us outside the core of capital cities, enabling us to pay heed to what else is happening along the corridor. It cuts through defined urban field-sites and decentres our gaze from the megacities. Only then do a series of ordinary places emerge along the coast, places whose development is intrinsically linked to (im)mobilities and circulations. Thinking infrastructurally and starting from the roadside embeds this view of mobility within current theorisations of extended urbanisation. Here, with its bumps and uneven surfaces, the road becomes the main protagonist of extended urbanisation, both as a physical infrastructure and a surface upon which everyday life unfolds. The road nudges theories of extended urbanisation to engage with mobility in more epistemolog-

ical terms to understand the transformation of urban territories through the lens of movement.

Observing how these processes play out along the corridor provides a clearer picture of how this larger scale of urbanisation is emerging. It also has the potential to better inform research on the cities themselves and their trans-local relevance. In the corridor, people draw on both the strong nodes of concentrated agglomerations and the threads of thinner extended urbanisation. Along the corridor, the capitals and megacities play a significant role as key nodes and major centralities, bringing together services, markets and infrastructure. However, the urban dynamics of these cities are not contained within their specific locations; they seep outside of their borders and resonate along the corridor, connected to other locations through various mobilities. Lagos and its 20 million inhabitants are transforming all kinds of places along the corridor well outside its boundaries. In neighbouring Benin, the arrival of Nigerian university students has created entire new areas with accompanying Nigerian shops, restaurants, barber salons, and evangelical churches. And as the wealth generated in Lagos fluctuates along the corridor, small tweaks in Nigeria's economic climate, import regulations and currency exchange rates produce shockwaves and shift trajectories of urban development along the coast, making a new business grow or well-established sectors crash.

Mobilising theories of extended urbanisation highlight the political implications of the current processes of urban development. Fractioned colonial legacies, combined with methodological nationalism and a euro-centric framing of movement and territory along the corridor, prevent practitioners and planners from considering the full extension of the corridor in terms of its development. Grounded fieldwork and empirical observations unearth contradictions between the regulation of these urban territories and the processes in play as everyday life seeks to produce and hang onto urbanity. The various state and regional instruments put in place to govern the corridor overlook the force of movement in reconfiguring extended urbanisation. This movement cannot always be channelled or determined. The roadside is a space where the state's authority is reconstituted and challenged.

The specific case of the West African corridor shines a light on how mobility is brokered in spaces of extended urbanisation. It also offers up insights into struggles elsewhere, notably in the north in times of austerity and recession. The first point of comparison is the roadside protests in France and the case of the Gilets Jaunes, whose mobilisations were sparked following a tax on fuel and crossed over traditional political divides. Its base was urban communities living outside of the city centres who rely on affordable car travel. As a movement, it positioned itself distinctly against classic forms of protest and occupied road infrastructures such as toll booths and roundabouts. These moments of infrastructure became key to reclaiming the urban, as in the tactics employed along the Lagos-Abidjan Corridor to create breakages in the road. The second point of comparison is with the rise of the "gig economy" in European and American cities. This relies on direct access to freelancers in the marketplace, allowing companies to remain competitive and flexible without employing in-house staff. Analysis of the West African corridor informs us of how, in the aftermath of Structural Adjustment Programmes, people remained on the move, hustling and engaging in informal trade or driving moto-taxis in the absence of formal labour. Talk to young people in the global North's cities, and they will speak of their hustle as they jump from gig to gig, clinging onto passing opportunities and driving Ubers as they struggle to craft decent livelihoods in their respective urban centres. On the brink of global recession, places like the West African corridor point to common urban futures where people must remain on the move in the absence of jobs.

With this in mind, we return to the toll booth one last time, where drivers and passengers slow down to be taxed and inspected, have a drink, and buy some fruit. For many along the corridor, slowing down traffic allows them to find a bargain, share some news, and maybe get something they didn't have before. And as people wind down windows and reach out to give a little, to take a little, to shake a hand, hand over a bribe, or a sleeping baby, urbanisation extends; it stretches out along the roadsides, reaching into all sorts of places outside of the city and its settlements. No one really lives here, there are no houses and no settlements. Most things get bundled up and packed away after sunset. But, during the day, as people move through, get tied down for lunch or a chat, and then set off again, differentiated encounters occur, and the urban fabric is stretched out a little further.

ENDNOTES

1 Current population estimates: Lagos 23 million, Abidjan 4.7 million, Porto Novo 0.9 million, Cotonou 2.4 million, Lomé 2.1 million, and Accra 3.4 million.
2 Moriconi-Ebrard, *Urbanisation Dynamics in West Africa.*
3 UN-Habitat, *The State of African Cities*, 94.
4 OECD, *Africa's Urbanisation Dynamic 2020*, 109.
5 Labbé, *Handbook of Megacities*, 1.
6 UN-Habitat, *The State of African Cities*, 98.
7 NEPAD, *Abidjan Lagos Corridor One*, 5.
8 Choplin, "Metropolisation et Gouvernance Urbaine."
9 International treaties have been signed by Benin that guarantee their right to circulation and residence (CEDEAO, 1975, Protocol A/P.1/5/79 de 1979).
10 Simone, "The Urbanity of Movement", 381, 388.
11 Adepoju, "Migrants and Refugees,"; Bredeloup, "Migrations entre les deux"; Jerven, "Poor Numbers."
12 Robin, "Panorama des migrations"; Simone, "The Urbanity of Movement."
13 Flahaux, "African Migration"; Landau, "The Future of Mobility"; CMPD, *A Survey on Migration.*
14 IOM, *West and Central Africa.*
15 Schmidt-Kallert, "Non-Permanent Migration."
16 Tacoli, "Urbanization, Rural-Urban Migration."
17 Bakewell, "Keeping Them in Their Place."
18 Potts, "Rural-Urban and Urban-Rural," 10.
19 Jedwab, "Rural Push, Urban Pull."
20 Bakewell, "Migration, Mobility," 5.
21 Bruijn, *Mobile Africa.*
22 Simone, "The Urbanity of Movement."
23 Bakewell, "Introduction: Forging a Study."
24 nccr, "The Migration-Mobility Nexus," para 1.
25 Melly, *Bottleneck*, 9.
26 Sheller, "The New Mobilities Paradigm," 214.
27 Büscher, *Mobile Methods.*
28 Sheller, "The New Mobilities Paradigm," 209.
29 Landau, "Urbanisms and Archipelagic Space-Time."
30 Law, "Between the Sea," 222.
31 Chouin, "Crisis and Transformation."
32 Law, "Between the Sea," 222.

33 Cornevin, *La République Populaire.*
34 Igué, *L'Etat-Entrepôt Au Bénin.*
35 Challenor, "Strangers as Colonial Intermediaries; Quintard, "Benin."
36 Brenner, "Planetary Urbanization," 12.
37 Lefebvre, *The Production of Space*, 313, 317.
38 Choplin, "The West African Corridor"; Choplin, *Matière grise de l'urbain.*
39 Gottmann, *Megalopolis*; Greenberg, "The Gauteng City-Region."
40 Agbiboa, "No Condition Is Permanent"; Sawyer, "Plotting the Prevalent"; Acey, "Rise of the Synthetic"; Lawanson, "Land Governance and Megacity"; Mendelsohn, "Making the Urban Coast."
41 Gough, "Land Markets in African Cities"; Pellow, *Landlords and Lodgers*; Grant, *Globalizing City;* Quayson, *Oxford Street, Accra;* Hart, *Ghana on the Go*; Paller, *Democracy in Ghana.*
42 N'Bessa, "Porto-Novo et Cotonu"; Ciavolella, Cotonou Histoire d'une Ville; Gervais-Lambony, *Lomé;* Spire, *L'Etranger et La Ville;* Choplin, "The West African Corridor."
43 Souaré, "Interview avec Mamady Souaré"; NEPAD, "Abidjan Lagos Corridor One"; Choplin, *Matière grise de l'urbain.*
44 Spire, *L'Etranger et La Ville.*
45 Merrifield, "The Urban Question under," 910.
46 Hertzog, "The Lagos-Abidjan Corridor"; Hertzog, "Heading to Town"; Hertzog, "Urban Migration in West Africa."
47 Hertzog, *Parcours de Migrants.*
48 Melly, *Bottleneck.*
49 Larkin, *Signal and Noise*, 329; Simone, "People as Infrastructure: Intersecting."
50 Harvey, "The Enchantments of Infrastructure"; Harvey, *Roads*; Klaeger, "Rush and Relax"; Klaeger, "Dwelling on the Road"; Manji, "Bulldozers, Homes and Highways"; Baptista, "The Road of Progress"; Filippello, *The Nature of the Path.*
51 Glele, "La Periurbanisation," 461.
52 Ciavolella, "Cotonou Histoire d'une Ville".
53 Melley, *Bottleneck.*
54 Melley, *Bottleneck.*
55 De Boeck and Baloji. *Suturing the City*
56 Kapuscinski, *Ebène*, 306–307.
57 Igué, *L'Etat-Entrepôt Au Bénin.*

58 Banque africaine de developpement, "Corridor Abidjan-Lagos."
59 Pike, "The Limits of City," Castriota, "Estudos Urbanos."
60 Ministère, "Projet d'Agenda Spatial."
61 Présidence, "Programme d'Actions Du Gouvernement."
62 Bakewell, "Keeping them in Their Place"; Collyer, "From Preventive to Repressive."
63 McGee, "The Emergence of Desakota."
64 Spire, *L'Etranger et La Ville*, 56.
65 Topalović, "Architecture of Territory."

BIBLIOGRAPHY

Acey, Charisma. "Rise of the Synthetic City: Eko Atlantic and Practices of Dispossession and Repossession in Nigeria." In *Disassembled Cities: Social and Spatial Strategies to Reassemble Communities*, edited by Elizabeth L. Sweet. Global Urban Studies. Abingdon, Oxon; New York, NY: Routledge, 2018.

Adepoju, Aderanti. "Migrants and Refugees in Africa." *Oxford Research Encyclopedia of Politics*, 25 June 2019. https://doi.org/10.1093/acrefore/9780190228637.013.723.

Agbiboa, Daniel E. "'No Condition is Permanent: Informal Transport Workers and Labour Precarity in Africa's Largest City." *International Journal of Urban and Regional Research* 40, no. 5 (2017): 936–957.

Bakewell, Oliver. "Keeping Them in Their Place": The Ambivalent Relationship between Development and Migration in Africa." *Third World Quarterly* 29, no. 7 (October 2008): 1341–1358.

Bakewell, Oliver, and Gunvor Jónsson. "Migration, Mobility, and the African City." Working Papers. International Migration Institute, December 2011.

Bakewell, Oliver, and Loren Landau. "Introduction: Forging a Study of Mobility, Integration, and Belonging in Africa." In *Forging African Communities: Mobility, Integration, and Belonging*, edited by Oliver Bakewell and Loren B. Landau. Global Diversities. London: Palgrave Macmillan, 2018.

Banque africaine de développement. "Corridor Abidjan-Lagos: Programme Phare Du PIDA et Catalyseur de Croissance Économique Pour l'Afrique de l'Ouest." Banque africaine de développement, 2016. https://www.afdb.org/fr/news-and-events/the-abidjan-lagos-corridor-a-pida-flagship-programme-and-catalyst-for-economic-growth-in-west-africa-16078/.

Baptista, João Afonso. "The Road of Progress: Individualisation and Interaction Agency in Southeast Angola." *Ethnos* 83, no. 3 (2016): 521–543.

Beck, Kurt, Gabriel Klaeger, and Michael Stasik, eds. *The Making of the African Road*. Africa-Europe Group for Interdisciplinary Studies, Vol. 18. Leiden; Boston: Brill, 2017.

Bredeloup, Sylvie, and Olivier Pliez. "Migrations entre les deux rives du Sahara." *Autrepart* n° 36, no. 4 (2005): 3–20.

Brenner, Neil, and Christian Schmid. "Planetary Urbanization." In *Urban Constellations*, edited by Mathew Gandy. Jovis, 2011.

———."The 'Urban Age' in Question." *International Journal of Urban and Regional Research* 38, no. 3 (1 May 2014): 731–755.

Bruijn, Mirjam de, Rijk van Dijk, and D. Foeken, eds. *Mobile Africa: Changing Patterns of Movement in Africa and Beyond*. African Dynamics 1. Leiden; Boston: Brill, 2001.

Büscher, Monika, John Urry, and Katian Witchger, eds. *Mobile Methods*. Abingdon, Oxon; New York, NY: Routledge, 2011.

Castriota, Rodrigo, and Bruno Siqueira. "Estudos Urbanos Ou Estudos Da Cidade? Notas Sobre o Citadismo Ou Cidade-Centrismo." In *Annals of the XVIII ANPUR Annual Meeting (Associação Nacional Dos Centros de Pós-Graduação Em Planejamento Urbano e Regional)*. Natal, Brasil, 2019.

Chabi, Moïse. "Métropolisation et Dynamiques Périurbaines: Cas de l'espace Urbain de Cotonou." l'Université Paris Ouest Nanterre La Défense, 2013.

Challenor, Herschelle Sullivan. "Strangers as Colonial Intermediaries: The Dahomeyan in Francophone Africa." In *Strangers in African Societies*, edited by W. A Shack and E. R Skinner, 67–84. Berkeley, CA: University of California Press, 1979.

Choplin, Armelle. *Matière grise de l'urbain: la vie du ciment en Afrique*. Geneva: Métis Presses, 2020.

———."Metropolisation et Gouvernance Urbaine: Le Réseau Des Villes Du Golfe de Guinée Au Défi Des Vulnérabilités et Inégalités (Accra, Lomé, Cotonou, Porto-Novo, Lagos)." Unpublished: IRD, 2015.

Choplin, Armelle, and Alice Hertzog. "The West African Corridor from Accra to Lagos: A Megacity-Region under Construction." In *Handbook of Megacities and Megacity-Regions*, edited by Danielle Labbé and André Sorensen. Cheltenham, UK: Edward Elgar Publishing, 2020.

Choplin, Armelle, and Olivier Pliez. *La mondialisation des pauvres: loin de Wall Street et de Davos*. La république des idées. Paris: Seuil, 2018.

Chouin, Gérard L., and Olanrewaju Blessing Lasisi. "Crisis and Transformation in the Bight of Benin at the Dawn of the Atlantic Trade." In *Power, Political Economy, and Historical Landscapes of the Modern World*. Albany: State University of New York Press, 2019.

Ciavolella, Riccardo, and Armelle Choplin. "Cotonou Histoire d'une Ville 'Sans Histoire.'" Catalogue d'Exposition. Cotonou: Fondation Zinsou, 2018.

Collyer, Michael. "From Preventive to Repressive: The Changing Use of Development and Humanitarianism to Control Migration." In *Handbook on Critical Geographies of Migration*, edited by Katharyne Mitchell, Reece Jones, and Jennifer L. Fluri. Research Handbooks in Geography. Cheltenham; Northampton, MA: Edward Elgar Publishing Limited, 2019.

Cornevin, Robert. *La République Populaire du Bénin des Origines Dahoméennes à nos Jours*. Paris: G-P Maisonneuve et Larose, 1981.

De Boeck, Filip, and Sammy Baloji. *Suturing the City: Living Together in Congo's Urban Worlds*. London: Autograph ABP, 2016.

Doherty, Jacob. "Life (and Limb) in the Fast-Lane: Disposable People as Infrastructure in Kampala's Boda Boda Industry." *Critical African Studies* 9, no. 2 (4 May 2017): 192–209.

Filippello, Marcus. *The Nature of the Path*. Minneapolis: University of Minnesota Press, 2017.

Flahaux, Marie-Laurence, and Hein De Haas. "African Migration: Trends, Patterns, Drivers." *Comparative Migration Studies* 4, no. 1 (22 January 2016): 1.

Gervais-Lambony, Philippe, and G. Kwami Nyassogbo, eds. *Lomé: Dynamiques d'une Ville Africaine*. Hommes et Sociétés. Paris: Karthala, 2007.

Glele, Gisèle Afiavi. "La Periurbanisation et Les Dynamiques Foncières Sur Le Plateau d'Allada (Sud-Benin): L'Espace Temoin de La Commune D'Abomey Calavi." Université d'Abomey-Calavi, 2015.

Gottmann, Jean. *Megalopolis: The Urbanized Northeastern Seaboard of the United States.* Cambridge, MA: MIT Press, 1961.

Gough, Katherine V., and Paul W. K. Yankson. "Land Markets in African Cities: The Case of Peri-Urban Accra, Ghana." *Urban Studies* 37, no. 13 (December 2000): 2485–2500.

Grant, Richard. *Globalizing City: The Urban and Economic Transformation of Accra, Ghana.* 1st ed. Space, Place, and Society. Syracuse, NY: Syracuse University Press, 2009.

Greenberg, Stephen. "The Gauteng City-Region: Private and Public Power in the Shaping of the City." *Politikon* 37, no. 1 (1 April 2010): 107–127.

Hart, Jennifer A. *Ghana on the Go: African Mobility in the Age of Motor Transportation.* Bloomington: Indiana University Press, 2016.

Harvey, Penny, and Hannah Knox. *Roads: An Anthropology of Infrastructure and Expertise.* Expertise: Cultures and Technologies of Knowledge. Ithaca: Cornell University Press, 2015.

———."The Enchantments of Infrastructure." *Mobilities* 7, no. 4 (1 November 2012): 521–536.

Hertzog, Alice. "The Lagos-Abidjan Corridor – Migration Driven Urbanisation in West Africa." ETH, 2020.

———."Heading to Town, Leveraging Migration for Development in Benin." Bern: Global Programme for Migration and Development, Swiss Development Cooperation, 2021.

———."Urban Migration in West Africa, Regional Patterns and Trends." Bern: Global Programme for Migration and Development, Swiss Development Cooperation, 2021.

———."Parcours de Migrants," 2021. http://www.parcours-de-migrants.ethz.ch/en

Hoehne, Markus Virgil, and Dereje Feyissa. "Centering Borders and Borderlands: The Evidence from Africa." In *Violence on the Margins: States, Conflict, and Borderlands* edited by Benedikt Korf and Timothy Raeymaekers, 55–84. Palgrave Series in African Borderlands Studies. New York: Palgrave Macmillan US, 2013.

ICMPD and IOM. "A Survey on Migration Policies in West Africa." Vienna & Dakar, 2015.

Igué, John, and Bio G. Soule. *L'Etat-Entrepôt Au Bénin.* Paris: Karthala, 1992.

Igué, John, and Kossiwa Zinsou-Klassou. *Frontières, Espaces de Développement Partagé.* Paris: Karthala, 2010.

IOM Migration. "West and Central Africa." Fact Sheets. West and Central Africa, 2020. https://www.iom.int/west-and-central-africa.

Jedwab, Remi, Luc Christiaensen, and Marina Gindelsky. "Rural Push, Urban Pull and… Urban Push? New Historical Evidence from Developing Countries." Working Paper. The George Washington University, Institute for International Economic Policy, 2014. https://ideas.repec.org/p/gwi/wpaper/2014-04.html.

Jerven, Morten. *Poor Numbers: How We Are Misled by African Development Statistics and What We Can Do about It.* Ithaca & London: Cornell University Press, 2013.

Kapuscinski, Ryszard. *Ebène – Aventures Africaines.* Paris: Editions Plon, 2000.

Klaeger, Gabriel. "Dwelling on the Road: Routines, Rituals and Roadblocks in Southern Ghana." *Africa: Journal of the International African Institute* 83, no. 3 (2013): 446–469.

———."Rush and Relax: The Rhythms and Speeds of Touting Perishable Products on a Ghanaian Roadside." *Mobilities* 7, no. 4 (1 November 2012): 537–554.

Labbé, Danielle, and André Sorensen, eds. *Handbook of Megacities and Megacity-Regions.* Research Handbooks in Urban Studies Series. Northampton: Edward Elgar Publishing, 2020.

Landau, Loren B, and Caroline Wanjiku Kihato. "The Future of Mobility and Migration Within and From Sub-Saharan Africa." EPAS Foresight Reflection Paper Series. European Strategy and Policy Analysis System, June 2018.

———."Urbanisms and Archipelagic Space-Time." African Mobilities (blog), 2 May 2018. https://archive.africanmobilities.org/discourse/2018/05/urbanisms-and-archipelagic-space-time/.

Larkin, Brian. *Signal and Noise: Media, Infrastructure, and Urban Culture in Nigeria.* Unknown edition. Durham: Duke University Press Books, 2008.

Law, Robin. "Between the Sea and the Lagoons: The Interaction of Maritime and Inland Navigation on the Precolonial Slave Coast." *Cahiers d'études Africaines* 29, no. 167 (1989): 209–237.

Lawanson, Taibat, and Muyiwa Agunbiade. "Land Governance and Megacity Projects in Lagos, Nigeria: The Case of Lekki Free Trade Zone." *Area Development and Policy* 3, no. 1 (2 January 2018): 114–131.

Lefebvre, Henri. *The Production of Space.* Oxford, UK; Cambridge, MA, USA: Blackwell, 1991.

Lentz, Carola. "'This Is Ghanaian Territory!': Land Conflicts on a West African Border." *American Ethnologist* 30, no. 2 (2003): 273–289.

Lopez, Sarah Lynn. *The Remittance Landscape: Spaces of Migration in Rural Mexico and Urban USA.* Chicago: The University of Chicago Press, 2015.

Manji, Ambreena. "Bulldozers, Homes and Highways: Nairobi and the Right to the City." *Review of African Political Economy* 42, no. 144 (3 April 2015): 206–24.

McGee, T. G. "The Emergence of Desakota Regions in Asia: Expanding a Hypothesis." In *The Extended Metropolis: Settlement Transition in Asia*, edited by Norton Sydney Ginsburg, Bruce Koppel, and T. G. McGee, 3–25. Honolulu: University of Hawaii Press, 1991.

Melly, Caroline. *Bottleneck. Moving, Building and Belonging in an African City.* Chicago: University of Chicago Press, 2016.

Mendelsohn, Ben. "Making the Urban Coast – A Geosocial Reading of Land, Sand, and Water in Lagos, Nigeria." *Comparative Studies of South Asia, Africa and the Middle East* 38, no. 3 (1 December 2018): 455–72.

Merrifield, Andy. "The Urban Question under Planetary Urbanization." *International Journal of Urban and Regional Research* 37, no. 3 (2013): 909–922.

Ministère la Décentralisation, de la Gouvernance Locale, de l'Administration et de l'Aménagement du Territoire. "Projet d'Agenda Spatial Du Benin." Schéma National d'Aménagement Du Territoire (SNAT), 2016.

Moriconi-Ebrard, François, Dominique Harre, and Philipp Heinrigs. *Urbanisation Dynamics in West Africa 1950–2010: Africapolis 1, 2015 Update*. West African Studies. Paris: OECD, 2016.

N'Bessa, Benoît. "Porto-Novo et Cotonou Bénin: origine et évolution d'un doublet urbain." Atelier National de Reproduction des Thèses, 1998.

nccr—on the move. "The Migration-Mobility Nexus." *The Migration-Mobility Nexus* (blog), 2019. https://nccr-onthemove.ch/about-us/the-migration-mobility-nexus/.

NEPAD. "Abidjan Lagos Corridor One Road – One Vision." Program on the Provision of Services and Assistance in the Preparation and Management of the Abidjan-Lagos Road Corridor Development Project, 2017.

OECD/SWAC (2020), *Africa's Urbanisation Dynamics 2020: Africapolis, Mapping a New Urban Geography*, West African Studies, OECD Publishing, Paris.

Paller, Jeffrey W. *Democracy in Ghana. Everyday Politics in Urban Africa*. Cambridge: Cambridge University Press, 2019.

Pellow, Deborah. *Landlords and Lodgers: Socio-Spatial Organization in an Accra Community*. Chicago: The University of Chicago Press, 2008.

Pike, Andy. "The Limits of City Centrism?" *British Politics and Policy at LSE* (blog), 2018

Potts, Deborah. "Rural-Urban and Urban-Rural Migration Flows as Indicators of Economic Opportunity in Sub-Saharan Africa: What Do the Data Tell Us?" *University of Sussex: Migrating Out of Poverty Research Programme Working Paper*, 2013.

Quayson, Ato. *Oxford Street, Accra: City Life and the Itineraries of Transnationalism*. Durham: Duke University Press, 2014.

Quintard, Mickael. "Benin." In *Dictionnaire Des Migrations Internationales Approche Géohistorique*, by Gildas Simon. Paris: Armand Colin, 2015.

Robin, Nelly. "Panorama des migrations en Afrique de l'Ouest." Grain de Sel, 2007.

Rodriguez, Michaël, and Fernand Nouwligbèto. "Taxi-Moto à Cotonou: Un Gagne-Pain Qui Coûte Des Vies." *RTS Decouverte* (blog), 2010. https://www.rts.ch/decouverte/dossiers/2010/en-quete-afrique-ville/benin/2579381-taxi-moto-a-cotonou-un-gagne-pain-qui-coute-des-vies.html.

Sawyer, Lindsey. "Plotting the Prevalent but Undertheorised Residential Areas of Lagos. Conceptualising a Process of Urbanisation through Grounded Theory and Comparison." ETH Zurich, 2016.

Schmidt-Kallert, Einhard. "Non-Permanent Migration and Multilocality in the Global South." *Die Erde* 143, no. 3 (2012).

Schwanen, Tim. "Towards Decolonised Knowledge about Transport." *Palgrave Communications* 4, no. 1 (3 July 2018): 79.

Sheller, Mimi, and John Urry. "The New Mobilities Paradigm." *Environment and Planning A* 38, no. 2 (February 2006): 207–226.

Simone, AbdouMaliq. "Inhabiting the Corridor." *Villes Noires* (blog), October 2016. https://www.villes-noires.tumblr.com/.

———."People as Infrastructure: Intersecting Fragments in Johannesburg," *Public Culture*, 16, no. 03 (2004): 407–429.

———."The Urbanity of Movement: Dynamic Frontiers in Contemporary Africa." *Journal of Planning Education and Research* 31, no. 4 (December 2011): 379–391.

Soja, Edward, and Miguel Kanai. "The Urbanization of the World." In *The Endless City: The Urban Age Project by the London School of Economics and Deutsche Bank's Alfred Herrhausen Society*, 54–68. London: Phaidon, 2006.

Spire, Amandine. *L'Etranger et La Ville En Afrique de l'Ouest*. Paris: Karthala, 2011.

Tacoli, Cecilia, David Satterthwaite, and Mc Granahan Gordon. "Urbanization, Rural-Urban Migration and Urban Poverty." Background Paper. World Migration Report 2015. IOM, 2014.

Topalović, Milica. "Architecture of Territory: Beyond the Limits of the City: Research and Design of Urbanising Territories." Inaugural lecture ETH Zurich, 30 November 2016.

UN-Habitat, ed. *The State of African Cities 2008: A Framework for Addressing Urban Challenges in Africa*. Nairobi: UN-HABITAT, 2008.

Urry, John. *Mobilities*. Reprint. Cambridge: Polity Press, 2012.

IMAGE CREDITS

All photography from author unless otherwise stated.

All maps from Philippe Rekacewicz with author unless otherwise stated.

F. 1   Martin Lozivit
F. 2   World Urbanization Prospects (United Nations)
F. 4   Stefane Brabant
F. 5   Air Côte d'Ivoire
F. 6   Anon. source: British Library
F. 7   Sources: Serge Grusinski, Les quatre parties du monde, Paris: La Martinière, 2004; P. Verger, *Flux et reflux de la traite négrière entre le golfe de Bénin et Bahia de Todos os Santos*, Paris: Mouton, 1968; Atlas Historique Larousse, Hachette et Bordas; P. Lovejoy, *Transformations in Slavery. A History in Africa*, Cambridge: Cambridge University Press, 1983 ; *Histoire générale de l'Afrique*, Unesco/Nouvelles éditions africaines, 8 vol., Paris, 1980–1998; J. Ki-Zerbo, *Histoire de l'Afrique noire*, Hatier: Paris, 1972.
F. 9   Christian Schmid
F. 18   BBC, The Guardian, Le Monde diplomatique, Le Monde, Migreurop, Migrinter (Poitiers)

Translocalisation and the Production of Space. West Bengal's Ex-Centric Territories

Fig. 1

GRAMER SHAHAR TERRITORIES, KANCHA–PAKA LANDSCAPES

We were heading towards Kolkata on the 7:30 am Bardhaman-Haora local train, and although this was only my third time there, I already felt like a regular. The embodied experience of dozens of similar train rides, all jam-packed with daily commuters, lent me confidence, but the special sense of familiarity had, no doubt, to do with Kartik. He had commuted daily between his village in Hugli district and Kolkata for 30 years now, and his accounts on the railway in south-western West Bengal could have filled books. Looking from the window, I saw the pits alongside the rail track and recalled his detailed description of how, in 2007, the soil was dug out with Caterpillars to build the foundations of the overhead line. "Farmers now cultivate paddy here," he had said, "no point growing potatoes or vegetables on low lands."

Shortly after we passed through the industrial plants of Dankuni, he diverted me from my musings. "You see, now the city has started.

F. 1   A paka-and-kancha landscape.

This is Belanagar Station; there are only little stretches of fields left here. It's still 12 or 15 kilometres to Haora. In a short while, you'll start seeing small factories. Some do ironworks, others manufacture different components for the rail, and there are many more small factories making gilded jewellery towards the interior." The scenery made me think of an old infrastructural landscape now devoid of human functions, forged who knows how long ago out of a governmental will to control the territory. Climbers and water plants covered the vacated factory shacks, deserted iron workshops, and decrepit houses. I replied that despite the new multi-storey housing complexes scattered here and there, this landscape didn't remind me of Kolkata, or Haora, for that matter. "Kolkata? Kolkata is another thing!" was Kartik's assertive reaction. "When you cross Haora [bridge], *that* city has a totally different feeling. This is *gramer shahar*."

The term "gramer shahar" is nearly untranslatable. One might render it as a city grown out of, from, or within the village, although the suggestive power of its literal translation, "the village's city," is hard to match.[1] Also, defining what it might stand for in the context of urbanising India is difficult. To be sure, the difference reclaimed by Kartik is not related to a temporal delay—he did not speak of something that wasn't there *yet*—but correlates with a problem recognised by urban studies scholar Ananya Roy. In her words, the "complex forms of rural-urban differentiation [in India] exceed our analysis of urban political economy and its patterns of accumulation and dispossession."[2]

Sometime later, I joined the "Territories of Extended Urbanisation" project, and from January to April 2018, I sought a better understanding of the processes that form gramer shahar. I got off the train at stations I had previously only passed, explored the towns and villages they served, interviewed elderly inhabitants, and listened to debates in tea stalls and market areas. I learnt about traditional and newly flourishing small or even micro-scale industries; about the increasing incidence of dengue fever, formerly an urban disease, in the

wake of ill-managed construction work and haphazard settlement growth;[3] about the closures of cinema halls built in the revolutionary enthusiasm of the 1980s. It was generous and trying fieldwork, marked by colossal traffic jams around Haora and by the precious clues from Ram, who worked for a bus company and knew every way of getting around them; by hilarious misunderstandings with co-travellers and the disconcerting silences of village women; by drastic clashes between party activists ahead of the local government elections; by blessed moments contemplating the Hugli River— *Ganga*, as people lovingly say in Bengal[4]—amidst the taciturn commuters on the Haldia-Nandigram ferry; by tedious technical mishaps and the seductive choreographies drawn by a green-eyed seller in his shop, chockfull of electronic devices down the alleys of Haora's Ganesh Market.

Two thought figures accompanied my explorations.[5] The first was Kartik's gift, gramer shahar; the second is a relational figure, *kancha–paka*. In Bengali, the adjective "paka"[6] connotes ranges of items that have undergone one or more phases of transformation; vis-à-vis their "kancha"[7] versions, they incorporate time and/ or labour. Paka refers to human and non-human things altogether, from ripe fruits to cooked food, bricks and brick-made houses to built structures made of asphalt or cement, and even skilled, "mature" workers. "Kancha," as one understands, applies to their relational opposites. [Fig. 1] Both words also recur in people's daily conversations about the city and the countryside, whereby "paka" is associated with the first and "kancha" with the latter. In the territory I studied, a large number of roads, workshops, makeshift manufacturers, houses, and granaries were becoming paka, and I frequently asked whether this could be a symptom of the countryside becoming urban. People always denied such a possibility in a way that was reminiscent of Kartik's insistence on the *difference* of gramer shahar. The paka elements, it must be said, were being added to the built environment without completely transforming it, and the kancha elements were certainly not disappearing. I also started to think about the advantages of being

Fig. 2

kancha. Settlements, like things, made solid, might be "reliable," yet not always variable or malleable enough.

In fact, the territory I am going to report on emerges from the continuous making, remaking, and even unmaking of paka and kancha in phases of developing, building up, fixing, tinkering, patching, fencing, enclosing, abandoning, and deterioration, which are determined by the seasons as much as by the initiative of the state and individuals. Similarly, at the level of dwelling and architecture, houses are adjusted, reorganised, divided, and amplified using paka and kancha materials—from corrugated iron sheets to cloth, from bamboo to plywood—that can be assembled, removed, and recycled on numerous occasions and for a myriad of reasons, such as on a daughter's marriage day, for any rite of passage, or in the hope of starting a business.[8] [Fig. 2] As I will explain later, this coexistence of paka and kancha elements correlates with the rhythms of (seasonal) migration, affecting the timing and pace of renovation works. In this chapter,

I propose two conceptual shifts from the analytical lens of Henri Lefebvre's spatial theory, helped by the kancha–paka and gramer shahar figures, to discuss how all these influences impacted this part of West Bengal.

SHIFT #1: BRINGING THE PRODUCTION OF SPACE BACK TO THE FORE

In satellite images, these structures becoming paka show the continually built-up belt stretching from West Bengal through Bihar, Uttar Pradesh, and Haryana to Delhi. For some, these internet images are evidence of what French sociologist and philosopher Henri Lefebvre called "the complete urbanisation of society."[9] Building upon that hypothesis, Christian Schmid and Neil Brenner put forward the controversial

F. 2   Houses in constant making
         in Begampur.

concept of "planetary urbanisation"[10]. Interacting with such expansions of Lefebvre's theory, I often feel that the focus on "urbanisation" leaves too many serious transformations unaddressed. I also doubt the validity of the idea that "the urban"— short for "the urban society" that, according to Lefebvre, was emerging from the current mode of production—connects with the concrete utopia of a fundamental societal change (one in which capitalism has been overthrown). The underlying suggestion, that "the city" facilitates "society's emancipation" through its constituting features of "centrality," "difference," and "mediation" is troublesome in its universalistic ambition. What city? In which society? Which inhabitants? It is evident that Lefebvre's notions rely quite uncritically on Western epistemologies, and this fact cannot be resolved through minor amendments. A thorough review, continuing the work undertaken by feminist, postcolonial, and decolonial authors towards more sensitive, plural, and effective theorisations, is in order.[11]

The *problématique* is rather how to critically analyse and make sense of current spatial and social phenomena impacting large but different territories worldwide from a postcolonial, non-stagist perspective that may accommodate a *grounded utopia*. I engage the word "utopia" to render a sense of possibility, of being able to cohabit with care on a non-homogeneous, non-ideal, damaged planet. But one can only use this word with wariness at a time when ecological destruction, climate change, socio-economic instability, and war are global— no longer resigned to the countries or regions regarded and exploited as Western peripheries. From this derives the need to keep it "grounded" and situate it, as feminist writer Donna Haraway would say, being aware of its limitations within its scope.[12] The scope lies in Lefebvre's emancipatory interpretation of the notions of urbanisation and urban society, which distinguishes them from usual understandings. He posits the progress of urbanisation and the emergence of an "urban society" inspired by the revolutionary events of May 1968 in France.[13] Against the backdrop of the Cold War, vis-à-vis the failure of Soviet communism and the dilution

and dispersion of the proletariat after the collapse of (Fordist) industrial production in Euro-America, this urban society in which women and men fought for hygienic and affordable housing, sexual liberation, gender rights, and self-determination offered a horizon of hope. Lefebvre collocated it in the transformation of city dwellers into a revolutionary subject (a role assigned by Marxism to the proletariat).

The limitations of this theory lie in the linear view of urbanisation as following (from) industrialisation and in the presumption that it could fit the whole world. As argued by historian Dipesh Chakrabarty,[14] the capitalist mode of production which was the backbone of the industrial revolution in Europe has impacted different societies at different points in their history; additionally, in colonised countries, its predominantly extractivist nature caused deep social, economic and ecological damages without the array of innovations and redistributive by-effects which capitalist development had in Europe. As different everyday experiences, societal responses, and crises were the consequence, non-Eurocentric epistemologies are needed. Apparently, Lefebvre never challenged the stagism inherent to the Marxist concept of Europe's capitalist transition. The projection of a global urban society is blind to the possibility that the social process, even if catalysed by capitalism, might be something other than "urbanisation" and its product—as well as its promise—something other than an "urban" society.[15]

While I align myself with those authors who are working towards reviewing and updating Lefebvre's theory through positions that give more thorough consideration to the effects and afterlives of colonialism,[16] the contribution I wish to make here is to revalorise his notion of the production of space. I deem this constructive and pertinent to the reflection of postcolonial critical urban studies because, by focusing on *how* space is produced, it asks about the historical inhibitors as well as the potential effectors of social change.[17] As Lefebvre understood it, social space is a "social product," never finished or given but constantly co-impacted by various factors and actors. This production

Fig. 3

process is catalysed by state- and corporate-led decisions (e.g., new monuments, infrastructure projects, operationalisations of large territories) on the global Level "G" and by the actions of people in everyday life (e.g., specific ways of inhabiting, cohabiting, and organising) on the private Level "P."[18] The developments on the two levels, permanently interacting, are mediated at Level "M," which, in this model, corresponds to the city.[19] The crossing and complicating of the production of space as it unfolds on the three levels includes 1) *representations of space*, i.e., social norms, cultural imaginaries, symbols, and narratives, the "codes" of subcultures ("conceived space"); 2) *spatial practice*, i.e., inhabitants' routines, mobility, communication, the built and non-built environment, etc. ("perceived space"); and 3) *spaces of representation*, i.e., negotiations and contestations of space ("lived space"). For spatial

analysis, this means that whether one is looking at the ways of dwelling, building, or working of inhabitants (Level "P"), at different manifestations of migration, economic growth, and shrinkage (Level "M"), or at the unfolding of urban development policies and operationalisation and extraction of landscapes (Level "G"), attention has to be paid to how space is perceived, conceived, and lived, and vice versa. As to whether the produced space is urban, this has to be answered from case to case. Then again, with all due respect, the question could finally take the backseat.

SHIFT #2: CONTEXTUALISING
THE PRODUCTION OF SPACE IN
AN INCREASINGLY
TRANSLOCALISED SOCIETY

There is a second reason my contribution entertains a tense dialogue with the presuppositions of the "Territories of Extended Urbanisation." I

F. 3   Women taking their morning
        bath in Singur.

Fig. 4

see the contemporary "production of space"—including questions around settlements, occupancy, and the "right to the city"—as a variable of lives and livelihoods based on *the logic of being on the move* rather than of "the urban phenomenon." As a result, I think of a modus operandi based on movement, not simply of mobility or migration between cities and "hinterlands."[20] This perspective was born empirically by living and travelling with "people-on-the-move" in parts of India and Bangladesh. They were daily commuters like Kartik, women moving between villages and cities to sell vegetables, agricultural workers, migrant labourers, etc. (not only specific professional groups or the most deprived but larger sections of the population as well). Observing how routinely they alternated work at home and shifting sites (not only in cities) just to make ends meet, and considering the more general mobilisation of society linked to increasing precarity in different world regions, including Europe,[21] I started to ask myself: What would it be like to live, struggle, and organise in a *translocalised* society? I learnt that whole territories could rhythmically lose and regain their populations as inhabitants follow the cycles of agriculture or respond to the fluctuating labour demand in practically all other sectors of the economy; as they move between megacities, towns, and villages (sometimes thousands of kilometres away from each other) in the hope of earning just a little more, improving their income marginally; as they adapt to environmental phenomena like the monsoon that has long become volatile.

In Indian development studies, the significance of temporary and circular migration is generally acknowledged but has rarely received dedicated attention from urban studies scholars.[22] Ananya Roy's book on Kolkata mentions the emancipatory potential that commuting between the city and its peripheries can entail for working women. In fact, studies on Mumbai's suburban train travellers and Chennai's urban-rural-urban commuters have discussed "circulatory lives" and "rural cosmopolitanisms," and the scholarship on peripheralisation has traditionally dealt with

F. 4   "Rajesh Cyber Café", Phulia.

questions of connectivity and mobility.[23] The perspective of these studies remains city-centric, and the movement they discuss is prevalently only rural to urban. However, the mobility patterns I have mapped speak to centrifugal, even thoroughly *ex-centric* movements going hand in hand with complex socio-spatial phenomena. In economic geography, the urban bias is at least relativised thanks to the discipline's territorial approach and studies that have addressed how state-led territorialisation and rescaling projects (eminently for extraction and the construction of infrastructures) "translocalise" people's lives.[24] Nonetheless, the discussion prioritises urban metaphors and horizons.[25] Also, the debate around India's "census towns" is undermined by this bias. The term connotes settlements that, by the official statistical classification, should fall into the category of "town" (population above 5,000, density above 400 persons per square kilometre, and a minimum of 75% of male inhabitants employed in non-agricultural sectors) but are still treated as "village." Densely populated West Bengal and Kerala have the highest number thereof. When the Census 2011 revealed that more than 30% of India's urban population growth since 2001 had occurred in newly listed "census towns," scholars scandalised the "unacknowledged urbanisation" of these settlements and demanded that they be declared towns to promote adequate development.[26] Few raised this question: If a large part of the national population in settlements of various sizes is increasingly involved in activities different from agriculture, but industrial development is lagging behind, how are people making a living? My answer is by moving.[27]

In an edited volume presenting case studies from all over India, Eric Denis and Marie-Hélène Zérah have explicitly questioned the (still predominant) idea that urban growth emerges from the convergence of globalisation and metropolitanisation.[28] They also suggest that today's increased circulation and movement are not sufficiently considered when assessing settlements' growth and shrinkage. Through the hypothesis of translocalisation, I intend to correlate the "marginal," apparently harmless phenomenon of people's increasing movement with the relations of production, which are slowly but surely transforming in a context of acerbating precarity. I am speaking of a transformation caused by extreme concentration of capital—so extreme that "normal" capitalist accumulation reverts to primitive accumulation[29]—and aggravated by ecological exhaustion and climate crises (see Nikos Katsikis' chapter in this volume). As its negative implications come to the surface, fears and alarmism, coupled in many cases with right-wing outbursts, are spreading globally. But viable answers already exist and even proliferate in the social and physical spaces produced by users-inhabitants who have no chance but to be on the move and improvise, negotiating questions of inhabitation, appropriation, resistance, and protest in new ways. [Fig. 4] They create unintended and utterly surprising outcomes, assemblages of multilevel and non-linear interactions, as Bruno Latour might have said.[30]

COLONIAL "STABILISATION," POSTCOLONIAL LAND REFORM, AND TODAY'S UNSTABLE ARRANGEMENTS

High population density, high connectivity, abandonment, and precarity are just a few labels I could use to explain the region.[31] Some of these attributes are geographical and historical, others contemporary in nature; throughout my fieldwork in West Bengal, I witnessed how they all interweave. Archaeological evidence in the Ganges Delta region attests to the continued development of human settlements since the fourth century.[32] Historical records show that by the twelfth century, complex land tenure patterns and taxation systems were in place. The growth of settlements was facilitated by a combination of factors: favourable climate, easy communications, and the fertility of the soil. Within a governmental regime that some have compared to European feudalism,[33] the competi-

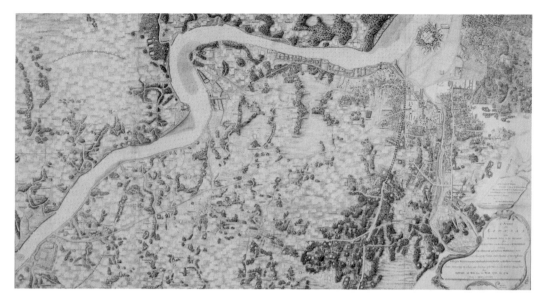

Fig. 5

tive coexistence of many landlords (rajas, thakurs, and from the Mughal period on, zamindars) and even more intermediaries ruling over relatively small estates gave shape to a constellation of bustling towns.[34] In the eighteenth century, the East India Company expanded its control in the Subcontinent and undertook violent moves to make the Delta's watery land "stable."[35] This fostered urban concentration: Calcutta, the initial British headquarters, passed from circa 10,000 inhabitants in 1700 to 500,000 in 1800 and about 1,000,000 in 1900.[36] Through channelling, embanking, fortifying, reclaiming, clearing, and connecting, the colonisers modified the territory to ensure quick shipments of raw export materials and promote agriculture and, therewith, the inflow of revenues through taxation. [Fig. 5] This entailed forced relocations of the population and large-scale dispossession, for which the selective and fragmented industrial development promoted by the colonisers could not compensate. As in other parts of the Subcontinent, most livelihoods increasingly depended on pauperised agricultural labour and a subsistence economy.[37]

From India's independence (1947) through the 1950–60s, Jawaharlal Nehru's government launched grand initiatives to foster industrialisation, with the main focus on extraction and metallurgy. However, the resulting damage to local economies and, in some cases, entire territories caused by the colonial regime was so severe that any slow, isolated improvements were utterly insufficient. To mitigate the pervasive rural poverty and agricultural distress, the government promoted agrarian as well as land reforms and the *panchayati raj* model of local self-governance.[38] In most places, the agrarian reform was mediated by "Green Revolution" initiatives based on monocultures and eventually fostered the centralisation of land ownership.[39] The land reform was implemented only in a few states, among them West Bengal, which from 1977 on was led by a "Left Front" headed by the CPI(M), or Communist Party of India (Marxist). Different authors have assessed this reform's mixed success, as the redistribution of land was severely undermined by local power games and individual interests. Most observers concurred that at least a tenancy reform was achieved, and, thanks to that, sharecroppers have enjoyed comparatively higher security of tenancy and protection from eviction in West Bengal, in contrast to other states.[40] The land reform

Fig. 6

discouraged monoculture, which in West Bengal—the region's topology is crisscrossed by rivers and dotted with waterbodies and seasonal flooding—remains far less common than in other Indian states. On a more symbolic level, the measures created confidence among the inhabitants. Apart from temporary moves during the lean months, West Bengal recorded altogether low levels of migration for almost 20 years, despite comparatively slow economic progress; long-term migration and permanent emigration only occurred in the districts where the land reform had been less successful. The city of Kolkata continued to grow, mainly due to the inflow of migrants from the neighbouring states and Bangladesh.[41] Today, the patchwork of bright greens (rice), yellows (rapeseed), deep greens (vegetables), and reds (sand), typical of its territory as seen from above, speaks to the reform's effects on local cultivation practices. [Fig. 6] As the contradictory methods and different phases of land distribution created highly fragmented landholding patterns, most families own fields at different sites and cultivate various crops in the same season: rice or jute in the low-lying fields, vegetables in the others.

After India's 1991 move to "liberalise" the economy, many states started to promote direct foreign investment and set up various types of Special Economic Zones (SEZ). In West Bengal, the Left Front held on to its rural legacy. However, the success of the agrarian reform had been short-lived, and agriculture's productivity was stable but not thriving. The agricultural sector, therefore, did not manage to absorb the available labour force—much to the contrary, the demand was sinking.[42] With increasing education levels, young people, especially, had little incentive to engage in rural labour (in West Bengal, the literacy level is among the highest

F. 5 Map of Calcutta and environs in 1785, showing "corrected" water bodies: rivers, embankments, tanks, broken ground, sands and soundings of the Hugli River at low water in spring tides.

F.6 A painter's interpretation of Bengal's territory: Ganesh Haloi, *Untitled*, gouache on Nepali paper pasted on board, 2014.

in India). Seasonal and permanent migration to the metropolises and states that liberalised their economies became widespread. In 2005, amidst an atmosphere of economic insecurity and abandonment, the state government opted for private investment-led industrialisation schemes. By this time, funds on the international market were starting to dwindle, and the desired shower of investments failed to arrive. Ever since the Left Front coalition lost the elections of 2011, successive governments headed by TMC (Trinamool Congress) have had difficulties attracting private investment and advancing industrialisation. Things have not been different in most parts of India. In fact, many observers maintain that the neoliberal turn has heightened regional disparities and competition, exacerbated environmental problems, and furthered the marginalisation of already discriminated social groups such as women, *adivasi*,[43] Dalits, and religious minorities, especially Muslims.[44] Moreover, the projects promoted in the neoliberal era have often been volatile, to say the least. The record of firms put up on a grand scale and dismantled as soon as the corporate logics or the moods of the global market commanded to do so is long in India.[45]

The state responded with innumerable subsidy schemes, various forms of loans, and the distribution of basic consumer goods or guaranteed employment—adding to and complicating the world's most convoluted (probably) quota system for members of oppressed communities. While all this only sufficed to hardly contain the damages, people soon learnt how to put the state's lobbyism and clientelism to work. In the words of political studies scholar Partha Chatterjee, the consequence was the emergence of a "governmentally managed informal social space." This social space is held together by small-scale private capital investments, a great deal of self-organisation and self-exploitation, activities on the edge of illegality, bribery, and all sorts of temporary, ad hoc, and unstable arrangements.[46] As Chatterjee also observes, this characteristic straddles and unites urban and rural settings. In the territory I investigated, it was *people* that made the best out of very little, regardless of their "urban" or "rural" location.

Many fought against caste and gender discrimination, opposed public officers' abuses of power, and contested development plans. The *andalon,* Bengali for "movement," with which virtually the whole state had blocked the government's plans to convert agricultural land into factories in 2007–08, was a case in point. Movement was another reaction to precarity. If multilocal livelihoods and translocal lives have existed for decades in India,[47] their incidence has grown exponentially since the 2000s.[48] In West Bengal, the frequent stories of brothers, fathers, fiancées, and daughters who toiled in western and southern India and came home for Durga Puja, or Eid,[49] to carry out the harvest, look after the house renovations, or get married, composed a storyboard of translocalisation. Even though they were absent in the season in which I conducted fieldwork, it was clear that many houses were turning from kancha to paka[50] and small businesses popped up thanks to their savings, confounding the statistical data on male employment in "census towns."

EXERCISES IN A PHENOMENOLOGY OF THE TERRITORY

The territory I researched, a region of approximately 33,000 km², was obtained by drawing a circle of 100 km around the centre of Kolkata. [Fig. 7] From former investigations, I knew that this delimitation corresponded to the maximum distance a daily commuter to/from Kolkata could cover and that beyond this radius, the effects of concentration-extension gradually disappeared, the more encompassing effects of movement generated by translocalisation became dominant. [Fig. 8] Agricultural areas like Bardhaman, West Bengal's "rice bowl," received seasonal workers in the harvest seasons;

F. 8   The fieldwork area was determined according to the maximum distance that could be covered by a daily commuter to/from Kolkata by public transportation.

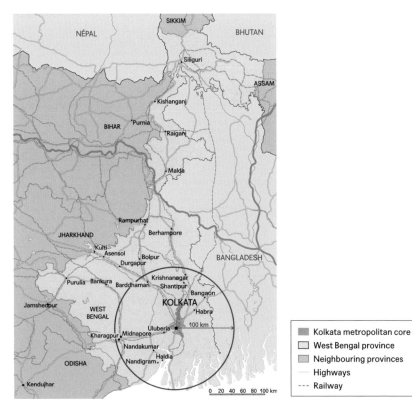

RESEARCH CONTEXT MAP: WEST BENGAL
Fig. 7

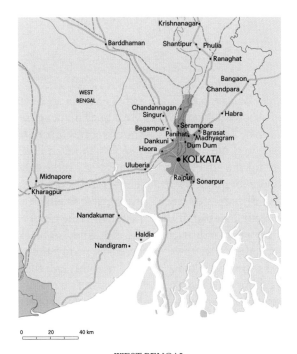

WEST BENGAL
Fig. 8

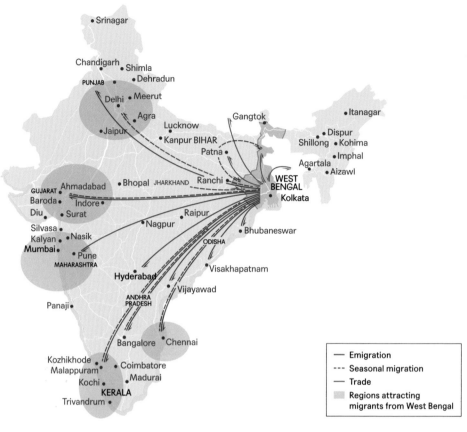

TRADE AND MIGRATION MOVEMENTS
TO AND FROM WEST BENGAL
Fig. 9

in mountainous northern West Bengal, past Malda, the tourism industry absorbed those who didn't engage in trade with Bihar, Bangladesh, Assam, Sikkim, or Nepal; Mumbai, New Delhi, and Bengaluru were magnets for the educated youth, who would often migrate for good, whereas the poorest and most dispossessed, such as the Muslim population of Murshidabad or the *adivasi* from West Bengal's dry western districts, mostly went to work in other states. [Fig. 9]

After carving my study's territory on the map I needed some time to calibrate my tools of observation because the Google Earth images I used to plan my visits collided with my general "sense" of the region. This type of familiarity with a territory grows gradually, enriched with local knowledge and consolidated by personal experiences in space and time. In the plains of West Bengal, the sense of the region may involve the memories of long-abandoned river ports and people's hopes and concerns about new railway connections and roads under construction. These recollections mark a (planning) history of improbable satellite cities built after armchair decisions;[51] the lower- and higher-lying areas and the red, sandy, or black soils, each fit for different breeds of paddy; the tradition of changing land uses through the seasons—there are six, not four or two in this part of the Subcontinent. I highlight this temporal variability, linked to environmental factors because satellite images generally fail to record it; a fatal problem for analysis, especially in monsoon regions. The permanent colours of satellite images, grey-rust-dust-green-maroon-whites, also conceal the myriad of things that users (residents, denizens, tenants, owners) constantly do and undo underneath their roofs—and in their fields, which are turned into buildable lots and then returned to nature when the investors fail to appear. Morten Nielsen and AbdouMaliq Simone have admonished that these activities may have nothing to do with the overarching processes of urbanisation, making it necessary to "detach ourselves from the familiar images and vernaculars and let the details speak another language."[52] One can learn that language by sticking to everyday life, resisting the temptation to interpret the extending urban fabric too hurriedly as a sign of Lefebvrian urbanisation only. (What makes a fabric "urban," by the way? The rust-grey of tin roofs, the new "vernacular" in the majority of self-built settlements in big cities, nowadays also prevails in satellite images of villages and *adivasi* hamlets or even in army camps in the forests.)

These considerations led me to experiment with a large spectrum of representations in the field. Parallel to exploring the territory "as a whole" by travelling and mapping extensively, I tried to grasp the production of space in everyday life through regular "zoom-ins" into a number of settlements, guided by the following questions: How does "the city grow from the village"? Which actors, ideas, and spatial practices are changing everyday life in gramer shahar, turning the fabric into paka, transforming its inhabitant's aspirations? I made it a habit to sketch constituencies, axes of circulation, and landmarks in a notebook, noting transformations (some occurring over decades) to the built and unbuilt environments that the locals reconstructed for me: growth/expansion of built structures, becoming paka/consolidation, emptying, new cultivation, etc.

Over the years, I learnt that our body sends us signals that can become useful when mapping the most subtle borders between public and private spaces—common transit space or *para* (residential cluster), for example. So, I also registered the sites where I had double-checked my *dupatta*[53] or taken off my sunglasses as the locals were looking at me (nobody coming from afar would go unnoticed) or where my pace had become slower either to synchronise with the pace of the majority or because the road was particularly rough. I compiled a personal atlas of "micro territories" that ranged from about 20 to 250 km², depending on what the inhabitants regarded as their settlement's catchment area. Once condensed, synthesised, and coloured, this information resulted in mappings of what I would call an "internalised" territorial experience: Bodily impressions, findings gathered through interviews, as well as casual conversations, along with Google Earth views adapted to my scope.

The somatic map of Begampur, reproduced here, mirrors memories of my movements impressed, as it were, "on the soil." [Fig. 10] Whether I was alone on the streets and lanes, ferries and fields, or talking with an interview partner, a traveller, or a tea stall owner, the small audio recorder hanging around my neck, underneath my dupatta and kurta, was permanently on. Once, while relistening to the recordings in search of a locality name that had already slipped my memory, I was struck by the quick interchange of the sounds produced by my steps on changing grounds: soft, muffled resonances when I was moving on *kancha rasta* (roads) and small embankments between fields; hard, rhythmic ones on *paka rasta*; staccatos when the surface was damaged or holey. I was curious as to what other details the sonic mappings could reveal. I printed out Google Earth maps of a number of localities I had visited, covered them with tracing paper, and started to report the sonic traces revealed by the respective audio tracks. This exercise re-imported the many activities that generally filled our environment into the silent cartographic space and helped me realise that kancha and paka did not just coexist but were overlapping in most settlements.

AN EX-CENTRIC TERRITORY

I generated this impressionistic transect towards the end of my fieldwork when, contrary to my habit of travelling only by public transport, I hired a driver and a car for some days. We followed two city-centrifugal trajectories, starting in Kolkata and driving for approximately 90 kilometres to the north-east on the National Highway 112, popularly known as *Jessore Road*. We crossed the district of North 24 Parganas up to Bangaon on the India-Bangladesh border.[54] We drove another 90 kilometres to the south-west from Kolkata to Nandigram, passing the districts of Haora and East Medinipur. Especially in the northward track, the built environment was turning paka, and the territory presented itself as haphazardly transforming under the effect of speculation on the land market and real estate investment; the fast connectivity with the metropolis was clearly a facilitator of these developments in the initial stretch. [Fig. 11] On the south-west track, the situation demonstrated how people's increased back-and-forth movement across urban and rural areas is reshaping old and new settlements and complicating the commonly accepted understanding of "centrality."

On our first 30 kilometres on Jessore Road, an axis of trade and communications with Bangladesh, the generic and "compressed" fabric (see AbdouMaliq Simone's definition of compression in this volume) was characterised by commercial premises, recently built and already dilapidated-looking shopping malls, workshops specialising in iron and woodworks, traditional dwellings side by side with small *new towns*, less than a decade old, and planned community housing complexes for the middle classes, generally developed with private funds.

"It's always such a mess from Belgharia to Barasat, ma'am! This place has totally transformed in the last ten years. It has become like Kolkata. Even the land prices are like in Kolkata! First, the investors came from there, and now the city people are buying the flats. And then they go to their offices by car every day!" snapped the driver in Hindi mixed with Bengali at Madhyamgram. I replied that this didn't surprise me since the road had only one lane in this stretch, and he answered: "What to do, each *member*[55] has got friends in their constituencies! Add all the people who file complaints whenever roadworks are planned or some temple committee opposing

the reclamation of its land—and there you see our situation!"

Even though the billboards advertising *Fortune Townships* and *Sports Cities* chased us until Chandpara, about 60 kilometres further north-east, the agglomeration effects soon waned. For the next 40 to 50 kilometres, the Jessore Road, now two lanes, resembled a corridor passing through an almost continual row of new paka structures, one- or two-storeyed, behind which the cultivated areas and paddy fields widened as we progressed. Although the small industries and manufacturers were slowly replaced by housing and commercial premises, the fabric retained a generic-by-compression appearance. Connections with the capital city were feeble now, and trade seemed fully oriented towards northern Bengal and Bangladesh. In Navapalli, the customers of the local tea stall all agreed that, with the exception of a few businesspeople and high-ranking public officers, nobody went to Kolkata regularly. Habra, at about 60 kilometres from Kolkata, constituted some sort of frontier. From there to the thriving and dense border town of Bangaon, the paka buildings left room for kancha structures, and agriculture-related activities became predominant. Also here, the roadsides were densifying through the addition of built structures, side by side with the small houses, many of them just shacks, carpentries alternated with stores selling construction materials or wood, while in the background, scattered brick kilns underscored the absence of other significant economic or business activities.

In contrast, the south-westbound track impressed me with a progressive decompression and emptying of the landscape. Already 20 kilometres from departure, the heavy metallurgic and light engineering factories and haulier companies, typical of Haora, became sparse; much smaller shacks selling wood, iron, and cement filled the landscape. We were driving through the paka territory of gramer shahar. Slowly, orchards and cultivated areas appeared; on the horizon only sparse recently built towns. After 15 to 20 kilometres, in Bagnan, I got out of the car and took a longer stroll. Served by

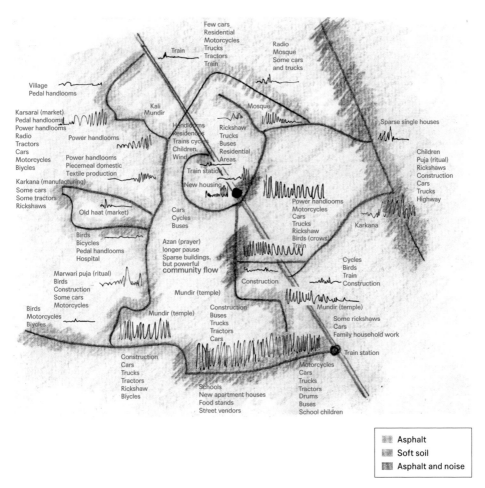

A SOMATIC MAP OF BEGAMPUR
Fig. 10

the highway and the highly frequented Kharagpur railway line, the locality is a hub for commuters—manufacturing workers from factories in the Haora district, sellers, employees in the public administration, and many others. I walked down Station Road, expecting to get to the centre. Yet, Bagnan did not seem to have any centre of sorts, and after asking and searching, I concluded that its "centres" were the railway station and two bus stops on the highway. These were places cohabited by people who aimed to be *somewhere else*.

 Like most other sites of my fieldwork, Bagnan was a "census town." Its fabric and infra-structures were not formally planned but well calibrated to cater to movement and, thus, a good example of spaces produced by translo-calisation. Although many of the spatial developments fostered by movement that I encountered in my research gave the impression

F. 10   The somatic map of Begampur was obtained by reporting the sonic traces of the author's movements on a sheet of paper during fieldwork. Soft, muffled resonances on the kancha roads and small embankments between fields; hard, rhythmic sounds on the paka roads; staccatos on damaged or holey surfaces.

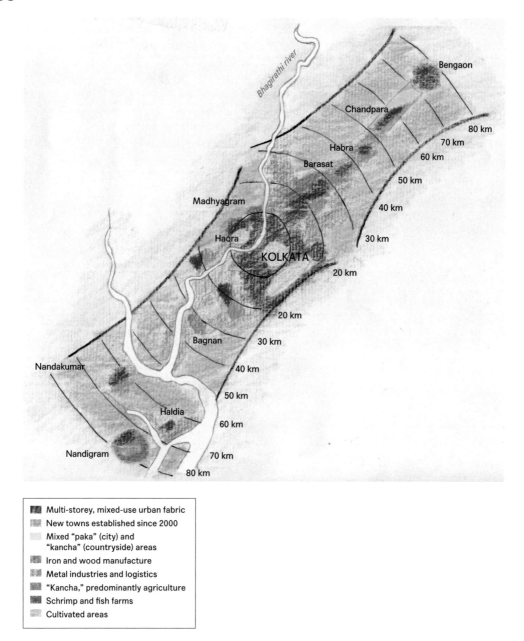

AN IMPRESSIONISTIC TRANSECT OF THE TERRITORY
Fig. 11

of being ex-centric, in Bagnan, staring at a "bus stop" that was actually the occupied highway, it occurred to me that I was moving in an altogether *ex-centric territory*. A territory in which new "competitors" add to the usual centralities (administrative centres, ancient towns, *haat*, or rural markets, etc.), which are bypassed or superseded by activities that occupy some places and empty others according to logics that are not immediately decipherable. To be fully clear, I am not simply positing that territories acquire additional centralities, competing with the old centralities. I am saying that since people increasingly cohabit in territories they occupy temporarily, centralities are losing relevance, be it due to inflation or exhaustion.[56] In Bagnan, the production of space was impacted by fugacious booms, short-term investments, and infrastructural improvements implemented sporadically by people not interested or able to afford to stay in one place. As in many other gramer shahar, social space seemed to follow an ambiguous trajectory and pointed to opaque relations, much like the inhabitants' activities that catalysed them (and simultaneously responded to them).[57] This is what, in my opinion, challenges the horizon of an "urban society." Impacted by many factors—media representations, communication technologies, the changing patterns of land ownership, old and new migration routes, as well as patterns, higher purchasing power and circulation of consumption goods, etc.—the city appears to lose one of its main features, "centrality." At the same time, "difference"— an additional feature regarded to be constitutive of the city—increases all over the territory by modes of occupancy that do not operate per extension from one point centrifugally.[58]

Past Bagnan, the paka environment waned, orchards and cultivated areas became prevalent, and sparse workshops, modest houses, and godowns[59] continued to alternate. At Kolaghat, we crossed the Hugli River and headed southwards onto the freshly asphalted four-lane National Highway 41. [Fig. 12] By the time the meter hit the 60-kilometre mark, we were looking at the open paddy fields and decongested landscape of East Medinipur. With every kilometre, the environment, dotted by shrimp

F. 11   The transect merges an extensive
         bird's eye view with the author's
         expansive-associative gaze of the
         landscape. Towards the north-east,
         the territory was seen transforming
         in haphazard ways under the
         effect of speculation on the land
         market and investment in real
         estate. To the south and west, it
         was faced with the dynamics
         of de-densification.

farms and okra-brown fields, appeared to be more rural. I was looking forward to Reapara and its canal built in 1880. However, upon arriving, we found the bridge crowded by an orange mob. I hinted to the driver to stop. In the previous months, I had repeatedly been caught in the middle of brutal clashes between parties, and now, just before the elections, the spirits were all the more likely to be high—especially here, in Nandigram.

NANDIGRAM: CONTESTED REPRESENTATIONS AND INHABITANTS' RESPONSES TO STAGNATION

"Are you from the state or the central government?" inquired the gracile old man firmly. I immediately guessed what he might be afraid of: Some 15 years ago, under pressure to promote industrialisation, the Left Front government planned to build an SEZ in partnership with the Indonesian conglomerate *Salim* in Nandigram. We were just a few kilometres from the port city of Haldia, a hub for refineries and related industries. I clarified that I'm no surveyor measuring land for some government programme but just a researcher grappling with questions around the development of settlements. He did not seem to be fully convinced but reciprocated my introduction by telling me, mixing Bengali and Hindi, that he had worked as a *coolie,* or porter, in a market in Ahmedabad (in the western state of Gujarat) for most of his life. He then spoke about the events of 2007, when the government tried to reclaim 20,000 acres of agricultural land, and the locals resisted. The details of the state's terrifying response were gruesome—murders, rapes, and infanticides commissioned to scare and repress those unwilling to cede their land. Journalists and intellectuals from the city, NGOs, and local, national, and international media flocked to the place, "and finally, the people won," he concluded. "The people of Nandigram have always fought against oppression."[60] I could

Fig. 12

not suppress the feeling that his words were a warning.

The past struggle seemed to have shaped a special identification with the place in Nandigram's inhabitants. In other localities, people appeared to relate the most to their village, if not just to their local para; they spoke of the larger aggregate of villages and cultivable land grouped under the administrative unit of the Community Development Block (CDB) as an abstract entity. [61] But in Nandigram, they regularly insisted that I visit this and that locality—the 7-kilometres-away ferry *ghat* (port) of Kendemari, the 10-kilometres-away ancient river port city of Terapekhia, etc. [Fig. 14] However, the answers to my question, "Is Nandigram rural or urban?" coincided with those I was given everywhere. "We're not urban. It's the people from outside, the city people, who started to call us a city." And, "Nandigram is a village, just with a lot of paka." Two factors immediately stood out as deterrents to becoming a "town," as the villagers discussed them very openly whenever the question of

"rural or urban" was on the table. [62] At the time, scholars and politicians were making a case for "upgrading" India's "census towns," and Nandigram, like Bagnan, fell into that category. From a practical, everyday-life point of view, living in a city means paying higher taxes on real estate and commercial activities. Additionally, India's subsidy system has historically benefitted rural areas more than urban ones, i.e., CDBs and gram panchayat are allotted more funds than municipalities. [63]

Nevertheless, representations of space are too multi-layered and dynamic to assume that inhabitants would only conceive of "village" and "city" depending on, or responding to, some state's denominations. Thus, for some, "city" promised at least a partial liberation from social control and caste identities that are difficult to elude in rural areas, whereas, for others, it was a synonym for undesirable features such as elitism, power games, and alienating social relations. All these are, in turn, common representations of "city" offered by popular culture, starting with the influential dream factory of Bollywood.

F. 12   View from the window, Chandpur,
          National Highway 41.
F. 13   A cottage industry for textile
          manufacturing in Phulia.

Fig. 13

When one tries and reads it through Lefebvre's model, in which conceived, perceived, and lived space are mutually correlated, the scepticism about being "urban" appears even more nuanced. The spatial practices ("perceived space"), mirroring an ongoing rearticulation of material fabric and everyday routines in connection with the introduction of new communications and means of transport, are changing much faster than the social relations in the realm of "lived space," where change is reluctant and prone to backlashes and unexpected detours. I am not thinking of explicit cultural resistance, although that plays a role too,[64] but of phenomena that would be simplistic and relate to the "urban phenomenon." In Nandigram itself, for example, I became aware of the emergence of a low-profile textile industry whose future developments were all but predictable. It took the material form of "generic" tin shacks adjoined to the brick or paka dwellings of lower-middle-income families.

"Are these all your sons working in the workshop?" I asked the young woman enjoying the evening breeze in the small yard before her house. "No, only my eldest son," she replied. "He used to work in factories outside, in Kolkata, Haora. Now he's married and has just settled down here. He gets the orders and the cloth from outside; they make jeans, shirts, and T-shirts. He employs three of his cousins. My smallest son is still in primary school, and one is in college. The third has gone to work in Tamil Nadu with my cousins a few years ago. He comes for Eid and stays with us only now and then. Would you like to take a look?"

In the neighbourhood, every third house accommodated such a workshop. Although this density was exceptional, people engaged in domestic textile production in many other villages within my study's territory. Closer to Kolkata, in North 24 Parganas, I found a capillary network of one-person enterprises, mainly women who hand-stitched or machine-sewed shirt collars, T-shirt sleeves, etc. They did this "on-demand," often on very short-term bases, from their one-room homes. Certain households complemented their regular income through it, while for others, it was the only source of livelihood. The business had developed very recently, in the last five to seven years. Thereby, the *karkana*, or workshops, were indistinguishable from the cottage industries typical of localities with a century-long handloom tradition in the more northern districts of Hugli and Nadia, which are traditionally integrated with the homestead. There, the old foot-treadle looms were being replaced by electric ones, but the work with and around them had resisted transformation. The weavers were caught in individualised relations with their commissioners, leaving minimal room for bargaining, and the labour relations were typical of traditional domestic systems, with women's and children's unpaid work taken for granted.[65] This represented another parallel to the newer manufacturers. [Fig. 13]

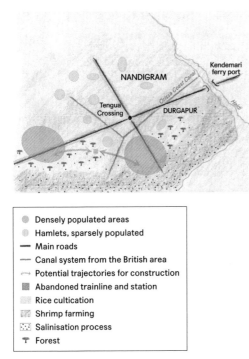

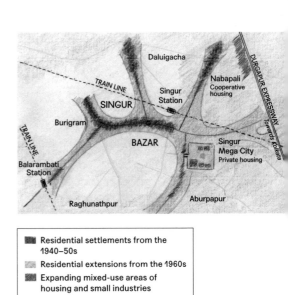

○ Densely populated areas
○ Hamlets, sparsely populated
— Main roads
⁓ Canal system from the British area
↢ Potential trajectories for construction
▦ Abandoned trainline and station
▦ Rice cultication
▦ Shrimp farming
∷ Salinisation process
⊤ Forest

▦ Residential settlements from the 1940–50s
▦ Residential extensions from the 1960s
▦ Expanding mixed-use areas of housing and small industries
--- Railway
— Expressway
⁓ Canals
▦ Rice cultivation
▦ Orchards and garden

FIELDWORK SKETCH OF NANDIGRAM
Fig. 14

FIELDWORK SKETCH OF SINGUR
Fig. 15

These self-employing, small-scale suppliers could be portrayed as agents of "the urban," bringing an industry from the city to the village, often via the mediation of NGOs as loan givers or contact makers, contributing to a transformation of production and consumption behaviours, causing debates about power blackouts, and perhaps even raising the question of child and female unpaid labour—adding a Lefebvrian difference, so to speak. Yet those who ran the workshops were regarded and regarded themselves as farmers—as they did engage in farming, some on their own land, others as wage labourers, others only in the harvest seasons. Looking closely, it was the new roads and incremental houses of the wealthy that created the impression of the built environment turning paka; in the "generic" fabric of the residential quarters, the karkana were hardly noticeable additions. The production process, finally, based on domestic work and individualised producer–commissioner relations, was difficult to identify as "industrial," per Marx, or "urban" in Lefebvre's terms.

Of course, I asked myself whether these garment manufacturers installed in villages weren't evidence against my hypothesis of trans-localisation and people's increased movement. Here, inhabitants were creating the conditions for working without having to move at all! Nonetheless, here the production of space appeared to correlate positively with movement—if due to levels of precarisation that people who had previously migrated to the city for better opportunities were now forced to abandon it as a place to live, and as the horizon projected by Lefebvre. Most of the current small textile manufacturers I interviewed (not only in Nandigram) had in fact lived and worked for years in textile factories, predominantly in Haora, or commuted back and forth. To advance hypotheses on which sort of "society" under the effect of which "phenomenon" might be taking shape, I should have analysed the social relations and productive forces on site more closely than the time available allowed. I could have investigated the relationships between producers and buyers, and how those were negotiated; the forms of ownership over mobile and immobile assets in place; the funds—remittances of migrated relatives, private lending, microcredit—backing the new karkana; and the impact of the modalities, times, and places of work on the family structures. If all this unfortunately exceeded the scope of my fieldwork, it is now clear to me that such a study could as well have turned into an investigation of non-capitalist class processes, in J. K. Gibson-Graham's terms.[66] Their non-capitalocentric perspective fractures the alleged identity and homogeneity of capitalism by highlighting economic diversity, that is, the variety of non-capitalist economic activities and different forms of organisation scattered over the economic landscape.[67]

Of course, I asked myself whether these garment manufacturers installed in villages weren't evidence against my hypothesis of translocalisation and people's increased movement. Here, inhabitants were creating the conditions for working without having to move at all! Nonetheless, the production of space appeared to correlate positively with movement—if due to levels of precarisation that people who had previously migrated to the city for better opportunities were now forced to abandon it as a place to live,[68] and as the horizon projected by Lefebvre. Most of the current small textile manufacturers I interviewed (not only in Nandigram) had in fact lived and worked for years in textile factories, predominantly in Haora, or commuted back and forth. The reasons they had decided to move back to the village were personal, and their conditions differed, but the conversations recalled the title chosen by Ananya Roy for her book about Kolkata, *City Requiem*. The city had failed to keep its promises. Movement played a significant role also on a more infrastructural point. The "ex-centric" production in the karkana was 1) enabled by improved mobility infrastructures, from highways to mobile phones, and 2) integrated with a complex supply chain, ensuring the movement of materials and goods through truck drivers, petty and bulk sellers, intermediaries, contractors, and

sub-contractors who did not reside in Kolkata or any city, at all. This resonated with the supply chain analyses produced in the 1990s by economic geographer Pierre Veltz.[69] To be clear, Veltz took the correlation between economic growth (of the West) and the growth of cities for granted and this correlation has never fully described the context of India, whose territorial developments and rearrangements (as shown, e.g., in the aforementioned book by Eric Denis and Marie-Hélène Zérah) are more ambiguous, multi-factored, non-linear. Nonetheless, I find the metaphors with which he described the territorial effects of globalisation interesting, as they perfectly apply to my understanding of how translocalisation affects the production of space. Globalisation, he wrote, led to a reinforcement of centrifugal forces and the emergence of an "archipelago economy," a "poly-centric space of simultaneities" rendered "relational" by the augmented movement of goods, money, and of people.[70]

SINGUR: INHABITANTS' STRUGGLE FOR SELF-DETERMINATION AND EXPERIENCES OF TRANSLOCAL SOLIDARITY

My decision to include Singur in the study was the least neutral. In 2007–08, Singur, a "census town" in Hugli district, had been the epicentre of a conflict over land that brought the Left Front its first failure at "industrialising"— Nandigram followed shortly—and eventually, its bitter demise in the 2011 elections after 35 years of uninterrupted rule.[71] The government wanted to acquire approximately 1,000 acres of high-yield land, part of which was common land used for grazing and foraging, to accommodate a car factory for the production of the Nano, a new cheap compact city car by the Indian corporation Tata Motors. The farmer compensation was unfair, and they united in demanding better conditions, yet the state ignored them and proceeded to expropriate the area. The farmers were joined by fellow villagers, including

Fig. 16

F. 16   Land evolving into kancha: weeds and birds reappropriating the fields once earmarked for the projected Tata factory in Singur.

many who did not own any land but worked as sharecroppers and/or grazed their cattle on the common land, and women for whom the area was a reserve of wild vegetables and herbs.[72] They became the protagonists of dramatic clashes, which soon circulated in the form of media images of peasants literally shielding the land with their own bodies against the public officers sent to fence it in. The *andalon*, or movement, had started. The Left Front was blind to those images and deaf to the voices raised not only from Kolkata and West Bengal but from elsewhere in India and abroad. Its reaction was unexpectedly violent and continued until Tata pulled out and chose to build its factory in Gujarat, in western India.

Although the major opposition party at the time, Trinamool Congress (TMC), was crucial for the mobilisation, this sort of event speaks to the inhabitants' potential to unite across social classes, religions, and party divides to oppose state decisions and effect long-term change.[73] Additionally, Singur's struggle, at least on paper, had a non-capitalist background: Even if the landowners were initially concerned about their returns from the "commodity" land, the movement took off and was maintained thanks to the numerous *users* of the collective land, and external supporters who denounced the Left Front's betrayal of the land reform it had once implemented. Another reason I took an interest in Singur's movement was its translocality, which was twofold. First, it was quickly adopted, expanded, and refracted in the rest of West Bengal and far beyond. As noted by

anthropologist Dayabati Roy, "Singur's land movement has … been translated in different places of the country wherever the respective governments have tried to acquire agricultural land for the interest of corporate capital."[74] Second, it was backed morally and materially by civil society groups, university students, and intellectuals from Kolkata and other cities, as well as the international diaspora.

As is often the case, the situation I found on site was less unambiguous than expected, starting with the state of the land the inhabitants had fought for, which lay idle and fenced in by cement slabs. Areas once envisaged to host factories and new housing, and to that end fenced in or covered with cement, were being reappropriated by weeds and birds and evolving into kancha. [Fig. 16] Villagers had hardly any access to it, and ten years on, many of the landowners were still waiting for legal compensation for the damages and losses caused by the government's violence.[75] In general, even though the events of 2007–08 were continuously recalled with a mixture of indignation and pride, disillusion about the present was by far the prevalent emotion. The new ruling party, TMC, had neither addressed the political, social, and developmental contradictions inherited from the previous regime nor lived up to its promise of bringing about "fair" industrialisation. With stagnant production and an overall unplanned and underdeveloped infrastructure for the storage, preservation, and transport of agricultural produce, farmers could hardly face rising costs while their productivity constantly decreased due to land fragmentation and soil exhaustion. As the younger generations (in particular) looked for different ways to ensure their livelihoods, the two most common options were becoming mobile or starting a small manufacturing unit. Not surprisingly, the middle/lower income class neighbourhoods of Singur "shahar,"—i.e., the core area of the settlement, but also parts of Singur "gram," the more agricultural areas—resounded with hundreds of electric looms and textile workshops like those I had become familiar with in Nandigram.

During my mapping exercises on foot, I observed an unmistakable ex-centric effect in and around Singur, with all current building activities—around houses mostly combining residential and commercial functions—gravitating around the main roads, departing from and "bypassing" both the town's old core with its dilapidated houses inhabited by entrenched local families and the newer residential quarters. [Fig. 15] The settlement illustrated the circumstances forging what Kartik had called gramer shahar—stagnation, abandonment, precarity, and people's initiatives, translating into everyday patterns and physical spaces that diversify *and* mix "rural" and "urban" features until these very concepts are completely transformed. At the same time, Singur featured a range of comparatively large construction endeavours. The middle-class neighbourhood of Nabapalli ("New Quarter"), for example, was developed 30 to 35 years ago by a "housing society," which was founded by state employees who commuted daily to Kolkata. Green Park, an alien-looking block of four-storey apartment buildings, was instead a developer's project built in anticipation of the Tata car factory. Only a few of its flats were inhabited, and I learnt that these were majorly occupied by childless working couples who commuted by car daily to Kolkata or other cities in the district. "Thanks to the Durgapur Expressway,[76] this is not a problem anymore," I learnt from one of them. He was employed in the industrial town of Durgapur, 135 kilometres away. So, ten years after the *andalon* with which they had opposed the state's top-down develop-ment plans, in both Nandigram and Singur, I found people entertaining or exploring livelihood strategies that accepted the state's incapability of promoting any "development" whatsoever. These strategies remarkably foregrounded movement.[77] In Nandigram, a majority had either opted for circular migration (mainly) to South India or started small enterprises that benefitted from the new mobility infrastructures. In well-connected Singur, the prevalent strategy was daily commuting.

HORIZONS FOR SPATIAL
PRODUCTION AND RESEARCH
BEYOND "THE URBAN"

In the context of this book, the case of West Bengal may be read as an ordinary example of decolonisation and development boosting a patchwork territorialisation under circumstances of dense population, low industrialisation, economic stagnation, and relatively high connectivity. By "patchwork territorialisation," I mean that the production of territory was constantly co-determined by the state's strategies—often partially implemented, mismanaged, or undermined by false promises, corruption, and interrelated local and global crises—and the inhabitants' responses. This text described two responses to this situation, with the diversification of local production in the form of small textile manufacturers in villages and towns, facilitated by the improved mobility and communication infrastructures, being one. Migration following a fluctuating demand for labour (farming and non-farming) is the other response. The latter isn't a new response nor one peculiar to West Bengal, but it takes new contours with the growing number of people opting for circular migration and translocal livelihoods, no longer only the rural landless, but thousands of fairly educated men and women from rural and urban areas. This speaks to a transformation of the modalities of the production of space—rural, industrial, urban, *x*.

The hypothesis of translocalisation, which shifts the hypothesis of urbanisation articulated by Lefebvre, cannot address all, but at least some of the multiscalar relationships responsible for the current production of space. It also proves more helpful in approaching a postcolonial context where, as discussed, the idea of rural–industrial–urban transition never really applied. The production of space evolving under circumstances of translocalisation, featuring dispersion and a sort of "vectoralisation" much rather than concentration-extension effects, has specific manifestations on the territory. In West Bengal, I observed built infrastructures that are growing "generic" in Nielsen and Simone's terms and centralities that are dissolving with the proliferation of ex-centric circulations, transactions, and exchanges. The domestic garment manufacturers and textile workshops—which were spreading in the state at the time of fieldwork—represent forms of production based on ways of organising non-corporate capital that, in the current historical moment, are producing an *other* social space that is non-urban, reliant on movement, and highly improvisational.[78] In whole economies, the scope of accumulation that is con*centr*ation has long become minimal. Parallel to, and caused by, unseen levels of enrichment of a very few people in very few places, the prospect or actual occurrence of expulsion is an everyday reality for the sheer majority and being on the move becomes a matter of survival. Yet the movement I am talking about, even though it is marked by indeterminacy and not always voluntary (on the contrary, often strictly necessary, compelled, or forced by utter poverty and dearth), relates to choices. People make decisions daily through down-to-earth appraisals of options, awareness of the pros and cons, and practical knowledge of their economic, social, and ecological environment. These choices, coming with specificities and opacities, render movement a horizon of humble, even battered, day-to-day possibilities, a promise of unexpected events, even reversals, of history as usual.

What are the requirements for an analysis of the translocalised production of space? The approaches vary. In previous research, I chose to follow people-on-the-move, whereas, during the fieldwork that backs up this chapter, I mapped the traces drawn by movement in the territory itself.[79] These were visible in the daily commuting of many inhabitants; in the experiences of temporary, circular, and permanent migration I was told about in every locality I visited; in the new and original socio-economic experiments through which small manufacturers accessed supply chains at national or even global scales; in the translocal influences of political struggle across India, and beyond. A particular mention should be made of the remittances sent by people-on-the-move from other Indian states or abroad, part of which was used to build new houses and businesses. Remittances represent an "abstract" but essential factor for the ongoing transformations of the environment in that they catalyse the kancha–paka interplay in the territory, the ex-centric growth of settlements, and the many opaque activities that ensure subsistence in "census towns." The "zoom-ins" into settlements allowed me to compile a tentative list of gramer shahar qualities. These include temporariness, or the temporal variability of people's presence and occupancy, linked to their increased movement; ex-centricity of physical and social developments; an environment whose paka and kancha elements mirror overlapping cycles of investment, abandonment, and re-inhabitation; and socio-economic precarity against the backdrop of deepening environmental exhaustion.

The hypothesis of translocalisation also responds to the desire for solidarity and collective organising in circumstances where "the urban" is not able to provide a concrete utopia and where top-down nationalist and classist/casteist versions of centralised power are experiencing a revival. Devastating structures of exploitation and deepening environmental exhaustion were not the only worrying circumstances I encountered during my fieldwork. In West Bengal and India-wide, widespread disenchantment and precarity have given a boost to right-wing ideology; hate speeches against activists, journalists, researchers,

Fig. 17

F. 17   When kancha–paka make up
ex-centric territories.

and crimes against minorities in the name of a skewed image of the nation are on the rise. The stories told to me over the past years by locals in many places across India and Bangladesh, those I heard in Singur and Nandigram in 2018, and scholarly and media discussions about the struggles that started there, demonstrate that the mobility and exchange of inhabitants across "urban" and "rural" territories enabled resistance and activated translocal solidarity. In other words, despite the risk of alienation that is permanently linked to it, movement (as "being on the move") can facilitate translocal solidarity and information.[80] Migrant labourers, "guest workers," young people studying abroad, diasporic communities, and those derogatorily called "economic migrants" all transpose and refract struggles happening elsewhere, making them at least shareable and, in the best cases, shared.[81]

AN ECOLOGICALLY GROUNDED MORE-THAN-HUMAN COHABITATION AS LEVEL "M"

My story started with one train conversation and will close with another. This one has stuck with me since its occurrence in the "ladies' compartment" of a local train to Haora.[82] I had gotten aboard in Singur when the sunset was just starting to colour the deep greens of the fields and silvers of the waterbodies in soft reds. I held myself on one of the compartment's doors, open as usual, my attention oscillating between the landscape and my co-travellers. There were some two hundred of us, teachers, schoolgirls, domestic workers, vegetable sellers, mothers with infants, and apathetic children, and I could tell that everyone (apart from me) commuted to Singur regularly. Some would go there for studies or tuition, others for work or family visits; they would get off within two or three stations in Diara, Seoraphuli, and Serampur. Among them was a student of Singur's girls' public school, currently in class 9,

as her uniform revealed. Partly to distract myself from tiredness and heat and partly to not leave her curious gaze unreciprocated, I entered into a conversation. We exchanged the usual information, then looking outside, I interposed: "I like this landscape of West Bengal so much!"

Her answer arrived like a cold shower: "In a few years, all these paddy fields will be covered with buildings." She spoke with no sentimentality, yet her jolly face had suddenly turned serious with a bitter shadow. Her words echoed something that the much older Kartik used to tell me about the crises confronting the region, from land fragmentation to ecological exhaustion, in a similar tone. As with him, I didn't know how to reply. Nevertheless, this interaction led me to articulate an urgent question: How is it possible to document, describe, and help circulate possibilities, and *other* viable approaches, to human and human-non-human cohabitation in times of ecological crisis?[83] My attempt to answer interweaves feminist philosopher Judith Butler's reflection on recent anti-capitalist movements and Anna Tsing's anthropological meditations on salvage accumulation and indeterminacy. Butler has long been concerned with the divides constructed by patriarchy, capitalism, and universalism along the lines of gender, race, class, nationality, city-countryside, colonial-decolonial (or global North-global South), and how these fragment the resistance of the oppressed. She has suggested that the problem could be overcome by calling into being an assembly or a tactically expandable time-space of cohabitation founded on the recognition of a deeper commonality— the differential distribution of precarity caused by capitalism.[84] The assembly she considered is the Occupy Movement, which in 2011 spread from New York to many other cities worldwide and, for Butler, was a re-elaboration and continuation of other struggles, like those sparked in 2010 in countries in North Africa and West Asia.

The necessity for human beings to stick together and cohabit on this planet, Butler argues, is "generalised" when owed to their *precariousness* (or vulnerability) but "unchosen" when it links to *precarity,* which is produced: "Our precarity is to a large extent dependent upon the organisation of economic and social relationships, the presence or absence of sustaining infrastructures and social and political institutions."[85] In such an understanding of precarity and its necessary consequence—cohabitation in a connected world—lies a contemporary, concrete utopia of the grounded, humble type I invoked above. An assembly's spatial and, above all, temporal expansion is tactical. After all, people occupy a square, a neighbourhood, a building, agricultural land, etc., to achieve certain demands for periods of time, which vary (also according to a state's levels of tolerance or oppression). As opposed to it, the time-space of cohabitation is durational; it evolves in everyday life. What logics and practices sustain such a cohabitation when each day is increasingly determined by the need to be on the move or to support others' mobilities?

Anna Tsing's work is based on her studies of the assemblages developed by expelled groups (in the specific cases of South East Asian migrants and Vietnam War veterans) in which the individual and collective options are curtailed, and the state support *and* control infrastructures are decreased, whether by neoliberal capitalism and austerity measures or by colonialism and its aftermaths. She shows that as a form of living and resisting, cohabitation is not limited by but benefits from translocality and indeterminacy.[86] In and through cohabitations that are temporary and tactical, chosen out of necessity and collectively devised in everyday life—different people are already developing practices fit for times of heightened mobility and multiple crises. I believe it is a task for contemporary research to study extant cohabitation practices and explicitly facilitate them through adequate solutions in architecture, urban planning, and mobility studies.

In both Butler's and Tsing's work, cohabitation correlates with an ethical commitment "to an equal right to inhabit the earth" for humans and non-humans.[87] This highlights an obligation to preserve the plurality of the world's popula-

tion and, read against the grain of Lefebvre's "right to (inhabit) the city," reminds us that it is not up to humans to "save" other species (the case has instead been the contrary so far), but for humans to endorse other species' rights to cohabiting a planet that is damaged, yet nonetheless worth living on.[88] My proposal is hence to further theorise cohabitation, updating Lefebvre's notion of "inhabitation" with feminist and ecological contributions. Inhabiting, according to his theorisation, is a practice of appropriation on Level "P" and, as such, entails an emancipatory potential that human beings may always upscale into appropriation on Level "G." The city plays a particular role there and Lefebvre projects it as the mediating Level "M," on which people exercise their right to self-determination, e.g., by demanding public amenities or opposing elitist urban development projects or by demonstrating and occupying streets and squares. The problem with this notion is that it does not sufficiently consider two aspects. It ignores the exclusion and oppression (sometimes utter violence) experienced worldwide by women, gays, non-heteronormative households, people of colour, indigenous peoples, and all other groups identified as "minorities." Nor does it pay enough attention to the consequences of humans' aggressive, extractivist attitude towards non-humans and the environment in general.[89] Due to this, "appropriation" remains an expansive, indeed expansionistic, approach (albeit counter-hegemonic), unavailable for too many. Rechannelling the efforts into cohabiting would foreground practices of care and paying attention in temporary, improvised, collective habitations, which are more widely available. Here lies the potential for emancipation from the hegemonic, white, male, and anthropocentric understandings, which for centuries have produced divisions in social space, gender relations, and the environment by dividing life into categories of less and more "worthwhile."

The inseparability of human and non-human cohabitation is relevant for the *problématique* of this chapter concerning the scope of a concrete utopia vis-à-vis the contemporary

phenomena of territorialisation and operationalisation of extended territories. From the stories
of Nandigram's and Singur's struggles, I learnt
that resistance and mediation under the contemporary circumstances of translocalisation take
different forms from those projected in earlier
times. People-on-the-move can and do participate in such struggles, in spite of or with their
being-on-the-move (last but not least, by sending
extra money to those mobilised in the struggle).
It is also important to remark that they can
assemble at many venues while on the move,
including social media, the networks of diasporas,
and so on. This is why I do not believe that
the role of the "mediating level" can be assigned
to "the city." This potential is common to all
places where humans and non-humans cohabit,
debate, negotiate, and stand up in solidarity, be
it against unjust land acquisition and extractivist
plans or privatisations and gentrification. This
resonates with the ideas of political scientist
Stefan Kipfer, reporting on the fight against the
extractivism of indigenous people in the country
known as Canada. Kipfer refused to reduce this
dynamic to a "new model of urbanisation" since
"political orientations among Indigenous groups
involved in pipeline politics vary, [and] few
would argue that they can be dissociated from
issues of Indigenous self-determination and land
control."[90] The struggle for self-determination
goes hand in hand with the reclamation of
territorial understandings and practices, which
are based on non-Western cosmologies. The
land is not regarded as an asset to commodify,
as per capitalist tradition, or to "protect" as
per the conservationist anthropocentric ecology
en vogue today—but common ground to cohabit
together, humans and other-than-humans.
In this spirit, the utopia needed today is humble,
situated, grounded, anti-colonial, and feminist;
it lies within decentralised but interlinked and
reciprocally informing assemblies of inhabitants,
and, vis-à-vis the deep ecological damage
faced by territories worldwide, it consists of the
task to collectively reconfigure the notions
and practices of cohabitation across the planet.

ENDNOTES

1   In the local language, Bengali,
    shahar means "city" and *gram*
    means "village."
2   Roy, "What Is Urban About Crit-
    ical Urban Theory?" 10.
3   The mosquito transmitting dengue
    fever proliferates where water is
    stagnant.
4   The Ganges River, holy to the
    Hindus, of which the Hugli River
    is one of many distributaries.
5   Thought figures, *Denkbilder* in
    German, are "montages" of images
    in the tradition of Walter
    Benjamin; for further discussion,
    see Taussig, *My Cocaine Museum.*
6   An online vocabulary for Bengali–
    English reads "পাকা: 1 Ripe, grown
    or mature (fruit squeezing, intelli-
    gence); 2 White (hair); 3 Full mass
    (boiled) … strong (ripe bamboo);
    … 5 Skilful, accomplished (ripe
    artisan, ripe thief); … 7 Perfect,
    pure (ripe gold); 9 Permanent,
    durable; … 11 Burnt (fire brick) in
    the fire or in the heat of the sun; …
    13 Paved, stacked with stone
    bricks, etc.; 14 Irreversible,
    unsteady (tired); 15 Edited (legal
    documents) … the words that do
    not alter or move."
7   "কাঁচা: 1 Raw, unfavourable (raw
    fruit); 2 Crushed, imperfect (raw
    meat); 3 Raw (raw bricks); 4 Mud
    (raw house, mud road); 5 Soft,
    green (raw grass); 6 Young; 7
    Immature (raw intelligence); 8
    Improperly done (raw text, raw
    work); … 10 Temporary, may vary
    (raw receipts, raw words); … 13
    Amish, pure (raw gold); … 17
    Available; … 19 Agricultural or
    unprotected, under normal condi-
    tions (raw material) … on the way
    to the path of fulfilment."
8   On this temporal "variability" of
    Indian spaces, see Mehrotra and
    Vera, *Kumbh Mela.*
9   Lefebvre, *The Urban Revolution.*
10 For a critique of this text that
    includes feminist and decolonial
    arguments, see Brenner and
    Schmid, "Towards a New Episte-
    mology of the Urban"; Buckley and
    Strauss, "With, Against and
    Beyond Lefebvre."
11 Santos, *Another Knowledge Is
    Possible.*
12 Haraway, "Situated Knowledges."
13 Lefebvre, *The Explosion.*
14 Chakrabarty, *Provincializing
    Europe;* for further discussion on
    the specific impact of capitalism in
    India, see Gidwani, *Capital, Inter-
    rupted.*

15   Its extreme compatibility with Western epistemologies could explain why, 50 years on, the horizon of urbanisation is deemed irrevocable by hegemonic agencies like the World Bank, IMF, UN, etc., which draw useful arguments from it in favour of their developmentalist programmes.

16   Buckley and Strauss, "With, Against and Beyond Lefebvre"; Kipfer and Goonewardena, "Urban Marxism and the Post-colonial Question."

17   Bertuzzo, "During the Urban Revolution."

18   Lefebvre, *The Production of Space*; for further discussion on this notion of production of space, see Bertuzzo, *Fragmented Dhaka*.

19   "In itself mediation, the city was the place, the product of mediations"; see Lefebvre, "The Right to the City," 107.

20   Bertuzzo, *Archipelagos*.

21   Sheller and Urry, "New Mobilities Paradigm"; Brickell and Datta, *Translocal Geographies. Spaces, Places, Connections*; Nail, *The Figure of the Migrant*; Smith, *Transnational Urbanism: Locating Urbanization*.

22   Deshingkar and Farrington, *Circular Migration in India*.

23   Roy, *City Requiem, Calcutta*; Echanove and Srivastava, "Mumbai's Circulatory Urbanism"; Gidwani and Sivaramakrishnan, "Circular Migration and Rural Cosmopolitanism in India"; for a pertinent study on Kolkata and West Bengal, see Mondal and Samanta, *Mobilities in India*.

24   Gururani and Kennedy, "The Co-production of Space, Politics and Subjectivities in India's Urban Peripheries."

25   For further discussion on regional developments that (like those that have concerned me in West Bengal) cannot be ascribed to state-led mega-projects and/or the effects of globalisation via the concept of "subaltern urbanisation" see Denis, Mukhopadhyay, and Zérah, "Subaltern Urbanisation in India."

26   Pradhan, *Unacknowledged Urbanisation*. Before the coronavirus pandemic, scholars projected that "because of the huge increase of agricultural labourers ... many new census towns might be reclassified as villages for the next census in 2021"; Guin and Das, "New Census Towns in West Bengal," 68. Since many migrant labourers have left the cities and stayed back in their localities since the pandemic, the prediction might have been matched.

27   Kundu, "Politics and Economics of Urban Growth." Demographer Amitabh Kundu is among the few to ask this question and come to my same conclusion.

28   Denis and Zérah, *Subaltern Urbanisation in India*.

29   Sassen, *Expulsions*.

30   Latour, *Reassembling the Social*.

31   "Ad hoc investments" would be a fifth feature, but here I shall remand to Bear, *Navigating Austerity*.

32   A region that broadly corresponds to today's Bangladesh, West Bengal, and parts of Assam.

33   Sharma, "The Origins of Feudalism in India."

34   Bandyopadhyay, *Land and All That*.

35   As Debjani Bhattacharyya's brilliant study points out, this stabilisation was from the very outset aimed at "propertising" the land. See Bhattacharyya, *Empire and Ecology in the Bengal Delta*.

36   The East India Company settled in Calcutta in 1696 and the city acted as capital of the British Raj from 1858 to 1911. Like other Indian cities, "Calcutta" was renamed "Kolkata" in 2003; in this chapter, I use this name when referring to events that occurred before that year. For other localities, I adopted the spellings used in the state's records.

37   Davis, *Late Victorian Holocausts*.

38   The basic unit of panchayati raj is the *gram panchayat* or village assembly, which unifies a varying number of village councils composed by elected councillors.

39   Shiva, et al., *Seeds of Suicide*.

40   Roy, *Rural Politics in India*.

41   Chatterji, *Ethnicity, Migration and the Urban Landscape of Kolkata*.

42   Rogaly, et al., *Sonar Bangla?*

43   Term used to classify ethnic tribal groups living all over South Asia.

44   Kennedy, *The Politics of Economic Restructuring in India*; Shah, et al., *Ground Down by Growth*.

45   A case in point is the departure of multinational companies, especially in the car industry sector, from Tamil Nadu—a state that, differently from West Bengal, has consistently promoted industrialisation—during the 2007–2008 crisis. For further discussion, see Homm, *Global Players – Local Struggles*.

46   Chatterjee, "Democracy and Economic Transformation in India"; Roy, "Why India Cannot Plan Its Cities."

47   Breman, *Footloose Labour*.

48   Deshingkar and Farrington, *Circular Migration and Multi Locational Livelihoods*.

49   Major religious celebrations for the Hindu and Muslim communities.

50   Bertuzzo, "The Changing Temporalities and Ecologies of House Production."

51   Bagchi, "Planning for Metropolitan Development."

52   Nielsen and Simone, "The Generic City. Examples from Jakarta, Indonesia, and Maputo, Mozambique," 138.

53   Thin scarf that most women wear over the *shalwar kameez* or *kurta* (a longish shirt).

54   Jessore is in Bangladesh.

55   Members of the local (municipal) government.

56   A longer discussion would concern the role of digitalisation of work in "dissolving" centrality.

57   Glissant, *Poetics of Relations*.

58   Benjamin, "Occupancy Urbanism."

59   Storerooms for agricultural produce or commercial goods.

60   IMSE, *Nandigram says NO to Neo-Liberalisation*; Sarkar and Chowdhury, "The Meaning of Nandigram."

61   In India's *panchayati raj* self-administration structure, variable numbers of *gram panchayats* form so-called community development blocks, shortened into CDBs, which are managed by community block development officers, CBOs.

62   On the not always smooth intersection of administrative boundary setting and inhabitants' actions in support of, or against, urban status, see Glover, "Living in a Category."

63   This ought to account for the demographic situation, as approximately 65% of India's population lives in areas denominated as rural, but, of course, it is also meant to contain migration to the big cities.

64   Ashis Nandy's analysis in *An Ambiguous Journey to the City* is still fitting, whereby in more recent years, the traditionally complex process of cultural transformation in India's multi-language, multi-religious, multi-ethnic context has been affected by the strengthening of political discourses with conservative (Hindu) nationalist tendencies. See Nandy, *Regimes of Narcissism, Regimes of Despair*.

65 Saith, *The Rural Non-farm Economy.*

66 Processes that "create the conditions under which individuals might appropriate their own surplus labor (rather than having it appropriated within capitalist firms) and at the same time enjoy a viable standard of living and decent working conditions. They also [could] promote noncapitalist commodity production and, more importantly, the existence of noncapitalist class processes as positive and desirable alternatives to capitalist employment and exploitation." See Gibson-Graham, *The End of Capitalism*, 170.

67 "Capitalocentrism is a dominant economic discourse that distributes positive value to those activities associated with capitalist economic activity however defined, and assigns lesser value to all other processes of producing and distributing goods and services by identifying them in relation to capitalism as the same as, the opposite of, a complement to, or contained within." See Gibson-Graham, *A Postcapitalist Politics*, 56. On the economistic fallacy, Adaman and Madra, "Theorizing the 'Third Sphere'".

68 High living costs and bad living standards are the reasons for that. For further discussion, see Kundu and Ray Saraswati, "Migration and Exclusionary Urbanisation."

69 Veltz, *Mondialisation, villes et territoires.* Christian Schmid is among those who used Veltz's analysis in support of theories of urbanisation. Schmid, "Specificity and Urbanization: A Theoretical Outlook."

70 Ibid, 220.

71 Bhattacharyya, "Left in the Lurch: The Demise of the World's Longest Elected Regime?"

72 On the consequences of enclosure from a gender perspective, see Federici, *Caliban and the Witch;* and Shiva, *Staying Alive.*

73 A change of political leadership in West Bengal, but also a change of policy through reforms both in West Bengal and the national level. For further discussion, see Roy, *Rural Politics in India: Political Stratification and Governance in West Bengal.*

74 Roy, *Rural Politics in India: Political Stratification and Governance in West Bengal*, 253.

75 Guha, "Have We Learnt from Singur?"

76 The Durgapur Express is officially registered as NH 19.

77 Dey, "The Suburban Railway Network of Kolkata."

78 Simone, *Improvised Lives.*

79 Apart from multi-sited research, the advantages of comparisons between cities, regions, cases—understood not as "global" or "planetary," but as "ordinary" in Jennifer Robinson's terms—are obvious. For further discussion, see Robinson, *Ordinary Cities.*

80 Brazilian economist Roberto Luís Monte-Mór advanced a similar argument within his framework of (extended) urbanisation and "the urban." See Amaral and Monte Mór, *Uma outra mobilidade.*

81 The role played by media in fostering translocal resistance is not to be underscored, and consists, again, in circulating images and information.

82 On the local trains of the Indian Railways, a few compartments are reserved for unaccompanied female passengers.

83 This crisis, as recognised by writer Amitav Ghosh, also points to a deep crisis of the imagination. For further discussion, see Ghosh, *The Great Derangement.*

84 Butler, *Notes Toward a Performative Theory of Assembly.*

85 Butler, *Notes Toward a Performative Theory of Assembly*, 119.

86 Tsing, *The Mushroom at the End of the World.*

87 Butler, *Notes Toward a Performative Theory of Assembly*, 114. In her own understanding, this commitment articulates an ecological supplement to solely anthropocentric views of cohabitation.

88 Tsing, et al., *Arts of Living on a Damaged Planet.*

89 Several authors in the emerging field of urban political ecology have highlighted the unequal distribution of environmental damage. For further discussion, see Swyngedouw and Kaika, "Urban Political Ecology."

90 Kipfer, "Pushing the Limits of Urban Research."

BIBLIOGRAPHY

Adaman, F. and Y. Madra. "Theorizing the 'Third Sphere': A Critique of the Persistence of the 'Economistic Fallacy.'" *Journal of Economic Issues*, 36/4 (2002): 1045–79.

Amaral, C.V.L., and Roberto Luis de Melo Monte Mór. "Uma outra mobilidade: movimentos, fluxos e metamorfoses nas cidades contemporâneas." *Revista UFG* 14, no. 12 (2013): 43–51.

Bagchi, Amaresh. "Planning for Metropolitan Development: Calcutta's Basic Development Plan, 1966–86: A Post Mortem." *Economic and Political Weekly* 22, no. 14 (1987): 597–601.

Bandyopadhyay, Parimal. *Land and All That: Land and Land Reforms in West Bengal: Perspective India.* Kolkata: Dey's Publishing, 2013.

Bear, Laura. *Navigating Austerity: Currents of Debt Along a South Asian River.* Redwood City: Stanford University Press, 2015.

Benjamin, Solomon. "Occupancy Urbanism: Radicalizing Politics and Economy beyond Policy and Programs." *International Journal of Urban and Regional Research* 32, no. 3 (2008): 719–729.

Bertuzzo, Elisa T. *Archipelagos: From Urbanisation to Translocalisation.* Berlin: Kadmos, 2019.

———."During the Urban Revolution: Conjunctures on the Streets of Dhaka." In *Urban Revolution Now: Henri Lefebvre in Social Research and Architecture,* edited by Akos Moravanszky, Christian Schmid, and Lukasz Stanek, 49–70. Farnham, UK: Ashgate, 2014.

———.*Fragmented Dhaka: Analysing Everyday Life with Henri Lefebvre's Theory of the Production of Space.* Stuttgart: Franz Steiner Verlag, 2009.

———."The Changing Temporalities and Ecologies of House Production in an Age of Translocalization: Instances in Kerala and West Bengal, India." In *The Transforming House,* edited by Rosalie Stolz and Jonathan Alderman. New York: Berghahn Books, forthcoming.

Bhattacharya, Snigdhendu. "Tribal Agitation Over Mamata Banerjee's Pet Mining Project Puts Bengal Govt in Fix." *The Wire,* 11 July 2020. https://thewire.in/rights/tribal-agitation-bengal-mining-deocha-pachami-mamata.

Bhattacharyya, Debjani. *Empire and Ecology in the Bengal Delta: The Making of Calcutta*. Cambridge: Cambridge University Press, 2018.

Bhattacharyya, Dwaipayan. "Left in the Lurch: The Demise of the World's Longest Elected Regime?" *Economic and Political Weekly* 45, no. 3 (2010): 51–59.

Breman, Jan. *Footloose Labour: Working in India's Informal Economy*. Cambridge: Cambridge University Press, 1996.

Brenner, Neil, and Christian Schmid. "The 'Urban Age' in Question." *International Journal of Urban and Regional Research* 38, no. 3 (2014): 731–755.

———."Towards a New Epistemology of the Urban?" *City* 19, no. 2–3 (2015): 151–182.

Brickell, Katherine, and Ayona Datta, eds. *Translocal Geographies. Spaces, Places, Connections*. Farnham, UK: Ashgate, 2011.

Buckley, Michelle, and Kendra Strauss. "With, Against and Beyond Lefebvre: Planetary Urbanization and Epistemic Plurality." *Environment and Planning D: Society and Space* 34, no. 4 (2016): 617–636.

Butler, Judith. *Notes Toward a Performative Theory of Assembly*. Cambridge, MA: Harvard University Press, 2015.

Chakrabarty, Dipesh. *Provincializing Europe: Postcolonial Thought and Historical Difference*. Princeton, NJ: Princeton University Press, 2000.

Chatterjee, Partha. "Democracy and Economic Transformation in India." *Economic and Political Weekly* 43, no. 16 (2008): 53–62.

Chatterji, Aditi. *Ethnicity, Migration and the Urban Landscape of Kolkata*. Kolkata: Bagchi & Company, 2009.

Davis, Mike. *Late Victorian Holocausts: El Niño Famines and the Making of the Third World*. London: Verso, 2017.

Denis, Eric, Partha Mukhopadhyay, and Marie-Hélène Zérah. "Subaltern Urbanisation in India." *Economic and Political Weekly* 47, no. 30 (2012): 52–62.

Denis, Eric, and Marie-Hélène Zérah, eds. *Subaltern Urbanisation in India. An Introduction to the Dynamics of Ordinary Cities*. New Delhi: Springer, 2017.

Deshingkar, Priya, and John Farrington, eds. *Circular Migration and Multi Locational Livelihoods: Strategies in Rural India*. New Delhi: Oxford University Press, 2009.

Dey, Teesta. "The Suburban Railway Network of Kolkata: A Geographical Appraisal." *The Indian Journal of Spatial Science* 3, no. 2 (2012): 3–15.

Echanove, Matias, and Rahul Srivastava. "Mumbai's Circulatory Urbanism." In *Empower! Essays on the Political Economy of Urban Form*, Vol. 3, edited by Marc Angélil and Rainer Hehl, 82–113. Berlin: Ruby Press, 2014.

Federici, Silvia. *Caliban and the Witch*. New York: Autonomedia, 2004.

Ghosh, Amitav. *The Great Derangement: Climate Change and the Unthinkable*. Chicago: University of Chicago Press, 2016.

Gibson-Graham, J. K. *The End of Capitalism (As We Knew It). A Feminist Critique of Political Economy*. Oxford: Blackwell Publishers, 1996.

———.*A Postcapitalist Politics*. Minneapolis: University of Minnesota Press, 2006.

Gidwani, Vinay. *Capital Interrupted: Agrarian Development and the Politics of Work in India*. Minneapolis, MN: University of Minnesota Press, 2008.

Gidwani, Vinay, and K. Sivaramakrishnan. "Circular Migration and Rural Cosmopolitanism in India." *Contributions to Indian Sociology* 37, no. 1–2 (2003): 339–367.

Glissant, Édouard. *Poetics of Relations*. Ann Arbor: University of Michigan Press, 1997.

Glover, William. "Living in a Category: A History of India's 'Census Town' Problem from Colonial Punjab," *Economic and Political Weekly* 53, no. 2 (2018): 55–61.

Guha, Abhijit. "Have We Learnt from Singur? A Retrospect." *Economic and Political Weekly* 52, no. 28 (2017): 18–22.

Guin, Debarshi, and Dipendra Nath Das. "New Census Towns in West Bengal: 'Census Activism' or Sectoral Diversification?" *Economic and Political Weekly* 50, no. 14 (2015): 68–72.

Gururani, Shubhra, and Loraine Kennedy. "The Co-Production of Space, Politics and Subjectivities in India's Urban Peripheries." *South Asia Multidisciplinary Academic Journal* 26 (2021).

Haraway, Donna. "The Science Question in Feminism and the Privilege of Partial Perspective." *Feminist Studies* 14, no. 3 (1988): 575–599.

Homm, Sebastian. *Global Players – Local Struggles: Spatial Dynamics of Industrialisation and Social Change in Peri-Urban Chennai, India*. Stuttgart: Franz Steiner Verlag, 2014.

IMSE. *Nandigram Says NO to Neo-Liberalisation*. Kolkata: IMSE, 2008.

Kennedy, Loraine. *The Politics of Economic Restructuring in India. Economic Governance and State Spatial Rescaling*. London: Routledge, 2014.

Kipfer, Stefan. "Pushing the Limits of Urban Research: Urbanization, Pipelines and Counter-Colonial Politics." *Environment and Planning D: Society and Space* 36, no. 3 (2018): 474–493.

Kipfer, Stefan, and Kanishka Goonewardena. "Urban Marxism and the Post-Colonial Question: Henri Lefebvre and 'Colonisation.'" *Historical Materialism* 21, no. 2 (2013): 76–116.

Kundu, Amitabh. "Politics and Economics of Urban Growth." *Economic and Political Weekly* 46, no. 20 (2011): 10–12.

Kundu, Amitabh, and Lopamudra Ray Saraswati. "Migration and Exclusionary Urbanisation in India." *Economic and Political Weekly* 47, no. 26–27 (2012): 219–227.

Latour, Bruno. *Reassembling the Social: An Introduction to Actor-Network-Theory*. Oxford: Oxford University Press, 2005.

Lefebvre, Henri. *The Explosion: Marxism and the French Revolution*. London: Modern Reader Paperbacks, 1969.

———.*The Production of Space*. Oxford: Blackwell Publishing, 1991.

———."The Right to the City." In *Henri Lefebvre. Writings on Cities*, edited by Eleonore Kofman and Elizabeth Lebas, 61–183. Oxford: Blackwell Publishing, 1996.

———.*The Urban Revolution*. Minneapolis: University of Minnesota Press, 2003.

Mehrotra, Rahul, and Felipe Vera (eds.). *Kumbh Mela: Mapping the Ephemeral Mega City*. Berlin: Hatje Cantz, 2015.

Mondal, Bhaswati, and Gopa Samanta. *Mobilities in India: The Experience of Suburban Rail Commuting*. Cham, Switzerland: Springer, 2021.

Nandy, Ashis. *An Ambiguous Journey to the City*. New Delhi: Oxford University Press, 2001.

———.*Regimes of Narcissism, Regimes of Despair*. New Delhi: Oxford University Press, 2013.

302

Nail, Thomas. *The Figure of the Migrant.* Redwood City: Stanford University Press, 2015.

Nielsen, Morten, and AbdouMaliq Simone. "The Generic City: Examples from Jakarta, Indonesia, and Maputo, Mozambique." In *Infrastructures and Social Complexity: A Companion*, edited by Penelope Harvey, Casper Bruun Jensen, and Atsuro Morita, 128–140. Abingdon, UK: Routledge, 2017.

Pradhan, K.C. *Unacknowledged Urbanisation: The Census Towns of India.* CPR Urban Working Paper 2. New Delhi: Centre for Policy Research, 2012.

Robinson, Jennifer. *Ordinary Cities. Between Modernity and Development.* London: Routledge, 2006.

Rogaly, Ben, et al., eds. *Sonar Bangla? Agricultural Growth and Agrarian Change in West Bengal and Bangladesh.* New Delhi: Sage, 1999.

Roy, Ananya. *City Requiem, Calcutta. Gender and the Politics of Poverty.* Minneapolis: University of Minnesota Press, 2003.

———."What Is Urban about Critical Urban Theory?" *Urban Geography* 37, no. 6 (2015): 810–823.

———."Why India Cannot Plan Its Cities: Informality, Insurgence, and the Idiom of Urbanisation." *Planning Theory* 8, no. 1 (2009): 76–87.

Roy, Dayabati. *Rural Politics in India: Political Stratification and Governance in West Bengal.* Delhi: Cambridge University Press, 2014.

Saith, Ashwani. *The Rural Non-Farm Economy: Processes and Policies.* Geneva: ILO, 1992.

Santos, Boaventura de Sousa (ed). *Another Knowledge Is Possible: Beyond Northern Epistemologies.* London: Verso, 2007.

Sarkar, Tanika, and Sumit Chowdhur. "The Meaning of Nandigram: Corporate Land Invasion, People's Power, and the Left in India." *Focaal European Journal of Anthropology* 54 (2009): 73–88.

Sassen, Saskia. *Expulsions. Brutality and Complexity in the Global Economy.* Cambridge, MA: Harvard University Press, 2014.

Schmid, Christian. "Specificity and Urbanization: A Theoretical Outlook." In *The Inevitable Specificity of Cities*, edited by ETH Studio Basel, 287–307. Zurich: Lars Müller, 2015.

Shah, Alpa, Jens Lerche, Richard Axelby, Dalel Benbabaali, Brendan Dongean, Jayaseelan Raj, and Vikramaditya Thakur, eds. *Ground Down by Growth: Tribe, Caste, Class, and Inequality in Twenty-First Century India.* New Delhi: Oxford University Press, 2018.

Sharma, R.S. "The Origins of Feudalism in India." *Journal of the Economic and Social History of the Orient* 1, no. 3 (1958): 297–328.

Sheller, Mimi, and John Urry. "The New Mobilities Paradigm." *Environment and Planning A* 38 (2006): 207–226.

Shiva, Vandana. *Staying Alive. Women, Ecology, and Survival in India.* New Delhi: Kali for Women and Zed Books, 1988.

Shiva, Vandana, Afsar H. Jafri, Ashok Emani, and Manish Pande, eds. *Seeds of Suicide: The Ecological and Human Costs of Globalisation of Agriculture.* New Delhi: Research Foundation for Science, Technology and Ecology, 2000.

Smith, Michael Peter. *Transnational Urbanism: Locating Urbanization.* Malden, MA: Blackwell, 2001.

Simone, AbdouMaliq. *Improvised Lives: Rhythms of Endurance in an Urban South.* UK: John Wiley & Sons, 2018.

Swyngedouw, Erik, and Maria Kaika. "Urban Political Ecology: Great Promises, Deadlock...and New Beginnings?" *Documents d'Anàlisi Geogràfica* 60, no. 3 (2014): 459–481.

Taussig, Michael. *My Cocaine Museum.* Chicago: University of Chicago Press, 2004.

Tsing, Anna. *The Mushroom at the End of the World. On the Possibility of Life on Capitalist Ruins.* Princeton, NJ: Princeton University Press, 2015.

Tsing, Anna L., Nils Bubandt, Elaine Gan, and Heather Anne Swanson, eds. *Arts of Living on a Damaged Planet: Ghosts and Monsters of the Anthropocene.* Minneapolis: University of Minnesota Press, 2017.

Veltz, Pierre. *Mondialisation, villes et territoires: une économie d'archipel.* Paris: PUF, 1996.

IMAGE CREDITS

All photography from author unless otherwise stated.

All maps from Philippe Rekacewicz with author unless otherwise stated.

F. 5   British Library (Public Domain); https://www.bl.uk/collection-items/survey-of-the-country-on-the-eastern-bank-of-the-hughly

F. 6   Copyright Ganesh Haloi. Courtesy of Akar Prakar, Kolkata.

The Territory and the State. The Urbanisation of Dongguan

During the course of its development,
the State binds itself to space
through a complex and changing relation
that passed through certain critical points …
Is not the secret of the State, hidden because
it is so obvious, to be found in space?
The State and territory interact in such
a way that they can be said
to be mutually constitutive.[1]

The city of Dongguan is a prime example
of extended industrial urbanisation in a contemporary form. It is located along the Hong Kong
to Shenzhen corridor, near the provincial
capital city of Guangzhou in the eastern part
of the Pearl River Delta. [Fig. 1] In the last few
decades, it developed into "the world's factory"
as a result of the rise of global production
systems. By plugging itself into Hong Kong's
international financial centre and its commercial
and port infrastructure, it launched a strategy
of export-led industrialisation that drove the
urbanisation of numerous towns and villages.
This resulted in large clusters of foreign enter-

prises, sub-contracting factories, and large
concentrations of Chinese migrant workers
in various labour-intensive manufacturing industries.[2] As a result, the entire once-rural county
of Dongguan was transformed into a manufacturing zone, with countless factories making
clothing, shoes, furniture, computers, electronics, household goods, mechanical and metal
parts, machinery, and so on. With the production of athletic shoes for famous brands and
computer and electronic components for global
companies, this world factory also became
a key player in global supply chains, one of the
important pillars of China's export economy and
a driver of Hong Kong's global business centre.

In Dongguan, it was not the traditional
centre of Guancheng that became the motor
of rapid industrialisation; rather, it was the
towns and villages. Travelling through the
endless urbanised territory of Dongguan is like
passing through countless contiguous industrialised towns and villages. Dongguan is a giant
hodgepodge of factories, village houses, condo-
minium towers, villas, shopping malls, hotels,

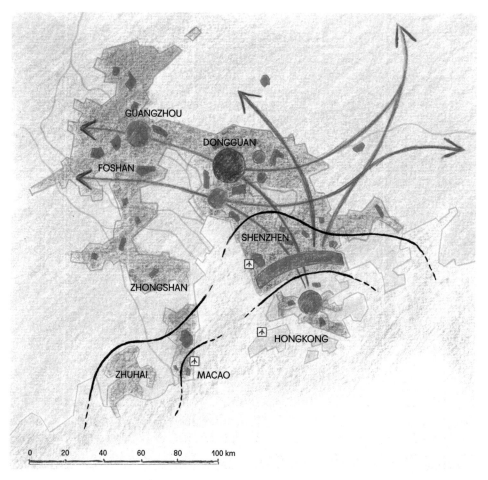

DONGGUAN'S EXTENDED URBANISATION
Fig. 1

street shops, wholesale markets, patches of farm-land, parks, and the like. It seems to be a world of different contingencies, people, buildings, logics, and practices that emerged spontaneously at different times and places.

F. 1 This conceptual map of Dongguan's extended urbanisation illustrates the relative position of Dongguan to Shenzhen, Hong Kong and Guangzhou as well as the general directions of urban corridors. The actual size of Dongguan's centre within this constellation is not to scale, but accentuated to distinguish it from other, more well-known centres in the region.

However, this seemingly fluid, amorphous, disorienting space of global production stands in stark contrast to the territorial power structure of Dongguan. It is a city-territory—with towns and villages—that forms a kind of "territory with many territories" based on village collectives and defined by complex and contradictory power relations. These territories tie all villagers to a communal landownership that determines the redistribution of land, income, resources, and, thus, everyday lives. The village collectives are not autonomous but form an extension of the state power with the task of managing local villagers, migrant workers, small entrepreneurs, and domestic and foreign capitalists in their territories. But these territories are also filled with land uses that do not conform to the legal framework of "rural land" but result from ambiguous and often illegal practices. Therefore, the villagers are constantly involved in land conflicts and have developed their own way of holding land and securing their village rights. This is a capitalist space deeply embedded in the Chinese state's territorial power, but it appears to be intrinsically contradictory and clearly different from what Henri Lefebvre conceptualised as a homogenising "state space," using the example of the French state in the 1970s.

In this chapter, I investigate how this contradictory space of *extended urbanisation* was produced in Dongguan during the 1980s and 1990s and how it was subsequently restructured and transformed into a space of *concentrated urbanisation*. My question is how the territorial power of the state materialised in this extended urban space and its various dynamics and contradictions. On a theoretical level, I argue that an analysis of extended urbanisation in China requires an analysis of the state space that goes beyond conceptions of a static and homogeneous nation. I approach this question from the perspective of China's changing relations between the state and the territory and their intersection with urbanisation processes.[3]

In China, the production of territories results from constant changes in state power and the political technologies that enable the party-state to achieve domination.[4] The central state reshuffles the levels of subnational governments and reorganises their administrative and territorial powers, thereby shaping different levels, forms, and processes of urbanisation. This enables the state to manipulate and encompass both concentrated and extended urbanisation processes at all subnational levels according to its national strategies and policies. However, this chapter shows that the exertion of the state's territorial power in China is neither a top-down nor a bottom-up process but has to be understood as a bundle of multiple contradictory processes. China's state space is not homogeneous; it can be heterogeneous, paradoxical, and conflictual.

At the same time, the analysis of spaces of extended urbanisation in Dongguan allows us to rethink the relationship between state power, the territory, and urbanisation, presenting the question: How are urbanisation processes, with their specific material, regulatory, and social characteristics, associated with the rise of particular forms of territorial powers? In the following section, I first raise the question of state-territory relations in the context of extended urbanisation in China. I argue that the popular concept of *desakota*, which is often applied to the analysis of China's extended urbanisation, gives no clue to understanding the significance between the territory and state power on the one hand and between state power and urbanisation on the other. The analysis of desakota leaves us with a simplistic economic model reflecting the transformation of vast rural areas under conditions of globalisation. It is based on thinking in binary oppositions, assigning top-down powers to the state and bottom-up reactions to the villages, and mapping the geography of power in terms of centre and periphery. It, thus, conceptually falls into a "territorial trap."[5] I suggest that it is essential to explore the specific relationships between the state and its territories in China to better understand its relentless process of urbanisation.

The second section explores the history of the state's manipulation of territories that emerged and developed in Guangdong. It focuses on the changes occurring in the transition from Mao to the post-Mao period and analyses the development of what Henri Lefebvre called a "state mode of production." The idea of the manipulation of territories by the state emerged during my cartographic research of Shenzhen in 2013, through which I discovered the shifting boundaries of this city-territory. To effectively grasp this systematic domination of state power over territory and urbanisation, I have chosen the scale of the entire Guangdong Province and traced all the changes in administrative boundaries, internal territories, and governments, and I analysed how this territorial apparatus mastered and manipulated the development of different cities, their forms, scales, and urbanisation processes. The maps show that the ongoing changes in Chinese territories are not only the results of state strategies and its regulation of urbanisation but also depend on the dynamics of the internal contradictions of the state space itself.

In the subsequent sections, I will present Dongguan as my case study in which I explore how these spaces of extended urbanisation were produced and evolved over decades and how state power occurred and reproduced itself through the urbanisation process. The case study shows how the city of Dongguan was re-territorialised into a three-tiered system of a city-territory, towns, and villages that all became institutional actors of extended urbanisation. This territorial arrangement constituted a specific form of state domination, which created various conflicts and contradictions, and finally initiated a fundamental shift towards concentrated urbanisation after 2000. The case study explores this shift in detail through fieldwork in several villages of Tangxia town. It shows that extended urbanisation followed neither the system of state-owned "urban land" nor collective-owned "rural land." Instead, it was the result of alternative strategies developed by the villagers in their struggles against the domination of towns and the abuse of power by local cadres associated with the expropriation and development of rural land at the expense of villagers. It also explores the question of agency and shows how local villagers and migrants shaped the process of the production of space.

This study is based on my intermittent fieldwork from 2013 to 2018 in Dongguan. The fieldwork included interviews and mapping sessions with local professionals (planners and scholars), villagers, and migrant workers. I used a specific method of mapping to understand the material production of these spaces of extended urbanisation.[6] I also conducted interviews with local informants to investigate territorial regulations, social relations, and modalities of everyday life, as informed by Lefebvre's theory of the production of space.[7] I analysed all of these aspects from a historical perspective and recon-

structed the pathways of urbanisation to better understand fundamental shifts and changes in the process itself, the power relations, and everyday life. As the questions concerning land and state power are sensitive for villagers, this research required building trust. Contacts with local villagers were therefore crucial for conducting this fieldwork: I stayed in the villagers' homes, hung out and discussed with young villagers, and conducted semi-open interviews with villagers and migrants, whom I found through snowball sampling. All these field methods were important for creating a deeper understanding of urbanisation processes because they often revealed a different reality than could be assumed from extant scientific literature or appearances at first sight. Furthermore, it also revealed stark contrasts from one villager to another and from one village to another. I gave a first account of this research in my article "Territorially-Nested Urbanization in China."[8]

Finally, I do not claim that this fieldwork represents China's urban development in general. There are considerable differences in the territorial regimes and the urbanisation processes across China. While the system of territorialisation is the key instrument of state power, multiple internal contradictions and effects of this system drive urbanisation processes, which can only be detected by detailed research on the ground.

STATE, TERRITORY,
    AND URBANISATION IN CHINA

THE CONCEPT OF DESAKOTA
    AS A TERRITORIAL TRAP
        In the scholarly discussion of extended urbanisation, the concept of desakota provided an important perspective on the massive urban change occurring in the wider urban regions of Asia, particularly in Indonesia, India, China, and Japan. According to Terry McGee, extended urbanisation in these areas materialised in intense rural-urban interfaces outside large urban agglomerations. It led

to extended urban regions composed of three typical urban forms: an urban core, peri-urban settlements, and desakota landscapes.[9] Thus, desakota designates large rural areas undergoing dramatic socio-economic change through industrialisation and urbanisation in the context of a globalising economy. Desakota studies explored how socio-economic changes led to geographical differentiation and a specific regional division of labour and provided a broader context for regional planning. Dongguan, amongst many other regions, served as a showcase for desakota. It was seen as resulting from urban expansion in the Pearl River Delta[10] and as a bottom-up process that contrasted with state-led urbanisation processes.[11]

Despite many criticisms, the concept of desakota provided a dominant perspective in the urban studies of China. For this research, I highlight two shortcomings when applying the desakota concept to analyse urbanisation in China. First, as argued by John Friedmann, desakota seeks a generalisation of extended urbanisation in Asia at the expense of the acknowledgement of specificities and complexities in different contexts and a more thorough theorisation.[12] Because of its core methodology of aggregating statistical data, the spatial analysis is usually based on a set of functional socio-economic indicators, thereby simplifying complex changes in social spaces in urbanising regions. It relies on a morphological analysis similar to the approach of the Chicago School and presents a generalised model of a region composed of just three morphological settlement types, depending on a locational theory for an explanation.

Second, the concept of desakota is caught in what John Agnew called a territorial trap because it adopts the perspective of global capitalism to account for the relentless urbanisation processes in China.[13] From this perspective, the territory is considered a container that changes with economic functions and transport infrastructure alterations. The analysis of the state is narrowed down to governments and planning systems. Such a static concept of the territory does not account for the fact that the reproduc-

tion of Chinese state power is strongly related to the *restructuring of the territory* in the context of ongoing urbanisation. There is also the question of how Chinese desakota studies could escape the problem of city-centrism if they adopt the assumption that "cities" are stable morphological units that could be understood as material spaces of capital accumulation. This assumption, however, contrasts with the Chinese understanding of the "city" as a politico-territorial unit that is systematically transformed before, during, and after the processes of urbanisation. In this context, these studies tend to perpetuate the idea of a rural-urban dualism with a "Chinese characteristic," which is either understood as a centre-periphery relationship or a dual power structure composed of the central state (top-down) and the villages (bottom-up).

This points to a general weakness in the analysis of the state in Chinese urban studies, which shows a strong tendency to apply concepts of "state-led" or "neoliberal" urban development derived from Western analyses. Consequently, such analyses were strongly criticised for de-contextualising China's history and state processes.[14] Thus, many studies focus on how planning is used as a governmental tool to propel urban development but lack an analysis of the state itself, or simply call this process state-led urbanisation. Finally, many studies focus on the Chinese dual-track rural-urban land system, highlighting the monopoly of the state in leading the development process.[15] Land is a critical means of production in this process, but it is different from the territory, which is the central state's encompassing instrument to control all levels of government power and their territorial relations, and also the key element in rural-urban relations, including the land and the hukou system (the local citizenship, see below). Therefore, it is the state's territorial power that guides urbanisation processes. My argument is that the usual conceptualisation of the Chinese state in urban studies became a "territorial trap" that prevented us from seeing how state power operated through the reorganisation of territories to produce specific forms of urbanisation and, thus, subsumed global capitalist activities under its modality of territorialisation (but not the other way around).

THE TERRITORIAL DIMENSION OF STATE SPACE

What are the specificities of the Chinese territorial system? My argument is built on a few important studies that critically interrogate the role of the Chinese party-state in guiding urbanisation processes.[16] In particular, as Laurence Ma argued, Chinese urbanisation cannot be understood, as in Western countries, through the lens of geographical rescaling processes generated by globalisation because the Chinese territory is politically defined and organised through a ranked administrative system of territorial levels.[17] It is this hierarchical system that propels urban development. Liu Junde pointed out how China managed economic changes by unhinging the Mao regime's highly centralised planned economy. This created what he called the "administrative area economy," wherein the central state delegates powers to local governments to develop the economy within their administrative territories, according to their rank.[18] Carolyn Cartier further developed the concept of "territorial urbanisation" to specify party-state interventions in the urbanisation process of Shanghai through territorial amalgamations.[19] Her studies opened up a new agenda of how the state constantly shaped and reshaped territories to propel urban development in China.

My theoretical concerns emerged from my mapping of Shenzhen in 2013, which raised the question of shifting territories and boundaries in relation to changes in state power. It opened up a different point of departure for theorisation, examining how Lefebvre approached the state's relation to space through the production of a territory.[20] The Chinese territorial division is not a mere administrative system but an encompassing institutional and territorial regime, managing capitalist accumulation and economic growth and facing contradictions and crises. The specificity of the Chinese state mode of production is that the ruling party manages both political and economic control. It entails the continuous domination and restructuring

of two key aspects: First, the entire national territory is hierarchised into a system of different rank-based territories, and the central state reshuffles all subordinated governmental levels—their rank-based territorially configured power relations. Second, in producing and reorganising the subnational territories, the governments are also advancing and shaping different urbanisation processes to support economic growth, linking the political to the urban space. As a result, the Chinese state mode of production has rapidly propelled different city-territories and urbanisation processes since the beginning of the post-Mao era.

The Chinese state space constitutes a complex and contradictory relationship between the state, the territory, and the urbanisation processes. Here, I highlight three crucial characteristics. First, this state space is not simply vertically articulated but *territorially nested*.[21] This means that the subnational governmental levels are organised according to political ranks and particular politico-territorial configurations, which complicate the geographies of state power—for example, when a decentralised territorial form has a multitude of lower-level governments or, conversely, when a centralised form has just one single government. The decentralised form of territoriality resulted from the political strategy conducted during the 1980s and 1990s to accelerate urban expansion, which led to divergent urbanisation processes and competition between governments of the same and different ranks. This strategy was then shifted during the 2000s by installing centralised governmental and planning systems, which contradicted the previous multiple territorial orders and rules and thus triggered all sorts of new conflicts.

The second characteristic of China's state space is that it materialises *through different urbanisation processes* because all territorial levels are advancing their own urbanisation strategies to increase economic growth in their areas. The outcomes of these urbanisation strategies shape the reconfiguration of the politico-territorial structure, the respective government relations, and territorial reach.

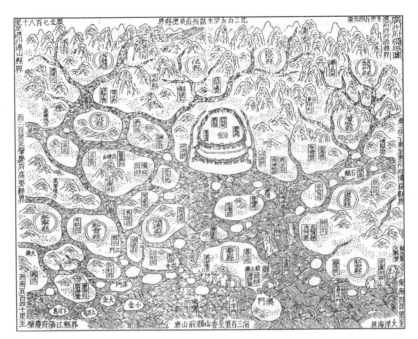

Fig. 2

Third, the state is constantly reshaping its space to engineer *new processes of urbanisation* to resolve the difficulties of governments in managing urbanisation. In doing so, the state needs to reshuffle its politico-territorial structure and reshape its internal geographies of power. However, these changes further trigger conflicts and tensions between local governments, which are already deeply involved in local economic interests.

The point is that "state centrism" remains an essential question in China because, as Brenner noted, it cannot be understood through a static, a-spatial, and non-territorial perspective.[22] Otherwise, we follow the party narrative of a powerful Chinese state. But this power is often over-emphasised because the full consequences of China's hierarchical territorial structure are neglected. Therefore, we have to adopt a dynamic *and* territorial perspective that considers the ambiguities, complexities,

and contradictions between the different governmental levels that generate massive consequences for the patterns and pathways of urbanisation. The relations between the state and its space are the "secret of the State," as Lefebvre notes in this chapter's introductory quote. We must problematise how the state historically reshapes itself to maintain its political domination and reproduce its power through social and economic changes. The complexities and transformations of the state space and the resulting contradictions that are determining its urbanisation need to be analysed. Both concentrated and extended urbanisation processes are intertwined with the changing geographies of state power. Thus, the extended urbanisation of Dongguan that this chapter explores was not the result of bottom-up forces that stood outside of state power. On the contrary, this form of urbanisation has been generated by the particular territorial form of state power and the multitudes of power relations, territorial regulations, and economic logic that it entailed.

F. 2   Chinese walled-cities (cheng 城) in the Kwangtung (Guangdong) province, Qing dynasty.

Fig. 3

TERRITORY AND THE STATE MODE OF PRODUCTION

This section analyses how territory is crucial for understanding the role of state power in the processes of concentrated and extended urbanisation. Here, I explore the state-territorial changes at the provincial level of Guangdong and show how a state mode of production emerged during the Mao period and rapidly unfolded after 1979. In this process, the territorial system of the Chinese state was used to push political change and shape urbanisation processes. China's territorial system allows the central party-state to manipulate and restructure all subnational territorial levels, reshuffle governmental power relations, establish new city-territories, and shape particular urbanisation processes. This is an encompassing, systematic, and malleable form of political technology that the party-state can use to control urbanisation and governmental action at all territorial levels.

A HISTORY OF GUANGDONG'S STATE—TERRITORY RELATIONS

To better understand the contemporary Chinese state-territorial power and its changing political geographies, it is important to highlight three pre-1949 historical conditions. First, historically, China did not have a concept of "territory" equivalent to the West. However, the Chinese term *jiangyu* (疆域) refers to the "boundary (*jiang*) of the imperial realm (*yu*)," including tributary and vassal states, but without a clearly defined boundary.[23] Relatedly, the concept of *tianxia* (天下), meaning "all under the Heaven," expresses a Sino-centric hierarchy of the world order between the Chinese emperor and foreign rulers in a suzerain-tributary system. Both terms signify the ruling power of the emperor as "the son of Heaven."

Second, the meaning of ancient walled cities called *cheng* (城) is completely different from the contemporary city-territory that is called *shi* (市), which designates not a morphological form (a "city") but a politico-territorial unit. Therefore, shi can contain dense settlements and large agricultural and sparsely settled areas. In contrast, cheng referred to a political centre of the empire that assumed military, defence, administrative, and social functions across many dynasties. [Fig. 2] Cheng had no autonomy or independent administration and did not develop any kind of civil society. It was the seat of a county government that administrated the city's territory and its rural surroundings, from which rural-urban relations developed.[24] However, although cheng were the centres of imperial power, this imperial power rarely extended below the level of the county, where villages and market towns were subjected to the powers of lineages and gentries, with their distinctive local and customary rules and practices.[25]

During the early twentieth century, this boundless, worldwide Chinese concept of the dynasty was supplanted by the Western concept of territory. The term *lingtu* (領土) was derived from the Japanese translation, meaning a "governed land," a sovereign state with a clear, fixed border.[26] This concept became an essential element in the nation-state formation when the empire and its tianxia system collapsed in the 1911 Revolution, and the Republic of China was founded. As I will show below, this modern concept of territory was further developed into the party-state apparatus through which the Communist Party could manipulate political, economic, and social processes and relations. Although the tianxia system collapsed, it survived as the state's ideology and later served as a tool to propagate China's hegemony in the world order.

In the first decade after the Republic of China's founding, new forms of cities also emerged in Guangdong alongside the historic walled cities and towns [Fig. 4]. This included the colonial cities of Hong Kong and Macau and the treaty ports for foreign trade, such as Jangmen. It also included new Chinese cities such as Canton (Guangzhou, originally a walled city) and Swatow (Shantou, a treaty port).

These cities designated as shi gained a kind of autonomous legal status with an independent city administration. This was a period of modernisation in which many walled cities demolished their walls and expanded their city areas. In this process, Guangdong's cities and towns remained the centres of international, regional, and domestic trade networks and governed, specialised, and commercialised agricultural systems in their rural hinterlands. After 1949, the meaning and the forms of Chinese cities and rural-urban relationships radically changed when the new version of a state-territorial apparatus was developed under the rule of the Chinese Communist Party (CCP).

The rise to power of the CCP after the Second World War led to the development of a new territorial regime through which Mao Zedong built a totalitarian party-state to realise the new "Socialist China." It was a centralised regime with a dual system to govern urban and rural areas. New city-territories (shi) were designated as sites of the socialist industrial production system that eliminated any capitalist commercial and consumption functions. *Danwei* (work units) helped reach this goal and were established as each industrial city's lowest political and social units. They had to meet state target values for industrial outputs, provide employment and social benefits, govern workers' social reproduction, and conduct surveillance.[27] Rural areas were re-territorialised into village collectives that served as encompassing political-economic units combining military, political, administrative, social, and economic functions.[28] They formed a three-tiered system of agricultural collectivisation, consisting of people's communes, production brigades, and production teams. Village collectives forcefully subjected all peasants, their bodies, and their labour forces to fulfil the state's quota of agricultural production without even leaving them enough food for themselves.

The *hukou* system was another state strategy to incorporate the people into the territorial control system. It implemented a compulsory household registration based

F. 3   The old city centre, Guancheng, Dongguan.

on residency permits linked to a place of birth. To this day, it constitutes an encompassing control mechanism of the population that differentiates between a rural and urban residential status and regulates entitlements to social services and welfare. It is also an instrument to control rural-urban migration and labour distribution.[29] Through these institutionalised distinctions between rural and urban realms, the state eventually established its power over all aspects of the social production and reproduction process.

In launching the "Great Leap Forward" in 1958, the central state introduced two major territorial processes to manipulate rural and urban relations. First, some rural areas were incorporated into large cities as their designated "countryside" (郊區). For example, Guangzhou (Canton) gained a large agricultural area to supply food and resources from village collectives. Second, a new territorial governing system was implemented called "city-leading-counties" (市管縣). This system forced the territorial subordination of counties under a city's jurisdiction, as exemplified in Guangzhou and Shaoguan. [Fig. 5] By 1976, Guangzhou administered seven counties to accelerate industrialisation and solve the food shortage problem. This territorial amalgamation transformed the historical form of the walled cities (cheng) into a city-territory, and the city was transformed into a politico-territorial form (shi) to encompass and control the urban-rural relations.

Accordingly, Mao's new territorial regime eliminated the pre-1949 administrative system and imposed a new state space by creating an all-encompassing, homogenising, and hierarchical territorial structure. It thus gave rise to a new state mode of production based on the political domination of the CCP. The state became the only agent exercising political and economic power and social control. As Wang notes, "People's land and assets, 'means of production,' basic supplies, and personal mobility were all thoroughly and institutionally centralised into the CCP-controlled people's communes, various units, and agencies."[30]

During the post-Mao era, the state-territory relationship changed again, but in a contradictory way. On the one hand, it had to adapt to the new political agenda of economic reforms under Deng Xiaoping. But, on the other, it had to maintain the politico-territorial system introduced by Mao in order to keep CCP's control of the political and economic realms. Although Deng advocated for economic *and* administrative reforms, the premier at the time, Zhao Ziyang, noted that Deng adovcated for economic reforms but it was an instrument to uphold the party's power in China.[31] If the party-state still dominated political and economic changes, we should ask how the creation of city-territories became a state strategy to promote economic growth in a way that the CCP could maintain its domination over all governments and urbanisation processes.

The answer is revealed in Figures 6 to 9. [Fig. 6–9] They show how the province of Guangdong underwent a constant reshuffling of territories and administrative boundaries during the post-Mao era. These territorial shifts articulated a direct relationship between the geographies of state power and urbanisation processes. The party-state became the central agent of the production of space through its manipulation of the administrative divisions of territories. The constant re-territorialisation of Guangdong led to a massive rise in the number of cities. From 1988 to 1994, the number of large cities (deputy-provincial and prefecture-level) increased from 9 to 21, and of the small cities (county-level) from 6 to 33. These processes also fundamentally restructured these cities and resulted in different urbanisation processes. As a result, all Chinese cities were territorially reconfigured and transformed into different large city-territories, which replaced the old forms of walled cities (cheng) or town settlements. These new city-territories (shi) incorporate both rural and urban areas within their jurisdictions and express a new rationale of governmental relations: "city-leading-countryside" (城市帶動農村). This means that cities and towns become the centres of development and govern both rural *and* urban relations. It can be understood

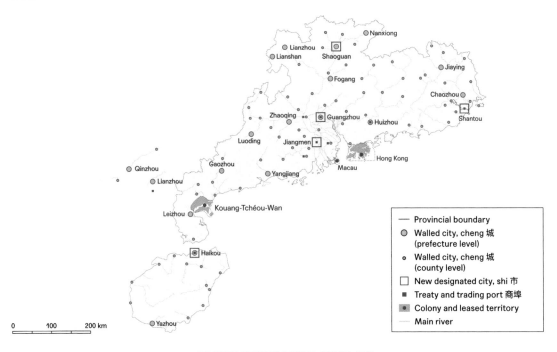

GUANGDONG'S WALLED CITIES AND
NEW URBAN SETTLEMENTS 1908–1943
FIG. 4

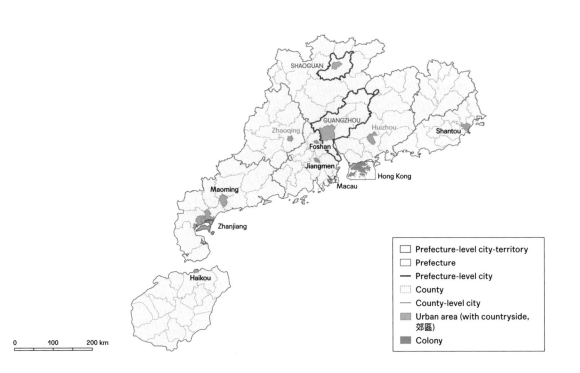

FORMATION OF CITY-TERRITORIES 1960–1976
Fig. 5

F. 7   The transformation of Guangdong
        through territorial splitting
        and boundary readjustment.

F.9   Consolidation of prefecture-level
        city-territories through
        transforming counties and county-
        level cities into "urban districts".

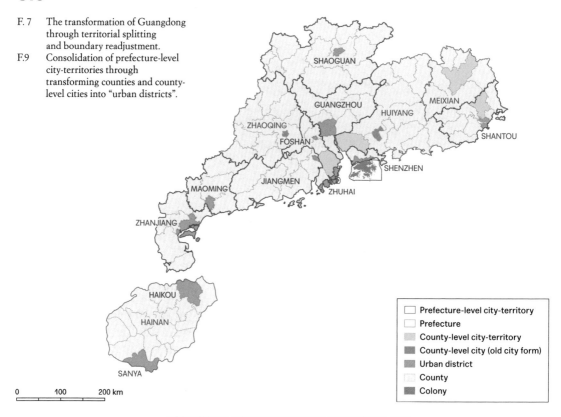

	Prefecture-level city-territory
	Prefecture
	County-level city-territory
	County-level city (old city form)
	Urban district
	County
	Colony

FORMATION OF NEW CITY-TERRITORIES 1977–1987
Fig. 6

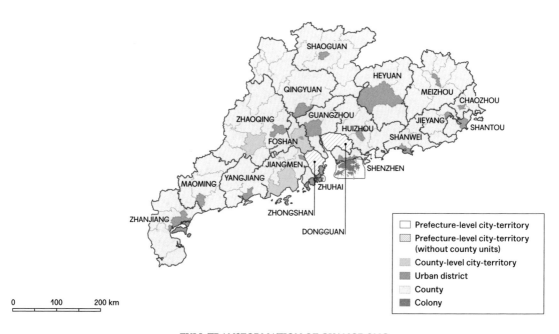

	Prefecture-level city-territory
	Prefecture-level city-territory (without county units)
	County-level city-territory
	Urban district
	County
	Colony

FULL TRANSFORMATION OF GUANGDONG
INTO CITY-TERRITORIES, 1988–1992
Fig. 7

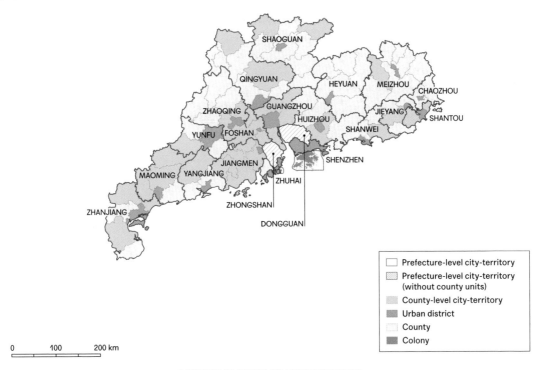

**MULTIPLICATION OF COUNTY-LEVEL
CITY-TERRITORIES 1993–1999**
Fig. 8

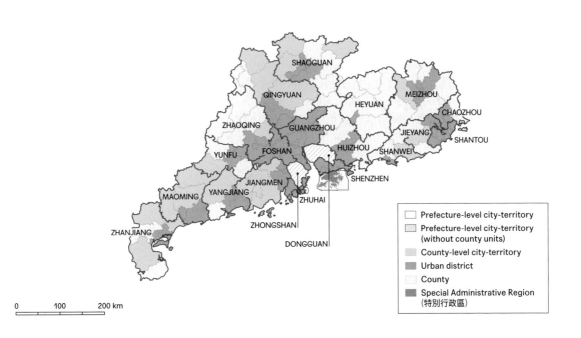

EXPANSION OF URBAN DISTRICTS SINCE 2000
Fig. 9

as an attempt to overcome the contradictions of the previous dual rural-urban system. This principle clearly contrasts with Mao's slogan of the "countryside-surrounding-cities" (農村 包圍城市), which was used to mobilise the rural masses.

Guangdong experienced several rounds of re-territorialisation to create these new forms of city-territories. In fact, Mao had already changed course in 1960 when he adopted the principle of "city-leading-counties" (see above). This principle was stipulated as the territorial form of large cities in 1982. [Fig. 6][32] In this way, the two largest cities in the Guangdong Province, Guangzhou and Shaoguan, further expanded their administrative jurisdictions to encompass more counties. Shenzhen and Zhuhai, China's first Special Economic Zones (SEZs), were founded in Guangdong in 1980 and transformed directly from rural counties to deputy-provincial and prefecture-level cities, respectively. Foshan, Jiangmen, Zhanjiang, and Maoming underwent a process of "city-prefecture amalgamation" by repealing the prefectures (an older administrative echelon initially managing counties) and then merging those counties and the old prefecture-level cities. Between 1988 and 1993, another round of territorial splits and administrative reshuffling took place that doubled the numbers of city-territories and readjusted their size: large city-territories (shi) were split into two or more city-territories, the Huiyang prefecture was repealed, its territory subdivided into four new city-territories, and the Hainan island was split from Guangdong and became a province. [Fig. 7] All these cities showed the various ways of territorial reorganisation and administrative reshuffling that shaped the size, form, and hierarchy of governmental relations in Guangdong.

Apart from the large cities, Guangdong's number of small cities drastically increased from six in 1988 to 33 in 1993. [Fig. 7–8] They were county-level cities to serve the state's strategy of developing small cities and towns in China. As the lowest rank, this new form of city was created by the re-territorialisation of rural counties (縣改市) (e.g., Dongguan in 1985) or through an amalgamation of an old county-level city and its historically related neighbouring county (e.g., Chaozhou in 1983). This territorial process facilitated extensive urbanisation by authorising lower-level governments to develop small cities and towns. Concomitantly, it hierarchised a multicentric form of a city-territory. A new form of territorial relations emerged by transforming counties into small cities: "city-leading-cities" (代管市). This means that a prefecture-level city-territory administers county-level cities on behalf of the provincial government. In this case, Guangzhou adopted the configuration of a "large city leading four small cities" that rapidly accelerated its multicentric processes of agglomeration and urban expansion during the 1990s. [Fig. 8]

However, since 2000 many cities have expanded their city centres by transforming counties and county-level cities into "urban districts" (市轄區). [Fig. 9] In Guangzhou, the four county-level cities were changed into urban districts to facilitate the metropolitan plan of "Greater Guangzhou." They immediately lost their city status while the Guangzhou government centralised its power over urban development, planning, and budgeting for the entire territory. It completely changed its urban development strategy from a decentralised, multipolar model to a centralised pathway of concentrated urbanisation.

STATE, TERRITORY,
    AND URBANISATION

Following the history of Guangdong presented above, three implications have to be highlighted to rethink the changing relationship between the state, its territories, and urbanisation processes. Firstly, the state organises territories and guides urbanisation in China to assert its domination in both the political and economic spheres. After 1978, the definition and designation of city-territories became the key instrument of the state to promote and control urbanisation. A "city" in China was no longer a dense urban settlement because it also contained large rural areas that served as support spaces and land reserves for future urbanisation. City-territories currently cover every inch of land in Guangdong. Regardless of whether areas were urban or rural at the beginning of this process, they were all reconfigured into a hierarchical territorial system that defined their status and rank and, thus, their political power relations. Any changes in the status and rank of the territory required the approval of the central state, which made decisions according to national urbanisation strategies. In this way, the urbanisation of the Chinese territory was internally organised according to a rank-based political-territorial system.[33] Under this new state mode of production, the state simultaneously controlled urbanisation processes and local governments at all levels while managing capitalist activities in space. Subsequently, it orchestrated, concentrated, and extended urbanisation and manipulated urbanisation processes to adapt to changing conditions and circumstances. On the ground, this led to very different patterns and pathways of urbanisation.

Secondly, with their complex and changing politico-territorial structures, all these city-territories determined the intertwining relationship between the urbanisation process and internal governmental relations. A prefecture-level city-territory comprises urban districts, counties, and county-level cities with sub-districts, towns, and villages at the lowest level. They are territorially nested inside one another according to their ranks. Ranks determine their level and scope of governmental (administrative, economic, fiscal, and legislative) powers, territorial form, and organisation. Thus, large cities are city-territories with urban districts, while small cities don't have districts. There is also a wide range of inter-governmental relations, such as "city-leading-counties" or "city-leading-cities." In this way, a city-territory can be understood as a constellation of numerous sub-territories with different statuses, multiple governments with different ranks, different territorial regulations, and political relations. The internal relations of a city-territory are like an inter-territorial matrix:[34] If a new strategy of urbanisation is launched, every territorial unit is subdivided, amalgamated, and rearranged to create a new configuration of relations appropriate to the implementation of the new strategy.

Thirdly, while this territorial regime was crucial for the reproduction of state power during the period of economic reforms (and the massive political and economic changes since), it also led to complex new geographies of state powers and to new contradictions that had strong impacts on power relations and urbanisation processes, which necessitated more changes to the territorial system. For instance, Shenzhen adopted a configuration of "city-leading-county" to manage its fast and massive urbanisation process during the 1980s, which led to subsequent contradictions. Since 1992, Shenzhen underwent two rounds of a "territorial fix" and abolished the county, town, and village systems to resolve various kinds of institutional fragmentation. And yet, large-scale contestations also emerged in each round of territorial restructuring, in which villagers could secure their land interests through plotting.[35]

THE URBANISATION
OF DONGGUAN

In the previous section, I explained how Guangdong's territorialisation has shifted from multicentric to concentrated forms of state power. Nevertheless, Dongguan, with its polycentric constellation of towns and villages, did not get the state's approval to change its administrative divisions to resolve its fragmented territorial structure and, thus, to coordinate its urbanisation processes better. In this and the following sections, I show how Dongguan's politico-territorial restructuring was played out and how it shaped a particular form of extended urbanisation. Dongguan's territorial structure did not show a clear vertical articulation of state power, and its urbanisation processes were dominated neither by top-down nor bottom-up strategies. Instead, I suggest that the urbanisation of Dongguan's villages was rooted in the multitudes of territorial powers and their contradictory practices. As a result, the villages rapidly transformed into fragmented urban spaces, each of which had a specific form of social relations, land politics, and villagers' consciousness.

Historically, Dongguan was an agrarian society, with the walled city of Guancheng as the county's seat. [Fig. 10] In the nineteenth century, Dongguan had three merchant towns, which were also trading ports (Guancheng, Taiping, Shilong), two additional ports, and many small market towns that served as trading places between the vast rural areas and some large cities like Guangzhou, Foshan, and Hong Kong.[36] The CCP's rise to power led to a radical territorial transformation of Dongguan that eliminated the pre-communist urban and rural economy and society.[37] In 1958, the entire county was divided into 13 people's communes with 190 brigades, and the three merchant towns were transformed into urban communes with state landownership and state-owned enterprises. [Fig. 11][38] Rural areas were likewise subject to massive changes with the elimination of the classes of the gentry, landlords, and wealthy peasants, who lost their land and property ownership. By abolishing rural townships, a three-tiered system of communes, brigades, and teams was established to implement agricultural collectivisation and collective land ownership under the control and exploitation of the party-state apparatus. The hukou system controlled internal migration, labour regulation, and food distribution in towns and villages (see above). By 1979, Dongguan was composed of three urban communes and 29 rural communes, with 545 brigades at the lower level.[39] However, this territorial structure would soon be subject to a new round of re-territorialisation.

During the post-Mao period, Dongguan experienced a rapid, extensive form of urbanisation that completely transformed vast rural areas into various industrialised towns and villages. On the highest level, several rounds of re-territorialisation led to the formation of new city-territories in the East Pearl River Delta. It was not only the historical centre of Huizhou that lost its importance, but also

many counties underwent a radical transformation. [Fig. 12] Bao'an County first became Shenzhen City at the prefecture level in 1979 and then the deputy provincial level in 1981.[40] In 1985, Dongguan became a county-level city to propel rural industrialisation. Thus, the walled city of Guancheng, with a city area of 15 km², was expanded to a city-territory encompassing 2,456 km² containing a great variety of urban and rural areas.[41] In 1988, the Huiyang prefecture was abolished, and its territory was subdivided into four prefecture-level city-territories with different territorial structures. Like the other three, Dongguan became a prefecture-level city-territory led by the provincial government without being amalgamated with or subordinated under Shenzhen or Huizhou's historical centre. In this process, Dongguan gained a lot of rural areas for urbanisation; but it did not have counties (like other cities) that offered land reserves for future urban expansion. Its territory was configured into a three-tiered governmental structure—city-town-village—that laid down the fundamental dynamics and politics of its ongoing urbanisation processes.[42]

Although export-led industrialisation and foreign investment from Hong Kong were the main economic forces of extended urbanisation, Dongguan's specific form of territoriality set the primary condition and dynamics of how these urbanisation processes and power relations played out and how they would change in the future. The city-territory of Dongguan consists of 29 towns and 542 village collectives[43] surrounding the old city centre of Guancheng. [Fig. 13][44] While the legal, governmental framework in China usually dictates that a city is leading counties (and not towns), the three-tiered administrative system of Dongguan was based on pragmatic political arrangements. While the city covered the whole territory, its administration was only responsible for the planning and development of the city centre. Without counties, the towns had greater discretion in fiscal policies, planning, economic development, and construction, and the village collectives were designated as "administrative districts" (管理區) by the

Fig. 10

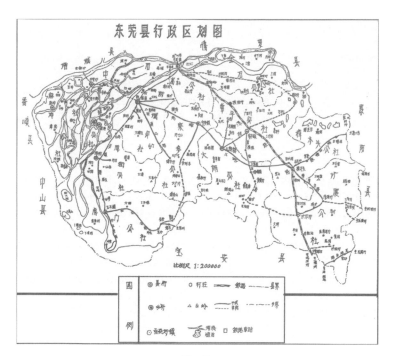

Fig. 11

F. 10   Dongguan's walled city,
        Guancheng, 1905.
F. 11   Dongguan's administrative
        divisions in 13 People's
        Communes, 1958.

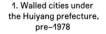

1. Walled cities under
the Huiyang prefecture,
pre–1978

2. First territorial split: formation
of new city-territories and Shenzhen
splitted from the Huiyang perfecture

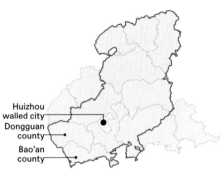

Huizhou
walled city
Dongguan
county
Bao'an
county

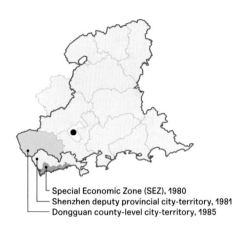

Special Economic Zone (SEZ), 1980
Shenzhen deputy provincial city-territory, 1981
Dongguan county-level city-territory, 1985

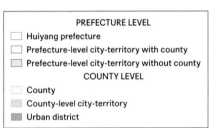

PREFECTURE LEVEL
☐ Huiyang prefecture
☐ Prefecture-level city-territory with county
▨ Prefecture-level city-territory without county
COUNTY LEVEL
☐ County
▨ County-level city-territory
■ Urban district

FORMATION OF CITY-TERRITORIES
IN THE HUIYANG PREFECTURE
Fig. 12

provincial government and continued to be politically mobilised as an extension of the town governments in charge of rural industrialisation.[45] Therefore, several administrative, economic, and planning tasks were devolved to lower levels, from the city to the town governments and from the towns to the village collectives. As noted by the then city party-secretary Li Jinwei, this was a three-tiered territorial government instead of four. This meant that all territorial levels—the city (Dongguan), the towns, and the villages—could have a larger share of profit from economic development.[46]

Instead of developing into a major city like Shenzhen, Dongguan's "mass mobilisation" strategy aimed at taking advantage of Hong Kong to attract foreign capital and industries. This strategy added to the explosive urban growth during the 1990s and 2000s. [Fig. 13] At the level of the villages, the industrialisation process led to a boom in new industrial areas.

They formed distinct, self-contained neighbour-hoods with factories, migrant workers, housing, social facilities, and related infrastructures. The rapid expansion of highways strengthened the north-south economic corridor between Guangzhou and Hong Kong. A range of ports (e.g., Zhongtang, Wangniudun, Machong, Shatian, Humen), Hongkong-Macau logistic control points (e.g., Fenggang, Chang'an), and railway hubs were built in different towns.

These centres and hubs grew with the rapid expansion of transportation networks to cope with the increasing flows of people, imports, and exports. These developments also reshaped the relationships between the city centre and the central and peripheral towns. Because the urban development of Dongguan's city centre was restricted within its small city district (市區), towns located along the north-south corridor soon had a much higher concentration of population, industries, and

3. Second territorial split: abolishing
the Huiyang prefecture and splitting
it into new prefecture-level city-territories

4. Reconfiguration of internal
territorial relations: expanding urban districts
and forming a county-level city-territory

Heyuen
prefecture-level
city-territory, 1988

Huizhou
prefecture-level
city-territory, 1988

Dongguan
prefecture-level
city-territory,
1988

Shanwei
prefecture-level
city-territory,
1988

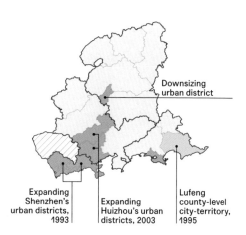

Downsizing
urban district

Expanding
Shenzhen's
urban districts,
1993

Expanding
Huizhou's urban
districts, 2003

Lufeng
county-level
city-territory,
1995

activities. In 2004, the migrant population of Chang'an town grew to 678,000, of which its three villages had 78,000, 83,000, and 84,000. The key industries in Dongguan included information and communications, computers, electronics, furniture, clothing, and metal and machinery. Numerous specialised and related industries formed clusters and networks in different towns and villages. Different social and economic activities flourished, including the construction industry, wholesale and retail markets, entertainment, transportation, and various consumer and producer services.

Dongguan's three-tiered, multicentric structure led to divergent political and economic trajectories and generated various contradictions and conflicts. The main problems were that territorial politics were intertwined with land interests and that the political actors were also the leading economic actors in their areas. Thus, on the lowest level, the village offices[47]

were responsible for local administration, including migrant workers and labour affairs, building, fire safety, sanitation, policing, and social stability. The village offices also developed the village land, constructed facilities and infrastructures, and directly connected to foreign investors. On the higher levels, though the city administratively leads the towns, the town governments were in charge of developing the land in their areas. Likewise, the towns should lead the villages, but the village collectives are the owners of the village's rural land, and the villagers have a right to land use. Thus, urban development was strongly complicated by these contradicting interests, which gave rise to various conflicts, particularly on questions of urban expansion and land expropriation.

F. 12   Several rounds of re-territorialisation of the Huiyang prefecture led to the formation of city-territories.

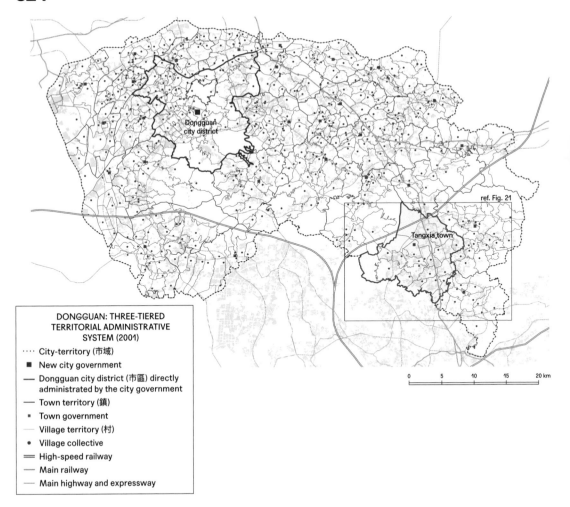

EXPLOSIVE URBAN SPACE:
DONGGUAN'S THREE-TIERED TERRITORIAL SYSTEM
Fig. 13

The following case study of Tangxia explores these contradictory processes and their power relations, which emerged in the processes of extended urbanisation and enabled a new stage of urban development.

TANGXIA: ONE OF DONGGUAN'S 28 TOWNS

Tangxia is located in the south-east of Dongguan, adjacent to Shenzhen at the former Kowloon-Canton Railway. In only two decades, this town transformed from a remote rural area to an important producer of manufactured goods exported to the world via Hong Kong. In 2005, it was one of China's "Top Thousand Towns" (千強鎮), accommodating a cluster of 1,083 foreign and 1,205 domestic factories and a total population of 372,300.[48]

The following section will present the urban transformation of Tangxia, initially through extended rural industrialisation during the 1990s. After 2000, it turned to real estate and the development of new centres, facilitated by the construction of highway networks and, later, a high-speed rail, following the pathway of urbanisation in other parts of the Pearl River Delta. In this process, Tangxia's extended urbanisation turned into concentrated urbanisation. Similar to other towns in Dongguan, Tangxia's 19 village collectives were the main actors in the urbanisation processes. This was related to a process of decentralisation of state power towards the town and village cadres. After 2000, a process of political realignment took place that again recentred the administrative power of Dongguan's city government. However, these changes in state power were not straightforward; instead, they resulted from the interplay between urbanisation and state power that created a fragmented, conflictual urban space.

Prior to 1948, Tangxia was a "rural township" (鄉), a basic-level rural administrative unit below the county, with a market and 132 village settlements. The township was governed by lineage villages and local gentries based on kinship and relations of proximity. However, this entire rural system was dismantled in 1958 when the CCP extended the new state order into rural areas under the new logic of collectivisation. In the wake of this territorial restructuring, Tangxia town was reorganised into a three-tiered territory composed of the Tangxia People's commune, 18 production brigades, and 161 production teams.[49]

In 1979, with the implementation of the new political agenda of economic reform under Deng Xiaoping, Tangxia adopted a strategy of rapid export-led industrialisation that started the process of extended urbanisation. During the early 1980s, rural industrialisation proceeded without large-scale land transformation. According to the national policy, the production teams managed the land, redistributing farmland, hill areas, housing zones, and self-reserved land to individual village households. Tangxia attracted foreign investors who set up processing and assembly manufacturing plants in old buildings and on vacant land. They were either members of the extended village families (most from Hong Kong), or they were introduced through the villagers' overseas networks.

The introduction of a new form of decentralised, three-tiered territorial arrangement in Dongguan in 1988 (see the previous section) delegated political power in Tangxia to the town and the village cadres. Tangxia became an "urban township" (鎮), leading 19 village collectives—the main actors dealing with foreign investors—to establish industries and businesses at the village level. Politically and administratively, the village collectives under the town's leadership were in charge of administration, development, and security. Each village collective was administered by a village office, usually composed of three to seven village party cadres. It was structured by a two-tiered system of land ownership and a collective administration consisting of brigades and production teams. Each brigade was led by the village party-secretary (the "first leader"), whose power was delegated by the town-level party committees that had the political task of managing the village territory. The production teams also had leaders chosen by the respective village households.

The new territorial structure of Tangxia accelerated the process of extended urbanisation. Rural industrialisation was further boosted by both the implementation of a new stage of national economic reform in 1992, and Dongguan's development strategy called the "second industrial revolution" in 1994. Backed by the town government of Tangxia, village offices started to expropriate farmland from individual households in the name of a policy of "integrated planning and development." They used large parts of rural collective land for urban uses, such as manufacturing, commerce, housing, social facilities, roads, and infrastructures. Large tracts of farmland were divided into plots for factories, and land adjacent to roads was used for self-built housing. Soon, each village had three or four large clusters of factories that the villagers called "industrial estates." [Fig. 14]

This process of urban transformation proceeded piece by piece without formal planning by selling "50-year land-use rights leases" to investors.[50] The village office was responsible for providing the land, roads, and basic infrastructure, as well as the leaseholder constructed factories, dormitories, and facilities. The leaseholding fee was usually settled by cash, which opened the door for various forms of corruption. None of these leases were acknowledged by the law, however, because farmland could officially only be transformed into urban land through acquisition by the government. Nevertheless, the leases were used as the main local tool for selling rural land for profit, and investors built their factories on this land in the name of the village collectives.

Initially, land for housing was for locals to construct self-built homes for personal use, but later it was sold to both villagers and non-villagers in a commodified manner. In many villages, hundreds of plots were demarcated for self-built housing,[51] and later, even the village offices themselves engaged in the construction of housing that they sold to non-villagers. This practice was illegal. Such large-scale land conversion violated the national law on the non-alienable and non-transferable nature of village housing land. As land revenue was the primary source of local government,[52] and the local GDP was the leading indicator of political performance, which was relevant for their position and annual bonuses,[53] local cadres strived to keep their housing development projects and land investments.

In this run for the commodification of land, various land conflicts emerged within the villages, as there was often no collective consensus on land expropriation, land transfer, investments, and the distribution of revenues. For example, in 1993, some people in a village protested to the town government against land commodification by their leader, which resulted in a "compromise." Half of the land was sold at a market price, and the other half was redistributed to all village households at a lower price. This massive land transformation supported by local policies and practices was clearly circumventing state regulations and laws. But regulation of the land was complicated because different government levels operated with their own interpretations of rules and laws.

For villagers, it was never clear which regulations were applied, which constructions could be counted as legal or illegal, and why a land transformation was possible in one village but not in others. But it was clear to them that different temporary measures or collaborative frameworks could be available to make things possible or get them legalised. Thus, local practices took advantage of ambiguity, and land deals and real estate projects were often undertaken in the name of state policies while violating national land regulations. As a result, the land of these villages became contested territories, full of buildings that were legally "problematic" or "non-conformable."

The rapid, extensive form of urbanisation in Dongguan also changed the villagers' relationships with their land. For the village collectives, land became an instrument for making huge profits, and village cadres expropriated land from individual households. This not only triggered land disputes but also formed the particular way villagers acted on the land. Although individuals could not change the dominant political structure, they could express their resistance and materially secure their land rights by constructing houses. By owning a building on a housing plot, villagers could secure the right to use that land.[54] Thus, villagers grasped opportunities each time land was auctioned by the village office to acquire plots by pooling money from their own savings, relatives in Hong Kong, land compensation, or by reselling village land to non-villagers.[55] The construction of individual houses that were rented out to migrants became a common practice of villagers. In this way, housing construction proceeded plot by plot, resulting in the individualised but large-scale urbanisation process of plotting.[56]

Village teams could also be an essential platform for villagers to intervene in the land development process and counterbalance the domination of village leaders. Some teams succeeded in pressuring village leaders to redistribute plots for collective investment in factory construction and leasing. Consequently, the investment of village teams became an important

Fig. 14

way of land development, and both individual villagers and village teams became involved in shaping their villages; they learned to invest and manage rental properties, pooled money, made leases, and collectively decided on the use of buildings, income redistribution, and savings. Even more importantly, they were circulating information and paying attention to anything related to the village's office and the situations and opportunities occurring in the immediate or broader surroundings. These activities and learning processes shaped the villages' internal dynamics and formed village politics.

In this way, local state power at the town and village levels made possible export-led industrialisation based on foreign investors, which drove Dongguan's extended urbanisation. In the 1990s, most of the village farmland was converted into industrial and housing land, and the vast agricultural landscape of Tangxia was utterly transformed into an urban-industrial zone.

F. 14   Clusters of factories: village's
industrial estates.

URBAN SPACES AND
EVERYDAY LIVES

In the late-1990s, a new industrial boom started in Dongguan when Taiwan undertook a profound economic restructuring and lifted restrictions for large-scale investment in China, which led to a massive move of Taiwanese enterprises towards Dongguan.[57] In the wake of this process, Tangxia experienced a substantial influx of Taiwanese enterprises, particularly in electronics, which further pushed the pace of urbanisation. Between 1997 and 2006, the number of migrant workers in Tangxia increased from 77,000 to 345,000.[58] Thus, several hundred to several thousand local villagers lived in each village, compared to 10,000 to 60,000 migrant workers.[59] This section shows how these spaces of extended urbanisation became the arenas of social change where a particular form of spatial transformation went hand in hand with fundamental changes in everyday life. Local villagers and migrant workers created their own spaces for making a living and earning profits during the booming economy.

Fig. 15

Fig. 16

Fig. 17

F. 15   Rural migrants in an old
         village settlement.
F. 16   Streetscape, Tangxia old town
         centre.
F. 17   A migrant street vendor
         in a village centre.
F. 18   A kinship-based workshop:
         manufacturing of electric cables
         and conductors.

As a result of the large-scale arrival of migrant workers, many village houses were transformed into rental housing. By 2010, the number of rental housing units in Tangxia reached 19,799, accommodating nearly 300,000 registered temporary residents.[60] In old village sites, villagers used—often subdivided—old houses for renting or constructed new houses with three housing units on empty plots. These often-dilapidated houses were densely placed next to each other, accessible only by small alleys, forming clusters of the migrant population within each village. [Fig. 15] Five- to six-storey self-built houses that villagers partially or entirely used for renting spread along roads and streets. The ground floors were used for shops, businesses, or workspaces, while the upper floors were dwellings.

As mentioned, it was through the resistance politics of plotting that villagers "took back" their land during the waves of land expropriation and commodification. On the one hand, villagers still owned large areas of collective land through land use and property rights. Although they were later disallowed from undertaking any construction on this land, it became a contested site on which villagers resisted the threats of expropriation by the town government or the village office. This explains why a large number of dilapidated, traditional houses continue to exist in many villages. On the other hand, the village collectives founded companies to manage and develop their collective property and assets. The founding of these companies was declared mandatory by the Guangdong provincial policy of 2004 to reorganise village administrations and collective assets to facilitate capital accumulation and resolve distribution issues. Hence, the villagers became shareholders and de facto "landlords," and for many of them, rent became the primary household income. In their own view, this constituted a turning point in their material and social life as they began to bind themselves to shareholding, land business, and speculation.

Thanks to the migrant population, these villages, once composed of old houses and farmland, were transformed into dense, lively, and

Fig. 18

productive neighbourhoods. As a large number of migrant workers could not be confined any longer to the discipline of factories and dormitories,[61] the reproduction of labour power was expanded to the wider surrounding of the village. Migrants worked in factories and related activities such as retail and wholesale, transportation, construction, restaurants, hotels, and entertainment centres. Thus, old village sites and multi-storey houses constituted the social space of mixed-use neighbourhoods, with a variety of small enterprises, subcontractors, workshops, hardware shops, and salons run by migrants. [Fig. 18] Old houses were used for working and dwelling, storing vendor carts and wagons, street vendors' food production, and recycling businesses for industrial waste. Around the market, makeshift structures were used for food stalls, lorry drivers were waiting for jobs, and taxi drivers were peddling for customers. [Fig. 17] These spaces contributed significantly to the booming neighbourhood economy, and migrants became their own producers of their everyday lives.

While the large influx of rural migrant workers became the engine of industrialisation, the state's hukou system continued to determine these migrants' "transient space" by denying their rights to access social welfare. It remained a heavy task for migrants to raise and teach their kids or leave them as "left behind children" in their hometowns; often, kids went to unauthorised schools or did not go to school at all.[62] Besides, village offices took the approach of "doing nothing in temporary dilapidated areas."[63] Thus, migrants faced everyday challenges such as the absence of streetlights, waste and sewage problems, or severe flooding during the rainy season. The social control of the labour force was subject to the discipline of the factory system and the policing of village offices, which were responsible for social stability, and claimed themselves as "arbiters" of conflicts between factory owners and workers in their areas. Such social control was effective until the outbreak of large-scale strikes in other towns led to their suppression by the respective town governments.[64]

Fig. 19

F. 19 City square of Nancheng CBD, Dongguan.
F. 20 A gated village apartment estate, concentrating villagers in high-rise towers.

This economic boom lasted for about a decade until the 2008 financial crisis led to factory closures and fundamentally changed these neighbourhoods. Migrants had to decide whether to stay or leave Dongguan. I talked to a private taxi driver who invested money to buy a car but no longer earned enough for basic expenses. However, some longer-term migrants with established social networks still anticipated opportunities. A workshop owner attained a local hukou because she purchased a flat in the new town centre, while a construction company owner surreptitiously built another rental house on the plot he had bought earlier to accommodate more migrants.

THE PARADIGM SHIFT TOWARDS CONCENTRATED URBANISATION

Since the early 2000s, the spaces of extended urbanisation have been regarded in the public discourse as a cause of the land shortage. The city of Dongguan started to implement new policies to realise a new vision of village space by "concentrating" villagers in high-rise residential areas. This went along with the national policy of "New Village Construction" (新農村建設) launched in 2004, which aimed at accelerating the urbanisation of rural areas, modernising villages, and maintaining social harmony. [Fig. 20] In Tangxia, five such village housing estates were constructed that seemingly fit into

the city's propaganda of "being a modern people, living a modern life, building a modern city." In the early 2000s, a village office began construction of one of these estates for 0.2 billion yuan.[65] It was a gated estate for 6,000 villagers, comprising medium- and high-rise apartment blocks and some villas. This project was advertised as a village model for the country in the context of the party's mass mobilisation and was therefore visited by many other villagers.[66] As noted by a villager, it became the "state's image building," a showcase of its achievements and economic success. It embodied a representation of the state space that established its authority and legitimacy in rural areas. The design of the new building for the village office, which had 200 villagers on its own payroll, imitated the government building of Dongguan, declaring itself as a political centre of the village landscape of Tangxia. The local villagers shared a collective aspiration for such modern living, and there was a strong sense of pride and privilege. As one villager said: "My apartment is just like a luxury mansion in Hong Kong."[67]

However, the new village housing estate failed to implement the national policy of "one household, one homestead." As villagers were reluctant to give up their foothold on their collective land, no land plots were returned to the village office as stipulated for eligibility for buying an apartment. Thus, the villagers still owned a property in the old village they rented out to migrants. Therefore, the spectacular gated

Fig. 20

village estate stands out in an industrial land-scape, imposing socio-spatial segregation between villagers and migrant workers and further reinforcing their uneven power relations. And at the same time, it was announcing another round of urbanisation in Tangxia based on a real estate–driven property development that ultimately led to a paradigm shift towards concentrated urbanisation.

The background of this shift was that in 1998, the Chinese government enforced more stringent land regulations on local governments, such as farmland conservation rules and land quotas for converting farmland to urban land to prevent further illegal urban expansion.[68] At the same time, Dongguan began reframing the dynamics of its three-tiered territorial structure through a realignment of the administrative power, which allowed the city government to advance urban restructuring. In this way, the city government resumed its responsibility for the territorial planning of the entire Dongguan territory, executed land-use control, and reshaped its relationships with the town governments. It also developed a new urban strategy to build more and larger centralities, new high-tech and high-end development zones, and to expand the highway and railway network. However, the city government could not get full control over urban development because it could not, like Shenzhen, transform the towns into its own urban districts. Only in 2015 was Dongguan finally granted its own legislative powers from the central state to resolve the contradictions of its government. Thus, the turn towards concentrated urbanisation was still strongly influenced by the old city-town-village administrative structure that had produced the fragmented and contradictory form of Dongguan's extended urbanisation.

Tangxia's strategic shift towards concentrated urbanisation followed the regional trend of building new centres as drivers to increase the exchange value of real estate developments. This trend ran parallel to the construction of new CBDs in Futian (Shenzhen), Nancheng (Dongguan), and the new University Town in Guangzhou. [Fig. 19] In Tangxia, however,

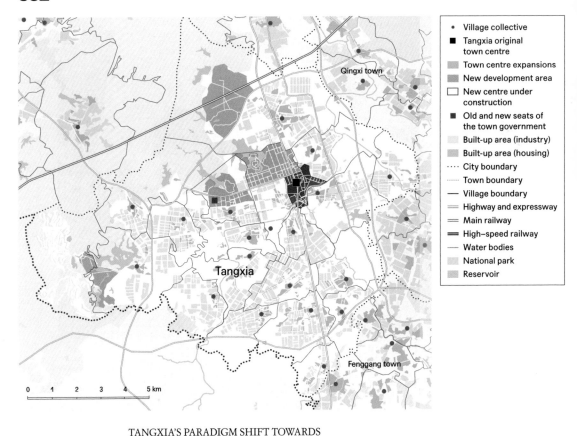

- • Village collective
- ■ Tangxia original town centre
- Town centre expansions
- New development area
- ☐ New centre under construction
- ■ Old and new seats of the town government
- Built-up area (industry)
- Built-up area (housing)
- ···· City boundary
- ······ Town boundary
- — Village boundary
- = Highway and expressway
- = Main railway
- ≡ High–speed railway
- — Water bodies
- National park
- Reservoir

Qingxi town

Tangxia

Fenggang town

0 1 2 3 4 5 km

TANGXIA'S PARADIGM SHIFT TOWARDS
CONCENTRATED URBANISATION
Fig. 21

the land had become increasingly scarce and fragmented. Therefore, in order to propel large-scale real estate development, the town government had to establish a master plan, seize the village land, and reassign it as urban land in conformity with new national regulations. The following accounts highlight some of the land conflicts in three villages at different times. [Fig. 21] It explores how local villagers, as the agents of extended urbanisation, also shaped the dynamics of the paradigm shift towards concentrated urbanisation.

LYCHEE TREES

The first example is the development of a new town centre for Tangxia in 2001, which required the implementation of large-scale land expropriation in one of the villages. This was

the first large development project by Tangxia's town government, taking advantage of the simultaneous new CBD development in the centre of Dongguan. It aimed at creating a new "administrative cultural centre" with government office towers, various cultural and leisure facilities, and a public square on an area of 58 hectares. It also was meant to function as a driver for real estate development along a new highway to the old town centre. [Fig. 22] This project was located in a hilly area around a reservoir that could be used for urban development through land levelling. This meant that a total area of 168 hectares, about half of the village land, had to be seized by the government.[69]

An agreement on the compensation scheme included the land price (owed to the village

Fig. 22

office) and the compensation for crops (owed to the individual farmers). The agreement was established between the town and the village party-secretary, and the village office as the landowner received a large sum of money for the land compensation—without having to redistribute it to the individual villagers. However, the largest pieces of land were still in the hands of individual villagers who held land-use rights. Each household had different amounts of land, and some used it to plant mandarin and lychee trees or left it idle. When the rumour of land expropriation spread in the village, all affected villagers began planting lychee trees to secure their interests at stake. A villager recalled the night before the land survey: "At midnight, the hill areas were full of villagers … everyone was planting lychee trees." The villagers made last efforts to claim their land interests without a common agenda. By increasing the number of trees, they attempted to maximise their compensation. They all had heard that land was going to be sold to a developer for building a five-star hotel and a cluster of villas facing the reservoir with a national park behind. The next day, the entire hills were covered with lychee trees. The tactic worked, and a village household could receive up to four million yuan in compensation. This story became the biggest news in town, and it also came as a shock to the town party-secretary who was in charge of this project. With the money received for the trees, some of the villagers constructed houses with up to five floors on plots they had previously acquired; others bought a car, started a business, or lost money in the gambling houses of Macau.

A few months later, villagers applied a similar tactic when the town considered redeveloping an old village area in front of the future government tower. Several rounds of meetings were held between the town party-secretary and the villagers. And yet, a villager recounted, "there was a 'rush to build' (搶建). It lasted for a week until the officials came to patrol and take

F. 22　Tangxia's new town centre, 2017.

Fig. 23

Fig. 24

pictures, and we stopped and restarted the construction at night. When I finished it, officials sprayed the word 'demolish' (拆) on the wall." In the end, the agreement failed. The town government accepted neither the villagers' request for a compensation of 3,000 yuan per square metre (in contrast to the official offer of 300 to 700 yuan) nor a land-exchange scheme after redevelopment. It finally built a long wall in front of the new government tower to block the view of the "ugly old village houses." [Fig. 23][70]

THE BACK GARDEN
OF SHENZHEN

The second example of the villagers' struggle is a land grab. It concerned about 67 hectares of village land that the village party-secretary sold to a speculator, who eventually put it to a public auction. It was offered for an opening price of 600 million yuan and finally sold to a national-level developer for an unprecedented price of 2.6 billion yuan. It became a cluster of single-family houses constituting one of the company's largest property projects in China. Originally, this poor village was regarded as remote. However, it was repositioned by the construction of a new highway that linked the new town centre of Tangxia to the PRD expressway. The village thus became part of a back garden of the CBD of Shenzhen, providing space for luxury housing next to the national park, a reservoir and a lake, and a large golf course. [Fig. 21] This attracted wealthy families from Shenzhen to buy properties and commute on the expressway to Shenzhen.

In this village, land grabs were common, even though all land transactions required the signatures of village representatives and did not necessarily lead to a mobilisation of villagers. In the words of villagers, the abuse of power was as easy as the "finger [of the village party-secretary] pointing [on a map]."[71] The village election had already turned into a game of corruption and bribery,[72] and various cases of complicities and co-optation between the village office and some villagers became known. This went hand in hand with a restrictive political climate and politicised social ties in the village office, which controlled the administration and the redistribution of villagers' incomes, opportunities, and welfare. This meant that mobilising villagers to oppose village cadres' appropriation of funds or land resources for personal gains faced serious hurdles.

However, as this land grab generated huge windfall profits, a few villagers succeeded in mobilising massive protests against the town government and demanding a fair share of the profit. At the same time, they revealed some hidden relations of interest between the village office and town and city officials. Their protests touched on the nerves of the officials that finally opened a path for a compromise between the town government and the villagers for "not letting the issue grow bigger."[73] It resulted in the distribution of the profit—0.5 billion yuan for the city, 1.5 billion for the town, and 0.32 billion for the village office.

After this success, villagers opposed the return of land revenues to the village office because of their distrust of the village party-secretary. The land revenues were finally turned into a material form of urbanisation by subsidising the construction of high-rise apartments for the villagers. A further impact of this protest was a change in the land policy in Tangxia, stipulating that 20% of the revenues of each land sale for real estate development had to be returned to the village collectives. This deal clearly incentivised both village offices and villagers to demand higher compensations for urban renewal projects, causing further land conflicts and a tremendous pressure against dissidents. Those villagers who led the protests experienced threats, violence, and imprisonment. By 2018, informed by villagers, the town government simply abolished the village election, and the village party-secretary also became the chairman of the village office.

A HIGH-SPEED RAILWAY
DEVELOPMENT

The last case is the construction of a national high-speed train station, including a proposal for a theme park, prompting different players to take advantage of the turn towards concentrated urbanisation. The train station is located in a large area of farmland, including some old village settlements, which were designated to be transformed into the train station. But the large tract of required farmland was protected by the 1998 National Land Management Law and, thus, was only rented to migrant peasant households. Several attempts to arrange land deals with investors failed because of the absence of construction-land quotas allocated by higher-level governments. In this situation, the high-speed railway construction became the key to releasing this farmland for urban development: Since the 2008 financial crisis, the national state had implemented a strategy of territorial restructuring to achieve regional integration and economic modernisation. As a result, the entire Pearl River Delta has been reconfigured by a whole range of new railway infrastructures, including high-speed rails, inter-city rails, and metro lines. These lines became instruments to open up rural land for high-end urban developments that would, in turn, increase land rents. In this case, the city government of Dongguan—not the town government of Tangxia—claimed the planning control over urban redevelopment.

Individual villagers were the first to claim their land interests, resulting in a common rush for house construction to maximise compensations. During my fieldwork west of this village in 2018, I did not find some old village houses and fishponds, as shown on the Google satellite image. I did, however, find a large group of empty, grey-walled houses in the middle of a large agricultural field. [Fig. 24] I walked through these empty buildings with only two workshops in operation. The same happened in another settlement nearby, where some workers were still laying bricks. I ended up at a huge construction site that turned out to be a high-speed railway station. It was then I realised that these houses were built for demolition, as the city government offered a compensation of about 3,000 yuan per square metre. They were owned by two of the 27 village teams,

Fig. 25

200 villagers each, who lived in a new village apartment area.

A simultaneous project was a large-scale, ten-year plan for urban renewal. A "500-year-old village" should be demolished to build a new centre close to the railway station. It was marketed as a "high-speed rail city" and "a city in the north of Shenzhen," with middle-class housing, condominiums, shopping malls, car parking, and various facilities. By collaborating with local developers, the village office combined administrative power, its own land, land rights, and also the capital. With these resources, it could incentivise the villagers to accept a scheme for a one-to-one exchange of building plots prior to and after redevelopment so that the office could consolidate the fragmented land of 400 properties. This turned unauthorised land (26.7 hectares without certification) into a property with market value.[74] The villagers called this deal "turning old tiles into gold" (瓦屋變黃金), and the village office became a developer according to the state regulatory framework, with the villagers becoming owners of alienable private properties. [Fig. 25]

This example shows no clear-cut boundary in the relationship between the state and the village. Different actors were drawn into this project at the national level and from the city government, the village office, and individual villagers and developers. Nevertheless, they created momentum in shaping this new round of concentrated urbanisation. However, this development eliminated a vibrant and heterogeneous space, which was initially developed by the villagers' efforts and by the migrant workers who created their own urban space. The urban renewal project completely destroyed this space and imposed a singular logic of space production and a single form of property management, following the urbanised pathway of urbanised villages in Shenzhen.[75]

F. 25   "Turning old tiles into gold": redevelopment of a 500-year old village.

THE POLITICS OF CONCENTRATED URBANISATION

The three examples presented above show different dynamics resulting in specific pathways of urbanisation. Understanding the different tactics and processes in the negotiations between villagers, village cadres, town officials, and higher-level governments helps to uncover the changing politics and power relations in the shift from extended to concentrated urbanisation. In the following discussion, I will highlight four key aspects of this new paradigm of urbanisation that emerged in this process, namely land politics, villagers' activism, territorial power relations, and the material element of urbanisation itself.

In Tangxia, the *power of control over the land* has played a vital role in the urbanisation process. Due to its three-tiered territorial structure (city-town-village), village land constituted a mechanism that linked social production and reproduction. By investing in land and the built environment, villagers could bolster the arenas of social reproduction. They constructed different facilities such as elderly centres, libraries, parks, parking structures, rental housing, and factories and redistributed the profit among villagers. Whereas the village land had been turned into a commodity through land leases during the phase of extended urbanisation, the focus shifted in the 2000s towards the appropriation of higher land value from real estate development. Tangxia expanded its town centre and also reorganised the messy village spaces. This new paradigm of concentrated urbanisation resorted to the instruments of master plans, land-use control and planning regulations, placing villages under centralised planning control and a regulatory framework. However, this new paradigm clashed with the extant territorial structure and created new conflicts.

In this change of land politics, the main problem was not a shortage of land as such, but the existing fragmented patchwork of the village territories, and particularly, the resulting *agency and activism of the villagers*. Engaging and negotiating in land became the terrain of claiming their vested interests and the reproduction of their social relations in the village. Villagers were well aware of the existing power relations from various experiences of land dispossession, corruption, and collusion. Through their own longstanding experiences, the villagers developed a strong understanding of local politics and the land economy. Confronted with a multitude of territorial powers and with the complicated power relations inside the village-collective system itself, villagers tended to look for individualised ways to secure their interests. Their actions were not coordinated and collective, but they learned from each other, multiplying their power. By planting more lychee trees, constructing bigger houses, or demanding higher land compensation, they claimed their right to the collective land.

From this point of view, I argue that there was not a binary and clear-cut state-village power relation that could have led to a kind of territorial autonomy in these villages. Only rarely could we see villagers deploying "collective action" by defending their land rights or developing a sense of "collective identity," as suggested by You-tien Hsing in reference to non-confrontational counter-strategies of "civic territoriality."[76] Instead, the case study clearly shows that villagers were still embedded in the *territorial power relations* of the city, town, and village levels as part of the extension of the state space.

Interestingly, the results of the interplays between the different levels were always linked to the *material aspects of the urbanisation process*. All actors maintained the momentum of urban change through confrontations, negotiations, collaborations, or complicities. One important example of this is that villagers gained land compensation and turned it into a material form by building their own multi-storey houses and high-rise apartments, extending their material influence on following rounds of urbanisation. In short, this material aspect of territory was the realm of ongoing contestations—farmlands, hills, old houses, and multi-storey apartment buildings. In this way, villagers actively engaged in the development of the paradigm shift towards concentrated urbanisation through their activism and engagement to keep their land.

THE PRODUCTION OF EXTENDED AND CONCENTRATED URBANISATION

By interrogating the territory, this chapter explored the complexities and contradictions of Chinese state space and provided an alternative account of extended urbanisation in Dongguan. It showed how the comprehension of the territorial question changes our view on the Chinese state space and transcends a dualist conception of territory and state power. In China, territorial control should be neither interpreted as a capitalist "territorial fix" nor as "state rescaling." Instead, Chinese territories are subjected to systematic, continuously shifting control and manipulation by the central state. However, "the territory" is largely absent as a concept in Chinese urban studies. The question of the territory is often assumed to be identical to the land question. But the control over land is a means to govern social relations and production processes, and both central and local governments are involved in this process within the national regulatory framework. However, the territory is controlled exclusively by the central state, while subordinated governments at different levels cannot change their territorial structure. My argument is that the central state uses this territorial regime to have a tight grip over all subordinated levels of government.

The continuous changes in Guangdong's territorial structure were directly related to the central control of the production of space and the implementation of national strategies of urbanisation. We thus saw a specific form of state space emerging during Mao's time and rapidly developing after 1979, when the state used the development of city-territories as motors of national economic growth and fast urbanisation. The continuous reorganisation and re-hierarchisation of the subnational territo-

ries enabled the state to control all governments and their interrelations and to produce and regulate different urbanisation processes and their dynamics of concentration and extension. This process of state territorialisation took place *prior to, during, and after* the unfolding of urbanisation processes and subsumed capitalist activities and the forces of globalisation under state territorial power. In this ongoing process, the state constantly changed its territorial structure to master socio-economic change and maintain and reproduce its political domination.

The case of Dongguan underscores how the specific process of extended urbanisation resulted from its specific territorial structure but in a contradictory way. The specificity of Dongguan was its three-tiered form of territorial power. This meant that village collectives were incorporated into the local government structure. This enabled local party cadres to execute political tasks and also circumvent certain regulations to pursue their economic interests, which caused fragmentation of political powers on the ground. The presence of state power was seemingly everywhere in this town-village landscape. Nevertheless, it was not a clear and consistent form of state power but a fragmentary, conflictual, and contradictory one that manifested itself in the production of space. The fieldwork shows us that these contradictions of state power were at the origin of the production of the fragmented spaces of extended urbanisation.

The control of state power over the urbanisation process became highly visible through the activities of the village offices, which were accountable to the town officials, and, thus, were fully embedded in the state territorial system. The village offices had to maintain social stability, binding villagers to the collective ownership system and managing a large number of people, activities, and land transactions. This was nevertheless a contested landscape because each round of urbanisation went hand in hand with land expropriations that sparked various conflicts. Despite the establishment of a redistribution system via investments into the built environment, improvements in social reproduction, and the formation of shareholding real estate companies, villagers were subjected to the politics of the village offices. They faced various forms of abuse of power, corruption, and collusion. Subsequently, instead of developing a consolidated identity, the villagers were caught in the dynamics of ambiguous, contested, and distrusted relationships that shaped the ongoing processes of urbanisation. Villagers developed their own way of getting hold of the land by developing and selling it piece by piece, which led to the process of plotting urbanism and the piecemeal production of space.

In producing these fragmented spaces, local villagers and migrant workers played crucial roles in making their own spaces and everyday lives. Despite their silent roles, migrant workers have established themselves in various local businesses, such as shops, construction firms, small workshops, trading, and transport. Despite their landlord-and-tenant relationships, local villagers and migrants found ways of co-existing and making their livelihoods in the villages.

The spaces of extended urbanisation were driven by various contradictions, which finally triggered a new round of urbanisation. On the one hand, the entire village territories had become urbanised in a fragmented and often chaotic manner. On the other hand, the overall urban dynamics in the Pearl River Delta turned towards centralisation and urban intensification to increase productivity and profits. Consequently, Dongguan's three-tiered territorial power structure and its mechanism of profit sharing between the three territorial levels were replaced by the territorial integration of state power and governmental relations. However, despite the introduction of centralised land regulation, the material spaces of the villages, whether legal or illegal, became the facts on the ground: The fragmentation of land allowed the villagers to negotiate the government's projects and land expropriations, considerably shaping the new forms of concentrated urbanisation.

Ultimately, the Chinese state reproduced its power through the production of space and, in turn, produced its own territorial contradictions with the fragmentation of space and power due to the linkages of the state to local economic interests. By taking into account the agency of the people in re-making space, it becomes obvious that the Chinese state neither shows a consolidation nor a fragmentation of power but rather a constant adaptation of territorial power to new challenges of economic development and urbanisation. This reveals a specific characteristic of the Chinese state: When unfolding the historical and contextual specificity of territories, this state mode of production is durable but simultaneously malleable and contradictory.

ENDNOTES

1   Lefebvre, *State, Space, World*, 224, 228.
2   Yeung, *Foreign Investment and Socio-Economic Development in China*.
3   Lefebvre, "Space and the State."
4   Elden, "Land, Terrain, Territory"; Elden, "Thinking Territory Historically"; Elden, *Understanding Henri Lefebvre*, 223.
5   Agnew, "The Territorial Trap."
6   Streule, "Doing Mobile Ethnography."
7   Schmid, "Specificity and Urbanization."
8   Wong, "Territorially-Nested Urbanization in China."
9   McGee, "The Emergence of Desakota Regions in Asia."
10 Sit, "Mega-city, Extended Metropolitan Region, Desakota, and Exo-Urbanization."
11 Lin, "Urbanization of the Pearl River Delta."
12 Friedmann, "The Future of Periurban Research."
13 Agnew, "The Territorial Trap."
14 Tang, "Governing by the State"; Buckingham, "Uncorking the Neoliberal Bottle."
15 Lin, *Developing China*.
16 Cartier, "Territorial Urbanization and the Party-State in China"; Cartier, "A Political Economy of Rank"; Chan, "Fundamentals of China's Urbanisation and Policy"; Lin, *Developing China*; Ma, "Urban Administrative Restructuring."
17 Ma, "Urban Administrative Restructuring"; Brenner, *New State Spaces*; Brenner, "The Urban Question as a Scale Question."
18 Liu, Jin, and Zhou, 中国政区地理 [*China's Administrative Geography*]; Liu and Fan, 中国市制的历史演变 [*A History of the City Administrative System in China*].
19 Cartier, "Territorial Urbanisation and the Party-State in China."
20 Lefebvre, *State, Space, World*; Brenner and Elden, "Henri Lefebvre on State, Space, Territory"; Schmid, *Henri Lefebvre and the Theory of the Production of Space*, Chapter 7.
21 Wong, "Territorially-Nested Urbanization in China."
22 Brenner, "Beyond State-Centrism?"
23 Hayton, *The Invention of China*, 189.
24 Tang, "Town-Country Relations in China."
25 Faure, *Emperor and Ancestor: State and Lineage in South China*.
26 Hayton, *The Invention of China*, 190; Yu, "The Concept of 'Territory' in Modern China."
27 Lincoln, *An Urban History of China*, 212–217.
28 Zürcher, "The Chinese Communes."
29 Chan, *Cities with Invisible Walls*.
30 Wang, *The China Order*, 178.
31 Zhao, *Prisoner of the State*, 247.
32 Pu, 中国行政区划改革 [*A Study of China's Administrative Division Reform*].
33 Ma, "Urban Administrative Restructuring."
34 Ma, "Urban Administrative Restructuring."
35 Karaman, et al., "Plot by Plot: Plotting Urbanism"; Wong, "Hong Kong, Shenzhen, Dongguan."
36 Dongguan Municipal Gazetteer Compilation Committee, 东莞市志 [*Dongguan Municipal Gazetteer*], 526.
37 Skinner, "Peasant Organization in Rural China."
38 Dongguan Municipal Gazetteer Compilation Committee, 东莞市志 [*Dongguan Municipal Gazetteer*], 85.
39 Dongguan Municipal Civil Affairs Bureau, 东莞市民政志 [*Gazetteer of Dongguan Municipal Civil Affairs*], 50.
40 Shenzhen Municipal Gazetteer Compilation Committee, 深圳市志 [*Shenzhen Municipal Gazetteer*], 259.
41 Dongguan's Guancheng Gazetteer Compilation Committee, 东莞市莞城志 [*Gazetteer of Guancheng of Dongguan Municipality*], 102.
42 There are four prefecture-level cities without a county-level unit in China. Administratively, a prefecture-level city has the county-level units, such as urban districts and counties. Dongguan is a city without county levels that allowed it directly to govern towns, and especially to appoint town offices; otherwise, power belongs to a county led by the provincial government.
43 These numbers were based on the year of 1988. By 1998, Taiping and Humen towns were merged to form a new Humen town. Thereafter, the total number of towns became 28.
44 Dongguan Municipal Civil Affairs Bureau, 东莞市民政志 [*Gazetteer of Dongguan Municipal Civil Affairs*], 51.
45 Village collectives are legally defined as non-governmental units. In 1982, the top-tiered communes were abolished, and village collectives remained a two-tiered organisation of collective ownership, in charge of political, economic, and social tasks within their areas.
46 Sanlian Lifeweek, 东莞30年巨变 [*The Great Transformation of Dongguan*].
47 Here, I use the term "village office" to simplify the complexity of the administration of a village collective.
48 Dongguan Institute of Urban Planning and Design, "Dongguan Tangxia Master Plan (2012–2022)," IX.
49 Dongguan's Tangxia Gazetteer Compilation Committee, 东莞市塘厦志 [*Gazetteer of Tangxia Town of Dongguan Municipality*], 49.
50 The term 50 years was just a common practice in this town and could be 20 or 30 years in other areas.
51 The size of these housing plots was mainly 40, 80, and 120 m² that followed the existent principles of housing construction in Dongguan.
52 Lin, *Developing China*, 174; Liu, "Land-based Finance," 36–58.
53 Whiting, *Power and Wealth in Rural China*; Whiting, "The Cadre Evaluation System at the Grass Roots."
54 Interview with a planner, 2015.
55 Interview with villagers, 2018.
56 Karaman, et al., "Plot by Plot: Plotting Urbanism."
57 Yang and Liao, "Backward Linkages of Cross-border Production Networks of Taiwanese PC Investment."
58 Dongguan Statistics Bureau, *Dongguan Statistics Yearbook*.
59 Dongguan Statistics Bureau, *Dongguan Statistics Yearbook*.
60 Dongguan Institute of Urban Planning and Design, "Dongguan Tangxia Master Plan (2012–2022)."
61 Pun, *Women Factory Workers*.
62 This is based on my home visits of migrants with a local social worker. See also Tan, "Temporary Migrants and Public Space."
63 Interview with a villager, 2014.
64 China Labour Bulletin, *Tensions Rise in Dongguan*.
65 Interview with a village officer, 2018.
66 Perry, "From Mass Campaigns to Managed Campaigns."

67   Interview with a villager, 2014
68   Yang and Wang, "Land Property Rights Regimes in China."
69   Interview with a village officer, 2018.
70   Interview with a villager, 2014.
71   Interview with a villager, 2016.
72   Interview with villagers, 2015. There were variations of villagers' election participation in different villages. See Wong, et al., "Village Elections, Grassroots Governance and the Restructuring of State Power."
73   Interview with a villager, 2016.
74   Interview with a village officer, 2018.
75   Jiang, et al., "Whose Village?"; Karaman, et al., "Plot by Plot: Plotting Urbanism."
76   Hsing, *The Great Urban Transformation.*

BIBLIOGRAPHY

Agnew, John. "The Territorial Trap: The Geographical Assumptions of International Relations Theory." *Review of International Political Economy* 1, no. 1 (1994): 53–80.

Brenner, Neil. "Beyond State-Centrism? Space, Territoriality, and Geographical Scale in Globalization Studies." *Theory and Society* 28, no. 1 (1999): 39–78.

———.*New State Spaces: Urban Governance and the Rescaling of Statehood.* Oxford: Oxford University Press, 2004.

Brenner, Neil. "The Urban Question as a Scale Question: Reflections on Henri Lefebvre, Urban Theory and the Politics of Scale." *International Journal of Urban and Regional Research* 24, no. 2 (2000): 361–378.

Brenner, Neil, and Stuart Elden. "Henri Lefebvre on State, Space, Territory." *International Political Sociology* 3, no. 4 (2009): 353–377.

Buckingham, Will. "Uncorking the Neoliberal Bottle: Neoliberal Critique and Urban Change in China." *Eurasian Geography and Economics* 58, no. 3 (2017): 297–315.

Cartier, Carolyn. "A Political Economy of Rank: The Territorial Administrative Hierarchy and Leadership Mobility in Urban China." *The Journal of Contemporary China* 25, no. 100 (2016): 529–546.

Cartier, Carolyn. "Territorial Urbanization and the Party-State in China." *Territory, Politics, Governance* 3, no. 3 (2015): 294–320.

Chan, Kam Wing. *Cities with Invisible Walls: Reinterpreting Urbanization in Post-1949 China.* Hong Kong: Oxford University Press, 1994.

Chan, Kam Wing. "Fundamentals of China's Urbanization and Policy." *China Review* 10, no. 1 (2010): 63–93.

Chen, Chao, and Hongling Chen. 中华人民共和国行政区 划沿革地图集,*1949–1999 [Atlas of Changes of Administrative Divisions of the People's Republic of China, 1949–1999].* Beijing: China Map Publishing House, 2003.

China Labour Bulletin. "Tensions Rise in Dongguan, China's Factory to the World," June 10, 2016. https://clb.org.hk/en/content/tensions-rise-dongguan-china%E2%80%99s-factory-world.

Dongguan Institute of Urban Planning and Design. *A Note of Dongguan Tangxia Master Plan (2012–2022), n.d.*

Dongguan Municipal Civil Affairs Bureau. 东莞市民政志 [*Gazetteer of Dongguan Municipal Civil Affairs*]. Guangzhou: Guangdong People's Publishing House, 2019.

Dongguan Municipal Gazetteer Compilation Committee. 东莞市志 [*Dongguan Municipal Gazetteer*]. Guangzhou: Guangdong People's Publishing House, 1995.

Dongguan Statistics Bureau. *Dongguan Statistic Yearbook.* Beijing: China Statistics Press, 1998, 2006, 2007.

Dongguan's Tangxia Gazetteer Compilation Committee. 东莞市塘廈志 [*Gazetteer of Tangxia Town of Dongguan Municipality*]. Guangzhou: Lingnan Fine Arts Publishing House, 2008.

Elden, Stuart. "Land, Terrain, Territory." *Progress in Human Geography* 34, no. 6 (2010): 799–817.

Elden, Stuart. "Thinking Territory Historically." *Geopolitics* 15, no. 4 (2010): 757–761.

Elden, Stuart. *Understanding Henri Lefebvre: Theory and the Possible.* London: Continuum, 2004.

Faure, David. *Emperor and Ancestor: State and Lineage in South China.* Stanford: Stanford University Press, 2007.

Friedmann, John. "The Future of Periurban Research." *Cities* 100, no. 53 (2016): 163–165.

Gazette Office of Guangdong People's Government. 广东省行政区划图志 [*Gazetteer of Maps of Guangdong's Administrative Divisions*]. Guangzhou: Guangdong Provincial Map Publishing House, 2016.

Hayton, Bill. *The Invention of China.* New Haven, CT: Yale University Press, 2020.

Hsing, You-tien. *The Great Urban Transformation: Politics of Land and Property in China.* Oxford: Oxford University Press, 2010.

Institute of Geographic Sciences and Natural Resources Research. 中华人民共和国行政区划变 迁地图集, *1980–2017 [Atlas of Changes of Administrative Division of the People's Republic of China, 1980–2017].* Beijing: China Map Publishing House, 2018.

Jiang, Yanpeng, Nalini Mohabir, Renfeng Ma, Lichao Wu, and Mingxing Chen. "Whose Village? Stakeholder Interests in the Urban Renewal of Hubei Old Village in Shenzhen." *Land Use Policy* 91 (2020): 104411.

Karaman, Ozan, Lindsay Sawyer, Christian Schmid, and Kit Ping Wong. "Plot by Plot: Plotting Urbanism as an Ordinary Process of Urbanisation." *Antipode* 52, no. 4 (2020): 1122–1151.

Landry, Pierre. *Decentralized Authoritarianism in China: The Communist Party's Control of Local Elites in the Post-Mao Era.* Cambridge: Cambridge University Press, 2008.

Lefebvre, Henri. "Space and the State." In *State, Space, World: Selected Essays*, edited by Neil Brenner and Stuart Elden, 223–253. Minneapolis: University of Minnesota Press, 2009.

Lefebvre, Henri. *State, Space, World: Selected Essays.* Edited by Neil Brenner and Stuart Elden. Minneapolis: University of Minnesota Press, 2009.

Lin, George. *Developing China: Land, Politics and Social Conditions.* London: Routledge, 2009.

Lin, George. "Urbanization of the Pearl River Delta: The Case of Dongguan." In *China's Urban Space: Development Under Market Socialism*, edited by Terry G. McGee, George C.S. Lin, Andrew M. Marton, Mark Y.L. Wang, and Jiaping Wu, 96–120. London and New York: Routledge, 2007.

Lincoln, Toby. *An Urban History of China.* Cambridge: Cambridge University Press, 2021.

Liu, Junde, and Jinzhao Fan. 中国市制的历史演变与当代改革 [*A History of the City Administrative System in China*]. Nanjing: Southeast University Press, 2015.

Liu, Junde, Runcheng Jin, and Keyu Zhou. 中国政区地理 [*China's Administrative Geography*]. Beijing: Science Press, 1999.

Liu, Yuyang. "Land-Based Finance: How Revenue Concern Drives Urbanization." In *Handbook on Urban Development in China*, edited by Ray Yep and June Wang, 36–58. Cheltenham, UK: Edward Elgar Publishing, 2019.

Ma, Laurence J. C. "Urban Administrative Restructuring, Changing Scale Relations, and Local Economic Development in China." *Political Geography* 24, no. 4 (2005): 477–497.

Mao, Zanyou. 东莞历代地图集 [*Dongguan Historical Atlas*]. Dongguan: Chinese People's Political Consultative Conference Dongguan City Committee Cultural and Historical Materials Committee, 2002.

McGee, Terry. "The Emergence of *Desakota* Regions in Asia: Expanding a Hypothesis." In *The Extended Metropolis: Settlement Transition in Asia*, edited by Norton Ginsburg, Bruce Koppel, and Terry McGee, 3–25. Honolulu: University of Hawaii Press, 1991.

Perry, Elizabeth J. "From Mass Campaigns to Managed Campaigns: Constructing a New Socialist Countryside." In *Mao's Invisible Hand: The Political Foundations of Adaptive Governance in China*, edited by Sebastian Heilmann and Elizabeth J. Perry, 30–61. Cambridge, MA: Harvard University Asia Center, 2011.

Pu, Shanxin. 中国行政区划改革 [*A Study of China's Administrative Division Reform*]. Beijing: The Commercial Press, 2006.

Pun, Ngai. *Made in China: Women Factory Workers in a Global Workplace.* Hong Kong: Hong Kong University Press, 2005.

Sanlian Lifeweek. 东莞30 年巨变: 前市长李近维郑锦滔的城市史 [*The Great Transformation of Dongguan in Thirty Years*], no. 46 (2008).

Schmid, Christian. *Henri Lefebvre and the Theory of the Production of Space.* London: Verso Books, 2022.

———."Specificity and Urbanization: A Theoretical Outlook." In *The Inevitable Specificity of Cities*, edited by Roger Diener, Manuel Herz, Jacques Herzog, Marcel Meili, Pierre de Meuron, Christian Schmid, and Milica Topalović, 287–307. Zurich: Lars Müller Publishers, 2015.

Sit, Victor. "Mega-City, Extended Metropolitan Region, Desakota, and Exo-Urbanization: An Introduction." *Asian Geographer* 15, no. 1–2 (1996): 1–14.

Skinner, G. William. "Peasant Organization in Rural China." *The Annals of the American Academy of Political and Social Science* 277, no. 1 (1951): 89–100.

Streule, Monika. "Doing Mobile Ethnography: Grounded, Situated, and Comparative." *Urban Studies* 57, no. 2 (2020): 421–438.

Tan, Yining. "Temporary Migrants and Public Space: A Case Study of Dongguan, China." *Journal of Ethnic and Migration Studies* 47, no. 20 (2021): 4688–4704.

Tang, Wing-shing. "Governing by the State: A Study of the Literature on Governing Chinese Mega-Cities." In *Branding Chinese Mega-Cities*, edited by Per-Olof Berg and Emma Björner, 42–63. Cheltenham, UK: Edward Elgar Publishing, 2014.

———."Town-Country Relations in China: Back to Basics." *Eurasian Geography and Economics* 60, no. 4 (2019): 455–485.

Wang, Fei-Ling. *The China Order: Centralia, World Empire, and the Nature of Chinese Power.* Albany: State University of New York Press, 2017.

Whiting, Susan. *Power and Wealth in Rural China: The Political Economy of Institutional Change.* Cambridge: Cambridge University Press, 2001.

———."The Cadre Evaluation System at the Grass Roots: The Paradox of Party Rule." In *Holding China Together*, edited by Barry Naughton and Dali L. Yang, 101–119. Cambridge: Cambridge University Press, 2004.

Wong, Kit Ping. "Territorially-Nested Urbanization in China: The Case of Dongguan." *Eurasian Geography and Economics* 60, no. 4 (2019): 486–509.

———."Hong Kong, Shenzhen, Dongguan" In *Vocabularies for an Urbanising Planet: Theory Building Through Comparison*, edited by Christian Schmid and Monika Streule, 84–107. Basel: Birkhäuser, 2023.

Wong, Siu Wai, Bo-sin Tang, and Jinlong Liu. "Village Elections, Grassroots Governance, and the Restructuring of State Power: An Empirical Study in Southern Peri-Urban China." *The China Quarterly* 241 (2020): 22–42.

Yang, Chun, and Haifeng Liao. "Backward Linkages of Cross-Border Production Networks of Taiwanese PC Investment in the Pearl River Delta, China." *Tijdschrift voor economische en sociale geografie* 101, no. 2 (2010): 199–217.

Yeung, Godfrey. *Foreign Investment and Socio-Economic Development in China: The Case of Dongguan.* New York: Palgrave, 2001.

You-ren Yang, and Wang, Hung-kai. "Land Property Rights Regime in China: A Comparative Study of Suzhou and Dongguan." In *China's Emerging Cities: The Making of New Urbanism*, edited by Fulong Wu, 44–61. London: Routledge, 2007.

Yu, Jingdong. "The Concept of 'Territory'
     in Modern China: 1689–1910."
     Cultura 15, no. 2 (2018): 73–95.
Zhao, Ziyang. *Prisoner of the State:*
     The Secret Journal of Zhao Ziyang.
     Translated by Pu Bao, Renee
     Chiang, and Adi Ignatius. London:
     Simon & Schuster, 2010.
Zürcher, E. "The Chinese Communes."
     Bijdragen tot de taal-, land- en
     volkenkunde 118, no. 1 (1962):
     68–90.

IMAGE CREDITS

All photography from author unless
otherwise stated.

All maps from Philippe Rekacewicz with
author unless otherwise stated.

Cartographic assistance Jan Zimmerman,
Ecce Emanetoglu and Aikaterini Katsouli.

F. 2, 10, 11
          Mao, *Dongguan Historical Atlas.*
F. 3, 19
          Christian Schmid
F. 4–9, 12
          Sources: Gazette Office of
          Guangdong People's Government,
          Gazetteer of Maps of Guangdong's
          *Administrative Division*s; Chen
          and Chen, *Atlas of Changes*
          of Administrative Divisions of
          the People's Republic of China,
          1949–1999; Institute of Geographic
          Sciences and Natural Resources
          Research, *Atlas of Changes of*
          Administrative Division of the
          Peoples's Republic of China (1980–
          2017).
F. 13   Sources: Dongguan Municipal
          Gazetteer Compilation Committee,
          Dongguan Municipal Gazetteer;
          Mao, *Dongguan Historical Atlas*;
          Footprint and transport data from
          the consultation of google satellite
          images and fieldwork.
F. 21   Data from fieldwork, 2018.
F. 22   Google Earth

The Highway Revolution.
Enclosure and
State Space in India

On 16 November 2021, a heavy-body Air Force aircraft carrying Indian Prime Minister Narendra Modi made a spectacular landing on a newly constructed six-lane motorway in a nondescript and remote agrarian hinterland in the Indian state of Uttar Pradesh. Following the landing, Modi delivered a speech to a large congregation of farmers and agriculture workers from the region, laying out the centrality of motorways and their world-class urbanisation in his vision for a "New India." In the backdrop to his speech, promotional videos of the motorway featured a series of free-floating architectural renderings that helped to conjure the abstract reality of the express urbanism yet to come[1]—what seems like a contradictory and distant everyday reality for this region of subsistence agriculture. The expressway is projected as a techno-fix that will bring prosperity and development to this "backward" agricultural region by unlocking agrarian land for more "productive" uses such as world-class investment parks, logistical centres, and industries.

In addition to offering express connectivity to metropolitan centres, such as Uttar Pradesh's capital, Lucknow, and the national capital, Delhi, the government narrative around the expressway claims that it would benefit farmers in the region through increased land prices and access to new employment opportunities.[2] Contrary to this narrative, the land for the expressway corridor was expropriated from the farmers at below-market rates using colonial-era eminent domain[3] laws for land acquisition. The involvement of the parastatal institution, the Uttar Pradesh Expressway Industrial Development Authority (UPEIDA), in this otherwise private project helped attach a public purpose (bringing development to the region) and thus allowed the project to unfold at a rapid pace, at minimum costs. Furthermore, this direct land-acquisition model has helped avoid unified farmer protests such as those that emerged during the heyday of India's land-acquisition projects in 2008.[4] In fact, no large-scale resistance emerged against land acquisition for highways, even at a time when one of the largest organised protests in India's history was unfolding against the agriculture privatisation laws in 2021, when the rate of highway construction in India stood at its highest, with 34 kilometres of lanes per day.[5] Despite the obvious accumulation by dispossession[6] that the construction of expressways facilitates, it has become an important political promise across India.

In his speech, Modi claimed that in the year 2021 alone, his government constructed over 12,000 kilometres of new highways to attract transnational capital investments to the most underdeveloped parts of the country.[7] His speech culminated in thundering applause, followed by a nationalistic chanting of *Bharat Mata ki Jai* (Hail Mother India) led by Modi. The plane soon took off, perhaps for another political congregation, on one of the 22 landing airstrips developed along newly constructed highways all over India. The rapid construction of highways and the express urbanism it catalyses are a kind of new opium for the masses, offering a state-created condition where rapid urbanisation, religious nationalism, and bellicose militarism undergo a toxic amalgamation.

INDIA'S HIGHWAY REVOLUTION

A profound transformation is underway in the Indian countryside that assumes nothing short of the complete urbanisation of India as its horizon. This is the transformation that is producing Modi's New India,[8] an India that is new not only in terms of its economic and religious nationalism and the erosion of social justice but also in its production of what Neil Brenner calls "new state spaces."[9] A new India is being produced through the extensive material extension of state infrastructure and urbanisation in territories previously bypassed by capitalism through the explosion and re-territorialisation of the "colonial state space." To put this process into perspective, at the height of the COVID-19 pandemic

in 2021, even as the country was reeling from a desperate lack of ventilators and hospital beds, the National Highways Authority of India (NHAI) constructed 34 kilometres of new highway lanes per day.[10] This translates to about 5.5 kilometres of standard six-lane highway built daily. This pace is unparalleled in history, even at the height of the US Interstate Highway System in the post-war period. The current government's stated ambition is for the construction pace to reach 100 kilometres of highway lanes per day by 2025, which will, in turn, catapult India into an elusive USD 5 trillion economy.[11]

The production of space through highway corridors has been a central feature of India's fast-paced growth trajectory under neoliberalism. It has emerged as the dominant mode through which "accumulation by dispossession"[12] functions in India, whereby the "land broker state" attempts to remove barriers for transnational capital to invest in rural land markets.[13] [Fig. 1] The construction of these corridors is not only rapid but also extensive. Under the ongoing highway development programme, curiously entitled *Bharatmala* (garland of roads around Mother India), 100 new highway corridors spanning 34,600 kilometres have been planned across the length and breadth of India at the cost of USD 74 billion.[14] The title of the highway programme builds upon the nationalist imaginary and contemporary mythology of *Bharat Mata,* or the nation as the mother goddess, where the highway corridors are presented as a garland on its mythical body.[15] The 100 new highway corridors include 44 primary economic and 56 inter-economic corridors. [Fig. 2–3] They are often implanted parallel to corridors that have only recently been constructed, some of which have not yet become fully operational. Together with other contemporary mega-infrastructure programmes, such as China's One Belt One Road initiative, India's highway revolution can be understood as a counter-revolution similar to the Green Revolution.[16] Raj Patel's analysis of the "Long Green Revolution" in India and the broader global South finds how direct links between

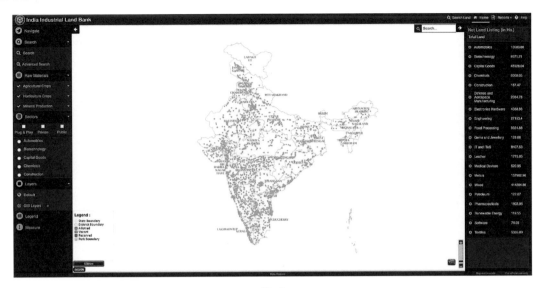

Fig. 1

governments and philanthropic institutions—such as the Rockefeller Foundation—ushered in the Green Revolution as a capitalist counter-movement to suppress the peasant rebellions in the countryside.

Similarly, the highway revolution is cata-lysing a very specific kind of large-scale extended urbanisation, which is distinct from what we encounter in the other chapters of this book. This form of state-driven extended urbanisation serves as a vehicle for the enclosure and commod-ification of rural land and its transformation into urban space rather than for the extraction of natural resources.[17] It often reaches beyond the nation-state borders, for example, with the construction of the Chabahar Port in Iran and the International North-South Transport Corridor in Central Asia by the Indian state.[18]

The "new state spaces" produced by the highway revolution are multi-scalar, reaching across local, metropolitan, regional, and inter-regional scales. Three examples are the six-lane, 150-kilometre Ring Road project around the city of Jaipur (USD 150 million), the double-storeyed, eight-lane, 29-kilometre-long Dwarka Expressway, which is an urban corridor between the cities of Delhi and Gurgaon (USD 1.3

billion), and the 1,320-kilometre-long Delhi-Mumbai Expressway (USD 12.4 billion). These new highway corridors often promise alternative faster and greener mobility to existing highways. Thus, the rapid construction of highway corridors across space and scales is no longer merely enabling a time-space compression,[19] but it is also turning Henri Lefebvre's thesis on a "complete urbanisation of society" from an abstraction into a concrete reality.[20]

However, as Brenner aptly points out, these new state spaces are ripe with "conflict, crisis, and contradiction as they exacerbate rather than alleviate the economic dislocations of post-Keynesian urbanisation. Therefore, they are also spaces of incessant regulatory experimentation and dynamic institutional searching."[21] The highway programme does not even try to avoid conflicts in the aggregation of agrarian land.

F. 1   The land broker state: a screenshot of the GIS-enabled India Industrial Land Bank Portal maintained by the Indian government, which allows transnational investors an overview of aggregated land banks available for investment.

Legend:
- — Existing highway networks
- — Golden Quadrilateral
- — North-South and East-West Highway
- — New corridors (Bharatmala Programme)
- ···· Dehli–Mumbai Expressway

THE HIGHWAY REVOLUTION AS EXTENDED URBANISATION
Fig. 2

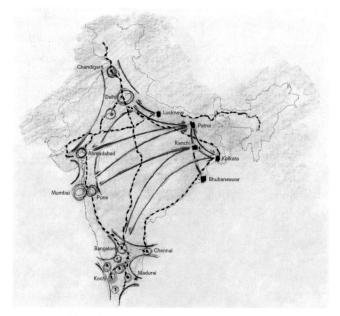

Legend:
- First economic corridors
- Internal migration towards the first corridors
- ···· Golden Quadrilateral NSEW

FORMATION OF ECONOMIC CORRIDORS &
MAIN MIGRATION MOVEMENTS
Fig. 3

The planning of new highway corridors into previously economically bypassed regions operates on a terra nullius assumption, ignoring the complexity of land ownership, cadastral negotiations, and practices of dwelling and occupancies on the ground. The abstract agrarian revenue cadastres substitute ground surveys for land acquisition, resulting in long-fraught legal conflicts that turn judicial courts into sites of struggle and negotiation.

On the one hand, marginalised groups exercise resistance by filing public interest litigations against highway development, citing a "Right to Life"[22] to expose the contradictions and arbitrariness in the planning and land acquisition process through the Right to Information Act.[23] On the other hand, the state invents new rationalities and narratives to legitimise highway projects.[24] The uncertainty imposed by such conflicts propels highway corridors into long phases of incompleteness, which, as discussed later in this chapter, becomes productive not only for the state and property-owning classes but also for the subaltern communities whose lives are disrupted by these highway corridors.

This chapter explores the production of new state spaces under India's ongoing highway revolution along four coinciding arguments. The first section presents a periodisation of highway development as a state works project in India since the late 1990s. The second section explores the dominant spatial strategies and the production of new state spaces. The third section highlights India's essential urban dilemma of continued low urbanisation rates despite these profound infrastructure transformations. This section also engages with the rich and varied scholarship on subaltern urbanisation in India, which tackles this question from a post-colonial perspective. The final section of the chapter brings us right into the everyday life of the new state spaces, full of conflicts and uncertainties, through the analysis of the production of a regional highway corridor on the periphery of Delhi.

This chapter draws upon extensive mobile and multi-sited ethnographic fieldwork conducted in the extended urban region of Delhi between 2017 and 2020.[25] In attempting to piece together India's political economy of highway corridors, I focus on the frictions and conflicts these projects generate on the ground. In particular, I employ the procedure of "dialectical transduction," which allows for a mutual interaction between concepts and empirical research,[26] combining an intimate observation of everyday life through critical ethnography with the analysis of state strategies driving large-scale processes of urban change.[27] The discussion draws upon interviews with experts and with communities displaced by highway construction, participant observation conducted at highway launches and state planning offices, as well as analysis of geospatial data, grey literature, and court archives. Additionally, this research used ethnographic film to draw upon the "urban sensorium" of the 2020 ethnographic documentary film *Not Just Roads*.[28]

A PERIODISATION OF INDIA'S HIGHWAY PROGRAMMES

In this section, I identify three distinct phases in India's neo-liberal highway revolution which marked important shifts in the political economy, public narratives, and governance of highway programmes in the country. The first of these phases, which I describe as the "foundational phase," emerged with the planning of the first nation-spanning greenfield highways under the National Highway Development Programme (NHDP), coinciding with the Asian financial crisis between 1997–1999. The second,

F. 2 The 34,800 kilometres of new highway routes proposed under the 44 economic and 56 inter-economic corridors as part of the Bharatmala Highway Program.

F. 3 Periodisation of the emergence of highway corridors across India and the migration patterns that resulted from the uneven development of these corridors.

the "expansion phase," saw the emergence of the first nationwide industrial corridors along the pathways laid out during the first phase. This coincided with the 2007–2008 global financial crisis and was marked by the emergence of parastatal corporations managing urban corridors. The third phase, which I describe as the "intensification phase," emerged in conjunction with the rightward, market-oriented shift in India's national politics since 2014. This ongoing phase is marked by a sharp acceleration in the pace of highway construction. The new highway corridors bypass the industrial corridors laid out in the earlier phases. I will elaborate on these three phases briefly in the following subsections.

THE FOUNDATIONAL PHASE
(1999 UNTIL THE MID–2000s)

Although the institutional foundations for the first phase of India's highway development were laid down at the beginning of the 1990s, the programme officially began under the first National Democratic Alliance (NDA) government in 1999, led by the right-wing Bhartiya Janta Party. In the narrative around the programme, highway development has been presented as an attempt to mitigate contagion from the 1997 Asian Financial Crisis.[29] The programme provided an avenue for international financial capital that was leaving East and South East Asian economies due to falling rates of profit.[30] It promised to catch up with its fast-growing neighbour, China, whose economy was built on a fast and efficient highway network.[31] Importantly, as Rupal Oza shows, the NDA used the promise of the reinvention of India through world-class infrastructures as a key argument of its India Shining election campaign.[32] This phase can thus be seen as the birth period of what Seth Schindler called the "infrastructure state": governments attempt to attract transnational investments for the transformation of the territory rather than for the production of urban space for the reproduction of an industrial proletariat.[33]

This phase cumulatively added over 49,260 kilometres of new roads and highways

to the existing network across the country with two distinct projects. The first, the Golden Quadrilateral Project, connected the four largest metropolitan regions of India—Delhi, Mumbai, Chennai, and Kolkata—whereas the second, the North-South, East-West Project, projected two central axes across India. While these highways were truly nation-spanning in their reach, their pathways followed the arc of fertile regions, which had experienced agricultural modernisation under the Green Revolution, producing an agricultural surplus.[34] The dominant agrarian castes in these regions were able to capture political power and thus guide decisions regarding the alignment of the highway corridors.[35] Therefore, according to Sai Balakrishnan, infrastructural choices in the neo-liberal era produced new uneven geographies, "like how irrigation canal projects socio-technically produced a geography of uneven agrarian capitalism."[36] This led to the production of uneven land markets whereby the regions through which these early highways passed were able to benefit from an above-average increase in ground rents. Therefore, "the distributive politics of who captures the surpluses from agrarian-to-urban land-use change depends on prior agrarian geographies."[37]

Another essential feature of this phase is the foundation of the National Highways Authority of India (NHAI), a parastatal institution whose main goal was, according to Liz Light, to cut the "red tape of bureaucratic accountability" and "bring a military-like urgency and command into the construction of highway infrastructure."[38] Founding members of the NHAI—such as Major General B.C. Khanduri—were taken from the Indian Army's engineering corps, and its decision-making was controlled by a narrow group of executives appointed by the Ministry of Road Transport and Highways.[39] Therefore, NHAI not only privileged the private sector with infrastructure development but also facilitated highway development as a "scalar fix."[40] The construction of these industrial corridors pushed inter-regional extended urbanisation, which predominated urbanisation processes at local and regional scales.

This phase resulted in proto-urban corridors, such as the Mumbai-Pune and the Bangalore-Mysore. They catalysed land markets and enclosures in territories of extended urbanisation but lacked regulatory bodies beyond the regional scale. They were largely regional-level experiments conducted by local governments acting in consort with the central state. In his excellent analysis of this period, Michael Goldman notes that there was an increasing intersection between neoliberal and world-city urbanisation through highway construction. Goldman finds that the "speculative urbanism" catalysed during this period shaped state-citizen relationships around a culture of real estate and land speculation.[41] As a consequence, a number of private townships emerged along toll highways in the agrarian peripheries around large Indian cities, such as DLF City (Delhi Land & Finance), which emerged on the periphery of Delhi in the early 2000s, and the private townships of the NICE Corridor (Nandi Infrastructure Corridor Enterprise Ltd) outside Bangalore.[42]

THE EXPANSION PHASE
(THE MID–2000s TO 2014)

While the foundational phase of India's highway development programme was forging initial pathways of extended urbanisation through agrarian hinterlands, the second phase was marked by efforts to enclose and commodify the land in these territories. By 2007–2008, planning the first genuinely inter-regional and nation-spanning urban corridors coincided with the global financial crisis. As Llerena Searle notes, there was a significant upheaval in the Indian real estate markets during this period as foreign investment funds, having invested millions into speculative urbanism, were exiting Indian markets.[43] The planning of these corridors can thus be understood as a state strategy to expand territories suited for speculative urbanism while also attracting further transnational investments into the country.

The first of these corridors, the Delhi-Mumbai Industrial Corridor (DMIC), was established through significant direct investment by the Japanese government, and it was modelled after the Japanese Tokyo-Osaka Taiheiyo Belt,[44] a 1200-kilometre-long urban corridor between the cities of Tokyo and Osaka along which a majority of Japan's manufacturing industries and urban centres are concentrated. For the management of the DMIC that cut across the jurisdiction of several regional governments, a state development corporation, DMICDC (Delhi-Mumbai Industrial Corridor Development Corporation), was established. As a parastatal corporation, it could simplify the palimpsest of jurisdictional boundaries and complexities in an extremely large territory stretching 150 to 200 kilometres on either side of an approximately 1,300-kilometre-long freight corridor. During this period, corridor urbanisation became an official state strategy to generate economic growth by directing large transnational investments into the conversion of land. Such urban corridors are often made up of several large-scale projects that emerge fluidly with the ebbs and flows of capital investment, which are often designed through the involvement of transnational consultants like the Jurong Corporation from Singapore.[45] There is, thus, a "worlding" of the experiences in East and South East Asian cities with such large-scale projects.[46]

Following the initial experimentation with the Delhi-Mumbai urban corridor, the DMICDC eventually planned and developed several other inter-regional urban corridors and was renamed the National Industrial Corridor Development Corporation (NICDC).[47] Thus, this second phase of India's highway revolution deployed extended urbanisation as a state strategy to capitalise on the ground rents generated in the first phase of highway programmes. While significant farmer resistance emerged during this period against land acquisition for smaller initiatives, such as special economic zones in Nandigram and Singur in West Bengal,[48] the territories of extended urbanisation opened through urban corridors were so vast and fluid that they faced little organised resistance. Furthermore, what becomes evident here is that contrary to the free-market myth often

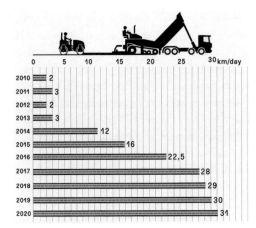

F. 4   The daily pace of highway
construction in India over the
last two decades.

THE UNPRECEDENTED PACE OF HIGHWAY
CONSTRUCTION IN INDIA
Fig. 4

attributed to speculative urbanism, state corporations played a significant role in facilitating these endeavours.[49]

THE INTENSIFICATION PHASE (2014–ONGOING)

The transition into the third and ongoing phase of India's highway revolution coincides with the political transition of central state power from the centre-left coalition United Progressive Alliance to the Hindu nationalist National Democratic Alliance-II coalition in 2014. In the first year following the political transition, the daily rate of highway construction jumped from 3 to 12 kilometres, finally reaching 34 kilometres in 2020–2021. [Fig. 4]

However, the increase in the pace of highway construction is not merely due to the mechanisation of construction (for example, through the introduction of very efficient asphalt paver machines), but it hints at the unfolding of a new political economy of land in India. Thus, a large number of highways were constructed in parallel to already existing highways in order to open up additional land for enclosure in previously bypassed regions. Their construction is often justified by the narrative of providing faster connectivity and bringing development to the "backward" and "tribal" regions of the country.

In 2017, the NHDP was officially transitioned into the *Bharatmala* Programme, which envisioned 100 *ex novo* urban/economic corridors (44 main corridors plus 56 inter-economic corridors). This programme literally strives for a complete urbanisation of the country. The territories of extended urbanisation that these corridors intend to open pass through some of the poorest subsistence agriculture and tribal regions of the country. While their construction is often premised on bringing development to regions that were previously bypassed by both agricultural modernisation and urban development, what they actually are facilitating is access to cheap land. The new Delhi-Mumbai Expressway, planned to bypass the existing DMIC, serves as a good illustration of this contradictory logic. [Fig. 5] It is promoted as a techno-fix, addressing previous uneven development in the regions passed through while simultaneously advertised as an opportunity for transnational investors to buy land that is far cheaper than in the DMIC. Under the promise of bringing development to disadvantaged regions, it expands territories of extended urbanisation in order to catalyse the formation of fully commodified land markets.

The phenomenal pace of highway construction has many additional consequences. It means that ground surveys are often not conducted, leading to highway corridors coming into conflict with existing practices of dwelling and resulting in extended periods of uncertainty. However, such uncertainty does not necessarily paralyse technopolitical action because state power increasingly acts through "governing through uncertainty," as Zeiderman et al. note. "Just as investment instruments like derivatives make it possible to capitalise on contingency, fluidity, and unpredictability in financial markets, other techniques for managing uncertainty in an urban context convert these conditions into forms of value that can be commodified and exchanged."[50] For example, instead of halting the construction of highway corridors until legal conflicts are resolved, parastatal companies continue land acquisition and construction in parts where they face little resistance. The real estate developers, on their side, hedge on the best time to complete their projects, maintaining enclosed agricultural land in a prolonged state of fallowness or leaving buildings and projects half-finished, speculating on future profitability.[51] Middle-class investors may hedge on differential property values, using uncertainty to buy into the future. In contrast, poor and less affluent communities can attempt to evade the foreclosing effects of the land enclosure by embracing practices of uncertainty and laying claim to urban space by squatting or intentionally investing in land or housing with unclear or illegal titles.[52] Uncertainty, thus, becomes something that is both produced and productive in very different ways and becomes a central constitutive feature of everyday life.[53] I will engage the generative potentials of uncertainty later in this chapter when discussing the regional urban corridor—the Dwarka Expressway, close to Delhi.

HIGHWAY REVOLUTION
AND NEW STATE SPACES

In the previous section, we saw how the Indian state significantly reshaped and redefined the highway programme at vital political-economic conjunctures, with one example being the global financial crisis bringing previously bypassed territories into its fold. This highlights the crucial role of the state in the production of space and in steering urbanisation, which can be critically analysed through Henri Lefebvre's concept of state space (*espace étatique*). Lefebvre introduced the term in his 1976 book *De l'État* to illustrate how the state binds itself to space through a complex and shifting relationship.[54] In other words, as Christian Schmid aptly points out, "The ever-increasing extension of urbanisation is only possible with an enormous expansion of state control and surveillance over the entire planet. The earth eventually becomes the new horizon of the production of space."[55] Therefore, as Neil Brenner and Stuart Elden highlight in their analysis of Lefebvre's writings, the state becomes the key actor of the production of space because: "only the state is capable of taking charge of space on a grand scale—highways, air traffic routes—because only the state has at its disposal the appropriate resources, techniques, and conceptual capacity."[56]

However, it is essential to recognise that for Lefebvre, the state stood not only for the nation-state but also for a multi-scalar state structure, spanning the planetary to neighbourhood scales. "It is the result of a long historical development in which the nation-state increasingly becomes dominant and finally becomes the principal actor in the production of space."[57] State space for Lefebvre encompasses the production of the territory of the nation-state in which capitalist social relations may unfold. It includes the symbolic representations of state power within such territories and develops state strategies to shape patterns of land use and circulation.[58] In this way, the state maps manage and manipulate the production of space, especially through attempts to extend capitalist social relations onto previously marginalised zones.

In her landmark 2010 book *Producing India*, Manu Goswami analyses the crucial importance of state works in distilling and communicating the ideology of state space in colonial India. Goswami finds that railways came the closest of any state infrastructure

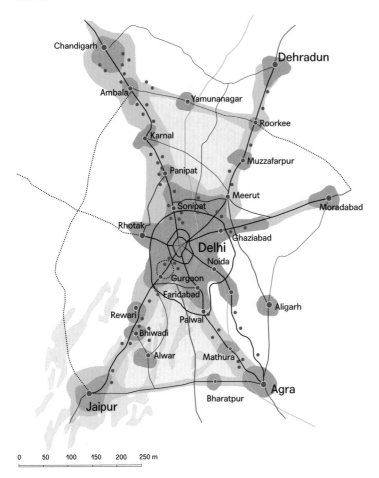

MULTISCALAR CORRIDOR
URBANISATION AROUND DELHI
Fig. 5

works in the production of colonial state space. She claims that the railways not only enabled the circulation of peoples and commodities within the boundaries of a state space but that the railways also emerged as a site of collective self-understanding and identity as Indian people, where new socio-economic differences were produced.[59] The Bharatmala highway programme as a state work similarly aims at producing a new state space, where "new" does not merely refer to the reimagination of India as *Bharat Mata* (nation-as-mother) but rather as a neoliberal state space that emerges through an explosion of colonial state space, no longer bound by the borders of the nation-state.

In his analysis of new state spaces, Neil Brenner finds that under neoliberalism, it is no longer capital that is moulded into the (territorially integrated) geography of state space, but it is state space that is moulded into the territorially differentiated geography of capital.[60]

However, as Lefebvre highlights, state space does not merely eliminate differences but also manages them. The modern state organises space to control the entire system, breaks up opposition

F. 4   The expanding network of highway axes leading to urban development and the enclosure of agricultural land.

by redistributing groups of people, and hierarchises places based on power relations.[61] We see these processes in the experience of extended urbanisation with highway corridors in India. While the state attempts to produce a homogenous commodifiable space by enacting eminent domain on agrarian land, its extensive urban fabric is highly differentiated and hierarchical. As I will discuss in the subsequent sections, this results in the production of "planned illegalities"[62] such as tenement towns and "unauthorised colonies," which concentrate masses of working-class people and urban poor in a socio-spatial difference to the legal spaces for the elite.

In this section, I discuss the narrative imaginaries and strategies that the Indian state employs to produce the national territory and manage socio-spatial differentiation, and I also look at their environmental consequences.

EXTENDED URBANISATION AND THE NATIONALIST STATE

"Not Just Roads, Building a Nation," the tagline of the ongoing Bharatmala highways programme, boldly suggests highway construction as a nation-building project. [Fig. 6] The programme imagines India's territory as the *Bharat Mata*, or Goddess India, her body (the nation-state) festooned with necklaces of roads and urban corridors.[63] This is similar to how road construction helps deploy and consolidate an image of a singular, abstract national territory or state space in Latin America, as Penny Harvey and Hannah Knox aptly highlight for Peru.[64] The Plan Puebla Panama in Central America and the Trans-Amazonian Highway in the Brazilian state of Amazonas have similarly allowed for the extension of state space.[65] Regular public spectacles like the landing and take-off of military aircraft on highways not only attempt to reinforce this imaginary and stimulate public thinking in favour of highway construction but also highlight how highways double as tactical military infrastructure.[66] In total, 22 landing airstrips have been planned along newly constructed highways in places that are both proximate and distant to India's political borders.[67]

Furthermore, a constant comparison of the Bharatmala Programme with the US Interstate Highway System is mobilised to locate its centrality in nation-building. John F. Kennedy's famous quote, "American roads are not good because America is rich, but America is rich because American roads are good,"[68] is often utilised in India's political discourse to make this point.[69] This imaginary of highways as a state space also serves the purpose of justifying the violence that the highway programme inflicts upon historically colonised and marginalised communities. In the case of the planning of the US Interstate, "officials routinely routed expressways through black neighbourhoods," as Rose and Mohl explain.[70] In contemporary India, this violence is exerted through the expropriation of land because it marginalises people inhabiting subaltern urbanisation.

STATE SPACE AND FOSSIL URBANISM

In his 2016 book, Andreas Malm notes how fossil capitalism allows the state to produce abstract space that is removed from the concrete qualities of space and time.[71] The consequent spatio-temporal fossil capitalism, which I term "fossil urbanism," finds its full expression in the abstract space produced historically through the US Interstate Highway System and India's ongoing highway programme. The state strategy to produce abstract space uses the image of a "car country"[72] with an upwardly mobile, aspirational, consumptive middle class that owns suburban property, commutes large distances using personal automobiles, and shops at highway malls.

Property relations in this abstract space are held together by fossil capitalism financially, materially, and socially. Just like the US Interstate, India's highway programme is primarily financed through taxes on fossil fuels.[73] The revenue collected through this tax in 2021 alone stood at $107 billion.[74] Materially, the rapid highway construction also offers an outlet for the en masse consumption of asphalt, a by-product of crude-oil refining.[75] However, the biggest promise of India's highway revolution has been "the invention

Fig. 6

of India as the world's fastest-growing car market."[76] A recent government report similarly notes that in addition to the highways adding to the gross domestic product through logistics, transport, and increasing capital expenditure, their "real promise" lies in the growth of commercial vehicle sales.[77] Under slow industrial growth, India's fossil urbanism not only fires the engines of economic growth but also helps uphold the property relations of the abstract space it produces.[78]

GREEN GROWTH AS A
STATE STRATEGY

Similar to the colonial view of land as state property that Goswami describes in the production of state space in India,[79] the ongoing highway programme attempts to settle and valorise primal forests and agrarian commons as "cheap green land," or wastelands, available for urbanisation.[80] The construction of highway corridors is thus leading to extensive socio-ecological damage and biodiversity loss on the one hand and an increase in carbon emissions

and accelerated climate change on the other. The state has invented narratives of sustainability and green growth in an attempt to soften these devasting environmental consequences. However, on the contrary, they present the construction of highway corridors as being beneficial to the environment. Existing corridors between urban centres are, therefore, reviled as a source of inefficient traffic circulation and congestion that produces excessive greenhouse emissions and air pollution. Against this backdrop, new highway corridors are presented as an alternative, offering possibilities for green growth in the form of savings in carbon emissions that are often quantified using international policy metrics and traded in international credit markets.[81]

F. 6   The political assemblage at the Bharatmala launch event. Seated from the centre to the right: the Minister of Finance, the Minister of Road Transport and Highways, and the Foreign Affairs Minister.

The Delhi-Mumbai Expressway offers an excellent example of these tactics; despite its disastrous environmental consequences,[82] the National Highways Authority of India claims that it will save an equivalent of 20 million trees worth of greenhouse emissions by opening an alternative, faster route between the cities.[83] An additional two million trees of strip forest will be planted along the expressway as compensatory forestation. Such strip forests are monocultural plantations of fast-growing trees along what is officially classified as government wastelands, such as on the sides of roads, canals, and railway tracks. Strip forests are quickly becoming a dominant category of forest cover in India and can be used by the state as cheap land when needed. Thus, the fossil urbanism of the highway corridors produces its own abstract space—a wasteland that can be called into the service of capital.

TERRITORIES OF EXTENDED URBANISATION FROM A POSTCOLONIAL PERSPECTIVE

The massive urban and agrarian change in India over the last two decades has provided a rich and generative terrain for postcolonial urban theory. A diversity of ideas and analytical frameworks have been developed and applied to analyse the transformations of the postcolonial state during the neo-liberal period and how it shapes urban space in Indian urban centres and beyond. The transformation of large metropolitan regions such as Delhi and Mumbai followed the lead of other global cities, which have been abundantly analysed in relation to the concomitant evictions of the marginalised, subaltern, and urban poor.[84] At the same time, the call to push urban and regional analysis beyond "metrocentricity"[85] has also inspired a rich body of scholarship. This research includes the analysis of the speculative transformations of agricultural land into real estate, its entanglements with the pre-existing structures of agrarian class and caste in the periphery of Indian cities,

and the formation of special economic zones and early urban corridors.[86] The broad scholarship also analysed the in-situ transformations of settlements across the Indian countryside (see also Elisa Bertuzzo in this volume) and attempted to reckon the urban and rural as categories of spatial classification.[87] The latter stream of scholarship is particularly interesting in the context of the territories of extended urbanisation discussed in the upcoming section.

THE POLITICS OF URBAN CLASSIFICATION

The governmental spatial classifications of "rural" and "urban" concretely determine the nature of governance and land use in India. Urban is usually defined by the Census of India using the tri-fold criteria of the total population, population density, and percentage of employment. If a settlement crosses the threshold of 5,000 inhabitants, a density of 400 people per square kilometre, and at least 75% of the male workforce is in the non-agrarian sector, then the settlement is considered urban. Failing to meet any one of these criteria results in the settlement remaining rural. Moreover, settlements are often not classified as "urban" despite crossing the tri-fold threshold. In fact, following political pressure, they are often classified back as rural, a phenomenon described as "census activism."[88] Furthermore, as I have written elsewhere, such static models of spatial classification fail to account for the seasonal mobility of labour migrants between spaces classified as rural and urban.[89]

Using the Census of India criteria, the level of urbanisation in 2011 stood at only about 31%. While similar statistics have not been released since then, according to a World Bank report the level stood at 35% in 2021.[90] Such a normative and narrow demography and male-workforce-focused methodology for urban classification helped portray India as a rural nation in need of urgent policy interventions that produce "fast cities of the urban age."[91] It also fails to register the evident urban transformations on the ground.[92] In their geospatial analysis of urban agglomerations across India published in a 2011 paper, Eric Denis and Kamala Marius-Gnanou disputed the low levels of urbanisation in India, finding the actual extent of urbanisation to be much higher. They registered these agglomerations as unacknowledged urban transformations (beyond urban regions) and called them "extended urbanisation in the Indian countryside" with rural-urban or *desakota*-like characteristics.[93] They called for a better appraisal of urbanisation in India and reported the existence of numerous census towns, which I will discuss in the following section.

CENSUS TOWNS—THE SETTLEMENTS THAT ARE NOT QUITE URBAN

Since the 1990s, Indian urbanisation has witnessed the peculiar trend of a remarkable rise in the number of so-called census towns. These are settlements that become urban according to the Census's tri-fold criteria yet remain rural in terms of their administration and service provision. This means that despite a large population that can often cross 50,000 inhabitants, census towns continue to be governed directly by an elected council of representatives with budgets analogous to small villages that cannot cater to municipal service provision. This trend of urbanisation through settlement reclassification, which also has been described as "in-situ urbanisation," accounted for as much as one-third of the total recorded urban growth between 2001 and 2011.[94] In absolute figures, the number of census towns has more than doubled every decade since 1991. Their number grew from 1,702 in 1991 to 5,315 in 2011. Moreover, it is predicted that this trend will continue to remain the predominant factor driving urban growth in India well into the next decades.[95]

The spectacular jump in the number of census towns has taken place concomitant to the shifts in the political economy of state space and large-scale urbanisation, as discussed in the previous sections. Furthermore, the terrains in which they emerge overlap with what I analysed as territories of extended urbanisation. Recent research has pointed to correlations between the hotspots of census town development and extended urbanisation of highway corridors, such as the DMIC.[96] As a settlement type, census towns emerge all over India but are highly varied in their character. Partha Mukhopadhyay proposes to distinguish them under the categories of proximate and non-proximate census towns, with the former being proximate to large urban centres and the latter being remote.[97] Similarly, Duijne and Nijman classify in-situ formations of census towns as emergent peri-urban formations, emergent highway formations, and emergent remote urbanisation, referring to their proximity to large cities, highway corridors, and remote locations, respectively.[98] Elsewhere, I have proposed differentiating census towns emerging in highway corridors as "tenement towns," as their transformation is often related to private landlords for housing workers.[99] As I elaborate in the following section, a rich body of scholarship is emerging under the umbrella of subaltern urbanisation that has attempted to explore the dynamics of census towns further.

SUBALTERN URBANISATION

Drawing upon and extending the work of Ananya Roy on subaltern urbanism beyond the city,[100] bourgeoning scholarship focuses on the experience of small towns and urbanising villages as the Indian countryside undergoes large-scale territorial change. The research attempts to draw attention to subaltern processes that are not dominant or fully capitalist in nature and are shaping poorer settlements at the urban-rural frontier.[101] Rather than the state, these settlements are shaped by the urban majority,[102] which operates through ambiguity and uncertainties in the agrarian land cadastre and ownership. The growth of these settlements is often in response to the lack of affordable housing, small commerce, small logistical operations, or rental tenements that are missed in the state's planning and provisioning. In response to such absences, local developers or land owners plot agricultural land without seeking requisite permissions and clearances.

Such settlements of improvised urbanism,[103] which are colloquially referred to as "unauthorised colonies,"[104] emerge not only around large cities like Delhi but also around distant small towns.[105]

Because the accumulation of capital through the production of space in these settlements is conditioned by existing landownership hierarchies, it reproduces existing relations of agrarian class and caste.[106] As Michael Levien has shown in his analysis of the transformation of rural settlements around special economic zones in the state of Rajasthan, the production of such subaltern urbanisation does not exclude capitalist urbanisation but is intersectional with it. He notes that the agrarian-to-urban transition, rather than serving as a pre-condition for the modernisation of the countryside, is reinvigorating pre-capitalist forms of brokerage and rentiership and turning farmers into entrepreneurs and land speculators.[107] It is not merely that the highway corridors are producing subaltern urbanisation as "agglomeration effects."[108] As I will discuss subsequently, the ongoing attempts to extend urban corridors and state space in previously bypassed regions have increasingly come into conflict with pre-existing subaltern urbanisation in often violent ways. Thus, the transformations in the socio-spatial structure and everyday life of subaltern urbanisation become particularly interesting in conjunction with the analysis of territories of extended urbanisation.

HEDGING THE DREAM HIGHWAY

As I drove along the narrow peripheral roads at the edges of Delhi on a foggy winter morning in early 2018, agricultural fields gave way to towering apartment blocks and narrow pathways abruptly transformed into an eight-lane expressway. Despite the fog, signs promoting rentiership and brokerage were everywhere to be seen. [Fig. 7] Real-estate salespeople were pitching brochures for new housing estates to passing cars. The flyers promoted more affordable but illegally plotted land in unauthorised colonies, and ads for the sale of agricultural farmland. I stopped beside one of the several salespeople, and as I wound down the window, he popped a brochure into the car and said, "Today is your lucky day, sir. Hero Homes is offering an inaugural 20% discount to the first 100 customers. What do you say—shall we go and visit the show flat at the sales office? Maybe that will change your mind." Although I was in no position to afford an apartment, I took the salesman up on his offer.

On the way, the salesman explained about the highway corridor, which was constructed to bypass the existing highway between Delhi and Gurgaon. [Fig. 8] Although it is only 29 kilometres in length, it is representative of the complexity in which the multi-scalar highway-corridors project is being executed across India. As we drove along the expressway's unfinished ruderal landscape, he painted the three-dimensional world of the "city yet to come" on the car's windscreen. He attempted to fill in the absences and gaps formed by large empty plots, unfinished facades, and patchy infrastructures with stories about the future of the highway. "The expressway will be two-storeyed with a metro train eventually running on the very top of it. There would be a convention centre and diplomatic enclave nearby, a commercial strip with shopping close by." There seemed to be no finality to the location or timeline of these urban dreams. However, the promise of proximity to this sizeable urban infrastructure, even though uncertain, started to look like a bet worth taking.

Only a few kilometres into our trip, the dreamscape came to a shattering end, and our journey was interrupted by what appeared to be an "unauthorised colony" at the end of the motorable road. A housing settlement emerged from the illegal plotting of rural land. The salesman asked me to go off-road, and we took an improvised dirt path around the colony for about two kilometres, after which the motorable sections of the expressway resumed. The salesman explained the roadblocks were temporary, and the legal litigation regarding houses

Fig. 7

falling onto the path of the expressway was nearing a resolution. He asserted that it would be wiser to buy the house now, claiming that the houses would be ready by the time the litigation was resolved. His point was that if I bet on the project's uncertainty, the profits that I stood to gain would be much larger.

In this way, the completion of the expressway was not only presented as a near-future prospect but also as a means to hedge uncertainty to potentially yield a greater return on investment. Thus, it is not just the land and the house that become speculative commodities but also the future completion of the expressway itself as a form of commodified value. In fact, none of the homes that were being sold through the sales office were actually built. They were fictional commodities against which middle-class investors could hedge. This lack of actual buildings is patched up with architectural renderings, master plans, and show flats, which attempt to recreate the distant but inevitable future.

SPATIAL DIFFERENCE

The Dwarka Expressway, initially planned in 2008 with the Delhi Commonwealth Games of 2010, was 14 years into the making at the time of writing this chapter. Millions of homebuyer investors have put bets on the uncertainty around its completion and have become entangled in its incompleteness and long-winded temporality. Although the house occupancy along the expressway remains low, at only about 20% according to the data collected by local real estate firms, about 300,000 families have lived daily improvised lives there for almost a decade now.[109] [Fig. 9–11] Then there are the lower-middle-class families that bought illegal plots in the unauthorised colony and now face the prospect of eviction when the expressway is completed. Then there are the former farmers from the region who were alienated from farming and could not find industrial work and now work as land brokers and tenement entrepreneurs in businesses, providing security and drinking water to the gated communities. Instead of successfully dislodging the pre-existing urban

Dense urban areas

Unauthorised settlements

Eviction zones

Resettlement site

Dwarka Expressway and new bypass roads

Dehli ring

National highways

State highways

Railway

Water bodies

Forests

LOCATION OF THE DWARKA
EXPRESSWAY CORRIDOR
Fig. 8

fabric and supplanting it with a new one, the state space of highway corridor seems to generate a spiralling conflict in which different social groups have become entangled in new hierarchical dependencies.

BUYING INTO THE FUTURE

It was a similar real estate pitch to the one presented above that hooked Mukesh and Sarita Khamboj into booking a house at the Ramaprastha (RP) City, one of the most significant gated projects along the Dwarka Expressway.[110]

F. 7 Billboards outside the sales office of an upcoming real estate project along the Dwarka Expressway.

F. 8 The Dwarka Expressway Corridor was proposed as a bypass to the corridor urbanisation along the National Highway 48. The lack of surveys meant that the corridor soon came into conflict with informally built unauthorized settlements. The families affected by the expressway construction were resettled after a decade-long legal battle.

Mukesh works as a travelling salesman for a farm products manufacturer. The family saw home ownership as an opportunity for investing in their retirement, thinking that they could invest in a house in a new urban extension and then, in a few years, trade it with something cheaper, making some savings in the process.

Mukesh narrates that the period before the Commonwealth Games (between 2008–2010) was a period of mass public investments. "There was suddenly a lot of construction activity, and everyone was looking to take loans and make investments. Pages upon pages of newspapers carried advertisements featuring new real-estate projects that were promising the so-called subvention scheme."

This scheme meant that after booking a house, one was exempt from paying equated monthly instalments (EMIs) for two to three years when the Dwarka Expressway and the housing projects were projected to be ready. As the entire landscape was merely agricultural fields back then, and the expressway was a mere fictional line, the subvention scheme

Fig. 9

Fig. 10

F. 9 From the belly of the infrastructure: a view of the city from under the Dwarka Expressway.

F. 10 A view from the house of Mr. and Mrs. Khamboj, in silhouette.

F. 11 Disparate settlement types coming together in the emerging urban fabric of corridor urbanisation in the Delhi region.

made the investment seem like a safe bet for the Khambojs and millions like them. It seemed like a safe buy into the future, especially for the millions of middle-class families who had missed out on the previous real estate boom in the early 2000s.

However, over a decade later, the Khambojs are still waiting for the promise of the expressway and its spectacular urban dreams to materialise. [Fig. 10] Despite the clear uncertainty around the project, new-homebuyer investors have kept investing. For example, a 2015 report on the Dwarka Expressway, prepared by the Bangalore-based realty firm Common Floor, presents this uncertainty as an investment opportunity for early investors.[111] Still, the pervasive uncertainty is not merely to do with the completion of the expressway but also with the patchy state of infrastructure in general. Instead of offering a networked municipal supply, the gated communities purchase drinking water from private water contractors, who, in turn, pump water illegally from canals and groundwater aquifers. The supply of drinking water is contingent on the continuation of the semi-legal/illegal sourcing of water by the water-tanker suppliers and is thus often uncertain. Moreover, the sharp socio-spatial polarisation between the affluent residents of the gated communities and the poorer residents, especially former farmers who lost their source of livelihood due to the project, often results in conflicts that manifest in the form of robberies and carjackings. The gated communities hire security companies to secure their compounds against the outside; however, the expressway itself, especially in its current incomplete state, becomes a flashpoint where these conflicts often break out. Thus, managing these forms of everyday uncertainty also becomes a commodity in which the consumptive residents of gated communities make significant investments. Moreover, local politicians also articulate their politics around managing this uncertainty.

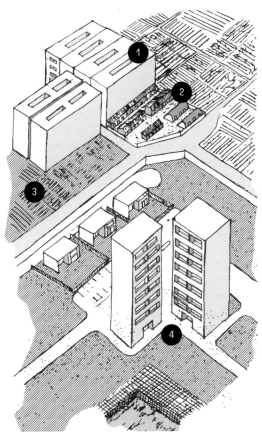

1   TENEMENT BLOCKS
(to house labour migrants)

Constructed and provisioned by tenement landlords. Insecure tenureship, high rental rates and covert local-corporate partnerships which hold migrants as a permanently temporary surplus labour.

2   TEMPORARY TENEMENTS
(for entry-level migrant tenants)

Help in solidifying claims over plotted colonies through occupancy.

3   ENCLOSED BUT CULTIVATED
(invisible enclosures)

Land is enclosed as real estate but still continues to be cultivated.

4   GATED UTOPIAS
(housing, shopping malls, entertainment, recreation)

Low occupancy rates, cater to the middle-classes and the bourgeois, amenities are provided and managed privately through resident Welfare Associations (RWAs). Based on an extensive resource consumption and cheap labour.

DISPARATE SETTLEMENT TYPES OF
CORRIDOR URBANISATION
Fig. 11

BOURGEOIS ACTIVISM AGAINST UNCERTAINTY

Mukesh claims that a major problem behind the conflict was that the requisite ground surveys were not conducted before the planning of the expressway. The source of his knowledge is his investigative work conducted with the[112] Dwarka Expressway Welfare Association (DXPWA).[113] This is an association of over 130,000 families living across 89 gated communities along the expressway. It works as a collective front of middle-class homeowners that exert collective political pressure to complete the Dwarka Expressway.

Since its formation in 2015, the DXPWA has been organising direct and collective action to manage the different forms of uncertainty surrounding the completion of the expressway. I followed their political mobilisations between 2018 and 2020 and had the opportunity to conduct key interviews with the group's core members. Pradip Rahi, the founder of the group, described that there was no incentive on the part of the state to seek a resolution with the plotted colony residents that lay in the path of the expressway. "It was as if they were letting the land prices rise sufficiently high before seeking a resolution, and it was us, who invested early into the project, who are paying the price for it in living through such prolonged uncertainty and everyday infrastructure disruptions."

To build public pressure for the express-way's completion, the individual RWAs along the expressway came together and formed DXPWA as an umbrella organisation. It organises symbolic protests to draw media attention and ridicule the protracted delays surrounding the expressway. Their protests often take the form of sit-in hunger strikes to facilitate the removal of barriers and roadblocks[114] and direct civic action, which can include laying off-road trails and even asphalt roads to close the gaps along the fragmented expressway.[115] The novelty of these protests and the bourgeois participation in them attracts significant media attention, leading to direct political interventions by powerful politicians. In one such hunger strike organised by DXPWA, the chief minister of the federal state of Haryana showed up with demolition teams and ordered direct action to remove a roadblock on live television.

One of the first public protests the DXPWA organised was at the prominent Jantar Mantar protest site in Central Delhi.[116] In the following, they launched a public interest litigation (PIL) in the High Court of Haryana.[117] In their PIL, the DXPWA argued that the prolonged uncertainty over the construction of the expressway violated their "Right to Life."[118] The incomplete nature of the project subjected them to a sub-standard quality of urban life compared to what had been promised at the time of booking their homes. The PIL facilitated the reopening of the court case between the plotted colony residents and the state, which had been under a stalemate for several years. I will elaborate upon the details of this court case in a successive section.

While the reopening of the court case led to the eventual settlement between the state and the residents of the plotted colony, it also led to a complete reshaping of the expressway itself. The expressway transformed from a regional road to a national highway, and the entire project was completely redesigned. The expressway was privatised and planned as an access-controlled toll road raised on stilts above the original road, thus closing off the urban poor who could no longer access it due to the physical barrier and exorbitant toll charges. The bourgeois activism[119] of DXPWA largely facilitated the expressway's final form, which

built upon their fears about urban insecurity.

Following the privatisation of the expressway and the settlement of the conflict with the plotted colony, several big-ticket projects were launched. One such project is the India International Convention Centre (IICC), planned as the largest convention facility in Asia at the cost of USD 4 billion.[120] Once the dust on the project had settled, several bigger companies started to enter the real estate market with high-value projects. Many of these are blue-chip companies such as Tata, Godrej, and the Hero Group. These brands have traditionally been associated with industrial manufacturing[121] and transnational conglomerates such as The Trump Organization and Emaar Properties, who acquired land aggregated by smaller local developers. [Fig. 12] These companies market their real estate ventures as premium and luxury projects, qualifiers that are not only employed as an assertion of the brand value, world-class materiality, and aesthetics of these projects but also to indicate their relative late entry into the market. The value of these projects is often several times higher than comparable projects, indicating how managing uncertainty also becomes financialised.

PLOTTING COUNTER-POLITICS

Caught at the other end of uncertainty around the Dwarka Expressway is the Kumar family, who reside in New Palam Vihar, the largest unauthorised colony in conflict with the expressway. It is, in fact, one of the unauthorised colonies in the entire Badhshahpur section of the Gurgaon district of Haryana, which was largely agrarian before 2008. Such colonies usually emerge on agrarian land outside the purview of the official master plans when an "aggregator" (colloquially referred to as a coloniser) buys rural land from individual farmers and divides it into plots that are then sold to individual homeowners.[122] The process through which such colonies are developed is colloquially referred to as "plotting" and shares close similarities with what Karaman et al. describe as "plotting urbanism."[123] What makes these housing colonies unauthorised or illegal is that while the purchase of land may be formal, it may not be legal due to the complexities in changing land use from agrarian to residential.[124] Thus, the land titles in these plotted colonies are usually not officially registered as residential, and their presence remains "off the map." This ambiguity in terms of ownership and land titles became a source of conflict between the residents of the New Palam Vihar and the expressway.

Construction of New Palam Vihar started in the mid-1990s in the rural outskirts of both Delhi and Gurgaon. [Fig. 5] A local politician belonging to the agrarian elite purchased several acres of farmland in Bhajghera village and began plotting it into plots of roughly 110 square metres in size. [Fig. 13] Nearly 10,000 plots were sold until the late-2000s; they were mainly purchased by lower-middle-class families like the Kumars. The Kumars migrated to Delhi in the mid-1980s when Mukesh Kumar took up a job in a car-driving company. After having rented houses across Delhi for over a decade, the Kumars decided to buy a plot in the colony in the mid-1990s as an investment into the future. Although the Kumars were crucially aware that their land purchase was illegal, the unauthorised colony was the only affordable housing option available to them. Furthermore, as the area was a *bahari elaka* (remote area) back then, they could not imagine a future possibility in which the state might need this land. However, in 2007, when the first chatter around the expressway emerged in the newspapers, their assumptions came crashing down. Even though the exact alignment of the expressway was still uncertain, many residents felt the state might exploit this opportunity to force evictions on their community. In 2008, when they really received eviction notices and the detailed plans of the expressway were made public, their worst fears were confirmed. Following the eviction orders, the roughly 450 affected families from New Palam Vihar formed a RWA and filed a PIL in the high court against the construction of the expressway, asserting their "Right to Life."

Similar to the investigative work by the DXPWA discussed earlier in this chapter, the litigant, RWA from NPR, began filing Right

Fig. 12

F. 12   Screen captures from an interview with Donald Trump Jr. about the launch of Trump Towers in Delhi NCR.

CONTESTATIONS
AND UNCERTAINTY UNDER
CORRIDOR URBANISATION
Fig. 13

F. 13 From top to bottom: the evolution
of 'plotting urbanism' in the
unauthorised colony of New Palam
Vihar (NPV), from agricultural
land in 2004 to the evictions
enforced by the Dwarka
Expressway between 2008 and
2019.

F.14 A view of demolished homes at the
unauthorised colony of New Palam
Vihar. The demolitions made and
evictions made way for the Dwarka
Expressway.

to Information (RTI)[125] requests to uncover the contradictions in the planning of the expressway. They addressed these requests to various government departments, such as the Delhi NCR Planning Board, the pollution department, and the Haryana Urban Development Authority (HUDA). These RTIs revealed the hidden but uncertain ways in which the state planned the Dwarka Expressway corridor. For example, no ground surveys were conducted before its planning, and environmental clearances were not sought at the regional level. Moreover, the litigants also found out that a crucially important step during the land acquisition process for the expressway was missed.[126] The litigants attempted to employ these contradictions to counter the tag of illegality that was thrust upon them by the state to justify the evictions by exposing the irregular ways the state conducted the planning of the expressway.

The state prosecution justified these irregularities and uncertainties in the planning of the expressway by falsely attaching the project to the preparation for the Commonwealth Games 2010 and claiming that this created a state of urgency, allowing for a suspension of "normal procedures."[127] Therefore, the state was unwilling to budge from its stance and wanted to undertake the evictions despite the apparent contradictions and irregularities on its part in the planning process. This led to a stalemate in the case, and the jury ordered a stay on the evictions. Nevertheless, the state continued to construct fragments of the expressway in stretches that were not under dispute. [Fig. 14] It was extended up to the edge of the colony, and a fragment of it was even constructed in a former village commons in the middle of the colony. It seems the continued construction served two intersectional purposes. Firstly, it kept drawing buy-ins from middle-class home-buyers betting on a future resolution to the conflict regardless of the uncertainty surrounding the project. Secondly, it signalled to the residents that evictions were an impending possibility.

The New Palam Vihar residents thus lived under a pervasive uncertainty and fear that the state may attempt to invent new rationalities to

Fig. 14

justify their eviction or be threatened with police violence. In my conversations with the Kumars and other members of the New Palam Vihar, it emerged that there were indeed moments when the state tried to employ police violence to enforce the evictions and that the uncertainty surrounding the evictions became an embodied and affective experience. Sushil Kumar, for example, mentioned that he suffered a major heart attack in 2012 due to prolonged uncertainty, and several others from the community complained of chronic depression. With the remaining stretches of the expressway constructed and evictions becoming an eventuality, the Kumars' struggle slowly shifted towards negotiating adequate compensation rather than seeking alternative alignments for the expressway to avoid the evictions.

IN THE PUBLIC INTEREST

The stalemate on the court case was broken only six years later, after the previously discussed PIL filed by the DXPWA. The actions undertaken by the state in the years following the stalemate allowed it to fabricate a new rationality of acting in the public interest. The state prosecutor argued that a change in the course of the project was no longer possible, as most of the stretches had been constructed and curving the road to avoid evictions would be against the "public interest." A curvy road, it was argued, citing expert opinion, would lead to a loss of fuel efficiency and a slowdown in traffic speeds.[128] Furthermore, the state argued, changing the course of the road would impede the right to property of investors who had aggregated land based on the promise of direct access to the expressway, thus leading to even more litigation from real estate developers who were hedging on the future of the project.[129]

After years of negotiations, almost 650 families from the unauthorised colonies were offered resettlement plots and compensation in accordance with the Resettlement and Rehabilitation (R&R) Policy of 2010. The resettlement plots were offered in a legally planned colony only a few kilometres from the original location. The Kumars were quite satisfied

Fig. 15

with this final outcome, and by the end of 2019, they had already constructed their new house on a plot awarded to them as part of the resettlement deal. Their emotion was echoed by several of the resettled residents because, with the resettlement, they could finally overcome the lifelong uncertainty of inhabiting the margins on land with unclear tenure. Several residents expressed that their children would not have to navigate the same kind of uncertainty of urban life as they did. Consequently, their investment in inhabiting the everyday uncertainty in the unauthorised colony had finally paid off. Furthermore, following the resettlement, several local politicians attempted to attach themselves to the success of the court case,

basing their election manifestos on the promise of managing the uncertainty related to the legal status of the colonies. A local politician, Rakesh Daulatabad, belonging to the local agrarian elite, was elected as Minister of the Legislative Assembly on the promise of legalising the colony through a process that is colloquially referred to as "regularisation."[130]

In the following years, New Palam Vihar experienced rapid upgradation. A high-shopping street evolved along the edges of the expressway, which is now used mostly by the residents of gated communities, as amenities such as small-scale shopping were not foreseen in the planning process. Moreover, local real estate agents, specialising in the sale of illegal plots, faithfully integrated the expressway in their sales pitch, with the plots closer to the expressway gaining property value. It was as if the resolution of uncertainty around the expressway and the consequent suturing of the urban fabric had opened new political and social possibilities. An interview that I conducted with a New Palam Vihar resident in the spring of 2019 best

F. 15   A traditional wrestling event (Dangal) in the former agrarian commons of Daulatabad village along the Dwarka Expressway. The urbanisation of the unauthorised colony, village, and highway corridor come into a spiralling conflict around such sites.

captures the double-edged nature of uncertainty imposed by the expressway. The resident, a former farmer from Bhajghera, claimed "the expressway brought both *sheher – keher* [urbanisation and destruction] and *aafat – paisa* [anxiety and wealth]. Although we know that we will never be able to afford to live in these towers [gated communities], and they are not even designed keeping us in mind, in the overall scheme of things, we have benefited from the coming of the expressway. Thus, altogether things are OK." [Fig. 16]

In the surveys that I conducted in New Palam Vihar, it emerged that the average monthly income of the residents was only between 10,000 and 12,000 Rupees (USD 120–170), while average property prices in the gated communities along the expressway were anywhere between 45,000–75,000 Rupees (USD 620–1,030) per square metre. Such strong difference puts formal housing and property in urban extension projects like highway corridors out of reach for the urban majority. That "things are OK" overall, despite the possibility that forces driving extended urbanisation might disrupt the lives of marginal communities, exposes what Goswami points to as the inherent contradiction in the production of state space, "the very practices that homogenised social relations also engendered new forms of differentiation and deepened socio-economic and cultural unevenness."[131] Thus, uncertainty and embracing practices of ambiguity in land titling and construction become a productive element for marginal communities in negotiating claims to urban space under extended urbanisation.

While the project described in this chapter is a regional-scale intervention, similar uncertainties operate in the extended urbanisation of urban corridors emerging at even larger scales. My research on the upcoming Delhi-Mumbai Expressway corridor that was conducted during the same period revealed similar patterns of patchiness and uncertainty over form and timeline.[132] As the ongoing attempts at corridor urbanisation continue to remain a defining feature of urbanisation in India and across the so-called global South,[133] it is perhaps necessary to pay attention to the immanent contradictions of the state space being produced through it.

NEW STATE SPACES AND THE URBANISATION YET TO COME

In concluding this chapter that journeyed through the political-economic transformations of India's ongoing highway revolution, it is perhaps pertinent to circle back to the nature of new state spaces under production. Throughout the chapter, we witnessed how the state employs highway corridors to facilitate extended urbanisation into previously bypassed agrarian regions, enabling the enclosure and commodification of land considered cheap compared to the regions that have experienced urbanisation previously. Moreover, we explored how the abstract space produced by the highway corridors is upheld through the state strategy of fossil capitalism, with the adverse environmental consequences masked under the narratives of green growth. However, as Neil Brenner aptly points out, these new state spaces are also spaces of conflict, crisis, and contradiction. We saw, for instance, how the attempts to open pathways for new highway corridors often come into conflict with a palimpsest of pre-existing claims, occupancies, and forms of dwelling, making uncertainty a constitutive feature of extended urbanisation. However, uncertainty does not necessarily paralyse technopolitical action. Instead, state power increasingly acts and governs through uncertainty. The state engages in incessant regulatory experimentation and dynamic institutional searching, inventing new rationalities for acting in the public interest to enforce such projects. Despite these attempts, the very ambiguities that produce uncertainty as a structure, such as uncertain land titles, non-formally constructed housing, and infrastructure precarity, offer possible hooks for contestation, becoming the grounds through which the "urban majority" make claims to urban space. There is thus a need to embrace the politics and practices of uncertainty in the continued efforts to push the

372

understanding of extended urbanisation beyond its narrow focus on state processes and commodification and resist its closing-down effects through diverse and imagined alternatives. This chapter did this by engaging with the burgeoning postcolonial scholarship on subaltern urbanisation focused on settlement transformations in the Indian countryside.

As I have written elsewhere,[134] in the scenario that the extensive entanglement of transport infrastructure, urbanisation, and production of state space at scales that defy commensurability is projected to continue, the question worth exploring is where these roads are heading and what kind of people and urbanisation is yet to come. Recent political events have shown how highways are not only the harbingers of urbanisation, but also flashpoints of protests and political struggles. In August 2020, farmers' unions representing millions of farmers from the states of Punjab, Haryana, and Uttar Pradesh (adjoining Delhi) occupied six major highways leading up to the city as part of the *Dilli Chalo* (March to Delhi) protests. These protests, reported to be one of the largest in global history, were organised in opposition to the introduction of new farm laws that attempted to privatise agriculture procurement in the country. The farmers built large encampments along highways, holding their ground for over a year, blocking crucial access to the city for commuters, visitors, and commodities, and ensuring the repeal of the privatisation laws. While the new state spaces under production through the highway revolution are currently characterised by militant nationalism, exclusion, and spectacles, they can also become plural, democratic, and inclusive by increasing cognisance about the extended political terrain they are producing.

Fig. 16

F.16 Stills from the film "Not Just Roads" from an interview with a resident from the unauthorised colony of New Palam Vihar. The resident speaks of the double-edged nature of urbanisation of the highway corridor, "how it has been destructive but has also brought money, so on the overall things are OK," he claims (the interview takes place between 17.30' and 18.30').

ENDNOTES

1   Simone, *For the City Yet to Come.*

2   ANI, "Purvanchal Expressway Will Become Lifeline of Development in Eastern UP: Yogi."

3   Eminent domain refers to the power of the government to take private property and convert it into public use. The law emerged during colonial India to further colonial interests, through the Land Acquisition Act (LAA) 1894. It was later enshrined into the postcolonial constitution in order to distribute land amongst the masses but ultimately became a tool to accomplish the opposite. For further discussion, see Balakrishnan, *Shareholder Cities: Land Transformations Along Urban Corridors in India,* 127–134.

4   Seth, "Explained: Politics of Uttar Pradesh Expressways."

5   FE Bureau, "Big Achievement."

6   Harvey, "Accumulation by Dispossession"; Levien, "The Land Question."

7   Transcript from PM Modi's speech at the political rally (16 November 2021). "PM Inaugurates Purvanchal Expressway, Says Earlier Govts Didn't Do Justice to UP."

8   Goswami, *Producing India.*

9   Brenner, *New State Spaces.*

10   FE Bureau, "Big Achievement."

11   PTI, "Highways Sector Can Help Nation Achieve $5 Trillion Economy: Nitin Gadkari"; Bathla, "India's Highway Revolution."

12   Harvey, "Accumulation by Dispossession," 149.

13   Levien, "The Land Question," 457; Balakrishnan, "Highway Urbanization and Land Conflicts."

14   Dubey, "Highway Construction Rate in India on the Right Track, More than Doubles in Five Years."

15   Ramaswamy, *The Goddess and the Nation.*

16   Patel, "The Long Green Revolution."

17   "The Land Question," 458.

18   PTI, "Chabahar Port's INSTC Link to Enhance Central Asia Reach: Sonowal."

19   Harvey, "Time—Space Compression and the Postmodern."

20   Complete urbanisation refers to the opening hypothesis of Henri Lefebvre in The Urban Revolution (Lefebvre, *The Urban Revolution,* 1 [1970]) where he states, "Society has been completely urbanised. An Urban Society is a society that results from a complete urbanisation. The urbanisation is virtual today but will become real in the future."

21   Brenner, *New State Spaces,* 304.

22   Although the "Right to Life" has also been misused by urban elites to force evictions of marginalised communities in Indian cities.

23   Bhan, *In the Public's Interest."*

24   Bathla, "Extended Urbanisation and the Politics of Uncertainty"; Bhan, *In the Public's Interest.*

25   Streule, "Doing Mobile Ethnography."

26   Schmid, "The Trouble with Henri," 38.

27   Schmid, 38; Hart, "Denaturalizing Dispossession."

28   Bathla and Papanicolaou, "Reframing the Contested City through Ethnographic Film"; El-Husseiny et al., "Not Just Roads."

29   A 1998 report by the IMF, "The Asian Crisis: Causes and Cures" lists falling rates of financial yields (rate of profits) for international investors as one of the major causes of the crisis.

30   This was highlighted during the speech of former Finance Minister Arun Jaitely at the launch of Bharatmala Programme (08.03.2019) and in several public speeches by Road and Transport Minister Nitin Gadkari.

31   Light, "The Golden Quadrilateral."

32   Oza, *Indian Elections: Mandate against Religious Nationalism and Neoliberal Reform.*

33   "Towards a Paradigm of Southern Urbanism," 54.

34   *Shareholder Cities: Land Transformations Along Urban Corridors in India,* 1–2.

35   Balakrishnan, 12.

36   Balakrishnan, 625.

37   Balakrishnan, "Recombinant Urbanization," 620.

38   Light, "The Golden Quadrilateral: Connecting India."

39   Nautiyal, "The Roads Ahead: Saga of Highway Development in India," 152.

40   Brenner, "The Limits to Scale?," 606.

41   Goldman, "Speculative Urbanism and the Making of the Next World City," 564, 567.

42   Levien, "The Land Question," 467.

43   *Landscapes of Accumulation,* 232.

44   Anand and Sami, "Urban Corridors: Strategies for Economic and Urban Development," 1.

45   DMIDC, "Metamorphosis."

46   Roy and Ong, *Worlding Cities.*

47   The official website of the NICDC provides the history of its transformation from DMICDC under the heading "Corporate Overview," https://www.nicdc.in/about-DMICDC.

48   Guha, "Peasant Resistance in West Bengal a Decade before Singur and Nandigram"; For further discussion, see Bertuzzo in this volume.

49   Shatkin, "The City and the Bottom Line"; Sawyer et al., "Bypass Urbanism."

50   Zeiderman et al., "Uncertainty and Urban Life," 299–300.

51   Seveilla-Buitrago, "Antinomies of Space-Time Value: Fallowness, Planning, Speculation."

52   Thieme, "The Hustle Economy," 542.

53   Zeiderman et al., "Uncertainty and Urban Life," 285; Simone, "Cities of Uncertainty."

54   Lefebvre, *De l'État*; Schmid, *Henri Lefebvre and the Theory of the Production of Space,* 464.

55   Schmid, *Henri Lefebvre and the Theory of the Production of Space,* 402–403.

56   Lefebvre, Brenner, and Elden, *State, Space, World: Selected Essays,* 238.

57   Schmid, *Henri Lefebvre and the Theory of the Production of Space,* 464.

58   Lefebvre, *State, Space, World: Selected Essays,* 20–21.

59   Goswami, *Producing India,* 103–104.

60   Brenner, *New State Spaces: Urban Governance and the Rescaling of Statehood,* 16.

61   Lefebvre, *State, Space, World: Selected Essays,* 24.

62   Bhan, "Planned Illegalities"; Bathla, "Planned Illegality, Permanent Temporariness, and Strategic Philanthropy."

63   Ramaswamy, *The Goddess and the Nation.*

64   *Roads: An Anthropology of Infrastructure and Expertise,* 187.

65   Wilson, "Plan Puebla Panama: The Violence of Abstract Space"; Monte-Mor, *Modernities in the Jungle.*

66 Rose and Mohl, *Interstate*, 98.

67 PTI, "22 Highway Stretches In India May Double Up As Airstrips: Nitin Gadkari."

68 PTI, "Delhi-Mumbai Expressway Set to Script New Age of Development for Tribal Areas: Gadkari."

69 Also highlighted during the speech of former Finance Minister Arun Jaitely at the launch of Bharatmala Programme (08.03.2019).

70 Rose and Mohl, *Interstate*, 96.

71 Malm, "The Origins of Fossil Capital," 308; Mitchell, "Carbon Democracy."

72 Wells, *Car Country: An Environmental History.*

73 Rose and Mohl, *Interstate*, 4.

74 PTI, "Govt Earned over Rs 8 Lakh Cr from Taxes on Petrol, Diesel in Last 3 Fiscals: FM Sitharaman."

75 Hein, "Oil Spaces."

76 "Mile by Mile, India Paves a Smoother Road to Its Future."

77 https://www.ibef.org/industry/roads-india.aspx.

78 Saluja, "Modi Govt Sets out on the Road to $5 Trillion with a Rs 8 Lakh-Crore First List."

79 Goswami, *Producing India*, 56.

80 Guha, "Forestry in British and Post-British India"; Sud, *The Making of Land and the Making of India.*

81 "Methodology for Estimating Carbon Footprint of Road Projects: Case Study: India."

82 Bathla and Singh, "The Delhi-Mumbai Expressway Is a Short-Cut to Socio-Ecological Disaster."

83 PTI, "Delhi-Mumbai Expressway Set to Script New Age of Development for Tribal Areas: Gadkari."

84 Dupont, "The Dream of Delhi as a Global City"; Ghertner, *Rule By Aesthetics*; Bhan, *In the Public's Interest.*

85 Bunnell and Maringanti, "Practising Urban and Regional Research beyond Metrocentricity."

86 Goldman, "Speculative Urbanism and the Making of the Next World City"; Searle, *Landscapes of Accumulation*; Gururani, "When Land Becomes Gold"; Levien, "The Land Question"; Balakrishnan, *Shareholder Cities: Land Transformations Along Urban Corridors in India.*

87 Denis, Mukhopadhyay, and Zerah, "Subaltern Urbanisation in India"; Pradhan, "Unacknowledged Urbanisation"; Samanta, "The Politics of Classification and the Complexity of Governance in Census Towns, Making a Show."

88 Samanta, "The Politics of Classification and the Complexity of Governance in Census Towns, Making a Show"; Guin and Das, "Spatial Perspectives of the New Census Towns, 2011"; Mukhopadhyay et al., "Understanding India's Urban Frontier."

89 Bathla and Duyne Barenstein, *THE [SEASONAL] ARRIVAL CITY.*

90 World Bank Group, *Demographic Trends and Urbanization.*

91 Datta, "Introduction: Fast Cities in an Urban Age."

92 Kundu, "Method in Madness"; Brenner and Schmid, "The 'Urban Age' in Question."

93 Denis and Marius-Gnanou, "Toward a Better Appraisal of Urbanization in India. A Fresh Look at the Landscape of Morphological Agglomerates," 68.

94 Pradhan, "Unacknowledged Urbanisation," 45.

95 Roy and Pradhan, "Census Towns in India," 7.

96 Duijne and Nijman, "India's Emergent Urban Formations," 14.

97 Mukhopadhyay, "Does Administrative Status Matter for Small Towns in India?"

98 Duijne and Nijman, "India's Emergent Urban Formations."

99 Bathla, "Planned Illegality, Permanent Temporariness, and Strategic Philanthropy."

100 "Slumdog Cities."

101 Mukhopadhyay, Zerah, and Denis, "Subaltern Urbanization: Indian Insights for Urban Theory," 14.

102 Simone, "Cities of Uncertainty."

103 Ghertner, "Improvised Urbanism in the Design of India's Unauthorized Colonies."

104 Karaman et al., "Plot by Plot."

105 Dubey, "Accumulation at Margins: The Case of Khora Colony."

106 Zerah, "Shedding Light on Social and Economic Changes in Small Towns Through the Prism of Local Governance."

107 Levien, "The Land Question," 480; Bathla, "Planned Illegality, Permanent Temporariness, and Strategic Philanthropy."

108 Punia et al., "Comparison of Peripheral Metropolitanisation in Haryana and Rajasthan, India"; Duijne and Nijman, "India's Emergent Urban Formations," 14.

109 Simone, *Improvised Lives: Rhythms of Endurance in an Urban South.*

110 RP City is spread over half a square kilometre (110 acres) of area with over 2,500 housing units. See http://www.ramprastha.com/.

111 Nagula, Gupta, and Singla, "Real Insights: Locality Snapshot—Dwarka Expressway."

112 Srivastava, *Entangled Urbanism*, xxi.

113 The DXPWA used to maintain a website (http://dxpwa.com) for collecting data around the delays on the expressway. However, the website is currently dysfunctional, and the group largely organises through social media channels such as Facebook—Dwarka Expressway & New Gurugram, and Twitter—DXPAssociation.

114 The Hindu, "Dwarka E-Way Homebuyers on Hunger Strike."

115 Tiwari, "Residents Build Road to Avoid Toll at Kherki Daula, Operator."

116 Singh, "Protest against Incomplete Dwarka E-Way Reaches Jantar Mantar."

117 Jha, "E-Way Delayed for 8 Years, Buyers Move High Court."

118 PILs were introduced in India in the 1970s to protect the fundamental rights of the marginalised. Communities and individuals fearing marginalisation due to state-led development projects or policies can file a PIL in the Indian court to claim their "Right to Life." Bhan, *In the Public's Interest*, 30, 111.

119 Baviskar, "Cows, Cars and Cycle-Rickshaws."

120 Sikarwar, "India Plans World-Class Convention Centre."

121 Levien, "The Land Question," 560.

122 Bhan, "Planned Illegalities," 59; Zimmer, "Enumeratig the Semi-Visible"; Bathla, "Planned Illegality, Permanent Temporariness, and Strategic Philanthropy."

123 "Plot by Plot."

124 Bhan, "Planned Illegalities," 61.

125 The Right to Information Act 2005 allows citizens to request the government for information in a time-bound manner. Its objective is to promote transparency and accountability in the working of the government. See https://rti.gov.in/.

126 Precisely, public objections regarding the land acquisition mandated under the Section 5A Land Acquisition Act (LAA) of 1870 were not followed.

127 Mittal and Sidhu, CWP-8055-2008 and connected matters (O&M), Hon'ble Mr. Justice Harinder Singh Sidhu at 23.

128 Mittal and Sidhu, Hon'ble Mr. Justice Harinder Singh Sidhu at 13, 18, 21.

129 Mittal and Sidhu, Hon'ble Mr. Justice Harinder Singh Sidhu at 12.

130 Periodically, the unauthorised colonies can be legalised through a "regularisation" process. Joseph, "Disquiet to Blame for Loss in Badshapur? BJP to Probe."

131 Goswami, *Producing India*, 9.

132 Bathla and Singh, "The Delhi-Mumbai Expressway is a Short-Cut to Socio-Ecological Disaster."

133 Balakrishnan, "Highway Urbanization and Land Conflicts," 786.

134 Bathla, "India's Highway Revolution."

BIBLIOGRAPHY

ADB. "Methodology for Estimating Carbon Footprint of Road Projects–Case Study: India." Manila: Asian Development Bank, December 2010.

Anand, Shriya, and Neha Sami. "Urban Corridors: Strategies for Economic and Urban Development." *International Growth Centre* (2015).

Angelo, Hillary. *How Green Became Good: Urbanized Nature and the Making of Cities and Citizens.* Chicago: University of Chicago Press, 2021.

ANI. "Purvanchal Expressway Will Become Lifeline of Development in Eastern UP: Yogi." *Times of India*, 16 November 2021. https://timesofindia.indiatimes.com/city/lucknow/purvanchal-expressway-will-become-lifeline-of-development-in-eastern-up-yogi/articleshow/87736101.cms.

Balakrishnan, Sai. "Highway Urbanization and Land Conflicts: The Challenges to Decentralization in India." *Pacific Affairs* 86, no. 4 (2013): 785–811.

———. "Recombinant Urbanization: Agrarian–Urban Landed Property and Uneven Development in India." *International Journal of Urban and Regional Research* 43, no. 4 (2019): 617–632.

———. *Shareholder Cities: Land Transformations along Urban Corridors in India.* Philadelphia: University of Pennsylvania Press, 2019.

Bathla, Nitin. "Extended Urbanisation and the Politics of Uncertainty: The Contested Pathways of Highway Corridors in India." *The Geographical Journal* (2022): 1–15.

———. "India's Highway Revolution." Special issue, *Architectural Review*, no. 1491 (2022): 88–91.

———. "Planned Illegality, Permanent Temporariness, and Strategic Philanthropy: Tenement Towns Under Extended Urbanisation of Postmetropolitan Delhi." *Housing Studies* (2021): 1–21.

Bathla, Nitin, and Jennifer Duyne Barenstein. "THE [SEASONAL] ARRIVAL CITY: Designing for Migrants' 'Transient Right to the City.'" *ETH MAS Housing* (2022). https://www.research-collection.ethz.ch/handle/20.500.11850/543590.2.

Bathla, Nitin, and Klearjos Eduardo Papanicolaou. "Reframing the Contested City through Ethnographic Film: Beyond the Expository on Housing and the Urban." *International Journal of Housing Policy* (10 March 2021): 1–16.

Bathla, Nitin, and Aman Singh. "The Delhi-Mumbai Expressway Is a Short-Cut to Socio-Ecological Disaster." *The Wire Science*, 6 June 2019, sec. Environment. https://science.thewire.in/environment/delhi-mumbai-expressway-nitin-gadkari-bharatmala-nhai/.

Baviskar, Amita. "Cows, Cars and Cycle-Rickshaws: Bourgeois Environmentalists and the Battle for Delhi's Streets." *Elite and Everyman: The Cultural Politics of the Indian Middle Classes*, 2011, 391–418.

Bhan, Gautam. *In the Public's Interest: Evictions, Citizenship, and Inequality in Contemporary Delhi.* Vol. 30. Geographies of Justice and Social Transformation. Athens: The University of Georgia Press, 2016.

———. "Planned Illegalities: Housing and the 'Failure' of Planning in Delhi: 1947–2010." *Economic and Political Weekly* 48, no. 24 (2013): 58–70.

Brenner, Neil. *New State Spaces: Urban Governance and the Rescaling of Statehood.* New York: Oxford University Press, 2004.

———. "The Limits to Scale? Methodological Reflections on Scalar Structuration." *Progress in Human Geography* 25, no. 4 (1 December 2001): 591–614.

Brenner, Neil, and Christian Schmid. "The 'Urban Age' in Question." *International Journal of Urban and Regional Research* 38, no. 3 (1 May 2014): 731–755.

Bunnell, Tim, and Anant Maringanti. "Practising Urban and Regional Research Beyond Metrocentricity." *International Journal of Urban and Regional Research* 34, no. 2 (2010): 415–420.

Datta, Ayona. "Introduction: Fast Cities in an Urban Age." In *Mega-Urbanization in the Global South*, edited by Ayona Datta and Abdul Shaban, 13–40. London: Routledge, 2016.

376

Denis, Eric, and Kamala Marius-Gnanou. "Toward a Better Appraisal of Urbanization in India. A Fresh Look at the Landscape of Morphological Agglomerates." *Cybergeo: European Journal of Geography* (28 November 2010).

Denis, Eric, Partha Mukhopadhyay, and Marie Helene Zerah. "Subaltern Urbanisation in India." *Economic and Political Weekly* 47, no. 30 (28 July 2012): 52–62.

DMIDC. "Metamorphosis." New Delhi: DMIDC, unknown. www.dmidc.com.

Dubey, Jyotindra. "Highway Construction Rate in India on the Right Track, More than Doubles in Five Years." *India Today*, 4 July 2019. https://www.indiatoday.in/diu/story/highway-construction-rate-in-india-on-the-right-track-more-than-doubles-in-five-years-1562333-2019-07-04.

Dubey, Shruti. "Accumulation at Margins: The Case of Khora Colony." In *Accumulation in Post-Colonial Capitalism*, edited by Iman Kumar Mitra, Ranabir Samaddar, and Samita Sens, 109–123. Singapore: Springer, 2017.

Duijne, Robbin Jan van, and Jan Nijman. "India's Emergent Urban Formations." *Annals of the American Association of Geographers* 109, no. 6 (2 November 2019): 1978–1998.

Dupont, Véronique D. N. "The Dream of Delhi as a Global City." *International Journal of Urban and Regional Research* 35, no. 3 (2011): 533–554.

El-Husseiny, Momen, AbdouMaliq Simone, Llerena Guiu Searle, D. Asher Ghertner, and Sandra Jasper. "Not Just Roads." *The AAG Review of Books* 9, no. 4 (2 October 2021): 39–52.

FE Bureau. "Big Achievement: Highway Construction in India to Hit Record Pace! To Touch 40 Km/Day in FY21." *The Financial Express*, 25 March 2021. https://www.financialexpress.com/infrastructure/roadways/big-achievement-highway-construction-in-india-to-hit-record-pace-to-touch-40-km-day-in-fy21/2219525/.

Ghertner, D. Asher. "Improvised Urbanism in the Design of India's Unauthorized Colonies." In *The New Companion to Urban Design*, edited by Tridib Banerjee and Anastasia Loukaitou-Sideris, 355–367. New York: Routledge, 2019.

———.*Rule By Aesthetics: World-Class City Making in Delhi*. 1st edition. New York: Oxford University Press, 2015.

Goldman, Michael. "Speculative Urbanism and the Making of the Next World City." *International Journal of Urban and Regional Research* 35, no. 3 (2011): 555–581.

Goswami, Manu. *Producing India: From Colonial Economy to National Space*. Chicago: University of Chicago Press, 2010.

Guha, Abhijit. "Peasant Resistance in West Bengal a Decade before Singur and Nandigram." *Economic and Political Weekly* (2007): 3706–3711.

Guha, Ramachandra. "Forestry in British and Post-British India: A Historical Analysis." *Economic and Political Weekly* 18, no. 44 (1983): 1882–1896.

Guin, Debarshi, and Dipendra Nath Das. "Spatial Perspectives of the New Census Towns, 2011: A Case Study of West Bengal." *Environment and Urbanization ASIA* 6, no. 2 (1 September 2015): 109–124.

Gururani, Shubhra. "When Land Becomes Gold." In *Land Rights, Biodiversity Conservation and Justice Rethinking Parks and People*, 1st edition, edited by Sharlene Mollett and Thembela Kepe, 107–125. London: Routledge, 2018.

Hart, Gillian. "Denaturalizing Dispossession: Critical Ethnography in the Age of Resurgent Imperialism." *Antipode* 38, no. 5 (2006): 977–1004.

Harvey, David. "Accumulation by Dispossession." In *The New Imperialism*. Oxford: Oxford University Press, 2003.

———."Time—Space Compression and the Postmodern." In *Modernity: After Modernity*, edited by Malcolm Waters, 98–118. London: Taylor & Francis, 1999.

Harvey, Penny, and Hannah Knox. *Roads: An Anthropology of Infrastructure and Expertise*. Ithaca, NY: Cornell University Press, 2015.

Hein, Carola. "Oil Spaces: The Global Petroleumscape in the Rotterdam/The Hague Area." *Journal of Urban History* 44, no. 5 (2018): 887–929.

IMF. "The Asian Crisis: Causes and Cures." *Finance and Development. International Monetary Fund*, June 1998. https://www.imf.org/external/pubs/ft/fandd/1998/06/imfstaff.htm.

Jha, Bagish. "E-Way Delayed for 8 Years,

Buyers Move High Court." *The Times of India*, 22 February 2017, sec. Gurgaon. https://timesofindia.indiatimes.com/city/gurgaon/e-way-delayed-for-8-yrs-buyers-move-hc/articleshow/57281208.cms.

Joseph, Joel. "Disquiet to Blame for Loss in Badshapur? BJP to Probe." *Times of India*, 27 October 2019, sec. Gurgaon. https://timesofindia.indiatimes.com/city/gurgaon/disquiet-to-blame-for-loss-in-badshapur-bjp-to-probe/articleshow/71780769.cms.

Karaman, Ozan, Lindsay Sawyer, Christian Schmid, and Kit Ping Wong. "Plot by Plot: Plotting Urbanism as an Ordinary Process of Urbanisation." *Antipode* 52, no. 4 (2020): 1122-1151.

Kundu, Amitabh. "Method in Madness: Urban Data from 2011 Census." *Economic and Political Weekly* 46, no. 40 (2011): 7.

Lefebvre, Henri. *De l'État*. Vol. 1049. Paris:Union générale d'éditions, 1976.

———.*State, Space, World: Selected Essays*. Edited by Neil Brenner and Stuart Elden. Minneapolis: University of Minnesota Press, 2009.

———.*The Urban Revolution*. Minneapolis: University of Minnesota Press, 2003.

Lefebvre, Henri, Neil Brenner, and Stuart Elden. *State, Space, World: Selected Essays*. Minneapolis: University of Minnesota Press, 2009.

Levien, Michael. "The Land Question: Special Economic Zones and the Political Economy of Dispossession in India." *The Journal of Peasant Studies* 39, no. 3–4 (1 July 2012): 933–69.

Light, Liz. "The Golden Quadrilateral: Connecting India." *E. Nz Magazine: The Magazine of Technical Enterprise* 4, no. 4 (2004).

Malm, Andreas. "The Origins of Fossil Capital: From Water to Steam in the British Cotton Industry." *Historical Materialism* 21, no. 1 (2013): 15–68.

Mitchell, Timothy. "Carbon Democracy." *Economy and Society* 38, no. 3 (2009): 399–432.

Mittal, Hon'ble Mr. Justice Satish Kuman, and Hon'ble Mr. Justice Harinder Singh Sidhu. CWP-8055-2008 & connected matters (O&M), Hon'ble Mr. Justice Harinder Singh Sidhu (High Court of Punjab and Haryana at Chandigarh 2015).

Monte-Mor, Roberto Luiz de Melo. "Modernities in the Jungle: Extended Urbanization in the Brazilian Amazonia." PhD diss., University of California Los Angeles, 2004.

Mukhopadhyay, Partha. "Does Administrative Status Matter for Small Towns in India?" In *Subaltern Urbanisation in India–An Introduction to the Dynamics of Ordinary Towns*, edited by Eric Denis and Marie-Helene Zerah, 443–69. New Delhi: Springer, 2017.

Mukhopadhyay, Partha, Marie-Helene Zerah, and Eric Denis. "Subaltern Urbanization: Indian Insights for Urban Theory." *International Journal of Urban and Regional Research* 44, no. 4 (July 2020): 582–98.

Mukhopadhyay, Partha, Marie-Helene Zerah, Gopa Samanta, and Augustin Maria. "Understanding India's Urban Frontier: What Is Behind the Emergence of Census Towns in India?" *The World Bank*, 19 December 2016. http://documents.worldbank.org/curated/en/378351482172055283/Understanding-Indias-urban-frontier-what-is-behind-the-emergence-of-census-towns-in-India.

Nagula, Vishal, Gaurav Gupta, and Meha Singla. "Real Insights: Locality Snapshot—Dwarka Expressway." *Bangalore: CommonFloor.com*, 2015. https://www.commonfloor.com/wordpress/wp-content/uploads/2015/09/Real-Insights-%E2%80%93-Dwarka-Expressway-Gurgaon-A-CommonFloor-Report-2015.pdf?utm_source=guide%2520commonfloor%2520survey&utm_medium=pdf%2520response&utm_content=1&utm_campaign=locality%2520report%2520-%2520guide.

Nautiyal, Santosh. "The Roads Ahead: Saga of Highway Development in India." *Indian Journal of Public Administration* 50, no. 1 (2004): 151–157.

Not Just Roads. DCP, Documentary. ETH Zurich, 2020.

Oza, Rupal. "Indian Elections: Mandate against Religious Nationalism and Neoliberal Reform." *Environment and Planning D: Society and Space* 22, no. 5 (2004): 633–638.

Patel, Raj. "The Long Green Revolution." *The Journal of Peasant Studies* 40, no. 1 (2013): 1–63.

Pradhan, Kanhu. "Unacknowledged Urbanisation: New Census Towns of India." SSRN Scholarly Paper. Rochester, NY: Social Science Research Network, 7 September 2013. https://papers.ssrn.com/abstract=2402116.

PTI. "22 Highway Stretches In India May Double Up As Airstrips: Nitin Gadkari." *NDTV*, 16 October 2016, sec. All India. https://www.ndtv.com/india-news/governments-latest-plan-planes-to-land-on-22-highways-across-india-1474802.

———."Chabahar Port's INSTC Link to Enhance Central Asia Reach: Sonowal." *Times of India*, 1 August 2022, sec. India. https://timesofindia.indiatimes.com/india/chabahar-ports-instc-link-to-enhance-central-asia-reach-sonowal/articleshow/93260369.cms.

———."Delhi-Mumbai Expressway Set to Script New Age of Development for Tribal Areas: Gadkari." *Outlook*, 16 September 2021. https://www.outlookindia.com/newsscroll/delhimumbai-expressway-set-to-script-new-age-of-development-for-tribal-areas-gadkari/2161437.

———."Govt Earned over Rs 8 Lakh Cr from Taxes on Petrol, Diesel in Last 3 Fiscals: FM Sitharaman." *The Economic Times*, 14 December 2021, sec. Economy. https://economictimes.indiatimes.com/news/economy/finance/govt-earned-over-rs-8-lakh-cr-from-taxes-on-petrol-diesel-in-last-3-fiscals-fm-sitharaman/articleshow/88281455.cms.

———."Highways Sector Can Help Nation Achieve $5 Trillion Economy: Nitin Gadkari." *Business Standard India*, 8 July 2019, sec. Economy. https://www.business-standard.com/article/economy-policy/highways-sector-can-help-nation-achieve-5-trillion-economy-nitin-gadkari-119070801260_1.html.

Punia, Milap, Rajnish Kumar, Laxman Singh, and Sandeep Kaushik. "Comparison of Peripheral Metropolitanisation in Haryana and Rajasthan, India." In *Subaltern Urbanisation in India—An Introduction to the Dynamics of Ordinary Towns*, edited by Eric Denis and Marie-Helene Zerah, 141–167. New Delhi: Springer, 2017.

Ramaswamy, Sumathi. *The Goddess and the Nation: Mapping Mother India*. E-Duke Books Scholarly Collection. Durham, NC: Duke University Press, 2010.

Rose, Mark H., and Raymond A. Mohl. *Interstate: Highway Politics and Policy Since 1939*. Knoxville: The University of Tennessee Press, 2012.

Roy, Ananya. "Slumdog Cities: Rethinking Subaltern Urbanism." *International Journal of Urban and Regional Research* 35, no. 2 (1 March 2011): 223–238.

Roy, Ananya, and Aihwa Ong. *Worlding Cities: Asian Experiments and the Art of Being Global*. Hoboken: John Wiley & Sons, 2011.

Roy, Shamindra Nath, and Kanhu Charan Pradhan. *Census Towns in India: Current Patterns and Future Discourses*. Delhi: Centre for Policy Research, 1 May 2018.

Saluja, Nishtha. "Modi Govt Sets out on the Road to $5 Trillion with a Rs 8 Lakh-Crore First List." *The Economic Times*, 24 October 2019, sec. News. https://economictimes.indiatimes.com/news/economy/infrastructure/nhai-likely-to-award-rs-8-lakh-crore-projects-over-3-years/articleshow/71711823.cms?from=mdr.

Samanta, Gopa. "The Politics of Classification and the Complexity of Governance in Census Towns." *Economic and Political Weekly* 49, no. 22 (May 2014): 55–62.

Sawyer, Lindsay, Christian Schmid, Monika Streule, and Pascal Kallenberger. "Bypass Urbanism: Re-Ordering Center-Periphery Relations in Kolkata, Lagos and Mexico City." *Environment and Planning A: Economy and Space*, 53, no. 4 (2021): 675–703.

Schindler, Seth. "Towards a Paradigm of Southern Urbanism." *City* 21, no. 1 (2017): 47–64.

Schmid, Christian. *Henri Lefebvre and the Theory of the Production of Space*. London: Verso Books, 2022.

———."The Trouble with Henri: Urban Research and the Theory of the Production of Space." In *Urban Revolution Now*, 43–64. London:Routledge, 2016.

Searle, Llerena Guiu. *Landscapes of Accumulation: Real Estate and the Neoliberal Imagination in Contemporary India*. Chicago: The University of Chicago Press, 2016.

Seth, Maulshree. "Explained: Politics of Uttar Pradesh Expressways." *The Indian Express*, 23 November 2021, sec. Explained. https://indianexpress.com/article/explained/politics-up-expressways-7634560/.

Sevilla-Buitrago, Álvaro. "Antinomies of Space-Time Value: Fallowness, Planning, Speculation." *New Geographies* 10 (2019): 18–23.

Shatkin, Gavin. "The City and the Bottom Line: Urban Megaprojects and the Privatisation of Planning in Southeast Asia." *Environment and Planning A* 40, no. 2 (2008): 383–401.

Sikarwar, Deepshikha. "India Plans World-Class Convention Centre." *The Economic Times*, 20 September 2018, sec. Industry. https://economictimes.indiatimes.com/industry/services/property-/-cstruction/india-plans-world-class-convention-centre/articleshow/65879866.cms?from=mdr.

Simone, AbdouMaliq. "Cities of Uncertainty: Jakarta, the Urban Majority, and Inventive Political Technologies." *Theory, Culture & Society* 30, no. 7–8 (2013): 243–263.

———.*For the City Yet to Come: Changing African Life in Four Cities*. Durham, NC: Duke University Press, 2004.

———.*Improvised Lives: Rhythms of Endurance in an Urban South*. Cambridge, UK: Polity, 2018.

Singh, Rashpal. "Protest against Incomplete Dwarka E-Way Reaches Jantar Mantar." *The Hindustan Times*, 25 April 2016, sec. Gurugram News. https://www.hindustantimes.com/gurgaon/protest-against-incomplete-dwarka-e-way-reaches-jantar-mantar/story-Odw7wHmRBgNLYk-7flPsN2N.html.

Srivastava, Sanjay. *Entangled Urbanism: Slum, Gated Community and Shopping Mall in Delhi and Gurgaon*. New Delhi: Oxford University Press, 2015.

Streule, Monika. "Doing Mobile Ethnography: Grounded, Situated and Comparative." *Urban Studies* 57, no. 2 (2020): 421-438.

Sud, Nikita. *The Making of Land and the Making of India*. Oxford: Oxford University Press, 2020.

The Hindu. "Dwarka E-Way Homebuyers on Hunger Strike." *The Hindu*, 11 January 2019, sec. Delhi. https://www.thehindu.com/news/cities/Delhi/dwarka-e-way-home-buyers-on-hunger-strike/article25964133.ece.

The Quint. "PM Inaugurates Purvanchal Expressway, Says Earlier Govts Didn't Do Justice to UP." *The Quint*, 17 November 2021, sec. Development and Environment. https://www.thequint.com/news/india/pm-modi-inauguration-purvanchal-expressway-up#read-more.

Thieme, Tatiana Adeline. "The Hustle Economy: Informality, Uncertainty and the Geographies of Getting By." *Progress in Human Geography* 42, no. 4 (2018): 529–548.

Tiwari, Siddharth. "Residents Build Road to Avoid Toll at Kherki Daula, Operator." *Times of India*, 1 October 2019. https://timesofindia.indiatimes.com/city/gurgaon/residents-build-road-to-avoid-toll-at-kherki-daula-operator-cries-foul/articleshow/71383016.cms.

Waldman, Amy. "Mile by Mile, India Paves a Smoother Road to Its Future." *The New York Times*, 4 December 2005, sec. World. https://www.nytimes.com/2005/12/04/world/asia/mile-by-mile-india-paves-a-smoother-road-to-its-future.html.

Wells, Christopher W. *Car Country: An Environmental History*. Seattle: University of Washington Press, 2013.

Wilson, Japhy. "Plan Puebla Panama: The Violence of Abstract Space." In *Urban Revolution Now*, 129–148. Routledge, 2016.

World Bank Group. *Demographic Trends and Urbanization*. Washington DC: World Bank, 2021. https://documents.worldbank.org/en/publication/documents-reports/documentdetail/260581617988607640/demographic-trends-and-urbanization.

Zeiderman, Austin, Sobia Ahmad Kaker, Jonathan Silver, and Astrid Wood. "Uncertainty and Urban Life." *Public Culture* 27, no. 2 (1 May 2015): 281–304.

Zerah, Marie Helene. "Shedding Light on Social and Economic Changes in Small Towns Through the Prism of Local Governance: A Case Study of Haryana." In *Subaltern Urbanisation in India—An Introduction to the Dynamics of Ordinary Towns*, edited by Eric Denis and Marie-Helene Zerah, 371–395. New Delhi: Springer, 2017.

Zimmer, Anna. "Enumerating the Semi-Visible: The Politics of Regularising Delhi's Unauthorised Colonies." *Economic and Political Weekly* 47, no. 30 (2012): 89–97.

IMAGE CREDITS

All photography from author unless otherwise stated.

All maps from author with Philippe Rekacewicz. Cartographic assistance Ecce Emanetoglu and Aikaterini Katsouli.

F. 1   https://iis.ncog.gov.in/parks/exploreParks
F. 2   National Highways Authority of India
F. 4   The Delhi Decongestion Plan – Ministry of Road Transport and Highways
F. 11   Field sketch, Nitin Bathla
F. 12   The Property Show – CNBC TV 18 (2018)
F. 13   Google Earth
F. 16   Film stills from "Not Just Roads" (2020), directed by Nitin Bathla and Klearjos Papanicolaou, www.notjustroadsfilm.com

When Extended
Urbanisation Becomes
Extensive Urbanisation

LENDING A HAND

In his elaboration of extended urbanisation, Henri Lefebvre sought, with some precision, to grasp how urban processes replicated themselves across various landscapes and historical and socio-economic situations. The conceptual conundrum was to identify how such processes entail a coherent series of manoeuvres and logics without reifying the intensely malleable, shapeshifting ways urbanisation functions to articulate and inter-calibrate divergent trajectories of spatial production. The conundrum is how to point to specific ramifications of relational density—the tying together and coordination of accumulation, resource distribution, political regulation, population movement, and territorial development—without necessarily fixing these ramifications to predetermined conceptual frameworks of exposition. It means allowing the unanticipated implications of urbanisation to feed forward into new understandings.[1]

Urbanisation not only becomes more extensive as an ongoing, increasingly dominant process of spatial production and realignment with a coherent set of constitutive dynamics but also *extends* itself into a wider multiplicity of situations and histories.[2] It offers a particular working-out of dilemmas, tipping points, and conjunctures faced by settlements. This working-out entails various equations of subsumption, adaptation, erasure, remaking, conciliation, and improvisation. Urbanisation is something that not only spreads out as a function of its own internal operations but is something contributed to through an intensely differentiated process of encounter, enabling it to change gears and operate through a wider range of appearances and instantiations. If urbanisation is extensive, it is not only in the sense that it covers more ground or becomes an increasingly hegemonic modality of spatial and social production but that it also "shows up" as a key facet in the vernaculars, institutional operations, and sectors not previously considered urban.

To be extensive is not only to impose or replicate, but also to extend, as in the sense of extending a hand and offering something to the functionality of places, bodies, and systems. Extended urbanisation, then, not only signals the progressive unfolding of urbanisation as a set of discrete processes but as a modality of extension, a means through which the operations of multiple systems and actors extend themselves to and through a world as a means to make themselves known as well as to endure.[3]

Extensivity is far from being simply virtuous or destructive. It is a process that continually repositions what exists in a particular place, at times dissipating the sense of boundedness that permits particular forms of self-recognition and, at other times, hardening boundaries as a defensive, immunological manoeuvre against the disturbances ushered in by a larger world of relevant connectivity.[4] The sufficiency of any place or territory relies upon metabolic functioning—i.e., inputs, flows, and regulations of materials and the generation of infrastructures of coordination and interoperability. As these are situated within the larger surroundings to which they are variously articulated, the compositions and character of connectivity play a decisive role in how a place maintains itself as a specific entity, a particular moment of "throwntogetherness."[5] For whom does a particular set of circumstances matter, and to what degree? How far do particular events and outcomes exert a particular impact? How does the thickening of such events and outcomes take place, and from where do they draw force and efficacy? These are fundamental questions informing the particular manners that become extensive ways of offering particular mechanisms for problem-solving.

The degree of urbanisation is not a matter of how particular instances conform or deviate from some kind of overarching normative functioning, but rather how the urban "shows up" in any specific instance of observation; that it is something potentially present in any place. The conceptual challenge, then, is not to decide upon whether something is urban or not, but rather to dynamically account for its oscillating appearances over time. In other words, any place

is articulated to something that exceeds its normative frames of recognition—its boundedness, categorisation, or sense of internal coherence. Even the most seemingly cut-off places derive their relative isolation or detachment from an engineered history of relations that act to maintain that detachment. Thus, what might be considered "rural" is partly a by-product of densities elsewhere, a hinterland perhaps on the surface, marginal to the operations of big city machines yet nevertheless possible because of them.

Relations are always materialised. They are not simply abstract, mediating frameworks but concrete objects. Relations are concretised, not as the interaction of definitive physical forms of life. Rather, they are concretised via the specific media in which they take place, the destination of the transmitted information, the name in which any messaging is enunciated, the content of that which is transmitted, and its particular procedural codification.[6] In other words, the process of *extending*—the very acts of touching, engaging, intersecting, inserting, and resonating—is the materialisation of the relation, the articulation of one place, one operation, and one functioning to another at the heart of urbanisation processes.

This chapter is largely descriptive, touching on the various modes of extending. Extending is not simply a matter of urbanisation overspilling its familiar forms or reaching out into various hinterlands. Extending also entails the expansion of the value form of the experience of residing and operating in urban contexts. It entails the extension of time from unilateral trajectories of past, present, and future into temporal experiences that thoroughly entangle these designations into a complex weaving of cycles, ruptures, continuities, and inversions. The objective of this chapter is to address the multiplicity of these extending processes as a means to better grasp the extensiveness of contemporary urbanisation.

TERRITORIES OF EXPERIENCE

The extending of relationality, so crucial to extended urbanisation, is continuously increased through various forms of calculation. Determinations of *who can do what, with whom, under what circumstances,* and what can be produced from these efforts are increasingly subject to a form of *relationship-making* taken over by integrated systems that convert experiences of all kinds into *interoperable data.* That is data that can be compared across different kinds of locations, bodies, protocols, and operations.[7]

The expansion of capital depends upon not only the colonising of specific resources located in particular places and the subsequent captivation of populations as labour for the extraction of those resources but also the colonisation of multiple operations of organisation and cognition as well. Value formation is not simply anchored in maximised access to cheap resources and labour but in forms of spatial production that entails not only the consolidation of territory but the proliferation of territories of experience as well.

These territories of experience entail the creation of experience as a commodity, as something bearing particular symbolic values. Urbanisation not only reflects the expansion of industrial production and consumption but also the increasing differentiation of space through the production of experience itself, in part made possible through the colonisation of the sensibilities and bodies of diverse peoples. Urbanisation reflects both a reaching outwards into a larger world and an intensive differentiation in the very character of a "locality"— its punctuation according to a more extensive grammar of experience and conceptualisation. In this way, the clear differentiation between a local and a global becomes blurred.

On the one hand, newly built environments are conceptualised and curated as promising the capacity to hold all kinds of experiences. Drawing on the notion of "recentration" posited some decades ago by Sassen, an urban core is expected to facilitate a wide range of synergies across sectors.[8] Rather than being siloed as discrete functions, experiential territories are imagined as an arena of continuous recalibration and mutual shaping that is supposed to reorient existing systems of valuation. As part of the general shift of surplus value away from labour to the production of "lifetimes,"[9] the loosely demarcated terrain of non-stop experience becomes a critical mode not only of commodification, but of the very ambiguation of what constitutes an "economic object." The access to "experience" and the always shifting, uncertain measures of its worth and substance, addressed largely through the ability to prolong and widen it, becomes an overarching priority.[10]

On the other hand, large swathes of urban regions are intensely segregated and particularised according to narrowly drawn backgrounds, interests, and capacities. For example, the popular practices of cosmopolitanism that had once characterised the everyday lives of working-class districts have become increasingly unaffordable. Access to experience becomes increasingly curtailed for many residents, thus instituting new kinds of divides and inequities that exceed income. The capacity to have relations, and thus experience, is something subjected to shifting criteria of eligibility, as well as something to be costed and worth the accrual of debt.

The politics of relation-making through data also becomes a critical facet of capitalist-practised urbanisation. Urban spaces may seem replete with standardised built environments and highly formatted management technologies and systems. Yet, their apparent homogeneity requires the work of many apparatuses, organisations, and actors capable of calibrating the volatilities of financial architecture with the specificities of a particular context.[11] Whatever the built environment may look like, its viability depends on the cultivation of mutable social entities capable of communicating new needs, desires, and practices that *continuously* remake what it means to "inhabit" the spaces being *redeveloped.*

The proliferation of relationality and territories of experience, while tying things down to particular formats of mutual causation and implication, also induces increased levels of uncertainty as to what particular facets of things are worth paying attention to. It becomes increasingly difficult to bind particular fields of relevance about what factors are important to attend to and what variables are actually at work constituting the disposition of any particular situation.[12] In a situation where everything is potentially relevant to consider and, yet, where decisions must be made and actions undertaken, ensuing events are much less subject to probabilistic calculations among already-weighted variables than they are to forms of pre-emption. For instance, anticipating contingency and instability and then folding that expectation into the very operations of production.[13]

Here, the question is, how do you hedge against the risks generated by exponential increases in the factors considered relevant to productivity and profitability? It is something that requires a way of visualising and calculating how behaviours, events, personal conditions, capacities, and inclinations exert particular effects—in various combinations of variables without the certainty of knowing which combination will be actualised on any given occasion.[14] Generating the multiplicity of such hedges, of such visualisations of the various interactive forces of an increasing number of variables, thus, drives the expansive production of interoperable data and a deep relationality.[15]

If continuous experience and its subsequent territorialisation, as in some instances the erasure and, in others, the hardening of boundaries, becomes increasingly important as the locus of value production, the very trajectories of "development" themselves must be reconsidered. As such, the future is not so much suggested by the present as something imbued within the very existence of any actual situation. Whereas urban development and expansionism remain driven by the attempt to maximise ground rent, as "land" itself becomes something more "social," in the sense of a continuously reconfigured terrain of effects, desires, propensity, and cognition; value is increasingly located

by securing the position to shape contingent future eventualities. Whereas risk management is centred on simultaneously hedging on and against particular unstable scenarios—through instruments such as collateralised debt swaps—the primary purveyors of urban development are increasingly seeking to manage a capacity to give rise to eventualities, no matter what shape or behaviour they might assume.

As such, urban infrastructural development not only constitutes a guess on where the city is "going," it also elicits the possibility of being part of a cascading and lateral chain of tropes, hedges, and realignments not necessarily imprinted with the weight of particular causations or history. It attempts to instigate a temporality "set loose" from calculation—a process of associating place, people, institutions, finance, and politics that ramifies in unanticipated ways. This indifference to an outcome, as the means to make use of any outcome, is, in turn, indifferent to its impact on the majority of urban inhabitants. Yet, speculation only skirts devolving into chaos because it depends on the fraught and increasingly vulnerable everyday efforts, ethical work, cooperation, devices, and experiments of the majority who "keep things together" but do not recognise themselves in any specific form or set of rights.[16]

THE PLURALITY OF TEMPORALITIES

RUNNING OUT OF TIME

When too many variables are potentially relevant to the success or failure of an initiative, and when computing speed and capacity simply generate additional uncertainty over what constitutes a fortuitous disposition, uncertainty itself becomes valorised as a critical resource.[17] With this, then, is an instigation of a temporality set loose from calculation, something that encompasses and exceeds speculation. Such temporality not only operates within the rubrics of the financialisation of risk as a means of hedging a multiplicity of probable futures for how a particular infrastructure will operate and the value it will have. This instigation also aims to posit infrastructure as *detached from reason* within a scenario that cannot be fully calculated now and which imbues it with adaptability to futures where no matter what happens, there is the possibility of recouping something that cannot be specified.

If, as Luciana Parisi points out, a programmatic calculation is not simply the execution of instructions but a machine ecology thoroughly infected with randomness, then digital infrastructures potentiate "unapprehendable" scenarios not easily subsumed to the dictates of techno-capitalism.[18] As soon as actualities come together, as soon as supposedly discrete events and objects feel each other out, are placed in some kind of relationship with each other, and are assessed in terms of their impact on each other or their respective genealogies of appearance, no matter how prescriptive or limiting their interactions might be, they always suggest a potential of what might have taken place, of non-denumerable dispositions. The compositions of gatherings, the particular ways they unfold, who can do what with whom, when, and how, are critical for how a worldly sensibility embodied within larger deployments of environmental sensing is rendered for a specific human endurance and of making the world appear to us in ways that open up multiple spaces for its reshaping.

This notion of worldly sensibility can be contrasted with the standardisation of time. Much has been written about the homogeneous character of time in a globalised world where every space appears accessible to scrutiny, where somewhere, trading floors are always open, and spatial products seem to adopt similar forms and modes of operation.[19] There is the well-worn image of the businessperson constantly in motion whose life plays out in a series of cities where airports, hotels, restaurants, conference centres, upscale residential communities, and leisure zones all look the same. Simply from the look of things, she would never know where she is located on any given occasion.

The disjointed circadian rhythms of the incessant traveller are the primary means through which she recognises the difference among her locations, evened out by the affective flatlines of pharmaceutical interventions. Within a universe of non-stop transactions, differentiations between night and day, work and play, friendship and commerce are frequently blurred, as are the objectives of social interchange. While instrumentality may prevail as the predominant modus operandi of action, it is often unclear for what purpose it is deployed. Certainly, self-aggrandisement may be an instrumental goal, but the *self* to be *aggrandised* becomes an increasingly elusive and vague entity, partially reflected by the incapacity of people to be alone and detached from their mediums of connectivity. Again, we find an urban resident who is permanently "activated," always needing new experiences and relationships.

As indicated earlier, the nearly decimated publicity of urban life gives rise to intensely divided and segregated cities. The "public city"—with its commitment to an equitable distribution of affordances, even when acknowledged as a nearly impossible goal—sought to imbue urban existence with a common orientation, a shared knowledge among different walks of life, where each person participated in a relationship that superseded those differences and anchored them in relevant, resourceful, and mutual interactions.[20] Now, throughout most of the urban world, residents view themselves as residing in divergent zones that have little to do with each other, even when it is structurally possible to chart out the interdependencies. Even as the rationales of urban administration fluctuate between more spatially encompassing territories of coordination and decentralising competencies and municipal power, the coherence of the city as a felt object and a locus of shared existence across a demarcated territory has largely dissipated. The commonality increasingly depends upon the trappings of large symbolic manoeuvres—megaevents, sports teams, or nationalistic invocations.

Institutions of any kind find it increasingly challenging to suture together the different spaces and times of urban residents. In some cities, shared religious identification might produce a strong sense of commonality, like the mega-churches in Lagos, even as they intensely compete with each other or, more typically, generate thousands of small units. Micro-territories become sites of intense competition over loyalties and trading opportunities. The wealthy and middle-class retreat to highly secured zones set apart from the unruly fabric of the "old city" as the poor find limited security in their own highly defended zones, often impervious to any official policing. Ironically, the semblance of what we might recognise as community life is increasingly the by-product of a situation where particular territories are "hemmed" in by insalubrious environmental conditions and poor transport infrastructure. They become the accidental pockets of continuity in a setting that has undergone a substantial spatial transformation.

As the working classes and the poor are pushed further into the periphery of urban regions or entrench themselves in areas of the urban core otherwise too expensive or complicated for upscaling development, their role as a hinge of connectivity—i.e., their provision of affordable inputs and services for residents across a city—also diminishes. So does the heterogeneity of time that the "majority districts" embodied, with their variegated rhythms of production, provision of services around the clock, the ebbs and flows of publicly enacted making, marketing, playing, socialising, worshipping, fighting, and deliberating. But this diminution is not a unilateral trend.

Many facets of life that have historically characterised "majority districts" continue to endure, albeit with the need to spend more time trying to sort out daily routines that ask too much from too many. These districts may be replete with intensely differentiated household compositions, entrepreneurial networks that hold too many one-room operations, or too many workers looking out for each other. Eating, sleeping, working, and deciding may increasingly occur in entangled spaces with no clear identities, which are sometimes fought over by clear sides. Residents may have to consider too many variables, watch out for too many potential interferences, and spend too much time avoiding

or resolving conflicts. They are constantly doing something but may be increasingly unsure about its meaning and value. Still, these districts provide the semblance of stability and seemingly inexhaustible resourcefulness. But time is less a backdrop here than something that has to be continuously reinvested. Endurance seems overly leveraged rather than a clear consolidation of discernible assets. Yet, it generates a life that cannot be considered precarious even when it affixes itself to sentiments and expectations that would seem to induce precarity.

As more residents are pushed out or voluntarily locate themselves at the physical peripheries of cities, time is increasingly measured in terms of commuting and traffic. In Mexico City and Jakarta, four hours is the average daily commute time. For families, maintaining a sense of household cohesion is measured in terms of small affective attainments,[21] e.g., the ability of a mother to return home in time to say bedtime prayers with her children. In Delhi's many poor neighbourhoods, male breadwinners are home only on weekends because available work is so far away, leaving the domestic management, as well as the maintenance of the district itself, to women. This is work that is not recognised by the men, who, when they return on the weekends, tend to act as if they are the ones in charge. There simply is not sufficient time to curate the once intensely textured social fabric that intertwined diverse lives with each other.

THE COMPLICITY AND INTERDEPENDENCY OF TEMPORALITIES

The heterogeneity of time is less a collective composition within specific places than a matter of highly stylised individual itineraries moving across urban spaces in the pursuit of better opportunities and resources. As the embodiment of a public enunciation of commonality, people in particular places being enjoined to a larger orbit of belonging, the state often seems to no longer have the legal, political, or financial means to produce a sense of belonging. If residents piece together a shared sense of identity with a city or region, it is increasingly because of their navigation of it through continuous circulation.

For urban youth in the global South, particularly, the ability to circulate becomes an overarching value.[22] Even though short-term employment contracts are the norm, and even though the belief that once one attains a job, it should be held onto at all costs, youth in cities such as Jakarta, Abidjan, and Hyderabad normally change jobs every couple of months, using an infrastructure of cheap boarding houses and rooms for rent to expand their orbits across wider swathes of the urban region. A more extensive circulation of individuals in search of better opportunities then, itself, constitutes an income opportunity for residents to convert space in their homes into short-term rentals. Particular places then exude an atmosphere of transiency, of people coming and going, which may destabilise local solidarities but also provide a medium of connections to the larger surroundings.

If the simultaneous erasure of time's heterogeneity and its particularisation through intensified spatial division appears to be an essential characteristic of contemporary urbanisation, the extension of urbanisation also underlines the simultaneous existence of many temporalities. Here, different ways of doing things, transacting, buying and selling, making and distributing, deliberating and deciding are *extended* to each other. Rather than a multiplicity of times being subsumed into a standardised version across much of the south, discrepant temporalities tend to coexist, even if the terms of coexistence tend to disallow the capacity of any one of them to posit their own trajectories of implication.

The time of bazaar, the festival, the factory, the neighbourhood, the coordinates of modernity, the time of extended family and kinship relations, the time of religious devotion, the time of diurnal and nocturnal markets, the time of administrative bureaucracies all coexist, not as individual tracts, not as the rhythms of autonomous worlds, but as pressure points that avail any operation to the exigencies and operational practices of the other. In a world of logistics, just-in-time production, and constantly recalibrated commodity chains, the bazaar—that multifaceted commercial system that integrated individual merchants and trades, that provided credit to those unable to access formal banking mechanisms, that mobilised political sentiment, that charted out specific geographies of articulation, that shifted resources across various kinds of social, geographic, and religious ties, that established the price of things based on considerations that far exceeded those of supply and demand, and that shaped the structure and settlement of built environments that continue to thrive. It thrives not on the basis of what it was and the implications of its own logics and operations but because those very logics and operations offer a resource to so-called modern economies and to advanced logistical operations when those economies and operations run into difficulty when they confront choke points or blockage.

The implicit design of urban economies elaborates on semi-permeable interfaces amongst varying temporalities. There is just enough of a solid, definitive boundary to enable the ongoing recognition of a specific time's coherence, but it is a porous boundary that can be "reverse engineered" into incorporating or adhering to discrepant times when needed.

In this instance, extensive urbanisation is not the unfolding of a single temporal format or the imposition of a standardised time—although there may indeed be elements of each—but rather the *extending* of diverse temporalities towards each other. Here is an urbanisation of temporality itself, a process of switching back and forth, changing temporal gears, accelerating, slowing down, and diversifying the rhythms of enactment so as to complexify the sensory field of urban life. This process engenders a broader range of implications and behavioural possibilities and, as such, modalities of valuation.

Capital works here less as the subsumption of life to the dictates of exchange and the financialisation of risk[23] than it does as the proliferation of times, caught in a compulsive dance, availing themselves to each other.

The implications of this availing are not always clear or measurable; it is not always clear what these times do for each other. In the case of the bazaar, it is evident that as the once predominant mode of the urban economy from Bombay to Tehran to Lagos to Cairo, it can no longer exist within its own terms. The bazaar must reinvent itself in other ways, such as participating in currency arbitrage or real estate investment to leverage the capital necessary to refund its own defining logics and recuperate from the loss of some of its functions to different "modern" institutions. At the same time, modern economies must turn to the bazaar as the most effective means of circumventing their own constraining regulations or excessive competition.

Not dissimilar, a fundamental consequence of the media is to not just simply link causes and effects, related circumstances and behaviours or connected causal processes and cultural practices. Instead, it is to constitute such distinctions for the collective that rely on such media to condition, stabilise, or transform what is understood to be a causal process versus a cultural practice, to draw a line between cause and effect or a circumstance and behaviour (and so forth). As Paul Kockelman points out: "Information is something that has been deeply transformed by particular modalities of science, technology, and economy such that the values in question seem to have become radically portable: not so much independent of context, as dependent on contexts which have been engineered so as to be relatively ubiquitous, and hence ostensibly and erroneously 'context-free'; not so much able to accommodate all contents but rather able to assimilate all contents to its media logics, and hence, ostensibly and erroneously 'open contexts'."[24]

Here, the experience of enclosure is not defined by a set of stable, unequivocal boundaries, but rather by its sheer open-ended nature, its capacity to make almost anything that exists, in the end, be about itself.

AMBIGUOUS BOUNDARIES

Still, the enfolding of space and populations by and through urbanisation processes generates a wide range of unanticipated outcomes, such as resistance, the diminution of social capital, waste, loss of productivity, and alienation. These are compensated through the resuscitation of something of a time already past. While the capacities of those resuscitated times may simply be reified as components or appendages of some overarching logic of capital accumulation, their endurance does signal the possibility of unanticipated apertures. While boundary lines may be constituted and policed to ensure a particular osmosis among different worlds and times, there is something about the very act of inscribing boundaries that potentially disrupts the very function they were intended to serve.

So, despite the ambition of scaling the urban in terms of the calculations of economy, there remain spaces of uncertainty that available symbolic and semiotic manoeuvres cannot suture. In part, the technologies of division and boundary-making required for the reflexive consideration of relations—i.e., the ability to trace the individuality of components and their interactions with each other—derive from a calculated blindness. If the urban is not so much a particular kind of space or time but rather a field through which both space and time can be differentiated simultaneously in all kinds of ways, then the urban is *indifferent* to any particular formation or content at any given moment. If this is the case, then our ability to consider specific spaces, people, and events that take place within the urban environment depends on being blind to this indifference.

Urbanity then operates on itself in and through these spaces of contingency. It is in the interstices between emerging constructs and whatever is withheld from the realisation that the urban works out its rhythms, narrative tendencies, and relational dynamics. Here, the idea that they *might have been actualised* haunts whatever is brought to life. This "might have been" is always there, always proximate, as some form of a "future past" that is to come but already operates in the present.

The implantation of the axioms of capital within specific contexts requires their translation into the local vernaculars of how things are done. Faced with the problematic disjunctions precipitated by the confrontation with capital, vernacular methods of doing things must find ways to individuate themselves within these axioms. If this is the case, the generalisability and singularity of urban formations can be narrated, but not without causing a particular spatio-temporal collapse. The resultant relations are not just integration, subsumption, or fragmentation. Something else happens through a complex mirroring process, a series of parallax recursions and gazes that add ambiguity to the differentiating inscription—i.e., is it local or global, here or there, them or us? It becomes difficult to determine *what time it is.* Is it the continuity of some "same old story," the reproduction of the endlessly "new," or the non-contradictory simultaneity of contradiction itself? We can be sure that relations both compose and are composed, depending on the scale of observation and the starting point of narration (e.g., Luhmann)[25]—we can never be certain about which of these dimensions we are observing at any given moment.

Here, the matter of time becomes critical, especially the extensiveness of temporalities. If capital has colonised space and bodies and the particularities of their operations and forms, it has also colonised time, not by subsuming it into a standardised format, but by enabling multiple temporalities to coexist as instantiations of flexible rhythms and continuous adjustment.

THE EXTENSION OF FORM

FINDING A PROPER FORM

Urbanisation has always been a matter of form. For in order to navigate the intensive relationalities of urban life, form was necessary as a delineation of space, as a means of precluding matters from simply becoming a blur, to maintain the sense of actors being able to go from "here" to "there," and of crafting particular domains that enabled actors to know what was expected of them and what to expect.

For, relationships are always moving across other relationships, turning themselves inside out and outside in, opening up possibilities and closing other ones down. At the same time, relations are twisting each other into particular kinds of knots. Sometimes they act as analogies or necessary contradictions for each other so as to pre-figure particular kinds of relations as essential to the exclusion of others. For example, there is no inevitable or necessary reason why kinship relations should be the predominant locus around which households are formed. But they become critical metaphors for each other. Kinship is turned into the household that continues to "turn" to kinship as its moral, expressive underpinning.[26] Similarly, neighbourhoods adapt "familial" feelings and obligations.[27]

But residents must also find ways to pay attention to or concretise the ensuing relationships based on these analogies. In Marilyn Strathern's ethnographies, relations can unfold without overarching reasons for doing so.[28] They can seemingly expand to encompass all kinds of actors and situations. But if relations are to be activated and recognised as operative in the daily lives of individuals and societies, then there must be some means for them to be recognised. This only occurs if they assume a particular *form*, an aesthetic that enables them to appear and be properly recognised.

While Western economies may make the terms explicit for recognising the specific characteristics of objects, for Strathern, objects exuded their own animate powers and means of personifying relations. Engagements had to be crafted, elicited, and designed so that people could see who they were so that there could be something to be exchanged—perspectives about things—that were products of the relationship itself. People have to be able to see rather than simply be within relationships, while visibility requires particular forms.

In cities, residents often initiate particular activities, such as making markets, improving the built environment, managing festivals, or undertaking small entrepreneurial activities to signal their willingness to explore collaborations beyond the function of these activities. These activities become devices for finding a proper form capable of exchanging perspectives. They explore ways of being together that rely upon making relationships visible in the moment. But they can also serve as a platform for residents to feel out the possibilities of collaboration that are not yet and perhaps never will be visible. As such, what they have in common is the interplay of the visible and invisible. It is not just a vision at work but also atmospheres of feeling and intuitive experimentation with relational devices and interfaces that often lack permanence and solidity.

The working out of the city's interweaving relationalities also involves actions *untaken*. Individuals have to establish a sense of proportionality: What is it about themselves and their capacities that are to be extended to others, and what do these acts of self-extending indicate about what is being withheld, in part, as a lure to incite the engagement of others? This working out of proportionality is not merely the calculations of self-interest. It is also the sculpting of a field of affordances that shapes the connections, interdependencies, and autonomies that people conceive and operationalise with each other. So, any social notion is always "out of joint," never assumed as a stabilised whole. Instead, it is an ongoing anamorphic deformation of systemic entities, as individuals are the carriers of social affordances and memory, and societies are the parts of ongoing transformations of personhood.[29]

This notion of affordances and working out of proportion is particularly evident in cities where the operations of formal governance institutions are sometimes constrained by limited consolidations of authority or by-laws and policies largely inapplicable to the characteristics of the populations and urban dynamics at work. These are places where residents must build residences, livelihoods, transportation, and administration on their own. These processes of auto-construction depend upon intricate ways of allocating land and opportunities and working out divisions of labour with complementary efforts. It is a matter of enabling individuals to experiment with their own singular ways of doing things but in concert with others.

What are the contemporary implications of such relational economies whose definition and scope may never be fully known? How do they play out in conditions where the dispossession of belonging, identity, and assets is very concrete? How do urban inhabitants mediate between the compulsion to turn bodies and lives into logistical instruments—being at the "right place at the right time" unimpeded by history—and slow circulation down sufficiently to be able to reflect on their own actions? How do they maintain some ground to build a sense of memory and a narrative about where they come from? Such are the means to anticipate possible forward trajectories to decide to act instead of succumbing to paralysis or constant anxiety.

The conundrum of urban life is managing the interstices between the accelerated and extensive circulation of things—a process that produces a density of dispositions and a continuous unsettling of identifications—*and* stabilising a population that renders bodies traceable and available for specific functions.[30] If the settling of accounts, that is, the capacity to tell how people are related to each other, is potentially unsettled by spiralling circuits of mobility and exchange, how do urban bodies coalesce in ways that incorporate the overall fluid densities of urban life? How do they deter expending inordinate amounts of energy defending particular modalities of being social from such urban volatility and thus enable them to recalibrate their coexistence with each other in ways that adapt to continuous movement, but in a manner where they continue to experience themselves as enjoined?

The elaboration of the social that mediates these questions cannot simply be the implementation of specific laws or structures of commonality. Instead, the social as an experiential milieu is an economic matter of combining whatever is at hand, whether the elements seem to go together or not, combining ways of tying things down and letting things go.

Such combinations are not the products of prescribed formulas; they are not pieces of a puzzle pre-designed to fit with others. They are, instead, combinations that reflect expenditures of effort, of an often inexplicable interest, enthusiasm, and patience on the part of individuals and groups to processes and events that they do not fully understand or view as relevant. In the context of urban life, with so many bodies, events, dimensions, and transactions that touch human and non-human residents in so many varying ways, the dilemma is always one of alignment with how one operates in the "crossfires" of such post-plural intersections. To be sure, adaptations cannot rely upon defensive or immunological manoeuvres alone. They also require active assertions of emplacement, opportunism, belonging, and risk in the face of all the things that can draw a person into various associations beyond their control. *It is a matter of things extending themselves to each other.*

STRANGE FORMS OF TIME

Extended urbanisation, as a process of urbanisation extending itself to and through various modalities of existence, also entails a reconsideration of the notion of "form." For urban form has long been the preoccupation of observers seeking to define urbanity's key components. The urban is expected to assume a specific look, to be availed of particular contents. But what happens when we consider urbanisation as a process extended beyond the centrality of particular "inhabitants" of the urban and beyond particular moments and modalities of reflexivity? In other words, who is doing the observing, under what conditions, and are they dependent upon what kinds of other labour or space-making? Form is the product of politics, of who gets to see and say what. The extensiveness of urbanisation then also entails the ways in which it is extended across the perceptions and geographies of those who have long been either disqualified as insufficiently urban or those who have, through the work they have done to support the reflexive consideration of the urban form, implicitly generated other forms removed from visibility.

While it is inevitable that comparative urban analysis will revolve around efforts to maintain the urban as a universal object of geographic focus and, as such, constitute the horizon-limit for the theory's revisability, any definitive identification of a given place or process as "urban" remains *both* elusive and possible. When Eduardo Kohn's Runa collaborators in Ecuador identified the vast surrounding rain forest—the domain of the spirit masters— as an underground "Quito," they were pointing to form as a strange but nonetheless worldly process of pattern production and propagation, one whose peculiar generative logic necessarily comes to permeate living things (human and non-humans) as they harness it.[31] While this forest has long been important to rubber and oil extraction, and has, in recent years, become intensely financialised in terms of both its "subtraction from extraction" in carbon credits and speculation on continued extraction, its urbanisation is not simply the degree of its external articulation, it also rests in its being experienced as "urban" by those who reside within.

Kohn emphasises the spontaneous, self-organising apperception and propagation of iconic associations in ways that can dissolve some of the boundaries we usually recognise both inside and outside. These are not symbolic connections requiring conventions of cultural meaning that generate and pattern differences. Instead, form blurs the lines of distinction as each action and entity flows into the other without cause or effect, without knowing what happened first. The ways particular sounds are associated with images connoting danger and the ways that subsequent reactions are signals for others to alter their behaviours, in turn, precipitate repetitions of the original sound.

Details here are less marks of distinction than they are conveyors of thoughts and feelings, "passing through," with resonance or a sympathetic charge. So, when Kohn says we no longer ask thought to produce a specific outcome or "return," our observations of what we "sense" in the world and in our minds become self-similar iterations. Even as Amazonian forests were objects of extractions and ruination, the capture of wealth could only take place by accessing these associations—i.e., the conjunctions of physical and biotic patterning in which this wealth was ensconced. The rivers were shaped by the forest embankments, which were, in turn, shaped by the flows of the river generating specific conditions to grow rubber trees. Through this very logic of patterning, the Runa experience the forest as Quito, an urban domain. While the "actual" Quito may look upon this forest as a domain of resource exploitation that is crucial to its own urban development, the Runa look upon Quito as an undeveloped city, a rudimentary imitation of the forest's vast "urban fabric." Here, the value of form is not that of a Platonic ideal but of matter emerging from its own complexity. It is the mimetic archives of an embodied sense, the propagation of self-similarity, and its constraints and potentials (how we are *inside form*—e.g., finding, dreaming, extracting something, anticipating how the world anticipates me anticipating it).

Just as notions of the urban are being extended across multiple spatial and temporal formations, so too are the modes of divergent inhabitation, no longer contained by or cohered within the once predominant form of the human as "Anthropos." The bracketing of cities as the embodiment, performance, and culmination of urbanisation processes while maintaining the façade of distinctive jurisdictions is subject to intensive porosities and fragmentation. Cities exhibit a protracted history as differentiation machines yet still seem obsessed with citing the "proper name" of their normative inhabitant, "the human," as an entity prohibitive of being anything else than what it is. In other words, the human is an inhabitant, a mere facet of a more extensive system, not potentially intertwined with various ecologies and life worlds.[32]

The city existed as the locus through which certain inhabitants could reflect on their being as a singular prerogative that is untranslatable across other modalities of existence. It was the place that formed a "we" unrelated to anything but itself. Yet this "we" was inscribed as the node whose interests and aspirations were to be concretised through the expropriation and enclosure of critical metabolic relations.[33] The city's formation of the "human" also required the occlusion of a wide range of human activities that could not be easily translated or reduced to labouring bodies.

Here, the figure of the black body looms large as something that cannot be settled even as it clears the way for settlement. Here, the unsettled, dismembered body, not immediately convertible into the figure of sheer labour, elaborates an almost phantasmagorical space of intersections—part human, part vegetative, monstrous, demonic, exotic, liminal, and libidinal. Here is the interweaving of the body with a bush, dirt, swamp, rain, and cacophonies of rhythm. This is a space beyond inhabitation, yet one that can be lived with.[34]

This is a geography that is displaced from any certain utterance or exposition. This is a geography constituted from the lapses in a surveillant and punitive gaze that cannot maintain its sovereignty if it looks too long or too longingly. It is constituted by the illusions of self-assurance of domination's efficacy, where the masters think there is no need to look upon what is essentially nothing anyway. The job of subjugation is already done.

The conversion of blackness into forced labour *and* a monstrous form of human exceptionality in the long march of "moderns" to a bell jar existence in the rarefied enclosures of sense and domesticity has kept cities alive. In contrast to the white urban body with its sense of individual responsibility and free will, black bodies were to intertwine themselves with thick fabrics of complementarity and affordances, of dust becoming flesh and flesh neon; without everything packed into a density of contact, of the discrepant rubbing up against each other in multiple frictions, sparks that ignite chain reactions. Without these webs of many crammed causations looking out for any possible vehicle of release, there would have been no city. Blackness was, then, not simply a vehicle to space things out, to engender order, but also to connote the chaos of intermingling, the loss of boundaries, and the dissipations of propriety.

The blackness of urban life is also found in the inexplicable instances of what might be seen as a form of rogue care. In the aftermaths of incessant evictions and evisceration of the attempts of black people to abide by the terms of normative urban existence, of being situated in the most toxic and uncertain environmental conditions, blackness also connotes an intertwining of ruined landscapes, making abodes, gardens, ceremonies, and infrastructures of support and communication that operate under the radar. This is not to underestimate the casualties or precarity of livelihoods, nor is it to turn attention away from the substantial accomplishments of alternative urbanisms that can be historically recorded. For instance, the Black Metropolis of Chicago, the vital Afrofuturist urban landscapes of pre-World War Two Detroit, and the black power movements of the 1960s and 1970s generated a wide range of new local institutions.[35] However, these progressive steps remind us that remainders do exist within the aftermaths of containment or the erasure of these more visible accomplishments.

THE EXTENSION OF THE POSSIBLE—WHAT IS AND WHAT MIGHT BE

IN PLAIN SIGHT

The activities of those converted to apparently sheer labour or relegated to labour in reserve give rise to the alternate forms that Moreno, referring to Lefebvre, calls the "residues hiding in plain sight."[36] In the third season of Italy's most popular television series, *Gomorrah,* the urban landscape is the main actor. Across abandoned factories, dilapidated housing projects, freeway underpasses, ruined seaside resorts, waste dumps, empty churches, unused parking garages, and jettisoned construction sites, an urban economy is pieced together and violently contested. While the proceeds from the amorphous *Camorra* are invested in gleaming office towers and offshore accounts, the everyday transactions that forge temporary alliances and betrayals, load and unload narcotics and other contraband, and act as venues for meetings between the licit and illicit all take place among the unused, wasted remainders of an urban fabric that is always moving on, seeking renewal and greater levels of abstraction.

In the wasted peripheries of Naples and Athens, a vast network of Chinese manufacturing unfolds largely in secret. The banlieues just beyond Gare du Nord are the sites of intricate home-grown real estate systems that house the barely documented, that operate as the interfaces and intersections among various diasporic commercial activities, all under the pretence of being car washes, petrol stations, box stores, delivery services, auto parts markets, recycling centres, and truck parts. Through these are the backdoors into a larger world, of goods and services moving outside official channels and of ethnicities being sutured into provisional complicities. Here, a "strange" urban geography emerges where it is not clear what things are, what they do, or what form they take. The apparent function of things, the ghostly spectres of their past identities shimmer into a blurred network of connections, both inviting and circumventing new modalities of urban control.

Whereas the objective of domesticating inhabitation—of situating urban residents in particular formats of everyday living, with their concomitant visibilities, responsibilities and attainments—may still prevail, acts of governing are no longer primarily predicated on the success or failure of these efforts. Instead, as Diren Valayden points out, a "society of targeting" emerges based on the tracking, monitoring, and targeting of mobilities.[37] This interception can take many forms, ranging from everyday harassment that forces a person to avoid certain areas at certain times, targeted assassinations of "suspected" terrorists, the use of urban designs such as anti-homelessness spikes and narrow benches (backed by laws against panhandling), the sudden demolition of "illegal structures" and temporary homes, and the use of private security guards and extensive border patrols. It is designed simply to make particular kinds of movement and inhabitation impossible and to *shift* problematic populations and practices elsewhere. But these strange geographies suggest that targeting has limits and cannot always penetrate the dissimilitude that these geographies engender unless it reverts to random firing all over the place.

This dispossession of clarity may increasingly be a prerequisite for the deployment of a collective effort that lives in conditions of *what might be taking place*—something that exceeds the available vernaculars of verification or affirmation—which is experienced as not all that far from *what is taking place*. The practical organisation of everyday life—the melding of different personal dispositions and ways of doing things—does require a sense of internal consolidation and coherence that is composed and communicated. Yet, the capacity of residents to get by, cooperate, and sometimes act in concert requires them to live as if they were always, at the same time, living somewhere else. So, the interface between the concrete empirical status of their identifiable location, their modes and practices of dwelling, *and* the ways their lives cut across territories and recognitions of all kinds—the *what might be taking place*—presents a particular problem. If there are facets of the urban that extend to a wide range of uses under the radar, then the question is how do we engage them, maximise their resourcefulness, and be cognizant of the importance of their opacity? Not rendering them visible in ways that increase their vulnerability is vitally important.

Certain practices of an urban majority may be useful for thinking strategically about this conundrum. Residents of cities across the global South have been recipients of many promises—for better livelihoods, democracy, and well-being. But they also avoided becoming preoccupied with whatever was promised. Through their own steady, incremental efforts to continuously work on their conditions, to turn them into resources, and to recalibrate relations of all kinds in the face of the volatilities of the larger city, promises became something else besides lures, manipulations, or meaningless inheritances of citizenship. Instead, promises were induced as the by-products of the districts' own efforts to prompt municipal governments to "show their cards" and divulge their weaknesses regardless of their capacity to attain a certain self-sufficiency. This self-sufficiency was manifested in the capacity of these districts to ensure large levels of variation in ways of doing things while not devolving into ongoing conflicts. The idea is to attain a sense of progress without being overwhelmed by specific measures or fears of failure. Promises were important more for what they offered than for their presence as a particular modality of disclosure, as something that kept matters open for deliberation rather than as the specification of a destination to which residents were committed.

In a practice that many residents in Rio de Janeiro refer to as *ficou na promessa* (staying with the promise), these are orientations to the future both staked out in clear terms of sufficiency and sustenance and an ability to not experience failure if those terms never were actualised. It was also a willingness to experience their realisation in unfamiliar forms. Residents may have continuously pushed their particular agendas and aspirations but were willing to be indifferent to them as well. For, endurance was an atmosphere of abiding, of willingness to "stand by" various trajectories of possible futures. Stand-by entailed both the sense of waiting to see how things unfolded and a commitment to see through various initiatives to improve livelihoods and the environment.[38] It is a willingness to operate "in reserve" of being prepared to make something from dispositions seemingly out of their control. There is a strategic indifference and detachment from the aspirations embodied in specific forms that address the problem of vulnerable opacities indicated before. As opposed to investing in particular forms that singularly embody specific attainments or aspirations, it is more important to think about the capacity of actors to recognise possibilities in the most seemingly banal or obscure landscapes.

In this context, the notion of compression, in terms of form, is useful. By compression, Alexander Galloway refers to asymmetric encounters, where things operate in the same space but have no obvious discernible relationships with each other.[39] Rather, the ground on which they are encountered and encounter each other embodies a generic orientation—a ground that has no particular definition. It is ground where things can show up in various formats without contradiction, that does not need to be realised empirically, according to specific criteria, but which engenders a sense of being in concert. For Galloway, compression is a mode of appearance that need not constantly "announce" itself and its networked positions. It is a mode of appearance that circumvents the imperative that everything must relate. As such, compression is not the simultaneous folding of the powerful or the weak.

COMPRESSED REALITIES

Compression produces a generic form that is not interested in how it relates to other things and stands apart from them. As such, it isn't interested in embodying or representing any particular value judgement. It is also unclear exactly what made it, how it was made or what it will do. It always shows up in "strange" ways, turns the expected into something bizarrely recognisable but, with some details always slightly "off" or "weird."

Many new sites of residence for working- and lower-class inhabitants—mostly at urban peripheries—are popularly understood to be transitory, a steppingstone to something else, a marker of passage rather than the culmination of a destination. Yet, they are accepted practices that often undermine recognition of any discernible status, refuse both past and future horizons, and are declined as measures of specific development processes or transformations.

Promises hold out a trajectory of the *transitive*—the prospect of going from here to there, of leaving one way of being to become something else. Promises then attempt to sweep people away, for their realisation culminates in an entirely different disposition for the person or place that was the initial recipient of that promise. But what if one were detached from such transitive conditions? What if a place or condition was self-sufficient? What if it required neither compensation for a failed past nor constructed aspirations for a better future? What if it was, instead, the very thing promised regardless

of the temporality of its delivery? What if a particular built environment allowed its users to "write themselves into" it in ways where they could recognise their needs and aspirations but where these particularities were not the exclusive characteristics of the place, where various kinds of divergent needs could be held within its confines?

Different kinds of money, residents, managerial practices, material readjustments, forms of ownership and tenancy encounter each other in an overarching atmosphere of indifference. It is a situation where it is difficult to work out how they all impact each other, *compressed* as they are in a space where so many distinct things seem to be happening. As such, the integrity of any of these elements—their distinctiveness as objects for comparison or integration becomes inoperable. This is not about the assemblage of hybrid urbanisations but rather a continuous proliferation of non-subsumable details incapable of being made *interoperable.*

Across Asia, high-rise vertical living has become the norm in the profusion of faceless megacomplexes. Seemingly, Africa will soon follow. Such modes of residence appear to be a standardisation of urban living and a means of domesticating the urban body to greater levels of individuation and self-preoccupation. But what if they held or could hold the incipient forms of new collective expression?

In the past several years, I have been involved in various research projects in megacomplexes that attempt to engage with what people do, who they do it with, where they go, for how long, and how. While it is possible to see an aggregate sense of stasis or stability, it is composed of wildly fluctuating differences in how residents attempt to make ends meet and deal with their fellow residents. Megacomplexes promise self-realisation, attainment, access, rewarding lifestyles, and security. Nevertheless, I found it rare that any prospective residents would buy into these promotions. Why sign a residential contract because the facility is simply there? It stood as an overarching fact devoid of affective registers, which is then perceived as enabling them to simply "get on with it"—

getting on, a methodology without much specification, and *"with it"* an accompanying objective that need not be anything but vague.

In other words, residents often implicitly express their preference not to be recognised. It is not anonymous in that no one pays attention, but rather that when it is paid to them, it does not know what to make of the results. A surfeit of scrutiny becomes an excess of diffraction. The resident may indeed leave their mark on the world—through a series of usually part-time service-provision jobs but then leaps across the assessment of relative success or failure by showing up somewhere completely discrepant, and the rent or mortgage gets paid, albeit barely, through use of another formula derived from these new lines of transit. Residents are far from being simply warehoused or disciplined. They may appear to be a long way from where the real action is, but nevertheless, they find all kinds of ways of associating with it, whatever *it* may be.

At the same time, the financial viability of these megacomplexes requires the ability for residents to write themselves into the landscape according to the practices that work for them and that make living within that landscape practical. So, in this plurality of instantiations of people residing in all kinds of settlement patterns, no one is precisely locatable, despite all the tech gear of surveillance and monitoring.

CONCLUSION

Recent analysis on extended urbanisation has productively demonstrated how urbanisation processes not only extend themselves across various landscapes through various forms of deterritorialisation and reterritorialisation, but also come to operate through an expansive set of logics and modalities. The extension is then not simply the expansionism of a coherent set of mechanisms for capital accumulation, and not simply the incursion of the city upon a periphery. It is also not merely the reformatting of space according to a coherent set of regulations, investments, or spatial products.

The extension of urbanisation processes may engender atmospheres of intense uncertainty and infuse places with volatile questions about the future for which urbanisation then becomes the "answer." As everywhere becomes situated in increasingly larger frames of reference in terms of how a place regards itself, its efficacy, and its prospects—or by how it is relegated to its margins, the standardised components of urbanisation— the maximisation of ground rent, the individuation of action and inhabitants, the multiplication of territorial operations, the financialisaton of materialities, and the mediasation of the social sphere become accessible problem-solving mechanisms and imaginaries for a future.

Regardless of the viability of specific dispositions of inhabitation and land in the present, there is increasingly widespread anticipation that, largely regardless of location, places will eventually find themselves within an urban orbit. This anticipation alone, and the concomitant actions informed by it, are converting many non-urban places into urbanised ones. Of course, there must be "recipients" of such anticipations, apparatuses prepared to speculate, invest, and marketise land at apparent peripheries. While the conversions of land use underway may not always seem to operationalise it in any discernible way, it is important to keep in mind that peripheries have historically long functioned as suturing mechanisms, even in liminal spaces that facilitate the articulation of divergent urban centres. Extended urbanisation, then, signals not only the more extensive operationalisation of diverse landscapes but also the engendering of "territories in waiting" in an interstitial temporality of waiting and seeing what something could become.

This chapter focused on the unequal processes of places and the operations "lending each other a hand" by availing to the other a series of affordances *and* constraints that mutually constitute urbanisation across a wide series of modalities. Important work has taken place in trying to be more precise and focused on the processes that seem to be at the heart of urbanisation across the world, albeit in different proportionalities. Still, such investigations leave

open the ways in which urbanisation is a
constantly mutating process that assumes new
forms of operation and recognition. "Lending
a hand" connotes the ambiguous duplicity
of both gift and debt relations and thus is in
accordance with the vital role that "gifting"
plays in the elaboration of social relations.

Various pathways of co-production, of
interchanges among patterning and practices
operative at different scales and temporalities,
potentially alter the forms through which
more astute political sensibilities might emerge
and through which enduring aspirations for
justice might be pursued. Instead of the urban
being tied to the models of reflexivity that are
historically embodied by the city, where particular
ways of doing things and social identities had
their own spaces of recognition, the implications
of an extended urban form generate possibilities
for an expanded opacity in and through which
multiple agendas and practices might be held.
Here, misrecognition, dissimulation, indifference, and forgetting become important urban
practices—ways of extending resistance
and experimental formulations through the
"minefields" of intensive surveillance and
commodification– and are thus a substrate
of subversive solidarity.

ENDNOTES

1   Buckley and Strauss, "With, Against, and Beyond Lefebvre."
2   Brenner, *Implosions.*
3   Schmid et al., "Towards a New Vocabulary."
4   Esposito, *Bios.*
5   Massey, *For Space.*
6   Hui, "Towards a Relational Materialism."
7   Crandall, "The Geospatialization of Calculative Operations"; Kitchin, "Big Data"; Luque-Ayala and Marvin, "Urban Operating Systems"; Leszczynski, "Speculative Futures."
8   Sassen, *The Global City.*
9   Adkins, *The Time of Money.*
10 Papadopolous, *Experimental Practice.*
11 Halbert and Attuyer, "Introduction: The Financialization."
12 Guironnet and Halbert, "The Financialization of Urban Develop-ment"; Rouanet and Halbert, "Leveraging Financial Capital."
13 Massumi, "Potential Politics."
14 Bryan, Rafferty, and Jefferis, "Risk and Value."
15 Muniesa, *The Provoked Economy.*
16 Gago, *Neoliberalism from Below*; Bear, *Navigating Austerity.*
17 Koonings, *Capital and Time.*
18 Parisi, *Contagious Architecture.*
19 Auge, *Non-Places.*
20 Ghertner, "India's Urban Revolution."
21 Lee, "Absolute Traffic."
22 Simone, "Precarious Detachment."
23 Marazzi, *Capital and Affects.*
24 Kockelman, *The Art of Interpretation.*
25 Luhman, *Introduction to Systems Theory.*
26 Cooper, *Family Values.*
27 Wagner, *An Anthropology of the Subject.*
28 Strathern, "Binary License."
29 Corsín Jimenéz, "Well Being in Anthropological Balance"; Corsín Jimenéz, "The Prototype."
30 Adams, "Natura Urbans."
31 Kohn, *How Forests Think*, 20.
32 Colebrook, "What is it Like to be Human"; Wagner, "The Chess of Kinship."
33 Cohen, *Telemorphosis*; Cohen, "Trolling 'Anthropos.'"
34 King, "The Labor of (re)Reading"; Spillers, "Mama's Baby."
35 Hunter and Robinson, "The Sociology of Urban Black America."
36 Moreno, "Always Crashing."
37 Valayden, "Racialization Feraliza-tion."
38 Kemmer, "Free Riding Rio."
39 Galloway, *Laruelle.*

BIBLIOGRAPHY

Adams, Ross Exo. "Natura Urbans, Natura Urbanata: Ecological Urbanization, Circulation, and the Immunization of Nature." *Environment and Planning D: Society and Space* 32, no. 1 (2014): 12–29.

Adkins, Lisa. *The Time of Money.* Stanford, CA: Stanford University Press, 2018.

Auge, Michel. *Non-Places: An Introduction to Supermodernity.* London: Verso, 2008.

Bear, Laura. *Navigating Austerity: Currents of Debt along a South Asian River.* Stanford, CA: Stanford University Press, 2015.

Brenner, Neil (ed.). *Implosions/Explosions: Studies in Planetary Urbanization.* Berlin: Jovis, 2015.

Bryan, Dick, Michael Rafferty, and Chris Jefferis. "Risk and Value: Finance, Labor, and Production." *The South Atlantic Quarterly* 114, no. 2 (2015): 307–329.

Buckley, Michelle, and Kendra Strauss. "With, Against and Beyond Lefebvre: Planetary Urbanization and Epistemic Plurality." *Environment and Planning D: Society and Space* 34, no. 4 (2016): 617–636.

Cohen, Tom. *Telemorphosis: Theory in the Era of Climate Change.* Ann Arbor, MI: Open Humanities Press, 2012.

———."Trolling 'Anthropos'—Or, Requiem for a Failed Prosopopoeia." In *Twilight of the Anthropocene Idols,* edited by Tom Cohen, Claire Colebrook, and J.H. Miller, 20–80. Ann Arbor, MI: Open Humanities Press, 2016.

Colebrook, Claire. "What is it Like to be a Human?" *Transgender Studies Quarterly* 2, no. 2 (2015): 227–243.

Cooper, Melinda. *Family Values: Between Neoliberalism and the New Social Conservatism.* New York: Zone Books, 2017.

Corsín Jimenéz, Alberto. "Well-Being in Anthropological Balance: Remarks on Proportionality as Political Imagination." In *Culture and Well-Being: Anthropological Approaches to Freedom and Political Ethics,* edited by Alberto Corsín Jimenéz, 187–197. London: Pluto Press, 2008.

———."The Prototype: More than Many and Less than One." *Journal of Cultural Economy* 7, no. 4 (2014): 381–398.

Crandall, Jordan. "The Geospatialization of Calculative Operations: Tracking, Sensing and Megacities." *Theory, Culture & Society* 27, no. 6 (2010): 68–90.

Esposito, Roberto. *Bios: Biopolitics and Philosophy.* Minneapolis: University of Minnesota Press, 2004.

Gago, Véronica. *Neoliberalism from Below: Popular Pragmatics and Baroque Economies.* Durham, NC: Duke University Press, 2017.

Galloway, Alexander. *Laruelle: Against the Digital.* Minneapolis: University of Minnesota Press, 2014.

Ghertner, D. Asher. "India's Urban Revolution: Geographies of Displacement Beyond Gentrification." *Environment and Planning A* 46, no. 7 (2014): 1554–1571.

Guironnet, Antoine, and Ludovic Halbert. "The Financialization of Urban Development Projects: Concepts, Processes, and Implications." *Document de travail du LATTS.* Working Paper 14–04, no. 44 (2014).

Halbert, Ludovic, and Katia Attuyer. "Introduction: The Financialisation of Urban Production: Conditions, Mediations and Transformations." *Urban Studies* 53, no. 7 (2014): 1347–1361.

Hui, Yuk. "Towards a Relational Materialism. A Reflection on Language, Relations and the Digital." *Digital Culture and Society* 1, no. 1 (2015): 131–147.

Hunter, Marcus Anthony, and Zandria Robinson. "The Sociology of Urban Black America." *Annual Review of Sociology* 42 (2016): 383–405.

Kemmer, Laura. "Free Riding Rio: Protest, Public Transport and the Politics of a Footboard." *City & Society* 32, no. 1 (2020): 157–181.

King, Tiffany Lethabo. "The Labor of (Re) Reading Plantation Landscapes Fungible(ly)." *Antipode* 48, no. 4 (2016): 1022–1039.

Kohn, Eduardo. *How Forests Think: Toward an Anthropology Beyond the Human.* Berkeley: University of California Press, 2013.

Kitchin, Rob. "Big Data, New Epistemologies and Paradigm Shifts." *Big Data and Society* 1, no. 1 (2014): 1–12.

Kockelman, Paul. *The Art of Interpretation in the Age of Computation.* Oxford: Oxford University Press, 2017.

Koonings, Martijn. *Capital and Time: For a New Critique of Neoliberal Reason.* Stanford, CA: Stanford University Press, 2018.

Lee, Doreen. "Absolute Traffic: Infrastructural Aptitude in Urban Indonesia." *International Journal of Urban and Regional Research* 39, no. 2 (2015): 234–250.

Leszczynski, Agniedzka. "Speculative Futures: Cities, Data, and Governance Beyond Smart Urbanism." *Environment and Planning A* 48, no. 9 (2016): 1691–1708.

Luhmann, Niklas. *Introduction to Systems Theory.* Cambridge: Polity, 2013.

Marvin, Simon, and Andrés, Luque-Ayala. "Urban Operating Systems: Diagramming the City." *International Journal of Urban and Regional Research* 41, no. 1 (2017): 84–103.

Marazzi, Christian. *Capital and Affects: The Politics of the Language Economy.* New York: Semiotext(e), 2011.

Massey, Doreen. *For Space.* London: Sage, 2005.

Massumi, Brian. "Potential Politics and the Primacy of Pre-emption." *Theory and Event* 10, no. 2 (2007): 10.1353/tae.2007.0066.

Moreno, Louis. "Always Crashing in the Same City: Real Estate, Psychic Capital, and Planetary Desire." *City* 22, no. 1 (2018): 152–168.

Muniesa, Fabian. *The Provoked Economy: Economic Reality and the Performative Turn.* London: Routledge, 2014.

Papadopoulos, Dimitri. *Experimental Practice: Technoscience, Alterontologies, and More-Than-Social Movements.* Durham, NC: Duke University Press, 2018.

Parisi, Luciana. *Contagious Architecture: Computation, Aesthetics and Space.* Cambridge, MA: MIT Press, 2013.

Rouanet, Hortense, and Ludovic Halbert. "Leveraging Finance Capital: Urban Change and Self-Empowerment of Real Estate Developers in India." *Urban Studies* 53, no. 7 (2014): 1401–1423.

Sassen, Saskia. *The Global City: New York, Tokyo, London.* Princeton, NJ: Princeton University Press, 2001.

Schmid, Christian, Ozan Karaman, Naomi C. Hanakata, Pascal Kallenberger, Anne Kockelhorn, Lindsay Sawyer, Monika Streule, and Kit Ping Wong. "Towards a New Vocabulary of Urbanisation Processes: A Comparative Approach. *Urban Studies* 55, no. 1 (2018): 19–52.

Simone, AbdouMaliq. "Precarious Detachment: Youth and Modes of Operating in Hyderabad and Jakarta." In *The Routledge Handbook of Anthropology and the City*, edited by Setha Low, 3–16. London: Routledge, 2018.

Spillers, Hortense. "Mama's Baby, Papa's Maybe: An American Grammar Book." *Diacritics* 17, no. 2 (1987): 64–81.

Strathern, Marilyn. "Binary License." *Common Knowledge* 17, no. 1 (2011): 87–103.

Valayden, Diran. "Racial Feralization: Targeting Race in an Era of Planetary Urbanization." *Theory, Culture & Society* 33, no. 7–8 (2016): 159–182.

Wagner, Roy. *An Anthropology of the Subject: Holographic Worldview in New Guinea and its Meaning and Significance for the World of Anthropology*. Berkeley: University of California Press, 2001.

———."The Chess of Kinship and the Kinship of Chess." *HAU: Journal of Ethnographic Theory* 1, no. 1 (2011): 165–177.

Biographies

NITIN BATHLA
is a lecturer and postdoctoral researcher at the Department of Architecture, ETH Zürich, where he also coordinates the Doctoral Programme at the Institute of Landscape and Urban Studies. His research practice actively combines academic research with artistic practices of filmmaking, and socially-engaged art. He is the director of the award-wining film *Not Just Roads*, which premiered at several important film festivals across the world.

ELISA T. BERTUZZO
is an urban ethnographer and theorist. Working with feminist, decolonial, and political ecology literature, she takes interest in underrepresented facets of everyday solidarity, resistance, and self-organisation. Having extensively published on urbanisation and migration in Bangladesh and India, she is currently mapping the European trajectories of seeds and edible plants imported from South Asia through the socio-material and ecological infrastructures enabling translocalised livelihoods.

RODRIGO CASTRIOTA
is a Postdoctoral Research Fellow on the ERC Project *Inhabiting Radical Housing* at DIST/ Politecnico di Torino. He holds a PhD in Urban and Regional Development from CEDEPLAR/UFMG (Brazil), where he did extensive research on urbanisation processes in the Brazilian Amazon. His main research interests also include popular economies, neo-extractivism, and postcolonial/ decolonial theory.

NANCY COULING
is an architect, Associate Professor at Bergen School of Architecture and Senior Researcher at the Chair of Professor Milica Topalović, Architecture of Territory, D-Arch, ETH Zürich. She is co-editor of *Barents Lessons: Teaching and Research in Architecture* (Zurich: Park Books, 2012) and *The Urbanisation of the Sea: From Concepts and Analysis to Design* (Rotterdam: nai010, 2020).

ALICE HERTZOG
is a social anthropologist whose work in the Republic of Benin examines the circulation of migrants and subsequent transformations within the urban fabric. Her current research addresses the (re)circulations of contested cultural heritage in West Africa. An alumnus of Cambridge University, Sciences Po, L'École Normale Supérieur Paris, and ETH Zürich, she was recently appointed to the Ethnographic Museum at the University of Zurich.

NIKOS KATSIKIS
is an urbanist and Assistant Professor at the Urbanism Department, TU Delft. His research seeks to contribute to a geographical understanding of the relations between cities and non-city landscapes that support urban life. He holds a Doctor of Design from Harvard Graduate School of Design, where he also served as Lecturer in Urban Planning and Design, and as editor of the *New Geographies* journal.

METAXIA MARKAKI
is an architect, urbanist, educator, and Lecturer at the Department of Architecture at ETH Zürich. Her ongoing PhD research delves into extended urbanisation in mountainous peripheral landscapes in Greece. Previously, she has been engaged in territorial research and teaching at the ETH Architecture of Territory with Professor Topalović, at ETH Studio Basel and Harvard Graduate School of Design with Professors Herzog and deMeuron, and co-authored the book *achtung: die Landschaft*.

PHILIPPE REKACEWICZ
is a geographer, cartographer, and information designer who graduated from Sorbonne University. He was the head of the cartographic department of *Le Monde diplomatique* (1988–2014) and associate researcher and lecturer at the University of Helsinki (Crosslocation programme, 2016–2022). He currently works on embedded ecologies at the Department of Social Sciences, University of Wageningen, Netherlands and co-animates the site Visionscarto. net with Philippe Rivière.

CHRISTIAN SCHMID
is an urban researcher, geographer, sociologist, and Professor of Sociology, Department of Architecture at ETH Zurich. His scientific work is on planetary urbanisation, comparative urban analysis and theories of urbanisation and space. He wrote a comprehensive reconstruction of Henri Lefebvre's theory of the production of space, and is a member of the International Network for Urban Research and Action (INURA).

ABDOUMALIQ SIMONE
is Senior Professorial Fellow at the Urban Institute, University of Sheffield, co-director of the Beyond Inhabitation Lab at the Polytechnic University of Turin, and Honorary Professor of Urban Studies at the African Centre for Cities, University of Cape Town.

MILICA TOPALOVIĆ
is an architect and Professor of Architecture and Territorial Planning at the Department of Architecture at ETH Zurich. Her work addresses territories beyond-the-city and the transformation processes they are exposed to through the movement of capital, social restructuring, and environmental change. She has studied remote regions, resource hinterlands, and countrysides in an effort to decentre and ecologise architectural approaches to the city, the urban, and urbanisation.

KIT PING WONG
is a geographer, urban researcher, and Research Fellow at the Urban Resilience Research Centre, Osaka Metropolitan University, Japan. Her research is on urbanisation in a comparative perspective and on extended urbanisation, with a focus on urban theories and urban histories and politics in Hong Kong, Shenzhen, and Dongguan.

Acknowledgements

This book is the result of the collaborative research project Territories of Extended Urbanisation. Initiated by the editors in 2017, the project aimed to bring together and sketch out vastly diverse territories characterised by different aspects of extended urbanisation in an open-ended, collaborative way. It was therefore also largely determined by the researchers themselves through workshops, conferences, and co-lateral discussions. These exchanges not only developed into stimulating and supportive collaborations and lasting friendships, they were also hugely enjoyable. The dedicated research and editorial team therefore gratefully acknowledges all those who supported and encouraged our project during our long and adventurous journey through the territories of extended urbanisation. We are particularly indebted to Nancy Couling for her crucial editorial, communication, and coordination work and for assembling this book.

We thank radical geographer and cartographer Philippe Rekacewicz for his engagement and collaboration in producing the unique maps that are a key element of this book. By applying his own expert knowledge, carrying out extra research, and embracing our conceptual proposals, Philippe has bought these previously unseen aspects of extended urbanisation to cartographic life. We are also grateful for his refinement of our cartographic approach and language through collaboration on the three exhibitions the *Shenzhen Bi-City Biennale of Urbanism / Architecture* in autumn 2015, *Cartographies of Planetary Urbanisation* in Bologna 2019, and the *Venice Architecture Biennale* 2021.

We thank Jennifer Robinson for her careful reading and editing of the introductory essay and her invaluable comments on Christian Schmid's text "Extended Urbanisation: A Framework for Analysis." Many thanks to Neil Brenner for his collaboration and insightful discussions on planetary urbanisation and extended urbanisation over many years, and in particular for the productive collaboration on the Venice Biennale 2021, together with the Urban Theory Lab team.

Goda Budvytytė has carefully crafted the book concept and the book design with the researchers since 2018 in a highly professional manner with enormous patience and creativity. We thank her for giving an enticing and coherent shape, structure, and aesthetic to this diverse material.

Without the expertise and support of Angelika Gaal and Baharak Tajbakhsh at Birkhäuser throughout the complex editing, printing, and publishing process, this project would not have come to fruition. Thank you for this exceptional collaboration.

We are also indebted to Evelyne Gordon for her administrative and organisational support; to copy editor Jake Starmer; to Ada St. Laurent for proofreading; and to E. Ece Emanetoğlu, Aikaterini Katsuoli, and Jan Zimmermann for supporting us in the final map adjustments. We also thank guest researchers Nazli Tümerdem and Giulia Torino who contributed to our workshops and discussions. We thank Pius Krütli and the USYS Transdisciplinary Lab ETH and Freek Persyn and the Newrope Design in Dialogue Chair ETH for hosting several of our Zurich meetings.

This project was carried out at the Future Cities Laboratory (FCL), Singapore-ETH Centre, as well as the Chair of Architecture and Territorial Planning and the Chair of Sociology at the Department of Architecture, ETH Zürich. This study was supported by the National Research Foundation Singapore as part of its Campus for Research Excellence and Technological Enterprise (CREATE) programme, as well as by the Department of Architecture at ETH Zürich.

We thank all our colleagues from FCL and from the Chairs of Architecture and Territorial Planning and of Sociology for their support, advice, and inspiration. Particular thanks to previous scientific director of the FCL, Stephen Cairns, and his team, who encouraged a stimulating dialogue with us, sharing ideas and research results. We also thank our collaborators in the ongoing FCL research project New Agendas Under Planetary Urbanisation, which builds on some of the findings discussed in this book; particularly Sacha Menz and Stephen Cairns for their crucial institutional support, our ETH colleagues and Co-PIs Adrienne Grêt-Regamey, Naomi Hanakata, Christoph Küffer, and Johan Six, and researchers Hans Hortig, Hiromi Inagaki, Karoline Kostka, Matteo Riva, and Kevin Vega.

NITIN BATHLA

Is grateful to his interlocutors, who allowed him to enter their lifeworlds despite the difficult circumstances that they are confronted with. He would like to especially thank Mazdoor Ekta Manch, the residents of Dwarka Expressway, the Commuters Welfare Association, and IamGurgaon. Additionally, he thanks Marie-Hélène Zérah and Shubhra Gururani, who have been important conversation partners. His gratitude also goes out to the Territories of Extended Urbanisation collective for their friendship and collegial intellectual exchange all these years. Lastly, thanks to Christian Schmid and Milica Topalović for providing such great input to the chapter and giving it good direction and form, and to Nancy Couling for the excellent guidance through the sometimes difficult coordination of the book.

ELISA T. BERTUZZO

Is grateful to all her interview partners and co-passengers for invaluable stories and sharing; and to the rains, blocked roads, sand banks, and train delays that had a part in occasioning them. She thanks Keya and Subhendu Dasgupta for the enriching and rigorous conversations and soothing meals; Labani Jangi for launching into the exploration of the Nadia district with as much spontaneity as dedication; and all the researchers and staff of the Centre for Studies in Social Sciences Calcutta (CSSSC). Anindita Ghoshal and Bhim Reddy provided crucial insights into the subcontinent's modern history and the agrarian question. Thank you also to Nancy Couling for her patient coordination throughout a very long publication process, and to Tammy Wong for being a most motivating and sincere peer.

RODRIGO CASTRIOTA

Is very grateful to all the participants in this research—peasants, activists, educators, shopkeepers, activists, and mining employees—in short, residents of the Carajás region who made this work possible. He is particularly indebted to the network of social movements in southeast Pará, particularly the MST (Landless Workers Movement), MAM (National Movement for Popular Sovereignty in Mining), CEPASP (Centre for Education, Research and Union and People's Advisory), CPT (Pastoral Land Commission), STTRCC (Rural Union of Canaã dos Carajás), as well as the Federal Universities of Pará (UFPA) and South/Southeast Pará (UNIFESSPA). Gratitude also goes out to the Territories of Extended Urbanisation team for vibrant discussions, continued engagement, and support, as well as PhD dissertation supervisor Prof. Roberto Monte-Mór, at the Centre for Development and Regional Planning (Cedeplar/UFMG) from where this book chapter emerged.

NANCY COULING

Would like to thank interviewees Gunleiv Hadland, the Norwegian Petroleum Museum; Daniel Ayala Høydal and Chriss Thomas Grimstad, CCB (NO);

Walter Brown, Gavin Mowat, and Alexandros Fotakis, Shell platforms (UK); shrimp fisherman Johann Looden (DE) and Paul Fetcher, Scottish Fishermen's Organisation (UK), for generously contributing their insights into offshore working life and operations in the North Sea fishing and oil and gas sectors. The research for this chapter was funded through the EU Horizon 2020 programme, Marie Skłodowska-Curie Individual Grant No. 753882. She also thanks Prof. Carola Hein, research supervisor during this fellowship, and her BAS students for their innovative design work tackling these issues, in particular Zoelie Millereau-Dubesset, author of "Bird Station."

ALICE HERTZOG
Is grateful to her fellow authors, who have been invaluable companions throughout this project. Much gratitude goes to Christian Schmid, Armelle Choplin, and Pius Krütli for their generous supervision of her doctoral thesis. Thanks also go to Milica Topalović and Christian Schmid for their commitment to this project, and to Nancy Couling for keeping everybody on the same page. Most importantly, this work would not have been possible without the many relationships forged along the Lagos-Abidjan Corridor with vendors, hustlers, drivers, and dwellers. Gratitude goes in particular to her friends at the Ahozon tollbooth for their hospitality and patience, and to Celestin Alloeiti for his valuable assistance. This research was supported by the Global Programme for Migration and Development of the Swiss Agency for Development and Cooperation.

NIKOS KATSIKIS
Is grateful to all members of the Territories of Extended Urbanisation research project for offering a unique intellectual environment, as well the ETH FCL program for supporting the necessary fieldwork. He is also especially grateful to Andrew Suiter and Don Vogel for facilitating multiple visits across Iowa in the most generous way, and for sharing their invaluable guidance and knowledge on the region. He would like to give special thanks to Neil Brenner and all members of the University of Chicago's Urban Theory Lab for contributing to the intellectual development of key concepts and theoretical frameworks.

METAXIA MARKAKI
Is deeply grateful to all her interview participants and co-travellers who generously shared their time, resources, and knowledge during her field trips in Arcadia, including Giannis Lagos, the Nikoloutsos and Striggos families, Panagiotis, Dimitris, Nena, Vaggelis, Maria, Manolis, George, and all those who wish to remain anonymous. She owes special thanks to Milica Topalović and the teaching team and students of the Architecture of Territory design studio ARCADIA for initiating this research together in 2015.

PHILIPPE REKACEWICZ
Is very grateful to the entire team that participated in the Territories of Extended Urbanisation project for having accepted and integrated him into their discussions and reflections on cities, urban space, and in particular spaces undergoing processes of urbanisation. The project enabled him to discover the immensely diverse types of urban territories and pathways of urbanisation, challenging all his preconceived ideas as a geographer and cartographer trying to understand the systemic links between the elements of human geography. There is indeed a before and after the Extended Urbanisation project.

CHRISTIAN SCHMID
Particularly thanks Jennifer Robinson for her unflinching support during the entire work on this research and book project and for being such a great companion during the not always easy task of bringing this project to a successful completion; he is also very grateful for her insightful comments on his book chapter. He thanks Phil Harrison for his valuable comments on the chapter and for the invitation to the exciting discussions on extended urbanisation in South Africa. The long-standing collaboration with Neil Brenner on planetary urbanisation was an indispensable basis and invaluable source for this project: thank you!

ABDOUMALIQ SIMONE
Expresses great appreciation for the ideas and friendship of all the members of the Territories of Extended Urbanisation collective, which embodies a much-needed way of researchers working together.

MILICA TOPALOVIĆ
Extends warmest gratitude to the friends and colleagues of the Territories of Extended Urbanisation collective. Getting to know you and following your work from the initial ideas through all stages of writing and cartography over several years has been a privilege and a great source of learning and inspiration. Thank you to all collaborators at the Chair of Architecture and Territorial Planning, Alice Clarke, Nancy Couling, Muriz Djurdjevic, Evelyne Gordon, Dorothee Hahn, Santiago del Hierro, Hans Hortig, Vesna Jovanović, Karoline Kostka, Metaxia Markaki, Nazli Tümerdem, Jakob Walter, and Jan Westerheide for supporting the project, the workshops and the exhibitions in various ways. She is particularly grateful for the shared teaching of territorial research and design studios on the countrysides and hinterlands of Asia and Europe for more than ten years. Many of the insights, ideas, and sketches created in those studios have been vital for the extended urbanisation project.

KIT PING WONG
Expresses deep gratitude to all interview partners and anonymous sources from institutions, universities, and villages that made her fieldwork in Dongguan fulfilling and meaningful. Special thanks to the young villagers for their invaluable assistance, sharing, and friendship throughout the years. Their support not only facilitated her contacts to local sources and the exploration of villages, histories, and people's lives, but also practical matters like accommodation, travel, and safety. She is also grateful to the local scholars and planners who generously shared their time, knowledge, and insights about Dongguan, as well as to the ordinary villagers and migrants who told their stories amidst enormous changes underway in Dongguan. She also extends her gratitude to Soloman Benjamin, Carolyn Cartier, Kam Wing Chan, Wing Yin Chan, Sylvie Fanchette, Geerhardt Kornatowski, Angela Stienen, and Wing-shing Tang for their encouragement, support, discussion, and feedback on the first research output in a special journal mentioned in the chapter. She also thanks all contributors to this book for their inspiration, discussion, and support during the workshops and conferences. Lastly, she thanks Christian Schmid deeply for his patience, openness, and rigorous supervisory work—it was crucially important throughout the entire fieldwork, mapping, writing, and editing process.

Colophon

EDITORS
Christian Schmid and
Milica Topalović
Department of Architecture,
ETH Zürich

ASSOCIATE EDITOR
Nancy Couling
Department of Architecture,
ETH Zürich/Bergen School
of Architecture

This research was conducted at the
Department of Architecture, ETH Zürich,
and the Future Cities Laboratory, Singapore-ETH Centre.

This research was supported by the
National Research Foundation Singapore
(NRF) under its Campus for Research
Excellence and Technological Enterprise
(CREATE) programme, and by the
Department of Architecture, ETH Zürich.

WITH CONTRIBUTIONS BY
Nitin Bathla, Zürich
Elisa T. Bertuzzo, Berlin
Rodrigo Castriota, Sao Paolo
Nancy Couling, Lausanne
Alice Hertzog, Zürich
Nikos Katsikis, Delft
Metaxia Markaki, Zürich
Christian Schmid, Zürich
AbdouMaliq Simone, Sheffield
Milica Topalović, Zürich
Kit Ping Wong, Hong Kong

CARTOGRAPHY
Philippe Rekacewicz, Oslo
Ece Emanetoglu, Zürich
Aikaterini Katsuoli, Zürich
Jan Zimmermann, Zürich

ACQUISITIONS EDITOR
Baharak Tajbakhsh, Birkhäuser
Verlag, CHE-Basel

CONTENT AND PRODUCTION
EDITOR
Angelika Gaal, Birkhäuser Verlag,
AUT-Vienna

COPY EDITING
Jake Starmer, Starmer
Communications, Inc.,
USA-New York

PROOFREADING
Word Up!, USA-Missoula

GRAPHIC DESIGN
Goda Budvytytė, with assistance
from Bernardo Rodrigues

IMAGE EDITING
Pixelstorm Litho & Digital
Imaging, AUT-Vienna

PRINTING
Holzhausen, the book-printing
brand of Gerin Druck GmbH,
AUT-Wolkersdorf

Printed in Austria

Library of Congress Control Number:
2023938803

Bibliographic information published
by the German National Library
The German National Library lists
this publication in the Deutsche National-
bibliografie; detailed bibliographic
data are available on the Internet
at http://dnb.dnb.de.

ISBN 978-3-0356-2297-3
e-ISBN (PDF) 978-3-0356-2303-1

© 2023 Birkhäuser Verlag GmbH, Basel
Im Westfeld 8, 4055 Basel, Switzerland
Part of Walter de Gruyter GmbH, Berlin/
Boston

9 8 7 6 5 4 3 2 1
www.birkhauser.com

ETH
Eidgenössische Technische Hochschule Zürich
Swiss Federal Institute of Technology Zurich

DARCH

(SEC) SINGAPORE-ETH
CENTRE

CORRIGENDUM

Inner cover, page 3.

The correct list of contributors is:

Nitin Bathla, Elisa T. Bertuzzo,
Rodrigo Castriota, Nancy Couling,
Alice Hertzog, Nikos Katsikis,
Metaxia Markaki, Philippe
Rekacewicz, AbdouMaliq Simone,
Kit Ping Wong

Edited by Christian Schmid and
Milica Topalović